THE UGARITIC BAAL CYCLE

SUPPLEMENTS

TO

VETUS TESTAMENTUM

EDITED BY
THE BOARD OF THE QUARTERLY

VOLUME LV

THE UGARITIC BAAL CYCLE

VOLUME I

INTRODUCTION WITH TEXT, TRANSLATION AND COMMENTARY OF KTU 1.1-1.2

BY

MARK S. SMITH

E.J. BRILL
LEIDEN · NEW YORK · KÖLN
1994

Library of Congress Cataloging-in-Publication Data

Baal cycle. English & Ugaritic.
The Ugaritic Baal cycle / [edited by] Mark S. Smith.
p. cm. — (Supplements to Vetus Testamentum, ISSN 0083-5889 ; v. 55-)
Includes bibliographical references and indexes.
Contents: v. 1. Introduction with text, translation and commentary of KTU 1.1-1.2.
ISBN 9004099956
1. Baal (Deity) 2. Ugarit (Extinct city)—Religion. I. Smith, Mark S. , 1955- . II. Title. III. Series.
BS410.V452 vol. 55, etc.
[BL1640]
221 s—dc20
[299'.2]

94-31618
CIP
r94

Die Deutsche Bibliothek - CIP-Einheitsaufnahme

Smith, Mark S.:
The Ugaritic Baal cycle / Mark S. Smith.- Leiden ; New York ; Köln : Brill
Vol. 1. Introduction with text, translation and commentary of KTU 1.1-1.2. – 1994
(Supplements to Vetus testamentum ; Vol. 55)
ISBN 90-04-09995-6
NE: Vetus testamentum / Supplements

ISSN 0083-5889
ISBN 90 04 09995 6

PRINTED IN THE NETHERLANDS

For Marvin H. Pope

rbt ʾilm lḥkmt
"Thou art great, O El, thou art wise"
KTU 1.4 V 3 (*EUT* 34)

TABLE OF CONTENTS

PLATES OF TABLETS

Acknowledgements

I owe a great debt of gratitude to many people and institutions, but I would like to begin by thanking scholars who have dedicated their energies to investigating the many mysteries of the Baal Cycle, other Ugaritic texts and relevant Near Eastern works. A commentary such as this one necessarily pays tribute to the labors of many predecessors and contemporaries.

This work was made possible through the aid of numerous institutions. I am grateful to the National Endowment for the Humanities, which awarded me a summer travel grant in 1986 for research on the Baal Cycle. During the spring and summer of 1987 and the summers of 1986 and 1989, I worked on this book in the hospitable surroundings of the William Foxwell Albright Institute and École Biblique et Archéologique Française de Jérusalem. For their generous hospitality I am grateful to these institutions and their members. I heartifully thank the American Schools of Oriental Research, the Association of Theological Schools and the Dorot Foundation for providing funding for the spring semester of 1987. As director of the West Semitic Research project, Professor Bruce Zuckerman was very generous in letting me use photographs of 1.1 and 1.2. It was a time-consuming chore to produce the photographs, and I wish to express my heartfelt thanks to Professor Zuckerman. I also am deeply indebted to the Département des Antiquités Orientales at the Louvre, which allowed me to examine the originals of KTU 1.1 and 1.2 in September of 1992. I thank the director of the department, Madame Béatrice André-Salvini, and I am grateful to the members of the department for their kind hospitality during my visit. I wish to express further my gratitude to Professor Bruce Zuckerman for permission to publish WSRP photographs of 1.1 and 1.2 and to the Louvre for permission to publish to publish these photographs as well a photograph of the Baal stele (AO 15.775).

I wish to thank friends who have aided this work over the years. Professor Benjamin Foster offered many criticisms and corrections to the Introduction. The members of the Old Testament Colloquium offered many criticisms of sections of this work, and they have been an inspiration to me. I have read the Baal Cycle with different classes which have given me new insights. I deeply appreciate my former students, especially Douglas Green, Richard Whitekettle and Wolfgang Hüllstrung. I also wish to thank my father, Donald

E. Smith, and my mother-in-law, Sonia Bloch, for providing me with recent newspaper reports pertaining to the domestication of horses. The members of the theology department of Saint Joseph's University have been gracious to me, and with their encouragement this work has finally come to publication. Paul Aspan, Gary Beckman, Richard Clifford, Aloysius Fitzgerald, Jonas Greenfield, Tryggve Mettinger, Dennis Pardee, Christopher Seitz, Karel van der Toorn, Robert Wilson and Bruce Zuckerman have sustained me with their interest, their help and their many acts of kindness. It remains to be added that I alone am responsible for the errors in this work.

My family has time and again earned my many thanks. My wife, Liz, and our children, Benjamin, Rachel and Shulamit, have given me many moments of joy, and these moments day in and day out whisper the wonder of life which the Baal Cycle expresses so eloquently and so deeply. I began work on this volume in the year of our Benjamin's birth, and I now come to its end eight years later in the third year of our Shulamit's life.

Finally, I reserve some words for my teacher, Marvin H. Pope, who has influenced this work more than any other person. I met Professor Pope in his office in the spring of 1980. The room was filled with shelves and boxes of books, papers, cards, drawings. In the middle stood a small seminar table with a blackboard of Professor Pope's own making with lines of some Ugaritic text. Little did I know that this would be the place where as a graduate student I would witness the resurrection of an ancient cosmos thanks to Professor Pope's imagination. Since graduate school I have continued to learn from Professor Pope through his works especially his ground-breaking *El in the Ugaritic Texts* (1955), his internationally acclaimed Anchor Bible commentaries on Job and the Song of Songs, and his most recent volume, *Probative Pontificating in Ugaritic and Biblical Literature; Collected Essays*.[1] In these and other works of his, I have frequently revisited Professor Pope's insights, his humor and expressions of humility. As a small expression of my thanks, I dedicate this work to this gracious man, my mentor and my friend.

25 January 1994
Bala Cynwyd, Pennsylvania

[1] Pope, *Probative Pontificating in Ugaritic and Biblical Literature; Collected Essays* (ed. M. S. Smith; Ugaritisch-Biblische Literatur 10; Münster: Ugarit-Press, 1994).

Citations, Abbreviations and Sigla

Biblical texts are cited according to Revised Standard Version (RSV) unless otherwise noted. The abbreviations, listed in *Journal of Biblical Literature* 107 (1988) 584-96 and *The Assyrian Dictionary. Volume 15 S* (ed. E. Reiner et al.; Chicago: Oriental Institute, 1984) vii-xxii, are used with following additions, changes and sigla:

I. Books, Journals and Series

ANET *ANET*. Third edition.

AO *Aula Orientalis*

AP A. Cowley. *Aramaic Papyrus of the Fifth Century B. C.* Oxford: Clarendon, 1923; reprinted ed.; Osnabruck: Otto Zeller, 1967.

Baal P. J. van Zijl. *Baal; A Study of Texts in Connexion with Baal in the Ugaritic Epics*. AOAT 10. Kevelaer: Verlag Butzon & Bercker; Neukirchen-Vluyn: Neukirchener Verlag des Erziehungsvereins, 1972.

Benz F. L. Benz. *Personal Names in the Phoenician and Punic Inscriptions*. Studia Pohl 8. Rome: Pontifical Biblical Institute, 1972.

Biella J. C. Biella. *Dictionary of Old South Arabic; Sabaean Dialect*. HSS 25. Chico, CA: Scholars, 1982.

BOS U. Cassuto. *Biblical & Oriental Studies; Volume 2: Bible and Ancient Oriental Texts*. Trans. I. Abrahams. Jerusalem: Magnes, 1975.

CEBCR U. Oldenburg. *The Conflict between El and Baᶜal in Canaanite Religion*. Supplementa ad Numen, altera series: Dissertationes ad historiam religionum pertinentes edendas curavit C. J. Blecker. Vol. III. Leiden: Brill, 1969.

CMCOT R. J. Clifford. *The Cosmic Mountain in Canaan and the Old Testament*. HSM 4. Cambridge, MA: Harvard University, 1972.

CMHE F. M. Cross. *Canaanite Myth and Hebrew Epic*. Cambridge, MA/ London: Harvard University, 1973.

CML[1] G. R. Driver. *Canaanite Myths and Legends*. Edinburgh: T. & T. Clark, 1956.

CML[2] J. C. L. Gibson. *Canaanite Myth and Legends*. Second ed. Edinburgh: T. &T. Clark, 1978.

CS S. E. Loewenstamm. *Comparative Studies in Biblical and Ancient Oriental Literatures*. AOAT 204. Kevelaer: Verlag Butzon & Bercker; Neukirchen-Vluyn: Neukirchener Verlag, 1980.

CTA A. Herdner. *Corpus des Tablettes en Cunéiformes Alphabétiques découvertes à Ras Shamra-Ugarit de 1929 à 1939*. Mission de Ras Shamra X. Paris: Imprimerie Nationale/Librairie Orientaliste Paul Geuthner, 1963.

CUL R. E. Whitaker. *A Concordance of the Ugaritic Literature*. Cambridge, MA: Harvard, 1972.

Dozy R. Dozy. *Supplément aux dictionnaires Arabes*. Two vols. Second ed. Leiden: Brill, 1927.

DW P. D. Miller. *The Divine Warrior in Early Israel*. HSM 5. Cambridge, MA: Harvard University, 1973.

Emar D. Arnaud. *Recherches au pays d'Aštata. Emar VI; Tome 3. Texts sumériens et accadiens. Texte*. Paris: Editions Recherche sur les Civilisations, 1986. Cited by text number.

EUT M. H. Pope. *El in the Ugaritic Texts*. SVT 2. Leiden: Brill, 1955.

Freytag G. W. Freytag. *Lexicon Arabico-Latinum*. Four volumes. Alle A.S.: Schwetschke et filium, 1830.

GA U. Cassuto. *The Goddess Anath*. Trans. I. Abrahams. Jerusalem: Magnes, 1971.

Jastrow M. Jastrow. *A Dictionary of the Targumim, the Talmud Babli and Yerushalmi, and the Rabbinic Literature*. New York: The Judaica Press, 1971.

KTU M. Dietrich, O. Loretz and J. Sanmartín. *Die keilalphabetischen Texte aus Ugarit; Einschliesslich der keilalphabetischen Texte ausserhalb Ugarits. Teil 1. Transkription*. AOAT 24/1. Kevelaer: Verlag Butzon & Bercker; Neukirchen-Vluyn: Neukirchener Verlag, 1976.

KU H. L. Ginsberg. *Kitve ʾUgarit*. Jerusalem: The Bialik Foundation, 1936.

Lane E. W. Lane. *An Arabic-English Lexicon*. In eight parts. London: Williams and Norgate, 1863-1893. Reprinted, Beirut: Librairie du Liban, 1968.

LAPO Littératures anciennes du Proche-Orient.

LC[1]	J. Gray. *The Legacy of Canaan*. First ed. SVT 5. Leiden: Brill, 1957.
LC[2]	J. Gray. *The Legacy of Canaan*. Sec. ed. SVT 5. Leiden: Brill, 1965.
Leslau	W. Leslau. *Comparative Dictionary of Geᶜez (Classical Ethiopic)*. Wiesbaden: O. Harrassowitz, 1987.
LS	C. Brockelmann. *Lexicon Syriacum*. Sec. ed. Göttingen: Max Niemeyer, 1928.
MARI	*Mari Annales de Recherches Interdisciplinaires*
MLC	G. del Olmo Lete. *Mitos y leyendas de Canaan segun la Tradicion de Ugarit*. Institucion San Jeronimo para la Ciencia Biblica 1. Madrid: Ediciones Cristiandad, 1981.
NJPS	*TANAKH* תנ״ך *The Holy Scriptures; The New JPS Translation According to the Traditional Hebrew Text*. Philadelphia/New York/Jerusalem: The Jewish Publication Society, 1988.
PE	Eusebius. *Praeparatio evangelica*, cited according to Attridge and Oden 1981.
PRU III	J. Nougayrol. *Le palais royal d'Ugarit. Vol. III*. Paris: Imprimerie Nationale, 1955.
PRU IV	J. Nougayrol. *Le palais royal d'Ugarit. Vol. IV*. Paris: Imprimerie Nationale, 1956.
PTU	F. Gröndahl. *Die Personnamen der Texte aus Ugarit*. Studia Pohl 1. Rome: Päpstliches Bibelinstitut, 1967.
PU 1 and 2	K. Aartun. *Die Partikeln des Ugaritischen*. Two vols. AOAT 21/1 and 21/2. Kevalaer: Verlag Butzon & Bercker; Neukirchen-Vluyn: Neukirchener Verlag, 1974, 1978.
RAI	Rencontre Assyriologique Internationale
RDAC	Reports of the Department of Antiquities of Cyprus
RHA	*Revue hittite et asianique*
RSP III	*Ras Shamra Parallels III; the Texts from Ugarit and the Hebrew Bible*. Ed. S. Rummel. AnOr 51. Rome: Pontifical Biblical Institute, 1981.
SPUMB	J. C. de Moor. *The Seasonal Pattern in the Ugaritic Myth of Baᶜlu; According to the Version of Ilimilku*. AOAT 16. Kevelaer: Butzon & Bercker; Neukirchen-Vluyn: Neukirchener Verlag des Erziehungsvereins, 1971.

SEL — *Studi Epigrafici e Linguistici*

Thespis — T. H. Gaster, *Thespis; Ritual, Myth, and Drama in the Ancient Near East*. New York: Norton, 1977.

TO — A. Caquot, M. Sznycer and A. Herdner. *Textes ougaritiques I. Mythes et legendes*. LAPO 7. Paris: Editions du Cerf, 1974.

UgM — J. Obermann. *Ugaritic Mythology; A Study of its Leading Motifs*. New Haven: Yale University, 1948.

Ug V — J. Nougayrol, E. Laroche, C. Virolleaud and C. F. A. Schaeffer. *Ugaritica V*. Mission de Ras Shamra XVI. Paris: Imprimerie Nationale/Librairie orientaliste Paul Geuthner, 1968.

Ug VII — C. F. A. Schaeffer et al. *Ugaritica VII*. Mission de Ras Shamra XVII. Paris: Paul Geuthner; Leiden: Brill, 1978.

UH — C. H. Gordon. *Ugaritic Handbook*. AnOr 25. Rome: Pontifical Biblical Institute, 1947.

UL — C. H. Gordon. *Ugaritic Literature; A Comprehensive Translation of the Poetic and Prose Texts*. Scripta Pontificii Instituti Biblici 98. Rome: Pontifical Biblical Institute, 1949.

UM — C. H. Gordon. *Ugaritic Manual*. AnOr 35. Rome: Pontifical Biblical Institute, 1955.

UT — C. H. Gordon. *Ugaritic Textbook*. AnOr 38. Rome: Pontifical Biblical Institute, 1965.

V — Virolleaud's *editio princeps* cited in textual notes.

WdM — H. W. Haussig. *Götter und Mythen im Vorderen Orient*. Wörterbuch der Mythologie I. Stuttgart: Ernst Klett, 1965.

Wehr — H. Wehr. *A Dictionary of Modern Written Arabic*. Ed. J. M. Cowan. Third edition. Ithaca, NY: Spoken Languages Services, 1976.

Wright — W. Wright. *A Grammar of the Arabic Language; translated from the German of Caspari and edited with numerous additions and corrections*. Two vols. Third edition. Rev. W. R. Smith and M. J. de Goeje. Cambridge: At the University Press, 1898.

WSRP — West Semitic Research Project of the University of Southern California.

WUS	J. Aistleitner. *Wörterbuch der ugaritischer Sprache*. Ed. O. Eissfeldt. Third ed. Berlin: Akademie-Verlag, 1967.
YGC	W. F. Albright. *Yahweh and the Gods of Canaan; A Historical Analysis of Two Contrasting Faiths*. Winona Lake, IN: Eisenbrauns, 1990. Originally published in 1968.

II. Terms

1. Languages and Dialects

Akk	Akkadian
Aram	Aramaic
Arb	Arabic
BH	Biblical Hebrew
ESA	Epigraphic South Arabic
Heb.	Modern Hebrew
MA	Middle Assyrian
MB	Middle Babylonian
NA	Neo-Assyrian
NB	Neo-Babylonian
OB	Old Babylonian
PS	Proto-Semitic
Syr	Syriac
Ug	Ugaritic
WS	West Semitic

2. Grammatical Terms

acc.	accusative case
C	causative stem (BH "hiphil")
cst.	construct state
D	double stem (BH "piel")
DN	divine name
Dt	double stem with *-t* reflexive or reciprocal (BH "hithpael")
fem.	feminine gender
G	ground or simple stem (BH "qal")
GN(s)	geographical name(s)
Gt	ground stem with *-t* reflexive or reciprocal
impf.	imperfect or prefix tense
impv.	imperative
inf.	infinitive

masc. masculine gender
N *N*-stem (BH "niphal")
p person
pass. passive voice
perf. perfect or suffix tense
pl. plural
PN(s) proper names(s)
prep. preposition
ptcp. participle
sg. singular
Št causative stem with -*t* reflexive or reciprocal

3. Other Terms

ANE ancient Near East or ancient Near Eastern
EA El-Amarna (cited according to Moran 1992)
LXX Septuagint
MT Masoretic Text
n(n). footnote(s)
RIH Ras ibn-Hani (text number)
RS Ras Shamra (text number)

III. Sigla

ʾ ʾaleph
ḏ Ugaritic sign 16 (see Fronzaroli 1955:24-30; Greenfield 1969:95)
ʿ ʿayin
ǵ ǵhain
v unknown vowel in vocalized text
* hypothetical form or root
/ ° / remains of an unidentified letter
/ x / remains of an identified letter
⟨ ⟩ restored letters
// parallel words or lines

PREFACE

The Story of the Baal Cycle

Greatest Astarte and Zeus, called both Demarous and Adodos, king of gods, were ruling over the land with the consent of Kronos.

With these words the late classical work, *The Phoenician History* attributed to Philo of Byblos[1] characterizes the political harmony in the West Semitic pantheon. Astarte and Baal, here called Zeus, jointly exercised power over the universe under the aegis of El identified in this text as Kronos. With the consent of El, the revered executive over the pantheon, Astarte and Baal ruled, the latter in the words of Philo, as "king of the gods." Philo of Byblos describes a peaceful rule which followed a divine struggle for kingship over the pantheon and the cosmos. The one extant indigenous source that details this struggle for kingship among the West Semitic gods is the Ugaritic Baal Cycle. This myth comes from the city of Ugarit, modern Ras Shamra, which lies near Latakia on the Syrian coast, approximately a hundred miles north of Beirut. It was during the first half of the fourteenth century that the extant form of the Baal Cycle, one of the classics of ancient literature, was committed to writing.

The six tablets[2] of the Baal Cycle[3] present a vivid story of conflict and kingship, love and death. The first two tablets present the battle of the storm-god Baal with his enemy, Yamm, whose name literally means "Sea." The next two tablets recount how Baal's palace, the mark of his kingship, came to be built. The last two tablets describe Baal's struggle against Mot, whose name means "Death." The god Athtar is also mentioned in two interludes as a possible rival to Baal. These four deities are warrior-gods who rule different realms of the universe: Baal, the god of the storm; Athtar, the god of the stars who

---

1 PE 1.10.31; Oden and Attridge 1981:55.

2 See pp. 2-15. The enumeration of Ugaritic texts in this volume follows KTU which employs four numbers for any given textual citation: first, according to the type of text; second, according to the number of the tablet in that classification; third, according to the column of that tablet; and finally, according to the line number in that column. The Baal Cycle belongs to the first group of texts in KTU, specifically the mythological or literary texts; it constitutes the first text of this group, and it comprises six tablets. Its number in KTU is therefore KTU 1.1 through 1.6, and its columns are cited in Roman numerals followed by line numbers.

3 The ancient name of this work is unknown except in the form of the superscription to 1.6 I 1, *lbˁl*, "concerning Baal," hence the modern name "the Baal Cycle.

is perhaps considered a natural irrigator[4]; Yamm, the god of the sea; and Mot, the god of the underworld (Gaster 1950:121-30; Smith 1985:115). Other deities take part in various parts of the narrative. El, the older king and executive over the pantheon, and Athirat, his wife and mother of the pantheon or "queen-mother" in Handy's formulation (1990:20), rule their divine family which is represented in narrow terms as "the seventy sons of Athirat" or in wider terms as the divine assembly patterned after the human royal council.[5] This older divine couple is generally construed as the parents of the pantheon who mediate the struggle among their sons making rival claims to the divine throne. The other characters in the cycle manifest other aspects of nature and society: Kothar, the middle-level specialist who serves other deities with his craftsmanship which includes spells (Smith 1985:464); Shapshu, the divine messenger who mediates among the rival claimants and travels between the realms of life and death; and Astarte and Anat, Baal's warrior allies.[6] The names of two of Baal's three women (*ʾaṯtm*) and "brides" (*klt*), Tallay ("Dewy") and Pidray ("Flashy"?) reflect their meteorological kinship with Baal, while the name of Arsay ("Earthy" or "Netherworldly"[7]) may evidence her chthonic relationship to him. The unnamed messengers of Yamm as well as Baal's messengers named Gpn w-Ugr, and Athirat's messengers, Qdš w-Amrr, occupy the lowest level of divine society (Smith 1984b). Based largely but not exclusively on the Baal Cycle, Handy (1990) sees four levels of rank among these deities: (i) highest

---

[4] For a survey of the evidence, see Excursus 3 (pp. 240-50) below.

[5] It is under the wider definition that Baal refers to El as "my father," although Baal bears the title *bn dgn*, "son of Dagan." For the issue of Baal's paternity, see pp. 91-94 below. For further definition of the family of El and Athirat, see pp. 92-93 below.

[6] Anat is also called Baal's sister. For discussion of Anat, see pp. 195-96 n. 147, 205, 311. For Astarte, see pp. 278-79, 311. It is often assumed that Anat and Astarte are also consorts of Baal, but this view of Anat has been disputed by P. L. Day (1991: 141-46; 1992:181-90) and Walls (1992:145-46). While both scholars note the absence of explicit sexual relations between Baal and Anat in clearly understood Ugaritic texts, Anat and Astarte are viewed as Seth's wives (*ANET* 15). This relationship may reflect a West Semitic association of these goddesses with Baal and may complicate the view of Day and Walls. The relevance of this evidence has been accordingly challenged by both Day and Walls following Te Velde (1977:29-30) since otherwise Anat is not called the consort of Seth. The very uniqueness of the rendering may militate in favor of its authenticity, however.

[7] See p. 72 for the evidence.

authority (El and Athirat); (ii) major active gods which form what Handy calls the managerial stratum of the cosmos (Baal, Yamm, Mot); (iii) craft-gods who have a "specialist responsibility" acknowledged and used by superiors in the divine organization (Kothar); and (iv) messenger deities. While the Ugaritic pantheon included a large host of other deities, the Baal Cycle shows a limited cast of characters in rendering its story of divine struggle.

The construction of the cosmos as represented by the divine abodes reflects aspect of their inhabitants. El's abode is cast in cosmic terms without explicit terrestrial referent.[8] As the wife of El, Athirat is not accorded a separate abode. Baal's abode is located on the mountain that receives the greatest rainfall in Syria.[9] His three "women" presumably live with him, although prior to receiving his own "palace," Baal and his three women apparently dwell with El and Athirat (KTU 1.3 IV 48-53, V 38-44, 1.4 I 9-18, IV 52-57). Mot dwells in the Underworld. Perhaps in accordance with his function as natural irrigator Athtar may live on earth.[10] Yamm presumably lives in the sea, although this fact is never made explicit. Anat's home is described in terrestrial terms in 1.3 II, although the text does not explicitly locate this palace at Inbb, the name of her mountain given elsewhere. Kothar's abodes at Memphis and Kaphtor may reflect trade in materials for crafts such as metals or trade in materials produced by crafts.[11] In sum, the Baal Cycle presents a royal society, with different deities and their abodes showing various aspects of the world known to the culture of ancient Ugarit.

For decades scholars have rightly emphasized the kingship of Baal as the main theme of the cycle. This volume modifies the general scholarly view of the cycle in three major ways. The first is to extend the political understanding of the text. It is well-known that political language dominates the Baal Cycle, but it should be recognized that the Baal Cycle presents the universe as a single political reality connecting different levels. This political reality of Baal's rule integrates three levels, cosmic, human and natural. First, the Baal Cycle concentrates on the interaction of the deities in the larger cosmos. Ritual texts and other mythological works involve deities, but no other text

---

8 See below pp. 230-31.
9 See below pp. 122-23.
10 See below pp 240-50.
11 See below p. 167.

focuses so strongly on the Ugaritic deities and the larger cosmos as the Baal Cycle. Second, the political events in the Baal Cycle reflect a concern for human society. The ramifications of Baal's struggles on humanity are occasionally expressed in the text. Indeed, the divine struggles represent life and death for Ugarit's society.[12] According to Mosca (1986:506-07), the Baal Cycle recapitulates the story of human life itself: "Even the individual life-cycle mirrors the myth's movement: before life, chaos; after life, death. This pattern, too, is built into the myth."[13] The struggles of Baal mirror the struggles of humanity against the vicissitudes of a dangerous world, but his victories re-invigorate not only the world of the divine pantheon but also human society. The dangers and defeats, the victories and the glories described on the divine level serve to give a religio-political interpretation of human experience. Third, the Baal Cycle uses natural phenomena, especially lightning, thunder and rains to underscore the political power of Baal the Storm-god. Through Baal's struggles for power, the Baal Cycle interrelates humanity, nature and divinity, and thereby yields an integrated political vision of chaos, life and death. As Kinet (1978:238) remarks, "Der Baᶜal-Zyklus birgt eine mythologische Deutung der Wirklichkeit, in der der Ugariter lebt." Finally, it is to be observed that given the extent and depth of martial language attributed to the West Semitic storm-god in human political texts outside of Ugarit, it seems quite plausible to stress the Baal Cycle's political importance and perhaps to suggest a political setting for the background of the Baal Cycle and its transmission.

The second modification concerns the general view of Baal in the cycle. Baal has often been compared with the powerful figures of Marduk in Enuma Elish and Yahweh in the Hebrew Bible, but the differences among these three deities are as significant as their similarities. Indeed, the Baal Cycle does not render the West Semitic storm-god in the exalted terms reserved for Marduk or Yah-

---

[12] Cf. Buckert's remarks (1979:98): "...civilized man, and monarchy, and warfare are not self-sufficient, as man is not the only representative of life; if he has managed to achieve dominance, this is by a violent tour de force, hope transcending the desperate borders of factuality."

[13] In this connection it may be noted Erich Neumann, a disciple of Carl G. Jung, interpreted some features in the Baal Cycle in terms of psychological development. See Neumann 1970:74, 97,160, 179; and p. 75 below.

weh. Nor does the Baal Cycle construe Baal as a champion who vanquishes his enemies for all time. Rather, Baal acquires a limited kingship and not primarily through his own exploits, but mostly thanks to the aid of other deities. His foes loom large not only in a single combat, but in repeated engagements, and without definitive outcomes. The threat of their return is never overcome entirely, at least in the case of Mot, and perhaps their return was as expected as the annual return of Baal's rains. Baal's kingship is indeed finite, won despite his own limitations and perhaps the limitations of the great deities as well. The cosmos of Baal's kingship is a universe nurturing life wondrously, but precariously. This universe is frequently, if not usually, overshadowed by chaos, the transient character of life and finally death. In its powerful vision of reality and its aesthetic accomplishment, the Baal Cycle is the greatest example of West Semitic myth.

The third scholarly view which requires correction involves the relationship between the Baal Cycle and the Hebrew Bible. Apart from its own importance, the Baal Cycle is central to the study of Syro-Palestinian religious literature in the Bronze and Iron Ages (2200-587 B. C. E.). The Baal Cycle manifests many of the religious ideas contained in the Hebrew Bible. Indeed, it may be said that the Baal Cycle expresses the heart of the West Semitic religion from which Israelite religion largely developed (Smith 1990:xxii-xxiv, 1-7). The original god of Israel was probably El (Smith 1990:7). Two deities, Baal and Athirat, who play major roles in the Baal Cycle, were worshipped and condemned in ancient Israel, according to 1 Kings 18 and other biblical passages. The depictions of Yahweh as enthroned king in Isaiah 6 and Daniel 7, or stormy warrior-god in Psalm 18 = 2 Samuel 22, resemble depictions of El and Baal respectively in the Baal Cycle (*CMHE* 13-75, 145-94). Many of the type-scenes and literary formulas in the Bible are found in the Baal Cycle (*BOS* 16-109). Several renderings of deities and literary features of the West Semitic milieu reflected in the Baal Cycle passed into ancient Israelite culture described by the Hebrew Bible and then into the New Testament and other Jewish works of the Second Temple period (6th century B. C. E. to 1st century C. E.). Numerous features of western civilization have their roots in West Semitic literature, best represented in its premier exemplar, the Baal Cycle. The message of peace of Christmas night, the heavenly banquet of the Last Supper, the depiction of God as "my heavenly father," the beast of Revelation and many other features familiar from the New Testament and rabbinic literature stem from a long history which includes the Baal Cycle.

The closing chapters of Revelation provide a glimpse of the future which recalls the three major themes of Baal's defeat of Yamm, the building of the heavenly palace for Baal, and his conflict with Mot. In the words of Rev 21:1-4,

> Then I saw a new heaven and a new earth; for the first heaven and the first earth had passed away, and the sea was no more. And I saw the holy city, new Jerusalem, coming down out of heaven from God, prepared as a bride adorned for her husband; and I heard a great voice from the throne saying, "Behold, the dwelling of God is with people. He will dwell with them, and they will be his people, and God himself will be with them; he will wipe every tear from their eyes, and death shall be no more, neither shall there be mourning nor crying nor pain anymore, for the former things have passed away.

This passage includes the death of Sea, the descent of the heavenly city and the final destruction of Death. The Baal Cycle describe a similar sequence, specifically Baal's defeat of Yamm, Baal's enthronement in his heavenly palace, and his battle against Mot. In both Rev 21:1-4 and the Baal Cycle these events issue in the rejuvenation of the earth and the proximity of divine presence. Baal assumes residence in his temple producing the rains which refructify the world. In Revelation 21 divine proximity is represented by the divine presence dwelling in the temple-city which signals the transformation of the world. It is no exaggeration to suggest that early forms of many, if not most, formative religious concepts of the western civilization may be found in the Baal Cycle.

Despite the importance of the Baal Cycle for biblical studies, this work and other Ugaritic texts have suffered in the assessment of at least a few biblical scholars, largely because of their personal convictions. The religious sentiments of U. Oldenburg (*CEBCR* xi) perhaps prevented him from appreciating the greatness of a Ugaritic work such as the Baal Cycle:

> That which impelled me to begin the study of Canaanite religion was my desire to investigate its relationship to Hebrew religion, to see whether the faith of Yahweh was a product of the soil of the Canaanite religion. The more I studied pre-Israelite religion, the more I was amazed with its utter depravity and wickedness. Indeed there was *nothing* in it to inspire the sublime faith of Yahweh. His coming is like the rising sun dispelling the darkness of Canaanite superstitition. (Oldenburg's italics)

As this quotation indicates, the Baal Cycle and other Ugaritic texts have served in the imagination of some biblical scholars as a foil to the advent of "true" Israelite monotheism. Indeed, this approach to Ugaritic literature replicates an older "scholarly" denigration of post-exilic Israelite religion. Mendenhall's work, *The Tenth Generation* (1973:226) impugns both post-exilic Judaism and the West Semitic religion of the Late Bronze Age in exalting both biblical prophecy and Christianity.[14] This attitude is unwarranted in the work of religious historians, especially as it may be argued that the Baal Cycle presents as deep and rich a religious vision of human existence as any biblical book.

This study represents the first volume of a commentary on the Baal Cycle, and it is my hope that it will contribute to a deeper appreciation of this work both on its own terms and in its relations to the Bible. A further goal of this work is to overcome the largely atomistic fashion of studying the Baal Cycle. Study of the Baal Cycle has long focused primarily on philological concerns, an understandable emphasis given the enormous etymological difficulties which Ugaritic literature presents. Apart from notable exceptions such as de Moor's *SPUMB* and van Zijl's *Baal*, longer works treating the whole of the Baal Cycle have been generally lacking. Studies dealing with the literary themes or structures of the Baal Cycle are conspicuous for their absence, except for del Olmo Lete's comments on the Baal Cycle (*MLC*). This first volume of this commentary contains the introduction and treatment of the first two tablets (KTU 1.1-1.2). A further volume(s) will address the other four tablets (KTU 1.3-1.6).

The Format of This Volume

This study follows the format of biblical commentaries in a number of ways. These are main features of this volume:

1. Introduction

Addressed in this section are general matters including the date of the tablets, their order, the development of the cycle, its literary classification, and the history of its interpretation with a critical assessment.

---

[14] I wish to thank Professor David Owen for bringing this passage to my attention.

2. Bibliography for each column

The study of each column begins with a bibliography of text editions, studies and translations.

3. Text

The readings of the text are based on a comparison of several sources: Virolleaud's *editio princeps* (cited as V); CTA and KTU; previously unpublished photographs of KTU 1.1 and 1.2 produced by Professor Bruce Zuckerman of the University of Southern California, director of the West Semitic Research Project (WSRP); and 20.5 hours spent on examining the originals (with two magnifying lenses) housed in the Département des Antiquités Orientales of the Louvre.

The siglum ° over a letter indicates a damaged but visible wedge. Damage consists generally of two sorts, either the loss of part of the sign in a lacuna or damage to the surface of the tablet. The siglum ° with no sign beneath it indicates the attestation of a wedge of a letter which cannot be identified. In contrast to the format of Virolleaud, CTA and KTU, spaces have not been placed between words (including those with proclitics or enclitics). Emendations are not made in the text, but are recorded in the textual notes and reflected in the vocalized texts. Reconstructions have been held to a relative minimum and have been based on generally accepted parallels.

4. The Textual Notes

It is my goal to present a minimal text which may serve as the reliable basis for interpretation and to inform readers as to the relative reliability or unreliability of different readings. The brief descriptions of the epigraphical views concerning the readings of signs may enable readers to appreciate the complexities involved. The textual notes survey the opinions of Virolleaud's *editio princeps* of each text, CTA, KTU, and less frequently the views of other scholars (e.g., *UT*, *SPUMB*, *CML*[2] and *MLC*). Further observations are made on the basis of comparison of the WSRP photographs with the originals in the Louvre. The remarks frequently refer to these photographs which have been produced as plates at the end of this volume. Disputes over reading word-dividers are not easily resolved, as they represent one of the greatest sources of diagreement among the editions. Some comments are made on the epigraphy of word-dividers in KTU 1.1 and 1.2, but readers may consult Horwitz 1972 for further details (see also Horwitz 1973).

For a number of reasons this edition of the text does not represent a marked advance. First, the tablets have suffered deterioration, and as a result some readings given by Virolleaud, CTA and KTU cannot be seen. This fact is especially evident in cases where Virolleaud was able to see more wedges than subsequent epigraphers. Second, the scholars who undertook these editions had far more experience with Ugaritic epigraphy than I do, and as a result, their readings represent an important witness even in cases where my readings differ. Third, the readings and the various proposed reconstructions could have been discussed at considerably greater length. Readers interested in pursuing less likely readings and reconstructions may consult *MLC*. Finally, due to my lack of drawing ability, this edition does not contain drawings which have rightly become *de rigeur* for the epigraphy of Ugaritic tablets.

5. *Translation*

Translations of Ugaritic texts have varied in style. Ginsberg's translation of the Baal Cycle (*ANET*) renders the archaic, epic flavor of the original. Coogan (1981) presents the cycle in a polished prose. Pope's translations, scattered throughout his articles and biblical commentaries, customarily keep the English translation as terse as the Ugaritic original. Parker (1990b:262-63) recommends that translations be rendered in traditional English meter. These translations are to be neither colloquial nor archaic. Rather, they should translate the picture, activity, idea or mood conveyed in a group of words (as opposed to word-for-word translations), and express the tension associated with great poetry.

A wooden translation has been avoided in this volume. Rather, a direct and terse translation has been attempted in order to form a bridge between the original text and modern readers. In passages where a word-for-word translation especially fails the original, I have tried to heed Parker's call for a translation which conveys the overall effect produced by groups of words. Parker calls also for a metrical translation. It has been argued that meter is not a feature of Ugaritic poetry (Pardee 1981a), and it is not clear that its reproduction in translation is the most appropriate means of rendering the original. The translation in this volume follows the generally recognized canons of Ugaritic poetry, namely various types of parallelism and terseness of lines (see Pardee 1988d). Furthermore, an attempt has been made to capture some of the paranomasia of the original. Finally, unlike Parker, I sense that the Baal Cycle was somewhat archaic to its audience. This view may be more intuitive than not, but some grammatical features seem to point in this direction.[15]

The words of Novalis (Friedrich von Hardenberg) in his Pollen (no. 68) capture the task facing the translator:

> A translation is either grammatical, transforming, or mythic. Mythic translations are translations of the highest sort. They realize the purest, most perfect character of the individual work of art. There does not yet exist, I believe, a complete model of this. . . It calls for a mind that has been permeated by the poetic spirit and the philosophic spirit to their full extent. . . Grammatical translations are translations in the ordinary sense. They require much scholarship but only discursive qualities. What is called for in the transforming translations if they are to be authentic is the highest poetic spirit. . . The true translator of this kind must in fact be the artist himself, capable of realizing the idea of the whole at will, in one way or another—He must be the poet of the poet, and thus capable of letting him speak in accord with his and the poet's own idea at the same time.

While this standard is impossible to achieve, it remains a goal, nonetheless. If it cannot be achieved in translation, it is sought more fully in the commentary; and if neither translation nor commentary "transforms" readers, then it is my hope that through the rest of this work readers may at least sense and appreciate the vast mythic world lying within and behind the translation.

A few matters of format and style in the translation should be mentioned. Line numbers appear at the left-hand side of the translation. This format departs from the custom of many editions of Ugaritic texts, which place line numbers at the precise points in the translation corresponding to the beginning of lines in the original text. Furthermore, the translation in this volume delimits major sections within a column by headings intended to indicate the plot for

---

[15] For the possibility of archaic language in the Baal Cycle, see below p. 36-58.

readers. These headings have been set in bold print to distinguish them from the translations. I have indented lines where parallelism between lines is clear in order to indicate the division of passages into bicolas (two-line poetic units) and tricolas (three-line units). Where the parallelism is unclear, no indentation has been made in the translation. Although the problem of "tense" in verbs in poetic narrative has not been resolved fully, verbs in narrative are rendered in the English historical present, as the present-future prefix form is the dominant one used in Ugaritic poetic narrative.[16]

6. Vocalized Texts

For those columns which are not too damaged, namely 1.1 III, 1.1 II, 1.2 III, 1.2 I and 1.2 IV, a vocalized text has been provided next to the translation. Texts that are very damaged, specifically 1.1 V, 1.1 IV and 1.2 II, remain unvocalized. This difference in format creates some inconsistency, but it is my hope that such inconsistency will be worth the gain provided by vocalizations. The *Ugaritica V* polyglot lists, Ugaritic loanwords into Akkadian texts from Ras Shamra and the three forms of ʾ in Ugaritic[17] provide information about the syllabic forms of Ugaritic words. Because of these sources, vocalizing texts involves more than comparing the syllabic formation of cognate words in other Semitic languages. There are, however, many hazards involved in vocalizing Ugaritic texts,[18] and I do not pretend that the vocalizations presented in this volume approximate the speech of the inhabitants of ancient Ugarit. Indeed, sometimes individual words cannot be vocalized with confidence. In some instances footnotes explain the vocalization. A lower case $_v$ (for vowel) is supplied to indicate the likelihood of the presence of a vowel although it is unknown which vowel is involved. Similarly, many passages cannot be vocalized with confidence, and readers will realize this fact by noting those lines in the translation which lack a corresponding vocalized text. KTU 1.1 III and II, while quite broken, have parallels elsewhere, and can be vocalized partially.

---

16 See below pp. 39-41.

17 For the first two categories, see Huehnergard 1987b. For the "three ʾalephs," see Marcus 1968. For further discussion of particulars, see notes to the vocalizations.

18 See the cautionary remarks of *CMHE* 21 n. 50; Pope 1977:181-82 n. 90; Pardee 1978b:75 n. 5, 1988d:1; Tuttle 1978:253-68.

KTU 1.2 I and IV are in better shape and are provided with vocalizations.

Despite the obvious and insurmountable problems facing vocalizations of Ugaritic texts, there are four advantages to presenting a vocalized text with a translation. First, it makes the commentary easier to follow. The vocalized text and translation can be read together as readers peruse the commentary. Second, a vocalized text makes explicit the grammatical analysis underlying the translations. Third, it indicates to an imperfect degree the assonance in each colon. While the assonance represented in a vocalized text remains purely theoretical, for the purpose of sensing the poetry a vocalized text appears preferable to a text without vowels. Indeed, the vocalization of a text read and heard many times may echo, albeit imperfectly, the great beauty of the original and may permit a deeper appreciation of its sonant quality. Fourth, a vocalized text provides readers with a general indication as to its difficulty.

7. Commentary

The commentary for each vocalized column begins with a poetic analysis consisting of a vocalization of each colon, followed first by a scanning of semantic parallelism (indicated by lower case letters) and then by word and syllable counts. The scanning of semantic parallelism renders construct phrases as a single unit, but where construct phrases in a second or third line correspond to a single word in the previous line within a colon, the siglum "x + y" is given in parentheses, following the practice of Pardee (1988d:9, 77-78). While the sigla for parallelism includes both grammatical and semantic parallelism (cf. Pardee 1988d:9-10 n. 15), some of the more distinctive features of grammatical parallelism are indicated in the remarks which follow the word and syllable counts.

The word and syllable counts indicate the length of lines within a colon. At times, a word count may be misleading in suggesting an imbalance in the length of lines in a colon, but the syllable count in the same colon not infrequently corrects this misimpression. The word count remains valuable, since the syllable count depends on the vocalization and is therefore purely theoretical. Some remarks bearing on various sorts of parallelism—syntactical, morphological and sonant (Hrushovski 1971:1201-02; Berlin 1985; Greenstein 1986-87)—often follow the presentation of cola, although syntactical parallelism is not treated according to any specific system. Rather, it has been my interest to indicate how these sorts of parallelism may bind and contrast lines of cola, especially in the absence of apparent semantic parallelism.

Berlin's treatment of sound pairs has advanced the understanding of sonant parallelism, and her definition of a sound pair (Berlin 1985:104; Berlin's italics) is followed in this volume: "*the repetition in parallel words or lines of the same or similar consonants in any order within close proximity*." Observations regarding various links between cola in this commentary are based more specifically on three criteria used by Berlin to delimit sonant parallelism (Berlin 1985:105): (i) "at least two sets of consonants must be involved"; (ii) "the sets must be in close proximity, within a word or adjacent words in both lines"; and (iii) "'same or similar consonant' means the identical phoneme, an allophone..., or two phonemes which are articulated similarly". I have not exhausted the observations which might be made about poetic features on the colonic and super-colonic levels in the meticulous manner presented by Pardee (1988d). Without denying the value of Pardee's approach, I have attempted instead to identify distinctive features especially within cola (see Berlin 1985:130-40; Parker 1990a:504). Furthermore, it is occasionally possible to suggest how formal features may affect the understanding of the content. They may shape the perspective given to the content or suggest further meaning. In these instances one may sense the performative character of the poetic medium. Indeed, the poetry of the Baal Cycle is sometimes so passionate and imaginative that even modern minds molded by sensibilities so distant from ancient Ugarit may be profoundly moved.

The poetic analysis is followed by some overall contextual remarks (labelled as "Introduction"). The commentary then presents detailed exegesis. The smallest unit of interpretation is the word followed in complexity by the syntax of a phrase; the clause; the sentence (often equivalent to a line); the colon (of which there are three general types, the monocolon, the bicolon and the tricolon); multi-cola units; and the larger setting of narrative or direct speech. Within these various units of length are other indicators of meaning: formulas varying in intricacy, form-critical elements, type-scenes, the intertextual relationships with other passages.[19] Each of the

[19] Ginsberg 1948:139; Parker 1989b:7-59; Fisher, *RSP III* 253, 260 n. 16; Whitaker, *RSP III* 209-11.

units of length and other features provide insights as well as check and balances on interpretation. In short, there is no philology without literary analysis; in turn, literary analysis has no foundation without sound philology. Literary structures and form-critical elements are noted in the section-by-section commentary which correspond to the divisions made in the translation.

Detailed philological notes for some words appear in the commentary proper. Otherwise, they have been relegated to footnotes to the translation when philological discussions are judged not to be central to the commentary. Readers will find further available philological options not discussed in this volume provided either in the notes of Caquot and Sznycer (*TO*), Cassuto (*GA*), de Moor (1988), the glossaries of *UT* and del Olmo Lete (*MLC*), the monographs of de Moor (*SPUMB*) and van Zijl (*Baal*), the list of Pardee (1987c; cf. 1980), or the many other studies provided in the bibliography for each column. It seems unnecessary to duplicate the philological information given in all of these works. Indeed, it appears misguided to list every proposed etymology, although a limited number of sound philological suggestions is obviously necessary in order to clarify a passage. The philological discussions in this commentary tend toward the scholarly consensus and avoid highly irregular interpretations although many of these are noted in the commentary. The context of a word, whether it involves the syntax of the line, the parallelism within a colon, or the fixed expression or *topos* or even its usage elsewhere within Ugaritic, represents the final determinant for suggested etymologies. While it is not always possible at this stage of knowledge to offer a solution which meets all the criteria suggested by the various levels of unit (line, colon, etc.), this standard remains the goal.

8. Bibliography

The bibliography at the end of this volume provides full documentation for the secondary sources cited in the text. The bibliography for Ugaritic studies is extensive,[20] and the Baal Cycle is no exception. The "social science" format is used for citing secondary literature,

---

[20] In general, see AOAT 21/1-5 for works up to 1971; for works after 1970, see the *Newsletter for Ugaritic Studies*.

thereby eliminating the need for many footnotes. The bibliography cited in this work indicates my great indebtness to the works of so many others.

9. Plates of Tablets

Photographs of the tablets appear at the end of this volume. The plates represent only a selection (which perhaps points to the need for published volumes of photographs for each tablet or group of tablets).

INTRODUCTION

The Data of the Tablets

The date of the tablets has been established by correlating textual and archaeological evidence. The colophon at the end of the Baal Cycle's sixth and final tablet, KTU 1.6 VI 54-58, mentions the name of king *nqmd*, supposedly Niqmaddu II, the contemporary of Amenophis IV and Shuppiluliuma I (Kitchen 1977; *SPUMB* 47).[1] According to Goetze (1975:6-19), Niqmaddu II reigned ca. 1380-1346. De Moor (*SPUMB* 47) proposes that the accessions of Niqmaddu II, Amenophis IV and Shuppiluliuma I may be calculated to approximately 1380. On the basis of this synchronization, de Moor argues that the extant tablets of the Baal Cycle may be dated more precisely to 1380-1360 (see Kinet 1981:67).[2] Other scholars prefer a wider range of 1400-1350, since the synchronization of the three monarchs' reigns may allow for a greater latitude in date (*CML*[1] 1; *CML*[2] 1).

The archaeological information pertaining to the tablets comports with a date in the first half of the fourteenth century. The tablets and fragments belonging to the Baal Cycle, generally regarded as KTU 1.1-1.6 (see the following section), were excavated between 1930 and 1933 from what has been called the "library of the High Priest," or scribal school situated between two temples, traditionally thought to belong to Baal and Dagan, which stand on the acropolis. The following synopsis indicates the relative provenance within the "library" and year of discovery of the six tablets[3]:

1.1: South-east, tranchée B 3, point topographique 9 at a depth of .65 cm (= point topographique 345). 1931.
1.2 I, II, IV: South-east, tranchée N 3, point topographique 3 at a depth of 2.10 cm, perhaps of the "terre ramenée" (= point topographique 203). 1931.

---

[1] There may have been more than two Ugaritic kings named *nqmd*, as the list of kings in KTU 1.113 contains many lacunas presumably containing the names of numerous unknown monarchs. Pardee (1988b:173) suggests that originally this text may have listed as many as fifty-two kings.

[2] For the dates of Amenophis' reign, given as 1379-1362, see Goetze 1975:7; cf. Astour 1989:5-9, 77.

[3] For this information, see Bordreuil and Pardee 1989:31, 32. See also Sasson 1981:89 n. 19; van Soldt 1991:212-20. The precise find sites were not published by Schaeffer (1956:252, fig. 216). On the basis of Schaeffer's excavation notebooks, Bordreuil and Pardee (1989) provide more precise information, at least for the first two tablets.

1.2 III: South-east, tranchée B 3, point topographique 3, 5, 7 at a depth of .30-.40 cm, perhaps of the "terre ramenée" (= point topographique 338, 343, 341). 1931.
1.3: South-east, tranchée C-E, K-L, point topographique 210-264. 1931.
1.4: North-east/South-east, tranchée C-E, K-L, point topographique 210-264. 1930/1931.
1.5: North-east/South-east, tranchée C-E, K-L, point topographique 210-264. 1930/1931.
1.6: North-east, tranchée C-E, K-L, point topographique 210-264. 1930/33.

Schaeffer (1956:252, fig. 216) stated that some of the tablets excavated in 1931 "were fixed in cement blocks from a demolished building; the blocks had been reused for buildings erected after the library." (Schaeffer 1932:22; North 1973:146 n. 114). De Vaux (1940:249; North 1973:146 n. 113) surmised that the tablets had been found in or near ash-layers dating to the first half of the fourteenth century.

The Order of the Tablets and their Narrative and Thematic Continuity

The initial issues facing the interpretation of the Baal Cycle involve the length of the cycle as well as the number, order and continuity of the tablets. It is presently impossible to determine the original length of the cycle. From the physical evidence of the tablets, Herdner's reconstructions of KTU 1.1-1.6 totalled about 1830 lines. Albright (1961:31) opined that "the Baal Epic contained at least 5,000 lines and perhaps even two or three times as much."[4]

The following chart produced by del Olmo Lete[5] represents a partial consensus of Ugaritic scholarship concerning the number and order of the tablets, KTU 1.1 – 1.6:

Herdner	1		2	3	4	5	6
Driver	1(+ 9?)		2	3	4	5	6
Jirku	1		2	3	4	5	6
van Zijl	1?		2	3	4	5	6
Gray	1?	2(+ 9?)		3	4	5	6

[4] It is unclear whether or not this estimate included tablets other than 1.1-1.6.
[5] *MLC* 83; cf. *Baal* 7; Vine 1965:277; cf. Fisher, *RSP III* 233.

Vine . . . . 1?	2(+ 9?)		3	4	5	6		
de Langhe	2	3	4	5	6			
Caquot-Sznycer	2	3	4	5	6			
Ginsberg 1	2(+ 8?)		4	3	5	6		
Cassuto 1	3	4	2	5	6			
Gordon . . . . . . 2(+ 9)		3 + 1(7)		4(+ 8)		5	6	
Kapelrud . . . . . 2(+ 9?)		3(+ 1?)		(7)	4(+ 8)		5	6
Rin . . . . 2(+ 9)		3 + 1(7)		4	5	6		
de Moor 3	1	2	4	5	6			
Gaster 2	4	5	6	3(+ 10)			1	
Løkkegaard . . . 7	3	2(+ 9)		4	5		6	
Aistleitner 5	6	3	1	4	2			

Attempts to assign other tablets (such as KTU 1.7 – 1.12) to the Baal Cycle have been generally rejected (*SPUMB* 3-8; *MLC* 81 – 88). KTU 1.7 – 1.12 contain material that overlaps with the Baal Cycle. For example, KTU 1.7 provides direct parallels with KTU 1.3 II-III. KTU 1.7 appears not to be a duplicate of 1.3 II-III, but a slightly different version written in a different hand (*SPUMB* 4; *MLC* 86). Dijkstra (1983:26 – 28) suggests that KTU 1.7 provides some parallels for reconstructing some of the lacunas in 1.3 II-III. KTU 1.8 likewise parallels parts of KTU 1.4 I, III, IV, V and VII (*SPUMB* 5; *MLC* 86) and, according to Dijkstra (1983:28-30), this tablet adds further information for lacunas in the Baal Cycle. There are a number of direct parallels between passages of the Baal Cycle and other texts (e.g., KTU 1.5 I 11-22 and 1.133), but these parallels do not indicate that 1.133 belongs to the extant text of the Baal Cycle (Pardee 1988b:160). Moreover, it is generally thought that the scribal hand of KTU 1.7 – 1.12 differs from that of *ʾilmlk* (usually called Ilimilku, but as or more likely Ilimalku[6]), the scribe of the extant texts of KTU 1.1 – 1.6.[7] Finally, it has been argued

---

[6] On the basis of the spelling *ma-al-ku* for "king" in the Ugaritica V polyglot, van Soldt (1991:21 n. 182) prefers to spell the name as Ilimalku. Van Soldt also observes (personal communication) that the only evidence from Ugarit for Ilimilku is the name of royal messenger *ᵖdinger—mil-ku* (*PRU IV*, 294:8), but "consonant-vowel-consonant signs like *MIL* can in principle be read with every possible vowel and *MIL* can therefore also be read, for example *mal*$_x$." All other syllabic spellings of names with *milku* belong to foreigners at Ugarit (e.g., Queen Ahat-milku). Ilimalku can be supported not only from the syllabic spelling *ma-al-ku* in the polyglot, but from other names (see *PTU* 157) including *[ᵖ] ʿaʾ-bi-ma-al-ku* in *PRU* VI, 79:17. I wish to thank Dr. Van Soldt for these points. On the background of this scribe, see van Soldt 1991:28-29.

[7] *SPUMB* 4-6; *Baal* 6-12; Sasson 1981:89 n. 19, 91-93; *MLC* 83-87.

that KTU 1.101 belongs to the Baal Cycle (Rummel 1978; de Moor 1987:1-2), but as Pardee (1988b:129 n. 20; 1989-90a:179) observes, this tablet does not resemble KTU 1.1-1.6. No material extant from 1.1-1.6 corresponds precisely to the text of 1.101.

The question of the degree to which KTU 1.1-1.6 represents a continuous narrative or a collection of texts lacking narrative continuity remains a controversial issue. The superscription, *lbᶜl*, in KTU 1.6 I 1[8] and the colophons at the end of KTU 1.4 and 1.6[9] would suggest that at least these texts were collected purposefully as a narrative concerning Baal.[10] The superscription *lbᶜl* indicates that Baal is the central topic of at least 1.6 (cf. *MLC* 89). There are, however, numerous lacunas in the cycle and there is certainly no proof of narrative continuity between KTU 1.1 and 1.2 or between KTU 1.2 and 1.3. Furthermore, some scholars doubt as well the continuity between KTU 1.3 and 1.4. which constitute variants of the same story.[11] Some scholars also view the cycle as three originally separate and discontinuous narratives, KTU 1.1–2, 1.3–1.4 and 1.5–1.6. The view of del Olmo Lete (1977:31) is not atypical. For him, KTU 1.1–1.6 constitutes the "basic cycle" of the myth, but it is not a "redactional unity." Rather, it is "a literary complex of similar compositions on either a subject or a character." Other commentators accept the narrative continuity of most of the cycle.[12] In order to evaluate the merits of these views, it is necessary to test the arguments about narrative continuity on a case-by-case basis.

1. First of all, no one questions the narrative continuity between KTU 1.5 and the larger fragment of 1.6.

2. The field of Ugaritic studies by and large accepts the narrative continuity of KTU 1.4 and 1.5.[13] Clifford (1984:189-191;

---

[8] *SPUMB* 1; Kinet 1981:66.

[9] The question of the relationship between the two fragments of 1.6, and its implications for this discussion, will await volume 2 of this work. My thanks go to Professor JoAnn Hackett, for urging caution on this question.

[10] Ginsberg 1950:159; Rainey 1969:127-129; *SPUMB* 181; Sasson 1981:91-92.

[11] Del Olmo Lete 1977:31; *MLC* 81-88; *Baal* 323-324; Clifford 1984:188-198.

[12] *UL* 9-11; *CML*[1] 10-21; Kapelrud 1952:135-45; *CML*[2] 2-3, 8, 14.

[13] *SPUMB* 1-2; *CML*[2] 10 n. 6; Gibson 1984:205; *MLC* 94-95; del Olmo Lete 1983:67-71; Kinet 1981:65; Fisher, *RSP III* 240.

1987:64), however, contests this view. His first argument is epigraphic in nature: there is not enough space in KTU 1.4 VIII for the length of description theoretically required before the commencement of KTU 1.5 I. KTU 1.5 I continues a message which Mot commands Gpn w-Ugr to deliver to their master, Baal. According to Clifford's count, the space required for continuity is approximately one hundred seventy-five letters. Yet the end of KTU 1.4 VIII can accommodate only one hundred and twenty-eight letters. It should be noted that Margalit (1980:87), from whom Clifford derives this argument, does not dismiss the narrative continuity between KTU 1.4 and 1.5, however. Abbreviated variants of speeches in the Baal Cycle vary in length, which jeopardizes the assumption that a speech and the following narrative describing the events mentioned in the speech are equal in length. One may compare KTU 1.1 III 10-16 with KTU 1.3 III 18-29 (the former omitting *ʾabn brq dl tdʿ šmm*); KTU 1.3 V 35-43 with KTU 1.4 I 4-18 and 1.4 IV 47-57 (the former omitting *mṯb klt knyt*); KTU 1.3 III 18-31 with 1.3 IV 11-20 (the latter omitting *bnʿm bgbʿ tlʾiyt*); and KTU 1.4 V 13-19 with 1.4 V 29-35 (the latter omitting *yblk ʾudr ʾilqṣm*). While these examples involve the omission of relatively few words, they demonstrate some variation in the repetition of passages. Either a great deal or little may transpire in a lacuna; how much material has been omitted cannot always be demonstrated only from parallel passages. Parallel passages indicate generally what events have transpired, but they do not show how many words or lines have been used to describe the events. This phenomenon might be invoked to account for the disparity between the number of letters for which there is space in KTU 1.4 VIII and the number of letters that Clifford argues is necessary.

There is a feature of 1.4 VIII which may explain better the disparity. De Moor (*SPUMB* 4-5) comments:

> The most interesting point is the fact that the double line after CTA 3:C.28 coincides with the beginning of a repetition of CTA 3.B.2ss in CTA 7. I venture to propose that by this double line Ilimilku wanted to indicate that he omitted a portion of standard text, in this case the repetition of CTA 3:B.2ss.
>
> A similar double line has been drawn between CTA 4.VIII.47 and 48. Of this column about 16 lines are broken off, about 14 of which may be supplied by CTA 5:I.14-27. From this it follows that between CTA 4:VIII.47 and 48 Ilimilku has omitted the transmission of the message of Baʿlu to Môtu by means of Gupanu and Ugaru (repetition of CTA 4:VII.55—VIII.46, *mutatis mutandis*).

> Finally, Ilimilku followed the same procedure after CTA 4:V.103, where he omitted the transmission of Baʿlu's message to Kôṯaru. In this particular case, however, he adds to the double line a specific direction...

This observation could explain the apparent disparity observed by Margalit and Clifford in the attempts to reconstruct the whole of Gpn w-Ugr's speech in the lacuna following 1.4 VIII.

Besides his epigraphic argument, Clifford advances a literary argument against the continuity between 1.4 and 1.5. He notes that KTU 1.5 I 1 displays signs of discontinuity with the preceding column especially in the use of the "when" (*k*-) opening of KTU 1.5 I 1, reminiscent of the opening of other "cosmogonies."[14] This fact might suggest that KTU 1.5-1.6 was originally a unit separate from KTU 1.4. It is clear from the ending of KTU 1.4 VIII and the rest of KTU 1.5 I, however, that this traditional way of opening "cosmogonies" has been reworked into a dialogue between Baal and Mot (transmitted through Baal's messengers). The word, "when" (*k*-), indicates that originally separate material may have been incorporated into a larger section of the Baal Cycle. Furthermore, the Baal-Mot section commences with KTU 1.4 VIII, not with KTU 1.5 I, as is commonly asserted, which would suggest that *k*- in 1.5 I 1 does not represent a formal break in narrative.

Finally, Clifford adduces a thematic argument against the narrative continuity between KTU 1.4 and 1.5. Clifford suggests that the reversal from Baal's victorious status in KTU 1.4 VIII to his defensive posture in KTU 1.5 I represents too abrupt a shift for there to be narrative continuity between the two columns. This assessment is a matter of opinion. It might be argued that there is nothing too abrupt or illogical about the narrative shift from KTU 1.4 VIII to KTU 1.5 I. After Baal defeats Yamm's challenge for kingship (KTU 1.1-1.2) and consolidates his kingship in the form of a palace for himself (KTU 1.3-1.4), Mot challenges Baal (KTU 1.5-1.6). Ancient Near Eastern monarchs often faced challenges to their crown, especially at the beginning of their reigns. In this respect, Baal is no exception.

---

[14] Such as Gen 1:1, 2:4b, Enuma Elish, and a Sumerian-Akkadian bilingual creation text dating at least to the reign of Tiglath-pileser I. For discussions of the Ugaritic and biblical texts, see *CMHE* 118-119; von Soden 1982; Wallace 1985: 66-67. For the Sumero-Akkadian bilingual, see Bottéro and Kramer 1989:503.

In sum, Clifford's reasons for questioning the conventional acceptance of the narrative continuity between KTU 1.4 and 1.5 are inadequate. As Ginsberg (1955:238) noted long ago, the speeches of Baal to Mot in KTU 1.4 VIII and Mot to Baal in KTU 1.5 I are easier to explain as two parts of a single narrative. KTU 1.4 VIII does not provide a conclusive ending to KTU 1.4, but it appears continuous with 1.5 I since its content fits the opening of KTU 1.5 I (see *SPUMB* 2). Furthermore, Clifford does not offer either an alternative logical ending to KTU 1.4 VIII or a sufficient understanding for the beginning of KTU 1.5 I. Therefore, it is reasonable to conclude that KTU 1.4-1.5-1.6 represents a continuous narrative.

3. KTU 1.3-1.4 likewise has been generally viewed as a continuous narrative.[15] A few questions about their continuity have been raised, however. De Moor (*SPUMB* 41-43) argues that the relationship between KTU 1.17 VI and KTU 1.3 and 1.6 indicates that 1.3 begins the cycle and 1.6 ends it. The themes described in the two texts may indeed be closely related.[16] That this proves that KTU 1.3-1.1-1.2-1.4-1.5-1.6 constitutes the only possible order is subject to dispute, as it assumes that the two events are related in a linear fashion. Following Gaster's insight that two sections of the cycle culminate in the autumn, it is possible to argue that the three sections of the cycle evoke phenomena associated with the same time of year, namely the early autumn.[17] The order of the tablets proposed by de Moor does not necessarily follow from the thematic proximity which he has correctly noted.

De Moor doubts the continuity of KTU 1.3 with 1.4 for another reason. Assuming that El does give permission to both Anat and Athirat for the building of the house in both KTU 1.3 and 1.4, de Moor argues:

> With regard to CTA 3:E-F [KTU 1.3 V-VI] we have seen that if Ilu actually did give permission for the building of Baᶜlu's palace there, which is by far the most probable supposition, the sequence CTA 3-4 [KTU 1.3-1.4] becomes dubious (B.b). But with the sequence CTA 3-1-2-4-5-6 [KTU 1.3-1.1-1.2-1.4-1.5-1.6] it may quite reasonably be assumed that Ilu revoked his initial decision because of the complaints

---

15 *CML*[2] 10 n. 16; Kinet 1981:66; del Olmo Lete 1983; Gibson 1984: 205.

16 For further discussion, see below pp. 64-69, 99-100.

17 For further explanation of this point, see pp. 97-100 below.

> lodged against Baʿlu in CTA 1:IV. Thereupon he gave the permission to build a palace to Yammu instead of Baʿlu (B.d and CTA 2: 'III'.7-10 [KTU 1.2 III 7-10]).

The first part of de Moor's argument is controvertible: it is equally possible that El does not give permission to Anat in 1.3, but he does give it to Athirat in 1.4. Like de Moor, Clifford argues for a narrative discontinuity between KTU 1.3 and 1.4 and assumes a specific reconstruction for the lacuna at the end of KTU 1.3 V, namely that El grants permission for the house to Anat (just as he does at the end of KTU 1.4 IV; so also *SPUMB* 38). In a similar vein, Margalit (1980:9) would argue that because Anat wins El's permission in the similar scene in KTU 1.17 VI, she wins the permission from El also in KTU 1.3 V, this time for the construction of Baal's palace. In all of these reconstructions, it is assumed but not demonstrated that like Athirat, Anat receives permission.

This argument for narrative discontinuity of KTU 1.3 and 1.4 rests on the unproven assumption that parallel motifs or plots indicate parallel stories or parallel resolutions at the ends of stories.[18] The further assumption that the parallel plots belong to an unconnected narrative is also left undemonstrated. There is another way to view the parallel plots in KTU 1.3-1.4. They may constitute two parts of a diptych, the first depicting Anat's failure to win El's permission for the house, and the second describing Athirat's success in gaining the very same permission.[19] This reconstruction would account also for the ending of KTU 1.3, which otherwise lacks a conclusion. Furthermore, a close comparison of 1.3 V with 1.18 I and 1.4 V indicates some differences suggesting that El's response in 1.3 V differs from his answers in 1.18 I and 1.4 V where he gives permission to the goddesses' wishes. The scene in KTU 1.18 I depicts El and Anat discussing the fate of Aqhat. In lines 17b-19 El admits that Anat will do what she intends, but the words in KTU 1.3 V 28-29 that correspond to 1.18 I 17b-19 appear as a question *mh tʾaršn lbtlt ʿnt*, "what do you desire, Adolescent[20] Anat?" In

---

[18] Clifford 1984:191; Margalit 1980:9-11; for further references, see *MLC* 94, n. 58; del Olmo Lete 1983:67.

[19] *Baal* 10; Mullen 1980:66 n. 108; *MLC* 93-94; del Olmo Lete 1983:67-69.

[20] The word *btlt* is often translated "virgin," but this is inaccurate (see Marcus 1970b:113; Pardee 1980:276; P. L. Day 1991; Walls 1992:78-79). Marcus suggests "maiden" and compares Akk *batultu*, "adolescent, young girl." The fact that *bĕtûlâ* in Joel 1:8 has a *baʿal nĕʿûrêhā* ("the husband of her youth"), shows that the term

KTU 1.18 I 17b-19, El acquiesces to Anat's designs to murder Aqhat, but in KTU 1.3 V 28-29 El's question suggests that he does not readily agree to Anat's demand for permission for the building of Baal's palace. Unlike 1.18 I 17-19, 1.3 V does not describe El telling Anat to "do what is in her heart."

Other differences between the speeches in KTU 1.3 V and 1.4 IV also suggest that El's response to Anat's request may have differed from his reaction to Athirat's supplications. While both goddesses declare how wise El is (KTU 1.3 V 30-31; 1.4 IV 41-43), Athirat's exclamation of El's wisdom follows his solicitous questions regarding her welfare, whereas Anat's declaration of his sagacity follows his observation about her bellicose threat, and then his question, "what do you want, Adolescent Anat?" (cf. 1.6 II 13-14). The different roles which El's beard plays in 1.3 V 24-25 and 1.4 V 4 also point to the different character of the two passages. In Anat's speech, El's beard appears as part as her threat to make his beard run with blood. For Athirat, El's beard serves as a mark of his wisdom. Although it is difficult to be sure, these differences in otherwise parallel scenes may issue in different outcomes. It seems more likely than not that El refuses Anat his permission for Baal's palace.

Clifford's doubts (1984:191-193) that KTU 1.3 and 1.4 belong to the same narrative rest on other thematic grounds. Mot is Baal's enemy in KTU 1.4-1.6, whereas Yamm is the enemy in KTU 1.2-1.3. The references to Yamm in KTU 1.4 IV 12 and 1.4 VIII 4 are too obscure for Clifford to indicate that Yamm remains Baal's threat until KTU 1.4 VII and that Mot becomes Baal's challenge only in KTU 1.4 VIII. Many, however, take these references to indicate at least that Yamm is still in the picture in KTU 1.4 VII (Ginsberg, *ANET* 134; *Thespis* 192-193; *DW* 34-37).

---

does not concern the status of marriage as such (P. L. Day 1991:145). Similarly, *bĕtûlâ* in Gen 24:16 would appear not to refer to a virgin as such since the word is qualified by the phrase *wĕʾîš lōʾ yĕdāʿāh* ("and a man had not known her," i.e., had not had sexual relations with her). Citing the BH and Akk cognates, Day (1991:144) suggests that *btlt* "refers to an age group, appromximately equivalent to the English term 'adolescent,' but applied specifically to females." Day proposes that a female could be called *btlt* until the birth of her first child. The application of this term to Anat indicates that she is "not (as defined by her patriarchal culture) fully an adult women. Adolescence is the time when males and females part ways in terms of their respective and normative social roles. Anat as perpetual *btlt* is suspended, as it were, at this crucial point in time". As a result, Anat engages in the characteristically male roles of warfare and hunting, according to Day. The discussion of Walls largely follows suit.

Margalit (1980:9 n. 1) raises another thematic point that could be an impediment to establishing narrative continuity between KTU 1.3 and 1.4. To Margalit it seems unlikely that Anat in KTU 1.3 VI would delegate a mission to Qdš w-Amrr, the servant of another goddess, Athirat. Margalit argues:

> Some scholars believe that Anat delegates the mission to Qdš-w-Amrr, but this seems unlikely. The latter, be it recalled, works for Asherah; and there is little love lost between Anat and Asherah! More probably, Qdš-w-Amrr dwells at a point along the way to Kṯr; by informing Asherah's servant, Anat circulated the news of El's decision without wasting time.

Margalit's reconstruction of events presupposes that either the narrative which he describes falls in the lacuna between KTU 1.3 and 1.4, or the narrative retains continuity without actually detailing all the events as he describes them. The first alternative would suggest narrative discontinuity between KTU 1.3 and 1.4. The premise to the first argument is, however, open to question. Miller (*DW* 16) observes that the two messengers, Gpn w-Ugr, carry a message for Mot in KTU 1.5 I although they are Baal's servants. Messengers can carry messages for deities other than their masters. The thematic observation raised by Margalit does not appear to be a serious objection for narrative continuity between KTU 1.3 and 1.4.

Rummel's discussion of the originally separate traditions in KTU 1.3 serves as a useful starting-point for seeing their larger integration within the narrative of the Baal Cycle. Rummel (*RSP III* 251) correlates elements of KTU 1.3 with those in KTU 1.2 and 1.4 (conflict, order, kingship, temple, banquet) and suggests that KTU 1.3 shows distinct traditions compared to the narrative centered on Baal in the rest of the cycle. Yet, the correspondences delineated by Rummel point to the connections between KTU 1.3 and the story of Baal's rise to power. The kingship in KTU 1.3 cited by Rummel is Baal's kingship, and the temple to which KTU 1.3 refers is Baal's temple. Rummel is probably correct in seeing in KTU 1.3 II a tradition of Anat's cosmogonic battle which originally differed from the tradition of Baal's cosmogonic battles, but Anat's battle in 1.3 II has been reworked into the larger framework of Baal's rise to kingship,[21] and may represent a secondary inclusion of an originally

---

[21] Cf. Peterson and Woodward 1977:242.

distinct story about Anat. Her battling described in KTU 1.83 and mentioned in KTU 1.3 III 37-IV 4 enhances this possibility (Smith 1986b:328-29). Anat's battle may have been placed in KTU 1.3 II for one of two reasons. It may be that when other deities come to them, deities are depicted in a mode typical of their character. Athirat is going about domestic chores when Baal and Anat come to her in KTU 1.4 III. El is seated in his watery abode when Anat and Athirat approach him in KTU 1.3 V and 1.4 IV (see KTU 1.17 V). When Baal's messengers travel to Mot in KTU 1.4 VIII, he is described as a ruler at home in his underworld city. Likewise, Anat is concluding a battle when Baal's messengers come to her in KTU 1.3 III.

Another possible reason for the present placement of Anat's battle in the story of Baal involves their relationship. The battle against the foes in KTU 1.2 IV and 1.3 II may take place simultaneously on heavenly and earthly levels: Baal fights a cosmic battle against Yamm in KTU 1.2 IV while Anat fights human soldiers in 1.3 II (Gray 1979:315, 323; see *DW* 44-48).[22] In sum, just as KTU 1.4 and 1.5 are considered parts of a single narrative, so also KTU 1.3 and 1.4 may be understood as a continuous narrative. Since a messenger is commanded to travel to Kothar at the end of KTU 1.3 and Kothar is receiving a message at the beginning of KTU 1.4, it appears unreasonable to disconnect KTU 1.3 and 1.4. Furthermore, it would be unclear how a message to Kothar provides a suitable conclusion to KTU 1.3. This review of the positions held by de Moor, Clifford and Margalit indicates that there is no serious impediment to viewing KTU 1.3-1.6 as a continuous narrative. At the same time, continuity for 1.3-1.6 cannot be fully confirmed due to the condition of the texts, and it is possible that they represent different texts involving Baal. Finally, it should be noted as before that 1.3-1.6 were not discovered in precisely the same area; this would cast some serious doubt on the assumption that the extant exemplars of 1.3-1.6 originally formed a single "text."

---

[22] Some depictions of Yahweh as "divine warrior" link heavenly and terrestrial levels. The earthly level is especially vivid in some biblical texts (Deut 32:42, Isaiah 34 and 63, Ezek 32:5-6, and Pss 50:13, 58:11 and 68), where the description of human blood is reminiscent of Anat's destruction of humans in KTU 1.3 II 9-15, 21-31. The "heads" and "corpses" heaped up in Ps 110:6 compare with the human "heads" and "hands" of those whom Anat slays in a bloodbath in KTU 1.3 II 9-15, 27-28 and cf. 34-35 (see Roberts 1982:102-106; Smith 1990:61-64).

4. KTU 1.1, 1.2 III and 1.2 I-II-IV were not found in precisely the same area, which raises a serious question regarding whether or not they also belong to the same narrative as KTU 1.3-1.6. Due to the lacuna in KTU 1.2, it is impossible to establish the narrative continuity of KTU 1.2 with 1.3-1.6. Meier (1986:241-54; 1989:154-55, 184-85) argues against direct narrative continuity on the basis of 1.2's physical character and internal evidence. The format of the tablet differs considerably from the other tablets of the cycle. According to Meier, the average number of alphabetic cuneiform characters in 1.2 I, III and IV is, respectively, 33.33, 40.0 and 28.8 while the lowest average in any column of 1.3-1.6 is 10.38 and the highest is 19.88. The longer length of lines in 1.2 points to fewer columns in this tablet and therefore at least a different copy or version, as tablets in the same series normally have the same number of columns. This physical difference between 1.2 and the other tablets of the cycle suggests that the "library of the chief priest" contained two versions of the Baal Cycle. In support of separating 1.2 from 1.3-1.6, Meier also cites the work of Horwitz (1973) showing that the small vertical wedges, customarily called "word dividers" in Ugaritic studies, appear differently in KTU 1.2 than in the other tablets of the cycle.[23]

---

[23] Meier also proposes that the different divine titles in 1.2 would indicate that it is a different composition from the rest of the extant copy of the Baal Cycle, but the argument is inconclusive. The differences might be attributed to the literary character of the text rather than problems of "distinct myths" (so Meier 1986:246), an approach which Meier does not consider. To take one example from Meier's presentation, he cites the poetic pair Yamm//Nahar only in KTU 1.2 but not in the other tablets; he contrasts this usage with the formulation *mdd ʾil ym* as well as the replacement of *ṯpṭ nhr* in 1.2 with *nhr ʾil rbm* in 1.3 III 39. Does this discrepancy indicate that 1.2 constituted a different version of the myth from the rest of the cycle? It is possible, but the differences in terms between 1.2 and the other tablets which Meier advances as evidence do not necessarily point to this solution. The phrases *mdd ʾil ym* and *nhr ʾil rbm* in 1.3 III 38-39 are irrelevant to his point since these lines belong to a passage which appears to have been redacted secondarily into the cycle. Furthermore, like 1.3 III 38-39, the version of 1.2 was redacted secondarily into the extant version of the cycle. In other words, the literary differences which Meier cites, including epithets, may reflect a separate prehistory and possibly a different scribal tradition, but not necessarly two extant redactions of the myth. The titles, *mdd ʾil* and *ydd ʾil*, which both mean "beloved of El," may represent further examples of epithets which point not to two extant versions of the same story, but to texts with separate prehistories redacted into the same single extant version of the Baal Cycle. The epithet *mdd ʾil* belongs to Yamm in 1.1 IV 20 1.3 III 38-39, 1.4 II 34 and VII 2-3. Mot is called *mdd ʾil* in 1.4 VIII 23-24 and *ydd ʾil* in 1.4 VII 46-47, 48, VIII 31-32, 1.5 I 8, 13, II 9, III 10, 26 and 1.6 VI 30-31. Hence tablets

Despite the evidence to the contrary, Meier allows that the themes of 1.2 belong to the cycle. Meier (1986:244) notes that the cosmogonic approach to the cycle would suggest the thematic continuity of 1.2 with 1.4 (*CMHE* 113-116; Rummel, *RSP III* 241-243) even if "such a general thematic condition is too loose to bind this particular tablet [KTU 1.2] to the rest of the cycle."[24] Hurowitz (1992: 93) also compares the two descriptions of divine victory and palace-building in Enuma Elish (Ea's defeat of Apsu followed by his building of a palace on him; and Marduk's defeat of Tiamat followed by his construction of a palace atop her) as well as Exodus 15. Hurowitz (1992:82) relates this pattern of divine battle and divine palace-bulding to the connection between temple building and defeat of the enemies in Assyrian and some Neo-Babylonian inscriptions:

> The linking of the two events may be related to the pattern of the 'victorious temple builder' or the 'divine warrior' frequently mentioned in the writings of biblical scholars ... This pattern in fact exists in all the Assyrian royal inscriptions in which the king's military victories are placed before the building account concluding the inscription.

Hurowitz suggests that this pattern appears also in the Idrimi inscription, 2 Samuel 7 and 1 Kings 5.

As these parallels suggest, the events of KTU 1.2 may connect thematically with the following tablets in other ways. In the present form of the text, the battles against the foes in KTU 1.2 IV and 1.3 II may take place simultaneously, as noted above. Similarly, the feast of Baal in KTU 1.3 I serves as a fitting aftermath to his battle in KTU 1.2 IV, and the sequence of battle and feast of Ugaritic tradition appears to underlie these motifs in biblical tradition represented, for example, in Isa 25:6-8. Marduk's battle is celebrated likewise with a feast of the great gods in Enuma Elish 3.136-38.[25] Given the possible thematic continuities between 1.2 I-II-IV and

---

1.1-1.3 appear to differ from 1.5-1.6 in the use of these titles. But 1.4 contains both epithets, and it is unlikely that two versions are to be posited in a single tablet. Moreover, the different epithets may be attributed to other factors. The story of Mot may have a different literary history as the narrative involving Yamm; it may be that the Baal-Mot section was patterned on the Baal-Yamm section, a theory explored below. The appearance of both *ydd ʾil* and *mdd ʾil* in 1.4 may reflect seams in the story where the narrative of Mot has been joined secondarily to the rest of the story, at a point possibly prior to the writing of the extant text.

[24] See below p. 15.

[25] Cf. J. Day 1985b:148-51; Levenson 1988:28-34.

1.3-1.6, it is possible that 1.2 represents part of another copy of the cycle, probably also copied by Ilimalku, to whom the tablet is commonly attributed. Ilimalku may have copied this tablet from an earlier copy that was like all the other tablets in its length of lines and other physical characteristics. Because of the highly fragmentary state of 1.2, it is impossible to adjudicate further the precise relationship of 1.2 to the rest of the cycle. As Meier states, neither continuity nor discontinuity can be proven,[26] and in view of the physical evidence, Meier's questioning of direct continuity is reasonable. In sum, KTU 1.3-1.6 could constitute one version of the Baal Cycle, which presumably is missing some narrative like the material in 1.2. KTU 1.2 may represent part of another version which perhaps included at least the palace-building material known also from 1.4, since the themes of battle and temple-building often go together.

5. Finally, there is the question of KTU 1.1's relationship to the rest of the tablets. Some degree of doubt has been expressed as to whether KTU 1.1 is connected even to 1.2. KTU 1.1 was discovered near neither 1.3-1.6 nor 1.2 I-II-IV (although it was found near 1.2 III). To explain the relationship of 1.1 to the other tablets, some scholars have argued that KTU 1.1 is a ''synopsis'' of the remainder of the Baal Cycle (*TO* 297-298; *CML*^{2} 3; Watson 1977:273). As support for this thesis, Caquot and Snzycer (*TO* 297-298) note the following correspondences:

KTU 1.1 column:	KTU tablet:
II	1.3
III	1.4
IV	1.2
V	1.6

Although these correspondences show that themes in other tablets appear also in KTU 1.1, they do not demonstrate that KTU 1.1 constitutes a synopsis of KTU 1.2-1.6. Furthermore, KTU 1.5 is absent from the synopsis.

Similarities do not establish narrative continuity. Gibson, who at one time subscribed to the synopsis theory (*CML*^{2} 205) has since re-

---

[26] The question of the relationship of the two fragments, KTU 1.2 I + IV and ''1.2 III'' is discussed below on p. 22. The latter fragment may not belong to 1.2, but may represent a text which contains a variant of part of 1.1 III plus a further episode involving Athtar otherwise unattested.

jected it (1984:205). De Moor (*SPUMB* 39) suggests the plausibility of the order 1.1-1.2, largely on the basis of the observation that the crisis described in 1.1 IV leads to the conflict like the one related in KTU 1.2 I and IV.

In sum, narrative continuity among 1.3-1.6 is possible (see Gibson 1984:206), but the relationship between 1.1, 1.2 I-II-IV and 1.2 III and the other tablets remains unclear. It is not unlikely based on the physical evidence that 1.2 I-II-IV and 1.2 III belong to a different copy of the cycle. It is possible that 1.1 belongs either to one of the same copies as 1.3-1.6 or to yet another copy. Although direct narrative continuity between 1.1, 1.2 and the other tablets seems unlikely, the continuity of material and themes may suggest that 1.1-1.6 represent different copies of the cycle.

The many correspondences between the Baal-Yamm and Baal-Mot episodes merit a reconsideration as to whether these two parts of the cycle reflect a thematic symmetry:

1.	Speech of enemy's messengers to Baal	1.2 I	1.5 I
2.	Baal's initial surrender	1.2 I 36-37	1.5 II 12-20
3.	Baal is "servant" (ᶜ*bd*)	1.2 I 36	1.5 II 12-20
4.	Baal fights the enemy twice	1.2 IV, 1.4 VII 1-4	1.6 V 1-4, 1.6 VI 12-22
5.	Battle on Sapan	1.2 IV; cf. 1.1 V 5, 18	1.6 VI 13
6.	Baal receives divine aid	1.2 IV (Kothar)	1.6 II (Anat)
7.	Baal fights with a *ṣmd*	1.2 IV	1.6 V 1-4
8.	The Athtar interlude	1.2 III 12-25	1.6 I 43-65
9.	Baal's enemy is "strong" (ᶜ*z*)	1.2 IV 17	1.6 VI 17-20
10.	Baal's two main enemies are both El's "beloved"	1.1 IV 20	1.4 VII 46-47 1.3 III 38-39 1.4 VII 31-32, cf. 1.4 II 34, 1.5 I 13
11.	Another deity declares Baal's victory	1.2 IV 32, 34	1.6 VI 17
12.	Expression of Baal's kingship	1.2 IV 32-34	1.6 VI 33-35
13.	Refrain: "how shall El hear you", etc.	1.2 III 17-18	1.6 VI 26-29

The thematic and verbal connections between KTU 1.1-1.2 and 1.3-1.4 are likewise noteworthy:

1.	Anat pours peace into the earth	1.1 II 19-21	1.3 III 11-14
2.	The message which the heavens do not know	1.1 III 12-16	1.3 III 21-31

		1.3 IV 13-20
3. Kothar summoned to build a house	1.1 III 26-30	1.4 V 51-57
	1.2 III 7-10	
4. Yamm fights Baal	1.2 IV	1.4 VII 2
5. Description of El's abode	1.1 III 21-25	1.3 V 5-9
6. "You delay, and I depart"	1.1 III 18-21	1.3 IV 32-36

The similar descriptions concerning palaces to be constructed for Yamm and Baal accounts for many of the correspondences (*UgM* 1-20). Indeed, the building narratives of 1.1 V-1.2 III and 1.3 III-1.4 VII may serve as foils to one another. While the building sequences share three elements, namely El's permission for the building project, the securing of Kothar's aid in building the palace and the announcement of the project to Anat, the two building sequences differ in some fundamental details. The story of the palace for Yamm opens with El's initiative in the matter, but no more is heard of this palace after Yamm fails to dispatch Baal in battle. In contrast, the sequence describing Baal's acquisition of a palace opens laconically: Baal secures El's permission for the palace only after the lengthy intervention of Anat and Athirat. Yet, once the permission is granted, the steps for the building project follow in short order. Baal's palace story ends where Yamm's begins: in the final scene of the building sequence (1.4 VII), Baal apparently strikes a further blow to Yamm. Such massive symmetries perhaps point to the secondary unification of originally unconnected narratives into a story with a basic symmetry: the palace of Baal, the crowning symbol of royal status, flanked on either side by a struggle over his kingship. Even if 1.1-1.6 do not belong to a single copy, it might be inferred by the themes shared by these tablets that they belong to different copies or versions of the same text.

Further features of the Baal-Yamm and Baal-Mot narratives might be used to argue that 1.1-1.6 belong to a single story. Both the Baal-Yamm and Baal-Mot stories have been classified as cosmogonies, as battles between a divine hero and his cosmic enemy issuing in cosmic order.[27] More specifically, the sequence of Baal's captivity, victory in battle and the proclamation of his kingship is prominent in both the Baal-Yamm and Baal-Mot narratives (Cross

---

[27] *CMHE* 120; Clifford 1984:184-98; cf. Peterson and Woodward 1977:241-42. See below pp. 75-87.

1968:3-5; Rummel, *RSP III* 234, 242, 249). Petersen and Woodward (1977:243, 241-42) comment:

> Whereas the Baal-Yamm episode deals with Baal's rise over the earth, the Baal-Mot conflict uses the same logical structure to address quite different issues, the flux between life and death, fertility and sterility. The differences in characters and theme between these two episodes should not however obscure the structural similarity in the myths.
>
> The relational structures of the Baal/Yamm and Baal/Mot conflicts are isomorphic, i.e. not only is there a one to one correspondence between the vertices of the two models, but also there is a similar correspondence between the relations linking these points. Since there are no points or relationships in one episodic model which do not have analogs in the other, each model may be understood to be a structural transformation of the other. By this we mean that while the two episodes of the myth may have different surface language, they share a common logical structure.

The argument that the Baal-Yamm and Baal-Mot stories are parallel and possibly genetically related would appear to be undermined by the fact that the features of a hero's captivity, victory and kingship are known in other ancient Near Eastern texts. The more specific structure observed by Wyatt (1986:137), however, supports a more particular relationship between the two parts. Wyatt notes the following correspondences[28]:

KTU 1.1-1.2	KTU 1.5-1.6
Yamm triumphant	Mot triumphant
Baal cowed and imprisoned	Baal killed
Athtar rejected	Athtar rejected
Yamm killed	Mot killed
Baal triumphant	Baal triumphant

The first and last elements of this schema for 1.1-1.4 involve divine lordship, first of Yamm (1.1 IV 17; cf. 1.2 I 37-38) and then of Baal (1.4 IV 42; cf. 1.2 IV 32, 34). The first and last elements of 1.5-1.6 declare divine fear, first of Baal (1.5 II 6-7) and then of Mot (1.6 VI 30-31). The most important evidence are the specific verbal links (listed above) which indicate that various parts of the cycle share much more than "surface language" or "structural similarities."

It is also possible that the symmetry between 1.1-1.2 and 1.5-1.6

---

28 Wyatt's view depends on taking 1.2 III after 1.2 I which is addressed in the next section.

may have resulted from the modelling of 1.5-1.6 after 1.1-1.2. This transformation may have included patterning the character of Mot in 1.4 VIII-1.6 after the figure of Yamm in 1.1-1.2 (Smith 1988). The distribution of evidence pertaining to Death may provide some basis for this view. The figure of Death differs in Mesopotamian literary tradition and West Semitic texts.[29] In general, Death does not appear in Mesopotamian literary tradition as a stock character, although Mesopotamian texts sometimes allude to Death personified (*CAD* M/II:318). In VAT 10057.3 (Livingstone 1989:7), "Death" (^{d}*mu-ú-t[u?]*) appears in a group of underworld figures. The relatively fewer West Semitic texts, in contrast, allude to Death more frequently and portray him as an important character, especially in the Baal Cycle. Death functions as a main character in KTU 1.5 I -1.6 VI, where the struggle between life and death is rendered as a personal one. While Death in the Baal Cycle lacks a clear analogue in Mesopotamian literary tradition, the stories of Dumuzi and Inanna/Ninhursag have been compared with the Baal-Mot narrative (see Smith 1986a:313-14; Walls 1992:71-74). The traditions about Dumuzi and Baal are similar in their deaths and perhaps in their returns to life. Both Dumuzi and Baal are related to agricultural fertility, albeit in different ways. Their divine consorts, Inanna/Ninhursag and Anat respectively, both mourn and search for them.[30] The Baal-Mot narrative contains other traditional elements found also in Mesopotamian texts. Such features include descriptions of the underworld; the descent of a main character to the underworld (Hutter 1985:130-46, 150-55); the description of Baal and Mot fighting like warriors in 1.6 VI (cf. Gilgamesh and Enkidu in Gilgamesh, OB version, 2[Pennsylavania tablet].6.15-25; Dalley 1991:14; *ANET* 78); perhaps the intervention of the sun-deity to give the hero the upper hand in fighting the enemy (1.6 VI 22-29; cf. Gilgamesh, Hittite recension of tablet 5.4, lines 10-20, *ANET* 83)[31]; and the description of the sun deity as the ruler over

---

[29] Walls (1992:183) argues that Ugaritic differs from other ancient Near Eastern mythological traditions in that "the god of the dead is not a member of the Ugaritic pantheon." Rather, "he is Death personified—the Grim Reaper—rather than simply a deity whose realm is the Netherworld."

[30] For Inanna's laments for Dumuzi, see especially Kramer 1982, 1983. For their similarities to the Ugaritic descriptions of Anat's laments for Baal, see Smith 1986a.

[31] I wish to thank Professor Aage Westenholz for bringing this parallel to my attention.

the dead (1.6 VI 45b-47; Healey 1980). The Baal-Mot narrative also exhibits some profound differences with the Dumuzi stories.[32] Dumuzi is no great god like Baal, nor does he engage in mortal combat as part of the description of the struggle between life and death.

Various explanations may be proffered for these similarities and differences. Perhaps the Baal Cycle used traditional elements well-known also in Mesopotamian literary texts in shaping its unique story about Baal versus Mot. Or, the tale of Baal's demise may have had an older form primarily consisting of traditional elements. It told the story of Baal's death which resulted in his descent to the Underworld, Anat's mourning for Baal and her searching for him, and his eventual return to life. If so, adding the figure of Death made Baal's death into a personal conflict. One might speculate further about the creation of Death. The epic figure of Mot may have derived from his personification as a demonic force, represented in texts such as KTU 1.127.29-31 and 2.10.11-14. Like Akkadian *mūtu* and BH *môt*, Ugaritic *mt* seems to have been a demon, associated especially with pestilence (Tawil 1980; Smith 1988; cf. Paul 1968). In the Baal Cycle he looms as a figure larger than life. This sort of development has Near Eastern analogues.[33] The cosmic and terrestrial levels are related in the Ugaritic texts as well. According to de Moor (1984) and Caquot (1988), *tnn*, Mot, and *brḥ*, a title of *ltn*, three of Baal's enemies known from the Baal Cycle, seem to appear in the very difficult text, KTU 1.82, as demonic forces which Baal was believed to be able to expel, perhaps in accordance with his ability to defeat cosmic enemies.

In closing, it may be suggested that if the character of heroes is revealed through the character of their adversaries and the nature of their conflicts,[34] then Yamm and Mot reveal aspects of Baal's character. Yamm and Mot are cosmic figures, and they show Baal's heroism in equally cosmic stature and proportion. Furthermore, as Yamm represents the chaotic waters and Mot signifies death in its cosmic proportions, Baal embodies order and life in equal, if not greater, universal proportions.

---

[32] For the many differences and some misleading assumptions in this comparison, see below pp. 69-74.

[33] To note one example, the figure of the *asakku*, initially a disease, appears as Ninurta's major enemy in Lugal-e (see Jacobsen 1988).

[34] For this point I am indebted to Professor Ron Hendel.

The Order of Columns in KTU 1.1 and 1.2

KTU 1.1 is the most broken tablet of the Baal Cycle, and as a result the placement and order of its columns are two highly debated issues. The tablet originally had six columns, three on each side. Two of the original columns have not survived and the edges of the other four columns are broken. L'Heureux (1979:19) has outlined three major options regarding the order of the columns in KTU 1.1. L'Heureux's listing, represented in the following schema, includes the views of Cassuto (*GA* 58) and Virolleaud (1938), as well as two alternatives considered by Herdner (CTA):

		Virolleaud/Herdner a	Cassuto	Herdner b
Recto	1st col.	missing	KTU 1.1 V	missing
	2nd	KTU 1.1 II	KTU 1.1 IV	KTU 1.1 V
	3rd	KTU 1.1 III	missing	KTU 1.1 IV
Verso	4th	KTU 1.1 IV	missing	KTU 1.1 III
	5th	KTU 1.1 V	KTU 1.1 III	KTU 1.1 II
	6th	missing	KTU 1.1 II	missing

The placement of the columns may be determined in part by the thickness of the tablet. The curvature of the tablet indicates that its narrowest portions are not extant; therefore it is not the middle columns that are missing, as in Cassuto's reconstruction, but the initial and final columns, as proposed by Virolleaud, Herdner a and Herdner b.

Unlike the issue of the placement of columns, their relative order has not been settled on epigraphic grounds. In their text editions, Virolleaud, Herdner and KTU suggested the order of KTU 1.1 II-1.1 V. Cassuto (*GA* 156) long held the opposite opinion contending that the events described in KTU 1.1 V and IV precede those of 1.1 III and II. Cassuto did not offer further reasons for his position, but Pope (*EUT* 96) and Oldenburg (*CEBCR* 123) follow his view. According to their interpretation, KTU 1.1 V constitutes Baal's dethronement of El, and the other columns contain his attempt at revenge through the agency of his son, Yamm. While this view of the tablet has been criticized (L'Heureux 1979:18-26), it has been modified by del Olmo Lete (1977:32-35). Del Olmo Lete takes his starting point from the words of 1.1 IV 23, *kd ynʾaṣn*, "when he reviled me." According to del Olmo Lete, this line presumes an attempt on Baal's part to supplant El as king of the pantheon. Then in 1.1 IV El decides to name Yamm as king. In order to support

Yamm's claims to kingship in 1.1 III and IV, El orders Kothar to build a palace for Yamm.

The arguments of Pope, Oldenburg and del Olmo Lete may be bolstered by some circumstantial epigraphic and thematic evidence. According to Dijkstra (1987:51, 53), the order KTU 1.1 V-IV-III-II appears preferable for epigraphic reasons:

> . . . a scribe was more often forced to divide a word on the reverse than on the obverse of a tablet. . . The two, possibly three cases of word-division on the alleged column suggests, however, that we have in reality to do with the fifth column of the reverse.

Furthermore, the order of events in ancient Near Eastern narratives describing the construction of temples and palaces also comports with the order of events in KTU 1.1 V-IV-III-II rather than vice-versa. According to Hurowitz (1985; 1992:137, 163-64), the feature of the summoning of the craftsman appears in building stories in a consistent manner. Whether the story involves the divine permission for the building project or divine initiation of the project, the summoning of the craftsman follows the permission for, or initiation of, the project. In the case of KTU 1.1, El's support for Yamm in 1.1 IV 20 and El's discussion of the palace in 1.1 IV 21 reflect his role in initiating the building project, which in compliance with the pattern of other narratives, precedes his summoning of Kothar in 1.1 III (see also Dijkstra 1987:54 n. 29).[35] On the basis of this evidence, the order advocated by Cassuto and considered by Herdner b is apparently correct. For this reason the order 1.1 V-IV-III-II is given in the arrangement of the commentary below, although the enumeration of KTU, based on Virolleaud and CTA, is followed.

The issues involving the order of columns in 1.2 differ in character. The main problem concerns the relationship of two fragments of 1.2. The larger fragment measures 125 millimeters in height and 101 millimeters in width. One side has the lower part of what Virolleaud designated III AB B (= CTA 2.1 = KTU 1.2 I), and the other side has the upper part of Virolleaud's III AB A (= CTA 2.4 = KTU 1.2 IV) plus fifteen lines of what CTA labelled as a second column (CTA 2.2 = KTU 1.2 II).[36] The smaller fragment,

---

35 This reconstruction also contradicts the view that KTU 1.1 constitutes a synopsis (see above p. 14).

36 1.2 II may be assumed to followed 1.2 I, although little else can be said about either the former's placement or its contents.

60 millimeters in height and 69 millimeters in width, has writing on only one side. Virolleaud originally placed this fragment which he called III AB C (= CTA 2.3 III = KTU 1.2 III) between 1.2 II and 1.2 IV. Del Olmo Lete (1984:48-49) defends the appropriateness of the themes and therefore the placement of 1.2 III between KTU 1.2 I and IV. More specifically, he explains the apparently disruptive appearance of Athtar in 1.2 III as a structural interlude similar to the one attested in 1.6 I.

There is no epigraphic reason for doubting that "1.2 III" belonged originally to 1.2. The number of alphabetic cuneiform signs per line in "1.2 III" corresponds approximately to the number of signs in 1.2 I and IV (Meier 1986:241-54; 1989:154-55, 184-85). However, the content of "1.2 III" partially matches the material in 1.1 III. Both 1.1 III 21-29 and 1.2 III 4-10 contain information detailing travel to El, obeisance before him, and El's commands that Kothar build a house for Yamm.[37] These similarities cannot be harmonized by viewing "1.2 III" as the sequel to 1.1 III; this would assume that the column following 1.1 III can be displaced by "1.2 III," but such an insertion is materially impossible. The order of either 1.1 II-III-IV-V or 1.1 V-IV-III-II cannot be interrupted on any basis. In other words, "1.2 III" may contain a variant of some material in 1.1 III in addition to a further episode involving Athtar. Ginsberg (*ANET* 129) noted that the placement of "1.2 III" between 1.2 I and 1.2 IV "seems strange; so, perhaps, it belongs to a tablet which preceded, and in outward disposition resembled, the tablet of which III AB B-A is a remnant." On the basis of these observations it would appear that 1.2 III 4-10 contains a variant to 1.1 III 21-29. Both variants may represent early parts in two versions of the Baal Cycle. The implications for the placement of 1.2 III seem clear: "1.2 III" would appear not to stand between 1.2 I and 1.2 IV, although epigraphically it belongs with them. Furthermore, 1.2 III is epigraphically separate from 1.1. Due to the many features shared between 1.1 III and 1.2 III, it would seem that "1.2 III" may belong prior to 1.2 I, II and IV.

Establishing the place of "1.2 III" requires an examination of the possible literary relationship among 1.2 and other Levantine texts describing similar episodes. On the basis of literary comparisons, it

---

[37] For another example of overlap of one column with another, compare 1.4 II and III.

might be argued that "1.2 III" is not to be placed between 1.2 I and 1.2 IV. Gaster (1952:82-85) and Albright (*YGC* 116) regarded 1.2 I + IV as a variant of the extremely fragmentary Egyptian text sometimes called "Astarte and the Tribute of the Sea" (*ANET* 17-18; see Wente in Simpson et al. 1973:133-36). In this story Astarte comes to Sea singing and laughing. Sea accepts the tribute from Astarte, and taken by her appearance he desires the goddess as an additional payment.[38] Astarte also makes a brief appearance before the divine council (*ANET* 18, iii y-2). The motifs shared by 1.2 I + 1.2 IV and "Astarte and the Tribute of the Sea" include: (1) the claim of tribute by the figure of Sea (1.2 I 21-35; *ANET* 17, i x + 8); (2) the payment of tribute (1.2 I 36-38; *ANET* 17, i x +); (3) the initiative against Sea (1.2 IV; *ANET* 18, xv y); (4) the response of Baal to fight against Sea (1.2 I 38-44 [?]; *ANET* 18 xv y); (5) Sea's title, "ruler" (1.2 I 17, 22, 26, 28, 30, 34, 41, 44; 1.2 IV 25, 27, 30; *ANET* 17, i x + 8, ii x + 3); and (6) the role of the goddess Astarte (1.2 I 40-43 [?]; *ANET* 17, x + 17; 18, iii y-2).

The Song of Ullikumi also incorporates the motif of the goddess' confronting the divine challenger from the sea within the larger narrative of this challenger's battle against the Storm-god. When the threat of Ullikumi becomes known, the goddess goes to the sea (Hoffner 1990:56; cf. *ANET* 123):

> Sauska kept on singing and put on herself a seashell and a pebble (for adornment). A great wave(?) ⟨arose⟩ out of the sea. The great wave(?) said to Sauska, "For whose benefit are you singing? For whose benefit are you filling your mouth with wind? The man (meaning Ullikumi) is deaf; he can[not] hear. He is blind in his eyes; he can-

[38] This addition apparently contains the further motif of the lecherous sea who pursues the goddess ending in her own dramatic escape (Redford 1990:831-33; 1992:45-47). Classical sources contain vestiges of other stories relating how the sea-goddess was desired by the Sea. Redford takes the story of Isis at Gaza in Plutarch (*De Iside*, 357D-E in Griffiths 1970) as a reflection of a cult-myth indigenous to Gaza. Redford also considers the Egyptian Story of the Two Brothers (Lichtheim 1976:203-10) as another variant, since the narrative detailing how the water monster chases the goddess is placed in the "Valley of the Cedar," known later as the river of Adonis in Lebanon. According to Redford (1992:45-47) this motif underlies the stories of Andromeda and Perseus and of Europa and Zeus as well (see p. 24). The difficulty is that the endings of these two stories dramatically differ: the hero saves the female; she does not need to make a desperate escape of her own. Hence it would appear that these two narratives echo at least partially the conflict between the Storm-god and the Sea.

> not see. He has no compassion. So go away, Sauska, and find your brother before he (Ullikumi) becomes really valiant, before the skull of his head becomes really terrifying.

The song has no effect, however, and as in the Baal Cycle, only a direct meeting between the divine males resolves the conflict. The explicitly West Semitic features in the text are limited. Mount Hazzi, known also as Mount Sapan, the home of the West Semitic Storm-god, Baal-Haddu, appears as the site where the Anatolian Storm-god spies his enemy. Another motif perhaps influenced by a West Semitic model is the brother-sister relationship between the Storm-god and the goddess. Other specifically West Semitic features are absent, perhaps reflecting modification of the type-elements in the Song of Ullikumi.

It is possible that this traditional episode was known further east as well. Lambert (1985b:535-37) compares the attestation of the deities ^{d}*ID* and ^{d}*aš-tár-ra-at* in a dedicatory inscription in the late Early Dynastic or early Sargonic bowl from Mari, although this evidence is minimal at best. Emar 373.92 attests to an offering made to the pair ^{d}*INANNA* (*Aštartu ša abi*) and the god ^{d}*Ya-a-mi* (Smith 1990:75 n. 110; Fleming 1992:300).

The classical story of Perseus' rescue of Andromeda may reflect the old West Semitic story of Astarte and the Sea.[39] According to Greek tradition, Andromeda, a daughter of the Ethiopian king, was bound to a rock in the sea at the Levantine port of Jaffa as tribute to a sea monster. On his return from slaying the Medusa, Perseus rescues Andromeda from the sea monster. Redford (1990:830) also compares the story of Europa carried by Zeus in the form of a bull, a tale placed on the Tyrian coast.

These narratives involve many of the same figures and events. The version in the Baal Cycle perhaps shaped a traditional story around the theme of Baal's place within the pantheon and cosmos. The divine council is not threatened by Sea's demands in the Baal Cycle. In 1.2 I the struggle does not belong to the divine council, as it does in the Egyptian version; rather, it becomes the story of Baal's own struggle placed in the setting of the divine council. Com-

---

[39] Apollodorus 2.4.3; Strabo 1.2.35; 16.2.28; Pliny, *Natural History* 5.14.69; Herodotus 2.91. See Yadin 1968:19; Fontenrose 1980:27; Redford 1990:831; cf. Wyatt 1989:376.

pared with the Egyptian version, 1.2 I Baal takes the place of the tribute in Yamm's demands. The extant Egyptian version gives a prominence to Astarte apparently absent from the Ugaritic version. Indeed, the Ugaritic version relegates Astarte to a secondary role: in 1.2 I 40-43 (?) she restrains Baal and in 1.2 IV 28-30 she rebukes him. Furthermore, unlike the Egyptian version which uses Astarte to convey Sea's demands to the Ennead, in 1.2 I Yamm has messengers who declare his demands before the divine council.

On the basis of some of these and other differences, Posener (1953:461-78) considered the Egyptian version indigenous to Egypt, with only superficial similarities to the West Semitic story (cf. Gardiner 1932). Te Velde (1967:122-23) sees some Semitic influence in this Egyptian treatment of Seth. While the views of Posener and Te Velde warrant caution, Gaster draws attention to a number of West Semitic expressions and motifs in the Astarte papyrus which would indicate some West Semitic influence. The mention of Astarte and Pa-Yamm and the substitution of Seth, the Egyptian equivalent of Baal, for Re, point in the direction of West Semitic influence during the New Kingdom period.[40] Furthermore, Redford (1990:833) labels the story of Astarte and the Sea as "clearly a translation of one version of the story... localized in some Levantine cult-centre and presumably owing much to the foreign community in Memphis."[41] Similarly, J. van Dijk (1986:32) remarks: "it is in my opinion hard to imagine that the Egyptian text could have been written without any knowledge of the Canaanite myth." From this survey of views by scholars of Egyptology, it would appear that the Egyptian story has been influenced by a West Semitic story involving Astarte, Baal and Yamm. The common plot would indicate that the scenes of 1.2 I and IV incorporated a story of the goddess and the Sea well-known along the Levantine coast from Anatolia to at least Joppa and borrowed into New Kingdom Egypt and possibly harmonized with indigenous Egyptian material. This survey would suggest that 1.2 I + 1.2 IV belong together and that 1.2 III may represent an interruption (although the text is very fragmentary). Given the epigraphic arguments as well as the thematic considerations, it would appear prudent to position "1.2 III" before 1.2 I.

---

[40] *ANET* 17; Stadelmann 1967:125-31; Wente in Simpson 1973:133.

[41] The type of translation envisioned by Redford (1990:833 n. 96) involved "oral tradition."

Literary Classification

The Baal Cycle (KTU 1.1-1.6) is generally considered a myth (Sasson 1981). The folklorist Heda Jason (1977:32) classifies the Baal Cycle as a "mythic epic" because of the epic elements involving the hero and his challenger especially in 1.2 I and IV.[42] Parker (1992:114) regards the Baal Cycle as a literary text which contains much myth. While scholars generally label the Baal Cycle as a myth, they disagree over the definition of myth. This disagreement is not only a matter of theoretical curiosity. Rather, it affects the interpretation of the text. For this reason some current views of myth require a brief discussion.

The term myth generally carries a negative connotation in western culture, but this attitude has changed in the fields of modern philosophy and theology, psychoanalysis, anthropology and history of religion which have examined myth in a more positive manner.[43] For anthropologists myths reveal important values or structures in the societies which produce them. Anthropological approaches toward myth tend to be functional rather than formal in character. Unlike formal definitions, functional definitions state what myths "do," such as "explain things." For some anthropologists, myths reflect social structure or resolve social conflict.[44] Following the insights of anthropologists such as B. Malinowski, the classicists G. S. Kirk (1970:41) and W. Buckert (1979:1, 23) regard myths as traditional tales that have a bearing on matters of cultural importance. Oden (1987:55) offers a similar definition of myths: (1) myths are narratives; (2) they are traditional, that is, transmitted almost always orally within a communal setting and for a long time; (3) they contain characters who are more than human in some way; and (4) they relate events from remote antiquity. According to Oden's definition, the Baal Cycle, Keret and Aqhat and many other texts are myths. Based on his work in the history of religions, Mirceau Eliade (1991:5) combines formal and functionalist criteria in

---

[42] So also Milne 1988:169-70. See below pp. 75-76, 337.

[43] See the surveys in Oden 1987:40-91; Batto 1992:1-14. The school of analytical psychology associated with the name of Carl G. Jung has shown a very positive attitude toward myth. For Jung and his disciples, myths are stories reflecting different stages in the development of human consciousness. See Neumann 1954.

[44] For Stith Thompson's criticisms of various functional approaches to myth, see Thompson 1965:171-72.

his definition of myths as stories about supernatural beings; these stories are considered both true because they refer to realities, and sacred because they involve supernatural beings. For Eliade myths describe origins of realities manifest in the world, and people who "live" the myths are able to affect these realities by knowledge of myths.

These views mark a major departure from the traditional definition of myths as narratives centering on divine beings. Indeed, these definitions do not differentiate myth from folktales, legends and sagas, although this distinction proposed by the Grimm brothers has played a role in biblical studies and other fields at least since Johann Gabler in the late eighteenth century.[45] Like myths, folktales, legends and sagas are narratives which were thought to hail from remote antiquity and which contain characters who are in some way more than human. Ugaritic texts such as Keret and Aqhat are sometimes considered myths, but the label of myth is controverted in these cases, and Eissfeldt and others have regarded them instead as saga.[46] Some scholars categorize narratives focusing on human deeds of remote antiquity as legend even though deities appear in them, while narratives focusing on deities are considered myths.[47] The definition of myth might be broadened to include narratives involving divine beings and not only ones centering on divine beings. Indeed, as the folklorist Stith Thompson (1965:169-80, esp. 173-74) as well as Kirk (1970:31-36) and Buckert (1979:22) note, many cultures do not make this distinction. When such a distinction appears problematic, the validity of the definition might be called into question, or it might even lead to jettisoning the category of myth.

Despite the valid criticisms of the older formal definition of myth, a narrower, formal definition retains some merit. In accordance

---

45 See Rogerson 1974:6-7. For the later form-critical adoption of this terminology, see Rogerson1974: 57-65.

46 Eissfeldt 1963:496-501; cf. Gibson 1975:60-68. For a discussion of Eissfeldt's views, see Rogerson 1974:146. Like the Pentateuch and the books of Joshua and Judges, Keret and Aqhat might be viewed as a myth of societal origins. In the case of Keret, it would appear that this narrative was considered the story of a distant ancestor of the dynastic line if the blessing in KTU 1.15 III is any indication. In this blessing Keret is to be blessed among the *pḫr ddn*, "the Assembly of Didanu," an ancestral figure known from both KTU 1.161 and Assyrian King List A. For discussion, see Smith 1990:76-77 n. 120; below pp. 112-13.

47 For this consensus form-critical definition of myth, see Eissfeldt 1965:35; Rogerson, 1974:145-73.

with Thompson's observations, using a narrower, formal definition rather than a functional one permits the identification of myths before moving to the question of identifying their functions according to different approaches whether they are form-critical, myth and ritual, anthropological, structuralist or whatever. Indeed, for ancient societies accessible chiefly through literary, iconographic and other archaeological remains, a formal definition of myth is necessary prior to making wider claims about different myths in relation to their cultural contexts. At the present state of knowledge of the ancient Near East, it can be said that myths are traditional tales preserved and modified in literary forms, and at least in many cases these texts center on deities. Moreover, the functions of myths in general and ancient Near Eastern texts in particular may have evolved considerably. Beginning with a functional definition may preclude the variety of functions which different myths may have enjoyed over a long period of time (see Buckert 1979:2, 4). A text such as the Baal Cycle represents a literary agglomeration of traditional material which functioned in a number of ways, as the following sections suggest.

Finally, Jacobsen's comments (1987:xiii) on Sumerian literary texts may serve as an apt starting-point for appreciating the Baal Cycle:

> The strictly literary Sumerian works can be defined generally as works of praise. The praise can be for something extant and enjoyed, a temple, a deity, or a human king. It can take narrative form as myth or epic, or descriptive form as hymn. The praise may also, however, be praise of something cherished or lost, a destroyed temple, a god who has died, or a dead human relative.

Jacobsen's comments apply in two ways to the Baal Cycle. First, the Baal Cycle represents a narrative of praise devoted to its main character, Baal. Second, the Baal Cycle reuses various forms as well including the spell, curse, lament and perhaps the hymn. The incantation tradition may lie behind the literary topos of the divine champion in the divine assembly in 1.2 I. The summoning of Kothar in 1.1 III and 1.2 III as well as the entire narrative in 1.3 III 8b-1.4 VII contains standard features of temple and palace building stories known from other West Semitic and Mesopotamian texts. All of these re-uses of forms suggest a complex development, as the next three sections suggest.

The Development of the Cycle

According to many scholars the Baal Cycle enjoyed a long oral history prior to its commitment to writing.[48] The dates proposed for the *terminus a quo* of the Baal Cycle range from the third millennium down to the middle of the second millennium. Albright (1933:19) argued that the earliest possible date of composition is fixed by West Semitic names and words transcribed into Egyptian and cuneiform during the early Middle Bronze Age.

Gordon (1958:109 n. 10) takes the absence of horses from the Baal Cycle as a sign of great antiquity (cf. Lambert 1960b). According to de Moor, this observation suffers from relying on an argument from silence (*SPUMB* 49). Furthermore, the argument from silence no longer holds. Recent excavations point to the domestication of the horse by the end of the third millennium. A Syrian site known as Tell es-Sweyhat has yielded a small clay figurine of a horse dating to about 2300.[49] T. Holland notes that the horse figurine has a hole through the muzzle, indicating that the horse is domesticated. Moreover, he also observes that the mane of this animal figurine "is laying down," unlike the manes on figurines of wild horses which "stand erect."

According to Vine (1965:119, 208), the cycle commemorates the founding of the so-called Baal temple at Ugarit by Amorites. Using the archaeological date assigned to this temple, Vine places the Baal Cycle toward the end of the twenty-first century. This date remains highly speculative.

Drower (1975:155) notes the great difference between the hierarchies of deities in the Baal Cycle and ritual texts, and suggests that this discrepancy points to the great antiquity of the Baal Cycle. De Moor (*SPUMB* 48) is rightly cautious about this criterion for dating because the deities in the Baal Cycle are mentioned in later Ugaritic texts. Indeed, the difference may be due as much to variations between genres.

---

[48] Albright 1933:19; 1934b:111; 1958:36; *YGC* 4; *CEBCR* 3; Whitaker 1970; *SPUMB* 48; *CMHE* 112-113; Horwitz 1979:390 n. 6.

[49] So John Noble Wilford, "Ancient Clay Horse is Found in Syria," *New York Times*, Sunday, Janaury 3, 1993. I wish to thank my father, Donald E. Smith, for bringing this article to my attention. See also Don Babwin, "Discovery by U. [University] of C. [Chicago] team sheds new light on antiquity," *The Chicago Tribune*, Sunday, 3 January 1993, section 2, pages 1, 3. I wish to thank my mother-in-law, Sonia Bloch, for sending me this article. The basis for dating the find remains unclear. Otherwise on horses in the ancient Near East, see the summary in Firmage 1992:1136.

De Moor (*SPUMB* 50-51) argues that the Baal Cycle shows signs of composition during the middle of the second millennium. He argues that Baal as the proper name of the storm god does not appear until the mid-second millennium (see also *YGC* 124).[50] De Moor (*SPUMB* 50-52) cites other features in the cycle in his argument for a mid-second millennium date. In incorporating the Amorite god, Amurru, the Baal Cycle has apparently demoted him from head of an Amorite pantheon to the lowly position as Athirat's lackey.[51] De Moor supposes that this change would have probably occurred during the middle of the second millennium. De Moor (*SPUMB* 49) points out that the so-called temple of Baal is not to be dated prior to the mid-nineteenth century since the two sphinxes found in the temple bear the cartouche of Ammenemes III (ca. 1842-1797). The cartouches do not provide, however, a date for the building of the temple, much less for the Baal Cycle. De Moor concludes that a tentative date of the nineteenth century would be suitable for the beginning of the Baal Cycle's composition.

Despite some of the difficulties in the evidence advanced by de Moor, his proposed dating for the cycle is compatible with its overall perspective, which reflects the financial support of, if not the urban, commercial setting of Ugarit, during the second millennium. Geographical references, such as Lebanon (*lbnn*), the Anti-Lebanon (*šryn*), Amurru (*ʾamr*), Sapan (*ṣpn*) and possibly also Byblos (*gbl*), point to ancient Ugarit as the backdrop for the cycle (Eissfeldt 1940). While the temple described in KTU 1.4 V-VII may not have been identified directly with the so-called temple of Baal excavated at Ras Shamra, it indicates an urban setting of a developed city-state.[52] On the basis of this approach, a date of the eighteenth century or later is possible (see *CMHE* 113), as Ugarit was already flourishing at this time (Drower 1975:132). This would correspond with the period of the early monarchs of Ugarit (Kitchen 1975; cf. Pardee 1988b:173). By this time Baal-Haddu may have become the divine patron of the Ugaritic dynasty as evidenced by the theophoric element **(h)d* in several royal names.[53] His place in the Ugarit pan-

---

[50] The argument of Pettinato (1980) to the contrary that the name of Baal is attested at Ebla, Abu-Salabikh and Mari is problematic. See Koch 1988:196, 204.

[51] See also Perlman 1978. The main difficulty with this argument is that the place-name, Amurru, is spelled *ʾamr* in Ugaritic while the servant's name is *ʾamrr*. See Pardee 1977:8 and esp. nn. 45-46.

[52] On this point, see below p. 79.

[53] On this point, see further below p. 90.

theon suggested by the Baal Cycle therefore may have represented an exaltation not only of the storm-god, but also of the king who named himself after Baal-Haddu. The time of Niqmaddu I and his line at Ugarit seems a plausible setting for the origins of at least some parts of the Baal Cycle.[54]

Scholars have used other features to date the Baal Cycle. D. Freedman (1970-71: 80-81) proposed that the formula for describing events of seven days in the Baal Cycle (KTU 1.4 VI 24-33) indicates a date ca. 2000. According to Freedman, the formula in the Baal Cycle is much older than comparable formulas in Aqhat and Keret. The Ugaritic versions predate the formulas in Gilgamesh 11 and the Sultan Tepe version of the Nergal-Ereshkigal myth, both dated to the first millennium. Albright (1933:19; 1958:36-38), Ginsberg (1946:46) and Held (1959) also suggested that the archaisms and archaic style in the Baal Cycle indicate its great age. De Moor (*SPUMB* 48) rejects this argument and suggests that apparent archaisms may represent scribal archaizing (cf. Lambert 1968a:124). Unfortunately, none of the criteria proposed for the early period of the Baal Cycle's composition is firm. Indeed, the grammatical evidence which has been marshalled is restricted. The following section provides a detailed discussion of the grammatical data which suggest a date older than the Ugaritic prose texts.

The material shared by KTU 1.3 IV-VI and 17 VI-1.18 I and IV points to the former's relatively secondary character (Parker 1989b:115). These passages describe how Anat travels to El and attempts to gain his permission for her plans. In the case of the passage in the Baal Cycle, Anat threatens El in order to win his permission for the construction of a palace for the Storm-god whereas in Aqhat, Anat threatens El in order to win his leave to avenge Aqhat's rejection of her advances toward him. Parker notes the well-known parallel between Aqhat and Gilgamesh 6 which describes Ishtar's threats before Anu induced by Gilgamesh's rejection of her. Based on this parallel Parker argues that the use of the material in Aqhat comports with its original context more suitably than it does in the Baal Cycle, suggesting that its usage of this traditional type-scene is secondary. Indeed, it does appear that the threat has been refitted

---

[54] See below pp. 33–34. This is also the period when Syrian seals depict together the weather god and the winged, armed goddess who are interpreted as Baal and Anat (so Tessier 1984:79).

in the Baal Cycle to support the pursuit of Baal's palace. At least one motif in Aqhat would then predate its counterpart in the Baal Cycle.

Before entertaining a hypothetical reconstruction of the cycle's development, it is necessary to mention the issue of the cycle's oral and written transmission which has been the subject of considerable discussion. The Baal Cycle contains a number of both oral and written scribal errors (Segert 1958; Horwitz 1977). Oral scribal errors (Segert 1958:211 n. 20; Horwitz 1977:124 n. 10) could have occurred at various stages of transmission or even at a late point of composition if one were to assume that the later stage of writing these texts entailed an oral recitation of some sort. Cross (*CMHE* 112-13, 117 n. 18, 127 n. 50) argues that the Ugaritic myths were transmitted by singing and orally dictated to a scribe. Cross' reconstruction has been challenged by Horwitz (1977:124) who argues:

> Not only does the evidence in the Ugaritic myths support Cross' theory of the transmission of the Ugaritic myths, but the procedure which he outlines has parallels in other literatures as well. Therefore, his theory may well be correct. But one can of course accept the theory of oral development and transmission without being bound to the view that the tablets which we possess are the first reductions of the myths to writing. The fact that the mythology as a genre generally requires dictation at some time is no proof that our present Ugaritic tablets were not copies of written texts. If such was the case, it is to be expected that some errors arose during dictation and others during copying.

An equally important issue for Cross' reconstruction is simply the general lack of evidence for late oral transmission. K. van der Toorn suggests the possibility that KBo 8.86//88 (Haas and Wilhelm 1974:260-63) and KUB 44.7 (which may be a copy of the same ritual) may bear on the question of the oral recitation of Baal's exploits.[55] The colophons for this text mention Mount Hazzi. It is unclear why Mount Hazzi gives its name to this ritual; the mountain could be either part of the subject or site of the ritual, or the recipient of the sacrifice. The ritual preceding the colophon in KBo 8 no. 86//88 alludes to the Storm-god (always written ^{d}U) and "the Song of Kingship (?)." Haas and Wilhelm transcribe and translate lines 8-12 of KBo 8.88, with restorations from KBo 8.86:

---

[55] Professor van der Toorn, personal communication. My thanks go to Dr. G. Beckman for his aid with the following discussion.

LÚ^{MEŠ} NAR šar-ra-aš-ši-ia-as [(SÌR)]
SÌR^{RU} nu ma-aḫ-ḫa-an GUNNI^{MEŠ}
kat-ta e-ša-an-da-ri nu EGIR-an-[(da)]
ḫa-an-te-ez-zi *A-NA* ^{D}U ke-el-di-[(ia)]
ki-iš-ša-an ši-pa-an-da-a[(n)-zi]

Die Sänger singen das Lied des Königtums.
Und sobald die Herdstellen
niederbrennen, opfert man danach
zuerst dem Wettergott zum Heile
folgendermassen

This ritual prescribes the "Song of Kingship (?)" before an offering to the Storm-god. The ritual in column i of KUB 44 no. 7 (which likely belongs with the colophon as part of the same text) mentions that "they sing the Song of the Sea" (*[Š]A A.AB.BA ŠIR$_3$ ŠIR$_3$RU*), although there is no allusion to the Storm-god in the little which is preserved of this text. Hurrian compositions attested in Hittite are not infrequently entitled "Song of so and so," named after their main character (Hoffner 1990:9, 38); perhaps in "the Song of the Sea," the figure of Sea is the main character. Given that the colophons to the texts mention Mount Hazzi, Baal might be also part of the topic of the two songs. They may refer to deeds of Baal, perhaps even his defeat of Yamm, but this is only a guess. Indeed, given the uncertainty as to which storm-god stands behind the ideogram ^{d}U, it is possible that these songs involve the storm-god known from Hittite mythology rather than Baal (Laroche 1975:63). Indeed, the god in question is more likely Tessub, given the Hurrian technical terms, but there has been considerable syncretism in late Hittite times, and the Storm-god here might have features of other storm-gods including West Semitic Baal. The scribed notation in KTU 1.4 V 42-43 may suggest a verbal recitation as well.

The evidence thus far discussed combined with internal evidence may permit a tentative and hypothetical reconstruction of four stages in the development of the Baal Cycle.

1. Originally various stories about Baal may have circulated separately. It may suggested that originally independent episodes perhaps included the story of Sea's demand of tribute from the divine council in KTU 1.2 I, the Baal-Yamm conflict in KTU 1.2 IV, the battle of Anat in KTU 1.3 II,[56] the audience of Athirat before

[56] Fisher, *RSP III* 240, 251; cf. Smith 1986b:326 n. 73.

El with Anat listening in the background in 1.4 IV, the building of Baal's palace in KTU 1.3 III-1.4 VII, the Baal-Leviathan struggle mentioned in KTU 1.5 I, and the death of Baal and his return to life in KTU 1.5 II-1.6 II. As noted above,[57] the figure of Mot himself may have been secondary to the development of the story. The development of the figure of Mot perhaps belongs to a later stage than the Baal-Yamm tradition.

Variants of these episodes in the cycle suggest their originally separate character. The story of Sea's demand of tribute from the divine council is attested in KTU 1.2 I, the Egyptian Astarte Papyrus of the 18th or 19th dynasty and other texts.[58] The episode of Athirat's audience before El in 1.4 IV appears also in the Elkunirsa story (*ANET* 519; Pope 1971). The two conflicts of Baal against his enemies, Yamm and Leviathan, constituted apparently separate traditions. Each of these stories perhaps served as a prelude to kingship. This reconstruction is compatible with the view of Cross (*CMHE* 120, 149; 1976:333) who understands the conflict stories of Baal-Yamm, Baal-Leviathan and Baal-Mot as "alloforms" or "variants" of the same type of cosmogonic story representing the victory of life over death (see also *CMHE* 58, 116, 156). A text from Mari appears to confirm at least a Middle Bronze date of the Baal-Yamm tradition. Durand (1993:45; cf. Charpin and Durand 1986:174) presents a text (A.1968. lines 1′-4′) that quotes the words of Nur-Sin of Aleppo to Zimri-lim of Mari: "I s[et] you on the thr[one of your father]; the weapons with which I had battled against Sea (*têmtum*) I gave to you" (*lu-t[e-e]r-ka a-na giš-[gu-za é a-bi-ka] ú-te-er-ka giš-tukul-[meš] ša it-ti te-em-tim am-ta-aḫ-ṣú ad-di-na-ak-kum*). Charpin and Durand (1986:174; Bordreuil and Pardee 1993) compare this passage with the Baal-Yamm conflict. The eighteenth century Mari text provides the earliest literary witness to the tradition of the Baal-Yamm conflict. The tradition could be considerably older than this date, but for the first time external data push back the date of the Baal-Yamm tradition at least to the Middle Bronze Age. The conflict tradition perhaps was not tied originally to the palace-building tradition of KTU 1.3 III-1.4 VII, although both the Baal Cycle and Enuma Elish have amalgamated the traditions of their

---

[57] See pp. 18-19.

[58] Gardiner 1932; Gaster 1952:82-83; Stadelmann 1967:125-31; Luft 1978: 217-18; J. van Dijk 1986:31-32. See above pp. 23-25 for further discussion.

divine heroes' battle, victory and proclamation of their kingship with the construction of a palace marking their sovereignty. The principle for the collection and integration for these diverse materials in the Baal Cycle is the exaltation of Baal much as the diverse materials in Enuma Elish served the purpose of exalting Marduk (Lambert 1965).[59]

2. The relatively early oral stage perhaps overlapped with a second stage when various stories about Baal were committed to writing separately. Internal evidence provides signs of originally separate written stories. The beginning of the fifth tablet (KTU 1.5 I) shows signs of having incorporated or alluded to an earlier version of a cosmogonic conflict between Baal and *ltn*. As noted above, the "when. . . then" opening in KTU 1.5 I has been compared with the beginning of a number of ancient Near Eastern stories and would appear to indicate an originally separate tradition about Baal and *ltn*.[60] This older material would have been redacted secondarily into the context of Mot's message to Baal. Furthermore, Anat's battle in KTU 1.3 II within the larger framework of Baal's rise to kingship may represent the secondary inclusion of an originally distinct story about Anat who battles alone in KTU 1.13 and 1.83 and whose martial exploits are cited in KTU 1.3 III 37-IV 4.

3. Writing errors detected in the tablets point to a third stage. These scribal mistakes indicate a prior written copy of the cycle from which the extant texts were copied.[61] Horwitz (1973:165-73; 1974:78; 1979:393-94) argues on the basis of the distribution of the small vertical wedge, called traditionally in Ugaritic studies the "word divider," that the scribe Ilimalku was a copyist of a prior written text. Instead of regarding the small vertical wedge as a word divider, Horwitz suggests that the wedge served as a metrical device designed to divide two words. From this feature Horwitz (1979:392-93) deduces:

> The use of the small vertical wedge as a metrical device is sophisticated enough to imply a thorough knowledge and analysis of the written forms of the myths. Thus, the manner in which Ilimilku distributed the small vertical wedge supports the hypothesis that he was a copyist.

---

[59] For further discussion, see below pp. 103-104.

[60] Albright 1924:364; *CMHE* 118-20, 149-50; Wallace 1985:66-67.

[61] Rosenthal 1939:216, 218; Segert 1958:205, 211 n. 20; 1971:415; Horwitz 1977:124 n. 10; Sasson 1981:93.

Parker's observations noted above on the relationship between 1.3 IV-VI and 17 VI-1.18 I and IV suggest that at this point in the literary tradition, traditional material known from other compositions was incorporated secondarily into the Baal Cycle and modified in accordance with its plot. This third stage may also represent the point at which originally separate stories were connected. Baal's declaration of his kingship in KTU 1.4 VII 45-52 functions both as the completion of the palace episode and the beginning of his conflict with Mot. The speech secondarily links together what were originally different materials about Baal.

4. The fourth and final stage in the development of the Baal Cycle involved the copying of the tablets which stemmed from an earlier written form of the cycle. The extant tablets date to 1400-1350, and perhaps more precisely to 1380-1360.[62]

In closing, this reconstruction remains highly hypothetical as it is deduced largely from internal evidence. Although the criteria are inadequate for dating (Held 1969:74 n. 32), some of them may suggest the relative antiquity of the Baal Cycle, or at least of some of its plot and motifs. Some of the grammatical features considered in the next section may suggest the antiquity of the Baal Cycle, if not relative to the other literary poetic texts, then to the prose texts.

Grammatical Dating of the Cycle

Various grammatical features have been invoked to support the high antiquity of the Baal Cycle (Ginsberg 1950:158; 1973:131-32; Held 1959:174-75; 1969:74 n. 32; *CMHE* 113). These features include: (1) the alphabet; (2) orthography and phonology; (3) various morphological items, especially the indicative verbal system; (4) syntax; and (5) vocabulary.

1. The Alphabet

Greenfield (1969:96-97) notes that the rise of the Ugaritic twenty-two letter alphabet developed by the time of the extant copy of the Baal Cycle, which like all the literary texts is written in a thirty-letter alphabet. The implications of this development are significant for

[62] See above p. 1.

understanding the character of the Ugaritic poetic texts, according to Greenfield (1969:96-97):

> A very plausible conclusion from the above considerations is that the main Ugaritic alphabet, with its panoply of possible phonemic realizations, was either archaic, obsolescent, or anachronistic during a good part of the period of its known use (1400-1200). At the time of its invention—better (for I follow in this Albright and Cross & Lambdin), at the time when a Canaanite model was 'cuneiformized'—the full graphemic-phonemic panoply was still in use (or was used in 'liturgical' recitation of the epics). It soon became a sort of etymological, historical spelling as found later in Hebrew, Aramaic and Arabic.

Dietrich and Loretz (1989) challenge the view that the shorter alphabet represents a reduction from the longer alphabet. According to Dietrich and Loretz, the longer alphabet was based on the shorter coastal or "Phoenician" alphabet and supplemented by letters of the "southern" tradition represented by the Beth-Shemesh tablet. If this reconstruction were correct, Greenfield's argument would be problematic, since the longer alphabet would be no older or archaic than the shorter alphabet. However, the reconstruction of Dietrich and Loretz remains highly hypothetical, as Sass (1991) has observed.[63] The older view as represented in Greenfield's remarks remains as likely, if not more so. Moreover, the orthographic and phonological evidence is consonant with Greenfield's view.

2. Orthography and Phonology

According to Greenfield (1969:95) and Garr (1986), originally unvoiced consonants in some words in the Baal Cycle did not shift to their voiced variants as found in other Ugaritic texts and therefore represent a retention of archaic spellings. Some variant spellings of the same words and roots in Ugaritic represent two sets of spellings, one an older and original set and the other a secondary set which reflect specific sound shifts. On the one hand, some words in the Baal Cycle reflect an archaic spelling. For example, *yṣʾa*, "he left," in KTU 1.2 IV 30 represents an older spelling, while the more contemporary spelling of the root is represented in *ẓʾi* in KTU 1.12 I 14, 19. Similarly, *yṣḥq* in KTU 1.4 IV 28 and 1.6 III 16 shows the older spelling of the word, while *yẓḥq* in KTU 1.12 I 12 represents

[63] For difficulties concerning the view of Dietrich and Loretz, see also Segert 1991:86-88.

the contemporary spelling affected by a voicing of the consonant. It may be noted that some genuinely archaic spellings occur only in the Baal Cycle (e.g., *tkšd*; *thrm*, "pure" in 1.4 V 19, 34).

On the other hand, Garr notes four words in the Baal Cycle that exhibit sound shifts due to voicing: *ybrd*, "he cuts" (KTU 1.3 I 6) 〈 **prd*; *lpš*, "garment" (KTU 1.5 VI 16, 1.6 II 10) 〈 **lbš*; *tkd̲d*, "it attracts" (?) (KTU 1.5 I 16)[64] 〈 **kšd* (?); and *d̲rt*, "vision" (KTU 1.6 III 5, 11) 〈 **šhr* (?). These forms reflects contemporary spellings of these words. In sum, the Baal Cycle contains both older and more recent spellings, in one case possibly of the same roots perhaps used for poetic contrast in the same bicolon (*tkšd* and *kd̲d* in 1.5 I 16-17).

3. *Morphology*

Garr (1986:52 n. 50) notes the contrast between *whn*, "and behold" 〈 **w-hn*, in Keret and Aqhat (KTU 1.14 II 14; 1.17 V 3) versus *wn*, "and behold," in the Baal Cycle (KTU 1.2 III 22; 1.4 IV 50). If *wn* in the Baal Cycle derives from **w-hn* (so *GA* 141), then the form *wn* in the Baal Cycle would be linguistically secondary to the form *whn* in Aqhat and Keret.

Held (1959) suggests that the *Gt*-stem form of the roots **mḫṣ* and **ḫṣb* only in the Baal Cycle represents an indication of its great antiquity. This view is unverifiable. *Gt*-stem forms are attested in West Semitic texts well into the first millennium, suggesting that these forms are not necessarily a mark of high antiquity.[65]

In his study of the older singular feminine ending *-(a)y*, Layton (1990:241-45) notes a clear example from the Baal Cycle. The form *brky*, "spring," in KTU 1.5 VI 16 has been recognized as equivalent to the form *brkt* in the copy of the same passage preserved in KTU 1.133.6. Another plausible case is represented by *nʿmy* in KTU 1.5 VI 6, paralleled by KTU 1.17 II 41. The word stands in parallelism with the variant feminine forms, *ysmt* (KTU 1.5 VI 7) and *ysmsmt* (KTU 1.17 II 42), and describes *ʾarṣ*, a feminine noun in 1.5 VI 6. The hypothesis that *-(a)y* formation contained in *nʿmy* represents an old feminine ending represents the most satisfactory

---

[64] So, based on *šbšt*, "it attracts," in the parallel copy, KTU 1.133. 8; see Garr 1986:47 n. 22; cf. "to long," so Held 1962:285 n. 4, 290; "to hasten," Pope 1978:27, 30 n. 9; cf. Held 1962:289 n. 1.

[65] See Greenfield 1969:97 n. 23. For Ugaritic *Gt*-stem forms in general, see Greenfield 1979.

explanation offered to date. The -*(a)y* ending in the divine names of *ʾarṣy*, *ṭly* and *pdry* has been viewed as either a hypocoristic or feminine ending. The old feminine ending -*(a)y* in the Baal Cycle and Aqhat reflects the archaic character of these two texts relative to prose texts, though not relative to the other epics.

The indicative verbal system has played a role in the discussion of the relative date of the Baal Cycle. Moran (1961:75) offers some cautionary remarks on this topic: "It is clear that the Ugaritic tense system is not that of contemporary Byblian Amarna. But what is it? The writer would make no pretensions of knowing. . ." With no less a disclaimer, an attempt is made in this section to clarify the Ugaritic verbal system in order to address its possible signficance for the date of the language in the Baal Cycle. Moran's reservations about knowledge of the Ugaritic verbal system are understandable. For while **yaqtulu*, **yaqtul* and **qatala* forms[66] are attested in the Ugaritic material, the usage and distribution of these forms have been a matter of great discussion.

The prefix forms are the norm for poetic narrative (*UT* 9.4; 13.32; Fenton 1973:365; Watson 1989). It remains unclear, however, why various verbal forms occur in the same or similar contexts in Ugaritic poetry. In other words, what different function does each different form have, especially in poetic passages where two of the forms occur together? According to many reconstructions of the indicative verbal system (see Verreet 1988), the **yaqtul* preterite past, **yaqtulu* present-future durative and the **qatala* past forms are attested. The verbal forms for narrative in Ugaritic poetry vary, but the prefix forms, especially **yaqtulu*, predominate. The Ugaritic evidence regarding the **yaqtul* preterite is problematic. Segert (1984: 62) and Sivan (1984b:147-49) omit any discussion of a **yaqtul* preterite in Ugaritic.

Greenstein (1988:13-14) doubts that a semantic distinction is to be drawn between Ugaritic **yaqtul* and **yaqtulu*:

> The very existence of a *yaqtul* preterite in Ugaritic is open to serious doubt. Rainey has himself been sensitive to this problem and has attempted to identify a very few instances. The form written *wyʿn*, "he spoke up," cannot be unequivocally parsed as a preterite, as Rainey

---

66 These *G*-stem forms are cited in the following discussion to represent the indicative forms of all stems.

> does, because it is only one of several final-*yod* verbs in Ugaritic that occur with the final *y* unwritten (e.g., *ybk*, *ymǵ*, *tšt*, etc.). In the clause *tiššaʾū ʾilūma raʾašātihuma*, "the gods raised their heads" (III AB B, 1:29), I see no reason to separate the verb from the ordinary prefixed form, which in the plural is commonly attested without the nun-augmentation. Again, the apparent lack of a semantic distinction between prefixed forms with and without nun in Ugaritic would be of little moment were it not that in a BH text like Exod 15:2. . . the distinction is likewise hard to maintain. The fact that the prefixed form of the verb never serves as a preterite in Phoenician also diminishes the plausibility of the notion that there was a YQTL preterite in Ugaritic.

This presentation of the issue contains two main arguments against **yaqtul* and **yaqtulu* as "corresponding in a one-to-one manner to two separate forms."[67] According to Greenstein, the variation between *yʿn* and *yʿny* (in their various persons) within identical environments points to a lack of semantic distinction corresponding in a one-to-one manner to two separate forms. The crux of the matter hinges on some III-*y* verbs which appear with and without final -*y* (not including forms with nunation) even in the same sort of context. For example, *wyʿn* and *wyʿny* both belong to what Verreet (1988:99-103) calls "Zitationsformeln," formulas introducing speeches. From Verreet's lists of these forms (1988:100-02; cf. *UT* 9.12), it is clear that *wyʿny* (including its first, second and third person forms) is relatively rare. *CUL* list eight long forms out of a total of sixty-four cases of both long and short forms. Verreet (1988:102) explains the eight instances as a special stylistic use: the long forms signal a contrast between the speeches preceding and following the long forms. While there is no means presently available to confirm Verreet's theory, this approach does not indicate a semantic distinction corresponding in a one-to-one manner between the short and long forms. Rather, the distinction suggested by Verreet is stylistic in character.

The second type of evidence in Greenstein's argument is that the plurals of some short forms seem to be used in an identical manner as the long forms. The short and long forms would therefore appear to be variants of the same verbal prefix-form. As with the III-*y* forms, the short and long forms of the same verbal prefix form offer

---

67 Professor Greenstein, personal communication, as a clarification to the interpretation of his position given in Smith 1991:65-67 n. 1.

no clear semantic difference corresponding in a one-to-one manner to short and long forms, but only a possible stylistic contrast. As Greenstein argues, **yaqtul* and **yaqtulu* are used similarly.[68]

There is a third context where both of the two prefix forms occur. The poetic texts use both **yaqtul* and **yaqtulu* after various adverbial particles (*ʾidk*, *hl*, *ʾaphn*, *ʾapnk*). The particles *ʾapnk* and *ʾaphn* take various prefix forms, for example **yaqtul* in the case of *yʿl* in 1.6 I 56, but **yaqtulu* in the case of *ytšʾu* in 1.19 I 21 (Fenton 1969:37).

Given these functional parallels between the two forms, it is possible that the preterite function of **yaqtul* was obsolescent already in the time of the written composition of the poetic texts. The prose texts show further obsolescence of **yaqtul*. Gordon (*UT* 13.32) and Mallon (1982:67, 77-78) note the relatively few examples of the **yaqtul* preterite in the prose texts relative to its occurrences in the poetic texts. According to Mallon, the **yaqtul* preterite is rare in the prose texts: *yph* (KTU 1.90.1); *ʾiph* (KTU 2.25.4); *yʿl* (KTU 1.127.29). Assuming that **yaqtul* is obsolescent in the prose texts, it would suggest that the frequency of the form in the poetic texts is relatively archaic. In sum, the **yaqtul* preterite forms seem to be indicated in numerous short III-*y* forms and III-ʾ forms ending in *ʾi* in the poetic texts. It appears from the similar usage of **yaqtul* and **yaqtulu*, that the two forms, though different originally in morphology, are functional variants as Greenstein suggests.[69] The distribution and usage of **yaqtul* forms also suggest that they are a regular feature of the Ugaritic poetic texts functioning in contexts equivalent to **yaqtulu*, but their rarity in prose texts seems to reflect their further obsolescence. Their more common occurrence in Ugaritic poetry compared to Ugaritic prose would seem to be a mark of archaism. Finally, Greenstein (1993) makes the intriguing suggestion that prefix forms are customary for poetic narrative because Ugaritic poetry deliberately renders narrative in the dramatic present, unlike biblical narrative which places the action in the past through the use of suffix forms as well as *waw*-consecutive forms.

The **qatala* form in Ugaritic poetry represents an equally difficult problem. Scholars have long noted the contrast in the distribution of **qatala* forms in Ugaritic poetry and prose. While **qatala* is the

---

68 Greenstein's appeal to the loss of **yaqtul* in Phoenician is controvertible as evidence for the same phenomenon in Ugaritic. See Smith 1991:67 n. 1.

69 Cf. Smith 1991:65-67 n. 1.

characteristic verbal form for past narration in prose texts, its usage diverges in poetic texts. As Fenton (1973:365) notes, the **qatala* form in narrative is confined to specific usages; otherwise the prefix forms are employed. Not including cases not entirely obscured by broken contexts, there are one hundred and fifty-two forms in the Baal Cycle plausibly identifiable as **qatala*.[70] The text of Keret contains fourty-nine instances.[71] Aqhat attests to at least twenty-one cases of the suffix form.[72]

Many **qtl* are generally presumed to be **qatala*, although whether some of the **qtl* forms are instead infinitives cannot be easily determined, as Gordon notes (*UT* 9.4 n. 1). For example, the infinitives, *šmḫ*, "she rejoices," and *ṣḥq*, "she laughs," in 1.4 II 28, V 20, 25 and 1.18 I 22 would suggest caution in assuming that *šmḫ*, "he rejoices," in 1.4 V 35 is a **qatala* form; it may be an infinitive. The forms, *wʿn* in 1.6 I 53 and *ʿrb* in 1.17 II 26, are likewise narrative infinitives. Similarly, the **qtl* forms in 1.4 VI 40-56 and 1.5 IV 12-16 might be infinitives.

Some forms of verbs I-*y* are also problematic since their consonantal spelling does not distinguish always whether they are prefix or suffix forms. As a result, they are omitted from consideration below, except in those cases where there is further evidence that helps to determine their form. The final ʾ of the verb **yṣʾ*, "to depart," clarifies forms of this root. In the case of *lyrt*, "you shall surely descend," in 1.5 I 6, the second person ending indicates assimilation /dt/ 〉 /tt/ in a suffix form. On occasion verbs in the immediate vicinity may suggest the form: the prefix forms surrounding *yṣq* in 1.3 II 31 may suggest that it is a prefix form rather than a suffix form.

As Watson (1989) observes, the usages of **qatala* may be distin-

---

[70] 1.1 III 18; IV 2, 4, 9, 15, 19, 28, 29, 30; V 8, 21; 1.2 I 3, 13, 19, 21, 24, 33, 38, 43, 45, 46; III 22 (2x); IV 6, 7, 8, 17, 32-33; 1.3 I 2-3, 4, 8, 18; II 3, 11-12, 19, 41; III 4, 38-46; IV 33, 40, 41, 44; V 17, 27, 30; 1.4 I 23; II 3, 8, 22-23; III 14, 17, 23-24, 30-31; IV 9 (2x), 10, 12, 16, 19, 31-32, 33-34; V 3, 6, 27, 35-36, 44-45; VI 13 (2x), 34, 35, 40, 41, 44, 45, 47, 48, 49, 50, 51, 52, 53, 54, 55 (2x), 56; VII 8, 9, 21, 23, 43 (2x); VIII 22; 1.5 I 6, 9, 17, 22, 23; II 7, 8, 13, 20; IV 12, 13, 15; V 17, 19, 23; VI 3, 5, 8, 9-10, 23; 1.6 I 6, 41-42; II 17, 19, 24; III 1, 14, 20; V 12, 13, 14, 15, 17, 18; VI 17 (2x), 18, 19, 20 (2x), 21, 22, 30.

[71] 1.14 I 14; II 39, 41, 43; III 55 (2x), 59; IV 2-9, 17, 19, 49-50; 1.15 I 1-2; IV 27; V 10; VI 4; 1.16 I 33 (2x), 39-41, 44, 51, 61-62; II 19-20//22-23; III 3, 12, 13-15; IV 2, 3; VI 13-14, 32, 35-36, 44, 51 (2x).

[72] 1.17 II 14, 31; V 31-32; 1.18 I 16 (2x); IV 33, 36; 1.19 II 26, 29 (2x); III 7, 9, 22, 23, 35, 37; IV 49, 51-52, 58.

guished according to their attestation in direct discourse and narrative within the Baal Cycle (KTU 1.1-1.6), Keret (1.14-1.16) and Aqhat (1.17-1.19). While **qatala* shows many of the same usages in both prose and poetic texts, it also exhibits additional functions in poetic usage.[73] Six basic usages known from Ugaritic prose and four additional usages in poetry unattested in the extant Ugaritic prose texts have been identified for **qatala*: (1) stative; (2) past report; (3) continuation of other perfects; (4) background information[74]; (5) subordination; (6) performative perfect; (7) optative perfect; (8) contrast with prefix forms; (9) report of action commanded commanded in imperative; and (10) delimitation of a section. Almost all the examples of **qatala* fit these categories. The Baal Cycle has a number of broken contexts which makes it impossible to assign precisely some possible **qatala* forms to any of the ten categories[75]; otherwise, all of the suffix forms in the Baal Cycle conform to the ten categories. Lest the discounting of problematic contexts appear to represent a case of special pleading, it may be noted that 128 of 152 of all forms plausibly identified as **qatala* in the Baal Cycle comport with the ten categories. Keret contains only two forms which do not fit the following ten categories; both forms involve a lacuna or some other interpretational difficulty (1.16 I 44, 50). Without exception, all of the forms identified as **qatala* in Aqhat conform to the ten categories. The following selected examples are divided within each category according to direct discourse and narrative (so also Watson 1989).

1. A number of stative **qatala* forms appear in Ugaritic narrative poetry: *ʿz*, "he is strong" (1.2 IV 17; 1.6 VI 17 [2x], 18, 19, 20 [2x]); and *šbʿt*, "she is sated" (1.3 II 19). The three-fold repetition of *ṣḥrrt* (1.3 V 17; 1.4 VIII 22; 1.6 II 24) is likely a stative **qatul(a)l* form.[76]

---

73 Prose functions for **qatala* unattested in poetry are omitted from the following discussion.

74 See Greenstein 1993. While prefix forms clearly are preferred for narrative in Ugaritic poetry, it is not clear that no **qatala* forms are used in narrative. Nonetheless, some of the forms discussed in categories one and two might be classified along the lines suggested by Greenstein. Previously I had referred to this category as a pluperfect (see below), but in view of some of the examples, Greenstein's view appears preferable.

75 1.1 IV 2, 4, 9, 15, 19, 28, 29, 30; 1.2 I 3, 38, 43, 46; 1.3 III 4; 1.4 II 3; 1.5 V 23.

76 Some BH words for colors may also derive originally from **qatull-* with reduplicated final radical; cf. Arabic IX and XI forms for colors and defects (T.

Instances from direct discourse are numerous. KTU 1.4 IV 31-34 contains two stative verbs in direct discourse: "Surely you are hungry (*rǵb rǵbt*). . ."//"Surely you are thirsty (*ǵmʾu ǵmʾit*). . ." In 1.4 V 3, El is praised: *ḥkmt*, "you are wise." In a parallel passage, 1.3 V 30, Anat praises El's decree: "your decree, El, is wise." Similarly, in 1.16 IV 2 an unnamed figure is praised: *ḥkmt kṯr lṭp[n]*, "you are wise like Bull Benefi[cent]."[77] In 1.2 IV 32 and 34, the proclamation of Baal as king is accompanied by the double proclamation of Yamm's death: *ym lmt*, "Yamm is surely dead."

To communiqués delivered by messengers Kothar in 1.1 III 18 and Anat in 1.3 IV 33 retort: *ʾatm bštm wʾan šnt*, "You are slow and I am fast" (*ANET* 137), or "While you delay I do quit" (*CML*^{2} 51).[78] Clifford (*CMCOT* 86 n. 59) notes that *bštm* is a stative perfect. Ginsberg (1944:27 n. 9) insists on the stative character of the second verb as well, but the cognates for the second verb are verbs of motion.[79] Thiṣ form is likely not a stative verb, as Gibson's translation suggests. The context would suggest that the messengers delay while their divine superiors respond quickly in accordance with the message.[80]

The verb **ydʿ* appears as a stative in direct discourse (1.1 V 8, 21; 1.3 V 27//1.18 I 16; 1.16 I 33; cf. future *wʾidʿ* in 1.16 III 8). To the verb **ydʿ* 1.16 I 33 adds *rḥmt*, "you are compassionate," and 1.3 V

O. Lambdin, personal communication). For this word, see Diest 1971; Rendsburg 1987b:625.

[77] For these three examples, see *EUT* 43.

[78] Many commentators compare *bštm* with BH *bōšēš*, "to delay" in Judg 5:28 and Exod 32:1 (*UT* 19.532; *CMCOT* 86 n. 59; *MLC* 530). Gordon, al-Yasin (1951:no. 93) and Caquot and Sznycer (*TO* 171 n. u) cite Arb *bassa*, "to drive (a caravan) slowly," but according to Kopf (1955:135) Arabic sources explain this word in various ways and therefore are not a good source to explain Ugaritic *bštm*. The vocalization of this word follows that of the Hebrew form. Comparison with Akk *bêšu*, "to depart" (*AHw* 123; *CAD B*:214), though semantically proximate (de Moor 1979:647 n. 54), suggests an originally middle weak root containing PS **h* or ʿ. Given that the middle weak forms appear semantically unrelated to Ugaritic *bštm* and BH *bōšēš*, this would appear to constitute a separate root. The BH forms of the word seem to reflect an analogous extension of **qatala* from middle weak roots to geminates, while the Arabic second form shows this extension to the strong verb as well.

[79] Akk *šanû*, "to change, depart" (*AHw* 1166-67a); Syr *šnʾ*, "to depart" (*LS* 789). See *CMCOT* 86 n. 59; *TO* 171 n. v; *CML*^{2} 158; *MLC* 630.

[80] Clifford (*CMCOT* 86-87 n. 59) suggests that the messengers' divine superiors travel faster due to their greater abilities. For other opinions, see Smith 1985:235-56.

27//1.18 I 16 adds *ʾanšt*, "you are irrascible."[81] Other cases of statives in direct speech appear in 1.4 IV 33-34, 1.5 V 17, 1.6 I 6, and 1.6 II 17.

2. The fientic **qatala* apparently refers sometimes to narrative past action. At the end of Baal's wrestling march with Mot in 1.6 VI 21-22, "Mot falls" (*mt ql*) and "Baal falls on him" (*bʿl ql ʿln*). This example may, however, belong to category ten.[82] The opening scene of Keret reports his various misfortunes with some **qatala* forms (1.14 I 7-14),[83] but Greenstein (1993) regards these forms as providing background information (see category four below). This use may apply to other apparent fientic **qatala* forms. For example, 1.15 I 1-2 describes how "she [Ḥry] extended (*mṯkt*) a hand" to the hungry and thirsty. Other instances of fientic **qatala* include 1.4 VII 9 and 21 (if this form is not an infinitive or does not belong to category ten), 1.14 IV 17 and 19, perhaps 1.4 II 3, 8 and 1.16 III 3 (if the form *sb* is not an imperative).

The forms, *šrḥq* and *št* in 1.3 IV 40-41, might be interpreted along these lines if they are not infinitive forms.[84] The verbs in the divine feasting topos in 1.4 VI 40-56 and 1.5 IV 12-16 may be narrative **qatala* forms if they are not infinitives.

In direct discourse, **qatala* refers to past action. Athirat asks in 1.4 III 30-31: *mgntm ṯr ʾil dpʾid//hm ǵẓtm bny bnwt*, "Have you beseeched Bull El the Benign// Or entreated the Creator of Creatures?"[85] Fenton (1969b:199) takes the four forms in 1.4 IV 31-34 as **qtl*, and he translates them in the past tense: "You have been hungry (*rǵbt*) so you came here (*wmǵt*)//You have been thirsty (*ǵmʾit*), so you came in (*wʿ-*)." The first verb in each clause is stative, which is frequently expressed by **qtl* (see category one above).

According to Fenton (1973:35; cf. 1969b:199 n. 4), there is another literary convention used to report past action in direct speech: "in conversations, that is, when the 'characters' of the poems address each other, they refer to, or inform of, past events in

---

[81] For discussion, see below pp. 311-12.

[82] See below p. 56.

[83] For the idiom of **tbʿ*, to depart," for "to die" in line 14, cf. BH **hlk* in Gen 15:2; Ps 58:9; see Rabin 1977:339.

[84] The **qatala* forms in 1.4 II 3 and 8 may serve to structure the description of Athirat working at her domestic chores.

[85] For Ugaritic rhetorical questions, see Held 1969.

the *qtl* form, not *yqtl*.'' The verbs in Anat's speech of KTU 1.3 III 38-46 are **qatala* forms apparently conforming to Fenton's rule (Fenton 1969b:199-200). In this speech Anat proclaims her martial prowess.

> I indeed smote (*lmḫšt*) the Beloved of El, Yamm
> I indeed destroyed (*lklt*) River, the Great God...
> I smote (*mḫšt*) the Serpent, the Twisty One...
> I smote (*mḫšt*) the Divine Bitch, Fire,
> I destroyed (*klt*) the Daughter of El, Flame...

In 1.5 I 22-23, Mot recounts how Baal invited (*ṣḥn//qrʾan*) his brothers and him to feast (cf. prefix forms in direct discourse in 1.5 II 21-22). In their search for the dead Baal, El's two servants report to him in KTU 1.5 VI 3-8 (Ginsberg 1944:29 n. 20):

> We went about (*sbn*)...to the watery ends,
> We two arrived (*mǵny*) at the beautiful outback of the Earth.
> To the beautiful fields of the shores of Death,
> We two came (*mǵny*) upon Baal fallen to the Earth.

El's messengers go on to inform him of Baal's condition: ''he is dead,'' *mt*//''he has perished,'' *ḫlq* (1.5 VI 9-10//1.6 I 41-42//1.6 III 1). Mot reports to Anat in 1.6 II how he arrived (*mǵt*) at the same location. Mot later recounts his destruction at Anat's hands with a seven-fold repetition, *pht*, ''I experienced...'' (1.6 V 12-18).

Keret's wife, Ḥuray, thrice tells the nobles that ''I invited you (*ṣḥtkm*) to eat and drink'' (1.15 IV 27; V 10; VI 4). In his attempt to withhold the truth of his illness from his daughter, Keret orders his son to tell her that he is busy feasting (1.16 I 39-40), which the son then relates to his sister (1.16 I 61-62). In his speeches directed first to himself and then to his father (1.16 VI 32//44-45), Yaṣṣib complains to Keret that in failing to keep justice, ''you have dropped your hand in weakness'' (?) (*šqlt bǵlt ydk*).

When Aqhat learns of his son's birth, he declares (1.17 II 14): *kyld bn ly km ʾaḫy//wšrš km ʾaryy*, ''for a son has been born to me like my brothers//a scion like my kinsmen.'' The topos of the report of the birth of a son, in this instance repeated by the father, usually uses a *G*-stem passive suffix form.[86]

3. The **qatala* forms continuing past action marked in the previous

---

[86] E.g., 1.23.53, 60. For other West Semitic examples, see Parker 1989b:63-70.

line by **qatala* have been listed by Watson (1989:439-40). Examples include *sʾid*, "he waiters" (// *ʿbd*, "he serves" in 1.3 I 2-3) and *šnst*, "she fastens" (//*ʿtkt*, "she binds" in 1.3 II 11-12). See also *ṯbr*//*ṯbr* in 1.19 III 22-23 discussed below in category seven.

4. The **qatala* used for background information might be rendered in English as a "pluperfect," as it constitutes one past action relative to a second past action (rendered as a historical present). 1.16 III 13-15 describes how food, wine and oil had been "consumed" or "used up" (*kly*) from their various containers at the time of the preceding **qatala* form, *nšʾu*, in line 12.[87] Similarly, *qm* and *yṯb* in 1.2 I 21 provide background information.

The idiom, *bph rgm lyṣʾa*. . . , "From his mouth the message had not left" (1.2 IV 6; 1.19 II 26, III 7, 35) might be included in this category, as the phrase provides background information for the following verb: before a word had departed from the mouth of one protagonist, then a second action transpired.[88]

5. The **qatala* in sentences with subordination is relatively rare and is controvertible. Blake (1951:80 n.1) interprets KTU 1.4 III 23-26 as a temporal sentence:

> Just when (*ʾaḫr*) Mightiest Baal arrived (*mǵy*),
> Adolescent Anat arrived (*mǵyt*),
> They bestowed gifts on Lady Athirat of the Sea,
> They entreated the Creatress of the Gods.

In this interpretation, two **qatala* forms stand in the protasis. KTU 1.4 V 44-48 shows the same usage: *ʾaḫr mǵy kṯr w-ḫss*. . . *tʿdb ksʾu wyṯṯb*, "after Kothar wa-Hasis arrives. . . , a seat is prepared and he seats him." If *ʾaḫr* may be regarded as an adverb, "afterwards," rather than a subordinating conjunction (see Pope 1986), then these cases might be interpreted as instances of simple past (category two above).[89]

---

[87] This example may provide a parallel for the BH "pluperfect." The BH prosaic equivalent of the verbal sequence of **qatala* plus **qatala* to express the pluperfect occurs regularly in clauses of the type **qatal* followed by *ʾăšer* + **qatal*. The BH poetic equivalent may omit *ʾăšer*.

[88] For other possible examples, see category two above.

[89] The sequence of a single suffix form followed by prefix forms in 1.17 VI 30b-31 has been understood also as temporal clause: "(when) he is brought to life (*ḥwy*), then one serves (*yʿšr*) and gives him drink (*wyšqynh*)." This sentence would appear to give support for the type of subordinate clause which Blake has identified

Blake (1951:80 n.1; cf. Cazelles 1947) also takes *qm* in KTU 1.3 I 4 as logically subordinate to *yṯʿr* and translates: "(after) he arose he prepares...".[90] This example may belong to category ten, however.[91]

6. A sixth function of the **qatala* known from both prose and poetic texts may be termed the "performative perfect." Some verbs of speech represent the performance of the action which they name.[92] Recanati (1987:46; see also 94-113, esp. 95-96, 216) discusses the nature of performative verbs: "The distinguishing characteristic of a performative verb is that when I use it in the first person present, I actually perform the act it denotes...To say 'I swear' is to swear...".[93]

Performative verbs in Ugaritic most commonly occur in the first person. The verb, *pʿrt*, in 1.1 IV 19 reflects El's royal naming of Yamm and constitutes an example of a performative perfect, and the form, *pʿr*, in line 15 introduces this naming section.[94] The phrase *ʾan rgmt* in 1.2 I 45 may also be a performative perfect, although it appears in a broken context. KTU 1.2 IV 7-8 provides two examples

---

in Ugaritic. The difficulty with this example is that the form *ḥwy* appears in this passage as the parallel term to *yḥwy* in the same bicolon and is dictated apparently by the convention of prefix and suffix verbal forms in parallelism (category eight), in this case in a subordinate clause (for this passage, see below pp. 64-65). Therefore, it is unclear that **qatala* is used as a characteristic form for subordinate clauses in Ugaritic narrative poetry. If it were so used, it would occasion no grammatical difficulty as this usage is known in Ugaritic prose texts and the Amarna letters.

[90] See below pp. 55-56.

[91] See below pp. 53-56.

[92] The epistolary perfect identified by Pardee and Whiting (1987) belongs to this category.

[93] Arabic also attests to first person performative verbs in the **qatala*. For Arabic examples see Wright 1898:2.1. For further discussion of the Ugaritic evidence, see Hillers cited in Lewis 1989:13 n. 27.

[94] In a similar biblical usage, Mettinger (1976:261) applies the label "perfectum performativum" to *yĕlidtîkā*, "I have begotten you" (Ps 2:7): "In this case the performative utterance initiates the king's status as son of God at the same moment that is pronounced." The "performative perfect" appears in BH direct discourse. Ecclesiastes uses verbs of speech in the **qatala* in this manner (see Fredericks 1988:58-59). Eccles 6:3 states: *ʾāmartî ṭôb mimmennû hannāpel*, "I say: 'Better than the miscarriage..." Similarly, Eccles 8:14 declares: *ʾāmartî šeggam zeh hābel*, "I say that this also is vanity." Fredericks (1988:36-46) makes a major point of the colloquial character of the language of Ecclesiastes, and similarly Isaksson (1987) stresses the autobiographical thread running throughout the book providing its structural continuity. These observations would comport with seeing the "performative perfect" as a feature belonging primarily to speech which could be used in more formal settings such as ritual or poetic narrative, as the Ugaritic cases illustrate.

of this usage in a poetic setting. In this passage, Kothar introduces his speech predicting Baal's impending victory:

lrgmt lk lzbl bʿl I indeed tell you, Prince Baal,
ṯnt lrkb ʿrpt I repeat, Cloud-rider.

The verbal usage here as elsewhere in the Ugaritic mythological texts[95] is derived from the language of letters where **rgm* serves to introduce the body of a letter. Like 1.2 IV 7-8, KTU 2.72 uses **rgm* and **ṯny* to introduce the body of a message: the initial message is introduced by **rgm* in line 6, and the further message is introduced by **ṯny* in line 12 (Pardee 1977:7). The beginning of the second part of the body of a letter in KTU 2.36.14 has been reconstructed *[wṯ]nty*, "secondly" (Dijkstra 1989:142). Kothar opens another speech to Baal also with *lrgmt* (1.4 VII 23).[96]

7. Cassuto (*BOS* 128 n. 56, 149) and Held (1962:283-85, 288-90) pointed to the parallelistic use of the indicative prefix and suffix forms.[97] The usage appears to be largely a narrative device, as it occurs rarely in direct discourse.[98] The following examples may be noted: *tskh//nskh* (1.3 II 40-41); *štt//ʾištynh* (1.4 III 14-16); *yʿdb//ʿdb* (1.4 VI 38-40); *kḏd//tkšd* (1.5 I 17); *yrʾaʾun//ṯtʿ* (1.5 II 7); *škb//tšʿly* (1.5 V 19-21); *yṯb* (**yaqtul[u]*)//*yṯb* (**qatala*) (1.5 VI 12-13); *yrʾu//ṯtʿ* (1.6 VI 30); *yḥwy//ḥwy* (1.17 VI 30-31[99]); *yṯbr//ṯbr* (1.19 III 8-9[100]); *mḫṣt//tmḫṣ* (1.19 IV 58-59). Some of these instances use the same root for both forms (Held 1962; *UT* 13.58; *CMHE* 115 n. 13).

The example from 1.19 IV 58-59 is notable for another reason, as it belongs to a sequence of curses. The sequence varies the format of the verbal forms, departing from the bicolon pair of *yṯbr//ṯbr* used in 1.19 III 8-9. The variations derive from the presence of the convention of the **qatala* used to report an order issued in the impera-

95 E.g., 1.1 III 14; 1.2 I 16; cf. the Assyrian version of the Myth of Anzu 2.103-104 in *ANET* 516.

96 The verbs in 1.161.2-12 reflect the performative perfect in a ritual context. For readings, see Pardee 1987b:211-12; for a discussion of this text, see Lewis 1989:5-46.

97 Cf. *UT* 13.58; Marcus 1969b:57; Fensham 1978; Freedman 1980:248; Watson 1989:440-41.

98 The corresponding phenomenon in direct discourse may be a jussive parallel to the precative perfect as in KTU 1.4 V 6-9, discussed under category nine below.

99 For translation, see Spronk 1986:151; below p. 65.

100 For further discussion of this example see below p. 52.

tive. As a result, the reports also use *ṯbr*, e.g., the **qatala* alone, as in 1.19 III 37, or *ṯbr*//*ṯbr*, in 1.19 III 22-23.

Cassuto (*BOS* 137; also *TO* 214 n. 1) plausibly reconstructed the **qtl*-**yqtl* sequence in three bicola in 1.4 VI 47-54:

špq ʾilm krm	He provides the gods with rams,
yšpq ʾilht ḫprt	He provides the goddesses with ewes;
špq ʾilm ʾalpm	He provides the gods with bulls,
yšpq ʾilht ʾarḫt	He provides the goddesses with cows;
špq ʾilm kḥṯm	He provides the gods with thrones,
yšpq ʾilht ksʾat	He provides the goddesses with chairs;
špq ʾilm rḥbt yn	He provides the gods with jars of wine,
špq ʾilht dkrt [yn]	He provides the goddesses with cruets [of wine].

This interpretation obviates the reconstruction of *[n]* and *[yn]* in alternating lines (e.g., *špq ʾilm krm y[n]*//*špq ʾilht ḫprt [yn]*). Based on this reconstruction, some commentators envision a scene of ram-gods, ewe-goddesses, etc.. Ginsberg (*ANET* 134), for example, translates the first bicolon: "He sates the he-lamb gods with w[ine], He sates the ewe-lamb goddesses [. . .?]." Del Olmo Lete (*MLC* 206-07) follows Ginsberg's lead and reconstructs *[n]* and *[yn]* in each bicolon. Other scholars have argued that the verb in each line of this passage takes one indirect object, namely the deities, and two direct objects, the reconstructed "wine" and a second noun, in the first two lines of the passage, "rams and ewes." So Gibson (*CML*[2] 63) renders the first two lines: "he did supply the gods with rams (and) with wine,//he did supply the goddesses with ewes [(and) with wine]." The parenthetically translated "and" points to a problem with this rendering: two uncoordinated direct objects would be rare in the Ugaritic poetic corpus. Unlike these views Cassuto's interpretation engenders no grammatical or thematic difficulty.

The attempt to view *tṯʿr*//*ṯʿr* (1.3 II 20-21) as another example of **yqtl*//**qtl*, perhaps most recently advocated by Marcus (1969b:57), founders on his assumption that stative verbs need not agree in in gender with their subjects. There is no reason not to expect the third feminine perfect form **ṯʿrt* to parallel imperfect *tṯʿr*, as Loewenstamm (1969b) argued. Marcus' rejoinder that the **yqtl*-infinitive sequence is otherwise unknown would militate against this solution, but poetic dictates do not nullify grammatical analysis. Indeed, *[ṯ]ʿr* in 1.3 II 36 would appear also to be an infinitive which comports with the suggestion of Gai (1982:55) that narrative infinitives may occur where the subject is clear from context; all of these cases follow a prefix form. The pair *tʾirkm*//*ʾark* in KTU 1.23.33-35 would represent another disputed instance of **yqtl*-infinitive sequence or **yqtl*-**qtl* (perfect) sequence (so Marcus 1969b:56).

It remains to be noted that Held (1962:286 n. 4) takes *yqtl-qtl* and *qtl-yqtl* sequences in the Baal Cycle, their relative rarity in Aqhat and their absence from Keret as an indication of the Baal Cycle's relative antiquity. As Held himself observes, however, this sequence appears centuries later in biblical poetry. This usage has been recognized also in the Amarna texts (Gevirtz 1973) and biblical poetry.[101]

8. Fenton (1969a; 1973:35) notes another function of **qatala* in Ugaritic narrative poetry. With commands issued in **tqtl*, the fulfillments of those commands are reported with **yqtl* forms; but if the command is expressed in the imperative **qtl*, the action is reported with the **qtl* past form. Examples of the latter include *mdl. . .št. . .ʿdb* (1.4 IV 9), *ʿrb. . .lqḥ. . .lqḥ. . .yṣq. . .wʿly. . .rkb. . . nšʾa. . .dbḥ. . .šrd. . .yrd. . .ʿdb* (1.14 III 55-IV 9), and *grnn. . .srnn* (1.14 IV 49-50). Fenton (1969:36-37) notes a few exceptions to this stylistic rule. It is possible to account for some of the exceptions. The sequence in 1.19 II 1-11 is commanded in the imperative, but recounted in the prefix form preceded by *bkm*, "then." This example belongs to a group of constructions which utilize either the particles *ʾidk*, *hl* (and in combination with other particles *-h*, *-k* and *-n*) and *ʾapnk* and *ʾaphn* with the prefix forms or suffix forms in order to begin new narrative sections. BH particles such as *ʾaz*, *bĕṭerem*, *ṭerem* and *ʿad* appear with the prefix form to express a past time-frame. Like the Ugaritic instances of this construction, the biblical examples may constitute a stylistic preference.

9. Ugaritic narrative poetry contains a few cases of the optative perfect.[102] Gordon (*UT* 13.28) takes the form *ḥwt* in the expression *ḥwt*

---

101 Held (1962:281) noted biblical examples without *waw* in Pss 38:12, 93:3, and Prov 11:7. According to Held, examples with *waw* include Isa 60:16, Amos 7:4 and Ps 29:10 (although this case has been questioned; see Fensham 1978:15-16). Other biblical examples of prefix-suffix parallelism with verbs of different roots have also been observed. Dahood (1970:420-23) notes numerous examples from the Psalter. Cross (*CMHE* 125 and n. 44; 139 n. 93) points to instances in Exod 15:5, 7-8, 14 and 15, and Ps 114:3, 5 and 6. Freedman (1980:46, 68, 210, 248, 299) has identified a score of other biblical cases.

102 The optative is well-known for Arabic **qatala* (on the problems of an optative or precative perfect in Akkadian, see Marcus 1969a). Similarly, BH examples

ʾaḫt (KTU 1.10 II 20) as an optative and translates "may you live, my sister." The verbal form has been regarded as a *D*-stem form (Marcus 1972), and if correct, it would suggest a *D*-stem passive optative, "may you be preserved."[103] The form *lyrt*, "you shall surely descend," in 1.5 I 6 may be regarded as an optative.[104]

The form *hlk* appears twice in 1.14 II 39 and 41. Given that their context is replete with commands and jussives, these two cases of *hlk* would seem to be optative if they are not infinitives. After El grants permission for the building of Baal's house, the Cloud-rider instructs Kothar wa-Hasis in KTU 1.4 V 51-57:

[ḥ]š bhtm [kṯr]	Hurry, the house, [Kothar],
ḥš rmm hk[lm]	Hurry, erect the pal[ace];
ḥš bhtm tbn[n]	Hurry, the house let it be bu[ilt],
ḥš trmmn hk[lm]	Hurry, let the pal[ace] be erected
btk ṣrrt ṣpn	Amidst the recesses of Sapan.
ʾalp šd ʾaḫd bt	A thousand acres let the house cover (*ʾaḫd*),
rbt kmn hkl	A myriad of hectares the palace.

The imperatives of the first bicolon and the jussives of the second bicolon suggest a precative force for *ʾaḫd* in line 56. Appealing to the infinitive's function of mimicing verbs that precede it (Gai 1982), Marcus (1970a:17-34; Greenstein 1988:9 n. 8) takes *ʾaḫd* as an infinitive, but *ʾaḫd* may be a precative perfect. Indeed, Marcus (1970a:17-34) denies the optative perfect in Ugaritic, yet elsewhere (1969b:57 n. 8) he takes *ṯbr* (*//yṯbr*) in 1.19 III 8-9 as jussive, "may [Baal] break." The form *ṯbr* in this instance may be an optative perfect.

Interpreting the first attestation of *ʿdn* in 1.4 V 6 as a precative perfect would clarify the stichometry in this passage. According to

---

of the optative **qātal* have been long noted. For a recent sound defense of the BH precative perfect in Lam 3:52-66, see Provan 1991. A case also occurs in Jeremiah 28 (Professor A. Fitzgerald, private communication). In verse 2 the prophet Hananiah speaks in God's name: *šābartî ʾet-ʿōl melek bābel*, "I shall break the yoke of the king of Babylon." Hananiah repeats the message in verse 11: *kākâ ʾešbōr ʾet-ʿōl nĕbūkadneʾṣṣar melek-bābel*, "Thus I shall break the yoke of Nebuchadnezzar, king of Babylon. . ." The parallel contexts in this chapter provide a control illustrating the future time-frame of the optative **qātal* in verse 2. For other proposed BH poetic examples, see Dahood 1970:404, 414-17, 422, 423; Freedman 1980:65 n. 17; 68; 299.

103 For discussions of the problem, see Marcus 1972; Walls 1992:91 n. 13.

104 The further example of *šlm* cited by Cunchillos (1986) from requests for information in Ugaritic letters is unconvincing. In this context *šlm* is more likely a nominal form.

1.4 V 6-7, Athirat exclaims these words after El grants permission for the building of Baal's house:

wn ʾap ʿdn mṭrh bʿl	And now may Baal also luxuriate with his rain,
yʿdn ʿdn *ṯrt bglṯ	May he luxuriate luxuriantly with abundant water in a downpour (?).

This bicolon is difficult. Some scholars emend *ṯkt* (a kind of ship) to **ṯrt* (precipitation of some sort, attested with *glṯ* in KTU 1.101.7-8; see Pardee 1988b: 145-46). The word *glṯ* remains difficult despite the helpful comparison with Biblical and Mishnaic Hebrew "to seethe, boil over" (of water) (Greenfield 1969a:99). Accordingly, *ṯrt* means watering in general and *glṯ* refers to the motion of water. The old view of Gaster (1933) that the root **ʿdn* in this passage means "to make luxuriant (with water)" has received support from **ʿdn* in a context refering to Hadad's rains in the Tell Fekheriyah inscription (see Greenfield 1984; Millard 1984; Cross cited in Tuell 1993: 100 n. 7). Other scholars reject the emendation as unnecessary and translate *ʿdn tkt bglṯ* as "the season of the ship on the wave" (see Tuell 1993), but KTU 1.101.7-8 militates against this view.

Like a number of the words in this bicolon, the stichometry has posed difficulties. Taking the first instance of *ʿdn* as the cognate accusative of *yʿdn*, some commentators understand this verb as part of the first poetic line (so *SPUMB* 148; cf. *CML*^{2} 60), but this approach would be stichometrically unbalanced. However, the initial *ʿdn* may be a verb of the first poetic line and *yʿdn* may be the verb of the second line (followed by the second occurrence of *ʿdn* which would be either the cognate infinitive or accusative of *yʿdn*). This approach provides superior balance. If it is correct, the bicolon contains a precative perfect parallel with a jussive expressing Athirat's hope for Baal's rains. This interpretation provides both a grammatical solution for the verbal forms and a stichometrical solution for the bicolon. The two lines may therefore exhibit parallelism of volitive suffix and prefix forms resembling the parallelism between indicative suffix and prefix verbs, noted in category seven above.

10. Fenton (1973:35) was the first scholar to observe that some cases of the suffix form signal the beginning of a new turn or a significant moment in the narration before the narrative reverts to its customary prefix verbal forms to continue the plot. Fenton (1973:35) remarks:

> when a significant stage in the narrative is reached, when there is a change in subject matter, or when the narrative turns to a "character" who has not been the focus of attention in the preceding lines, the first verb or verbs of the new episode may be in the *qtl* form before the narrative reverts to *yqtl*.

Fenton's description includes two different usages: one is to mark the beginning of a new section and the second to mark highpoints in the narrative. At the outset, it needs to be mentioned that these two categories are *prima facie* subjective and difficult to establish.

Narrative sections involving travel begin with **qatala* and then revert to suffix forms. The verb *tbᶜ* occurs in 1.2 I 19, 1.4 IV 19, 1.5 I 9 and II 8 and 13 to open a travel section which then reverts to prefix forms. 1.17 II 31 uses the same form to close an episode. Likewise, the verbs of motion, *sb//nsb* in 1.4 VI 34-35, close a section otherwise narrated with prefix forms. In this example both the use of the **qatala* forms and the parallelism of two different stem forms highlight the closure of this unit.[105] In contrast, the prefix forms, *ytbᶜ* (1.14 VI 35; 1.16 VI 39) and *ttbᶜ* (1.6 IV 6; reconstructed in 1.18 I 19 and 1.18 IV 5 in *CML*² 111), do not open new sections. In the unreconstructed cases, there may be no intention to demarcate the section beginning with *ytbᶜ* or *ttbᶜ*; indeed, there is no change in subject in these cases, except in 1.14 VI 35, as opposed to the examples with *tbᶜ*.

Another example of a **qatala* verb of motion beginning a section is **ᶜly*, "to ascend," in 1.4 I. Kothar "goes up," *ᶜly*, to his bellows in 1.4 I 23 and then fashions a series of gifts for Asherah, described by verbs *yṣq*, "he pours,"...*yšlḥ*, "he casts,"...*yṣq*, "he pours,"...*yṣq*, "he pours," in lines 25-29.[106] The second verb, *yšlḥ*, would suggest that the other three verbs are prefix forms.

The forms *yṣʾat* in 1.16 I 51 and *mǵy[t]* in 1.19 IV 49 appear also to commence new sections. The **qatala* form in *bkm [ᶜ]rb* (so CTA; see *DW* 34-35) in 1.4 VII 13 may also mark a new point in narration. The reading of the line is in question, however; KTU reads *bxxxb**. As verbs of motion not infrequently begin sections describing travel, it might be suspected that the two occurrences of *yrd* in 1.6 I 63-64 are suffix forms and not prefix forms.[107] The two **qatala*

---

[105] For this particular example of parallelism involving two different stem forms of the same root, see Held 1965a:273.

[106] The nominal clauses in the remainder of the column are syntactically dependent on the last verb.

[107] Cf. *bkm yṯb* in 1.4 VII 42.

forms in 1.4 II 3 and 8 belong to the description of Athirat at her domestic chores. Thc scctions of lincs 3-7 and 8-11 begin with **qatala* and then revert to prefix forms; in this manner, the two **qatala* forms provide structure to the description. 1.4 V 35-36 also begins a new section with two **qatala* forms, *šmḫ* and *ṣḥ* (if these are not infinitives); the narrative then reverts to the standard prefix forms. Similarly, *šmḫ* in 1.5 II 20 and 1.6 III 14 begins a new section, but this form may be an infinitive in these two passages.[108]

KTU 1.2 I may contain six **qatala* forms. Bracketing for the moment occurrences in direct discourse[109] and the forms which provide background information, the following four **qatala* forms remain: *tbʿ* in line 19; *rgm* in line 33; and *ʾanš* in lines 38 and 43. These forms may mark a new departure in the narrative. The word *tbʿ* begins the travel section; immediately after this verb, the verbal forms revert to the prefix verbal forms customarily found in the travel clichés attested elsewhere. The form *rgm* commences the speech section, and the two instances of *ʾanš* start short sections detailing Baal's response.

KTU 1.3 I uses the **qatala* form three times in an unusual fashion (Watson 1989:441). The first example in line 4 begins a tricolon[110]:

qm yṯʿr wyšlḥmnh	He arises, he prepares and feeds him,
ybrd ṯd lpnwh	He slices a breast before him,
bḥrb mlḥt qṣ mrʾi	With a salted knife a cut of fatling.

The first line of this tricolon does not correspond syntactically to any other line within this colon. In using only verbal forms, the syntax in this initial line also differs from not only the other lines in this tricolon, but from any other line in Ugaritic poetry, except for two other cases in this same column.[111]

The next example occurs in this passage in the immediately following lines (1.3 I 8-11):

---

108 Those instances of Ugaritic **qatala* beginning a new narrative section which reverts to prefix verbal forms correspond to the BH prose construction of initial **qātal* followed by converted imperfects.

109 See *ypʿt* in line 3 and possibly *ṯbr* in line 13; the latter form sometimes is viewed as a precative (*CML*^{2} 40 n. 4).

110 As the third example below illustrates; cf. Pardee 1988d:6, 9, 16-17.

111 Watson (1989:441) also lists 1.17 I 3-4, but the context is difficult and *yd* may be interpreted as a prefix form.

ndd yʿšr wyšqynh	He arises, he serves and gives him drink,
ytn ks bdh	He places a cup in his hand,
krpnm bklʾat ydh	A goblet in both his hands.

The two tricola in 1.3 I 4-11 manifest similar syntax: three verbs in line one, verb-direct object-prepositional phrase in line two, and prepositional phrase-direct object in line three (though in reversed order compared with the second example). The comparable syntax of the two tricola perhaps signals their parallelism with one another. This is also the case semantically: the singer serves food according to the first tricolon and drink in the second, the typical order of service in Ugaritic literature, as Lichtenstein (1968-69) observes. As a further observation, the identical structure of the two tricola would appear to help resolve the form of *ytn* in 1.3 I 10. Like *ybrd* in the syntactically parallel position in 1.3 I 6, *ytn* in 1.3 I 10 seems to be a prefix form.

The third instance occurs in 1.3 I 18: *qm ybd wyšr*, "he arises, chants and sings." Lichtenstein notes that the traditional order of the feast describes music after food and drink. The section continues with a description of singing in lines 19-21. This passage reflects in some ways then the most unusual usage of **qatala* in all Ugaritic poetry. Blake (1951:80 n.1; cf. Cazelles 1947) takes *qm* in KTU 1.3 I 4 as logically subordinate to *yṯʿr* and translates: "(after) he arose he prepares...". Gordon (*UT* 9.8) calls these instances of the **qatala* auxiliary verbs. These examples may belong to category ten, **qatala* to begin or end a section, with an additional feature of structuring the description of the feast.

The use of **qatala* to draw special attention to a narrative highpoint is more difficult to identify with certitude. 1.17 IV 36 would appear to provide an example. Through her agent, Yatpan, Anat achieves revenge against Aqhat. The last clear tricolon of 1.18 IV 36-37 represents the climax of action leading to Aqhat's demise: *yṣʾat km rḥ npš[h]*, "his life-breath departs like wind." Another passage manifests a similar progression. KTU 1.6 VI 17-20 reports how Baal and Mot are "strong" (*ʿz*) in their combat against one another, and 1.6 VI 21-22 proceeds to relate that Mot "falls" (*ql*) and how Baal then "falls on him" (*ql ʿln*).

In conclusion, the **qatala* form in the poetic texts is more restricted than its occurrences in the prose texts. Whereas **qatala* is the general form for the past in prose texts, **qatala* occurs generally in poetic narrative either to mark various sorts of disjunction in the narrative (Smith 1991:67-69 n. 3) or to produce specific stylistic effects. While this definition does not apply to all the forms of **qatala* in Ugaritic poetry, especially in direct discourse, perhaps it provides a glimpse of an earlier stage of **qatala* in Ugaritic poetry relative to Ugaritic prose; if so, it would represent a further sign of the archaic character of Ugaritic poetry. Some other differences between the Baal Cycle on the one hand, and Keret and Aqhat on the other hand, are conspicuous. The use of special particles plus the prefix forms appear in Keret and Aqhat, but not in the Baal Cycle. Where the Baal Cycle tends to use the suffix form to mark the opening of a new section, Keret (1.14 I 26, III 50, IV 31; 1.15 III 25; 1.16 I 46, II 17) and Aqhat (1.19 III 50 and IV 1) occasionally shows a prefix form. This particular difference may reflect either a stylistic preference or a more archaic usage.

4. Syntax

A few syntatical features suggest the relative antiquity of the poetic language. Loewenstamm (1969a:173) argued for the archaic character of "a day" (*ym*) for the first day in Ugaritic mythological texts. Here the expression for "a first day," may be contrasted with the prosaic *bym prᶜ*, "on the first day," which appears in a rations list (KTU 4.279.1; cf. *UT* 19.2113). Although this root occurs in the Baal Cycle (KTU 1.4 VII 56), its use in the formula for "the first day" is restricted to the prose material.

The syntax for time also differs. The poetic seven-day formulas use the adverbial accusative without a preposition while a rations list uses *bṯlṯ*, *brbᶜ* and *bḫmš* (KTU 4.279.3-5). This particular feature may be a matter of poetic and prosaic style and not a question of archaic style.

Loewenstamm (1969:175) also suggests that the predominance of *l-* for composite forms of numerals in the mythological texts "creates a more archaic impression."

5. Vocabulary

A number of lexical items have been cited to support the antiquity of the Baal Cycle. Held (1959:174-75) noted how *ʾalp* and *ṣʾin*, used for large and small animals, appear only in the literary texts while their counterparts, *gdlt* and *dqt*, are attested only in the ritual and economic texts (Levine 1963). Similar contrasts obtain in *ʾimr* versus *š* for sheep, *ǵlm* versus *nʿr* for a "youth," *mṣbṭm* versus *mqḥm* for a sort of tool for metallurgy. Ginsberg (1973:131-32; cf. 1950:158) observed that the Ugaritic pair, *ʿr//pḥl*, "donkey"//"jackass" (so *ANET* 133), occurs in the Baal Cycle but never the later equivalent *ḥmr*, "donkey." This word appears only in later texts including Aqhat and Keret, and Ginsberg took its omission as evidence for the great antiquity of the Baal Cycle. Ginsberg (1973:131) similarly argued that **ḫlq*, "to perish" in the Baal Cycle is replaced by the less archaic **ʾbd*, "to perish," in Keret. The B-words for these two verbs show a similar substitution: **mwt* in the Baal Cycle is replaced by *l* + **ḥyy* in Keret.

From these comparisons, Ginsberg and Held argued that the Baal Cycle represents the oldest literary text, followed in age by Aqhat and Keret. This position at times seems an argument from silence, which in some cases may not be invalid. Perhaps some old grammatical features which appear only in the Baal Cycle, while not providing a date for the cycle, suggest its relative antiquity. The use of the longer alphabet was probably archaic for the date of the extant Baal Cycle. One may regard the attempt to preserve such an alphabet as archaizing in intention, but such a preservation may reflect the retention of a genuinely old practice. The same may be said for the lexicographical items attested only in the older literary texts. The inconsistent spellings of the same roots in the Baal Cycle would indicate that some of the spellings are genuinely archaic, as the newer spellings would have been eliminated if a conscious attempt at archaizing were at work.

In sum, the indicative verbal system of all the three major literary texts appears quite archaic compared to the prose texts, and some items of phonology, morphology and vocabulary may suggest that the Baal Cycle is the most archaic of all three of the major Ugaritic literary texts. Given the apparently long development of the Baal Cycle, it is also possible that some of its sections were composed after Aqhat or Keret, but many elements of the Baal Cycle appear to be older.

Interpretations of the Baal Cycle

Six and a half decades of Ugaritic studies have witnessed numerous views of the Baal Cycle which in the words of Walls (1992:185) "remains largely impervious to comprehensive interpretation."

Approaches to the cycle include seasonal and ritual interpretations, historical and political views, and cosmogonic theories. These views have been prominent for decades and continue to exert considerable influence on how the Baal Cycle is understood. They have also guided the interpretation of details in the Baal Cycle. Each one illuminates various aspects of the Baal Cycle and each has significantly advanced its understanding as a whole. Indeed, the most serious interpretations offer profound syntheses integrating the themes of kingship, temple building and divine conflict within the Baal Cycle.[112]

It should be observed at the outset that virtually all interpreters agree that the Baal Cycle narrates a basic story of conflict and resolution.[113] On one side of the Baal Cycle stands Baal, the source of life in the cosmos, and on the other side are Yamm ("Sea") and Mot ("Death"), the sources of destruction and death in the universe. Yamm embodies the chaos that threatens the life of the world. Mot is Death incarnate. The struggle between Baal and his opponents represents the conflict between life and death. The building of Baal's house represents the victory of life over chaos. Baal's final meeting with Mot in KTU 1.6 VI celebrates life's overcoming of death.

Scholars also recognize the royal nature of the conflict and resolution (Smith 1986b:322). Baal's battles with Yamm and Mot are cast in terms of kingship in KTU 1.1 IV 24-25, 1.2 IV 10, 32, 1.6 V 5-6, and 1.6 VI 28-29, 33-35. Likewise, Yamm's epithet, *ʾadn*, "lord," indicates his royal character. Baal is described as Yamm's "servant" (*ʿbd*), which reflects Baal's subservience, much as one monarch subservient to a second referred to himself as *ʿbd*, "servant" (Greenfield 1967:117; Fensham 1979a:272-273). Yamm's title, *ṯpṭ*, "judge," reflects a function of kingship.[114] Baal and Mot are struggling for *mṯpṭ*, "rule," also a royal quality (Cazelles 1984:177-182). The titles of Yamm and Mot, *ydd* and *mdd*, "beloved," may be royal titles (*Thespis* 125). Wyatt (1985:117-125)

---

112 Professors F.M. Cross and L. Boadt (personal communications) rightly criticize the survey of Smith (1986b:313-39) for construing too narrowly the interpretation of some scholars whose views combine a number of approaches. For an older survey, see Kapelrud 1952:13-27.

113 *GA* 174-177; cf. *CMHE* 116, 120, 149; 156; *MLC* 143-153; Margalit 1980:202-205. In a more comparative vein, see Stannard 1992:227-53, 285-86, 295-96.

114 Gevirtz 1980:61-66; Fensham 1984:65; Muntingh 1984:7-8; cf. Stol 1972.

suggests that these titles point to these two gods as the blood princes of El who were expected to succeed him as monarch. Scholars have noted that Baal's palace perhaps holds a political significance akin to the temple of Solomon (*SPUMB* 59-61). In numerous ways, the Baal Cycle alludes to the royal nature of the struggle between Baal and his adversaries, Yamm and Mot. The Baal Cycle concerns the process of recognition that Baal wins for his own kingship through his battles against Yamm and Mot and through his acquisition of a palace.

Given the general acceptance of the royal character of the Baal Cycle, various approaches have been proposed to explore its underlying meaning. These views are addressed in the following order corresponding to their relative appearance over the history of the Baal Cycle's interpretation: (1) Ritual and Seasonal Theories; (2) Cosmogonic Interpretations; and (3) Historical and Political Views. A synthesis of these views is offered in (4) The Limited Exaltation of Baal.

1. Ritual and Seasonal Theories

Since the decipherment of the Baal Cycle, Baal's conflicts with Yamm and Mot as well as his palace have received ritual explanations. Virolleaud, Dussaud, Gaster, Hvidberg, Gray, de Moor (*SPUMB* 9-24), Schaeffer-Forrer (1979:42-43) and Yon (1989) have articulated ritual theories involving most or all of the Baal Cycle. In the formulation of the ritual interpretation's most significant proponent, Gaster (*Thespis* 17, 19, 24-25; cf. *UL* 185-186),

> seasonal rituals are accompanied by *myths* which are designed to present the purely functional acts in terms of ideal and durative situations. The interpenetration of the myth and ritual creates *drama*...The texts revolve around different elements of the primitive Seasonal pattern, some of them concentrating on the ritual combat, others on the eclipse and renewal of kingship, and others again on the disappearance and restoration of the genius of topocosmic vitality ...myth is not...a mere outgrowth of ritual, an artistic or literary interpretation imposed later upon sacral acts; nor is it merely...the spoken correlative of "things done." Rather, it is the expression of a parallel aspect inherent in them from the beginning; and its function within the scheme of the Seasonal Pattern is to translate the punctual into terms of the durative, the real into those of the ideal.

According to Gaster (*Thespis* 124-125), the proper names of the major deities reflect their roles in the Baal Cycle. The "land of

Baal'' refers to soil watered by rain in Arabic.[115] Yamm, literally ''sea,'' embraces the seas, lakes, rivers ''and other inland expanses of water,'' while Mot, meaning, ''death,'' is the god of all that lacks vitality or life, as reflected by Arabic *mawat*, ''dead soil which remains arid and infertile.'' Each deity was sovereign over his own domain.

Gaster's theory involves ritual drama. Baal's fight against Yamm mirrors the cosmogonic battle with the ''dragon'' (or ''monster'') (*Thespis* 128-129). The house of Baal is the durative counterpart of the annual installation of the king. The Baal-Mot conflict introduces the motif of the dying and reviving god. The end of the cycle describes ritual wailing for Baal (''a projection of the seasonal ululations''), usurpation by Athtar (''a projection of the interrex''), the restoration of Baal through Shapshu (''a projection of the solar aspects of the seasonal festival''), and the final defeat of Mot (''a projection of the Ritual Combat''). Gaster (*Thespis* 129) concludes:

> *On both internal and external grounds, therefore, there is every reason for seeing in the Canaanite* Poem of Baal *a seasonal myth based on the Traditional drama of the autumn festival.* (Gaster's italics)

In his study of the ritual underpinnings of myths, Gaster (*Thespis* 18) groups features common to myths from various areas: ''What is at issue is, in fact, the history of the literary genre as a whole, not of the particular compositions.''

The explanatory power of Gaster's interpretation was immense. It achieved a total synthesis tying cosmic and royal dimensions of the Baal Cycle to the human and seasonal realities facing Ugaritic society. Gaster's ritual approach was paralleled or followed in great part in the works of Hvidberg (1938), Dussaud (1941), Engnell (1943), Kapelrud (1952), Gray (*LC*[1]; *LC*[2]; 1979:324), de Moor (*SPUMB*), van Zijl (*Baal*), Toombs (1983) and others (see *SPUMB* 8-24).

Many criticisms of Gaster's work on the Baal Cycle have been voiced and may be rehearsed in brief.[116] First, Gaster's approach assumes elements unattested in the Baal Cycle, but based on other literatures (such as the equation of Yamm with ''the Dragon''). Second, his theory offers unsupported speculations about some

---

115 Cf. b. Taʿan. 6b: *myṭrʾ bʿlʾ dʾrʿʾ*, noted by Ginsberg 1935:328.

116 See *SPUMB* 13-19, 30; Robertson 1982:335. For more general criticisms of the myth and ritual approach, see Fontenrose 1966; Kirk 1970: 12-28; Buckert 1979:35-39, 56-58.

texts. According to Gaster, KTU 1.4 VIII leads to the banishment of Mot, but the text says nothing of the kind, and it apparently issues in a very different outcome, namely Mot's challenge to Baal in KTU 1.5 I. Third, Gaster's view of the seasons reverses the order of the texts. KTU 1.2 and 1.4 are autumnal, KTU 1.5-6 I summer, KTU 1.6 II-VI late summer, 1.1 III is a subsidiary text corresponding to the fall (*Thespis* 128-129; cf. *SPUMB* 19). Even if these correlations were correct, such an approach does not explain the texts in their present order. Fourth, the Baal Cycle purportedly reflects the autumnal New Year festival, and yet none of the extant ritual or administrative texts attest to such a festival.[117] There are additional difficulties in using either a hypothetical biblical New Year Festival or the Babylonian Akitu festival as supporting evidence.[118] Even those who otherwise maintain ritual interpretations, such as de Moor (*SPUMB* 162-163) and Robertson (1982:319, 335), dissent from this cornerstone of Gaster's reconstruction. Fifth, the explicit terms of the narrative are rarely either ritual or seasonal in character. The themes of the cycle bear out this point: in KTU 1.2 I and 1.2 IV Yamm demands not water or flooding, but kingship. As Loewenstamm (*CS* 350) observed, "it is just the name of the god of the sea which draws the reader's attention to the connection with the cosmic element of the water." Both the characters and the plot are removed from a purely seasonal setting. The cycle sometimes draws on seasonal and ritual elements for descriptions, but this usage need not indicate a seasonal or ritual setting for the cycle. Sixth, Gaster's comparative framework tends to diminish the historical dimensions of the material.[119] Finally, Gaster's view implies that the Baal temple excavation at Ras Shamra is the temple mentioned in the Baal Cycle (*Thespis* 128-129; cf. Schaeffer 1939:68). This view continues to be expressed,[120] but without much textual support. As Cunchil-

---

[117] See *Baal* 326; de Tarragon 1980:184. For problems with positing a hypothetical Ugaritic New Year's festival at Ugarit, see Marcus 1973 and Grabbe 1976.

[118] See Smith 1986b:330-31. For cautions against comparing the Akitu festival, see Lambert 1968b:106-08; Nakata 1968; cf. J. Z. Smith 1982:90-96. For a balanced comparison of the Akitu festival and purported biblical evidence for an autumnal New Year festival, see van der Toorn 1991a.

[119] On the comparative method, see the instructive remarks of J. Z. Smith 1982:22-35.

[120] Kapelrud 1952:17-18, 87; *SPUMB* 59-61; Miller 1981:126; see Clifford 1979:145; 1984:198.

los (1984-85:232) stresses, the text of the Baal Cycle explicitly locates this palace on Mount Sapan, which lies to the north of the city of Ugarit. Correlating the palace of Baal in the Baal Cycle with the so-called temple of Baal excavated in Ras Shamra would assume that the cycle's audience equated the two structures.[121]

A number of points may be offered in Gaster's defense. First, the hypothetical New Year festival has yet to be disproved. While the evidence does not support Gaster's reconstruction of a New Year festival, there is at present little evidence against this view. The rejection or acceptance of Gaster's view relies on an argument from silence. Second, Gaster recognized the "depth dimension" of the language of the cycle; the cycle presupposed on the part of its audience aspects of religious thought barely accessible to modern commentators. While interpreters may have some idea of the cycle's ancient significance thanks to data gleaned from other Ugaritic and Near Eastern texts, a great deal of information now unaccessible to modern interpreters was assumed on the part of the cycle's audience. Third, his interpretation of the seasons in the Baal Cycle represents a natural reading of the texts, for both the Baal-Yamm and Baal-Mot conflicts lead up to the autumn rains. This view would sugggest that the cycle is not arranged according to the order of a single annual cycle. Finally, despite the general lack of evidence, it remains theoretically possible that parts or all of the Baal Cycle were recited in ritual form.[122] In sum, the ritual underpinnings presupposed by Gaster lack for evidence both inside and outside of the Baal Cycle.

Following the lead of Gaster, de Moor has developed most fully the seasonal dimension of the ritual approach. While ritual interpretations presuppose a correlation between the Baal Cycle and the annual cycle of weather on the Syrian coast, de Moor's theory represents the most comprehensive effort to coordinate the events reported in the Baal Cycle with the weather of the Syrian coastal climate within a single annual cycle (see also Yon 1989). The interpretation assumes that the rites or cultic acts celebrating the divine deeds reflect the vicissitudes of the seasons (*SPUMB* 61, 67):

---

[121] As well as the gods, *bʿl ʾugrt* and *bʿl ṣpn*. This equation seems quite likely, although the two gods are distinguished in ritual texts (e.g., KTU 1.109.9, 16).

[122] For possible evidence, see above pp. 32-33.

> The myth of Baʿlu is a combination of a nature-myth and a cult-myth because it wanted to explain the origin of the alternation of the seasons as well as the origin of the Ugaritic cult which was largely based on rites determined by the same seasons.
>
> In accordance with the principle laid down in the preceding chapters I shall now try to demonstrate that the Ugaritic Myth of Baʿlu contains a large number of references to datable seasonal events that follow the course of Ugaritic cultic year which coincided with the Syrian agroclimatic year.

The seasonal interpretation correlates the three phenomena of seasons, rites, and myths.

De Moor situates passages in the cycle in specific ritual and seasonal settings. He treats thirty-seven passages that constitute a sampling sufficient in his opinion to demonstrate his theory. Perhaps he made his most fundamental correlation in connecting KTU 1.3, which he considers the beginning of the cycle, and the end of the cycle, 1.6, to the beginning and end of the year during the autumn. As support de Moor (*SPUMB* 42-43; cf. 1987:4 n. 7) compares KTU 1.17 VI 28-33 with KTU 1.3 I. KTU 1.17 VI 28-33 alludes to resurrection involving Baal followed by a feast with music; under one view the passage includes a singer called *nʿm*. De Moor locates in this setting both 1.3 I 18-22a, which narrates *nʿm*'s musical entertainment at a feast for Baal, and 1.6 III which describes El's vision of Baal's return to life. KTU 1.17 VI 28-33 would then suggest a religious background shared by KTU 1.3 I and 1.6 III. As noted by de Moor and others, KTU 1.3 I 18-22a and 1.17 VI 28-33 share common wording and ideas. KTU 1.3 I 18-22a is translated by de Moor (1988:4):

qm ybd wyšr	He rose, improvised a poem and sang,
mṣltm bd nʿm	The gracious lad (held) the cymbals in his hands,
yšr ǵzr ṭb ql	The sweet-voiced youth sang
ʿl bʿl bṣrrt ṣpn	Before Baʿlu in the heights of Sapanu.

KTU 1.17 VI 28-33 celebrates the return to life and divine celebration[123]:

ʾašsprk ʿm bʿl šnt	I will make you count the years with Baʿlu,
ʿm bn ʾil tspr yrḫm	With the sons[124] of El you will count the months!

---

[123] De Moor (1987:238-39; *SPUMB* 42) and Spronk (1986:151-61) take Baal as the subject of *yḥwy* and *ḥwy*.

[124] Either singular or plural is theoretically possible. If the former, the reference may be to Baal as suggested by the parallelism, as Professor Nicholas Wyatt re-

kbʿl kyḥwy yʿšr	Like Baal when he is revived,[125] he is served -
ḥwy yʿšr wyšqynh	(When) he is revived, one serves and gives him drink,
ybd wyšr ʿlh	Chants and sings before him -
nʿmn [dy?]ʿnynn	A gracious one (?)[126] [who is?] his servant (?),[127]
ʾap ʾank ʾaḥwy ʾaqht [ǵz]r	So I too can revive Aqhat [the her]o!

According to de Moor the correlation between 1.17 VI 28-33 on the one hand, and 1.3 I 18-22a and 1.6 III on the other hand

> proves conclusively that the events of CTA 6 were followed very shortly by those of CTA 3. This is possible only if we assume a cycle ending with CTA 6 and beginning with CTA 3. It is impossible, however, to reconcile CTA 17:VI.28ss with a series consisting of the sequence, CTA 1-2-3-4-5-6.

Hence for de Moor 1.3 begins the cycle and 1.6 ends it.

In favor of de Moor's thesis, KTU 1.4 V 6-9 and KTU 1.4 VII 25-31 clearly refer to the rains of Baal that rejuvenate the world. In

---

minds me. The phrase is elsewhere, however, stereotypical for the deities of the Ugaritic pantheon.

125 Literally, "is made to live" (i.e., *D*-stem passive). De Moor and Spronk takes these forms as active transitive and assume that Baal is the subject, but the absence of an object does not militate in favor of this view (van der Toorn 1991b:46). Van der Toorn's translation of the occurences of **ḥwy*, "he comes to life" is unlikely, since, as Marcus (1972) shows, **ḥwy* in these cases is a *D*-stem (see the Ugaritic *D*-stem infinitive syllabic form *ḫu-PI-ú* = /huwwû/ in Huehnergard 1987b:123). The translation, "comes to life," would not appear to be within the usage of the *D*-stem of this verb. Like other commentators van der Toorn deletes *ḥwy* (before *yʿšr*) due to dittography. The line-length in the parallel line suggests retaining the word as it has been here.

126 Given the suitability of the context, it is difficult not to consider Cassuto's view (*GA* 111-12) that Ug *nʿmn* is related to BH **nʿm*, "to sing, chant." For this meaning Cassuto cites 2 Sam 23:1, Pss 81:3, 135:3 and 147:1. Sarna 1993:213 n. 8 adds Ben Sira 45:9 and this meaning in various forms of the root in rabbinic Hebrew. The Arabic cognates constitute the obvious difficulty for this view of Ugaritic *nʿm*. Arabic **nʿm* means "to live in comfort , to enjoy"; related are the nouns *niʿma*, "benefit, blessing favor, grace, *nuʿma*, "favor, good will, grace," *nuʿma*, "happiness," and particles *naʿm*, "yes" and *niʿma* "what a perfect, wonderful, truly" (Wehr 980). Arabic **nǵm* means to "hum a tune, sing" with the cognate nouns *naǵm* and *naǵam*, "tune, air, melody" as well as *naǵma*, "tone, sound, musical note" (Wehr 981). Fronzaroli (1955:19) notes some cases of Proto-Semitic **ǵ* ⟩ Ugaritic ʿ, but does not discuss Ugaritic *nʿm* in this connection. Cf. *CMHE* 185 n. 169.

127 The reconstruction *[dy]ʿnynn* is suggested by Spronk. For **ʿny* in this sense, see KAI 202:2 discussed below p. 294. Pope (1981:162) renders: "One sings and chants before him/ Sweetly [and they] respond." Given the lacuna, any suggestion remains most tentative.

the first of these passages, Athirat exclaims these words when El finally grants permission for the building of Baal's house:

wn ʾap ʿdn mṭrh bʿl	And now may Baal also luxuriate with his rain,
yʿdn ʿdn *ṯrt bg̣lṯ	May he luxuriate luxuriantly with abundant water in a downpour (?).[128]
w〈y?〉tn qlh bʿrpt	And may he give his thunder in the clouds,
šrh lʾarṣ brqm	May he flash to the earth lightning.

When the house is completed, a window is installed, and from it Baal utters his holy voice in KTU 1.4 VII 25-31:

ypth̩ h̩ln bbhtm	He opens a window in the house,
ʾurbt bqrb hk[lm]	A window in the midst of the pala[ce].
[yp]th̩ bʿl bdqt [ʿrp]t	Baal open[s] a break in the [clou]ds,
qlh qdš b[ʿl y]tn	Ba[al g]ives his holy voice
yṯny bʿl ṣ[ʾat š?]pth	Baal repeats the is[sue of?] his [li?]ps,
qlh q[dš t?]r ʾarṣ	His ho[ly?] voice, the earth [sha?]kes.

Few scholars, if any, would deny that these two passages refer to Baal's luxuriant rains that fertilize the earth.

De Moor's interpretation has been criticized on a number of grounds. First, athough de Moor (*SPUMB* 150, 162-163) assigns the manifestation of Baal's thunder and rain in these passages to the spring, a number of scholars who espoused a seasonal interpretation took these passages to refer to the fall rains.[129] It was precisely this type of ambiguity for the apparently clear references to the weather that led to criticism of de Moor's seasonal interpretation. Second, the few passages that explicitly refer to the weather constitute a limited base of data. The more ambiguous references to the seasons as well as to the many passages in the Baal Cycle that make no reference to weather further complicate de Moor's hypothesis. In several instances Grabbe (1976:57-63) criticizes de Moor's assignment of specific non-meteorological phenomena to particular times of the year. Third, de Moor is faulted for relying too heavily on broken passages to sustain some important correlations between the text and the seasonal pattern. He interprets some Ugaritic words in relation to the seasons although the same words are susceptible also to non-meteorological interpretations. According to Grabbe, these criticisms affect the interpretation of twenty of the thirty-seven texts that de Moor analyzes. These criticisms do not disprove the idea of a seasonal pattern in the Baal Cycle. They demonstrate, rather, the

---

128 For this bicolon, see above p. 53.

129 Dussaud 1932:298-300; *Thespis* 195; Hvidberg 1962:51-55; *LC*[1] 70.

difficulties in sustaining a comprehensive seasonal interpretation. Fourth, the Baal Cycle has few correspondences with Ugaritic ritual texts,[130] and weather plays little explicit role in other Ugaritic mythological or ritual texts.

Fifth, Gordon argues that the seven-year drought caused by Baal's death in KTU 1.6 V 7-9 directly contradicts a one-year seasonal interpretation.[131] If the seven-year period is simply a metaphor for "a long time" as de Moor (*SPUMB* 238) argues, then other allusions to weather in the Baal Cycle may be metaphorical as well. Gordon (1977:103) also notes that the summer is not the time of utter sterility, as de Moor's seasonal interpretation apparently suggests. Gordon (*UT* 19.37) argues:

> The fact that Baᶜl, as a god of fertility-giving water, is associated with the dew as well as rain in 1 Aqht:44 rules out any seasonal interpretation of his role. . . Dew in Canaan is a round-the-year phenomenon. It condenses most when the rainfall is least. . . Dew is connected with fertility (e.g., Gen 27:28 and ᶜnt: II: 39. . .) quite like rain. For the concept that dew in summer takes the place of rain in winter, note the Jewish prayer for dew which states *lk l̆šlwm gšm wbʾw bšlwm ṭl* 'depart in peace, O rain, and come in peace, O dew' anticipating the rainy season and start of the dewy summer.

The Gezer Calendar (KAI 182; *ANET*, 320), and Amos 7-8 (Talmon 1963) attest to summer fertility as well.

Finally, de Moor and Spronk (1986:152-54) assume that in 1.17 VI 28-33 Anat draws the analogy between Baal and herself, but van der Toorn (1991b:46) suggests that Anat draws the analogy between Baal and Aqhat: in exchange for his bow, Anat promises to give to Aqhat the return to life commonly associated with Baal. Under this view Baal is the recipient of resurrection and not the cause of others' resurrection as envisioned by de Moor. Hence the role of Baal's resurrection remains unclear.

Although other criticisms of de Moor's seasonal interpretation have been made,[132] his treatment represents an important contri-

---

130 De Tarragon 1980:39, 44, 56-60, 71, 123-125, 144, 184. For a comparable difficulty on the Mesopotamian side, see Hecker 1974:22; Damrosch 1987:64. Hecker observes that Mesopotamian myths appeared in writing several centuries before rituals began to be committed to writing and that ritual connections are rarely suggested in the myths.

131 Gordon 1949:4. See also Buckert 1979:188 n. 14.

132 *CS* 110-165, 236-245, 426-432, 503-516; Margalit 1980:204; Robertson 1982:335; Healey 1983:248-251; Gibson 1984:204-205.

bution in a number of respects. First of all, its comprehensiveness exceeded that of its predecessors. Second, it is the only major seasonal interpretation that does not rearrange the sequence of KTU 1.4-1.6.[133] Third, de Moor's study showed the depth of seasonal information embedded in the cycle as well as the limits of the seasonal approach.

Fourth, de Moor's argument about the relationship between KTU 1.17 VI and KTU 1.3 I is fundamentally correct insofar as the two passages appear to be closely related. That this relationship proves that KTU 1.3-1.1-1.2-1.4-1.5-1.6 constitutes the order of tablets is subject to dispute, as it assumes a linear reading within the scheme of a single year. Following Gaster's insight that two sections of the cycle culminate in the autumn, the three sections of the cycle may be viewed as parallel, each evoking phenomena associated with the same time of year, specifically the early autumn. KTU 1.1-1.3 I, especially Baal's battle with Yamm, evokes the arrival of Baal's rains in the fall. KTU 1.3 II-1.4 VII conjures up the image of the autumnal inauguration of a temple and the rains it is to provide (cf. 1 Kgs 8:36[134]). KTU 1.4 VIII-1.6 suggests the end of the period of the summer, perhaps manifest in Mot as the personified scirocco or east wind, and the return of the Cloud-rider to life (so de Moor 1987:97 n. 470; Yon 1989:462). Each of these sections evokes a meteorological wonder based on Baal's powers, and each one ends in the acknowledgement of Baal's kingship (see Rummel, *RSP III* 234-35). De Moor's own arguments for a single annual cycle in the Baal Cycle provide the basis for seeing autumnal imagery in each of the three major sections of the cycle. De Moor dismissed the possible autumn background of Baal's manifestation of rain in KTU 1.4 VII, because he assumed a single annual cycle (*SPUMB* 162 n. 1). De Moor (1987:97 n. 470; *SPUMB* 238-39) argues, nonetheless, that the battle between Baal and Mot was inspired by the autumn setting: "The ensuing fight is the mythological representation of the 'fight' between hot dry east winds and moist west winds in September." Although de Moor rejects an autumnal setting for either Baal's clash with Yamm in 1.2 IV or his meteorological manifestation in 1.4 VII, the background which he assigns to 1.5-1.6 may ap-

[133] To be sure, de Moor's identification of KTU 1.3 as the first tablet of the Baal Cycle has not met with acceptance; see above p. 7.

[134] Kapelrud 1952:29-30;1963; Fisher, *RSP III* 284; Hurowitz 1983.

ply as well to these sections. It may be argued that his analysis, like the work of Gaster before him, has provided the evidence and general direction for viewing the three major sections as drawing on meteorological imagery of the early autumn.

Some subsequent ritual and seasonal interpretations have been founded on the basis of parallels between the Baal Cycle and traditions associated with Tammuz and Adonis.[135] Robertson (1982) interprets the Baal Cycle as the outgrowth of rituals which he detects in the Adonis traditions. Robertson reconstructs an ancient ritual background by using *aitia* about Adonis, that is, the classical explanations given for the traditions associated with him. Robertson extends this approach to the Baal Cycle. For him, the Baal Cycle contains reflexes of Baal/Adonis rituals: the winnowing of Mot in KTU 1.6 II corresponds to a threshing rite of the gardens of Adonis, which in the summer flourished, only then to expire.[136] Robertson's interpretation of the Baal Cycle does not account for both the differences and similarities between the Baal Cycle and the Adonis traditions (cf. Loretz 1980). The application of the Greek *aitia* and their *Sitz im Leben* to the Ugaritic myths is assumed and never demonstrated. Robertson's approach (1982:315-320, 339) also reverses the sequence of events in the Baal Cycle in some cases. His perspective is atomistic, as it reduces the episodes of the Baal Cycle to numerous units reflecting rituals. Robertson does not address the numerous chronological and thematic differences between the Baal and Adonis traditions. Robertson's theory about the comparison between 1.6 II and the death of Adonis inherent involves a further difficulty: it would be expected that Adonis' counterpart in the Ugaritic tradition, Baal, would be the victim of winnowing and grinding. However, it is Mot who is subject to this fate in the Baal Cycle.

The problem of whether Baal is "a dying and rising god" affects Robertson's reasoning. It has been long assumed that Baal is a "dying and rising god" like Tammuz, Adonis and Osiris, and this view continues to be expressed (Mettinger 1988:77, 83-84; 1990:401 n. 44; Day 1992:549).[137] A number of scholars, including Lambrechts

---

135 See *Thespis* 129; Ribichini 1981; see also Loretz 1980.

136 On this point Robertson (1982: 347) incorrectly states that "Everyone agrees that the manner of [Mot's] death reflects the threshing and the winnowing of grain" (see Healey 1983a:251).

137 See the survey and critical discussion of Barstad 1984:84 n. 45, 148-51.

(1952, 1955, 1967), Buckert (1979:100-1), Barstad (1984:150), J. Z. Smith (1987), Redford (1992:43-44) and Walls (1992:5-6, 68), question the category of the "dying and rising god" and the textual foundations on which it was based. Buckert's comments (1979:101) are characteristic of the criticisms:

> The evidence for resurrection is late and tenuous in the case of Adonis, and practically non-existent in the case of Attis; not even Osiris returns to real life, but instead attains transcendant life beyond death.[138]

In view of the many difficulties, it is presently impossible to accept a general category of a "dying and rising god" in the ancient Mediterranean and Levantine world. Indeed, the similarities need not be explained on the basis of a shared ritual background. Redford (1992:44) argues that some similarities may be due not to a common type of god involved, but to a history of shared plot structures and roles. Some Adonis traditions may be related to the Late Bronze Age Ugaritic traditions of Baal. For example, KTU 1.12 represents the clearest Ugaritic antecedent to the classical tradition about the boar goring Adonis (Redford 1990:828). The relationship may, however, be entirely literary in character.

A general literary approach to the similarities may also help to explain the many, important differences between Baal and the so-called "dying and rising" gods. Baal is a high god, unlike Tammuz and Adonis. Furthermore, Baal shows major meteorological functions unlike Tammuz and Adonis. Indeed, it might be argued that Baal shares less with Tammuz and Adonis than with the Hittite disappearing gods, the Storm-god and his son, Telepinu (Kapelrud 1952:38-39; *Thespis* 215; Parker 1989a:295-95; 1989b:186-87). The disappearance of the Storm-god causes the withering of vegetation (Hoffner 1990:20-22). Similarly, Telepinu's absence on a journey and sleep causes the destruction of vegetation and his return restores fertility (*ANET* 126-27; Hoffner 1990:14-17). Baal's absence likewise threatens vegetation and his return fructifies the world, as El foresees in a vision in 1.6 III 1-13 (Barstad 1984:84 n. 45). Divine absence and sleep are two of the taunts which Elijah directs against the prophets of Baal in 1 Kgs 18:27 according to Parker (1989a:

---

[138] Buckert goes on to question the dying and rising of Dumuzi, but the case can evidently be made. See Kramer 1966:31; Scurlock 1992.

295-96): "But he may be in a conversation, he may be detained, *or he may be on a journey, or perhaps he is asleep and will wake up.*" (NJPS; my italics).[139] This source does not, however, mention Baal's death. Indeed, it may be no coincidence that although Philo of Byblos' *Phoenician History*, the longest late classical source for West Semitic religion, mentions Adonis,[140] it also shows no evidence of Baal as "a dying and rising god."

Finally, some of the language used to establish Baal's so-called death and resurrection in the Baal Cycle has been interpeted in other ways. The attempt to take *ḥy ʾalʾiyn bʿl* (KTU 1.6 I 2, 8, 20) as a reference to Baal's resurrection has scant support. Barstad (1984: 150-51) comments: "The usefulness, and even possibility, of isolating one formula like *ḥy aliyn bʿl* and giving it a content of such wide-reaching consequences as has been done is dubious, to say the least." The attempt to view takes the BH expression, "the living god" (*ʾĕlōhîm ḥayyîm*) as an anti-Baal title because Baal is a "dying and rising" god (Mettinger 1987:82-91) is equally problematic and other views are plausible. Halpern (1991:73), for example, prefers to read this biblical title as a polemic against the cult devoted to deceased ancestors.

The Ugaritic text sometimes invoked as support for Baal as a "dying and rising god" is 1.17 VI 30 where Baal appears to "be brought to life (*yḥwy*)."[141] The contacts between this text and 1.3 I indicate a relationship with the notion invoked in 1.17 V 28-33, but it is clear from the many differences that the Baal Cycle does not explicitly show the idea of "being made alive." Furthermore, the relationship between 1.3 I and 1.17 V 28-33 may be a literary one and not a ritualistic one: the first may re-use an old plot structure cited explicitly by 1.17 V 28-33. As for the language of Baal's death, this does appear in the Baal Cycle (1.5 VI 8, 23; 1.6 I 6, 41). Baal descends to the underworld (1.5 V 14-15) and Mot attacks and con-

139 The first three verbs in this verse have been interpreted quite differently, however, and may be irrelevant to the point at hand. The first three verbs are interpreted in scatological terms by Young 1993:172-73. This issue does not change the plausibility of the comparison between the last two verbs and the notion of Telepinu's sleep.

140 PE 1.10.29; Attridge and Oden 1981:54-55, 91 n. 123.

141 The form is *D*-stem 3 masc. sg. impf. It remains a controverted point as to whether the form is active or passive (see above p. 65). For the proponents of the active voice, the form implies not only Baal's resurrection, but also Baal's ability to make humans (primarily kings) alive. The view is problematic, however.

sumes him (1.6 II 21-23). Moreover, one of his three "daughters" or "women" is Arsay, literally "Earthy," but plausibly "Netherworldly,"[142] given the equation of this goddess with Allatum (*UgV*:44-45),[143] an underworld figure in Mesopotamian myth.[144] As Pidray and Tallay, Baal's other two "women," seem connected with his meteorological functions, Arsay's characteristics might be taken as an indication of some chthonic aspect of Baal. Gaster (*Thespis* 156) argued that the imagery of Baal's death and return to life in the Baal Cycle was related to the seasonal imagery. This image may not derive from a specific ritualistic understanding of Baal as "a dying and rising god."[145] Rather, the notion of Baal's death may reflect the power of the storm eclipsed by the power of Death in the form of the east wind. Using this language for Baal's disappearance, perhaps like that of Telepinu, does not make Baal a "dying and rising god" like Adonis and Tammuz, but only a weather-god whose powers and presence wax and wane in language

---

142 For Ugaritic *ʾarṣ* as both "earth" and underworld," see below p. 178 n. 118.

143 Noted by *CMHE* 56 n. 49; *TO* 79. Equations do not always rest on a single characteristic, and perhaps in this case the basis for the equation is not the underworld. The other argument that Arsay is "Underworldly" derives from the equation drawn between her title *bt yʿbdr* interpreted as "daughter of wide world" (< Arb **wʿb*, be large, big" [Lane 2954] plus **dwr*, "circuit" [cf. Arb *madar*, "celestial orb" in Lane 931]; so *CML*[1] 165), and Akk *irṣitu rapaštu*, "broad land," a designation for the underworld (cf. Astour, *UgVI*, 13). Other views of *yʿbdr* have been proposed: "ampleness of flow," assuming Arb **wʿb* and **drr* (Lane 862-63; so *SPUMB* 84 n. 6; *CML*[2] 48 n. 8); "great rain," assuming Arb **wʿb* plus *badray*, "rain that is before...or in the first part of winter" (Lane 166; so Smith 1985:290). Either of these two derivations would assume a meteorological characteristic of Arsay in accordance with those of Pidray and Tallay. Finally, commentators observe that of Baal's three women, it is Arsay who does not descend to the Underworld with him in KTU 1. 5 V 10-11 (*CML*[2] 48 n. 8), the assumption being that as a netherworld figure, there is no point in describing her as descending to the Underworld. So Gibson (*CML*[2] 72 n. 5) following de Moor (*SPUMB* 83) construes this feature in meteorological terms: "her role is not affected by the summer drought."

144 According to Lambert (1980b:64), this goddess may be the spouse of Alla who is "a dying god, a type of Tammuz." For Allatum, see also the treaty of Ramses II with Hattusilis (*ANET* 205). Emar 383.11' contains the phrase ^{d}*Al-la-tu*$_4$ *ša kib-r[i]*, "Allatu de la ri[ve]."

145 It is possible that Baal's apparent death and return to life is reflected in some biblical texts as argued by Mettinger and Day. According to Day, the imagery of death and resurrection of "a dying and rising fertility god" is reflected in Hos 5:12-6:3 and the parallel imagery of national death and resurrection in Hosea 13-14 should be read against this same background, as 13:1 mentions Baal. Whether or not a specific ritualistic notion of "dying and rising" inheres in these texts is a matter of presupposition.

reminiscent of the seasons. Given the difficulties with correlating at Ugarit rites and literary texts, and the numerous differences between these gods and Baal, it would appear unwarranted to assume that Baal is "a dying and rising god," at least not one like Adonis and Tammuz. The first millennium cult of Hadad-Rimmon might be invoked to support the notion of Baal-Hadad as "a dying and rising god," but this cult is poorly understood (Greenfield 1976), and it is possible that it was influenced secondarily by the cults of Adonis and/or Tammuz. In sum, Baal may have been thought to return to life in accordance with his meteorological character, and this return may have been formulated in literary terms possibly influenced by the Ugaritic royal cult of the dead. At the present state of knowledge[146] it would seem that Baal's return to life does not reflect a ritualistic concept of the Storm-god as a "dying and rising" god.[147]

Hvidberg-Hansen (1971) borrows Dussaud's ritualistic idea that the destruction of Mot in KTU 1.6 II (cf. 1.6 V) symbolizes the agricultural ritual of the sacrifice of the last sheaf (cf. Yon 1989:464). Healy (1983a:251) raises three criticisms of the theory espoused by Hvidberg-Hansen. First, Mot is alive soon after he has been killed. Second, the details of such rituals differ from any other evidence contained in the Ugaritic texts. Third, there is no evidence of such traditions of the last sheaf in ancient Syria or Palestine. The immediate narrative context of 1.6 II likewise militates against a ritual theory. Commenting on the consumption of Mot's limbs by birds in 1.6 II 36-37, Gibson (*CML*² 7 n. 7) observes: "It is particularly difficult to see the point of this action for any agrarian rite." These problems illustrate that if 1.6 II drew on traditional sacrificial language known to its audience, it has rearranged this material to suit its own narrative ends in presenting Anat's destruction of Mot. The weapons which Anat uses to destroy Yamm apparently are specifically agricultural implements (Healey 1983a; 1983b; 1984a), and it would appear that the passage evokes realia of the agricultural world familiar to the ancient audience. Whether or not a specific ritual of the last sheaf also stands behind this description, the text does not correspond to a known Ugaritic ritual. Loewenstamm (1972:382) is

---

146 In the second volume of this commentary I will return to the question of the similarities among Baal, Adonis and Dumuzi in greater detail.

147 This direction of influence might underlie descriptions of Melqart's death which may draw on the Phoenician practice of cremation (Bonnet 1988:173; M. S. Smith and E. Bloch-Smith 1990:591).

critical of the approach represented in the work of Robertson and Hvidberg-Hansen: "Farfetched associations to heterogeneous sources are welded in order to ascribe to the killing of Mot the sense of a ceremony in a fertilizing rite, i.e. a meaning thoroughly different from that of a punishment inflicted on a hated enemy." It may be said at most that the passage may draw on agricultural language in order to heighten the dramatic effect of Mot's destruction.

Livingstone (1986:162-64) provides further comparative evidence for Hvidberg-Hansen's view by noting the motif in two other texts. In the neo-Assyrian text known as "Marduk's Ordeal" (Livingstone 1986:207-53), the abundance of grain following the harvest in the month of Nisan is explained as the result of a god, probably Marduk, having been taken as prisoner (Livingstone 1986:163). Livingstone (1986:162) also cites the identification of Dumuzi with grain among the Sabeans of Harran in an Arabic text dating to the middle of the first millennium:

> In the middle of the month is the festival of the *būqāt*, that is, of the wailing women. It is also called Taʾuz, as it is the festival performed for the god Taʾuz. The women lament for him, and that his master murdered him, ground his bones in a mill and winnowed them in the wind. The women do not eat anything ground in a mill, but only moistened wheat, chick pea paste, dates, raisins, and similar foods. On the twenty-seventh of the month the men performed the mystery of the North for the jinn, satans and deities. They make many loaves of bread cooked under the cinders, out of flour, terebinth, "*mais*" raisins, and shelled walnuts, in the manner made by the shepherds. They sacrificially slit the throats of the nine lambs to Hāmān, the chief, the king of the gods, and there are sacrifices to Namriyyā. On this day the chief takes from every man among them two dirhams, and they eat and drink.

Following Ebeling and Jacobsen, Livingstone takes this text as referring to a myth in which the death of the god Dumuzi is understood in the processes of winnowing and grinding grain. Livingstone's discussion shows both the range of attested material for this ritual language and restraint in suggesting no more than that the Baal Cycle has used this imagery in 1.6 II.

In retrospect, the emphasis of the seasonal approach, like that of the ritual approach, falls heavily on explaining the setting and therefore the origins of the cycle. Neither seasonal nor ritual interpretations place as much stress on what is unique to the Baal Cycle.

Rather, by their very character they tend to focus on what the Baal Cycle shares with other compositions thought to belong to the same "type" or genre. In sum, although seasonal or ritual settings or patterns explain neither the overall diachronic formation nor the larger synchronic narrative of the Baal Cycle, it would appear the Baal Cycle used and assumed a wide range of seasonal and ritual information on the part of its audience.

2. Cosmogonic Interpretations

As noted at the outset of this survey, many interpretations of the Baal Cycle include the observation that on one side of the Baal Cycle stands Baal, the source of life in the cosmos, and on the other side are Yamm ("Sea") and Mot ("Death"), the sources of destruction and death in the universe. This approach may be called in most general terms the cosmogonic view, as it interprets the Baal Cycle primarily in terms of the conflict of the major figures, Baal, Yamm and Mot which issues in the Storm-god's divine kingship. This view has been expressed by numerous scholars, especially Mowinckel (1962:1.134), Cassuto (*GA* 174-77), Fisher, Cross and Clifford. Like these scholars, Margalit (1980:202) offers the view that 1.5-1.6 reflects the struggle between life and death:

> For like it or not, Death is the ultimate ruler of all that lives. However Mot has a very serious problem, to wit, guaranteeing his source of supply. Stated differently: Mot's enormous strength, symbolized by his unlimited ability to take away life, is circumscribed by his inability to grant or restore it. In order to ensure his supply of food, Mot needs Baal—the agency of life-giving precipitation, especially of the winter rains.

While Margalit's remarks parallel Cassuto's emphasisis on the inexorable struggle between life and death, Margalit further notes their interdependence. Similarly, for the disciple of Carl Jung, Erich Neumann (1970:97), Baal and Mot are twins reflecting two aspects of the same cosmic reality. Neumann identified the two gods as expressions of psychological development. Recent descriptions of the Baal Cycle by folklorists comport with the cosmogonic interpretation. Jason (1977:32) classifies the Baal Cycle (as well as Enuma Elish) in the following terms: "In the mythic epic positive mythic forces (deities) create the order of the world in a struggle with negative mythic forces. The struggle has a strong element of physical warfare." This ethnopoetic classification and description conforms to the cosmogonic interpretation of the cycle. The "mythic epic" also renders Baal as a divine, monarchical hero. Like the work of Cassuto, Fisher, Cross and Clifford, the ethnopoetic classification of "mythic epic" also points to the underlying unity connecting the cosmogonic and royal perspectives on the cycle.

The basic view of the cosmogonic approach is well-founded. While not allies, Yamm and Mot may be seen as comparable forces treated as rivals to Baal for divine kingship, albeit not simultaneously.[148] Other Ugaritic texts would appear to support this view of Yamm and Mot. In KTU 1.2 IV 3 and KTU 1.14 I 19-20, Yamm is characterized as a source of destruction. One Ugaritic letter, KTU 2.10.11-14 refers to Mot to describe the speaker's difficult circumstances.[149] Pardee renders these lines:

(11) wyd	Also, the "hand
(12) ʾilm p kmtm	of a god" is here, for Death (here)
(13) ʿz mʾid	is very strong[150]

Another Ugaritic text, KTU 1.127.29-31, describes Mot as one who attacks humanity (Rainey 1973:51):

(29) hm qrt tʾuḫd hm mt yʿl bnš
(30) bt bn bnš yqḥ ʿz
(31) wyḥdy mrḥqm

(29) If the city is (has been) taken, (or) if Mot should attack man,
(30) the house of the son(s) of man(kind) will (should) take a goat
(31) and will (should) look to the future (lit. afar).[151]

Viewing Yamm and Mot as comparable forces rivaling Baal suits Cross' view of the Baal-Yamm story and the Baal-Mot narrative as variants forms or "alloforms." In short, on one level Baal embodies life for the cosmos, while Yamm and Mot are characters of chaos and death.

---

[148] Dividing the characters of the Baal Cycle into forces of fertility and powers of destruction has two limitations. First, as Loewenstamm (*CS* 350) has observed, the battle of Baal and Yamm would never have been interpreted as a battle of order over chaos, except that the name of Yamm ("Sea") suggests such a possibility. The names of the protagonists of the Baal Cycle should not be ignored, however. Second, Cassuto's interpretation envisions Yamm and Mot as allies against Baal.

[149] Pope 1977b:668; Lipiński 1983:124-1235; Pardee 1987a:66-68.

[150] Pardee 1987a:66-68.

[151] Cf. an Akkadian text from Ugarit which reads: *ultu pî mu-ti ikimanni* "he snatched me from the mouth of death." *Ug V*, #162: 40, pp. 268-9; *CAD* M/2, 317-8.

In the work of Fisher, Cross and Clifford, the cosmogonic approach has taken a more particular expression. Building on the work of Mowinckel (1962:1.134), Fisher (1965: 314-15) proposes that the Baal Cycle constitutes a mythological description of the creation of the world:

> Is this conflict theme related to kingship, temple building, or creation? I think that this is an improper question. . . conflict, kingship, ordering of chaos, and temple building are all related to an overarching theme that I would call ''creation.'' However, this is not theogony or a creation of the El type. Rather it is cosmogonic and is of the Baal type.

Fisher (1965:317-18) bases his view of creation in the Baal Cycle on a number of points.

First, Fisher (1965:318) argues that the palace of Baal constitutes a microcosm of the whole world or cosmos. That the palace symbolized Baal's place in the world as its fructifier is evident from the window in Baal's house, according to Kapelrud (1952:29-30; 1963) and Fisher (1963:40; 1965:318; cf. Rummel, *RSP III* 284). That the language of creation, in Fisher's terms, underlies the description of the building of the palace in KTU 1.4 V-VII appears plausible when it is compared to Ps 78:69: *wayyiben kĕmô-rāmîm miqdāšô kĕʾereṣ yĕsādāh lĕʿôlām*, ''He built his sanctuary like the high heavens, like the earth which he has founded for ever'' (see Hurowitz 1992:332, 335). Levenson (1988:87) observes that creation and temple-building in biblical texts such as this one serve as a ''homology'' which interpenetrate descriptions of one another: creation can be rendered in terms of temple-building and vice-versa (see also Hurowitz 1992: 242).

For the interpretation of the Baal Cycle, it is important to determine the significance of the ''interpenetration.'' While the Ugaritic passage evokes cosmic dimension and importance by drawing on cosmic imagery, this usage does not indicate that the building of Baal's palace constitutes an act of the creation of the cosmos. Indeed, the ''homology'' in the Baal Cycle perhaps renders cosmic fructification (but not creation) in terms of temple-building and vice-versa. Furthermore, Fisher's thesis that the temple-building episode in KTU 1.4 V-VII describes creation is not confirmed, however, by the passage's other features. What Fisher calls the ''creation'' language of Baal's palace evokes the cosmic grandeur of his role in maintaining the cosmos. The divine palace has cosmic ramifications: it is the source of well-being for the cosmos. It also may have been understood as enthroned on top of the known cosmos. The house is clearly cosmic in importance, but this fact does not indicate that Baal is a creator. If fructifying the world and maintaining it qualifies as cosmogony, then there is no denying that the Baal Cycle contains these features, but then the definition of creation is imprecise. Fisher's own formulation of cosmogony at Ugarit (1965:320) is ambiguous: "At Ugarit we have no description of the process of ordering the cosmos, but nevertheless we have it."

Second, according to Fisher (1965:319; cf. 1969:204), the motif of "seven days" in both Genesis 1 and KTU 1.4 VII further indicates that the temple-building constitutes a type of creation. Fisher might have also mentioned that the tabernacle was thought to have been built over seven months (Hurowitz 1992:227), and Solomon spent seven years building the Temple (1 Kgs 6:38). As Hurowitz' discussion (1992:242-43 n. 3) of temple-building indicates, these examples suggest not that temple-building is a metaphor for creation in the Baal Cycle, but that creation in Genesis 1 uses the language of temple-building. It might be questioned further whether the motif of the seven-day period is too common (Freedman 1970-71; *CS* 192-209) to be considered a basis for inferring creation or cosmogony from the biblical account of Genesis 1 to KTU 1.4 VII. Finally, Fisher suggests that Baal's setting of the "season" (*ʿdn*) in KTU 1.4 V 6-7 represents an act of creation, but this view is based on a faulty understanding of **ʿdn*.[152]

For some proponents of cosmogony in the Baal Cycle, cosmogony represents a kind of creation different from theogony. Cross (1978: 333-34) focuses attention on this aspect of the definition of cosmogony:

> The Ugaritic cosmogonic cycle (in which Baʿl battles with Sea and Death to secure kingship) is not prefaced by a theogony. Indeed no theogonic myth is extent in the Canaanite cuneiform texts. This circumstance has led certain scholars to claim that there is no creation myth at Ugarit. Such a view is wholly wrong-headed in my judgement.

[152] See above p. 53.

> The absence of a theogonic prologue is merely a primitive feature of the Ugaritic cosmogonic cycle. Otherwise, it bears all the traits of the cosmogony. The conflict between Baᶜl and Yamm-Nahar (Sea and River), Môt (Death), and Lôtan are alloforms reflecting the usual conflict between the olden gods and the young gods of the cult. The primary focus of the cycle is the emergence of kingship among the gods. Baᶜl the divine warrior returns victorious to the divine assembly, receives kingship, builds his royal temple on Mount Sapon, and invites the gods to the royal banquet. The pattern of the cosmogonic myth could not be more evident.

In a theogony the events are described as having occurred in the distant past. However, the Baal type of creation is a cosmogony, which pits a young god in battle against a divine force representing chaos or death; it may or may not locate events in time. It delineates primordial events and structures, such as kingship.

Clifford (1984) expands on the ideas of Fisher and Cross. According to Clifford, cosmogony is not a creation from nothing (*creatio ex nihilo*), but the ordering of chaos. Clifford (1984:186-87, 198) suggests:

> Ancient cosmogonies were primarily interested in the emergence of society, organized with patron gods and worship systems, divinely appointed kings or leaders, kinship and marriage systems.
>
> Baal's move to a central place among the gods contributes to the establishment of the world. Baal arranges the heavens and earth as a source of life for humans. In the myths the perspective is heavenly. From the earthly perspective, Baal's palace is reflected in the temple in the city of Ugarit. It is the place where the king is identified as the regent of the god. The stories are thus cosmogonies, stories which describe how the society came to be established and how it continues to remain supportive of human community.

According to Clifford, Genesis 1-3, Psalms 77, 78:41-55, and 104, Enuma Elish and Atrahasis also constitute cosmogonies issuing in conditions requisite for a stable human society. Genesis 1-3 and Enuma Elish also describe the formation of order for human society and the creation of the world. Creation follows Marduk's defeat of Tiamat in Enuma Elish, and numerous biblical passages recount the defeat of cosmic foes in the primordial time of creation. Genesis 1 plays on this tradition, asserting the divine omnipotence by omitting mention of any cosmic opposition to the divine plan of creation (Levenson 1988:3-77). While older treatments of this question occasionally posited a creation account in a lacuna of the Baal Cycle,

Clifford (1984) has changed the basis for the argument for the Baal Cycle as a cosmogony. He redefines cosmogony in a manner which fits the Baal Cycle by arguing that cosmogony does not constitute creation out of nothing (*creatio ex nihilo*) or primarily creation of the physical universe, but the formation of conditions suitable for human society. By this logic Clifford classifies the Baal Cycle as a cosmogony. Finally, for both Fisher and Clifford, the absence of one element from a cosmogony (such as kingship, temple building or the rendering of order from chaos) is not crucial. For an ancient cosmogony may concentrate on "one element without explicit reference to the whole." It is "a kind of synecdoche, the part stands for the whole" (Clifford 1984:188).

Several commentators have criticized the cosmogonic approach developed in the work of Fisher, Cross, Clifford and other scholars.[153] The most common objection to their approach involves the terms of creation and cosmogony.[154] Greenfield (1987b:557) regards creation as a major criterion for defining an ancient Near Eastern cosmogony:

> In the Ugaritic tale Baᶜal must defeat Yamm in order to achieve rule, but there is nothing more than that in the text, notwithstanding scholars' efforts to interpret those texts as indicating that Baᶜal imposed order on a chaotic world, and the battle with Yam as thus taking on cosmogonic significance. There are two reasons for this line of thought, the first being that in the Hebrew Bible the theme of the defeat of the sea is connected with creation, as in Psalm 74:16-17...Defeat of the monster symbolizing chaos, followed by creation and the ordering of the universe, is known also from the Babylonian creation epic [Enuma Elish], a work which may have come under western influence before it was written down, which happened after the composition of the Ugaritic texts. Be that as it may, this creation theme is lacking in the Ugaritic texts that have reached us.

Battle conflicts like 1.2 IV appear in other ancient Near Eastern texts in the context of creation. The Egyptian Instruction of King Merikare lines 13f. read: "Well directed are men, the cattle of their god. He made heaven and earth according to their desire, and he

---

[153] Fisher 1963, 1965, 1969, *RSP III* 240, 242, 249-50 n. 5; Gaster, *Thespis* 137; Wakeman 1969:313, 1973: 37-39; Komoróczy 1973:32; Cross 1978:329-338; Miller 1981:125; J. Z. Smith 1982:98, 134; Grønboek 1985:27-44; Wyatt 1986; cf. Caquot 1959:182.

[154] Caquot 1959; McCarthy 1967; Kapelrud 1979, 1980; Margalit 1981; Korpel and de Moor 1986:243-44; Cunchillos 1987.

repelled the water monster'' (*ANET* 417; Lichtheim 1973:106; Faulkner in Simpson 1973:191). This passage contains a ''reference to the concept of a primordial water monster, defeated at the time of creation'' (Lichtheim 1973:109 n. 29; cf. *ANET* 417 n. 49). In his discussion of creation in the Coffin Texts, Allen (1988:33-35) notes the role which the language of battle plays in conveying the struggle between the forces of development and inertia, between life and lifelessness. This struggle began in creation and is replicated in daily life. According to Korpel and de Moor (1986:244), biblical narratives sometimes combine conflict with creation not because the two motifs necessarily belonged together in all cases, but because the two were attributed to a single deity in biblical tradition (cf. Levenson 1988:10; Smith 1990); the same point applies to Marduk in Enuma Elish.[155] Caquot (1959:181-82; cf. J. Day 1985b:12) suggests that although the Ugaritic texts do not include any examples of cosmogony as such, the West Semitic literary tradition knew such cosmogonies because of the biblical texts (Psalms 93, 95-99) attesting to the combination of battle and creation. It is unclear whether cosmogonies constituted a general genre of the West Semitic literary tradition. The combination of battle and creation may have been secondary within Israelite culture, or it was simply absent from Ugaritic literature. Indeed, Curtis (1978:255) notes a number of psalms where the theme of Yahweh's subjugation of the waters is separate from creation, and he argues that in the Psalms the former is at least as prominent a theme as the latter. In sum, if the Baal Cycle constitutes a cosmogony, it must be asked why creation material is absent from the Baal Cycle (or from the other Ugaritic texts as well).

The difficulty in definition is the primary crux in the cosmogonic approach. The Baal Cycle is unlike many of the ''cosmogonies'' which Clifford compares to it. Clifford (1984:185) notes that scholars have taken Enuma Elish as ''the standard'' of cosmogonies, and he also classifies Atrahasis and biblical poems with creation motifs as cosmogonies (see Clifford 1984:185-86 n. 8). The argument that the Baal Cycle is a cosmogony has depended on comparisons with Enuma Elish. There are many parallels between the two texts, as commentators have long noted.[156] The dissimilarities between

---

155 Kapelrud (1952:28) called this development ''absorption.''

156 See pp. 13, 34-35, 79, 82, 95, 96, 101, 103-05, 110-12, 130, 150, 231, 288, 296, 300, 314-15, 319, 335, 340, 353 and 358-61. Enuma Elish is too complex in its composition (Lambert 1965:287-300; cf. Komoróczy 1973:32) to serve as ''the standard'' against which cosmogony in the Baal Cycle is to be assessed.

Baal Cycle and Enuma Elish are equally instructive. Unlike Enuma Elish, the Baal Cycle relegates the deeds of the older generation of deities to the background and only alludes to old events such as creation in the form of divine epithets. The Baal Cycle does not describe primordial events such as the creation of the cosmos, but rather its maintenance through the power of the storm-god. The Baal Cycle concerns a more "recent" series of divine events compared to either the opening tablet of Enuma Elish or the opening chapters of Genesis, and in this sense the Baal Cycle differs sharply from well-known "cosmogonies." Because of comparisons with texts such as Genesis 1-3 and Enuma Elish, the cosmogonic interpretation focuses on the human dimension of the Baal Cycle, but this story concentrates on the affairs of deities; it is theocentric in its perspective, although its concerns sometimes reflect human needs (KTU 1.4 VII 49-52; 1.6 I 6-7, II 17-19, V 25-26[157]). As a result, in order to understand the Baal Cycle in Clifford's terms, it is necessary to impose the features of ordering society, explicit in texts like Enuma Elish and Atrahasis, onto the Baal Cycle which is silent on these matters. The Baal Cycle therefore appears to be fundamentally different from any of these texts in its expression of "cosmogony." Furthermore, Albright classifies the text of Illuyankas as a cosmogony, but like the Baal Cycle, this text has no creation or ordering of human society.[158] While Fisher, Cross, Clifford and others distinguish between theogony and cosmogony, still other scholars such as G. Komoróczy (1973:31) categorize Enuma Elish as a cosmogony with two parts, the theogony and the theomachy, and elsewhere Komoróczy (1973:36) calls the opening portion of Enuma Elish a cosmogony which Fisher and others label as theogony. These different uses in terminology and classification therefore require further clarification and refinement.

Hillers (1985: 266) also addresses the problem of terminology, especially Cross' application of the terms "theogony" and "cosmogony" to Ugaritic texts:

> But the support for such a view of Canaanite religion in general. . .is derived from the lists of divine witnesses in Anatolian treaties and what we could call the "late-late show," Eusebius and Damascius. Against this choice of a center for Canaanite religion we may set the attested diversity visible in Ugaritic texts: god-lists arranged on

---

[157] See pp. xviii-xix.

[158] Albright 1936b:18; cf. Komoróczy 1973:33. For recent treatments of Illuyankas, see Beckman 1982; Hoffner 1990:10-14.

> neither theogonic nor cosmogonic principles, but by cultic rank (with many vagaries), or by theological principles, or geographically or in ways that baffle us; and the obvious prominence not just of myths of various sorts, but also of rituals, divination, and prayer. For that matter, it is easier to find in Ugaritic texts something like "Hebrew epic" than it is to find cosmogonic myths.

It is commonly objected that the terminology of creation in the Baal Cycle itself militates against the approach of Fisher, Cross and Clifford. Some of the epithets attributed to El and Athirat suggest that they, and not Baal, are the creators of humanity and hence the agents of cosmogony or "world-building."[159] Two of El's titles are *ʾab ʾadm*, "father of humanity," and *bny bnwt*, "creator of creatures." Athirat is *qnyt ʾilm*, "creatress of the gods." These epithets suggest that the generation of El and Athirat is responsible for the creation of humanity.[160] According to Lambert (1985b:537), this dimension of El's character underlies one inscription of Yahdunlim of Mari. The inscription states that "El (*ilum*) built the city of Mari."[161] Roberts (1972:32-33) would see a similar depiction of El evident in a number of Akkadian personal names (cf. Millard 1974:89). El performs actions indicative of his creative power (e.g., the creation of Shaʿtaqat in KTU 1.16 V 23-30) in the image of the potter nipping clay, precisely the language of creation in Mesopotamian,[162] Egyptian[163] and Israelite literatures.[164]

El's character raises a serious issue as to Baal's role within the cosmos. The Baal Cycle does not assert that Baal "creates" or even "arranges" the cosmos. It suggests, rather, that Baal is its preserver and savior. As Korpel and de Moor (1986:244) summarize the evidence, "Baal may have been the champion among the gods able to

---

159 *CML*¹, 21; *EUT* 49-50; Schmidt 1961:49-52; Kapelrud 1952:138; 1979: 407-412; de Moor 1980b:171-187; Gibson 1984:207-208; see Miller 1980: 43-46.

160 Cf. El's role in the theogony, in KTU 1.23; cf. Ugaritic DN, *ybnʾil*, "El builds/creates" (*PTU* 96).

161 For the issue whether *ilum* is El or a generic usage meaning "god" and involving another deity, see Hurowitz 1992:333.

162 E.g., the creation of humanity in the Assyrian version of Atrahasis in *ANET* 100, related to the OB composition called "Creation of Man by the Mother Goddess," in *ANET* 100; creation of Enkidu by the goddess Aruru in Gilgamesh 1.2.34-35 in *ANET* 74. See Moran 1970.

163 See the creation of humanity by Khnum in *ANET* 441; see Gordon 1982.

164 Isa 64:7; Job 33:6; 1QH 13:14-15. See Ginsberg 1946:48; Pope 1973:217; Margalit 1981:144.

subdue the forces of evil, yet he was unable to create anything new.'' In the Baal Cycle the Cloud-rider revives the world. This is clear from the effects of his rains that fructify the earth (KTU 1.3 IV 25-27; 1.4 V 6-9; 1.4 VII 26-31) and his feast that nourishes the gods (KTU 1.4 VI 38-59). KTU 1.4 VII 49-52 relates the primary function which the divine king is expected to exercise on behalf of the pantheon and humanity:

ʾaḥdy dymlk ʿl ʾilm	I alone am the one who rules over the gods,
lymrʾu ʾilm wnšm	Indeed commands/fattens gods and men,
dyšb[ʿ?] hmlt ʾarṣ	Who satis[fies?] earth's multitudes.

Baal's death lamented in KTU 1.5 VI 23-24 and 1.6 I 6-7 threatens the continuation of human life:

bʿl mt my lʾim	Baal is dead! What of the people?
bn dgn my hmlt	The son of Dagan! What of the multitudes?

These passages demonstrate that Baal is the fructifier of the earth, the source of well-being for the pantheon and humanity alike, and only in this sense, the ''recreator'' of the cosmos. While El is the creator of the cosmos, it is Baal who gives life to the world.[165] Although the old generation of creator-deities appears in the Baal Cycle, their original act of creation is not the concern of the Baal Cycle. Rather, the accent falls entirely on Baal's conflict with his enemies, Yam and Mot, and his kingship in the cosmos.

The express differences between the Baal Cycle and other ancient Near Eastern ''cosmogonies'' may suggest another approach to the appearance of ''cosmogonic'' elements in the Baal Cycle. As opposed to creation accounts described in the idiom of the battle conflict, the Baal Cycle reuses elements of creation accounts in its rendering of the battle between Baal and Yamm. Yamm as the embodiment of chaos or destruction on a cosmic level may represent a vestige of a creation background. It has been claimed that the natural conditions of the storm constituted the source for the symbolization of Yamm as chaos. Various views, such as flooding (*ANET* 135 n. 28; Kloos 1986:170; cf. Coogan 1981:81), and inter-

---

[165] Hvidberg 1962:62-63; Kapelrud 1979:407-12; *Baal* 145; *CS* 353 n. 106; see also Kaiser 1959:76; Schmidt 1961:38; Mowinckel 1962:1.241 n. 21. See Lambert 1985a:538.

ruption of shipping (*SPUMB* 141; *CML*^{2} 7), have been suggested. According to Kaiser (1959:65), the waters whipped up by the storm were viewed as a symbol of resistance to the the storm-god whose "own season in the fall marked the cessation of Sea's hostility." Commenting on this particular version of the argument, Greenfield (1961:91) questions "if the battering of the Syro-Palestinian coast by the waters of the Mediterranean... does not really have enough motivating force to have engendered the mythological material..." For all their threat to human living conditions, the storm may not lie directly behind the representation of Yamm as chaos. A direct natural interpretation may be insufficient to explain the symbol of Yamm as the divine enemy embodying chaos and destruction (KTU 1.2 IV 3; 1.14 I 19-20); rather, a more complex natural interpretation may be involved.

Like Tiamat, Yamm may represent a deity from an older theogonic tradition. Creation stories regularly describe the primeval chaos as watery. Allen (1988:63) notes the oldest concept of creation in Egypt: "The first concepts may well have been those with obvious roots in the experience of Egyptian life—the image of a first sunrise over the first mound of earth to appear from the receding waters of pre-existence." In one Egyptian text (from CT 714), the primeval waters constitute "the milieu within which the creation unfolds" (Allen 1988:14). The image of the god Atum floating in the primeval waters at the moment of creation serves to convey this process (Allen 1988:13): "See, the Flood is subtracted from me (Atum): see, I am the remainder." As Allen (1988:14) notes of this description: "Creation involves the distinction between this primordial mass and the surrounding waters." Traditions from Hermapolis, Heliopolis and Memphis depict creation as the primeval hillock arising from the waters of chaos (*ANET* 3, 8; cf. 4a n. 7, 4b n. 6; Allen 1988; Plumley 1975:25-29). As early as the Coffin texts, the primeval waters bear the epithet, "father of the gods" (Allen 1988:21).

Greek and Levantine seem to follow suit. The Iliad (14:201, 246; cf. 23:607-08) calls Okeanos "the genesis of all." According to PE 1.10.1, at the beginning of the cosmos there was "chaos," which Baumgarten (1981:106-07) interprets as watery chaos and equates with BH *tĕhōm*, "Deep." Given the absence of an attested Ugaritic tradition regarding creation, Yamm perhaps constituted the primeval waters in older traditional material or was related to these waters in some manner. According to Baumgarten (1981:106), a remnant of an older cosmogony may lie behind the descriptions of

El's abode in the Baal Cycle. El's abode has been compared with the home of Ea (*EUT* 71; Lipiński 1971), built over the watery Apsu according to Enuma Elish 1.71f. (see *ANET* 72, 111, 342, 390). The creation of Ea's abode shortly after the first conflict following the theogony and anticipates the later creation of Marduk's palace atop the carcass of Tiamat in Enuma Elish 4.137-39. A similar situation may be operative in the Baal Cycle. According to Baumgarten, like Ea's creation of his abode on top of Apsu, El's home at the source of the "Double-Deeps," *thmtm* (*EUT* 71) may reflect an element of an old cosmogony.

It may be noted further that if the figure of Yamm goes back to an older, unattested West Semitic theogony, it would have an analogy in the Mesopotamian theogonic traditions. The first millennium theogony known as "the Harab myth"[166] includes both "Sea" (*tâmtum*) and "River" (^{d}*ID*) in the earliest divine generations. In this account "Sea" is the mother of "River." It might be suggested further that the storm on the Levantine coast may have constituted the ultimate background to the West Semitic traditions about the sea, and therefore indirectly the figure of Yamm as a source of chaos and destruction in the Baal Cycle. By the same token, the setting for this development is so removed in time[167] from the extant text of the Baal Cycle that it only partially addresses the meaning of the Baal Cycle for the Ugaritic society which produced, transmitted and added to it.

Despite these problems, it is important to note that the cosmogonic approach makes a number of significant contributions. First, this interpretation accounts for the whole of the Baal Cycle, and it finds support in the effects that the death of Baal brings to the earth in KTU 1.6 I 6-7 and KTU 1.6 IV 1-2. As noted above, Baal's house and the opening of the window is expected by Athirat to produce a luxuriant, green earth in KTU 1.4 V 6-9. Second, the language of creation, in Fisher's terms, underlying the description of the building of the palace in KTU 1.4 may point not to an implicit account of creation, but to the reuse of the language of creation designed to serve the concerns of this particular text, which is not creation but

[166] *ANET* 517-18; Lambert and Walcot 1965; Lambert and Millard 1965:#43; Jacobsen 1984.

[167] For Lambert (1988:128) fundamental myths involving nature derived from pre-historic times:

Baal's power. Third, the cosmogonic approach offers a rich explanation and larger context for understanding the themes of kingship, temple building and divine conflicts. Fourth, the cosmogonic view of the Baal Cycle shows how the conflict in 1.2 IV and temple-building in 1.4 VII thematically belong together and are thus plausibly parts of a single work.[168] Finally, Clifford's statement that an ancient cosmogony may concentrate on one element without specific reference to other parts of even the whole is significant, because it can show what is special about one cosmogony as opposed to another. What the Baal Cycle means depends on those elements and themes upon which it concentrates in a way that no other "cosmogony" does. Or, to make the point differently, the question that remains is the theme which the Baal Cycle emphasizes and the materials and strategies which the cycle deploys to underscore it.

3. Historical and Political Views

Although ritual and seasonal interpretations dominated discussion of the Baal Cycle from the 1930s through the 1960s, a number of scholars proposed historical settings or factors to account for the formation of the Baal Cycle. Virolleaud (1946) and Obermann (1947) argued that the background of the Baal's conflict with Yamm in KTU 1.2 IV was to be located in the arrival of the Sea Peoples to the Syrian littoral in the late Bronze Age. Obermann (1947: 205-06) remarks:

> For the present, however, it is all but impossible to escape the impression that—unlike the enmity between Baal and Mot, which may be best understood as one of cosmological character—that between Baal and Prince Sea should be considered as having originated under definite conditions. In other words, in the light of the fragment which we have analyzed, the narrator of 3AB [KTU 1.3] would appear to have incorporated in his version of the building saga a myth designed

---

It seems to the present writer that the creative period lies in prehistory. That was the time of genuine mythic creativity, so that the basic material was spread everywhere from the Aegean to India before our written evidence begins. When the earliest myths and allusions known to us were written down, the basic concern of myth had already lost some of its force. But there was still a good measure of respect both for these powers and the traditional stories about them, so the stories were maintained, but often with new uses.

[168] See also p. 13.

> to explain, etiologically how the people of Ugarit succeeded in expelling a hostile invasion effected by the inhabitants of a sea region, say, on the eastern shore of the Mediterranean, how they routed and deranged the invader's forces, how they destroyed his ranks into ruin. That, by the medium of folklore, the struggle between two peoples may easily have come to be remembered as the struggle between their respective gods—and, in the present instance, between Baal, the most active and the most popular god of Ugarit, and Prince Sea, the real or popularly assumed name of the god worshipped by the invaders from the sea region—is too well-known a phenomenon to need being discussed here.

The evidence for this historical background is minimal at best.[169]

Some scholars followed the historical lead of Virolleaud and Obermann. A student of Obermann, Pope (*EUT* 92-93) argues that the narrative of the Baal Cycle reflects the replacement of El by Baal. For Pope (*EUT* 103-104) this theme had historical implications:

> The social and political forces that caused El to be displaced before Baal at Ugarit can only be surmised. The displacement of one god by another is probably brought chiefly by the influx of new cultural and ethnic groups, whether by conquest or peaceful infiltration. At Ugarit there was a large Hurrian element mixed with the Semitic population. For the Hurrians, Kumarbi, like El, was the father of the gods, but Hittite texts of about the 14th century B. C. or earlier mythologize the displacement of this god before the Storm-god, and the Ugaritic texts, we believe, do the same in regard to El and Baal. In the Amarna and Ramessid period, the storm-gods, the Hurrian Teshub and the Semitic Hadad-Baal, are the major deities—their identification with one another and with the Egyptian Seth in the Ramessid period is patent—while Kumarbi and El have passed out of the picture.[170]

---

[169] Gray (1979b:323) offers a historical interpretation for 1.2 IV and 1.3 II comparable to the view of Obermann. Gray begins with the valid observation that 1.2 IV may reflect on a cosmic level what the 1.3 II represents on a terrestrial level. He then suggests that these two episodes may have commemorated the supplanting of the cult of Yamm by that of Baal. On the historical level, these passages in the Baal Cycle might reflect Ugarit's assertion of independence from Beirut under Egyptian hegemony. Gray proposes that the address in an Akkadian letter from the king of Beirut to his "son, the governor of Ugarit" reflects a period of Beirut's hegemony over Ugarit, and that KTU 1.2 IV and 1.3 II would then reflect an attestation to these political conditions. Gray admits that this hypothesis is conjectural and he offers a ritual interpretation for KTU 1.3 II in addition to his historical reconstruction. Fensham (1979: 272-274) offers a similar historical interpretation of the Baal Cycle. According to Fensham, the treaty terminology in 1.2 I 36-38 and 1.5 II 12 suggests the possibility that Yamm and Mot may have represent invaders from the west and east.

[170] Mann (1977:96-100; cf. Wyatt 1979:826-27) also describes the exaltation of Baal in these terms.

Coogan (1981:81) echoes Pope's view:

> The transfer of power from an older god to a younger storm god is attested in contemporary eastern Mediterranean cultures. Kronos was imprisoned and succeeded by his son Zeus, Yahweh succeeded El as the god of Israel, the Hittite god Teshub assumed kingship in heaven after having defeated his father Kumarbi, and Baal replaced El as the effective head of Ugaritic pantheon. A more remote and hence less exact parallel is the replacement of Dyaus by Indra in early Hinduism. These similar developments can be accurately dated to the second half of the second millennium B.C., a time of prosperity and extraordinary artistic development, but also of political upheaval and natural disasters that ended in the collapse or destruction of many civilizations, including the Mycenaean, Minoan, Hittite, and Ugaritic. In such a context a society might suppose that its traditional objects of worship had proved ineffective, that the pantheon in its established form had, like entrenched royalty, become incapable of dealing with new challenges. At this point it might choose an extradynastic god, as Ugarit chose Baal, son of Dagon and not of El; and, beset by invasions from the sea and tidal waves arising from earthquakes, it might construct a mythology in which the new god demonstrated his mastery over the sea.

Vine (1965) offeres a more precise historical view of the cycle. Distancing his position from the earlier historical interpretations of Virolleaud and Obermann, Vine (1965:vi-vii, 148) argues that the Baal Cycle reflects the rise of the Amorites at Ugarit in the twenty-first or twentieth century B.C. With the emergence of the Amorites, Baal, the new god of the Amorites, replaced El, the local god. In a similar vein, Oldenburg (*CEBCR* 101-42) suggests that the rivalry between Baal and the family of El and Athirat reflects a tension in their cults at Ugarit during the second millennium. Like Vine, Oldenburg views Baal-Haddu as an Amorite god. According to Oldenburg (*CEBCR* 143-63), the cult of Baal progressively spread into Mesopotamia and along the Levantine coast and came into conflict with the cult of El during the Middle Bronze Age.

The interpretations of Vine and Oldenburg have been criticized for their lack of evidence (*Baal* 325). However, two Ugaritic texts published since Vine's study have established the Amorite background of the Ugaritic dynasty of "Niqmaddu II," under whose royal patronage the extant copy of the Baal Cycle was produced. According to Levine and de Tarragon (1984:655), the references to *ddn* in KTU 1.161 and *dtn* in 1.124.2 (cf. lines 4 and 11) demonstrate the Amorite background of the Ugaritic dynasty: "At Ugarit, there was a tradition which traced the origin of the Ugaritians and their kings and heroes to the Didanum-people who flourished in what is today North-East Syria, long before a rise of a dynasty at Ugarit.''[171] In view of these texts, Vine's proposal may be rehabilitated and revised. The Baal Cycle may be understood to reflect not the rise of the Amorites at Ugarit, but the origins of Ugaritic kingship under the Amorite dynasty of Niqmaddu (see Kitchen 1977:131-142). To extend this speculative reconstruction, ''Niqmaddu II'' took the name of the early Ugaritic leader, Niqmaddu. The name of both rulers may reflect their devotion to the Baal-Addu, given that the name Niqmaddu is an Addu name meaning ''Addu has vindicated'' (*PTU* 17, 168). A third monarch had the name *yᶜḏrd*, ''Addu helps'' (see Kitchen 1977:132, esp. n. 12; *PTU* 41, 113, 133). As Pardee (1988b:140) observes, *(h)addu* is the only theophoric element in royal names from Ugarit, which would suggest that this god is the dynastic god (Garbini 1983:57[172]). The importance of Baal may be measured also from his iconography at Ugarit. Seeden (1980:106) observes that Baal ''was in greater demand at Ugarit than any other male deity, since his representations are by far the most numerous.''

To support his dynasty at Ugarit, ''Niqmaddu II'' sponsored the scribal production of the Baal Cycle, as indicated by the colophon at the end of KTU 1.6 VI. The description of Baal's rise to kingship might have been understood as a divine reflection of the emergence of the Ugaritic dynasty of ''Niqmaddu I.'' Without advancing a specific theory about Amorite invasions or the arrival of specific deities to Ugarit, the Baal Cycle may have served to support the rise of Niqmaddu's line in the Middle Bronze Age or the maintenance of the line during the Late Bronze Age.[173] The rise of the dynasty was traced back to the early figures of Niqmaddu I and Yaqaru, as shown by the king list in KTU 1.113. The royal seal bearing the words, ''Yaqaru, son of Niqmaddu, king of Ugarit,'' *ya-qa-rum mâr ni-iq-má-du šàr* ^{al}*ú-ga-ri-it* (*PRU III*: xli) comes from ''Level II'' of Ugarit, which might suggest the Middle Bronze Age as the general period for the rise of Baal and the dynasty of Niqmaddu. Presuma-

---

171 For a phonological explanation of the variation in dentals in *ddn* and *dtn*, see Garr 1986.

172 This point and reference were brought to my attention by Professor K. van der Toorn.

173 So-called ''Level II'' = ca. 2100-1500 according to the excavator; see Courtois 1974; North 1975.

bly this process continued into the Late Bronze Age when Baal and the dynasty of Niqmaddu were entrenched firmly in the city-state of Ugarit. The Baal Cycle may reflect the culmination of this development. Thus the broad cultural context for the emergence of Baal at Ugarit as described by Pope and Coogan may be correlated with specific texts reflecting the rise of the dynasty of Niqmaddu such as KTU 1.113 and 1.161, the Yaqaru seal and perhaps the Baal Cycle itself.

Stolz (1982) argues for a more precise political interpretation. Baal not only represents the rise of Ugaritic dynasty; El and his distant abode represent Ugarit's overlords during the fourteenth and thirteenth centuries. One possible difficulty with the element of El's symbolization of the foreign empires resides in the Ugaritic use of a Ugaritic god to symbolize a non-Ugaritic power. Nonetheless, Stolz's view rightly emphasizes that Baal wields limited power, which reflects Ugarit's relative position among the great powers of Egypt and Hatti.

The thesis that the Baal Cycle reflects the rise of a new dynasty at Ugarit may help to explain why Baal, although not a son of El and Athirat, is selected king of the cosmos. Indeed, the tension between the family of El and Baal belongs to the theme of kingship in the Baal Cycle (cf. *EUT* 55-56, 93, 97; Pope 1989:228-30). Although Baal calls El "father" in both Ugaritic texts (KTU 1.3 V 35; 1.4 IV 47; cf. 1.4 I 5) and in the Elkunirsa story (*ANET* 519), Baal is also the "son of Dagan," for example in the Baal Cycle in 1.2 I 19, 35, 37, 1.5 VI 23-24 and 1.6 I 6, which would suggest that his status as El's son represents a secondary divine lineage. The Cloud-rider's title, *bn dgn*, "son of Dagan," suggests that El was not considered his father by blood. In view of the derivation of Dagan's name based on Arabic **dgn*, "to be cloudy, rainy,"[174] Baal the Cloud-rider would appear naturally the son of Dagan rather than a son of El.[175]

---

174 Lane 853-54; Albright 1920:319 n. 27; Pope, *WdM* 277; Roberts 1972:18; Renfroe 1992:92.

175 On Dagan, see Roberts 1972:74-75 nn. 95,151; Healey 1977; Lambert 1985a:538; cf. Wyatt 1980. For Dagan at Ebla, see Pomponio 1983:149; Xella 1983:289. For Dagan at Emar, see Fleming 1992:169-71, 203-08, 240-56. Fleming (1992:247) speculates that Dagan and Baal were originally both heads of pantheons. At Emar, Fleming argues, the confrontation of the two pantheons was "resolved by placing Dagan at the top, with ^{d}IM given the next position." According to Fleming Baal's title "son of Dagan" may reflect a means of reconciling the two cults.

Moreover, Roberts notes that a fragment from northern Mesopotamia gives Dagan as the father of Addu.[176] In a number of god-lists discovered at Ugarit, the position of Dagan corresponds to that of Kumarbi, likely indicating an identification between the two gods (Laroche, *UgV* 523-24; 1968:150). The equation may be ascribed to their common status as fathers of the storm gods,[177] who are also identified at Ugarit (*UgV* 249, #137, IVb, line 17[?]); otherwise, the comparison would appear problematic since Kumarbi and the storm god are adversaries (*ANET* 120-25) while Dagan and Baal are not.

Philo of Byblos reports a tradition bearing on Baal's parentage:

> Thus, Kronos waged war against Ouranos, expelled him from his dominion, and took up his kingdom. Ouranos' favorite mistress, who was pregnant, was also captured in the battle and Kronos gave her in marriage to Dagon. While with the latter, she gave birth to the child conceived by Ouranos, whom she called Demarous.[178]

The use of this tradition to reconstruct a conflict within the Baal Cycle might been criticized since the witness of Philo is layered heavily with elements of Phoenician and Hellenistic religion (L'Heureux 1979:42; Barr 1974). As Pope (*EUT* 47 n. 95) notes, the tradition of Philo of Byblos, however complex, reflects an attempt to render order from the conflicting traditions about Baal's irregular paternity. It would appear that this account reflects Baal's secondary relationship to the family of El and Athirat.[179] According to KTU 1.4 VI 46, this divine couple had seventy children, or as the Elkunirsa myth (*ANET* 519) says, seventy-seven//eighty-eight offspring.[180] Athirat's sighting of Baal provokes her to inquire in KTU 1.4 II 24-26 if Baal is the killer of her children. Her question implies that

---

176 Roberts 1972:75 n. 98. See *CRRA* 3 (1954) 129.

177 Laroche, *UgV* 523-24; 1968:150; Roberts 1972:75 n. 98.

178 PE 1.10.18-19; Attridge and Oden 1981: 48-51.

179 Lipiński (1983:308, 309) argues that Kronos in this passage is to be identified with Dagon and not El and that the identification of Kronos wth Elos in PE 1.10.29 (Attridge and Oden 1981:54-55) is secondary.

180 This mythological enumeration appears to be related to the expression attested at Emar: "all the seventy gods of Emar" (Emar 373.37-38; Fleming 1992:73, 242). It is also a standard for a royal family (Fensham 1977:113-15). Panammu refers to his seventy brothers (KAI 215:3). Jerubbaal likewise had seventy sons (Judges 9) as did Joram (2 Kings 10). Similar enumerations of divine groups appear also in Egyptian material (Massart 1954:85, 101). It is unclear whether the seventy-seven//eighty-eight siblings in 1.12 II 48-49 belong to Baal's family or Athirat's clan.

Baal does not belong to her brood.[181] Baal, born of parents different from the children of El and Athirat, but adopted secondarily into the central divine family, competes with them for kingship. In short, the Baal Cycle explains how Baal the outsider came to assume kingship in the divine family of El and Athirat.[182]

As a result of Baal's status as an outsider to the family of El, it has been thought that the Baal Cycle reflects tensions between El and Baal (*EUT* 55-56, 93, 97). Indeed, the notion of Baal's kingship as the outcome of two rival lines might be seen to have parallels in Hittite texts. Hoffner (1975:138-139) argues that the theme of the four generations of divine kingship in Hittite literature, in particular the Kumarbi cycle consisting of the Kingship in Heaven myth, the myth of the kingship of the god KAL and the Ullikummi myth, involves two competing rival lines. Hoffner (1975:139) diagrams the two lines as follows:

Alalu	Anu
Kumarbi	Storm god (Teshub)
Ullikumi	

Hoffner argues that these two rival lines compete for divine kingship. Hoffner (1975:139) concludes: "it is indisputable that we have two rival dynasties here with the kingship alternating between them in their struggles. Each deposed father is avenged by his son, who then becomes the new ruler." This struggle culminates in Teshub's successful defense of his kingship.[183]

The remarks of Hoffner may be suggestive for the interpretation of the Baal Cycle. The pattern of divine kingship appears in comparable form in Hittite and Ugaritic traditions, though in a truncated manner in the latter. On one side stand El and his two "beloved" ones (*ydd ʾil/mdd ʾil*), Yamm and Mot, and the other side stands their rival, Baal. The theme of the rival lines never emerges in full form in the Baal Cycle (L'Heureux 1979:3-70). El is never

181 According to Greenfield (1985:193 n. 1; cf. Kapelrud 1952:64; 77-78), the brood of El and Athirat does not include Yamm and Mot.

182 Cf. Pope 1987:228-29.

183 Beckman (1986:18-20) notes that this pattern differs from Hittite secular texts, including the statements of Shuppiluliuma I to two vassals (KBo 1.5 i; 5.3 i) and the "Edict of Hattusili" (CTH 6). According to these texts, any of the royal sons were eligible for kingship; the reigning king made the decision, and he sometimes changed his mind on the subject This pattern perhaps compares with El's choices of Athtar and *ydʿ ylḥn* as the new king in KTU 1.6 I.

explicitly opposed to Baal; indeed, he mourns the death of the Cloud-rider (KTU 1.5 VI) and later supports his kingship (1.6 VI 35-36). Indeed, it might be argued, following Schloen (1993), that the family issue is not so much one of tension between El and Baal but of sibling rivalry between Baal, the son only indirectly related to El, and the two "beloved" of El, Yamm and Mot. Other Ugaritic sources which Pope (1988) cites to support the tension between El and Baal, namely 1.12 (and by implication, 1.1 IV and V), reflect emnity among brothers according to Schloen (1993:219-20):

> Fratricide or parricide, and not regicide, is the issue in the Hurrian and Ugaritic myths and in Hesiod's *Theogony*. But this is to be expected if second-millennium political structures were closer to what Max Weber called "patrimonial" regimes than to professionalized bureaucratic states. In a patrimonial state the kingdom is simply the patriarchal household writ large, and the struggle for power is analogous to the factional rivalry for property and privilege between patrilaterals in extended patrilineages that is so well known in Middle Eastern anthropology. Thus in Ugaritic mythology the stories of internecine warfare between Baʿl and his "brothers" in the household of ʾEl—who is both patriarch and king—are not simply a picture of days gone by but a living tradition reflecting the workings of a complex patrimonial state in which the struggles between "kin" were a determinant of social relations at all levels of society, from the patriarchal household of the villager to the royal household itself.

Under this view El would appear more removed from the field of rivalry. It is true, however, that El takes more than a casual interest in the struggle among the brothers. El seems to support Yamm's cause in 1.1 IV and V. In either case the model of the family and its tensions are raised to a cosmic, political level in the Baal Cycle. This view is consistent with Gaster's view (1946-47:288) that El presides over a household of divine children who rule over their own realms. Gaster (1950:121-30) stresses the tripartite division of the cosmos corresponding to the realms of Baal, Yamm and Mot: Baal rules the heavens, Yamm the seas and waters, and Mot the underworld, like Zeus, Poseidon and Hades in Greek myth.[184]

---

[184] So also Toombs 1983:613-23; for further discussion, see Smith 1985:115-18; Handy 1990:21-22. These observations are echoed in structuralist discussions of the pantheon in the Baal Cycle. Petersen and Woodward (1977) suggest that the Baal Cycle reflects a universe consisting of three "tiers" ruled by different deities. In these three tiers, El rules the macrocosm, Baal the microcosm and Anat the human world, a view partially reflected in the parallelism between Baal's heavenly

The division of the cosmos into different realms appears in literature from not only Ugarit and Greece, but also Mesopotamia. Marduk's assumption of control not only over the cosmos as a whole echoes that of Baal. Baal and Marduk assume their place in their palaces (KTU 1.4 V-VII; Enuma Elish 5.119-22) as well as dominion over the cosmos. The comparison between the two texts also highlights some central differences between the Baal Cycle and Enuma Elish: whereas Marduk has entirely supplanted the rule of the older generation of gods such that he assumes their place in assigning their places in the order of cosmic creation, Baal does not assume El's full rank. El remains the executive director of the pantheon and the cosmos. Furthermore, Yamm and Mot hold a rank represented spatially on par with Baal's own insofar as they hold power over a specific realm like Baal. In contrast, Marduk is not identified with a specific realm; rather, his strength transcends specific realms. These differences illustrate that the exaltation of Baal in the Baal Cycle remains a partial one at best.[185]

Handy (1988) suggests that the differences between the kingship of Baal and El can be understood in part as a matter of realms: Baal's kingship extends over his heavenly realm, corresponding to the kingship of Yamm and Mot in their respective realms. According to Handy, Baal is also king over the city of Ugarit. Handy (1988:59) offers the following schema to represent the different expressions of kingship:

Title	Level	Example
mlk	Highest Authority	El
mlk	Patron Deity	Baal
mlk	City Ruler	Niqmaddu

Identifying different domains constitutes an important point for understanding Baal's kingship in tandem with the kingship of El. Baal moves from being king over his own heavenly domain to becoming king over the cosmos and the pantheon (so KTU 1.3 V 32; 1.4 IV 43-44). As the new king, Baal serves in conjunction with the old king of the gods, El; Baal may be viewed as his "co-regent."[186] Both El

---

battling in 1.2 IV and Anat's terrestrial warfare in 1.3 II. In a similar vein, Wyatt (1985; 1986; 1988; 1989) and Waterston (1988; 1989) also categorize into "tiers" the deities and the realms which they represent and rule.

185 See below pp. 104-05.

186 Cf. PE 1.10.31 translated above on p. xxii.

and Baal are called "king" (*mlk*) though in complementary ways: El remains the executive over the universe and Baal is the sustainer of the cosmos (Mullen 1980:84-85; cf. Handy 1988, 1990). El is not deposed in an active struggle with Baal; nor is El degraded or demoted by Baal. El retains his dignity in a way comparable to Ea in Enuma Elish. As Greenfield (1985:196) suggests, El is the aging head of the pantheon not unlike Ea.[187] El and Baal differ more in function than in realm. Baal's traditional heavenly domain expands to embrace the entire pantheon and cosmos in conjunction with El. Baal's kingship is realized in terrestrial terms by providing rains for the earth, which differentiates him from Yamm, Mot and Athtar, who may desire dominion over the earth, but do not attain it. While the Baal Cycle presents Baal's kingship over pantheon and cosmos alike, the text also manifests constraints on Baal's kingship; he is "king" (*mlk*), but not "king of kings" (*mlk mlkm*), a title attested in the letter RS 34.356. Indeed, the limitation on Baal's exaltation is a central feature of the following synthesis.

4. The Limited Exaltation of Baal

The theme of Baal's kingship provides an appealing starting-point for interpreting the Baal Cycle, as royal language permeates the cycle. Moreover, this political framework accounts well for the whole of the cycle. It can also explain the references to the seasons without being indebted to a specific, reconstructed setting that has little corroborative evidence. However, there remains important considerations of why Baal and not another deity is king, and what the nature of his kingship is (Smith 1986b). Baal is monarch precisely because he is the deity who can mediate the blessings of the natural cosmos both to human society and to the company of the pantheon. The means of providing blessings are his rains, which the seasonal interpretation has emphasized. These rains revivify the world, duly noted by proponents of the cosmogonic approach. Indeed, without the rains, there is no life. Baal's kingship brings life to the world, prevailing over the forces of death and destruction, as stressed by those who view the Baal Cycle as a struggle between the forces of life and death. The theme of kingship is the explicit topic of the cycle, but its expression and meaning depend on information

---

[187] Both gods also display wisdom and inhabit watery abodes (*EUT* 43, 45, 71; Lambert 1985a:538; cf. Pope 1987:228-30).

stressed by various interpretations. The various phenomena emphasized in the different approaches, whether they be seasons, ritual elements or expressions of cosmogony, play a significant role in the cycle, and their importance is not to be underestimated only because they may be subsumed under the rubric of kingship.

Diverse elements, such as meteorological phenomena, cosmogonic traditions and the character of other deities advance the theme of Baal's kingship.[188] Gaster, de Moor and other proponents of ritual and seasonal interpretations rightly emphasize how the use of language undoubtedly held tremendous religious, social, economic and political significance for the culture of Ugarit; rains at the correct time affected all dimensions of this agrarian society. Some elements of weather have been incorporated to dramatize Baal's kingship (KTU 1.3 IV 25-28 and 1.4 V 6-9). Other internal indications that the Baal Cycle draws on meteorological elements include Baal's epithet, *rkb ʿrpt*, "Cloud-rider" and his meteorological entourage in KTU 1.5 V 6-11 (*BOS* 160). The weather elements often serve as indications of Baal's power. The Baal Cycle is not arranged, however, according to a single annual cycle. This is evident from the present sequence of texts which differs from the order advocated by proponents of the seasonal and ritual approaches. The order proposed by Gaster corresponds to a view of KTU 1.1-1.2 and 1.4 VIII-1.6 as texts with parallel plots climaxing in the period of autumn rains (see Millar 1976:71-81; Clifford 1984:190). From this evidence Gaster builds a circumstantial case for an autumn festival that celebrated the kingship of Baal.

A different approach is perhaps indicated by the difficulties incurred by Gaster's view. Instead of examining the meteorological references for information which they may provide about a theoretical ritual setting which is then read as the background of the text, the meteorological references may have been used and adapted to the literary framework of the text. As Gaster's arrangment of the seasons in the Baal Cycle partially suggests, each major part of the cycle uses the imagery of the fall interchange period (Gibson 1984:216; Smith 1986b:331; cf. Mosca 1986:506-07). This period witnesses the alternation of the eastern dry winds of the scirocco with

---

188 The following discussion was inspired in part by conversations with Professor Robert R. Wilson, and I wish to thank him. For traditional roles of deities placed in service to the theme of Baal's kingship, see also Walls 1992:177.

the western rain-bearing winds coming off the Mediterranean Sea until the western winds finally overtake the eastern winds (Nash 1989:18-19).[189] KTU 1.1-1.2 reaches its climax in Baal's victory over Yamm in KTU 1.2 IV. The meteorological phenomenon of Baal's coming in the storm over Yamm could be correlated with the coming of the fall rains. Scholars have long viewed Baal's battle with Yamm as inspired by the eastward procession of the rain-storm from the Mediterranean Sea to the coast. According to Gaster (*Thespis* 164-165), Lipiński (1967:253-282), Yadin (1970:211-214) and J. Day (1992:545), Baal's weapons in KTU 1.2 IV symbolize lightning.[190] These weapons may represent Baal's lightning and herald the coming rains, perhaps reflecting the Palestinian proverb that at the time of the fall interchange "the lightning is a sign of rain."[191] KTU 1.3-1.4 reaches its crescendo in the opening of the window in KTU 1.4 VI. Up to this point the rains have been lacking according to 1.4 V 6-9, and thus the opening of the window would mark the beginning of the rainy season during the period of the fall interchange. Scholars have compared the inauguration of Solomon's temple in the autumn; perhaps Baal's temple held a similar political significance (*SPUMB* 59-61). Finally, KTU 1.4 VIII-1.6 describes Baal's disappearance from, and return to, the realm of life. El's dream in 1.6 III implies Baal's meteorological powers, for El interprets the rain in his dream as a sign of Baal's return to life. The struggle between Baal and Mot in KTU 1.6 VI may draw on the imagery of the alternation of the eastern and western winds in the fall interchange, and Baal's tenuous victory over Mot at the end of this column may suggest the end of the summer dry season and the beginning of the early autumn rainy season. The narrative so inter-

---

[189] See above p. 68. The following remarks not only draw on the work of Gaster, de Moor and Mosca, but also the insight of A. Fitzgerald (apud Nash 1989) that the setting of some biblical texts is the fall interchange period when after alternation of westward dry winds (sirocco) and eastward rain-cloud bearing winds, the rains finally arrive from the Mediterranean. Based largely on the observations of Dalman and other visitors to the Holy Land during the late nineteenth and early twentieth centuries as well as their native Palestinian informants, Fitzgerald identifies the imagery of numerous biblical compositions with meteorological phenomena known during the fall interchange period. Particularly successful is the interpretation of the book of Joel along these lines which has been developed in the dissertation of Nash (1989).

[190] Cf. the similar arguments of Rendsburg (1984:18) regarding the Tell Asmar seal noted below on pp. 348-49.

[191] *Thespis* 238 citing Dalman; see Dalman 1928:114.

preted does not demonstrate that an autumn festival was the background for the Baal Cycle and its celebration. Rather, it suggests only that the Baal Cycle used the background of the fall interchange period to dramatize Baal's power. If an analogue may be suggested, Amos 4:6-13 and 7:1-9:6 climax in the storm theophany of Yahweh using imagery connected with the autumnal festival of Sukkot (see Talmon 1963; Coote 1981:56-57).

This approach affects the understanding of ritual information in the cycle. De Moor and Spronk propose a New Year's festival as the setting for the Baal cycle (cf. Dietrich and Loretz 1980). For de Moor (1988:238 n. 101) the religious setting is Baal's effecting of human resurrection, specifically "the revivification of the spirits of dead kings and heroes in the course of the New Year festival." Some scholars also use the closing lines of the cycle, 1.6 VI 42-53, to reconstruct a major New Year celebration involving Baal.[192] Dijkstra (1974:68) initially suggested that the final lines of the cycle, KTU 1.6 VI 42-53, represent an instruction from Baal to Shapshu to guide the shades to a sacrifical banquet. Dijkstra (1986: 152) subsequently re-interpreted this passage as a liturgical address to the audience[193] to participate in the autumnal festival which celebrated Baal's return and re-instatement as king. These reconstructions are highly controversial because the extant data are too problematic to confirm the background (Marcus 1973). The Baal Cycle evoked the associations of vivid religious language, even if the particular cultic setting of a hypothetical New Year's celebration did not underlie the cycle itself (Smith and Bloch-Smith 1988). While it is difficult to establish this specific ritual background, de Moor may be correct in detecting some religious background relating to the Ugaritic beliefs about the dead behind the related language in 1.17 VI 28-33 and 1.3 I 18-22a.[194] The language of 1.3 I 18-22a ob-

192 See Kapelrud 1952: 29-30, 36, 97, 117, 123, 128, 131-33, 143; *Thespis* 31; *SPUMB* 244; cf. Spronk 1986:150-51.

193 Rather than to Shapshu as most commentators propose.

194 Later texts have played a role in this discussion. An Aramaic royal inscription, KAI 214:15-17, 20-22, reflects an apparently related belief about royal afterlife, as recognized by Greenfield (1973:46-52). Greenfield translates the passage:

> He will take the sceptre and he will sit on my throne [as king of Yaʾdiy] and he will acquire power. . . and he will sacrifice to Hadad. . . and he will sacrifice to Hadad and invoke the name of Hadad. . (then he will say) "may the soul of Panamu eat with you and the soul of Panamu drink with you". . . he will invoke the soul of Panamu with Hadad. . . may the offering be acceptable to

served by de Moor may draw on the powerful royal background of the cult of the dead to communicate and advance the theme of Baal's kingship.[195] Indeed, as noted above,[196] the description of Baal's death and return to life was perhaps influenced by the royal cult of the dead and not vice-versa.

Further circumstantial evidence may be cited to suggest the plausibility of this view. KTU 1.113 may bear on the royal cult of the dead (Pardee 1988b:170-78) as attested in 1.3 I and 1.17 VI. The front of the text describes musical instrumentation perhaps played by a figure called *nʿm* (Pardee 1988b:172); the same word is used for the player in 1.3 I 19 and the personage seems to be called by a similar appellation, *nʿmn,* in 1.17 VI 32. The back of 1.113 contains a list of kings originally containing at least thirty-two names (Kitchen 1975) and perhaps as many as fifty-two (Pardee 1988b:173). Despite the differences in details among the texts in question (Pardee 1988b:170-78), it would appear that the royal cult of Ugarit invoked the dead ancestors (KTU 1.161) and perhaps this cult is reflected in the musical instrumentation in KTU 1.113. KTU 1.3 I and 1.17 V 28-33 may have drawn on this imagery from the Ugaritic cult devoted to the dead monarchs. This religious background might also involve 1.108.1-5, if *rpʾu mlk ʿlm* who plays music in this text were to be identified with *nʿm* or viewed as the eponymous tribal figure (Yaqaru?) corresponding or related to the royal figure of *nʿm*. Indeed, it has been suggested that *ḥbr kṯr ṭbm* in 1.108.1-5, whom *rpʾu* musically entertains, may be the Rephaim (so Smith apud Pardee 1988b:100 n. 111).

In addition to seasonal and ritual data, the Baal Cycle has incorporated older traditions of "cosmogony," or battles pitting a divine hero against a cosmic enemy to achieve its picture of Baal. While the Baal Cycle may be understood as cosmogonic in a general sense,

---

> Hadad and to El and to Rakib-El and to Shamash. . . Who[ever of] my sons grasps the sceptre and sits upon my seat as king [of Yaʾdiy] and confirms his rulership and sacri[fices to this Hadad and menti]ons the name of Panamu, let him say, "May the soul of Panamu e[a]t with Hadad, and may the soul of Panamu drink with Ha[dad]."

This text may suggest a royal setting for the theology of immortality in KTU 1.17 VI 28-33 (Healey 1984b; Spronk 1986:207). This background was perhaps presupposed for KTU 1.3 I and 1.6 III as well.

[195] It is also important to note one narrative difference between 1.3 I 18-22a and 1.17 VI 28-33. 1.3 I 18-22a makes no mention of Baal's return to life.

[196] See above p. 73.

strictly speaking the cycle has re-used the traditions of cosmogonic battle to highlight Baal's power. KTU 1.3 III 38-47 alludes to the tradition of Anat's victory over Yamm. The Baal Cycle perhaps re-uses some of this material to stress that it is Baal's role to defeat Yamm. KTU 1.5 I 1-8 likewise alludes to an old battle between *ltn* and probably Baal.[197] The tradition of the battle against the seven-headed serpent, of which *ltn* and Leviathan are the Ugaritic and biblical reflexes, goes back at least to the late third millennium, as suggested by the Tell Asmar seal.[198] The Baal Cycle refers to these older conflicts perhaps as preludes to the victories of Baal over Yamm and Mot (*CS* 353). This use of older tradition might be compared with Ea's defeat of Apsu which anticipates Marduk's victory over Tiamat in Enuma Elish (Bottéro and Kramer 1989:658, 666-67).

The descriptions of Baal's enemies in the Baal Cycle may have developed at least in part to exalt the storm-god. As noted above,[199] Mot may have been modelled literarily after Yamm. The depiction of Yamm, too, may represent a literary creation. While traditions of battles against various creatures in the sea are known to antedate the Baal Cycle, there seems to be little if any evidence for the cosmic sea as an enemy of the storm-god beyond West Semitic tradition. In Greek tradition Zeus' enemies include Typhon (Weinfeld 1973), but not Poseidon who rules the sea. Similarly in Hittite mythology, Teshub defeats Ullikumi who arises out of the sea. When Indra fights the great cosmic battle, it is against Vrtra (Rgveda 1.32; *Thespis* 164-165). "Sea" is personified in Mesopotamian tradition, for example in the "Harab myth,"[200] but the references to Sea appear largely in theogonies and not in "cosmogonies" (to use the terminology of Fisher, Cross, Clifford and others). The exaltation of Baal through his conquest over Yamm is also realized in a specific

---

197 Binger (1992:144-45) would prefer to attribute this role to Anat. Either is grammatically feasible although in a dialogue involving Baal as the addressee, it would seem more likely that Baal is the referent (see Clifford 1987). While one might bracket the evidence of 1.5 I 1-8 and one may agree with Binger that Anat's battles mentioned in 1.3 III 37-46 show her to be the slayer of the dragon, there is no reason to assume that Baal never manifested this role. Iconographic evidence, including the Tell Asmar seal (noted on pp. 346-47), would tend to support Baal as the hero of KTU 1.5 I 1-8.

198 See below pp. 346-47.

199 See above pp. 18-19.

200 See above p. 86.

shift of Yamm's title *ṯpṭ* (KTU 1.2 IV 15, 16, 22, 25) to Baal (KTU 1.3 V 32; 1.4 IV 44). Baal receives recognition by Anat and Athirat as the figure who embodies "rulership." Thus Baal's defeat of Yamm contributes directly to a heightening of Baal's character: Baal is magnified through Yamm.

Anat's role as warrior and Baal's ally also exalts him, as her battling in the valley in KTU 1.3 II and her conflict with Mot in KTU 1.6 II contribute to Baal's victory over Yamm and Mot, respectively. Walls (1992:184, 185) presents Anat's defeat of Mot in terms of her character:

> Anat's mythic identity as a nubile young female is essential to her unique ability to defeat Death and restore fertility to the cosmos. This symbolism acknowledges that females have the ability to create life—to overcome death—while males do not. . . Anat overcomes Death by the creative potential stored within her as an adolescent maiden.

Van Rooy (1979) observes that Anat's relationship to Baal is not a static one in the Baal Cycle. Rather, the text shows a change from her restraint of Baal at the end of 1.2 I to her warfare and intercession on his behalf (cf. Walls 1992:163 n. 1). Furthermore, while Anat's battling in 1.3 II may have originated outside of the traditions associated with Baal, it perhaps functions in its present setting as the terrestrial counterpart to Baal's cosmic battling in 1.2 IV (Gray 1979:323). Other material in the Baal Cycle associated traditionally with Anat serves the narrative function of exalting Baal. As discussed above,[201] Parker (1989b:115) notes the material shared in common between KTU 1.3 IV-V1 and 17 VI-1.18 I and IV. Parker shows that the material from Aqhat comports with its context more suitably than in the Baal Cycle, implying secondary usage of traditional material in the Baal Cycle. The material assumes a different function in the Baal Cycle than it holds in Aqhat: it serves to advance the theme of Baal's kingship through the pursuit of his palace.

Just as the characters of Yamm and Mot as well as Anat ultimately exalt Baal, so also El and Kothar contribute to Baal's success as the new king of the cosmos. El's title of king is applied to Baal. El is called king in the formulas, *mlk ʾab šnm*, "king, father of years"

---

[201] See pp. 31-32.

(KTU 1.1 III 24; 1.3 V 1; 1.4 IV 24; 1.6 I 36), and *ʾil mlk dyknnh*, "El, the king, who created him" (KTU 1.3 V 35-36; 1.4 I 5-6). Baal, however, is hailed by Anat and Athirat as the new king (KTU 1.5 III 32, 1.4 IV 43). In receiving the title of "king," Baal grows in stature in terms of his authority within the pantheon and in the cosmos. As the new king, Baal serves in conjunction with the old king of the gods, El.[202]

Like El, Kothar (Smith 1985) contributes to the glory of Baal. Kothar's magical weapons bring Baal victory over Yamm in KTU 1.2 IV and then later the gifts necessary to bribe Athirat in KTU 1.4 I so that she might help to convince El of Baal's need for his own palace. Athtar and *ydʿ ylḥn*, two candidates nominated in KTU 1.6 I to replace Baal as divine king, likewise contribute to exalt Baal's kingship, for their inadequacies, manifest upon their attempts to assume the divine throne, serve as foils to underscore the strength and size of Baal (Greenfield 1985).[203] In sum, every major figure of the Baal Cycle contributes to the theme of Baal's kingship.

This overview of the diverse materials and traditions including meteorological phenomena, ritual information, cosmogonic battles and the characters of various deities, raises the question of the rationale behind this amalgamation and ordering of these materials. The answer lies in part with the central theme of the cycle, Baal's kingship. All of these different sets of material have been shaped to contribute to the story of Baal's rise to power and thereby magnify him. This development finds an analogue in Enuma Elish (see

---

202 There is minimal evidence for El as a warrior (Roberts 1972:95-96 n. 233). If any such traditions for El as warrior existed in Ugaritic, they are attested vestigially at best and appear to have been displaced at Ugarit by the martial exploits of Anat and Baal.

203 The poetic structure of 1.5 VI-1.6 III is pertinent to this point. The passage exhibits the large structure of a concentric pentacolon (ABCB'A'):

A Discovery of Baal's death (1.5 VI 3*-25)
    B Anat searches for Baal and mourns him (1.5 VI 25-1.6 I 31)
        C Nominations to replace Baal (1.6 I 32-67)
    B' Anat searches for Baal and destroys Mot (1.6 II)
A' Discovery of Baal's life (1.6 III).

This arrangement not only illustrates the balance and relationships among these columns; it also focuses attention on the events of the central section indicating that Baal is irreplaceable. Once the central section illustrates this point through the negative portraits of the two nominees for kingship, the narrative moves inexorably toward Baal's return to life and kingship (Waterston 1988:363). The word-pair *yrʾaʾun//ṯtʿ* in 1.5 II 7 is repeated as *yrʾu//ṯtʿ* in 1.6 VI 30, and thus marks the episode of Baal's demise and its reversal.

Lambert 1965), a text frequently compared to the Baal Cycle. Like Marduk, Baal is a figure raised to a position of primary importance. The manner in which the text describes Baal also represents a significant departure from prior tradition. Baal resembles Marduk in Enuma Elish in that both gods are fitted with the attributes of other deities. Similarly, Baal compares with Yahweh in Israelite tradition who displays the characteristics associated with deities such as Baal, Asherah and Mot although biblical traditions are equally insistent on the distinction between Yahweh and the other deities of Israel (Korpel and de Moor 1986:244; Smith 1990). The collection of both older, traditional materials and the introduction of new features about Baal and the rest of the pantheon serve to exalt him over the cosmos. This manner of rendering Baal transforms him from being one contender for divine kingship to being literally the natural choice for the royal role. This development may be reflected also in his name. While Baal is identified with Haddu/Addu, the West Semitic storm-god, the reason for the dominance of his title *b*ᶜ*l* in the Baal Cycle is unclear. In the Baal Cycle the name of Baal is shorthand for his longer title *b*ᶜ*l ṣpn*, "Baal of Sapan," but it could additionally represent the embodiment or personification of divine "lordship" or "ownership," or in Koch's formulation (1988:201), "Innewerden der numinosen Kraft von Autorität."

While Baal's kingship is glorious, it is also fragile. The Baal Cycle describes a circumscribed or limited exaltation of the storm-god. This limited exaltation is indicated by the differences between the Baal Cycle and those texts which it is thought to resemble most closely. Major differences between the Baal Cycle and Enuma Elish indicate that the kingship of Baal is a hard-won reign, fraught with peril (cf. Lambert 1988:140). First, Baal fights on his own behalf and without the assembly's support. Lambert (1988:140) argues that unlike Marduk in Enuma Elish, the stature of Baal recalls Tishpak in the Labbu myth and Ninurta in the Anzu myth:

> ... a junior god does battle with a demonic being or monster on behalf of elders unable to face the challenge themselves, but the promised reward does not include abdication in favour of the young victor.

The position of Baal in 1.2 I is even weaker than that of Tishpak and Ninurta, because unlike them the Cloud-rider fights on his own without the assembly's support. Second, Baal's victory in KTU 1.2 IV requires the aid of another deity, Kothar. In contrast, Marduk needs no help from an outsider. Third, while Marduk's palace is virtually concomitant with his victory, Baal's palace requires a lengthy process of help and negotiations dependent on the aid of Anat and Athirat (1.3 III-1.4 VII). Furthermore, securing Athirat's aid additionally requires Kothar's help to make gifts so that she would be persuaded to intercede on Baal's behalf before El. Hurowitz (1992: 96) notes that different building stories emphasize different elements:

> Just as the 'historical' temple building stories displayed a tendency to emphasize a certain motif or segment in the story at the price of brevity in describing other segments, so in the myth: one story element has been blown out of proportion in such a way that it occupies most of the story.

While the quest for El's permission does not occupy "most of the story," it is the main issue governing seven extant columns. When this amount of text is contrasted with the relatively few number of columns or lines devoted to any other theme, for example Baal's status as king or his victory over Yamm in 1.2 IV, then it suggests his relatively weak status in the Baal Cycle. Fourth, Baal is proclaimed king after his defeat of Yamm, while Marduk is acclaimed king before his engagement with Tiamat. Moreover, the older gods including Ea proclaim Marduk as king while the old executive of the Ugaritic pantheon, El, acquiesces to Baal's kingship only after a lengthy process following his defeat of Yamm. Fifth, the Baal-Mot narrative represents a challenge to Baal's kingship and indicates the fragility of his royal status; there is no comparable sequence in Enuma Elish. Upon Baal's death, El and Athirat select candidates to replace Baal. Sixth, it is not by his own power that Baal returns to life in 1.6. Rather, Anat's destruction of death accompanies and apparently enables Baal's reappearance. Finally, the end of the cycle also reflects the fragility inherent in Baal's power. Baal's struggle with Mot in KTU 1.6 VI is ultimately a stalemate. Neither foe defeats the other, and Baal gains the upper hand only through the intervention of another deity. In sum, the general equilibrium of forces in the universe is achieved thanks not only to Baal's power, but perhaps more remarkably to all the help which he receives from the other deities.

This limited exaltation of Baal may correspond in some manner to Ugarit's limited political situation lying between the great powers of the ancient Near East, as Stolz (1982) quite correctly suggests. Through the myth Baal gains his own throne in his own palace

(Uehlinger 1992:355). As Baal's palace is located terrestrially at Mount Sapan, his kingship at Ugarit is identified with his kingship over the cosmos. The political ramifications were presumably immense. The cycle was developed under the royal aegis of the dynasty of Niqmaddu at Ugarit (Miller 1982:125). Divine kingship not infrequently paralleled human kingship in the Near East (Mann 1977), and the association between divine and human kingship sometimes involves expressions of the storm-god's support for the monarch. A famous stele from Ugarit now housed in the Louvre (RS 4.427 = AO 15.775) may link the human and divine dimensions of kingship. The stele (on facing page) depicts the god Baal wielding a weapon and standing on top of what scholars have taken as either Baal's mountain (Frankfort 1954:256), the sea or possibly both (Yon 1985:180; 1991:295; Bordreuil 1991:21-24).[204] There are two sets of undulating lines, one set beneath the figure of the standing god and another set further below. The separation of the two sets of undulating lines as well as the different mode of rendering these sets of lines would suggest that the two sets of lines represent two different features. For this reason the notion of the storm-god standing on mountains which lie above the waters is a reasonable interpretation. Bordreuil understands the four crests in the top set of undulating lines as the mountain range encompassing Mount Sapan. According to Ginsberg (1945a:53), Amiet (1980:201), Yon (1985:181) and Bordreuil (1991:21), the smaller figure standing before Baal and facing in the same direction as the god is the Ugaritic king.[205] Yon suggests that the stele expresses the close relationship between the god and the king; the god stands as the king's patron and protector. This depiction may encapsulate the political significance which KTU 1.1-1.2 held for the dynasty of Niqmaddu.

Other descriptions of the king couched in the language of the West Semitic storm-god hail from Egypt, Mari and the Levantine littoral.

---

[204] Williams-Forte (1983:30) consider mountains or a writhing serpent as possibilities. For a beautiful picture of this stele, see Amiet 1980:201 # 75. For a complete description, see Yon 1991: 294-99. For a discussion of this stele with the iconographic evidence for Baal standing on double mountains, see Dijkstra 1991. For other iconographic representations of the storm-god at Ugarit, see Seeden 1980:102-06.

[205] In contrast, Frankfort (1970:257, 396 n. 58) and Williams-Forte (1983:30) take the smaller figure as a goddess allied with the storm-god.

Baal and the Ugaritic King. Louvre AO 15.775 = RS 4.427.
Used with permission of the Musée du Louvre.

These examples illustrate the political application of the West Semitic conflict-myth. EA 108, 149:7, 159:7 and 207:16 (partially reconstructed) compare the pharaoh to Baal. EA 147:14 goes further, describing the Egyptian king as one "who gives forth his cry in the sky like Baal" (Moran 1992:233). In Egyptian texts, too, the pharaoh was not infrequently compared to Baal. One text (*ANET* 249) proclaims: "His battle cry is like (that of) Baal in the heavens."[206] According to Gaál (1977) lines 15 and 18 of the victory stele of Tutmosis III renders this king in terms reminiscent of Baal-Haddu:

> I have come that I may cause You to trample on the eastern land and to tread down those who are in the regions of Tonuter; that I may cause them to see Your Majesty as a lightning flash, strewing its levin-frame and giving its flood of water. . . I have come that I may cause you to trample on the Islanders in the midst of the sea, who are possessed with your war shout; that I may cause them to see Your Majesty as the Protector who appears on the back of his wild bull.[207]

Line 15 perhaps recalls Athirat's words to El that when the palace of Baal is constructed, the Storm-god's lightning and waters shall appear (1.4 V 6-9). As Gaál (1977:31) notes, line 18 recalls the imagery of the West Semitic storm-god astride the bull in a relief from Arslan Tash. The imagery comports with the description of Baal mating with a heifer in 1.5 V, which presupposes a characterization of him as a bull.

Mari texts likewise witness various types of associations between the West Semitic Storm-god and the king. In one text Addu is invoked to march at the side of Zimri-Lim: *i-la-ak ad-du-um i-na šu-me-li-šu*, "March, Addu, at his left side" (Charpin 1987:661). Another text from Mari (A.1968.1′-4′) also uses the conflict between the storm-god and the cosmic sea to support royal power.[208] Nur-Sin of Aleppo reports to Zimri-Lim the words of Addu: "I s[et] you on the thr[one of your father]; the weapons with which I battled again Sea (*têmtum*) I gave to you" (*lu-t[e-e]r-ka a-na giš-[gu-za é a-bi-ka] ú-te-er-ka giš-tukul-[meš] sa it-ti te-em-tim am-ta-aḫ-ṣu ad-di-na-ak-kum*; Durand 1993:45). These weapons are known from another text (A.1958): they are said to have been installed in Dagan's temple at Terqa

---

[206] For an Egyptian example of the parallelism of cosmic and royal enemies, see the myth of Apophis in *ANET* 6-7 and esp. 7 nn. 19, 21.

[207] For the fuller context, see Faulkner in Simpson 1973:286-87.

[208] For full citation, see above p. 34.

(Durand 1993:53). As commentators (Charpin and Durand 1986: 174; Durand 1993; Bordreuil and Pardee 1993) have observed, the Ugaritic witness to Baal's conflict with Yamm corresponds to A.1968.1′-4′ which pits Addu against Tiamat. The most impressive biblical example of divine empowerment of the monarch expressed in terms of the West Semitic conflict-myth is Ps 89:26 (RSV 25): *wĕśamtî bayyām yādô ûbannĕhārôt yĕmînô*, "And I shall set on Yamm his hand, and on River(s)[209] his right hand" (*CMHE* 258 n. 177). All of these texts indicate that the monarchies of Egypt, Levantine cities and Mari utilized the imagery of the West Semitic storm-god to dramatize royal power and legitimacy.

The Mari letter (A.1968. lines 1′-4′) reflects the notion that the power of the West Semitic storm-god manifest through the king's defeat of his cosmic enemies recapitulates on the cosmic level the king's own power against his enemies. Perhaps the Baal-Yamm conflict, and perhaps the whole of the Baal Cycle, functioned at Ugarit along the lines explicitly mentioned in the Mari text: the divine kingship of Baal mirrors and reinforces the human kingship of the royal patron of the Baal Cycle.[210] This relationship between the kingship of Baal and Niqmaddu, the royal patron of the cycle, may be reflected further in the fact that Baal is the divine patron of the dynasty.[211] It is logical to suppose that if the heartland of Baal's cult such as Mari and the Levantine littoral as well as the periphery in Egypt used the imagery of Baal to support its sovereign, so too Ugarit, a center of his cult, understood this concept of divine and human kingship in its longest and most developed text devoted to

---

[209] In view of the regular use of the singular in Ugaritic, the plural form in this instance may be a plural of majesty.

[210] Similar arguments about the political background of Enuma Elish have been offered. Enuma Elish has been thought to functioned as political apology for the Amorite dynasty at Babylon. Lambert (1964:3-13) argues that Marduk's kingship over the pantheon finds a ready explanation in the events during the reign of Nebuchadnezzar I (ca. 1124-1103), especially in his victory over Elam and the celebrated return of the statue of Marduk to Babylon. An earlier date may be indicated. According to Dalley (1989:229-30), one part of the list of names of Marduk in tablet 7 of Enuma Elish is dependent on the lexical text An-Anum which shows that Enuma Elish or at least this portion of it predates the reign of Nebuchadnezzar I. Jacobsen (1975:76) suggests that the battle between Marduk and Tiamat reflects the political tension between Babylonia and the Sealand that began in the early second millennium. Whatever the origins for the composition of Enuma Elish, it later served as divine confirmation for the king of Babylon when it was recited at the New Year's festival (Nakata 1968; Dalley 1989:231-32; van der Toorn 1991a).

[211] See above p. 90.

Baal. In sum, it appears that the Baal Cycle expresses the political exaltation of the divine king, and by implication that of the human king, as well as the limits of their kingship.

The tradition of the West Semitic conflict myth may be attested not only at Ugarit, Mari and Egypt, but also in the Mesopotamian heartland. According to Jacobsen (1968; 1975:75-76), the Marduk-Tiamat conflict in Enuma Elish derived ultimately from a West Semitic prototype, represented by the Baal-Yamm struggle. Jacobsen bases his view on the observation that the climatic conditions of the thunderstorm and the sea underlying the battle between the storm-god, Marduk, and the cosmic sea, Tiamat, are to be found in the Levant and not in Mesopotamia. He argues that the West Semitic tradition as found in the Baal-Yamm story provided the basis for the East Semitic version of the story. Jacobsen suggests further that the story would have been imported into Mesopotamia by Amorites during the Old Babylonian period. On the basis of putative iconographic evidence, Kaplan (1976) argues for an older date, possibly even the Old Akkadian period.

The text from Mari (A.1968. lines 1′-4′) may provide a link between the Baal Cycle and Enuma Elish. The Ugaritic witness to Baal's conflict with Yamm provides an exemplar of the primary version, while the Mari text pitting Addu against Tiamat constitutes a secondary attestation, and the Enuma Elish depicting Marduk's struggle against Tiamat yet a tertiary witness. The names of the protagonists in the three texts are equated in a variety of sources. One of Baal's standard Ugaritic epithets, *hd*, Haddu, is equivalent to Akkadian Addu. Furthermore, in two corresponding lists of divinities discovered at Ugarit, ^d^*adad bēl ḫuršân ḫazi* corresponds with *bᶜl ṣpn* (RS 20.24.4; KTU 1.118.4; cf. 1.47.5; see Nougayrol, *Ug V*:44-48; Herdner, *Ug VII*:1-3). The same list provides the correlation of ^d^*tâmtum* with *ym* (Nougayrol, *Ug V*:44-48; Herdner, *Ug VII*:1-3).[212] The Mari text (A.1968. lines 1′-4′) apparently witnesses to the West Semitic conflict tradition with the local names of the deities of Addu and Tiamat. The weapon mentioned in the Mari text also suggests the parallel with the Baal Cycle.

There is wide disagreement over Jacobsen's proposal. Lambert (1965; 1977; 1986) disputes Jacobsen's view and argues that the

---

[212] For further evidence for the cult of Yamm in the second and first millennia, see below pp. 151-52.

account of Marduk's conflict with Tiamat derived from indigenous Mesopotamian traditions concerning the god Ninurta.[213] According to Lambert (1986; cf. Lambert and Walcot 1965:69), the story of Ninurta's battle against the monstrous Anzu bird could have provided the background for the meteorological weaponry of Marduk.[214] J. Day (1985b:12) supports Lambert's position:

> Such common themes as exist between Enuma elish and the Baal-Yamm conflict cannot be attributed to direct influence, but rather be attributed to a common intellectual background. The upshot of all this is that one cannot postulate a West Semitic background to Enuma elish...

Jacobsen has his followers as well. Komoróczy (1973:31-32), Cross (*CMHE* 93, 113), Kaplan (1976), Greenstein (1982:208) and Dalley (1989:230) support Jacobsen's theory (cf. Greenfield 1985:195 n. 7; Malamat 1992:215). Although Assyriologists agree that Marduk's battle over the cosmic Sea was modelled largely on the indigenous Anzu traditions, this battle-scene may have incorporated some West Semitic material. Dalley argues (1989:230) that no Sumerian prototypes contain and therefore explain the cosmic Sea as the enemy in Enuma Elish. The Anzu traditions contain many of the antecedents for Enuma Elish but not the motif of the cosmic Sea.[215] This text also exhibits Marduk's assuming both the name and role of the storm god, Addu. This replacement is mentioned expressly in Enuma Elish 7.119 where Marduk's fourty-sixth name is *dAddu*.[216] The replacement of Marduk for West Semitic Addu is not without parallel. Line 10 of the obverse of CT 24 50 (BM 47406) likewise exhibits the replacement of Adad with Marduk in its delineation of various deities as aspects of Marduk: "Adad (is) Marduk of rain" (Böhl 1936:210; Lambert 1975b:198). The Mari letter A.1968 would suggest that the West Semitic conflict-myth existed within the larger Mesopotamian cultural sphere. Therefore, it is plausible that

---

[213] See Jan J. van Dijk 1983:1.9-23; Bottéro and Kramer 1989:659, 661, 668, 674.

[214] See *ANET* 111-13, 514-17; cf. the cautionary remarks of Dalley 1989:230-31.

[215] A different ecological background has been proposed for the Anzu traditions; see Hempel 1987.

[216] Böhl 1936:210; cf. Enuma Elish 5.47-54 and Bottéro and Kramer 1989:664. According to Dalley (1989:277 n. 52), the phonetic writing of the name is "specifically west-semitic."

the complex development of the rendering of Marduk and Tiamat in Enuma Elish involved primarily East Semitic elements, but possibly West Semitic ones as well.

The argument that West Semitic traditions made their way into Mesopotamia is by no means without parallel. Lambert (1982) demonstrates that some West Semitic features in Mesopotamian literature are to be attributed to an "Amorite"[217] importation during the Old Babylonian period. For example, the mount of divine assembly is located in the area of the Anti-Lebanon and Lebanon mountain ranges according to a fragment of the OB version of Gilgamesh and the Cedar Forest. More specifically, *mu-ša-ab a-nu-na-ki*, "the dwelling-place of the Anunnaki" is located in the area of *Ša-ri-a ù La-ab-na-na*, "the Sirion (Anti-Lebanon or Hermon range) and the Lebanon (range)."[218]

The use of the West Semitic conflict myth by the dynasties of Ugarit, Mari and Babylon may have derived from a common cultural heritage. KTU 1.161 invokes a long line of deceased heroes and kings in support of the kingship of Ammurapi and the city of Ugarit.[219] The deceased monarchs include king Niqmaddu, probably a later king than the ruler named in the colophon of the Baal Cycle or the figure by the same name who stands at the beginning of the Ugaritic dynasty (Kitchen 1977:134, 138). Line 10 calls the summoned heroes the "Assembly of Didanu" (*qbṣ ddn*), the same group[220] that KTU 1.15 III 2-4, 13-15 mentions in the blessing pronounced by El on the occasion of king Keret's wedding:

mʾid rm krt	May Keret be exalted greatly
btk rpʾi ʾarṣ	Among the Rephaim of the Underworld,
bpḫr qbṣ dtn	In the Gathering of the Assembly of Ditanu.

The figure of Ditanu appears also in KTU 1.124.1-4: *kymǵy ʾadn ʾilm*

[217] By this term I do not mean specifically the kingdom of Amurru, but more generally the second millennium West Semitic stock known especially from Mari.

[218] T. Bauer 1957:255 rev. lines 13, 20; Lambert 1960a:12; *ANET* 504. Examples of specifically East Semitic influence on West Semitic texts are known as well. Texts influenced directly by Mesopotamian models are attested at Ugarit (for a list and discussion, see Mack-Fisher 1990:68-70, 75); these include a piece of Gilgamesh, the Flood story and the "counsels of Shubeʾawilum." Lucian's *De Dea Syria* contains motifs considered to show contacts with the Gilgamesh epic (Oden 1977:36-40). Cultural contacts between east and west carried literary traditions in both directions over a long period of time.

[219] For references, see Bordreuil and Pardee 1982; Pitard 1987:75 n. 2.

[220] For the variation in the spellings, *ddn* and *dtn*, see Garr 1986.

rbm ˁ*m dtn wyš*ʾ*al mṯpṭ yld wy*ˁ*ny nn dtn*, "when the lord of the great gods go to Ditanu, and asks (of him) the ruling of (regarding) the child, then Ditanu answers him. . .".[221] In this instance, Ditanu, a distant ancestor of the dynasty, is consulted for information.[222] Ugaritic *ddn* also occurs in the broken text, RIH 78/11.2. De Moor (1968:332-33), Lipiński (1978:94) and Pardee (1981b:133) compare Ugaritic *ddn*/*dtn* with *Di-ta-nu* in the genealogy of the Hammurapi dynasty of Babylon and with *Di-ta-na* and *Di-da-a-nu* in Assyrian King List A. As these sources indicate, *ddn*/*dtn* is a name belonging to an old genealogical stock to which the first Babylonian, Assyrian and Ugaritic dynasties traced their lineages. According to Kitchen (1977:142), *ddn*/*dtn* was an old West Semitic princely ancestor of approximately the twenty-second century and Keret a western descendant who came to be remembered in Ugaritic tradition.[223] In conclusion, the storm-god's battle against the cosmic sea may have been cherished long before the Amorite dynasties at Ugarit, Mari and Babylon enshrined them in the extant traditions of Baal-Haddu and Marduk.[224]

---

221 Pardee 1981b; 1988b:179-92; Cazelle 1984:177-82.

222 This mode of gaining divine information is found also in Israelite society (Deut 18:11; 1 Samuel 28; 2 Kgs 21:6).

223 See Astour 1973; Levine and de Tarragon 1984:655; Pardee 1988b:165-78.

224 Scc Mendenhall 1992:240. Some Indianist scholars believe that the West Semitic conflict myth moved further eastward from Mesopotamia to India (see Smith 1990:76 n. 117). According to Lahiri (1984), the West Semitic conflict myth was transmitted through Mesopotamia to India, and this influence is reflected in the Rgveda. In some texts from the Rgveda (1.32; 1.85; 1.165, 1.170 and 1.171; translated in O'Flaherty 1981:148-51, 167-72; see Velankar 1950), the storm-god, Indra, defeats the cosmic enemy, Vrtra with the aid of weapons made by a divine craftsman, Tvashtr just as the storm-god, Baal, vanquishes the cosmic enemy, Yamm, with the help of weapons fashioned by a divine artisan, Kothar. Wyatt (1988:391-98) suggests other parallels with the Rgveda. He compares Baal's meteorological entourage, "your seven youths (*šb*ˁ*t ǵlmk*), your eight lads (*ṯmn ḫnzrk*)" in KTU 1.5 V 8-9, to the seven Maruts, assistants to either Indra or Rudra Siva, for example in Rgveda 8.28.5:

> The Seven carry seven spears;
> seven are the splendours they possess,
> seven the glories they assume.

The theory of borrowing from west to east has been made in various forms, ranging from theories of a direct borrowing to a more complicated model of various influences, with the Semitic conflict-story representing one influence on the development of the Indian narrative (Lahiri 1984; cf. Wyatt 1988:391-98). The proposals have been criticized on various grounds (Lahiri 1984; Santucci 1988). Besides the temporal and spatial distance involved in the theory, only thematic similarities between the Baal Cycle or Enuma Elish, on the one hand, and the Rgveda, on the other hand, can be adduced to support the idea of a borrowing. Furthermore, the opposite theory has been proposed to account for the similarities. According to Wyatt (1988), the West Semitic conflict myth derived ultimately from the Indian myth of Varaha. There are a few problems also with this theory. Wyatt's criteria for this position are thematic. There are no unquestionably Indo-European elements in the Baal Cycle which point in this direction. Despite the thematic parallels between the West and East Semitic conflict myths and the Indian traditions of Indra, the suggestions of both Lahiri and Wyatt are highly speculative. For further comparative analysis, see Stannard 1992:227-53, 285-86, 295-96. On such parallels, see the comments above of Coogan (1981:81) cited on p. 89, and Lambert (1988:128) cited on pp. 86-87 n. 167.

TEXT, TRANSLATION AND COMMENTARY

KTU 1.1

Other numbers: CTA 1 = UT ʿ*nt*, plates ix, x = VI AB = RS 3.361 = AO 16.643 (museum number).

Measurements: 86 by 61 by 38 millimeters.

Physical condition: The tablet is beautifully preserved. The surface is damaged only at the edges; otherwise it is smooth and the signs are especially clear.

Find spot: house of the Great Priest, "tranchée" B 3, point topographique 9 at a depth of .65 cm. = point topographique 345 (Bordreuil and Pardee 1989:31).

KTU 1.1 V

Bibliography

Text Editions: Virolleaud 1938:100-02 + plate X; CTA pp. 4-5 + figure 2 and plate I; KTU pp. 5-6.

Studies and Translations: Aistleitner 1964:35; Caquot and Sznycer, *TO* 311-14; Cassuto, *GA* 160-61, 170; Driver, *CML*[1] 76-77; Gese 1970:56-57; Gibson, *CML*[2] 131; Ginsberg, *ANET* 129; Gordon, *UL* 25-26; 1977:88-89; Jirku 1962:18; L'Heureux 1979:9-26; de Moor 1987:27-28; Mullen 1980:92-109; Oldenburg, *CEBCR* 185-86; del Olmo Lete, *MLC* 157; Pope, *EUT* 30-32, 93-94.

Text and Translation

		El Speaks to Yamm (?)
1	[...]b̊	...
2–3	[...wym.ym]m̊ [yʿtqn]	["...and a day,] two [days] [will pass]...
3	[...ym̥ǵy.]npš	[...he will arrive] with a life...
4	[...h]d̊.tngṯn	[...Ha]ddu (?), you will meet him...
5	[...].bṣpn	[...]at Sapan...
6	[...]nšb.bʿn	[...]a cut...when he sees..."
		Yamm (?) Speaks to El
7	[...]b̊kmyʿn	[... he speaks: "...
8	[...ydʿl]ẙdʿt	[...truly] I know
9	[...]ʾasrn	[...]will bind him (?) [Bull El]
10	[...]t̊rks	[...]you (?) will bind...
11	[...]°°bnm.ʾuqpt	[...]stones (?)...I/you am/are (was/were) constrained (?)
12	[...]l°ǵrmtnẙ	[...]and he (?) will attack (me) in my loins
13	[...ḏ(?)]rq.gb	[...red st]uff (?), back...
		El Responds to Yamm (?)
14	[...]k̊l.tgr.mtnh	[...]you shall drive (?) (him) in his loins...
15-16	[...]ḇ.wymymm [yʿtqn]	[...]a day, two days [will pass]
16	[...]˚.ymǵy.npš	[...]he will arrive with a life
17	[...]t.hd.tngṯnh	[...]Haddu...you will meet him
18	[...]ḫmkbṣpn	[...]your (?) [...f]lood (?) on Sapan...
19	[...]ʾišqb.ʾaylt	[...]a doe
		Yamm (?) Responds to El
20	[...]g̊mbkm.yʿn	[...]then he speaks: "...
21	[...].ydʿ.lydʿt	[...]truly I know...
22	[...]tʾasrn.ṯrʾil	[...]you (?) will bind him (?), Bull El...
23	[...]rks.bn.ʾabnm	[...] will bind...stones...
24	[...]ʾupqt.ʿrb	[...]I/you am/are (was/were) constrained (?)...enter...

25	[. . .]r.mtnyʾatzd	[. . .]attack (me) in my loins. . .I will be provisioned. . .
26	[. . .]tʿrb.bšʾi	[. . .]you will enter when he lifts [his head/eyes?]
27	[. . .]°̥ zd.l̊tptq	[. . .]with provisions you will indeed be fed. . .
28	[. . .].g̊[. . .]lʾarṣ	[. . .]to the earth. . .
29	]°[	

Textual Notes

Line 1. *b̊*: CTA and KTU read *b* while V has *b*(?). The photo shows all of the sign except the head of the top left-hand vertical wedge. The sign is not a *d* since no third horizontal wedge is visible despite the room for it.

Line 2. *m̊*: The top left-hand portion of the head of the horizontal wedge is on the broken left-hand edge of the tablet.

Line 3. *n*: All read *n*. The very top left-hand corner of the head of the most left horizontal wedge falls on the broken left-hand edge of the tablet.

Line 4. *d̊*: All read *d*. Only the most right-hand of the vertical wedges is visible from the photograph. The heads of two horizontal wedges are clear, but a third is not distinguishable. On this basis, one could argue that the reading is *b* and not *d*. Context, however, suggests *d* (cf. line 17).

Line 6. All read a word divider at the beginning of this line, but this word divider shows damage and it does not look like the word divider later in the same line. Furthermore, there is considerable space at the beginning of the line. If there is a word divider at the beginning of the line, one might expect to see some indication of a letter before the left-hand break.
n: This sign is written with four wedges (so also *n* in line 7).

Line 7. *b̊*: All read *b*, but it is difficult to make out more than one wedge (although there is space for the wedges to form the letter *b*). The reading *b* is suggested by context (cf. line 20). If *b* is not the correct reading, then this is not a temporal particle, as interpreted by Caquot and Snzycer (*TO* 312: "ainsi"). A translation based on the root **bky*, "to weep," would also be excluded.
k: Although the reading is clear, there is damage to the top left-hand wedge. Against CTA and Horwitz (1972:48), the WSRP photograph shows no word divider after *m* (so V).

Line 8. *ẙ*: The reading is legible, but the three vertical wedges of the left-hand side of the sign fall on the left-hand break in the tablet.
d: All read *d*. The sign has only two horizontal wedges.

Line 9. *s*: All read *s*, which is slightly damaged due to a crack that runs through the sign. The reading is also suggested by context (cf. line 22).

Line 10. *t̊*: All read *t*, but the sign is so damaged that the reading is not secure. The sign also falls along a small crack on the tablet.
KTU's reading of *x(?)x(?)* at the end of this line is apparently no more than damage on the surface of the tablet.

Line 11. .:: All read *ʾa*, but the photographs reveal so much damage that the reading is in doubt. Context might suggest the reading (cf. line 23).
KTU reads *x* before *ʾa* (against V and CTA). The photo shows that the space for

a sign and the damage there is sufficient so that a sign cannot be ruled out.
t: The sign goes through the scribal double lines that mark the edge of the column.

Line 12. *l*: There is a small break in the tablet which obscures the body of the left-hand vertical wedge. Otherwise the sign is clear.

Line 13. °: V and CTA read *w*, KTU *w**. The sign is considerably damaged. Only the two most right-hand horizontal wedges can be read with confidence. The sign may be *ʾa*, *n* or *w*. If the reading is *ʾa* or *n*, perhaps a verb (first sg. or pl.) from the root **g(w)r* is involved (see *MLC* 608).
y: The right-hand wedges are unclear.

Line 14. .: This word divider is written quite high.
r: The sign, especially in the two bottom left-hand horizontal wedges, is a little obscure.
n: The heads of the two right-hand wedges are indistinct.
h: The middle horizontal wedge is barely visible (cf. *h* in line 4).

Line 16. .̊: The word divider is now hardly visible, although all read it.
p: The top wedge comes right up to the edge of the winckelhocken of *š*.

Line 17. *d*: The left vertical wedge is off to the left.
h: The middle wedge is barely visible.

Line 19. *ʾi*: The heads of the two lower horizontal wedges are on top of one another.
š: A break on the tablet runs between the left-hand and middle wedges and it obscures the body of the left-hand wedge.
CTA reads a word-divider after *ʾišqb*, while V and Horwitz (1972:48) do not. The WSRP photograph shows a somewhat damaged word-divider.
l: The middle vertical wedge is only faintly visible.

Line 20. *g̊*: Before *mbkm* is a single vertical wedge which has been read as a word divider (so KTU; cf. V and CTA which read nothing before *mbkm*). Compared to the considerably smaller word divider later in this same line, this sign would appear not be a word divider. It is also unconnected to any other wedge(s) and therefore is likely *g*.
The word divider after the first *m* in this line is no more than a small crack.
Line 21. *d*: The middle and right-hand horizontal wedges of the second *d* in this line cannot be distinguished clearly in the photo. Perhaps as with some other *d*'s in KTU 1.1, this sign has only two horizontal wedges.

Line 22. *ʾi*: The middle horizontal wedge is barely visible.

Line 23. *s*: The wedges have a little space between them, unlike *s* in the preceding line.
n: The sign runs together with the following *m* sign and through the double scribal lines that mark the edge of the column.

Line 24. *ʾu*: The tablet has a break obscuring the body of the middle vertical wedge.

Line 25. *r*: The only portion of the sign which is not easily read is the middle upper horizontal wedge. KTU reads *g** before *r*, but there is no evidence in the photo for such a reading.
m: The bottom of the vertical wedge is partially damaged.
n: The bottom of the vertical wedge is partially damaged.
d: The sign is slightly damaged although the heads of all three wedges are visible.

t: All read *t*. The overall length of the wedge would suggest ^{c} (though this is a crowded line), but the stance favors *t*. In ^{c} the angle of the left edge to the horizontal edge of the letter tends to be about 45° and the horizontal edge is truly horizontal. The left edge of *t* generally has a higher angle to its horizontal (about 70°) and the horizontal edge goes (left to right) slightly diagonally upwards.

Line 26. *r*: The upper middle horizontal wedge is damaged.

Line 27. °: KTU reads *x* at the beginning of the line. There is room for a sign and enough damage to the space that a sign may be in the space. It may be conjectured that the orientation of the wedge is horizontal.
l̊: V reads *l* (?) while CTA and KTU read *l*. The heads of all three vertical wedges and the bodies of the middle and right-hand wedges are visible.

Line 28. *.̊g̊*: Both CTA and KTU (with an asterisk) read *.g* at the beginning of this line while V does not read anything in these spaces. A slim head of a vertical wedge apparently indicates the presence of a word divider. The single head of a vertical wedge (twice as wide as that of the word divider) follows, suggesting the sign for *g*.
r: The lower two wedges are slightly damaged, but the reading is clear.
ṣ: The body of the left-hand wedge is slightly damaged.

Line 29. °: There are remains of a sign below *r* and *ṣ* in line 28.

Commentary

Introduction

As Virolleaud observed in his *editio princeps*, it may be inferred from the words repeated in KTU 1.1 V that the column contains two sections consisting of lines 1-14 and 15-28 (*MLC* 98 n. 70, 157). Moreover, the lacunas in one section may be reconstructed on the basis of the more complete portions in parallel lines in the other section. The two major sections open with the standard formula for the passing of time, *ym ymm [y^{c}tqn]*, "a day, two days [will pass/passed]." The presence of *y^{c}n*, "he answered," in the middle of each section (lines 7 and 20) indicates that each of the two major parts, 1-14 and 15-28, may be subdivided into two further units, lines 1-6 and 7-14, and lines 15-19 and 20-28(?). With the exception of lines 7 and 20, the column may represent direct discourse, as first and second person suffixes or first or second person verbs in lines 4, 8, 10, 12, 14, 17, 18, 21, 22, 25, 26, 27 indicate (cf. opinions noted in *MLC* 98 n. 70). The two major sections, presented under the rubrics A and B, may be delineated and reconstructed in the following way:

	A		B
line			
2-3	ym ym]m[yʿtqn]	15-16	ymymm[yʿtqn]
3	ymǵy]npš	16	ymǵynpš
4	h]d.tngṯnh	17	hd.tngṯnh
5	lḥmk].bṣpn	18	l]ḥmkbṣpn
6	]nšb.bʿn	19	ʾišqb.ʾaylt
7	]bkmyʿn	20	bkm.yʿn
8	ydʿl]ydʿt	21	ydʿ.lydʿt
9-10	t]ʾasrn[ṯrʾil]	22	tʾasrn.ṯrʾil
10	]trks	23	]rks
11	ʾa]bnm.ʾupqt	23-24	ʾabnm ʾupqt

If line 11 is reconstructed correctly on the basis of lines 23-24, it may indicate the approximate length of lines in this column. The word *ʾupqt* in line 24 apparently follows *ʾabnm* in line 23, which appears likely in view of the parallel in line 11. The amount of space in the lacuna preceding *ʾupqt* in line 24 would be very small; perhaps only a word divider falls in this gap. If so, then the lacunas at the beginnings of the lines in this column would be short. Unfortunately, there is no further evidence to corroborate this reconstruction.

Lines 1-5

Line 1 offers no information. Lines 2-3 and 15-16 mention the passage of "days." The verb **ʿtq* refers to the passage of time in KTU 1.6 II 26 which uses the same formula as in 1.1 V 2-3.[1] 1.6 II 26-27 reads:

ym ymm yʿtqn	A day, two days passed;
lymm lyrḫm	From days to months
rḥm ʿnt tngṯh	Young Anat sought him.

The phrase *ymǵy npš* in lines 3 and 16 is syntactically difficult. The

[1] Pardee 1973; *MLC* 157. Cf. *ʿattîq yômîn/yômayyāʾ*, "(the) Ancient of Days," in Dan 7:9, 13, 22.

verb is one of motion, specifically of travel.[2] The noun in Ugaritic may refer to "desire, appetite," "throat" or "lung" as a type of offering; and "person(s)." Perhaps the noun might be understood in the third sense: "he will arrive with a *npš*" (see below). Or, the two words may not belong to the same syntactical unit. Line 4 refers to the purposed meeting of El or Yamm with Baal, presuming that Baal serves as the referent of the pronominal suffix—although this view may be disputed.

As lines 5 and 18 suggest, the location of the meeting between Baal and his enemy may be the mountain known in Ugaritic by both *ṣpn*, Sapan, and *ʾil ṣpn*, "divine Sapan,"[3] in Hittite as Mount Hazzi,[4] in Akkadian as *baʾliṣapûna*,[5] in Greek as Kasios and in Latin as mons Casius,[6] in modern Arabic as Jebel ʾel-Aqraʿ and in modern Turkish as Keldag.[7] The Ugaritic and Hittite names for the mountain, *ṣpn* and *ᵈḫursân ḫazi*, are equated in line 14 of KTU 1.118 = RS 20.24 (see Herdner, *UgVII*:1-3). Standing at a height of 5660 feet (1780 meters), the peak lies about twenty-five miles to the north of Ugarit and 2.5 miles from the coast (Hunt 1991:112).

Sapan is a well-known site of divine conflict. In 1.3 III 35-47 Anat's claims to have engaged various cosmic enemies include an

---

[2] Held (1962:289 n. 1; 1969:74 n. 32) takes the root as an allograph of *mṣʾ/mẓʾ* (cf. Aram *mṭʾ*; BH *mṣʾ*).

[3] The most common proposal for the etymology of Sapan is third weak **ṣpy*, "to look out" plus the *-ānu* adjectival morpheme, hence "look-out point" or the like (*Baal* 332-36). This view sometimes presupposes the root **ḥzy*, "to look" behind the Hittite name. One appeal of this approach is that the Storm-god is described as looking out from Mount Hazzi in the myth of Ullikumi: "Then they all joined hands and went up Mount Hazzi. (Tessub), the King of Kummiya, set his eye. He set his eye upon the dreadful Basalt. He beheld the dreadful Basalt, and because of his anger his appearance changed." (Hoffner 1990:55-56). Cross (*CMHE* 28 n. 87) takes *ṣpn* from middle weak, **ṣwp*, "to flow, overflow" with the *-ānu* sufformative which he calls the "adjectival morpheme." Lipiński (1971:62) claims that the middle weak root means "to float," and that Baal Sapan is the "lord of floating," which he considers a suitable title for a patron god of sailors. For criticisms and alternative proposals, see Grave 1980:225; 1982; de Savignac 1986.

[4] Güterbock 1951:145; *ANET* 123 and n. 8; cf. 205 and n. 3; Lambert 1985b:443 n. 42. Cf. Emar 472.58; 473.9; 476.21 (Fleming 1992:271). See also Dijkstra 1991.

[5] For the Akkadian references see *ANET* 282; *CEBCR* 106.

[6] See the survey of classical references in Fauth 1990. Lipiński (cited in Hunt 1991:107) derives Kasios from the Hittite form of the name, Hazzi.

[7] For the modern names of the mountain, see Bordreuil 1989. For the biblical *baʿal ṣĕpōn* located in Egypt (Exod 14:2, 9, and Num 33:7), see Fauth 1990.

allusion to divine battle at Sapan (*CMCOT* 59). The foe in question is difficult to determine, but Yamm, the first enemy in the list of enemies, represents a possible candidate. In any case, this passage attests a tradition of divine battle against Baal at Sapan. KTU 1.6 VI 1-2, 33-35 also situates Baal's conflict against Mot at the site of Sapan. The Hurrian-Hittite myth of Ullikumi places the conflict between the Storm-god and Ullikumi at Mount Hazzi.[8] Zeus also fights Typhon and other monsters on Mount Kasios (Apollodorus, *Bibl.* I, 5, 3.7f.; cf. Iliad 2:782f.; Hesiod, *Theogony*, 820f.).[9] Given the allusion to Sapan in KTU 1.1 V 5, 18, the conflict between Baal and Yamm in 1.2 IV may take place on this mountain. Oldenburg suggests that Baal, now having superseded El, dwells on El's original mountain. Oldenburg (*CEBCR* 125) comments: "Since the attack [in 1.1 V] happens upon Mount Sapân, it is clear that it is El's mountain from where he rules the world." The context does not require that Baal attacks El on Sapan; rather, in this passage Yamm is to meet Baal on Sapan. To judge from the widespread attestation of the various textual traditions, the motif of the Storm-god's conflict at Sapan is old, and as the allusion to this tradition in 1.3 III 35-47 would suggest, it predates the extant copy of the Baal Cycle. It is fitting that Sapan was known as the mountain of the great storm-god, as this mountain receives the heaviest annual rainfall on the Levantine coast at over fifty-seven inches (Hunt 1991:113).

If El is addressed in line 8, then perhaps Yamm, or less likely Baal, is the addressee of line 5. If so, line 4 reports El's wish that Yamm meet and defeat Baal, perhaps at Sapan. Lines 1-5 would appear to represent El's directions to Yamm to attack Baal. After a period of time (lines 2-3), Baal will arrive (line 3); at that time, Yamm should attack Baal, apparently at the site of Sapan (line 5). The picture of one party lying in wait for another has few parallels within the Ugaritic corpus, but the similarities of KTU 1.1 V-IV to 1.12 I are patent (*EUT* 30). KTU 1.12 I 29-37 reads[10]:

---

[8] Güterbock 1951:145; *ANET* 123 and n. 8; cf. 205 and n. 3; Lambert 1985b:443 n. 42.

[9] Zeus' similarities to Baal extend also to epithets, i.e. Baal's title, *rkb ʿrpt*, "Cloudrider" (Weinfeld 1973) and Zeus' epithet, *kelainephēs*, "the one in a black cloud" (Iliad 2:412, 6:267, 15:46, 21:520; Weinfeld 1983a:145).

[10] *Baal* 255-64; *TO* 341-42; *MLC* 482.

ʾilm ypʿr šmthm	El pronounces their names[11]:
bhm qrnm km ṯrm	"On them may there be horns like bulls,
wgbṯt km ʾibrm	And humps like buffaloes,
wbhm pn bʿl	And on them the face of Baal."[12]
bʿl ytlk wyṣd	Baal goes about hunting,
yh pʾat mdbr	He is at the edge of the outback.
wn ymǵy ʾaklm	Then he comes upon the Eaters,
wymẓʾa ʿqqm	He encounters the Devourers.

There are five similarities between 1.1 V-IV and 1.12 (*EUT* 30). First, El initiates a plan directed against Baal. Second, this plan is to be effected through a third party, the "eaters" (*ʾaklm*) and "rippers" or "devourers" (*ʿqqm*)[13] in the case of 1.12 II. Third, in both 1.1 IV 17-20 and 1.12 I 29 El formally endorses the third party by "pronouncing the name" (**pʿr šm*). Fourth, the conflict is to transpire while Baal is travelling; in both texts "he will arrive" (*ymǵy*). Fifth and finally, the confrontation is described with the verb **ngṯ*, "to seek."[14] The word **ngṯ* describes how Anat "seeks" Baal in 1.6

[11] Most commentators take the following lines as narrative, but Oldenburg (*CEBCR* 200) renders them as speech. The idiom **pʿr šm* elsewhere introduces direct discourse (1.2 IV 11, 18).

[12] So most commentators (*TO* 341-42 n. o). De Moor (1988:131 and n. 23; cf. de Moor and van der Lugt 1974:21) adopts this approach and comments: "They were hybrid creatures with an anthropoid face like the bull men of ancient Syrian art. . . Of course their facial likeness to Baʿlu was intended to provoke a mutual curiosity". The psychological dimension of this interpretation is at once intriguing and problematic: what was the source of the idea of animals with the face of Baal? Might these animals be hypostases of Baal who himself is elsewhere characterized as a virile young bull (1.5 V 18-23; 1.10 III 19-21, 35-37; cf. 1.12 II 54-55)? The word *pn*, "face," is one of the technical terms for hypostasis in West Semitic religion, although as a hypostasis, it usually applies to a goddess (cf. below pp. 281-82). Caquot and Sznycer (*TO* 341-42 n. o) take *pn(y) b* as adversative: "Et Baal se tournera contre eux."

[13] See Renfroe 1992:24, 107.

[14] See *EUT* 30. Ugaritic **ngṯ* is cognate with BH **ngš*, "to approach," as indicated further by the Ugaritic noun *mgṯ*, "offering" (Dietrich and Loretz 1986a:452; for the parallel semantic development, cf. BH **qrb*, "to be near," in the *C*-stem, "to bring near, offer"; *qorbān*, "offering"). See de Moor 1987:131. There has been some discussion over this root and Ug **ngš*. Ug **ngṯ* and **ngš* have been related to Arb roots **ngṯ* and *ngš* meaning "to approach" and "to seek" (so *CML*[1] 111, 156; *UM* 294; Dietrich and Loretz 1986a:452). Ug **ngš* and **ngṯ* have been compared also to BH **ngś*, "to press, drive, overwhelm," and BH **ngš*, "approach" respectively (Ullendorff 1962:340). The root **ngš* probably refers in 1.114.19 to Hby's "approaching" and not "attacking" El (de Moor 1969:173; 1970a:350; Pardee 1988b:60; cf. Dietrich and Loretz 1986a:452), and **ngš* in 1.23.68 describes the ap-

II 6 (*SPUMB* 208-09) and how Baal "stalks" beasts on foot in 1.12 I 40. The intended result, realized in the case of 1.12 II 54-55 but not in 1.1 V, is the defeat of Baal. Similarly, the Elkunirsa myth, especially in fragments 3 A iii 1-19 + 4 A iii 1-15, seems also to reflect an adversarial role for Elkunirsa, that is, El[15] (*ANET* 519; Hoffner 1975:141-42). Hoffner (1990:70) suggests for these broken lines that "Elkunirsa and Ashertu succeed in injuring Baal, for in the next fragment Baal is treated for injuries." The evidence in 1.1 V is most difficult; it may be suggested with all due caution that the point of Yamm's speech in 1.1 V is to induce El to produce a strategy against Baal, just as El does in 1.12 I and the Elkunirsa myth.

Like 1.1 IV 17-20 and 1.12 I 29, the Hurrian-Hittite Song of Ullikumi contains the motif of the older god's naming a new divine champion to attack the storm-god (*CEBCR* 128). In this text Kumarbi speaks (*ANET* 122):

> Kumarbi began to say to his soul:
> "What name [shall I give] him?...
> ...let him go and let his name be Ullikummis!
> Let him ascend to heaven for kingship!
> Let him vanquish Kummiya, the beautiful city!
> Let him attack the Storm-god and tear [him] to pieces like a mortal!
> Let him tread him under foot [like] an ant !

It may be noted that there are some similarities among major divine protagonists in the Ugaritic and Hurrian-Hittite texts (Pope 1989:227-28). The older gods, El and Kumarbi, are the putative heads of the pantheon both challenged by younger storm-gods. The two older gods, both called father of the gods (*ANET* 122), promote and name younger challengers to the storm-gods. The new challengers are related to the sea: Yamm is Sea personified and Ullikumi arises from the sea when he attacks the storm-god. As noted above, the narratives of both texts use the same mountain, Sapan/Hazzi as a backdrop. Direct conflict between the old god and

---

proach of the "beautiful gods" to the watchman of the sown. Both examples would support the interpretation that in 1.6 II 21 **ngš* refers to Mot's "approach" of Baal (see de Moor 1987:87; L'Heureux 1979: 20; cf. *Baal* 199-200, 259).

15 A form of the name of El meaning "El, Creator of Earth." See *CMHE* 16; Miller 1980; cf. **qny*, "establish" in KTU 3.9.2.

the storm-god is not involved in either Ullikumi or the Baal Cycle. Perhaps the motif of conflict between an older god and a younger god, effected through a third party, has been incorporated into the plot as the vehicle to describe the background leading to the combat in 1.2 IV. This type-scene suits the larger context of the Baal-Yamm conflict as El favors Yamm for kingship and opposes Baal who is an outsider to the family of El and Athirat.

Seeing this type-scene behind 1.1 V 1-5 may provide further clarification of *npš* in 1.1 IV 4. 1.12 I presents Baal hunting; perhaps the same scene is presumed in 1.1 V 1-5. Baal may be hunting, and when he comes, perhaps "he will arrive with a *npš*." The *npš* in this case would be an unnamed animal, perhaps game which he captured during his hunt.[16] This interpretation comports with *nšb* in line 6. The term *nšb* is the divine game described in KTU 1.114.10-11 (cf. line 13):

ᶜṯtrt tᶜdb nšb lh	Athtart offers a *nšb* to him,
wᶜnt ktp	And Anat a shoulder-cut.

As Pardee (1988b:50) notes, the precise meaning of *nšb* is unknown, but as KTU 4.247.16-19 indicates, it is a slaughtered item (cf. Gray, *Ug VII*, 95). On the basis of this interpretation of *npš* and *nšb*, it would be feasible to reconstruct *[l]ḥmk* in lines 5 and 18, as Virolleaud and Cassuto suggested. Oldenburg (*CEBCR* 186 n. 1) reads instead *[t]ḥmk*, "your decree."

Lines 6-14

Line 7 marks the beginning of a new speech. One reconstruction is to render *bkmyᶜn* as "...then he speaks." In any case, this line and its counterpart in line 20, may constitute the only narrative elements in this column. In line 8 Yamm perhaps responds to El and suggests that he should bind Baal (lines 9-10). El's handing over Baal to Yamm finds an analogue or perhaps more precisely anticipates KTU 1.2 I when El does indeed surrenders Baal to Yamm's messengers.[17]

"Stones" (*ʾabnm*) in line 11 was taken by Pope (*EUT* 30, 31) to

---

[16] The word has a wide range of meanings in Ugaritic including human persons (KTU 4.338.1). For other meanings, see Murtonen 1958; Pope 1978; Zevit 1990.

[17] In the Elkunirsa myth the god Elkunirsa hands over the Storm-god to be punished by Ashertu (*ANET* 519; Hoffner 1975:141-42; 1990:69-70).

refer to El's "testicles," which might be supported by appeal to BH *ʾăbānîm*, "stones," used for male genitalia in Qoh 3:5 (Kaufman 1979:157 n. 113). The notion of *ʾabnm* as "testicles" might be feasible, given further the appearance of "my loins" (*mtny*) in line 12 (cf. line 25) and "his loins" (*mtnh*) in line 14. If *ʾabnm* refers to bodily parts, they belong not to El, but to Baal; he is the intended victim of the discussion in this column. Indeed, Pope (*EUT* 31) invokes a parallel from the Kumarbi cycle which would militate against the notion of El's demise. Pope notes the words of Kumarbi, El's counterpart: "Give me my son, I want to devour my son" (*ANET* 121).[18]

The term *ʾupqt* in line 11 is exceptionally difficult to determine; *prima facie* it is a fem. sg. or pl. noun belonging to the root **ʾpq*, which occurs in Ugaritic as *ʾapq*, "channel," a term used regularly in the description of El's abode,[19] and often so understood in this passage (Mullen 1980:105). Given the morphological difference the word may be a verb, however.[20] If it is, it may be *G*-stem passive pf., "be restrained," possibly refering to El's or Yamm's restraint (while the other is expected to deal with Baal?).

Line 12, *]l°grmtny*, is likewise terribly difficult. It corresponds to *kl. tgr.mtnh* in line 14. In view of the verbal form in line 14, the prefixed *l-* in line 12 may be asseverative; given this interpretation of line 12, *kl* may be viewed not as the substantive, "all" or "every," but the conjunction *k-* plus asseverative *l-*. Line 12 may be translated accordingly "for he will surely X my loins" (assuming **mtn* is loins[21]), and line 14 may read correspondingly, "because you shall surely X (to) his loins." In other words, **gr* involves an action between two adversaries. The notion of an attack might be based on either BH **g(w)r*, "to attack, quarrel, stir up strife" (*BDB* 158) or **grh*, "excite, stir up, strife" (*D*-stem), "to engage in strife with" (with *b-*), "to excite onself, wage war" (*Dt*-stem) (*BDB* 173). Either root would comport with the context of line 12.

---

18 Yet as Pope (*EUT* 31) stresses, "the text is so fragmentary that any guess is hazardous."

19 On El's abode, see below pp. 227-36.

20 Cf. *ʾapq tʾapq* in RIH 78/20.12 (Caquot and de Tarragon in Caquot, de Tarragon and Cunchillos 1989:58 n. 147; cf. Watson 1983b:12); BH **ʾpq*, "be constrained or restrained."

21 Cf. Ak *matnu*; Eblaite *ma-da-nu* (= /matnu/, "tendon" (Fronzaroli 1984:144); BH *motnayim*. For the suggestion that this word in 1.1 V 12, 14 and 25 may mean "gift" (< **ytn*, "to give"), see *MLC* 585.

Line 13 *]rq.gb* is likewise difficult. The second word may mean "back" as elsewhere in Ugaritic, in view of *mtny* in the previous and following lines. Possible reconstructions for the first word include *[b]rq*, *[d̲]rq*, *[y]rq*, and *[p]rq*, all roots extant in the Baal Cycle. It is unclear how any of these roots, except perhaps the second, would fit this context. The second reconstruction, in connection with *gb*, "back," might resemble *d̲rqm ʾamtm* in 1.5 I 6 as a phrase for either a part or an aspect of Baal's forearm or a different part of his body. If so, *[d̲]rq gb* would refer to some part of Baal's body which like his loins in the previous and following lines may be the object of attack.

Lines 15-28

Lines 15-25a repeat many words attested lines 1-14 and add little new information. The name of El[22] as well as his title, *t̲r*, "bull" occur for the first time in the Baal Cycle in line 22 (1.2 I 16; 1.3 IV 54; 1.3 V 35; 1.4 I 4; 1.4 II 10; 1.4 IV 47; etc). The word *t̲r* occurs as PN in KTU 4.360.3, possibly as a hypocoristicon for **ʾilt̲r*, "El is bull." KTU 1.15 IV 6, 8, 17 and 19 use *t̲r* to describe one group of nobles within Keret's kingdom. According to Philo of Byblos (PE 1.10.31; Attridge and Oden 1981:54-55), the head of the bull was an "emblem of kingship." The description of Yahweh as having horns "like the horns of the wild ox," *kĕtôpōt rĕʾēm*, in Num 24:8, represent reflexes of this imagery to El (see Smith 1990:51). The imagery also serves to represent power or leadership within West Semitic society according to Miller (1970a). Curtis (1990:31) suggests that El's title as bull "would suit the head of the pantheon admirably in the eyes of people who were familiar with herds. The bull was the head of the herd, the strongest and most fearsome of all the group, just as El was the head of the gods and, originally at least, the strongest and most to be feared."

Line 24 fills out the apparently parallel line 11 with the word *ʿrb*,

---

[22] For bibliography pertaining to El, see Pardee 1989-90b:434-36. Given the Ugaritic alphabetic form *ʾil*, the syllabically spelled forms *iʔ-luʔ* and *DINGER-lu*$_4$ (Huehnergard 1987b:107) and BH *ʾēl*, the simplest etymology is middle weak **ʾy/wl*, "to be strong" of the stative formation analogous to BH *gēr*, "resident alien" ⟨ **gwr*, "to sojourn" (for a survey of views of the name of El, see *EUT* 16-19). This root is attested in the word *ʾawl* in 1.12 II 56, variously rendered as "first" or "prince" (for discussion, see Huehnergard 1987c:276). Oldenburg (*CEBCR* 164 n. 2) compares *hē dunamis*, "the Power" (Matt 26:64; Mark 14:62) with the name of El, but this NT expression may reflect the BH hypostasis of *derek*, "power, dominion," cognate with Ug *drkt*.

"to enter."[23] The significance of this word in either this line or line 26 is unclear.

The relationship between lines 25-28 and the previous section is also unclear. Line 25 contains *ʾatzd*, perhaps "you are presumptuous" (*CEBCR* 186), or given the collocation of *tzd* and *ltptq* (*Gt*-stem of **pwq*) in line 27, *zd* may be connected with eating, perhaps even provisions.[24] Line 26 may further describe a prelude to conflict: "you will enter; when he raises [his eyes?]." If so, line 28 may be understood as a prediction that [he will fall?] to the earth" (cf. 1.6 VI 22). If this approach to lines 25-28 is correct, then they might be viewed as the continuation of previous lines.

In general, the contents of the column remain unclear. Pope (*EUT* 30-32, 50, 91-94) and Oldenburg (*CEBCR* 124-25, 1875-86) argue that this scene refers to Baal's castration of El and his removal from kingship of the pantheon. This view has been criticized severely for the lack of evidence (L'Heureux 1979:21-26; Mullen 1980:92-101). From the verbs **ʾsr*, "to bind" (lines 9, 10, 22 and 23) and **rks*, "to bind" (lines 10 and 23), it would appear that some sort of conflict is discussed although the protagonists remain unclear (L'Heureux 1979:21-26; Mullen 1980:105). Line 17 mentions Haddu, a title of Baal in the Ugaritic texts meaning "thunderer,"[25] and an unnamed subject of the verb in *tngṯnh* (possibly"you" [sg. or pl.], "she"or "they"). If the suffix of the verb refers to Baal, then Yamm may be the subject of the verb. However, if the *hd tngṯh* were to be understood as a syntactic unit, then *hd* might be vocative and Yamm the referent of the object. It may be suggested tentatively that the former seems more appropriate to the context. The following column, KTU 1.1 IV, includes a speech apparently of El informing Yamm that he needs to dispose of Baal. The topics of the two columns might be connected: both involve conflict between two divine protagonists. 1.1 IV perhaps provides the general setting for 1.1 V: Baal stands in opposition to Yamm, whom El supports for kingship.

---

[23] On the irregular correspondence of Ugaritic **ʿrb*, "to enter," and Arabic *ǵrb*, "to go away," see Fronzaroli 1955:19, 68; *UT* 19.1915.

[24] Muller (1970:233 n. 48) compares Arab **zwd*, "provisions for travelling" (Lane 1267).

[25] On the basis of the Arb root **hdd*, "to thunder." See Pope, *WdM* 254; *Baal* 350; *CEBCR* 59. One danger in such etymologies is that deity may be the source for the attested meaning. Even so, the putative etymology would then reflect a function or aspect of the deity. For bibliography pertaining to Hadad, see Pardee 1989-90b:448-49.

De Moor (1987:27) makes Baal and El the interlocutors in this column. According to de Moor, Baal speakers the words of line 22:

> I know for sure, [o Ilu],
> [I perceive with certainty]
> [that] you would imprison me, Bull Ilu...

It is arguable, however, that Baal is not a participant in this conversation. Perhaps it is Yamm who speaks in the vocative to El, "you shall bind him, Bull El." In either case, it seems that El is not deposed in this column; rather, he sponsors Yamm's kingship. The thrust of Yamm's speech may be that he expects El to dispose of Baal for him. Indeed, there is no indication that Baal castrates or has castrated El. Pope notes friction between El and Baal, especially in KTU 1.12 II, but there is no indication that a conflict erupts between them in 1.1 V, especially not one that results in El's demise. Indeed, El appear enthroned in 1.2 I and later El supports Baal's kingship after the Cloudrider proves himself against Yamm (1.2 IV) and after some cajoling of El by Anat and Athirat (1.3 III-1.4 V). Explicit conflict between El and Baal is not described in the extant Ugaritic material, although it may have existed in Ugaritic tradition besides the extant Baal Cycle's attestation to otherwise peaceful relations between these two great gods. L'Heureux (1979:3-108), Mullen (1980:92-101) and Schloen (1993) rightly question the nature of conflict between El and Baal, yet L'Heureux (1979:17) states that it "may not be possible to exorcize all traces of rivalry between Baal and El." The indirect character of the friction between El and Baal may be deduced also from 1.12 I and the Elkunirsa myth (*ANET* 519).[26]

This rivalry may underly the special character of Yamm's relationship with El compared with cosmic foes in other ancient Near Eastern narratives involving the Storm-god. Unlike Tiamat in Enuma Elish, Yamm presents a threat only to Baal and not to the entire divine assembly. Tiamat threatens the divine council, including Ea, El's counterpart. Furthermore, Marduk is Ea's choice for champion (Enuma Elish 2.98-99). Tiamat is unrelated to Ea and is inimicable to Ea's purposes. In sharp contrast, El calls Yamm "my son" in 1.1 IV 14. Hence Enuma Elish and the Baal Cycle present the relations

---

[26] For the question of relations between El and Baal, see above pp. 91-94.

among the high god, the Storm-god and the cosmic enemy in very different terms. In the Baal Cycle the divine conflict between the Storm-god and the cosmic foe has been brought into line with other themes, especially the divine family and the precarious character of Baal's kingship.

In sum, it may be guessed that in the first part of 1.1 V, El tells Yamm to dispose of Baal, and Yamm responds that El should do it. In the second part, El agrees to help and Yamm affirms this arrangement. Although there is no firm evidence for this reconstruction, it is consistent with El's adherence to Yamm's demands to surrender Baal in 1.2 I.

KTU 1.1 IV

Bibliography

Text Editions: Virolleaud 1938:96-99 + plate X; CTA p. 4 + figure 2 and plate I; KTU pp. 4-5.

Studies and Translations: Aistleitner 1964:34-35; Caquot and Sznycer, *TO* 306-11; Cassuto, *GA* 161-62, 171-72; Driver, *CML*¹ 74-77; Gibson, *CML*² 39-40; Ginsberg, *ANET* 129; Gordon, *UL* 26; 1977:87-88; Jirku 1962:16-17; de Moor, *SPUMB* 116-23 (cf. 106-08); 1987:24-27; Oldenburg, *CEBCR* 127-28, 186-87; del Olmo Lete 1977:35-41; *MLC* 158-60; 1984:39-47.

Text and Translation

Invitation to El's Feast

1	[. . .]°.ṣ[. . .]°[. . .]	. . .
2	g̊m.ṣḥ.lqb̊[ṣ.ʾilm (?)]	Aloud[27] they summon the ass[embly of the gods (?)],
2–3	[ṣḥ (?)] lrḥqm.	[. . . They summon (?)] the distant ones,
3–4	lp[ḫr.ʾil. (?)] ṣḥ.	The as[sembly of El (?)] they summon:
	ʾil.yṯb.bm̊[rzḥh?]	"El sits in [his] ma[rzeah (?)]
		. . .
5	b̊ṯt.ʿllmn.[. . .]	The shame (?) of the Eternal One (?)
		. . .

27 No clear Semitic etymology for the monoconsonantal noun *g*-, "voice," is known. *MLC* 531 cites Sumerian gu_3, "voice."

6	ʾilm.bt.bʿlk[. . .]	O Gods, to the house of your lord (?)
		. . .
7	dl.hlkn.ḥš.bʾa[rṣ (?)]	Who surely travels quickly through the l[and (?)],
8	bʿpr.ḫbltṭm°[. . .]	[who goes (?)] in the dust of (?) destruction. . .
9	šqy.rṯʾå.tnmy.yt[. . .]	He drinks curdled milk overflowing,
	ytn[.ks.bdh]	He takes [a cup in his hand],
10	krpn.bklʾatyd.°	A flagon in both hands.
11	[. . .]kmll.	. . . like pulp
	kḥṣ.tʾusp[. . .]	Like. . .is gathered. . .
12	tgr.ʾil.bnh.	El appoints his son
	ṯr[. . .]	The Bull. . .
		El's Proclamation of Yamm
13	wyʿn.lṭ⟨p⟩n.ʾild[pʾid. . .]	And Latipan El the Benefi[cient] speaks:
		. . .
14	šm.bny.yw.ʾilt[. . .]	The name of my son (is?) Yw, O Elat
		. . .
15	wpʿr.šm.ym[. . .]	And he pronounces the name Yamm
		. . .
16	tʿnyn.	. . .they answer
	lzntn[. . .]	for sustenance. . .
17	ʾat.ʾadn.tpʿr[. . .]	You, O Lord, (may?) you proclaim [his name (?)]
		. . .
18	ʾankltpn.ʾil[. . .]	I, Latipan El. . .
		. . .
19	ʾl.ydm.pʿr̊t̊[. . .]	Upon the hands. . .I pronounce. . .
		. . .
20	šmk.mdd.ʾi[l. .]	Your name. . .beloved of E[l. . .
		. . .
21	btkspy.dt̊[. . .]	My house of silver which (?). . .
		. . .
22	bdʾaliynb[ʿl. .]	In the hand of Aliyan B[aal]
		. . .
23	kdynʾaṣn̊[. . .]	Thus he reviles me (?). . .
		. . .

24	gršnn.lk[sʾi.mlkh.]	Drive him from [his royal] thr[one],
25	[lnḫt.lkḥṯ]drkth.	[From the resting placc, the throne] of his dominion,
	š°[. . .]	. . .
26	whm.ʾap.l[tgršh. lksʾih (?)]	And if then [you] do not [drive him from his throne (?)],
	[lkḥṯdrkth (?)]	[From the throne of his dominion (?)],
27	ymḫṣk.k[. . .]	He will beat you like [. . .]
		. . .
		El's Feast
28	ʾildbḥ.[. . .]	El sacrifices. . .
		. . .
29	pʿr.b°[. . .]	He proclaims. . .
		. . .
30	ṭbḫ.ʾalp[m.ʾap.ṣʾin]	He slaughters large st[ock, also small stock].
31	[šq̌l]ṯrm.w[mrʾi.ʾilm]	[He fells] bulls and [divine fatlings],
	[ʿglm.dt.šnt]	[Yearling calves],
32	ʾi̊m̊r̊[q]m[ṣ.llʾim]	Sheep by the fl]o[ck], [kids].

Textual Notes

Line 1. V does not read this line. CTA has: *[—]m. (ṣ/y) [ ]*. KTU reads: *[ ]m.ṣ*/y* t*/p*r* [ ]*. *CML*[2] suggests *[g]m.ṣ[ḥ]* as a possibility. The line shows the bottoms of four vertical wedges, which appear to represent one vertical wedge, two word dividers and finally an *ṣ*. Then there is a space, and finally either remains of a letter and/or damage to the tablet. CTA's reading of *m* is apparently based on slight evidence of a horizontal wedge before the first vertical wedge. But what may be taken for the barest remains of a letter in the photo may just be due to the poor condition of the tablet. In comparison to the *m* in line 2, one would not expect to be able to see the horizontal wedge of the *m* in line 1, since the horizontal wedge of the *m* in line 2 is written above the head of the vertical wedge of the *m* and the space above the body of the vertical wedge falls in upper broken edge of the tablet (see also *m* in lines 3, 5, 6, 8, 9). Therefore, the reading *m* is by no means likely. The apparent source for the reading *y* lies with the most right-hand of the four vertical wedges. Compared with the other three vertical wedges to its left, the fourth wedge is wider at the top at the edge of the tablet. From the photograph one cannot determine whether or not this is due to the head of a wedge falling within the extant portion of the tablet. This may be part of a sign which is vertical and has more than one wedge, thus *y* (but possibly also *z*, *h*). Yet the alternate reading *ṣ* may be preferable as there is no indication of two or three vertical wedges (as required by *z*, *h* or *y*). Rather, one wedge is apparent from the photograph. The right-hand wedge of *ṣ* is considerably smaller than its left-hand wedge (see *ṣ* in line 4).

Line 2. *ğ*: Only the top right-hand corner of the head is visible. Context suggests the reading.

°: V and CTA read *r* as part of the reconstructed portion of the line. V suggests *lq[rbm*. CTA Appendix (p. 292), KTU and *CML*² 39 note the possibility of reading *q[ṣm ʾilm]*, a phrase found in KTU 1.114.2. The WSRP photo shows, however, parts of two wedges; the bottom one seems to be a horizontal wedge. This reading would exclude *q[ṣm]* as a possible reconstruction, and leaves *r* as a possible reading. Most tentatively *qb[ṣ]* has been reconstructed in the translation above, but this is only a guess.

Line 3. *p*: CTA and KTU read *p* without qualification while V places a question mark after the reading. The photo shows the letter clearly. Only the tip of the body of the upper horizontal wedge is damaged.

Line 4. *ḥ*: The head of the horizontal wedge is slightly damaged.
ʾi: The vertical wedge is separated from the lowest horizontal wedge (cf. *ʾi* in line 6).
m̊: V reads no space after *b*, while CTA (p. 292) and KTU read a possible *m* (so also *MLC* 158; cf. del Olmo Lete 1984:41). Like V, others read *b[mrzḥh]* on the basis of KTU 1.114.15 (so *SPUMB* 116). In either case, many accept the reconstruction (Gordon 1977:87; *UT* 19.2312; Barstad 1984:138; *TO* 307 n. 6). The WSRP photo barely shows the head of a horizontal wedge.

Line 5. *b̊*: The sign is damaged. The damaged wedges appear to be filled in with only part of their outline remaining (cf. a similar case in the *d* of line 28, etc.). The right-hand diagonal edge of both horizontal wedges is partially visible.
ṯ̊: This sign is somewhat damaged. V places a question mark after reading *ṯ* (= V's *š̀*). Both CTA and KTU read *ṯ* though with qualification. The sign looks similar to *ṯ* in line 9.
°?: KTU places an *x* at the end of the line signifying space for a sign which is at present illegible. The space there is no greater or less than at the end of the next line where KTU does not read *x*. In either case, it is likely that if any sign is involved here, it includes a horizontal wedge.

Line 6. *ʾi*: The head of the upper horizontal wedge is damaged but legible, and parts of the two other horizontal wedges can be seen from the photo.
l: The middle vertical wedge of this sign is damaged and cannot be read clearly from the photo.
b: Compared to the first *b* in this line, the vertical wedges' heads of the second *b* are written a bit apart.
ʾi: The left and middle wedges are apart (cf. *l* in line 5).

Line 7. *d*: There are only two horizontal wedges.
l: The left vertical wedge overlaps with the middle vertical wedge.
ʾå: At the right-hand edge of the line, the heads of two horizontal edges are visible. The letter *n* would also be a possible reading.

Line 8. °: This could be a word divider as read by V and CTA. Yet this sign looks little like the word divider in the same line or in the preceding or following lines. Moreover, the head of a vertical sign is visible; *h*, *t* and *m* are possible readings.

Lines 9-10a are reconstructed partially on the basis of 1.3 I 10-11.
Line 9. *ʾå*: All read *n*, and KTU offers *ʾa* as an alternative. There is no indication of a middle horizontal wedge making *ʾa* the correct reading. As de Moor (*SPUMB* 118) notes, the reading *rṯn* would be a bi-form of *rṯ*, "mud," which epigraphically is less probable. As in V's hand-copy, *rṯʾa*, "curdled milk," or the like, is more likely (see *GA* 99; *CML*² 39).
y: Compared with *y*'s in line 8, the wedges' heads are not distinct.

t: Only the tip of the body of the wedge is obscured by the right-hand edge of the tablet.
n̊: CTA and KTU (with an asterisk) read *n* after *t*. There is something which might be interpreted as the head of the most left-hand horizontal wedge of an *n*. However, this *n* is not formed like left-hand wedge of the *n* in line 10. The head of the third wedge is smaller than those of the first two wedges.

Line 10. °: KTU reads *x* after the second word divider in this line. There may be the left-hand part of the head of a large horizontal wedge. It may be *m* (but not *p*; cf. *p* in lines 15 and 17).

Line 11. *m*: V has *m*(?), CTA *p*, and KTU *p**. It is a horizontal wedge (cf. *s* in the same line). (The stance of the sign differs considerably from the ᶜ in line 13, and is probably not a winkelhocken. It is clearly not a vertical wedge.) The wedge after the single horizontal wedge cannot be determined as it falls on the broken right-hand edge of the tablet. The head of the horizontal wedge appears too big to be either the horizontal wedge of *p*, but it fits well with the head of the horizontal wedge of *m*. If the reading were *p*, however, one would expect to see the second horizontal stroke. It is certainly not above the extant horizontal stroke, for then it would be way above the line. There is no indication of it below the extant horizontal stroke, either. Besides *m*, *t* is a possible reading. The root may be *ʾ*sp* (see del Olmo Lete 1977:38).

Line 12. *h*: This letter is written with four wedges.
r: The most right-hand vertical wedge is slightly damaged. The top left corner of the head and the body of the wedge are obscure.

Line 13. *ṯ*: The head of the horizontal wedge and the winkelhocken are both clear. The right-hand edge of the head of the vertical wedge can be seen, but the rest of the vertical wedge cannot be seen.
⟨*p*⟩: CTA reads *lṯn* and emends to *lṯpn*. According to KTU the letter is written under *n*. What KTU takes as a *p* does not appear to be a sign.
n: The left-hand wedge's head is damaged, but it is partially visible from the WSRP photo.
All read a word divider after *l*, but compared to the preceding word divider in the same line, what remains could be either scratches on the tablet or a damaged word divider.
CTA and KTU (with an asterisk) read *p* after *d* at the end of the line, while V relegates *p* to the portion of the reconstructed portion of the line. The photo shows neither *p* nor room for any sign.
The end of the line might reconstructed *wy*ᶜ*n.lṯ⟨p⟩n.ild[bḥ]*, "And Bene⟨fi⟩cent El answered: 'Sa[crifice...]" on the basis of ʾ*ildbḥ.[...]* in line 28.

Line 14. *t*: All read *l*, but the left-hand edge of an adjoining vertical wedge, if it existed, would be obscured by the right-hand edge of the tablet. The single horizontal wedge read by all as *t* could be an *m*.

Line 15. *w*: The two left-hand wedges are separated from the rest of the sign.
m: All read *m*. Only the horizontal wedge survives of this sign, justifying V's question mark after it.

Line 16. *n*: Over the most left-hand horizontal wedge, there is something that appears to be a small, vertical wedge. It may represent an inadvertent scribal error. KTU reads a word divider at the end of the line, but this is not visible in the photo.

Line 17. *d*: This sign has two horizontal wedges.

n: The sign is legible, but has slight damage.
ʿ: This winkelhocken is smaller than normal for this letter.
r: V and CTA read *r*, KTU *r**. The body of the most right-hand horizontal wedge falls along the right-hand side of the tablet and cannot be seen from the photo.

Line 18. ʾ*i*: The vertical wedge is slightly damaged.

Line 19. *r̊*: In the photo this sign consists of a damaged area and a horizontal wedge that follows. Just before the horizontal wedge, there are two tips of horizontal wedges. The length of *r* here (which is the largest letter this scribe makes) matches well with *r* in line 15.
t̊: V reads *t*(?), CTA *t* and KTU *t**. The photo shows a clear head of a horizontal wedge (the body is obscure). The reading is possible although the head is rather small for a *t* (other letters with horizontal wedges could be considered.)

Line 20. *k*: The right wedge is separated from the rest of the sign (cf. *k* in line 18).
m: The wedges are close together (cf. *m* in line 19).
d: This letter has only two horizontal wedges.

Line 21. *t*: The head of a single horizontal wedge is visible; other readings besides *t*, are possible. Against V and CTA, KTU reads word divider after *t*. There is no word divider in the WSRP photograph.
t̊: V and CTA read nothing after *d*, but KTU reads *t**. The photo shows clearly the head of a horizontal wedge. Readings other than *t* are feasible, however.

Line 22. All read a word divider after *d*, but the photo only shows scratches. They do not look like the word divider in the preceding line, and they lack the form of the word divider.
b: All that remains of this sign is the top left-hand vertical wedge and the head of the bottom left-hand horizontal wedge. Context suggests the reading *b*, adopted by all (KTU reading with an asterisk).

Line 23. *d*: This sign has only two horizontal wedges.
All read a word divider after *d* (though CTA's drawing does not indicate this word divider). It may be just a scratch on the tablet.
n̊: All read *n*, but the sign looks more like an ʾ*a* than *n*. The three horizontal wedges are barely distinguishable in the photo compared to the wedges in the two *n* signs in the same line. The third wedge may lie in the broken edge of the right hand side of the tablet, although the heads of the second and third wedges of *n* are closer than such a reconstruction usually presupposes. The ʾ*a* reading might be considered as likely as *n* based on epigraphic considerations. If *n* is not the correct reading, then the speaker is not claiming the "he (Baal?) has abused me/us" (see del Olmo Lete 1977:32, 36).

Lines 24-25. These lines are reconstructed on the basis of KTU 1.2 IV 12-13, 20 and 1.3 IV 2-3.
Line 24. *k*: All read *k*. All that remains of the sign are the top and bottom left horizontal wedges' heads and part of their bodies. The reading *k* is indicated by context.

Line 25. °: Only KTU reads anything after *š*, namely *x*. In support of KTU, the area before before the right-hand edge of the tablet shows the head of a horizontal wedge, perhaps *t*.

Line 26 is reconstructed on the basis of 1.2 IV 12b-13a, 20 (cf. 1.1 IV 24-25a). See *MLC* 160.

Line 27 has been reconstructed on the basis of 1.3 V 1 (*MLC* 160), but the verb governing the reconstructed clause in line 27 differs, however, from the verb in 1.3 V 1.

Line 28. CTA and KTU read a word-divider after *ʾil*. As V and Horwitz (1972:48) argue, the WSRP shows no word-divider after *ʾil*.
d: The sign can be read despite some difficulty.

Line 29. °: Only KTU reads anything after *b*, namely *t**/*n**. The WSRP photo shows the head of a horizontal wedge. Many readings are possible.

Lines 30-32. These lines are restored according to the parallel texts, KTU 1.4 VI 40-43 and 1.22 I 12-14.

Line 31. .: Against V and with CTA and KTU, the WSRP photograph shows a word divider after *m*.

Line 32. *ʾi̊*: V and CTA read *ʾi*, KTU *i**. All that clearly remains of this sign is the uppermost horizontal wedge. There may be the barest evidence of a second horizontal wedge. The remains compare favorably with some other *ʾi*'s in this tablet, for example in line 26.
m̊: The head of the horizontal wedge and all of the vertical wedge are visible. Some of the body of the horizontal wedge can be seen as well.
r̊: The heads of the upper horizontal wedges can be seen from the photo. All read *r*.
m̊: All read a word divider. There is the head of a vertical wedge which is possible a word divider. Based on the parallels to this line (1.4 VI 40-43 and 1.22 I 12-14), the reconstruction after *ʾimr* would be *[qmṣ.lḷʾim]*. The head of the visible vertical wedge would fit the position expected to be filled by *m* in *[qmṣ]*. Therefore, *m* is read tentatively instead of a word-divider.

Commentary

Introduction

It is difficult to identify the overall structure(s) of this fragmentary column.[28] Three main parts may be inferred. First, a section describes an invitation to a feast, perhaps with a reference to El's drinking in progress in (lines 1-11). Del Olmo Lete (1984:39) describes this section as a "Lamento por Yammu" while others generally characterize this section as a description of the poverty of El's circumstances. Second, El discusses with Athirat the naming of *yw* as Yamm and El commissions Yamm to defeat Baal (lines 12-27). Third, El carries out a feast (lines 28-32).

The location of El's feasting is unclear. The houses mentioned in lines 6 and 21 are different, the first belonging to El and the second to Yamm (cf. Murtonen 1952:91). Indeed, Gibson (*CML*[2] 39 n. 3)

---

[28] For a massive reconstruction of this column, see del Olmo Lete 1984:39-47.

takes the house in line 21 as that of Yamm indicating that his house is already built. Gibson thus presumes that 1.2 III preceded this column. Palace-building appears later in the Baal Cycle as a mark of victory (1.4 V-VII following 1.2 IV), and at the point when El instructs Yamm to defeat Baal in lines 24-25 of this column, Yamm does not yet have a house (del Olmo Lete 1977:34). The house mentioned in line 21 is that of Yamm, but it has yet to be built.

Lines 1-4

This section contain the hallmarks of a divine feast. According to Lichtenstein (1968-69), the feast in Ugaritic and biblical literature may contain four elements: (1) the preparation of food; (2) the summons to the feast; (3) the service of drink; and (4) the service of food.[29] KTU 1.4 VI contains the four elements in Lichtenstein's schema: Baal prepares the food (lines 39-43); Baal summons deities to his feast (lines 44-46); Baal serves them wine (lines 47-54); and the deities are supplied with food (lines 56-58).[30] Some of these elements do not appear in El's feast in 1.1 IV. Moreover, the motif of the preparation of the meal does not appear prior to lines 28-32 which would seem to constitute a second feast given that the preparation precedes the invitation.

Del Olmo Lete (1977:33) notes that lines 1-12 contain a dialogue between El and some goddess(es), as he is addressed in line 6. Del Olmo Lete (1977:36) and Gibson (*CML*[2] 39) treat the initial few lines as narrative which introduce a speech at the end of line 4 proclaiming that El sits in his marzeah. This view reconciles the placement of *ṣḥ*, "he/they called," immediately prior to *ʾil y̱tb bm[rzḥh]*, "El sits in [his] ma[rzeah . . .]". It also accords with the topos of the divine feast: mention of summons (lines 1-4a) followed by the invitation itself (lines 4b-7?). De Moor (1987:24) takes all of lines 1-12 as the speech of Athirat who complains of the poor condition of El and his family and advocates El's naming of Yamm as king. The fault of El's condition lies with the usurper Baal who treats poorly El and the other members of the pantheon. Gibson (*CML*[2]

[29] Sexual activity, or at least an offer of sexual intercourse, may have constituted an optional fifth element, perhaps implied at the end of KTU 1.3 I when Baal eyes his girls following feasting, or in 1.4 IV 31-39 when El offers to Athirat first food and drink and then sexual pleasure. In the parallel in the Elkunirsa myth (*ANET* 519; Hoffner 1990:70) Elkunirsa engages in sexual relations with Ashertu.

[30] Line 55, which includes mention of both drinking and eating, represents a cliché which may connect the feast to the next episode.

4, 39) interprets these lines as part of a speech which includes lines 3 through 8 as well; indeed, lines 1-12 contains some direct discourse indicated by *-k*, "your," in line 6. Hence some sort of feast is already *in medias res*. Since the summons is the only part of feasting preparations where speech customarily occurs, then perhaps line 6 and the section to which it belongs, lines 4b-7 (?), constitute the summons. Del Olmo Lete (1977:36) reconstructs two feasts in lines 1-12; the first is El's feast which is a larger context for lines 1-12, and the second, described in the summons, relates the degraded situation of Yamm's fare. There seems little warrant for postulating two feasts in this manner. Drawing on Lichtenstein's scheme as the background of lines 1-12, a tentative outline may be offered for these lines: (1) invitation in lines 2-8 (?); and (2) drink and food in lines 9-11. However, it is unclear whether the invited guests have arrived yet since they are not mentioned thus far, or whether El has begun drinking prior to their arrival.

El, mentioned by name in line 4 or his servants, may summon deities "near" (?) and "far" in lines 2-3 (cf. *rḥq//*qrb in Isa 33:13; 57:19) according to de Moor (*SPUMB* 116). The phrase *lq[ṣ ʾilm]* has been reconstructed with KTU 1.114. 2 in mind: *ṣḥ lqṣ ʾilm* (see Pardee 1988b:22, 33-35). The reconstruction *qṣ*, is taken to mean "remotest" in parallelism with *rḥqm* by del Olmo Lete (1977:37), but the epigraphical support for *qṣ* is lacking.[31]

Lines 2-4a might be reconstructed in the following manner:

gm ṣḥ lqb[ṣ ʾilm]	Aloud they summon the ass[embly of the deities (?)][32],
[qrʾu] lrḥqm	[They invite] the distant ones,
lp[ḫr ʾil (?)] ṣḥ	[The assembly of El (?)] they summon.

If *qb[ṣ]* in the first line is unmatched in the subsequent lines, then the term parallel to *lrḥqm* in the second line might fall in the lacuna in the third line. One might suggest terms beginning with *p-*; a substitute might be *pḫr* (or *pḫr ʾil*?), a term used elsewhere for the collectivity of the pantheon. There is, however, no particular warrant for this reconstruction of the third line, and the parallelism for this proposed reconstruction is lacking.

---

[31] See above p. 134.

[32] Cooper (1991:834) takes *ʾil* in line 1.114.6 as the ancestral spirit.

El appears seated "in [his] ma[rzeah]" in line 4. Several commentators[33] suggest this reconstruction on the basis of the same expression in KTU 1.114.15.[34] For the following parallel line del Olmo Lete (1977:36) plausibly reconstructs: *[yšt ʾil yn ʿd šbʿ]*. This reading is likewise based on 1.114.16. De Moor (1987:24) reconstructs the subject and verb governing the first words of line 5: "[Ilu does not notice] *the shameful conduct of the usurper*!" These differences of opinion regarding line 4b illustrate the great difficulty in reconstructing this and subsequent lines: it is clear from parallels to lines 24-25 that maximally only half of each line may be extant, but there is no way to determine how short some of the lines may have been.

Excursus 1: The Marzeah[35] in the Ugaritic Texts

The marzeah was a social institution attested perhaps as early as the late third millennium at Ebla (Pope 1981b:179 n. 65), in the late second millennium at Ugarit (KTU 1.114.15; 3.9; RS 15.88; cf. KTU 1.21 II 5) and Emar (446.92; Fleming 1992:269, 276), in ancient Israel (Jer 16:5; Amos 6:4-7), in one Transjordanian (Moabite?) papyrus dating some time after the mid-sixth century (Bordreuil and Pardee 1990),[36] in a fifth century ostracon from Elephantine in Egypt (Porten 1968:179-86), in a fourth century Phoenician inscription inscribed on a drinking-bowl (Avigad and Greenfield 1982), in Palmyran (CIS II:3980; Ingholt 1955:138-42) and Nabatean inscriptions (Barstad 1984:132), in the Marseilles Tariff deriving from the temple of Baal Sapon in Carthage (KAI 69; *ANET* 656-57), in a first century inscription from Piraeus (KAI 60), and in rabbinic sources.[37] Non-textual evidence is less well-at-

---

[33] See above p. 134.

[34] See Pope 1972. For this text see Excursus 1 below on pp. 142, 144.

[35] This common spelling represents an Anglicized form derived from *marzēaḥ*, the common English transliteration for the BH form. Ugaritic *mrzḥ* provides little basis for a modern spelling, but three syllabic forms, *mar-za-i*, *mar-zi-i* and *ma-ar-zi-ḫi* appear in Akkadian texts from Ras Shamra. The first form points to a base **marzaḥu* while the second and third forms suggest a base, **marziḥu*, which corresponds to the BH form. Huehnergard (1987b:178) suggests that the Ugaritic was originally **marzaḥu* with the secondary development of the form **marziḥu* due to "the effect of vowel harmony around the gutteral".

[36] The question of whether or not this text is a forgery has been voiced privately by some scholars.

[37] For various surveys, see Bryan 1973; Porten 1968:179-86; Pope 1972, 1981b; Friedman 1980:200; Avigad and Greenfield 1982; Barstad 1984:127-42; McLaughlin 1991; Ackerman 1992:71-79. For the biblical material, see especially Greenfield 1974; Barstad 1984:127-29, 138-42; Ackerman 1992:76-79. For the variation in spelling between Ugaritic *mrzḥ* and *mrzʿ*, see Garr 1986:46.

tested. According to Barnett (1982), the banquet scene depicted in Assurbanipal's palace in Nineveh showing him reclined on a bed in the presence of his queen represents a marzeah. Palmyra also provides some iconographic evidence in the form of tesserae which depicts cultic personnel standing before various deities (for a summary, see Barstad 1984:135).

Four elements characterize the marzeah in both sacred and secular texts. First, it comprised a limited social group. KTU 3.9 reflects a private association; the marzeah in this text is "the marzeah which Shamumanu established in his house" (*mrzḥ dqny šmmn bbtw*). RS 15.88 (PRU III:88).2-8 is explicit about this feature: "Niqmepa, son of Niqmaddu, king of Ugarit, has established the house of the marzeahs and he has donated it to these marzeahs (i.e. the men of the marzeah) and to their sons forever" (*níq-me-pa mâr níq-ma-adu šàr ^{al}u-ga-ri-it it-ta-ši bît ^{amil}mar-za-i ù id-di-šu a-na ^{amil}mar-za-i-ma a-na mâri^{M}-šu-nu a-na da-ri-ti*).[38] Similarly, KTU 3.9.13 mentions "a man of the marzeah" (*mt mrzḥ*).[39] That the members of the marzeah association were landed and belonged to the upper-class may be inferred from RS 18.01 (*PRU IV*:230) which mentions fields belonging to them (see Barstad 1984:139). In divine representations of the marzeah, the precise nature of the group is unclear. Given its restricted use in divine contexts and its absence from numerous descriptions of the divine council, it would appear that the marzeah was not synonymous with the divine assembly. The Rephaim in 1.21 II may be the invited members belonging to this association; certainly if this were the case, the guests would reflect a limited segment of the divine population.

Second, the marzeah met in a private domicile. In KTU 3.9 the marzeah seems to gather in the home of one of its members, Shamumanu. According to RS 15.88.2-8 the king donated a house for another marzeah association. RS 15.70 (*PRU III*:130) mentions "the house of the marzeah-members of Shatrana" (*bit ^{amil}mar-ze-i ša ša-at-ra-na*), perhaps the same figure named in RS 16.157 (*PRU III*:83). 5. Based in private houses, the human marzeah was not a public institution. If the marzeah called *[m]zrʿy*, "my marzeah," in 1.21 II 1, 5 and 9 were Danil's, as suggested by Pope (1981b:174),

---

[38] Cf. $^{lú.meš}$*mar-za-ḫu ša mi-KI* (Emar 446.92); cf. ^{iti}*mar-za-ḫa-na* in Emar 446.85 See Fleming 1992:269, 276.

[39] The number of the *nomen regens* is clarified by the verb, *ydd*, which is singular, while the plural would have been **tdd* as Dobrusin 1981 argues.

then the location of this marzeah might be his home. Barnett proposes that the house of ivory which Ahab built (1 Kgs 22:39) was perhaps a *bêt-marzēaḥ* or "marzeah house."

Third, the marzeah had a leader. KTU 3.9.11-12 names Shamumanu as leader: *wšmmn rb*, "and Shamumanu is chief." RS 15.70 (*PRU III*:130) refers to "the marzeah-members of Shatrana." The Palmyrene texts speak of a symposiarch of the marzeah. In the Ugaritic mythological texts, the figure functioning as the *rb* could vary theoretically, but in 1.114 and 1.1 IV 4, the *rb*, though left unnamed as such, is El, as the marzeah in KTU 1.114, is called "his." Perhaps El serves the role of *rb* of the marzeah in KTU 1.21 II 1, 5 and 9, but there are other possibilities (see below). Morever, the marzeah called *[m]zrʿy*, "my marzeah," in 1.21 II 1, 5 and 9 may represent represents El's marzeah or in the view of some scholars, Danil's (Pope 1981b:174). As in the case of the marzeah described in KTU 3.9, the invitees in 1.1 IV are apparently to meet in a locale called El's marzeah; he is presumably its chief. It is unlikely that the site of El's marzeah was also his domicile described in KTU 1.1 III, 1.3 V and 1.4 IV, as KTU 1.114 distinguish the two places.

Fourth, the marzeah had a divine patron: El in some Ugaritic texts (KTU 1.114); *šmš* (Avigad and Greenfield 1982); Eshmun (KAI 60), and *bʿl ṣpn* (KAI 69) in Phoenician inscriptions; Bel (Ingholt 1955:138-42), ʿAglibol and Malakbel (CIS II:3980) in Palmyrene texts. This point may clarify the setting of 1.20-1.22. Pope (1977b:166) suggests about 1.20 II that "it is a fair guess that this MRZḤ feast is for Aqhat." In a manner analogous to how the royal ritual of KTU 1.161[40] presents the living king invoking the Rephaim on the behalf of the dead king, so El invites the deceased to his banquet in KTU 1.114 according to Cooper (1991:833-34). El may be its chief, and for this reason it may be El who calls the marzeah *[m]zrʿy*, "my marzeah," in 1.21 II 1, 5 and 9. This marzeah is also called *ʾaṯry*, literally "my place,"[41] *hkly*, "my palace, temple," and *bty*, "my house" (see 1.22 II 1-12). So also Danil might conduct a meal, possibly on behalf of his dead son in 1.20 II

---

40 See Pope 1977:177-82; Levine and de Tarragon 1984; Pardee 1987b; Pitard 1987.

41 Cf. BH *māqōm*, "place," for a sanctuary.

7. In any case, the figures of Danil and his son, Aqhat, belonged to the long line of ancient heroes, the Rephaim, as the marriage blessing of 1.15 III 3 and 14 indicates: "Greatly exalted be Keret, Among the Rephaim of the Earth, In the Assembly of the Gathering of Ditanu."[42] For the society of ancient Ugarit, the main protagonists of Keret and Aqhat were heroes of old. It would appear that their ancient lineage accounted for the treasured place which these two narratives held in the religious literature of ancient Ugarit (cf. Parker 1989b:142-43, 210). That ancient lineage might be traced to a northern Mesopotamian locale (so Astour 1973; Kitchen 1977) may be reinforced by other bits of evidence.[43] The marzeah and the cult of the dead, evidently overlapping in 1.20-1.22, were imputed to be near and dear to the ancient hero, Danil.

Biblical parallels supplement the Ugaritic information about the marzeah. On the basis of the longest biblical allusion to the marzeah, Amos 6:4-7, Greenfield (1974; cf. Barnett 1982:3*) gleans the following elements of the feast. Lying on ivory beds, the participants eat lambs and fattened calves, drink wine from a cup (called *mrzq* in a Phoenician text; see Avigad and Greenfield 1982) to drunkenness, sing and play music, and anoint themselves with oil.

The marzeah was a social association which served a variety of functions. Friedman (1980:200-01) describes the marzeah at Ugarit:

> The term *mrzḥ* refers to banqueting which became regularized, formally or loosely, by virtue of a regular membership, schedule or meeting-place. The occasions of meeting might be sorrowful or joyous, a mourning meal or a holiday feast. The term *mrzḥ* may variously denote the association of participants, the banquet or possibly the meeting place.

Avigad and Greenfield (1982:125) comment in a similar vein:

> Although the biblical and rabbinic sources do connect the marzeah with the funerary cult, it had a wider function as an institution, for it was a place for sacred repasts and memorial meals, and it also served as social institution since the leaders of the community were members.

In contrast to these views, it has been argued that the marzeah served primarily as a funerary association. Based on 1.20-1.22 and Jer 16:5, Pope (1981:170-75) suggests that the marzeah was first and

---

[42] See above p. 112.
[43] See above pp. 89-90.

foremost devoted to commemorating the dead. Pope (1981:170-75) further hypothesizes that the marzeah involved a type of ritual marriage. Following Pope (1981b), Cooper (1991:833-34) emphasizes the funerary character of the marzeah especially in KTU 1.114.[44] Ackerman (1992:96) likewise claims that the "purpose of the banquet, when specified, is funerary." Pope's occasional emphasis on the marzeah as a funerary feast has been criticized (Lewis 1987:3, 80, 93-94; McLaughlin 1991), but few, if any scholars, deny that a funerary feast was celebrated at times in the marzeah. In sum, while one might not entirely equate the marzeah with the cult of the dead, it appears that the marzeah provided a context for it.

There is some debate as to the precise sense of *mrzḥ* in 1.1 IV 4 (if correctly reconstructed) and in KTU 1.114.15. According to Gordon (*UT* 19.483) and de Moor (*SPUMB* 117), the marzeah is a place such as a "banquet hall." As Friedman (1979-80:192, 200-01) argues, it refers to both the association and the locale where it takes place; in other words, the place took its name from the association. A locale is involved in 1.1 IV 4 and 1.114.15. This interpretation is further required by the verb-preposition combination **yṯb b-*, which means "to dwell, be enthroned in" a place (Pope 1977:170). Finally, it should be noted that in KTU 1.114 drinking receives greater emphasis, while feasting receives great attention in 1.1 IV especially in lines 9-10 (cf. lines 30-32). Despite the similarities between 1.114 and 1.1 IV and the many interpretive advantages gained by reconstructing *bm[rzḥh]* in 1.1 IV 4, it remains a reconstruction, and other reconstructions are possible.

Lines 5-12

These lines are notoriously difficult to interpret. Line 5 provides two words. The first is sometimes read *bṯt* and translated "shame" (cf. 1.4 III 19, 21). The second word, *ᶜllmn*, might be a divine title. De Moor (*SPUMB* 117; cf. *CML*² 39, textual note to 1.1 IV 5) notes the possibly comparable term, *ᶜllmy*, in 1.22 I 10 (cf. 1.22 II 12) which follows the titles *zbl mlk*. De Moor (*SPUMB* 116) translates the term, "usurper" (literally *ᶜll*, child," plus *my* or *mn*, "whom"). Del Olmo Lete (1977:38) views it as parallel to *bᶜl* in line 6 and

[44] See the various views discussed by Pardee 1988b:57-58.

derives it from *ᶜ*ly*, elsewhere the basis of Baal's title, "Exalted One." A simpler derivation would involve the root *ᶜ*lm*, "eternal one" with final *-n*, perhaps as a title of El.[45] The title in 1.22 I 10 belongs to *mlk*, perhaps to be identified with *rpʾu mlk ᶜlm* in KTU 1.108.1,[46] but there appears to be no further warrant for introducing this figure into 1.1 IV. Gibson (*CML*² 39) perhaps wisely prescinds from an interpretation of *ᶜllmn*. The two words of line 5 are taken to refer to the condition of El's status by many commentators,[47] but it is unclear whether it is El's status or his physical condition which may be shameful.

The meaning of the words in lines 7-8 is clear. The expression *ḥš ylkn* seems to correspond to the word-pair **hlk//*ḥwš* in Job 31:5. Akk **ḫāšu* and **alāku* likewise fall in the same semantic field. They are parallel in Gilgamesh, Pennsylvania tablet, 2.4.18-19 (*AHw* 343) and equated in BAW 1, 72, 56 (*AHw* 343). Ugaritic **ḥš* and Akk **ḫāšu* may be related despite the irregular correspondence between their initial letters.[48] The formation of word-pairs into syntactically parallel units is attested elsewhere in the West Semitic poetry (Melamed 1961). The larger significance of lines 7-8 is less transparent. "Those who pass quickly in the land" in line 7 could echo the theme of the dead *ᶜōbĕrîm* described in Ezekiel 38 according to Ratosh and Pope (see Pope 1977a:173). Del Olmo Lete (1977:36-41) takes the line literally as a picture of El walking through the underworld (cf. *TO* 307 n. e). The allusion to the dead could be a description of El being "dead drunk," an image used precisely for his sodden state in KTU 1.114.21-22: "El is like a dead man, like those descending to the underworld" (*ʾil km mt//ʾil kyrdm ʾarṣ*). The language in both contexts may be not only metaphorical, but also ironic, as the marzeah serves as the setting for feasts for the dead in KTU 1.20-1.22 and for the living mourning the dead in Jer 16:5. The context of 1.1 IV is so difficult that it cannot determined whether this line is literal or metaphorical. The minimally recon-

---

45 Del Olmo Lete 1984:42. For the formation, see Good 1981.

46 Pardee (1988b:64) takes *rpʾu* as an title of *mlk*, but the opposite may be the case, or the two names may be epithets of a third deity (see Smith 1990:31-32 n. 45, 140 n. 14; cf. 129, 136-37, 143 n. 63) or the divinized Yaqaru (?). For bibliography on *mlk* and *rpʾu*, see Pardee 1989-90b:460-61, 476.

47 *SPUMB* 117-21; del Olmo Lete 1977: 38-39; *CML*² 4.

48 So Fronzaroli 1955:18; Held 1965:277 n. 26; cf. *MLC* 549. Fronzaroli also observes the same irregular correspondence between Ug **rḥṣ* and Akk **raḫāṣu*, "to wash."

structured translation offered above is compatible with a metaphorical description of El as dead drunk.

Gibson (*CML*[2] 39) offers a different view of this line. He argues that *bᶜprḫbl*, "in the great destruction" refers to the lowly condition of El's banquet. This reconstruction founders on the likelihood that the two words do not belong together syntactically. The large lacuna at the end of the line suggests that two words precede precede *bᶜpr* (//*ʾarṣ* in line 7) and thus *bᶜpr* ends the poetic line (Pardee 1980:271). *TO* (307) renders line 8 "dans le poussière de la destruction affamés," perhaps suggesting a scenario that those coming through the land arrive hungry at the feast in line 8. There is, unfortunately, little to confirm these views, although it may be stated in Caquot and Sznycer's defense that their view imputes less to the text than the interpretations of either del Olmo Lete or Gibson. What is also distinctive about Caquot and Sznycer's interpretation is the observation that these lines describe those summoned to the feast, an unusual feature for the topos of the feast. The apparent grammatical impediment to this approach is that the verb *ylkn* in line 7 is not plural but either singular or dual (so Dobrusin 1981). If the verb is dual, then perhaps it refers to El's messengers perhaps going out to announce his feast. If the verb is singular, the apparent subject would be El himself, and perhaps El is too indisposed to conduct himself well. If so, these lines could present a picture of the drunken El parallel to KTU 1.114.17-22, though the wording is different. If the words belong to a description of El and if the words are to be construed together syntactically, one might translate "who indeed goes quickly through the earth. . .", but the significance remains unclear. Given the grave uncertainty of these lines and their interpretation, it appears advisable to refrain from basing any larger view upon them.

The nature of drink and food in lines 9-11 is unclear, but on the basis of the topos of the divine feast, drink precedes food, casting doubt on del Olmo Lete's reconstruction of food before drink in line 8b. According to de Moor (*SPUMB* 118), these lines describe a feast of mud and filth. This interpretation depends on the reading *rṯn* for *rṯʾa* in line 9, which is untenable. De Moor himself notes that Virolleaud's hand-copy has *rṯʾa*, but suggested that the photograph of CTA reads *rṯn*. Building on the work of de Moor (*SPUMB* 116; cf. 1987:25), del Olmo Lete (1977:36) reconstructs lines 9-11:

šqy rṯn tnmy	he drinks silt to overflowing.
ytn [ks bdh]	There is put [a cup in his/one hand],

krpn bklat yd	a goblet in both hands;
[ ] kmll	[its contents (?) are] like ordure,
kḥṣ tusp [ ]	like gravel what gathers [into it (?)].

The reconstruction of the second line[49] is sensible given the parallel in another Ugaritic passage (1.3 I 10-11), but the last two lines are impossible to reconstruct with confidence. The words are so problematic that little is certain about their interpretation. The main problem with this line of interpretation remains the reading, *rṯn*, as the photographs of WSRP confirm *rṯ*ʾ*a*. Divine drinking, reflected in the term, *rṯ*ʾ*a*, "curdled milk," would appear to begin in line 8. Divine food, in terms familiar from other divine feasts, does not appear in this column, but *rṯ*ʾ*a*, "curdled milk," would not necessarily point to degradation; a high-class divine banquet is also possible. It is arguable then that the feast represents an exalted occasion, one involving neither degradation nor filth nor the dead. Rather, El has consumed on a superhuman scale. Indeed, de Moor (*SPUMB* 118) takes *tnmy* as "flooding" or "overflow" with an ecological interpretation, but it may refer to El's great consumption.

Lines 9b-10 use clichés of drinking known from 1.3 I 10-11, but the words of line 11 are less clear. The word *kmll* may be parallel to *kḥṣ*, especially given their apparent syntatical parallelism. Given the preceding context of drinking, these terms may characterize the type, content or manner of drink or food. De Moor (*SPUMB* 116) translates: "like crumbs, like gravel. . ." He notes the verb *tmll* in KTU 1.101.6 where it means "to rub" (Pardee 1988b:144). The *G*-stem of Akk *malālu* means "to eat, consume" and the *D*-stem "to provide with food" (*CAD M*/1:160-61; Watson 1982:9). BH *mĕlîlōt* refers to ears of standing grain (Deut 23:26). In post-BH the verb means "to crush or squeeze, esp. to rub ears for husking the grain," but also "to stir a mush, make a pulp" (Jastrow 792). De Moor (*SPUMB* 118) compares post-BH *milmûl*, crumb" (Jastrow 793). Perhaps *kmll* should be understood in light of this last meaning as "like mush" or "like pulp," referring to a type of drink or food or the manner of preparation. The phrase *kḥṣ* might be viewed similarly in view of Syriac *ḥayeṣ*, "to bind, compress." De Moor

[49] For Ug *ks*, cf. Akk *kāsu*, BH *kōs*, Aram *kāsāʾ*, Arb *kās* (*UT* 19.1276) and Egyptian *ku-ṯi* in the Leiden Magical Papyrus. The Egyptian word is a West Semitic loan according to Albright and Lambdin (1957:123) and Ward (1961:39-40). For *krpn*, see Akk *karpu*, *karpa(t)tu* (so *UT* 19.1312). For *klʾat*, cf. BH *kilʾayim*, "twofold," Arb *kilaʾ*, "both," Eth *klʾ*, "two" (so *UT* 19.1231).

(*SPUMB* 118) takes *ḥṣ* as "gravel" based on cognates with the geminate root, **ḥṣṣ* (Jastrow 496); this view is based on de Moor's predisposition to a seasonal view of the terms of El's feast. Line 11 perhaps describes the food of El following the drink, in accordance to the order of elements in feasts outlined by Lichtenstein. These elements are followed by the narrative link to the following section. Line 12 mentions "El," "his son" and *ṯr*, perhaps an epithet of El. The unclear term in line 12 is *tgr*, for which de Moor (*SPUMB* 118) reconstructs *[y]tgr*, 3 masc. sg. *tD*-stem of **gry*, "to appoint a deputy for oneself," comparing Arab. *jarra(y)*, "to appoint a deputy." The view would lead aptly to the following section.

Lines 13-20

A feast provides the context for the central act of the column, the naming of Yamm in lines 13-27.[50] Line 13 introduces El's speech with the notice that he "speaks up" (*wyʿn*[51]). Line 13 provides the first occurrence of El's epithet, *lṭpn*. H. Bauer (1933:83; *SPUMB* 191) compared this title with Arabic *laṭif*, "friendly" (with the *-ānu* ending).[52] This scene also involves Athirat, presumably in a manner similar to the selection of *ydʿ ylḥn* and Athtar in 1.6 I 43-55. In 1.1 IV the emphasis apparently falls on El, while in 1.6 II Athirat seems to play a greater role. In line 14 Athirat appears under the name *ʾilt* for the first time in the Baal Cycle (cf. 1.3 V 37; 1.4 I 7, IV 49; 1.6 I 40; cf. *ʾilt* for Anat in 1.3 II 8). The word *ʾilt* in the thirteenth century Lachish Ewer probably also refers to Athirat. Elat of Tyre (cf. KTU 1.14 IV), depicted as a goddess of the sea on Tyrian coins, may be Athirat (*CMHE* 31).

The text is very fragmentary, but it may be deduced that *yw* and Yamm in lines 14 and 15 are the names of the same deity. Murtonen (1952:91) remarks: "For if we presume that *Yw* and *Ym* are names of separate deities, the poem would fall into two parts entirely un-

[50] Cf. the feast for a king provided by the patron-deity, a common motif in Mesopotamian tradition (Barré and Kselman 1983:105).

[51] The verb of speech **ʿny* is usually rendered "to answer," but it also occurs in a number of instances where no preceding speech is involved. In these cases the root means not "to answer," but "to speak up" or the like. This meaning is attested also in BA (*BDB* 1107, #2), Ahiqar and other Aramaic texts (see Steiner and Nims 1984:104 n. 62). For a proposed Egyptian cognate, see Ward 1961:37.

[52] Garr (1986:49) views the second letter of El's title, *lṭpn*, as a scribal or orthographic practice retaining the original etymological spelling (versus the spelling with *ẓ* in KTU 1.24.44). The intervocalic shift in the spelling with *ẓ* implies a vocalization of **laṭipānu* or the like rather than **luṭpānu*. See the PN attested at Mari *la-ṭí-pa-an* (*SPUMB* 191).

[l ypʿr] (14) šm bny yw ʾilt	My son [shall not be called] by the name of *Yw*, o goddess,
[k ym smh (?)]	[but *Ym* shall be his name! (?)]
(15) wpʿr šm ym	So he proclaimed the name of Yammu.
[rbt ʾaṯrt (?)] (16) tʿnyn	[Lady Athiratu (?)] answered,
lzntn [ʾat npʿrt (?)]	"For our maintenance [you are the one who has been proclaimed (?)],[53]
(17) ʾat ʾadn tpʿr	you are the one who has been proclaimed 'master'"
[wyʿn ṯr ʾil (?)]	[And the Bull Ilu answered, (?)]
(18) ʾank lṭpn ʾil [dpʾid]	"I myself, the Benevolent, Ilu the good-natured,
[lqḥtk] (19) ʾl ydm	[have taken you] in my hands,
pʿrt [šmk]	I have proclaimed [your name].
[ym šmk]	[Yammu is your name],
(20) šmk mdd ʾi[l ym]	your name is Beloved of I[lu, Yammu]."

The central act of this scene is El's naming (**pʿr*) of Yamm. The form, *pʿr*, "he names," in line 15 introduces this section, and the verb, *pʿrt*, in 1.1 IV 19, is a performative perfect.[54] Other examples of special naming occur in the Ugaritic texts. The weapons in 1.2 IV receive special names which the ultimately unsuccessful naming in 1.1 IV may anticipate. KTU 1.12 I 29-37 describes El's scheme to bring Baal down by recourse to strange beasts. The opening description of these beasts is preceded by the point in lines 28-29: *ʾilm ypʿr šmthm*, "El pronounces their names."[55] In this case, "naming" designates an assignment of mission or task by a superior to an inferior.[56] Biblical examples involve the divine calling of humans for specific tasks, e.g., the craftsman Bezalel as "called by name" in Exod 35:10 (Cohen 1968:32-34).

Like this passage of the Baal Cycle, the Hurrian-Hittite Song of Ullikumi describes an older god naming a new divine champion to

---

53 The translation of line 16 assumes that *znt* is to be compared with Akk *zinnatu*, "support, maintenance" (*SPUMB* 120).

54 See above p. 48. For the root de Moor (*SPUMB* 119; so also *MLC* 61) compares BH **pʿr*, Syr *pĕʿar*, Arb *faġara*, "to open the mouth" (Wehr 722), despite the irregular correspondence of gutterals.

55 For citation of this passage, see above p. 124.

56 Inferiors' calling by name to superior denotes entreaty or prayer; for the further possibility that naming the beasts constitutes an act of creation for a specific purpose, see Cohen 1968:34; for further discussion, see below p. 341.

attack the storm-god. As noted above,[57] both texts use as a backdrop Mount Sapan, known as Baal's home in Ugaritic tradition and called Mount Hazzi in Hurrian-Hittite tradition. Furthermore, the relationship between Kumarbi and Ullikumi is analogous to that of El and Yamm. In both texts, the older gods have sons. Like Ullikumi, Yamm is called "son" in 1.1 IV 14, which represent either a standard reference to El as the father of divine progeny (like Baal's reference to El as his father in KTU 1.3 V, 1.4 I, IV), or as it seems more likely in this case, an expression using divine adoption for the royal figure. Indeed, the explicit declaration of Yamm as "my son" (*bny*) in line 24 is not a stereotypical expression like Baal's allusions to El as his father. Like Ullikumi, Yamm, the divine son, is given a name as part of parental commission to destroy the Storm-god. If de Moor's translation cited above is correct, Yamm is also named *ʾadn*, "lord."[58] As line 24 states, Yamm is to drive Baal from the royal throne. Kingship will then pass to the divine son.

The language of relationship between the divine son and father may have been modelled on royal language, which imagined the king as the divine son of the divine father. Keret, for example, is called *bn(m) ʾil*, "the son of El" (KTU 1.16 I 10, 20).[59] Indeed, the feature of Yamm's naming has been compared to the conferral of a regnal or throne-name at the accession of a new monarch. As examples, de Moor (1987:25 n. 117) cites Enuma Elish 5.109f., Atra-hasis 1:245f., Gen 17:5, 15, and 32:29. Similarly, Tiglath-Pileser III and Shalmaneser V assumed new names upon ascending the throne in Babylon (*ANET* 272) and the Judean monarchs, Eliakim and Mattaniah took new names (2 Kgs 23:34; 24:17). Yamm's title, *mdd ʾi[l]*, "beloved of E[l]," in line 20 may belong as well to the depiction of Yamm as the royal son of El. This epithet belongs to Yamm not only in this line, but also in 1.3 III 38-39, 1.4 II 34 and VII 2-3. El's other "darling" is Mot, called *mdd ʾil* in 1.4 VIII 23-24 and *ydd ʾil* in 1.4

---

[57] See above pp. 123-24.

[58] The word consists of *ʾad*, "father" in KTU 1.23.32, 43, plus the *-n* sufformative (*UT* 19.352). Cf. the equation of Ug syllabic *a-da-nu* with Akk *a-bu*, "father" in *UgV*, text 130 ii 9′ (Blau and Greenfield 1976:16; Huehnergard 1987b:48 n. 2, 104, 289). For further references, see Pardee 1987c:369.

[59] Similar notions are attested in Judean royal ideology (2 Sam 7:14; Pss 2:7; 89:27-28; 110:3; see Mettinger 1976:259-75; Paul 1979-80).

VII 46-47, 48, VIII 31-32, 1.5 I 8, 13, II 9, III 10, 26 and 1.6 VI 30-31. Wyatt (1985:120-25) argues for the phrases' specifically royal connotation which would suit their usage in the Baal Cycle.

The name of Yamm is attested first in the late second millennium in the form of Mari personal names with *ym* as the theophoric element: *abdiyamm*, "servant of Yamm" and *ilym*, "Yamm is god" (Huffmon 1965:120, 124, 210; Gelb 1980:272-73; Durand 1993: 57-60). A tablet from Tell Taanach attests *aḫiyamm*, "Yamm is brother" (Glock 1983:60). Malamat (1987:184-88; 1992:211-15; cf. 1965:367) argues that the sacrifice which Yahdunlim of Mari offered to the "Ocean" (*A.AB.BA*) at the Mediterranean Sea reflects the West Semitic cult of Yamm. According to Malamat, this Sumerogram underlies the reading ^{d}*tâmtum* in RS 20.24.29 (cf. *ym* in the parallel texts, KTU 1.47.30//1.118.29; see *UgV*:45, 58; Herdner, *UgVII*:1-3). The Sea in the West Semitic tale of "Astarte and the Tribute of the Sea" is called Tiamat (*ANET* 17). The cult of Yamm may have continued in the first millennium Phoenician cities, to judge from late classical sources. Third century coins attest to Poseidon as the sea-god of Beirut.[60] Some classical stories recounting Perseus' rescue of Andromeda from the sea-monster place the story at Jaffa.[61] That Yamm continued to be understood as a deity in first millennium Israel might be argued on the basis of b. Hul. 41b which prohibits even profane slaughtering by which blood flows into lakes, rivers and the like so that such an act would not interpreted as an offering to *śrʾ dym*, "Prince of the Sea" (Tsevat 1954:47; Jacobs 1977:2).

The background of the name *yw* in line 14 has been debated.[62] Eissfeldt (1952:85) identified this name with the god Ieuo attested in Philo of Byblos' *Phoenician History*.[63] In this passage, this figure is said to be the god of a priest named Hierombalos who dedicated his work to the king of Beirut (see Baumgarten 1981:41, 54). If the correlation were correct, it would provide additional evidence for the cult of Yamm in the first millennium. A number of scholars have

---

60 See Gray 1979:323; Hill 1914:pls. VII, 12; VIII, 17. Some scholars (Teixidor 1977:43; Betlyon 1991:151) take this evidence as an indication of a cult of Baal Sapan and not Yamm.

61 For discussion see above p. 24.

62 Murtonen 1952: 49-50, 90-92; Gray 1953; *SPUMB* 119; Attridge and Oden 1981:24 n. 22; Hess 1991:182-83.

63 PE 1.9.21; Attridge and Oden 1981:20-21. See also *CML*^{2} 4 n. 2.

fied either *yw* or Ieuo with the name of Yahweh, however. Albright (*YGC* 228) and Barr (1974:37) accept the identification of Ieuo with Yahweh. Despite the fact that there is no extra-biblical reference to Yahweh prior to the Mesha stele (KAI 181:18), de Moor (1987:116; 1990:113-18) considers cautiously and seriously the possibilities that *yw* is to be identified with Yahweh or that *yw* is a caricature of Yahweh. De Moor nonetheless notes that given the explicit identification of *yw* with Yamm in 1.1 IV, it seems unlikely *yw* is historically connected with Yahweh. Assuming the historical accuracy of PE 1.9.21, Ieuo is more likely to be a deity indigenous to Phoenicia than to Israel, and the identification of Ieuo with Yamm/*yw*, though by no means assured, is preferable to an equation with Yahweh.

Lines 21-32

Line 21 begins the topic of *bt kspy* "my silver house." In this line, either Yamm refers to his own house, or El refers to the house which he will have built for Yamm (so *SPUMB* 120; *CML*² 39 n. 9). A similar sentiment occurs in 1.4 VI 36-37, either as part of Baal's expression at the completion of his own house: 〈*b*〉*hty bnt dt ksp*, "my house I have built of silver" (so *CML*² 63), or addressed to Kothar, "you have built a house of silver for me" (so D. N. Freedman 1981:22 n. 1, taking the suffix as dative). KTU 1.4 VI 36-37 may parallel 1.1 IV 21 in both formulation and intent, but the contexts are slightly different, since the craftsman-god is not present. Rather, El expresses the wish that "[he (Kothar) will build] a silver house for me" (which would seem to support Freedman's translation of 1.4 VI 36-37). Since the suffix on *kspy* in 1.1 IV 21 does not refer to El's house, but to Yamm's, the suffix is dative (providing some clarification for the otherwise ambiguous 1.4 VI 36-37).[64] In sup-

---

64 Freedman compares the issue of 1.4 VI 36-37 with textual variants in 1 Kgs 8:13:

> The reading should be, not "I have built my house" but rather "you have built a house for me." Compare the passages in 1 Kings 8 [verse 13] where we have alternate readings in MT and LXX: "I built (MT)"—"You built (LXX)." The difference is not only textual but conceptual: "I built" must refer to the earthly temple built with human hands, while "you built" is a reference to God's action in building his heavenly temple.

The reading "I built" would correspond to Gibson's translation of 1.4 VI 36-37 as Baal's boast, while the interpretation "you built" would correspond to Baal's

port of Gibson's view of line 21, El appears to name Yamm for the purpose of establishing his kingship, which will be reinforced first by his intiating a palace-building project for Yamm, and second, by the act of Yamm's defeat of Baal. Hence El may propose that a silver palace of Yamm's own is to be built.

The significance of line 22, *bd ʾalʾiyn bʿl*, "in/by the hand of Mighty Baal,"[65] is unknown. Given that the weapon is *bd bʿl*, "in the hand of Baal," in 1.2 IV 13, 15, 21 and 23, the phrase in 1.1 IV 22 may anticipate the later battle between Baal and Yamm. Yamm's palace depends on Baal's demise, and the theme of Baal's defeat follows in lines 23-25. A conversation may be involved at this point. Either El or Yamm refers to someone, presumably Baal: "thus he reviles (me?)" (*kd ynʾaṣn*).[66] Following other commentators, del Olmo Lete (1977:36) reads *ynʾaṣn* and takes lines 24-25 as evidence for El's opposition to Baal.

The phrase *ks[ʾi mlkh]* in line 24 is to be understood literally as "the thro[ne of his kingship]," parallel to Akk *kussû šarrūti*[67] and BA *korsēʾ malkûtēh* (Dan 5:20).[68] The parallel bicola in 1.2 IV 12-13 Kothar, the Ugaritic craftsman-god, involve an incantation over the two weapons which Baal will use to vanquish his enemy, Yamm. Just as El empowers Yamm with new names against his enemy,

---

congratulations to Kothar, as Freedman's view suggests. The sentence in 1.4 VI 36-37 could be read either way, but the context of 1.1 IV 21 would favor the latter view since in this passage the palace is strictly speaking not El's house. Freedman's conceptual model is, however, imprecise. Divine temple-building in 1.4 VI is described on analogy with human temple-building, and Kothar corresponds to human builders in this passage (Hurowitz 1985). In the case of 1 Kings 8 the Septuagint may reflect the notion that Yahweh could be a divine craftsman like Kothar in 1.4 VI, but this seems unlikely given the explicit mention of human craftsmen in 1 Kings. More likely, the Septuagint reflects the notion of Yahweh as the divine sponsor of the construction project.

65 Taking *ʾalʾiyn* as an elative of **lʾy*, to be mighty," with the *-ānu* ending, with most commentators (*CEBCR* 58 n. 58; *MLC* 513). Del Olmo Lete (*MLC* 513) compares the title of Erra, ^{d}*Erra qarrad DINGER*^{meš}, "Erra warrior of the gods." According to Albright (1938:19) and Cross (*CMHE* 66-67), *ʾalʾiyn* is the hypocoristicon of **ʾalʾiyu baʿl*, while *ʾalʾiy qrdm*, is a sentence-name meaning "I am the mightiest of warriors." For bibliography on this title, see Pardee 1989-90b:438.

66 Murtonen (1952:53) compares Ugaritic *kd*, "thus," to other words with the two "deictic particles," **k* and **ḏ*: BH *kāzô*, *wĕkāzēk*, *kāzōʾt*, Aram *kidnāʾ* and Arabic *kadaʾ*.

67 De Moor and van der Lugt (1974:16) take *ksʾu mlk* as a translation of Akk *kussû šarrūti*. The derivation of Ug *ksʾu* and Akk *kussû* from Sumerian *GU.ZA* is generally accepted (*UT* 19.1277).

68 The Ugaritic form would therefore be vocalized **mulki-hu*, "his kingship," rather than **malki-hu*, which would mean "his king."

Baal, so Kothar empowers Baal against his adversary, Yamm, with incantations over weapons designated with names. Both scenes use the verb **pʿr*, "to name": El "names" of Yamm in 1.1 IV 15, 17, 19 (cf. 29), and Kothar "names" the weapons in 1.2 IV 11, 18. Yamm's new name is a sign of his royal power; so also the names of the weapons serve to empower them. In the use of the bicolon of line 24-25, the context of 1.2 IV may be more than parallel; 1.1 IV 24-25 may foreshadow and anticipate Baal's victory in 1.2 IV.

Lines 28-32 describe El's preparations for a feast, apparently the second one in this column. This scene begins with the god El slaughtering. Gibson (*CML*[2] 39, textual note to line 28) compares 1.114.1-2, which begins *ʾil dbḥ*. The scenes of KTU 1.114 may reverse the sequence of 1.1 IV: El feasts in his marzeah, then in his house. Line 29 shows the verb *pʿr* as in 15, 17 and 19. Perhaps this usage implies that lines 13-26 represent a discussion between El and Athirat over "naming" Yamm, while line 29 represents El's formal act of "naming" Yamm in the midst of the assembly. Parallels for lines 30-32 are found in other scenes depicting deities feasting, for example in 1.4 VI 40-43 and 1.22 I 12-14. The sequence of animals elsewhere follows *ʾalpm ʾap ṣʾin*, namely large animals followed by small animals (Levine 1963; Lichtenstein 1979: 205 n. 352). That these words do not constitute the first two items in a long list of animals may be inferred also from the two different verbs which govern them, indicating parallel but not identical meaning (Loewenstamm 1973:210). The verb *ṭbẖ* governs *ʾalpm ʾap ṣʾin*, while *šql*, "to fell" (literally, "to cause to fall"[69]), governs the following list of animals. Like 2 Sam 6:13 and 1 Kgs 1:9, lines 31-32 contain a list of individual sorts of animals, here beginning with *ṯrm*, "bulls," and *mrʾi*, "fatlings."[70] In this instance *ʾilm*, "literally "god(s)," here may be a superlative in the singular with mimation,[71] here rendered "divine." The next animals, *[ʿglm dt šnt]*, are year-old calves, or veal. Lines 32 closes the extant portion of the list with *ʾimr*

---

[69] Cf. the semantic development of the *C*-stem of **npl*, "to fall," which in 2 Sam 20:15 means "to execute" (cf. Akk *nuppulu*, "to demolish, maim," discussed by Greenfield 1958:215-17).

[70] The word *mrʾi* is cognate with Akk *marû*, "well-fed, fat" and BH *mārîʾ*, "fatling."

[71] See p. 166.

[q]m[ṣ lʾim], which has been taken as "[sk]ip[ping] sheep" and "kids" or "sheep by the flock" [or more literally, "sheep of the flock"], kids.[72]

KTU 1.1 III

Bibliography

Text Editions: Virolleaud 1938:93-96 + plate IX; CTA p. 3 + figure 1 and plate I; KTU pp. 3-4.

Studies and Translations: Aistleitner 1964:33-34; Caquot and Sznycer, *TO* 303-04; Cassuto, *GA* 164-67, 172-74; Clifford, *CMCOT* 48, 123-311; Cross, *CMHE* 36; Driver, *CML*[1] 74-75; Gibson, *CML*[2] 130; Ginsberg, *ANET* 129; Gordon, *UL* 24-25; 1977:85-87; Jirku 1962:13-15; de Moor 1987:22-23; Mullen 1980:92-109; Oldenburg, *CEBCR* 187-90; del Olmo Lete 1977:41-44; *MLC* 160-63.

Text

1 [kptr].̊ks[ʾu.ṯbth.ḥkpt.ʾarṣ.nḥlth]
2 b̊ʾålp.šd.r̊[bt.kmn.lpn.kṯr]
3 h̊br.wql.t̊[štḥwy.wkbd.hwt]
4 w.rgmlk[ṯr.wḫss.ṯny.lhyn]
5 dḥrš.ẙ[dm.tḥm.ṯr.ʾil.ʾab]
6 hwt.lṭpn̊[.ḥtkk?]
7 yh.kṯr.b[ ]
8 št.lskt.n[ ]
9 ʿdb.bǵrt.[ ]

[72] All the other nominal forms for animals in this list show a plural ending except *ʾimr*, which indicates that it stands in construct to *[q]m[ṣ]*. Gibson takes **qmṣ* from Arb *qamaṣa*, "to leap, spring" and Mishnaic Hebrew *qamṣūṣ*, "squatting" (*CML*[2] 157), and *lʾim* from Akk *laliʾu* and *lalû*, "kid" (*CML*[2] 150; the gemination of the first two consonants is rare in Semtic languages and might point to a non-Semitic loan, as observed in Greenberg 1950). Assuming this meaning for **qmṣ*, this word is unlikely to be in construct to *lʾim* as Gibson renders the line; rather, it is to be taken with *ʾimr*. This construal would also obviate the lack of final *-m* on *ʾimr* in Gibson's translation of the form in the absolute state. Ginsberg (*ANET* 134) did not translate *qmṣ*. Citing Gen 41:47 for "abundance" for **qmṣ*, Tuttle (1978:255, 265 n. 23) argues for the translation "kids of the abundance of lambs." The usage in Gen 41:47 appears to reflect an inner BH semantic development, however. Others relate the word to Arb *qamaṣa*, "to bind" and BH **qmṣ*, "to grasp," and assume the meaning "to be strangled" (for summary, see Tuttle). Although the BH verb appears in sacrificial contexts (Lev 2:2, 5:12, 6:18), it is not with this meaning, but with the sense of sacrifices brought "in hand." For a defense of "flock" for *qmṣ* based on Akk *kamās/ṣu* A, "to collect, gather," see Lichtenstein 1979:125 n.200.

10 ḥšk.ʿṣk.ʿ[bṣk.ʿmy.pʿnk.tlsmn]
11 ʿmy twtḥ.ʾi[šdk.tk.ḫršn]
12 ǵr.ks.dm.r[gm.ʾt.ly.wʾargmk]
13 hwt.wʾaṯnyk[.rgm.ʿṣ.wlḫšt.ʾabn]
14 tʾunt.šmm.̥ʿm̊[.ʾarṣ.thmt.ʿmn.kbkbm]
15 rgm.ltdʿ.nš̊[m.̥wltbn.hmlt.ʾarṣ]
16 ʾat.w.ʾank.ʾibǵ[yh]
17 wyʿn.kṯr.wḫss[.lk.lk.ʿnn.ʾilm]
18 ʾatm.bštm.wʾan̊[.šnt.kptr]
19 lrḥq.ʾilm.ḥkp[t.rḥq.ʾilnym]
20 ṯn.mṯpdm.tḥt.[ʿnt.ʾarṣ.ṯlṯ.mtḥ]
21 ǵyrm.ʾidk.lyt[n.pnm.ʿm.lṭpn]
22 ʾildpʾid.tkḫrš[n.ǵr.ks]
23 yglyḏd.ʾi[l.wybʾu.qrš.mlk]
24 ʾab.šnm.l̊[pn.ʾil.yhbr.wql]
25 yštḥwẙ[.wykbdnh
26 ṯr.ʾi̊l[.ʾabh
27 ḥšb̥[htm.tbnn.ḥš.trmn.hklm]
28 btk.[
29 bn.[
30 ʾa[

Textual Notes

Lines 1*-6 are reconstructed largely on the basis of 1.3 VI 12-25.
Line 1. .̊: Only KTU reads the word divider before *ks*. The photograph shows the right-hand side of a vertical wedge.

Line 2. *b̊*: Only the two horizontal wedges are visible. CTA and V read this sign without qualification and KTU reads *b**. Context suggests the reading of *b* as well. The relative length and size of the two horizontal wedges compare well with the horizontal wedges of *b* in the following line.
l: All three vertical wedges are visible. A break or damage to the tablet has taken place just to the very right of the most right of the three vertical wedges. This damage obscures the head of this wedge, but the body of this wedge is clearly distinguishable from the middle vertical wedge. Context requires the reading as well. The two right-hand wedges are quite close together.
r̊: The bottom part of the head of the upper left-hand wedge can be read, as can the head of the lower left-hand wedge.

Line 3. *h̊*: The three horizontal wedges can be read, but the letter has suffered damage.
r: The head of the upper middle wedge is slightly damaged.
t̊: Only the head of the sign can be read. The rest of the sign falls within the broken right-hand side of the tablet. Context requires the reading.

Line 4. *k*: All read *k*, and KTU goes further in reading *ṯ** after *k*. The upper left-hand horizontal wedge's head of *k* is clear. There is space for the *ṯ* following *k*, but the damage along the right hand side of the tablet obscures the reading.
CTA reads a word-divider after *k*, but there is no word-divider.

Line 5. *ẙ*: The three right-hand vertical wedges of the *y* are barely visible while the three left-hand vertical wedges are legible. The reading is indicated by context.

Line 6. *n̊*: The head of the left-hand horizontal wedge is clear, but the rest of the sign is only partially visible. The reading is indicated by context.

Line 7. *y*: As with the *y* in line 5, the left-hand three vertical wedges are more compressed in length than the three right-hand vertical wedges. The reading is clear, except that it is difficult to distinguish clearly the head of the bottom left hand wedge.
b: Only the body of the bottom right-hand horizontal wedge is slightly damaged. A break in the tablet near the sign slightly overlaps with the area of the body of the bottom right-hand horizontal wedge.

Line 8. *n*: V and CTA read *n*, KTU *n**. Two of the three heads of the horizontal wedges are distinguishable, and perhaps a third can be discerned.

Line 9. .: The second word divider is unclear.
The end of the line has space for another sign, but the damage is too great to discern the reading. The reading *t* is possible. The shape looks like the head of the wedge here with the left corner of the *t* in line 20. It is uncertain, however.

Lines 10-16 are reconstructed on the basis of 1.3 III 18-29, IV 11-19; cf. 1.1 II 1-3, 21-23.

Line 11. *w*: V reads *w*, CTA *w!*, and KTU *w**. The head of middle horizontal wedge is large. Instead of *twtḥ ʾišdk* in this line, Dahood (1958:67-69) proposed to read *tptḥ ʾišdk*, literally "to open the legs," comparable to the Akk expression *pitû puridê*, "to open the legs, to hasten" (noted by *UT* 19.813). According to Dahood the most right-hand horizontal wedge is to be read as *t* and the initial three wedges to its left are to be read as a *p* rather than reading all four wedges as a *w*. Although the most proximate instances of *w* in the passage (in line 13) show the most right-hand wedge to be considerably closer in the putative *w* in line 11, other examples of *t* in lines 6, 8 and 13 are as close to other letters as the *t* in Dahood's reading *tpptḥ*. This issue cannot be resolved epigraphically.
ʾi: The sign is visible, but slightly damaged (especially the middle horizontal wedge).

Line 12. *d*: There are only two horizontal wedges.

Line 13. *k̊*: Only the body of the right-hand horizontal wedge cannot be seen, as it falls on the broken right-hand edge of the tablet. Context suggests the reading.

Line 14. *m̊*: Only the left-hand horizontal wedge's head can be seen. The rest of the sign falls on the broken right-hand edge of the tablet. Context requires the reading.

Line 15. *l*: Unlike other *l*'s (see lines 8 and 21), the left and middle wedges do not join at the heads.
d̦: There are only two horizontal wedges.
š̥: V reads *n/šm*, but CTA records *š* and KTU *š**. The WSRP photo shows only the left hand winkelhocken of the *š* sign. The sign is required by context, and is virtually certain due to the stance of the surviving wedge. The only wedge in this stance is the left-hand wedge of *š*.

Line 16. *ʾi*: The sign is legible, but not as clear as *ʾi* in line 19. The head of the middle horizontal wedge is a little obscure.

ǵ̊: Only KTU does not assign this sign to the reconstructed portion of the line. What the photo does show of this sign is the head of the single horizontal wedge of *ǵ*. The rest of the sign falls on the broken right-hand edge of the tablet. Context requires the reading.
The lacuna at the end of the line perhaps contains a reference to the location of where El will reveal the message to Kothar (perhaps using language in line 12a), to judge from the parallels in 1.3 III 30-31, IV 19b-20 (perhaps *ḫršn ǵr ks*?).

Lines 17-21a are reconstructed on the basis of 1.3 IV 32-36. See also the poorly preserved version in 1.2 III 2-3.
Line 17. [.]: KTU reads a word divider after *ḫss*, but the WSRP photo shows no word divider.

Line 18. *n̊*: V reads [*n*, CTA *n* and KTU *n**. The WSRP photo shows a head of a horizontal wedge, but the rest of the sign falls on the broken right-hand edge of the tablet. Context requires the reading.

Line 19. *ʾi*: The head of the lowest horizontal wedge is obscured by the head of the vertical wedge (cf. *ʾi* in line 21).
p: Compared to the *p* sign in line 20, the *p* sign in line 19 lacks only the ends of the bodies of the two horizontal wedges, which fall on the broken right-hand edge of the tablet. Context requires the reading.

Line 20. *t*: The head of the final *t* in this line is large compared to other *t*'s.

Line 21. *k*: All read this sign without comment. The right-hand horizontal wedge is distorted by damage on the surface.

Lines 21b-25 are reconstructed on the basis of 1.4 IV 20-26 and 1.6 I 32-38. See also the less well-preserved versions in 1.2 III 4-6, 1.3 V 5-8 and 1.17 VI 46b-51.
Line 22. *ʾi*: See the remarks on *ʾi* in line 19.
d: The middle horizontal wedge is unclear (see *d* in line 15).
k: The head of the lower left horizontal wedge falls in a break in the tablet.
š̊: V and CTA read *š*, KTU *š**. All the WSRP photo shows is the head of the left-hand winkelhocken. Context requires the reading.

Line 24. *l̊*: V and CTA read *l*, KTU *l**. The photo shows the left-hand vertical wedge, and part of the middle vertical wedge. Context indicates the reading.

Line 25. *ẙ*: V reads *[y*, CTA *y*, and KTU *y**. The photograph shows only the head of the top left vertical wedge. Context requires the reading.

Line 26. *l̊*: V reads *ʾi[*, CTA *ʾil[*, and KTU *ʾil**. *ʾa**. The photograph shows space for the reading (against V). The left-hand edge of the left-hand vertical wedge is visible; the bottom of the body of this wedge falls on the broken edge of the tablet. The context requires the reading *ʾil*.

Lines 27-29, or at least line 27, may be reconstructed on the basis of KTU 1.4 IV 51-55 = CTA 4.5.113-117 (Held 1965:273-74). See below for further discussion.
Line 27. *b̊*: V reads nothing, CTA *b*, KTU *b**. The WSRP photo shows the top left-hand vertical wedge and the head of the lower left-hand horizontal wedge. The reading is likely from context.

Line 28. .: Note the size of this word divider (cf. the word divider in line 29).

Line 30. KTU adds a space after *ʾa*, while V and CTA do not. The photograph indicates no such space.

Translation and Vocalized Text

El's Two Messengers Journey to Kothar

1*	[Then they surely head]	[ʾiddaka ʾal tatinā[73] panīma]
	[Toward the whole of divine Memphis]	[tôka ḥikupta ʾila kulla-hu]
1	[- Kaphtor] is the thro[ne of his sitting,]	[kaptā]ru kussi[ʾu ṯibti-hu]
	[Memphis his inherited land.]	[ḥikuptu ʾarṣu naḥlati-hu]
2	From a thousand acres, ten thou[sand hectares],	bi-ʾalpi šiddi ra[bbati kumāni]
	[At the feet of Kothar] they bend over and fall,	[lê[74]-paʿnê kôṯari] huburā wa-qîlā
3	They [prostrate themselves and honor him.]	ti[štaḥwiyā wa-kabbidā huwata]

The Speech of El's Messengers to Kothar

4	And they speak to Ko[thar wa-Hasis]	wa-ragamā lê-kô[ṯari wa-ḫasīsi]
5	[They address the Skilled One] of the Handicrafts:	[ṯanniyā lê-hayyāni] di-ḥarrāši[75] ya[dêmi]
	["Decree of Bull El, your Father,]	[taḥmu ṯôri ʾili ʾabī-ka]
6	Word of the Beneficient One, [your Scion]:	hawatu laṭipāni [ḥatiki-ka]
7	"...Kothar...[...]	...kôṯar$_{v}$...
8	Prepare to pour (?) [...]	šit lê-sikti (?)...
9	Prepare in the mountains (?) [...]	ʿudub bi-ǵūrāti (?)...
10	You hasten! You hurry! You r[ush!]	ḥāšu-ka ʿāṣu-ka ʿa[bāṣu-ka[76]]
	[To me let your feet run,]	[ʿimma-ya paʿnā-ka talsumāni]
11	To me let [your] l[egs] race,	ʿimma-ya tiwtaḥā[77] ʾi[šdā-ka]
12	[To the mountain,] Mount Ks.	[tôka ḫuršāni] ǵūri k$_{v}$si
	For a me[ssage I have, and I will tell you,]	dam ri[gmu ʾêṯa[78] lê-ya wa-ʾargumu-ka]

---

73 The dual number for El's legation is indicated by *bštm* in line 18.

74 For the vocalization *li* based on *le-*⌈e⌉ in Ugaritic syllabic form, see Huehnergard 1987c:142. Pardee (1988d:2) uses the vocalization *lê*.

75 The form is **qattāl* (*nomen professionalis*) as suggested by BH *ḥārāš*, "artisan"; Jewish Aramaic *ḥārāšāʾ*, "artist, artisan, carpenter."

76 These verbs are infinitives used as imperatives with second person sg. suffixes (Pope 1952:135; *CMCOT* 35-36, esp. n. 4). For *ḥš*, see above p. 145. Grelot (1956:202-05) compares Ugaritic **ʿṣ* with Syr **ʿṣṣ*, "compresit" as a biform of BH **ʾwṣ*, "to press" in Exod 5:13, but also "to hurry" in Josh 10:13. Grelot (1956:202-05; 1957:195) posits PS **ʿbḏ*, "to hasten" 〉 Ug **ʿbṣ* and **ʿbq* attested in Old Arm 〉 *lʿwbʿ* (Genesis Apocryphon 20:8-9) 〉 **ʾbʿ* (Jewish Arm). This development corresponds to the one proposed for PS **ʿḏ* 〉 Egyptian Arm *ʿq* 〉 **ʿʿ*〉 BA *ʾaʿ*, "wood" (*BDB* 1082).

77 For the form and vocalization, see *CMCOT* 37 n. 4.

78 According to de Moor (1965:357-58) and Rainey (1971:169), this word conjugates as a suffix verb, as is evident from the fem. sg. *ʾiṯt*.

13	A word and I will repeat to you:	hawatu[79] wa-ˀaṯanniyu-ka
	[The word of tree and the whisper of stone,]	[rigmu ˀiṣṣi wa-laḫšatu ˀabni]
14	The converse of Heaven [to Hell],	tuˀunatu[80] šamīma ᶜimma [ˀarṣi]
	[Of Deeps to Stars];	[tahāmātu[81] ᶜimmana kabkabīma[82]]
15	The word peop[le] do not know,	rigmu lā[83]-tidaᶜū našū[ma]
	[And earth's masses do not understand.]	[wa-lā-tabīnu hamulātu ˀarṣi]
16	Come and I will [reveal it]...'"	ˀati-ma wa-ˀanāku ˀibǵa[yu-hu]

Kothar's Answer

17	And Kothar wa-Hasis answers:	wa-yaᶜnî kôṯaru wa-ḫasīsu
	["Go, Go, Divine Servants!]	[likā likā ᶜananā ˀilīma]
18	You, you delay, but I, I [depart]	ˀattumā bāšatumā wa-ˀana [šanītu]
19	[Kaphtor] is indeed far, O Gods,	[kaptāru] la[84]-raḥāqu ˀilāmi
	Memphi[s is indeed far, O Deities:]	ḥikup[tu la-raḥāqu ˀilāniyyāmi]
20	Two lengths beneath [Earth's springs]	ṯinu maṯpadāmi taḥta [ᶜênāti ˀarṣi]
21	[Three], the expanse of caves."	[ṯalāṯu mataḥī] ǵayarīma

Kothar's Journey to El's Abode

	Then he indeed h[eads]	ˀiddaka la-yatī[nu panīma]
22	[Toward Beneficent] El the Kindly One,	[ᶜimma laṭipāni ˀi]li di-paˀidi
	Toward the mounta[in, Mount Ks]	tôka ḫuršā[ni ǵūri k$_v$si]
23	He enters E[l]'s mountain [and he comes	yagliyu ḏada ˀi[li wa-yabuˀu[85]]

---

79 The word is cognate with Akk *awatum*, "word." Obermann (*UgM* 37, 50) related the word also to Arb *hawwata*, "to call, shout" and to BH *tĕhôtĕtû* in Ps 62:4. Ward (1969) offers as cognates the Egyptian forms *hwt*, "to speak, shout" attested in the Coffin texts and Late Egyptian *hwt* meaning "to lament, wail."

80 The form *tˀant* is also attested (KTU 1.3 III 24). Blau and Loewenstamm (1970:22) note the problem of *ṯˀat* and *ṯˀut*. One might suggest that *tˀunt* is either a different form from *tˀant*, a "grafia arcaica" (Fronzaroli 1955:40), an oral (?) scribal error, or even less likely, an instance of regressive assimilation, i.e. **tuˀanatu* 〉 **tuˀunatu* (only the opposite form of vowel assimilation is attested in other Ugaritic nouns; *UT* 5.19).

81 The Ugaritic word is spelled syllabically *ta-a-ma-tu*$_4$ (*UgV*, 137 iii 34") indicating the vocalization *tahāmatu* (Huehnergard 1987c:184-85). Cf. Akk *tihāmatum* and Eblaite *ti-ˀà-ma-tum* (= *AB.A*); so Fronzaroli 1984:151. The first vowel in the Ugaritic form is due to vowel harmony with the following vowel, a phenomenon attested in a number of other Ugaritic nouns (see *UT* 5.19).

82 While Arabic, Ethiopic, Hebrew and Syriac show the dissimilation from **kabkabu* to *kawkab/kôkab* , Ugaritic and Mehri retain the reduplicated form (Fronzarolli 1955:67). Fronzaroli calls attention to the Ugaritic form *kkbm* which appears to be similar to the Akkadian assimilated form *kakkabu*.

83 For the vocalization based the Ugaritic syllabic form *l[a]-a*, see Huehnergard 1987c:141.

84 For the vocalization of the asseverative *l-*, see Huehnergard 1983:584.

85 The middle theme vowel is reconstructed on the basis of the same theme vowel in the Arabic prefix form. Cf. BH *yābōˀ* (〈**yabuˀu*). See Joüon 1991:1.221.

24	To the domicile of the King,] the Father of Years.	[qarša malki] ʾabī šanīma
	A[t El's feet he bows low and falls]	lê[-paʿnê ʾili yahburu wa-yaqîlu]
25	He prostrates himself [and honors him...]	yištaḥwiyu [wa-yakabbidanu-hu]

El's Speech to Kothar

26	Bull El [his father speaks (?)...]:	ṯôru ʾi[lu ʾabū-hu yaʿnî (?)...]
27	"Hurry, a ho[use may it be built,]	ḥūš ba[hatūma tubûna]
	[Hurry, may there be erected a palace]	[ḥūš turāmimuna hêkalūma]
28	In the midst of [...]	bi-tôka [...]
29	Build/son (?) [...]	b$_{\text{v}}$n [...]
30	I (?) [...]	ʾa[nāku?...]

Commentary

Poetic Parallelism and Word/Syllable Counts

	semantic parallelism	word/syllable count
1* [ʾiddaka ʾal tatinā panīma]	a b c	4/10
[tôka ḥikupta ʾila kulla-hu]	d e f g	4/10

There is sonant parallelism between the otherwise non-parallel terms, *ʾal* and *ʾila*. Furthermore, the consonants *k* and t resonate through the second line and echo the single use of these consonants in the first line.

1 [kaptā]ru kussi[ʾu ṯibti-hu]	a b c	3/9
[ḥikuptu ʾarṣu naḥlati-hu]	a′ b′ c′	3/9

The syntactical and morphological parallelism of this bicolon provides also strong sonant parallelism. The same formulas, though with different words for place, are attested in comparable form in 1.4 VIII 12b-14a and 1.5 II 15b-16. The two-place names in this case add further sonant parallelism, due to the three consonants which they share (*UT* 19.860).

2 bi-ʾalpi šiddi ra[bbati kumāni]	a b a′ b′	4/11
[lê-paʿnê kôṯari] huburā wa-qîlā	c d e e′	4/12
3 ti[štaḥwiyā wa-kabbidā huwata]	e″ e‴ d‴	3/11

Despite the semantic differences between them, the prepositional phrases connect the first two lines, while the verbs bind the second and third lines. The pronoun in the third line also refers back to the DN in the second line.

4	wa-ragamā lê-kô[ṯari wa-ẖasīsi]	a b (= x + y)	3/12
5	[ṯanniyā lê-hayyāni] di-ḥarrāši ya[dêmi]	a′ b′ b″	4/14

It would be possible to construe this unit as a bicolon by counting the second line as two lines, each with counts of 2/7. This count would differ from that of the first line significantly more than the count of 4/14 which results from construing the unit as a bicolon.

	[taḥmu ṯôri ʾili ʾabī-ka]	a b c	4/9
6	hawatu laṭipāni [ḥatiki-ka]	a′ b′ c′	3/11

The two lines have identical syntax, not counting the additional appositional term in the first line. Semantic parallelism likewise extends throughout. This strong balance is further enhanced by the relative proximity in line length. Although the first line has an additional word, the words in the second line are longer, thus maintaining balance in the length of lines.

7 . . . kôṯar$_v$. . .
8 šit lê-sikti (?). . .
9 ʿudub bi-ǵūrāti (?). . .

10	ḥāšu-ka ʿāṣu-ka ʿabāṣu-ka	a a′ a″	3/10

The unusual syntax of three commands in a row, each one with the same personal suffix, has a jolting effect that perhaps emphasizes the urgency of the message. Each one of three words bears the unusual form of imperative plus pronominal suffix referring to the addressee. The alliterative effect of the letters ʿ and *k* in the line is equally striking. This monocolon is prefixed to the following tricolon.

	[ʿimma-ya paʿnā-ka talsumāni]	a b c d	3/10
11	ʿimma-ya tiwtaḥā ʾi[šdā-ka]	a b d′ c′	3/9
12	[tôka ẖuršāni] ǵūri k$_v$si	a′ b′ (= x + y)	4/9

	dam ri[gmu ʾêṯu lê-ya wa-ʾargumu-ka]	a b c d e	5/12
13	hawatu wa-ʾaṯanniyu-ka	b′ e′	2/9

While the first line contains many more elements than the second, the second shows longer words: *hawatu* for three syllables compared to two for *rigmu*, and *ʾaṯanniyu* for four syllables compared to three for *ʾargumu*. The syntactical parallelism is close in this bicolon, and there is strong sonant parallelism between the otherwise unrelated sequences, *ʾêṯi lê-ya* and *ʾaṯanniyu*.

	[rigmu ʾiṣṣi wa-laḫšatu ʾabni]	a b a′ b′	4/10
14	tuʾunatu šamīma ʿimma [ʾarṣi]	a″ c d e	4/11
	[tahāmātu ʿimmana kabkabīma]	c′ e′ d′	3/11

Morphology provides an coherence in the first line in that all of its nouns belong to the type **qvtl*. This morphological features carries over into the second line with the forms *ʿimma* and [*ʾarṣi*] and in the third line in *ʿimmana*. Though the third line has fewer words than the second line, the third line balances with longer words.

15	rigmu lā-tidaʿū našū[ma]	a b c	3/9
	[wa-lā-tabīnu hamulātu ʾarṣi]	b′ c′	3/11

The two relative clauses governed by the negative particle *lā* and the verbs with the same prefix *t-* are the outstanding markers of coherence between the two lines.

16	ʾati-ma wa-ʾanāku ʾibǵa[yu-hu]	d e f	3/11

Given the parallels to this unit (KTU 1.3 III 28-31, IV 18-20; cf. 1.7.33), this colon likely concluded with the location of the revelation of the word, most likely on El's own mountain.

17 wa-yaʿnî kôṯaru wa-ḫasīsu

This unit is a speech-opening formula which appears to be extra-colonic.[86]

	[likā likā ʿananā ʾilīma]	a a b	4/10
18	ʾattumā bāšatumā wa-ʾana [šanītu]	c d c′ d′	4/13

While the two lines are disparate in most types of parallelism, sonant patterns provide some continuity between them: *ʿananā*. . . *wa-ʾana [šanītu]*; *ʾilīma* . . . *ʾattumā bāšatumā*; and *likā likā* . . . *ʾilīma ʾattumā bāšatumā* [*šanītu*].

19	[kaptāru] la-raḥāqu ʾilāmi	a b c	3/10
	ḥikup[tu la-raḥāqu ʾilāniyyāmi]	a′ b c′	3/12

The syntax and semantics are closely parallel. Besides the repetition

---

86 Such rubrics are regularly regarded as "extra-metrical." Given the problem of whether Ugaritic poetry is metrical in the technical sense (Pardee 1981a), I prefer to use the term "extra-colonic" for "extra-metrical."

of one of the same phrase, *la-raḥāqu*, sonant parallelism extends to the place names which share three consonants and the words for deities which also share three consonants.

20 ṯinu maṯpadāmi taḥta [ʿênāti ʾarṣi]	a b c	5/13
21 [ṯalāṯu mataḥī] ǵayarīma	a′ b′ c′	3/10

The syntax and consonance of the first two words in each line are the major features of parallelism in this bicolon.

ʾiddaka la-yati[nu panīma]	a b c	3/10
22 [ʿimma laṭipāni] ʾili di-paʾidi	d e f	4/12
tôka ḫuršā[ni ǵūri $k_v$si]	d′ e′ f′	5/9

23 yagliyu ḏada ʾi[li wa-yabuʾu]	a b c a′	4/11
24 [qarša malki] ʾabī šanīma	b′ c′ (= y + y)	4/9

Ugaritic parallelism customarily dictates the placement of the second verb with the second line, producing semantic parallelism: a b c//a′ b′ c′. In such a reading the length of line in this bicolon would be imbalanced, however, yielding counts of 3/7 for the first line and 5/13 for the second line.

lê[-paʿnê ʾili yahburu wa-yaqîlu]	a b b′	4/12
25 yištaḥwiyu [wa-yakabbidanu-hu]	b″ b‴ a′	3/11

The longer verbal forms in the second line balance the prepositional phrase in the first line, yielding proximate syllable-counts.

26 ṯôru ʾi[lu ʾabū-hu yaʿnî (?) . . .] a (= x + y). . .

27 ḥūš ba[hatūma tubnûna]	a b c	3/8
[ḥūš turāmimūna hêkalūma]	a c′ b′	3/10

28 bi-tôka [. . .]
29 b_vn [. . .]
30 ʾa[nāku? . . .]

Introduction

This column presents the mission of El's messengers to Kothar wa-Hasis, the Ugaritic craftsman-god, in three basic parts. The first part, lines 1* (reconstructed)-16, begins with the messengers' journey to Kothar's abode and their obeisance before the craftsman-god (lines 1* [reconstructed]-3). The rest of the first part (lines 4-16) relates El's message to Kothar that he should travel to the divine patriarch's mountain. The second part, lines 17-25, gives Kothar's response. He first tells the messengers that he will respond immediately and go to El, and then he departs. The third and most fragmentary part, lines 26f., seem to depict El relating specific instructions to Kothar for the construction of a palace, in accordance with the craftman god's role known also from 1.4 V-VII.

The first two parts might be viewed as exhibiting formal symmetry, more specifically an "envelope" structure:

A′ El's instructions to his messengers to travel to Kothar (lines 1*-3)
B El's message to Kothar to hurry to El's abode (lines 4-16)
B′Kothar's verbal response that he will go immediately to El's abode (lines 17-21a)
A′ Kothar travels to El (lines 21b-25)

Lines 1*-5

In this section El's messengers travel to deliver a message to Kothar, the Ugaritic craftsman-god. From the parallel formula found in 1.3 VI 12-14, it is possible to reconstruct a full line before the extant line 1: *ʾidk ʾal ttn pnm tk ḥqkpt ʾil klh*, "Then you shall surely head toward all divine Egypt." The phrase, **ytn pnm tk*, is an expression for departure towards a location which occurs about twenty-five times in Ugaritic. The verb-noun phrase literally means "to give face," and it has been rendered "to set the face toward." Here it is glossed by the more idiomatic English phrase "to head towards." Layton (1986:177) notes some Akkadian examples of this idiom (see EA 148:26-34; 151:37-40; cf. *AHw* 702). Layton (1986:175-76) also compares two biblical passages. Gen 31:21 reads: *wayyāśem ʾet-pānāyw har haggilʿād*, "and he [Jacob] headed toward Mount Gilead." According to the Qere of Dan 11:18, the king of the north "will head towards the islands and capture many of them" (*wĕyāśēm pānāyw lĕʾiyyîm wĕlākad rabbîm*). BH **ntn rʾš* in Num 14:4 might be compared as well: *nittĕnâ rōʾš wĕnāšûbâ miṣrāymâ*, "Let us face (literally, give the head) and return to Egypt."[87]

Lines 1*-1, reconstructed on the basis of 1.3 VI 12-16, provide the location of Kothar's homes (cf. 1.17 V 20-21, 30-31). The first is

[87] See *NJPS* 229 and n. a-a which compares this idiom in Neh 9:17.

called *ḥqkpt* and *ḥkpt*, two variant spellings for Memphis.[88] Like Amarna *aluḫi-ku-up-ta-aḫ* (EA 84:37; 139:8), the Ugaritic spellings are based on the Egyptian expression for Memphis, *ḥ.t k3 ptḥ*, meaning "the house of the ka of Ptah" (see Faulkner 1976:166; Rendsburg 1987a:94-95). The West Semitic form of the word (as represented by the Ugaritic) shows the loss of the final consonant. This apocopated form was the source of the Greek name, *Aiguptos*, which provided the basis for the modern English word, Egypt (Muhly 1977; see also Rendsburg 1987a:95 n. 23). The place is further called "all divine" (*ʾil klh*) and "the land of his family estate" (*ʾarṣ nḥlth*). The expression *ʾil klh* shows the piling of epithets to glorify the locale (for other examples, see KTU 1.3 III 29-31; Ps 48:2-3). The first is *ʾil*, the usual word for "god," but in this case it is a means of expressing superlative quality as in KTU 1.3 III 29, 1.4 I 31, 33, 34 (with emendation), 36, 38 and 41, and 1.17 VI 23 (cf. Thomas 1953:209-24). Gordon (*UT* 13.22) renders this use of *ʾil* as "glory" or splendour."[89] Gibson (*CML*^{2} 107) translates the word as "broad," which is similar to Clifford's rendering, "the whole land" (*CMCOT* 92; *TO* 178 n. g). The phrase *klh* is a postpositive expression, literally "all of it." Cassuto (*GA* 153) and Loewenstamm (*CS* 36-37) argued that *ʾil klh* represents "the god Kulla," but unlike this deity, the postpositive constructive is known not only in Ugaritic (KTU 1.6 I 37), but in other West Semitic languages as well.[90] Here attributed to a god's abode, the expression *ʾarṣ nḥlth* draws on traditional terminology for patrimonial land (see also 1 Sam 26:19; 2 Sam 14:16, 20:19, 21:3, etc.).[91]

---

[88] So Albright (1938:22), Ginsberg (1940), Eissfeldt (1944:84-94), de Moor (*SPUMB* 51) and Rendsburg (1987:95 n. 23).

[89] For this use of *ʾil* as a superlative, see 1.4 I 30-41; Pss 36:7; 51:19 (Dahood 1965:37); 80:11. For Akk *ilu* as superlative, see EA 35:20; *CAD* I:98. In general, see Thomas 1968.

[90] Coogan (1978:96) renders *ʾidk ʾal ttn pnm tk ḥqkpt ʾil klh* "then head toward Egypt, the god of it all". This rendering makes Kothar the referent of *ʾil klh*, but this interpretation ignores the immediate antecedent and the use of postpositive *kl*- plus pronominal suffix for places. For postpositive *kl* with suffix following place-names, see 1.6 I 65. BH examples include 2 Sam 2:9; Isa 16:7; Jer 18:31; Ezek 29:2; 35:15; Job 34:13 (de Moor and van der Lugt 1974:9). The construction also underlies Ps 29:9c. Aramaic cases are also attested: KAI 215:17; 222 A 5; Peshitta Lev 8:21; Peshitta Num 14:21 (Avinery 1976). KTU 1.14 IV 20 shows the temporal use of this construction. For further discussion, see Avinery 1976:25; Dietrich and Loretz 1984; Smith 1985:227.

[91] See Malamat 1962; Forschey 1973; Lewis 1991.

The GNs *ḥqkpt* //*ḥkpt* are appropriate for Kothar's residence in Egypt, as the names include the name of Ptah, the Egyptian god responsible for the crafts. The name of Kothar's Egyptian abode has been cited as evidence that the Ugaritic craftsman-god was probably identified with Ptah (Albright 1956:82, 210 n. 98; Coogan 1978: 118). There is some evidence that Kothar was known in Egypt. An ambiguous spelling of his name may appear in a late magical Egyptian text (Stadelmann 1967:123-24). According to "the Phoenician mythology according to Mochos" cited in Damascius' *De principiis* (Attridge and Oden 1981:102-03), Chousor was the first "opener." Assuming the West Semitic root**ptḥ*, "to open," Albright (*YGC* 196) argued that this title represents a word-play on the name of the Egyptian god, Ptah (see Eissfeldt 1944:94-100). Kothar's second home *kptr* is called *ks[ʾu ṯbth]* which expresses Kothar's dominion over the place. Kaphtor (BH *kaptōr*; Akk *kaptāru*) is generally identifed with Crete.[92] The double abodes have been explained as reflexes of metal or craft trade from Egypt and the Mediterranean Sea to Ugarit, as Kothar is imputed to be their divine patron.[93] Similarly, it has been argued on the basis of his foreign homes that Kothar was a god originally foreign to the Levant, but was secondarily imported. If so, this import was old relative to the Ugaritic texts. The texts from Ebla also attest to Kothar, spelled ᵈ*ka-ša-lu*,[94] which would suggest that this god was known in Syria as early as the late third millennium.

In line 2-3 the messengers bow down after a reference to a great distance. Gibson (*CML*² 55), Coogan (1978:96) and del Olmo Lete (*MLC* 161; cf. *TO* 178) view the distance as one which the messengers are to traverse. Noting the parallel between this passage and 1.4 VII 24-26, Ginsberg (*ANET* 138 n. 20) and Pardee (1975:344) see the reference to distance as the position from which the messengers are to bow down to Kothar (also Smith 1985:279). Pardee (1976:227) appeals to the context of 1.4 VIII 24, where the reference to distance occurs without **ytn pnm*; in this case the reference to distance is syntactically dependent on the following verb **hbr*, "to bend

---

[92] Strange (1980) argues for Cyprus as *kptr*, a conclusion which has been criticized by Astour (1982), Kitchen (1982) and others.

[93] For this theory, see *UgM* 14, 84; Rendsburg 1987a:95.

[94] Lambert 1988:143; Pettinato 1979:106; Pomponio 1983:145; Xella 1983: 282-90.

over.''[95] Yet the opposite syntactic situation obtains in 1.3 IV 38 = CTA 3.4.82; there the phrase, *bʾalp šd rbt kmn*, is dependent on **ytn pnm*, as the command to obeisance is absent from this context. It is evident that *bʾalp šd rbt kmn* constitutes a poetic line that could augment a bicolon into tricolon, either by fronting or following the bicolon. It could modify bicola describing either obeisance or duration of travel. The context of 1.1 III 2-3 and its parallel, 1.3 VI 24-26, may further illustrate the poetic malleability in the use of this line. The preceding bicolon referring to Kothar's abode elaborates the goal of the messengers' travel; this bicolon also interrupts syntactically the connection of *bʾalp šd rbt kmn*. Therefore, either *bʾalp šd rbt kmn* hinges syntactically on **ytn pnm* despite the interruption of the bicolon, but it is more likely that *bʾalp sd rbt kmn* is dependent upon **hbr*.

Loewenstamm (*CS* 246-48) compared this distance with the diplomatic gesture of obeisance ''at a distance'' (*mrḥqtm*) before royal figures mentioned in two Ugaritic letters, KTU 2.12.6-11 and 2.64.5-8. He also noted two literary contexts which use this language. In Gilgamesh 6.152-55, Gilgamesh and Enkidu ''drew back and did homage before Shamash'' (*ANET* 85). Exod 24:1 likewise contains the motif: ''The he said to Moses, 'Come up to the Lord, you and Aaron, Nadab and Abihu, and seventy of the elders of Israel, and worship afar off.''' These two passages reflect a correspondence of behavior exhibited before gods and kings. Like many other motifs in Ugaritic and biblical literatures, deities are revered as divine kings, and treatment appropriate for monarchs is accorded dei-

[95] Although this verb lacks a sound cognate, the root in 1.23.49, 55 refers to El's position in kissing, a prelude to copulation. The verb parallel in instances of obeisance is **qyl*, ''to fall,'' cognate with Akk *qiʾālu*, ''to fall'' (so von Soden 1967:295-96; *AHw* 918b) and paralleled by *maqātu*, ''to fall,'' in EA epistolary formulas (so Rainey 1974:304-05; for references, see Knudtzon 1915:2.1461). Arb *habru*, ''depressed land'' has been compared with Ugaritic **hbr* (*UT* 19. 745). Renfroe (1992:42-44) justifies the comparison as the Arabic and Ugaritic usages of **hbr* ''refer to 'depresssed' or 'lowered' physical and geophysical features.'' BH (hapax) *hāběrû* (ketib)/*hōbrê* (qere) in Isa 47:13 has been compared with Arb **hbr*, ''to divide'' (assuming no text-critical difficulty), but its relationship to Ugaritic **hbr* is unclear (see Blau 1957:183-84; Ullendorff 1962:339-40; cf. Dahood 1965:56). The forms *hštḥwy*/*yštḥwy* have been derived from the *C*-stem of **šḥy*, based on *šěḥî* in Isa 51:23, ''to bow down'' (Emerton 1977; *CML*^{2} 158), or **ḥwy*, ''to coil oneself,'' in the *Št*-stem (Lambdin 1971:254; *MLC* 546; Davies 1979; Gruber 1980:1.90-92; see also Kreuzer 1985:54-59). If the root were **šḥy*, the letter *w* in the plural forms remains to be explained, while there is no morphological problem with the root **ḥwy*.

ties in heightened form. In the Baal Cycle the command to make obeisance at a great distance is not in every instance a display of royal deference: in 1.4 VII 24-26 the messengers of Baal are warned to keep at a distance from the god of death, Mot, for the sake of protecting themselves from his deadly appetite. Yet as Ginsberg observes, the reason for obeisance before Kothar in 1.1 III 2-3 is not to be traced to some malevolent feature of his character. It would appear that the desire to secure Kothar's aid in building the palace of Yamm in 1.1 III 2-3 and the palace of Baal in 1.3 VI 24-26 inspires an act of divine courtesy. The great distance of a thousand *šd*'s and ten thousand *kmn*'s suits the superhuman scale of the divine realm, a feature attested also for the length of divine travel (1.3 IV 38 = CTA 3.4.82; 1.17 V 9-11) and the size of divine architecture (KTU 1.4 V 56-57 = CTA 4.5.118-119).[96]

Lines 4-6 relate first the messengers' speech to Kothar and then introduce the communication from El. The formulas in these lines echo Ugaritic royal correspondence. Reflecting epistolary idiom attested in Akkadian, the lingua franca of diplomatic correspondence, the formula, *l-X rgm tḥm Y*, "to person X speak: decree of person Y," opens numerous Ugaritic letters. Many of these texts contain formulas of prostration (see *CS* 256 nn. 4 and 4a).[97] One letter, KTU 2.13.1-8, illustrates the epistolary usage of the formulas contained in 1.1 III 2-6:

lmklt ʾumy rgm	To the queen, my mother, say:
tḥm mlk bnk	"Message of the king, your son:
lpʿn ʾumy qlt	'At the feet of my mother, I bow down.
lʾumy yšlm	To my mother may there be peace;
ʾilm tǵrk tšlmk	May the gods guard you and give you peace.'"

These letter formulas have been adapted to the correspondence between deities in the Baal Cycle.[98] The message to Kothar in 1.1 III,

[96] The terms *šd* and *kmn* compare with Akk *šiddu* and *kumānu*, which refer to measurements of land. At Nuzi they are approximately the same size (see Oppenheim 1946:238 n. 3; Speiser 1935:441; *CS* 36-37; *CAD* K:532a; Zaccagnini 1979:849-56). For *šiddu* at Emar, see Emar 2.12; 3.2, etc. Mishnaic Hebrew uses *kmn* for "soil, land" (S. and S. Rin 1967:184). Ward (1962:4-07-08) compares Egyptian *śdy*, "field," as well as *śdy.t*, "a kind of land," and *śdw*, "plot of ground."

[97] For cognates to Ug **rgm*, Rosenthal (1953:83-84) and Rabin (1963:134-36) cite Akk *ragāmu*, "to shout; bring legal action against," BH **rgn*, "to complain," Eth *ragama*, "to curse," and Arb *rajama*, "to curse."

[98] For discussion, see Rainey 1969:142; cf. *CS* 256-61.

like other openings to divine messages in the Baal Cycle, uses the epistolary terms *rgm* and *tḥm*. The introduction to the message to the craftsman-god here is further augmented by *ṯny* and *hwt*. An Ugaritic letter, KTU 2.72, illustrates the epistolary background of the word-pair, **rgm//*ṯny*: **rgm* is used for the initial message in KTU 2.72.6, followed in the next section by **ṯny* "to send a further message to" in KTU 2.72.12 (Pardee 1977:7).

In lines 4-5a the pair, *rgm//ṯny*, announces the addressee of the message, namely Kothar wa-Hasis, a "double-barrelled name" (Ginsberg 1944:25; *EUT* 44). Double-names are common in Ugaritic, and they refer to both single and double figures. Individual deities with double-names in Ugaritic mythology[99] include Qdš w-ʾAmrr (KTU 1.4 IV 13; Ginsberg 1944: 25; *EUT* 44), Nkl w-ʾIb (KTU 1.24.1), Mt w-Šr (KTU 1.23.8) and possibly Lṭpn w-Qdš (*EUT* 44, 55).[100] Gpn w-Ugr, as Ginsberg (1944) noted, constitute two figures like Shahar wa-Shalim in 1.23.52.[101] The god's first and main name, Kothar, was augmented with wa-Hasis, like some other double-names in Ugaritic religious literature. This process is evidently at work in the DN Nikkal w-Ib as well. The Sumerian goddess Ningal (literally "great lady"), corresponding to Ugaritic Nkl, bore the epithet *ilat inbi*, "lady of fruit," which provided the basis for the second element in her Ugaritic double-name (so *CML*², 31 n. 1; cf. *TO* 391 n. b). This process differs from the assimilation of two deities to a single figure, as argued for some of the double names noted above (de Moor 1971). Gordon (*UT* 8.61 n. 1) calls this latter phenomenon the "fusing of two names into one" (so also *CMHE* 49 n. 23; Barstad 1984:173).[102] Olyan (1988:10 n. 29, 40 n. 6, 55) variously labels this phenomenon a "fusion deity," "fusion-hypostasis" or "double-fusion hypostasis."[103] Olyan (1988:10 n. 29) comments further: "The 'combination' deity produced by this

---

[99] Double-names occur also at Ebla (see Pardee 1988b:146-47).

[100] Cross (*CMHE* 49 n. 23) includes Athirat wa-Rahm⟨ay⟩ (1.23.13, 24 [partially reconstructed], 28), but the second title may belong to Anat, as it does in 1.6 II 27, 1.15 II 6 and perhaps in 1.23.16.

[101] For further discussion of Ugaritic double-names, see de Moor 1970; for double-names in the Iron Age, see *EUT* 55-56; Barstad 1984:173; Olyan 1988:10, 40, 48, 55-56.

[102] Later instances of double-names may include *ʿštrkmš* in KAI 181:17. Both *ʿštrt* and *kmš* are known separately in other Iron Age texts (cf. Ugaritic *ʿṯtrt* and *kmṯ*). Cross (*CMHE* 49 n. 23) also lists *ʾtrʿtʾ* (Atargatis) and *ʾršp mlqrt*.

[103] Is Erragal in Enuma Elish 11:101 (*ANET* 94) a "fusion hypostasis" of Erra and Nergal? Speiser (*ANET* 94 n. 205) identifies him with Nergal, while Damrosch (1987:112) suggests Erra or Nergal.

fusion has independent existence from both of the two deities whose name it carries.'' Philo of Byblos (*PE* 1.10.11; Attridge and Oden 1981:44-45) interprets Kothar's double-name as two brothers.[104] The craftsman-god's names mean literally ''Skilled and Wise'' or a little less literally (taken as a hendiadys), ''Wise Craftsman.'' The first element of this double-name means ''Skilled Workman,'' like *mkṯr*, the ''skilled work'' which Kothar presents to Athirat in 1.4 III 30 after fashioning it in 1.4 I.[105] The second part of the name means ''wise'' one, like the second element in the name of Atrahasis, ''Exceedingly Wise.'' Ea, the craftsman of the Mesopotamian pantheon, is also called *ḫasīsu*, ''wise.''[106]

Line 4 also calls Kothar, *hyn*, ''deft'' one, which like his name *ḥṣṣ* reflects one of his professional qualities. H. Bauer (1934:245) noted the appropriateness of Arb *hayyin*, ''easy,'' to the craftsman-god. In the Targum to Prov 28:16, Aramaic *hawnāʾ*, ''ability, strength,'' translates *tĕbûnâ*, ''understanding,'' one of the qualities of the human craftsman Bezalel (Exod 30:3) who makes the furnishings for the tent of meeting (Gaster 1946:21 n. 4). According to Cassuto (1967:402), Bezalel is designed to stand in contrast or opposition to the idea of divine craftsmanship embodied by Kothar. Whether or

---

104 Clapham 1969:108; Attridge and Oden 1981:84 n. 69; Baumgarten 1981:170. Cf. the citation of El and Baetylos as two brothers in PE 1.10.16, perhaps reflecting Bethel as a hypostasis of El, as argued by Barré 1983:48-49; cf. van der Toorn 1992.

105 Cf. the syllabic form *ku-šar-ru* (for the spelling with double resh, see Huehnergard 1987b:210). The form is to be normalized /*kôṯaru*/ or less likely /*kuṯaru*/. Besides the evidence of Arb *kawṯar* and BH *kôšārôt* (Ps 68:7) noted by Huehnergard (1987b:141), the Amorite PN *kwšr* is attested in the Execration texts (Sethe 1926:46), as noted by Albright (1926:46; 1940:296-97 n. 47; 1956:81; 1968:136) and Goetze (1958:28), which militates in the favor of the first alternative. Cf. Eblaite DN ^{d}*ka-ša-lu(m)*. Cognates include: Akk *kašāru*, ''to repair; succeed, achieve; replace, compensate'' (*CAD* K:284-86); Amorite **kšr*, ''to be proper'' (so Gelb 1980:23); BH **kšr*, ''to be proper'' (Esth 8:5; Hebrew fragments to Ben Sira 13:4), ''to prosper'' (Qoh 11:6), ''to cause success'' (*C*-stem in Qoh 10:10), ''skill'' (Qoh 2:21, 4:4), ''advantage'' (Qoh 5:10); Palmyrene, Syriac, Mandaic, etc. **kšr*, ''to be proper,'' etc.; Arb *kaṯura*, ''to be or become much, numerous'' (Kraemer, Gatje and Ullman 1960:60-69). Due to the unexpected sibilant instead of the expected dental in the Aramaic forms, they appear to be a loan, either from Akkadian or from another West Semitic language with the sibilant. The basic meaning of the root appears to refer to ''skill'' or ''labor'' which have developed analogical meanings, ''to be proper'' or ''to prosper.'' For a full survey, see Smith 1985:51-79. For further bibliography on Kothar, see Pardee 1989-90b:454-55.

106 See Akk *ḫasāsu*, ''to think, remember; *ḫasīsu*, ''ear, understanding''; *ḫassu*, ''intelligent'' (*CAD Ḫ*:126). For discussion, see Smith 1985:51-81, 85-90.

not such opposition was deliberate, Kothar may have been the divine prototype for Bezalel. The two are West Semitic wise craftsmen summoned specially to build the divine abode.

The expression *dḥrš y[dm]* in line 5 means "skilled with two hands" (so *CML*² 55 n. 5), or "the one of handicrafts" or less literally "Handyman" (*Thespis* 163). It is either a separate epithet of Kothar, or it is part of a larger epithet linked to the preceding word, meaning "Hayyan of the Handicrafts" (so *ANET* 138; Rainey 1962:67-68). The relative particle *d-* would seem to indicate a construct phrase, and all of the occurrences of the epithet *dḥrš ydm* show *hyn* before it which might suggest that the phrase did not constitute an epithet separate from *hyn*. However, *hyn* is used without *dḥrš ydm* in 1.4 I 24, which might imply that these titles could be used separately or jointly. In administrative texts, *ḥrš* is commonly used for human craftsmen (Rainey 1962:67-68; *CUL* 265-66). The root may suggest not only craftsmanship in general, but also its magical character. Two ambiguous contexts containing **ḥrš* in Ugaritic mythological texts (1.12 II 61 and 1.16 V 26) suggest either craftsmanship in a narrow sense or a broader sense of magical craftsmanship. A semantic range of this sort is by no means unique. Akkadian *nēmequ* combines both "skill" and "sorcery" (Lichtenstein 1972:109 n. 99). Kothar's weapons in 1.2 IV are magical in character, and the artistry of other divine craftsmen such as Ea and Hephaistos sometimes shows magical properties.[107]

Lines 5-9

Following the introductory formulas of El's message to Kothar in lines 1-4, lines 5-9 present the first part of the body of the letter. A series of commands may be involved; unfortunately, the lines are too fragmentary to provide a sure description of their contents. The form *lskt* in line 8 may be the infinitive of the verb **nsk*, "to pour," which is attested in KTU 1.105.8 (RS 24.249.22′) and in line 2 of an unnumbered tablet published by Bordreuil and Pardee (1991-92:42-53). In these two instances, the root **nsk* refers to metallurgical activity (Bordreuil and Pardee 1991-92:48-49), which would suit Kothar in this context. It may be only guessed that if *bǵrt* in line 9

---

107 See below pp. 336, 341-43, 352.

means "mountains" or "hills" like *ǵr* in line 12,[108] then perhaps it refers to the location of Yamm's future palace, more explicitly mentioned in 1.2 III 7-11, or the source of the materials for the building as in 1.4 VI 18-21.

Lines 10-12a

These lines command Kothar to hasten to El's abode, for El has a further message to relate to the craftsman-god. Based on parallels in 1.3 III 8-31 and 1.3 IV 11-20, this passage expresses the message of cosmic peace to be achieved through Baal's demise and Yamm's victory and kingship. The fuller versions, even while allowing for variations, provide a reasonably detailed reconstruction for lines 10-16. The various versions also indicate that lines 10-12a and 12b-16 constitute two basic compositional units, since they appear separately. When the message is sent to Anat, it contains yet a third unit (1.1 II 19-21a; 1.3 III 14b-17).

The second part of El's speech to Kothar in lines 10-16 is one of the most beautiful compositions in Ugaritic literature. The passage, with more developed parallels in 1.3 III 20-31 and 1.3 IV 13-20 (*SPUMB* 106), informs Kothar to hurry to El, for El has a message of cosmic significance to impart to him. The first part of the speech in lines 10-12 forms a poetically dramatic message. First, there is the unusual monocolon of three words commanding Kothar to hurry himself (Watson 1977b:274). The rhythm of the monocolon perhaps conveys the urgency of the message. The emphasis is placed on Kothar's hurrying, introduced with the colon showing an unusual series of three infinitives (?) serving as imperatives with second masc. sg. suffix, prefixed to a colon stressing the parts of the body

---

108 The general meaning of Ug *ǵr* is evident from its parallelism with *gbᶜ* and *ḫlb* (*UT* 19.1953; de Moor 1965:362). The noun *ǵr* is often related to BH *ṣûr* (*UT* 19.1953; de Moor 1965:363; *MLC* 607), but Ug *ǵr* may be related to ESA *ᶜr*, "mountain" (Good 1981:119 citing CIH 74.4; cf. *BDB* 786) while BH *ṣûr* may be cognate with Ug *ṣrrt* (so Good 1981:119). If these etymologies are correct, it may resolve the etymology of BH *ᶜār*. It is a place-name in some passages (Num 21:15; Isa 15:1), but in other texts it is not a place-name, but a topographical feature, as in Num 21:18 where it is parallel with *bāmôt*, "high places." (*ᶜĀr* in Deut 2:9, 18 and 29 is ambiguous, although the third verse seems to reflect a place-name.) In either case, BH place-names based on natural phenomena such as hills is common and BH *ᶜār* may be derived from a noun meaning "height." For further discussion of Ug *ǵr*, see de Moor 1965:362-63; *SPUMB* 134.

which produce locomotion, namely "feet" (*pʿn*[109]) and "legs" (*ʾišd*[110]).

Using synecdoche to substitute a part for the whole (Segert 1979: 734), the tricolon names El as the goal of Kothar's hastening. While the word-order emphasizes El, the synecdoche focuses on the parts of the legs in accordance with the message of El. The legs are the parts of the body most visibly involved in producing locomotion and the synecdoche thereby emphasizes the urgency of Kothar's hurrying to El's abode.

A significant departure in 1.1 III 10-16 from the parallel passages is the name of El's mountain, called *ks* in line 12. The name of the mountain is often translated as "cup" on the basis of BH *kōs* and Akkadian *kāsu*. The usage has been explained variously as "possibly the cup of destiny which Ilu takes in his hand when he is going to bless someone" (de Moor 1987:20 n. 103). Or, *ǵr ks* is the mountain where El pronounces decrees, that is, the mountain where destinies are fixed.[111] Aistleitner (*WUS* 1350), Oldenburg (*CEBCR* 125), and Dietrich, Loretz and Sanmartín (1973:99 n. 21) identify *ks* with Greek Kasios and Latin Casius, the classical names for Baal's mountain, Mount Sapan; this view is rejected by Lipiński (1970:86, 88) and Clifford (*CMCOT* 39). This identification is defended on the theory that Baal took over El's mountain and gave it a new name. The Ugaritic texts do not provide any evidence for this reconstruction. Indeed, *ks* and Sapan occur as separate mountains belonging to two different gods in a single tablet, KTU 1.1, unlikely evidence that the two mountains were equated.[112]

A number of scholars identify El's mountain, *ks* with Mount *ll*, known from 1.2 I 20 as the meeting-place of the divine assembly, the Ugaritic Mount Olympus.[113] Two different names, *ks* and *ll*, would presumably represent separate mountains, although it is

---

[109] See *UT* 19.2076. According to Fronzaroli (1955:67, 80), Ugaritic *pʿn* shows phonological dissimilation of two bilabials from original **pʿm* as in Hebrew. Gordon (*UT* 19.1998) suggests BH *paʿam* is the result of congeneric assimilation of two originally different roots **pʿn*, "foot" and **pʾm*, "time," now conflated into a single form. For the verb **lsm*, see below p. 314; for **yḫy*, see *GA* 80; Renfroe 1992:156.

[110] Cf. Ugaritic syllabic spelling *iš-du₄* to be normalized /*ʾišdu*/; Akk *išdu*, "leg"; BH *šēt*; Syr *ʾeštāʾ* (*UT* 19.384; Huehnergard 1987b:111).

[111] So Lipiński 1970:86-88 who compares *kōsî*, "my cup"//*gôrālî*, "my lot" in Ps 16:5.

[112] For further discussion and criticisms, see below pp. 230-32.

[113] See below p. 285.

possible that the same mountain had two names. The descriptions of El's abode differ so markedly from the mountain of the divine assembly that the identification of the two peaks appears strained. It seems equally logical to interpret mount *ll* as the name of the mount of assembly and mount *ks* as the peak of El's abode. Biblical descriptions place the home of the divine council at the abode of El (see Ezek 28:2; Isa 14:13). According to Cross and some of his students,[114] this juxtaposition occurs not only in the biblical material, but also in Ugaritic tradition. The biblical identification may represent, however, a secondary development postdating the Ugaritic mythological texts (so *EUT* 68; cf. Lipiński 1971:35, 65-66), an alternative explanation which Cross (1981:171 n. 8) considers but rejects. Two names for the same mountain in the same corpus of Ugaritic texts seems unlikely unless multiple traditions about divine abodes are involved.

Lines 12b-16

Lines 12b-16 proclaim the cosmic importance of El's message, without revealing its content. The initial unit, a bicolon in lines 12-13a, begins with the particle *dm*, which links the previous commands to hurry and the following description of the message's universal significance. The particle functions perhaps like the English conjunction, "for." The noun, *rgm*, which refers to the message, fronts the poetic line. The word-choice echoes the diplomatic diction of **rgm* and **ṯny* in lines 4-6.[115] The relative clauses *wʾargmk*//*wʾaṯnyk* ending the two poetic lines of the initial bicolon in lines 12-13a reinforce that the message is El's.[116] The verbs have a further function, and that is to dramatize the unveiling of the message. It is a message reverberating around the universe, but not yet revealed. El is poised, ready to inform Kothar of the dramatic message. The prefix verbal forms at the end of the lines might be seen accordingly as ingressive in force: El is about to tell to Kothar.

The tricolon of lines 13b-14 elaborates the character of El's message, that it is one echoing throughout the cosmos. This unit con-

---

114 So *CMHE* 36-39; Clifford 1972:35-57; Roberts, *IDBS* 256; and Mullen 1980:146-47. See further below pp. 232-33, 286.

115 In 1.3 III 20-27 and IV 13-15 (reconstructed) following *brq*, *rgm* may have the further connotation of "thunder" (Pardee 1980:277).

116 Co-ordination with *w*- in these lines corresponds to relative *d*- in the parallel text, KTU 1.7.30 = CTA 7.2.18.

tinues the diplomatic language with the term, *hwt*, but abandons the diplomatic terminology by introducing a fourth term, *tʾunt*, "converse" (*GA* 127; *CMCOT* 68) or "murmuring" (de Moor, *TDOT* 6:32-33).[117] Rather than use the word *tḥm* as the fourth term for communication as in line 5 (albeit reconstructed), line 14 utilizes, *tʾunt*, a term unattested in Ugaritic diplomatic correspondence. This word shows that lines 12-15 transcend the immediate diplomatic context of El's communication with Kothar. Rather, they constitute a message which travels throughout the universe. The term *ʾarṣ* is ambiguous in this context. Elsewhere it refers to either "earth" (e.g., 1.3 VI 16; 1.5 VI 10, 14; 1.6 I 43, 65; 1.6 II 19; 1.6 III 9, 21; 1.14 I 29) or "underworld" (1.5 V 16).[118] The chiasm matches heavens with stars, and *ʾarṣ* with deeps. From these correspondences it would appear that underworld rather than earth is the more congruent match.[119] Despite the fact that the concept of Hell and some of its features developed considerably later than the Ugaritic texts, "Hell" has been chosen for the translation here because of its familiarity to English readers, its assonance with "Heaven" and its relative shortness in contrast with the usual translations of "underworld" and "netherworld." The merisma in lines 13b-14 cover the entire universe, including the regions named explicitly and the unnamed realms lying between them.

The "message" or "announcement" (*rgm*) of tree and the whisper (*lḫšt*) of stone is nature's secret language which conveys El's message. According to de Moor (1969:172 n. 31; *SPUMB* 108 n. 1), the ritual text KTU 1.82.43 cites the speech of trees and stones as favorable omens: *kʿṣm lttn kʾabnm tʾiggn*, "when the trees do not give (sound), when the stones do not murmur."[120] According to Watson (1988:43), "a tale of trees and whisper of stones" represents an

---

[117] Given the other parallel nouns, it would appear that another term for communication is indicated rather than "meeting" (see the proposals in Pardee 1975:378). For the variation in spelling, see Tropper (1990:366).

[118] Although the meaning "land" is the patent meaning in 1.5 II 16 and 1.6 II 19, paranomasia is involved as the "land" of Mot is the underworld. The double connotation of land and underworld underlies the word in 1.5 V 15, VI 8-9, 25, 27 (29 and 31 reconstructed), 1.6 I 8, 18, 1.6 II 16 (see Smith 1986a). For "earth" as underworld in Egyptian myth, see Hornung 1982:228. Many biblical examples have been noted (e.g., Exod 15:12; see *CMHE* 129 n. 62).

[119] So Dahood 1965:42; 1969; Scullion 1972:122.

[120] See also line 40 which de Moor reconstructs along similar lines.

instance of "metathetic parallelism," a form of synonymous parallelism where objects and their corresponding predicates are transposed. For Watson, "the imagery here is of the wind rustling the leaves of the trees and making them whisper." While this natural explanation is reasonable, the resulting "noise of the stones" remains unexplained. The reason for the references to "tree" (*ʿṣ*) and "stone" (*ʾabn*) as opposed to other natural phenomena is unclear.

Pope (1978) argues that these two words in KTU 1.23.61 refer to the distant reaches of civilization, but doubts that the two nouns in KTU 1.1 III 12-15 indicate that El's word is to cover the entire human world. Such a notion would comport, however, with the larger context of El's message. Batto (1987) compares the reference to stone in 1.1 III 13 to Job 5:17-23. The biblical passage lists numerous evils from which Eloah//Shaddai delivers the just one; these include death, the sword and famine. In the final verse the absence of these evils is linked to the covenant involving creation: "For with the stones of the field is your covenant, and the beast of the field makes peace with you." The personified stones enter into an agreement of peace, which marks the new and wonderful relationship between Eloah and humanity. Similarly, the stone and the tree in 1.1 III 13 communicate the peace which is to result from Yamm's dominion, signalled by the construction of his royal palace (*CMCOT* 69 n. 46). The aftermath of the announcement of divine peace and fructification inspires praise on the part of nature, including the trees of the forest (cf. Ps 96:12 = 1 Chron 16:33).

Like KTU 1.1 III 12-15, Jer 33:3 perhaps expresses the theme of the secret, divine message:

> Call to me, and I will answer you,
> And I will tell you wondrous things,
> Secrets you have not known. (NJPS)

Hos 2:21-22 has an elaborate form of this message (Batto 1987:189, 200):

> And in that day, says the Lord,
> I will answer (**ʿny*) the heavens
> and they shall answer the earth;
> and the earth shall answer
> the grain, wine, and the oil,
> and they shall answer Jezreel
> and I will sow him for myself in the land.

Both this passage and KTU 1.1 III 12-15 involve a message of divine fertility bestowed upon the universe. Hosea 2 locates the divine message in a different time and place than the Baal Cycle, however. For Hosea, the message of natural discourse involves a specific reference to Israel, embodied in the allusion to Jezreel. The time-frame also differs, for this message belongs to the future as in Jer 33:3. In the Baal Cycle there is no geographical particularity. Unlike Hosea 2:21-22, the message of the Baal Cycle is already "answering" around the cosmos; its realization is imminent. Isa 50:24 presents a description contrasting that of Hos 2:21-23. There is no "answering" of the heavens, as they lament infertility.

Other biblical passages alluding to nature's language are hymnic in character and might suggest a hymnic background for the Ugaritic language as well.[121] In Psalm 148 numerous parts of nature, including "all the stars of light" (*kol-kôbĕbê ʾôr*), "the highest heavens" (*šĕmê haššāmāyim*), "the waters beneath the heavens" (*hammayim ʾăšer mēʿal haššamāyim*) and "all the Deeps" (*kol-tĕhōmôt*), are to praise Yahweh because of the good which his dominion provides for "his people" (v 14). This theme is implied in El's message to Kothar: the message proclaimed in nature heralds Yamm's royal reign of peace. One biblical hymn often compared to this Ugaritic passage is Ps 19:1-4. As Cassuto (*GA* 128), Jirku (1951) and others observed, Ps 19:1-4 alludes to nature's secret speech which anticipates the revelation of the divine word: "The heavens are telling the glory of God..." (v 1), "their voice is not heard..." (v 4). The differences between KTU 1.1 III 12-15 and Psalm 19 are equally instructive (Donner 1967:327-31). The cosmic realm in 1.1 III 12-15 is rendered in less mundane terms than in Ps 19:1-4. The Ugaritic passage includes the dramatic image of the Deeps and the Underworld. Unlike the Ugaritic passage, this biblical passage refers to the firmament as well as the speech of personified Day and Night. From these and other texts, it might be argued that Ugaritic poetry seems more at home than biblical tradition with more descriptive renderings of the Underworld (see Tromp 1969).

Some rabbinic texts may offer parallels to 1.1 III 15's divine language expressed to nature. Cassuto (*GA* 127) and de Moor (*SPUMB* 108) cite Johanan ben Zakkai's knowledge of the language of palm-

---

[121] Cf. Pss 42:8, 96:10; and Isa 44:23, 45:19a and 48:16.

trees (b. Sukk. 28a; b. B. Bat. 134a). Of Hillel the Elder it was recorded that he learned the speech of mountains, hills and valleys, of trees and herbs (Sop. 16:7, cited in *GA* 127). De Moor (*SPUMB* 108) also compares b. Taᶜan. 25b: "When the libation of water takes place during the feast (of Tabernacles), one flood (*thwm*) says to the other: 'Let your waters spring, I hear the voice of the two friends.'" This passage may suggest that in Israel the water libation rite served as the ritual context for these descriptions of nature's secret speech which anticipate the impending appearance of natural fertility.[122]

The Ugaritic passage, its biblical and rabbinic parallels indicate that the language of nature presages cosmic well-being. Fertility is explicitly connected to the parallel of KTU 1.1 III in the divine message in 1.3 III and IV. Reacting to the message of cosmic importance, Anat responds in part with a wish for the appearance of fertility (1.3 IV 25-26a). While the contexts of 1.1 III and 1.3 III and IV differ in the means intended to achieve cosmic well-being, this concern underlies both instances of this message. El will inform Kothar of a message of cosmic importance; the building of Yamm's palace will inaugurate his divine reign and thereby facilitate cosmic peace (Batto 1987:199-201). When Kothar completes the palace of Yamm, his kingship will be established fully, and as a result harmony and fertility will be channelled to the cosmos. The explicit connection between fertility and temple-building is known from Mesopotamia, Ugarit and Israel. This association is explicit in Gudea Cylinder Seal 1, column xi (Thureau-Dangin 1907:100-04; Jacobsen 1987: 401-02)[123] and in Hag 1:7-11 and Mal 3:10, and this theme underlies KTU 1.4 V 6-9. In sum, the speech of nature anticipates cosmic harmony and well-being.

Line 15 does not contain one line attested in the two parallels from 1.3 III 26 and IV 17-18: *ᵓabn brq dl tdᶜ šmm*, "I understand the lightning which the heavens do not know."[124] The absence of this line from 1.1 III 12b-16 may stem from more than a variation in phraseology (Grabbe 1976:82). Rather, this line may be applicable only in a message concerning Baal, but inappropriate for a commu-

---

122 For this ritual in 1 Sam 7:6, 1 Kgs 18:30-35, and possibly Lam 2:19, see Barstad 1984:72 who also includes 2 Sam 23:16 and Jeremiah 14-15.

123 I wish to thank Professor Victor Hurowitz for bringing this passage to my attention.

124 For a defense of this view as well as the alternatives, see Smith 1984a.

nication regarding Yamm. The content of the line would suggest that Baal's lightning will accompany the building of Baal's palace but not that of Yamm (Smith 1984a:297-98). Otherwise, the two parallel messages share the secret of the divine palace, which will stand as a sign of divine kingship and prelude to cosmic peace.

Line 16 contains the final unit of the message. The initial word *ʾat* may be a noun such as "sign" in apposition to the preceding *rgm* in line 15 (*UgM* 50). Or, El orders Kothar to "come," which recapitulates the imperatives of line 10a. The following clause of line 16 begins with the first person pronoun, *ʾank*, before *ʾibǵ[yh]*, the 1 c. sg. prefix form (with 3 sg. suf.). The pronoun was unnecessary to make the statement intelligible; rather, the fronted pronoun emphasizes El's role in communicating the message.[125] The verb *ʾibǵ[yh]* in line 16 and in the parallel passage, KTU 1.3 III 29, has been often compared to the rare BH **bʿh*, "to ask" (Isa 21:12; Obad 6), Aramaic **bʿh*, "to seek," and Arb **bǵy*, "to seek, desire" (Wehr 68). The verb has been taken to refer to the process of "seeking" (*CMCOT* 70 n. 46; Dahood 1981) or "searching for" (*CML*[2] 49) "it," namely the antecedent, *rgm*, in line 15. According to Clifford (*CMCOT* 70 n. 46), *rgm* refers to a royal palace in 1.1 III 16 and in the parallel passages, 1.3 III 29 and IV 19 which the speaker "seeks":

> Baal does not yet have the temple, so is not in a position to reveal anything. Rather, he is about to seek it through Anat's intercession. So he is seeking the temple. . . and all the trapping of royal power. Such an interpretation fits also in 1.3.16 [= KTU 1.1 III 16] where El is going to arrange with Koshar wa-Khasis for the building of Yamm's palace.

Clifford assumes that *rgm* refers to the palace, but it is unlikely that it is a message which El seeks. Moreover, El does not seek a house in the same subservient manner which Baal must endure in 1.3 II-1.4 V. Nonetheless, this view remains plausible. Commenting on *ʾibǵyh* in 1.3 III 29, Pardee (1980:277) notes the contextual difficulty of Gibson's rendering, "I will search it out":

[125] See line 18 below and 1.2 IV 11, 19; cf. *ľikt ʾank* in KTU 2.72.20. In KAI 26 A II 5 Kilamuwa stresses his role in his achievements by proclaiming that they came to pass *wbymty ʾnk*, "in my days, mine" (for BH examples of this construction, see Muraoka 1985:61-66).

> For the life of me I cannot fit this translation in with G.'s [Gibson's] interpretation of the preceding lines, where the emphasis has been throughout on Baal's knowledge. It appears to me that we must either assume an ellipticised prepositional phrase: 'I will seek it out (for you)'—perhaps taking the verb as a D stem: 'I will have it sought (for you)...

Another approach renders the verb "to relate" (*GA* 128), based on Arb **nbᶜ*, "to flow" (Wehr 939)[126] or "to reveal" (*ANET* 136) on the basis of Arabic *fağa*, "to be revealed" (of a secret) (Caquot 1974:203; *TO* 166 n. l). While the latter proposal assumes a consonantal shift of bilabials, it admirably suits the context. Contrary to Clifford's objection that El would have nothing to reveal, *rgm* would then refer to El's message about the palace to be built. The lacuna in the second half of line 16 presumably gives the location of El's mountain as *ǵr ks*, provided already in line 12 and as suggested by the parallels with 1.3 III 28-31 and IV 18-20 (so *MLC* 161)

In sum, line 16 may be viewed as summarizing El's communication to Kothar in lines 10-15. The first verb ordering Kothar to come (*ʾat*), if correct, recapitulates El's instructions to hurry to him in lines 10-12a and the second verb focusing on the revelation of the word (*ʾibǵ[yh]*) reiterates the description of the cosmic word in lines 12b-15. In short, El seeks to reveal to Kothar the message of the palace and the universal fertility and peace which Yamm's new reign, marked by his new palace, will engender. While El's message conveys paradisial connotations, its content remains veiled. Kothar awaits further information in order to learn El's great secret involving the new palace.

Lines 17-21

These lines relate Kothar's response in formulas found in Anat's answer to Baal's messengers in 1.3 IV 31-36. Kothar first orders the messengers to "go, go," a double command paralleled in form in biblical literature, for example in Judg 5:12 and Song of Songs 7:1 (Pope 1977b:595). In the following bicolon in line 18 Kothar declares that the messengers delay while he himself departs. The fronted position of the pronouns, "you" (*ʾatm*) and "I" (*ʾan*) highlights the contrast between Kothar and El's messengers. The verbs

---

[126] *GA* 128 also cites Arb **nbg*, "to arise, emerge, come into sight" (Wehr 940) as a cognate, but this root would appear to be unrelated for semantic reasons. The claim that Arb **nbᶜ* is related to the Ugaritic form also appears unlikely given the irregular correspondence between gutterals.

likewise contrast the two parties, specifically the messengers' delay versus Kothar's departure.[127]

The next bicolon of lines 18b-19 presents a second statement of Kothar specifically regarding his homes in Kaphtor and Memphis, which are largely reconstructed in this column in lines 1*-1 and paralleled in 1.3 IV 34-35. The meaning and syntax in line 19 are difficult to interpret. Ginsberg's rendering of 1.3 IV 34-35, which is parallel to 1.1 III 19, reflects one approach. Referring to Anat's mountain, Ginsberg's translation (*ANET* 136; cf. Watson 1984: 334) points to the great distance to El's abode: "From (my) Mount to the godhead afar, Enbiba to distant divinity." Clifford (*CMCOT* 86-88, esp. 87 n. 59) suggests that the bicolon contains two rhetorical questions: "Is not Kaphtor distant from El, Memphis distant from the gods?" For Clifford, Kothar's home is distant from El, who has summoned Kothar and the other deities to the divine assembly. While Clifford's view assumes that other deities are in attendance with El, scenes of deities going to El's abode do no refer to other deities in attendance; this may attributed to either ellipsis or the absence of any divinities in attendance (Pardee 1980:279). Pope (1971:402) takes *ʾilm* and *ʾilnym* in 1.3 IV 34-35 as vocatives referring to the messengers of El. The words may represent not a question, but a statement, since the standard means of indicating a rhetorical question, zero-element before the first line and *hm* before the second (so Held 1969), is missing from the parallel to this bicolon in 1.3 IV 34-35. Furthermore, as Ginsberg's translation indicates, the parallelism of *ʾil*//*ʾilnym* may suggest generic meanings for both forms; the parallelism of "El"//"divinities" is unattested otherwise in Ugaritic texts.[128] Taking *ʾilm* and *ʾilnym* as vocatives avoids the awkward syntactic problem of Clifford's translation of *rḥq ʾilm*//*rḥq ʾilnym* as "distant from El"//"distant from divinities." Following Pope, the statements may be taken as declarative clauses with prefixed asseverative *l-* (so also Huehnergard 1983:583): "[Kaphtor] is indeed distant, O Gods"//"Hikup[ta is indeed distant, O Divinities]."

---

[127] For the verbs, see above p. 44.

[128] Cf. Ezek 28:2: "I am El, in the dwelling of the gods (*ʾĕlōhîm*); I dwell in the midst of the seas" (see *CMHE* 38 n. 151, 44). This passage is susceptible to other translations for *ʾĕlōhîm* (such as "divine," or less likely as a superlative).

Falling on the heels of Kothar's description of his own distant domiciles is a bicolon in lines 20-21a describing the distance between them and El's abode. The meaning of *mṯpdm* and *mtḥ* is not entirely clear although commentators generally agree that measures of distance are involved. Oldenburg (*CEBCR* 189 n. 1; cf. 118) takes *mṯpdm*, as "marches" from **ṯpd*, to stamp" (KTU 1.4 IV 29), although the verb has been taken to mean "to set" (Greenfield 1969:99; Renfroe 1992:112, 154). For *mtḥ* Oldenburg (*CEBCR* 189 n. 2) notes BH **mtḥ*, "stretch out" (Isa 40:22) and Arb *mataḥa*, "to be long." Less promising etymologies suggest topographical notions about *mṯpdm*. Pope (1977:581) cites Arabic **ṯpd* "used of lining a garment or reinforcing a coat of mail with an inner lining, suggests the sense of layers or strata." De Moor (1981:30-4) relates *mṯpdm* and *mtḥ* to BH *mšptym* and *špytm*, "donkey-packs" and BH *ʾmtḥt*, "saddle-bags," despite the irregular consonantal correspondence between the dentals in the first comparison. De Moor comments that these terms "may well have been used here as poetical designations of curved regularly layered geological formations." Renfroe (1992:112-13) is highly critical of de Moor's cognates. Renfroe notes that the two terms are strictly speaking not parallel and offers the following translation to illustrate his point:

> Two layers below the furrows of the earth,
> Three [layers below the furrows of the earth are]
> the expanse of caves/stretches of hollows.

With this rendering Renfroe follows the view that *ṯn mṯpdm tḥt [ʿnt ʾarṣ]//ṯlṯ mtḥ ǵyrm* in lines 20-21a and their parallel in 1.3 IV 35-36 refer to subterranean travel (*CMCOT* 86-88). According to Clifford (*CMCOT* 88), this "passage was created originally for Koshar wa-Khasis and then applied to Anat, hence the reference to the underground." According to this view, Kothar travels underground, perhaps on the understanding that the craftsman-god has an underground forge and therefore travels by subterranean routes to his destinations. De Moor (1981; 1987:13 n. 67) suggests that an underground route is taken in order to go unnoticed. Furthermore, de Moor takes *ʾilnym* in this passage as underworld deities in Ugaritic (1.6 VI 47; cf. 1.20 I 2; 1.20 II 2, 6, 9; 1.21 II 4, 12; 1.22 II 4, 6, 9, 11, 19, 21, 26), a meaning which might further suggest subterrranean travel since the dead were thought to dwell in the Netherworld below the surface of the earth. Whatever the interpretation of *ʾilnym* in this passage, the underground route may suggest the secret character of the travel. Clifford (*CMCOT* 88) points to underground travel in the myth of Ullikumi.[129] Watson (1984) points to Gilgamesh as another example.

E. Gordon (1967:70-88) has noted a geological formation which may have served as the basis for the notion of underground travel. He suggests that *dKAŠKAL.KUR*, an ideogram which appears in OB itineraries and Hittite treaties, stands for "road" plus "netherworld," and thus means "underground water-course."[130] In one treaty it stands between springs and the Great Sea. Gordon believes that underground water-courses, well-known especially in Turkey and northern Syria, form the basis for the idea of Etana's descent to the underworld. This formation may have served as the basis for underground travel in Hittite and Ugaritic sources. Given Renfroe's interpretation of *ǵyrm* as caves or hollows,[131] it may be that a subsurface feature may be indicated for *ʿnt* as well. If so, this word may mean "springs" rather than "furrows." This interpretation of subterranean travel has not met with universal agreement. Pardee (1981:27-28) translates the passage differently: "...by double strides (down) among the furrows of the earth, By triple stretches of lowlands." The evidence is not clear, but a subterranean route would be fitting, especially if El's plan is a secret as suggested by his speech to Kothar in 1.1 III 12-16. Moreover, it would fit the more common meaning of *tḥt* as "under" as opposed to "(down) among."

Lines 21-25

Immediately after his speech to the messengers, Kothar "then heads towards" (*ʾidk ytn pnm ʿm*) El, who in lines 21-22 is called *lṭpn ʾil dpʾid*, a phrase denoting his benevolence and sympathy (*EUT* 44). Bauer (1933:83) explained *dpʾid* based on Arabic *ḏu fūʿad*, "one who has a heart."[132] Personal names in a number of languages, meaning "El (God/the god) is gracious," convey a similar picture: Ugaritic *ḥnʾil*, *ḥnnʾil*, "El is gracious" (*EUT* 87; *PTU* 136); Akkadian Enna-Il, "Mercy-O-Il" (Roberts 1972:31); Phoenician *ḥnnʾl*,

---

[129] KUB XII 65 iii 2-4. See Güterbock 1951:155, lines A46'-C8'; Sieglová 1971:50-51. I wish to thank Dr. Gary Beckman for these references.

[130] Cf. the underworld deities called in *dKASKAL.KUR.ra.(meš)* in Emar 373.153 and 378.35′, 43′.

[131] For Arabic cognates, see Renfroe 1992:37, 112.

[132] For the first title *lṭpn*, see above p. 148.

ḥnwʾl (Benz 313); and BH *ḥannī-ʾēl*. This picture of kindly beneficient El appears in the longer biblical expression, *ʾēl rāḥûm wĕḥannûn* "God the Compassionate and Merciful," in Exod 34:6 and Ps 86:15 (*EUT* 15; Roberts 1976a:257).

Another standard epithet of El, *ʾab šnm*, appears for the first time in the Baal Cycle in line 24. The title is rendered by many scholars as "father of years" (*CMHE* 16; *TO* 59-60; Ullendorff 1978:23*; cf. Ginsberg 1936:164), despite the attestation of the Ugaritic feminine plural, *šnt*, for years. Cross (*CMHE* 16 n. 24) and Dahood (1965:49) suggest that the word has two plurals. According to Cross, the masculine is a frozen form in this title. Other translations include "father of exalted ones"[133] and "father of Šanuma."[134] The latter view is based on the figure of *šnm* in 1.114.18-19 who accompanies El in his drunken state; that the son is the one holding the father's hand when he is drunk is assumed from this filial duty as described in 1.17 I 30, II 5 and 19. This son is sometimes identified as a Cassite god, Shumaliya, but this interpretation is unnecessary and generally lacks for evidence. Citing the parallelism of "sons of God" and "the morning stars" in Job 38:7, Gray (*Ug VII* 90-91) insteads regards *šnm* and his brother *ṯkmn* in 1.114.18-19 as astral deities who are sons of El. It is plausible that El has sons with astral characteristics. Indeed, *šḥr* and *šlm* in 1.23.52-53 are astral children of El, and Job 38:7 would appear generally supportive of this idea. If the astral character of El's son, *šnm*, were clear, then the interpretation of *ʾab šnm* as "father of the exalted ones" would be supported further. Unfortunately, there is no other evidence for the astral character of *šnm*.

The interpretation of *ʾab šnm* as the "father of years" would comport with other information known about El. The great age of the god is conveyed in 1.10 III 6 (*EUT* 51; *CMHE* 15) where El is called "the ageless one who created us," *drd⟨r⟩ dyknn*. In 1.3 V 25 and 1.4 V 4, Athirat and Anat refer to El's grey beard, another indication of his advanced age. Athirat says to El: "your hoary beard indeed instructs you," *šbt dqnk ltsrk*. One stele from Ugarit has been taken to depict El as an ancient figure seated in his throne (*ANEP* 493; *EUT* 45-47; Niehr 1992). The Greek god, Kronos, equated with El in PE 1.10.16, 44, bears the epithet *ageraos*, "ageless" (*EUT* 35).

---

133 *EUT* 33, 61, 81; de Moor 1969:79; *CEBCR* 17-18; Wieder 1974:108-09. Wieder interprets *bqrb šnym* in Hab 3:2 as "in the midst of the exalted ones" analogous to *bqrb ʾlhym* in Ps 82:1.

134 Jirku 1970; Gordon 1976; cf. *ANET* 129 n. 1; Pardee 1988a:59 n. 274;1988c.

The biblical titles, *ʾēl ʿôlām*, "God/El the Eternal One" (Gen 21:33; *CMHE* 46-50) and *ʾăbî ʾad*, "eternal father" (Isa 9:5), and the picture of the white-haired "Ancient of Days, *ʿattîq yômîn/yômayyāʾ* (Dan 7:9, 13, 22; cf. Isa 40:28) are considered survivals of the Ugaritic picture of the aged El (Montgomery 1933:102; *EUT* 33; *CMHE* 16).[135] El's epithet, *ʾab*, "father," is widespread in the Ugaritic corpus. He is regularly called *ṯr ʾil ʾaby/ʾabh*, "Bull El, my/his/her father." The Ugaritic personal name, *ʾilʾabn*, also expresses the sentiment that "El is father" (so *PTU* 87).

These titles belong to lines 21-24 describing Kothar's arrival at El's abode. The description of arrival in these line has several lacunas, and the parallel passages do not completely fill these gaps. Lines 21-22a give El as Kothar's destination, and lines 22b-23 describe El's location more precisely. The first phrase, *tk ḫršn [ǵr ks]*, "to the midst of the mountain, [mount *ks*]," is reconstructed in part on the basis of the name of El's mountain given in line 12. That the name of the mountain suits this position within the topos of arrival may be seen from comparison with 1.2 I 20; in this instance *tk ǵr* + PN likewise parallels *ʿm* + title (cf. 1.5 II 14).

Little additional information concerning El's abode can be gleaned from the word, *ḫršn*. Akkadian *ḫuršānu* means "mountain" and "underworld," but it is thought that underlying the two meanings are two etymologically unrelated words, the latter being a loan from Sumerian *ḪUR.SAG* (*AHw* 359-60; *CAD* H:253-54). Eblaite attests *ᵈḫur-ši-in* (Pomponio 1983:144; Xella 1983:290), but little else is known about this divinity. Akkadian *ᵈḫuršanu*ᴹ are equated with Ugaritic *ǵrm*, "mountains" in KTU 1.118 = RS 20.24 line 18 (Herdner, *Ug VII*, 2). Ugaritic *ḫršn* is not unlikely a loanword from Akkadian, and despite their possible distinct etymological origins, they may have come to be associated. Pope (*EUT* 69-72) notes both meanings in his discussion of Ugaritic *ḫršn*. Cross (*CMHE* 39) also inquires into the relationship between the two meanings of the word: "One wonders what connotations it carried beside the usual meaning 'mountain.' Can it refer also to the place of the river ordeal (at the entrance to Sheol) as in Mesopotamia?" Similarly, McCarter (1973:407) suggests that "the river ordeal is

[135] Ps 102:25 presents a similar picture of the aged god; the verse proclaims "your years are throughout all generations," *bĕdôr dôrîm šĕnôtêkā* (Montgomery 1933:111; Greenfield 1987:555; de Moor 1987:16 n. 83). Job 36:26, Pss 10:16 and 90:1-4 also reflect Yahweh's old age (Roberts, *IDBS* 257; Greenfield 1987:555; de Moor 1987:16 n. 83).

understood to take place at the foot of the cosmic mountain, the source of the waters and the entrance to the Underworld." Neither Akkadian nor Ugaritic texts use this word in both of its meanings (cf. *CAD* Ḫ:255; Frymer-Kensky 1977:1.156); indeed, there is no Ugaritic text clearly describing the river ordeal.[136] Biblical references to the Netherworld with terminological parallels to El's abode, such as Job 28:11, 38:16-17, and Ps 18 (2 Sam 22):16,[137] could be explained by the idea that El's abode lies at the headwaters leading to the Netherworld.

The second stage of Kothar's arrival involves his entering the mountain of El in lines 23-24a. Both words in the phrase *ygly d̲d* have spawned numerous interpretations. The verb *ygly* is a verb of motion, perhaps best known for the BH meaning, "to go into exile," and its nominal form, *gōlâ*, is a standard BH term for exile. The background to this meaning lies in its usage primarily as a verb of travel. Pope (*EUT* 64) comments: "As a verb of motion *gly* usually refers to departure, but it may also refer to arrival, Amos i 5, or to both departure and arrival, Amos v 27 and Jer xxix 7, 14." This view accords with the Arabic cognate, *jālâ*, "to emigrate" (so *CML*² 144). The collocation of this verb with **bwʾ* in the next line likewise suggests a verb denoting arrival.

The noun *d̲d* in line 23 has been thought to represent a term describing El's home, like the parallel term, [*qrš*], in line 23b. Aistleitner (*WUS* 2712), Blau (1968:523 n. 5) and Greenfield (1969:97) relate *d̲d* to Akkadian *šadû*, "mountain."[138] Greenfield (private communication; cf. *EUT* 67) suggests the form *d̲d* was used instead of *šd* for Ugaritic "mountain" because Ugaritic *šd* (cf. BH *śādeh*, "field") was used for "field." Cross (1962:249-50; cf. *CML*² 145; Dahood 1965:56) reads the noun as *t̲d*, meaning "breast," as referring to El's mountain on the basis that "breast" and "mountain" are comparable in form. Clifford (*CMCOT* 52), subsequently followed by Cross (*CMHE* 36, 55 n. 43; 1981:171), understands *ygly d̲d* as "rolling back a tent(-flap)," based on the supposition that *ygly*

136 Cf. the Akkadian-Hurrian bilingual text attested at Ugarit, *PRU III*:311-33; see Frymer-Kensky 1977:1.248-51.

137 See below p. 227.

138 Ward (1962:408) relates Egyptian *śdy.t*, "mound, refuse heap, lump," to Akk *šadû*.

d̲d ʾil semantically parallels the following construction *wybʾu qrš mlk ʾab šnm*. The etymological basis for this view of *d̲d* is lacking (Renfroe 1992:97-99), however, and **gly*, "to roll back" (a tent-flap) is semantically distant from the meaning of this root in other West Semitic languages. Clifford's appeal to 1.19 IV 50 assumes a scribal error of *lhlm* to *lʾahlm* which is debated, though accepted by some scholars (e.g., *CML*² 121; *MLC* 399; Watson 1978).

Arb *d̲wd*, "to protect," has also been compared to Ugaritic *d̲d*. On the basis of this root, the translations "parapet" (*CEBCR* 106 n. 6) and "corral" (Dijkstra and de Moor 1975:192) have been suggested, and meanings with an architectural sense would suit the context. Renfroe (1992:99-102) criticizes appeals to Arb **d̲wd* , however, as the meaning "to protect" overstates the Arabic sense of the root. Renfroe suggests instead "encampment" on the basis of the rarely attested Akk *šadādu*, *sadādu*, "to camp." Like the comparison with Akk *šadû*, "mountain," Renfroe's proposed cognate supposes the correspondence between an Ugaritic *d̲* and an Akkadian *š*/*s*. Less convincing are comparisons of Ug *d̲d* with Arb *sadda*, "cold," hence "refrigerium" (*EUT* 68; Lipiński 1971:65-66); Hebrew *zdh* (Siloam tunnel inscription, KAI 189:3), putatively "fissure" (del Olmo Lete 1978:43; 1984:156-58); Egyptian *dʾdʾ*, "skull, head, peak (of roof, tent)" (so Watson 1978).

The entrance into El's *qrš* represents the last stage in travel before the standard gesture of obeisance. That *qrš* represents an architectural term, more precisely a tent of some sort,[139] appears evident from three types of evidence. According to Cassuto (1967:323) and Clifford (1971; *CMCOT* 52, 54), Ugaritic *qrš* and its BH cognate, *qĕrāšîm*, represent architectural terms describing the divine domicile. Following Cross, Clifford argues further that the descriptions, albeit different in type—the Ugaritic one being in the divine realm and the biblical one belonging to the human realm—are culturally related, since the biblical description of the tent of meeting (Exodus 36) may be traced to the presentation of El's home (*CML*² 53 n. 5). According to Cross (*CMHE* 321-22), the biblical "description of the Tabernacle goes back ultimately to Canaanite models of the (cosmic) tent shrine of ʾĒl with a solid framework, *qéreš*, Ugaritic *qaršu*". Second,

---

[139] *ANET* 133; *CMCOT* 52, 54; *CMHE* 36-39; Cross 1981:171.

the fuller description of El's abode in 1.3 V 26-27a also indicates that *qrš* is an architectural expression. After Anat enters El's mountain, she foregoes obeisance before El in this passage, perhaps because she is angry with him.[140] In any case, their conversation ensues at a distance, for "El answers from seven chambers, from eight closed doors" (*yʿny ʾil bšbʿt ḥdrm//bṯmnt ʾap sgrt*).[141] The words *ḥdrm* and *ʾap* point to the architectural character of El's abode. Finally, Pope (*EUT* 66), Cross (*CMHE* 72 n. 122; 1981:171 n. 9) and Weinfeld (1983:104) note that the West Semitic tale of Elkunirsa preserved in Hurrian-Hittite tradition (*ANET* 519) describes the home of Elkunirsa as *GIŠ.ZA.LAM.GAR* = Akkadian *kuštaru*, "tent," lying at the source of the Euphrates. The determinative *GIŠ* also indicates that the structure is wooden in character. The tent of El recalls other biblical descriptions of Yahweh's dwelling besides "the tent of meeting" (*ʾōhel môʿēd*), a technical term for the divine domicile. Biblical poetry attests the divine tent also in more generic terms. Greenfield (1987:551-54) compares Ps 15:1, which asks: "O Yahweh, who shall sojourn in your tent (*ʾohŏlekā*)? Who shall dwell on your holy mountain?" (cf. Pss 24:3; 27:6). The evidence from the Elkunirsa story bearing on the tent-structure of El's abode goes unnoted by Renfroe (1992:99) who compares *qrš* with Akk *karaš/su*, "encampment," which accords with his interpretation of *ḏd*. This suggestion suffers further in requiring a phonological irregularity between Ugaritic *q* and Akkadian *k*. In sum, coming to (**gly*) the *ḏd* may represent a stage of movement prior to the entrance (**bwʾ*) to the *qrš*, in which case *ḏd* may mean either "mountain" or or less likely "encampment" while *qrš* refers to El's tent.

Finally in lines 24-25, Kothar performs obeisance before El. The lines, partially reconstructed on the basis of parallel in 1.4 IV 23-26 and 1.6 I 34-38, are stereotypical. There is nothing distinctive about Kothar's bowing down before El, a sign of his superior rank. The West Semitic story of "Astarte and the Sea" offers a description of obeisance precisely as the act of lesser gods before their superiors. In this narrative, Astarte enters before the divine assembly, and members of the pantheon offer gestures of servitude before her (*ANET* 18):

---

140 See Smith 1984b.

141 KTU 1.3 V 25b-27a. For the semantic relationship between body-parts and architecture, see also Semitic **ṯǵr*, which often means "gate" (so Ug *ṯǵr* and BH *šaʿar*), but also "mouth" in Syr *tarʿāʾ* (with metathesis) and Arb *ṯaǵr* (*UT* 19.2721).

> And Astarte heard what the Sea [said] to her, and she lifted herself up to go before the Ennead, to [the] place, where they were gathered. And the great ones saw her, and they stood up before her. And the lesser ones saw her, and they lay down on their bellies. And her throne was given to her, and she sat down.[142]

The prostration of Kothar in 1.1 III 24-25 is precisely that of a lesser god before a superior god, in this case El.

Lines 26-30

Line 26 seems to introduce El as the subject, presumably of the speech that follows. In lines 27-29 El apparently commands Kothar to erect a palace for Yamm, to judge from additional evidence supplied by 1.2 III.[143] Lines 27-29, or at least line 27, may be reconstructed on the basis of KTU 1.4 IV 51-55 = CTA 4.5.113-117 (Held 1965:273-74):

[ḥ]š.bhtm.[kṯr]	"Hurry the house, Kothar,
ḥš.rmm.hk[lm]	Hurry, erect the palace.
ḥš.bhtm.tbn[n]	Hurry, the house you shall build,
ḥš.trmmn.hk[lm]	Hurry, you shall erect the palace
btk.ṣrrt.ṣpn	Amidst the recesses of Sapan."

On the basis of this parallel as well as KTU 1.4 V 18 = CTA 4.5.80, Obermann (1948:21; cf. Ginsberg 1948:144) reconstructed 1.1 III 27-29:

ḥš [rmm hklm]	"Quickly [erect a palace]
btk [ṣrrt ṣpn w]	In the midst [of the recesses of Sapan and]
bn [bt ksp wḫrṣ]	Build [a house of silver and gold.]"

In a more precise adaptation of the parallel of 1.4 V 51-55, CTA proposes to reconstruct:

ḥš b[htm tbnn]	"Hurry, let a ho[use be built]
[ḥš trmm hklm]	[Hurry, may a palace be erected.]"

Unlike the treatment by Obermann, CTA's reconstruction accounts for *b[* in line 27. Del Olmo Lete (1984:36) reconstructs *b[rq]*

For another word referring to both body-parts and architecture, see below pp. 349-51 regarding *tmnt*. A similar usage is attested by BH *regel*, "foot," which is applied to a part of a table (Exod 25:26; 37:13).

[142] The behavior of the great ones in this passage parallels Baal's posture before El in 1.2 I 21.

[143] See *ANET* 129. For a massive reconstruction, see del Olmo Lete 1984:36-38.

sent from El's message to either Kothar in KTU 1.1 III 10-16 or Anat in 1.1 II 17-23, compared to Baal's message to Anat in KTU 1.3 III 26 and reconstructed accordingly in 1.3 IV 17 (Smith 1984a).

Line 28 attests only *btk*, which would appear to designate the location for Yamm's palace, just as *btk* in 1.4 V 55 introduces the site where Kothar is to construct Baal's palace. What is to be reconstructed in the lacuna following *btk* can only be guessed, as the name for Yamm's site of enthronement is lacking from the Ugaritic corpus. It might be guessed that the building site is El's own mountain or another mountain, just as the parallels in 1.3 III 18-31 and IV 11-20 mention Mount Sapan as the site where Baal is to have his palace where he will manifest his rain and thunder.

Line 29 contains the word *bn*, either a further command to "build," or a reference on El's part to Yamm as his "son." All of these reconstructions assume that Kothar is commanded to construct a palace for Yamm. The import of *ʾa* in line 30 is impossible to determine.

KTU 1.1 II

Bibliography

Text Editions: Virolleaud 1938:91-93 + plate IX; CTA pp. 2-3 + figure 1 and plate I; KTU p. 3.

Studies and Translations: Aistleitner 1964:32-33; Caquot and Sznycer, *TO* 301-03; Cassuto, *GA* 166-69, 174; Driver, *CML*[1] 72-75; Gibson, *CML*[2] 130; Ginsberg, *ANET* 129; Gordon, *UL* 24; 1977:84-85; Jirku 1962:11-12; de Moor 1987:20-21; Oldenburg, *CEBCR* 189-90; del Olmo Lete, *MLC* 163-64.

Text

1 [. . .]ṃ̊ẙ.̊p̊ ʿ̊n̊k̊
2 [. . .]ḥ̊.ʾišdk
3 [. . .]r[. . .]ḥmk.wšt
4 [. . .]ẓ[. . .]rdyk°
5 [. . . . .]qnʾim
6 [. . . . .]šʾu.bqrb
7 [. . . . . .].ʾasr
8 [. .]m.ymtm
9 [. . .]°[. . . . .]kʾiṯl
10 [. . .]m[. . .]ʿ̊db.lʾarṣ

11 [. . .].špm.ʿdb
12 [. . .].tʿtqn
13 [. . .]šb.ʾilk
ḥẓr
14 [. . .]ʾin.bb.bʾalp
15 [. . .]n.ʿnt
16 [. . .]hwẙn.wy
17 [. . .]ṣ̊ḥ.tḥm
18 [. . .l]ṭpn.ḥtkk
19 [. . .]m̊t.štbʿp
20 [. . .].lkbd.ʾarṣ
21 [. . .]dm.ḥšk
22 [. . .]n̊k.tlsmn
23 [. . .]k̊.tk.ḫršn
24 [. . .]b̊dk.s̊pr
25 [. . .]°nk

Textual Notes

Lines translated and vocalized (below) prior to line 1 are reconstructed on the basis of the message in lines 14-23 and parallels in 1.3 III 20, 29. There is one question about the reconstruction. It is unclear whether *[ṯny lybmt lʾimm]* is to be reconstructed since the corresponding narrative omits this line, although it appears in the parallel in 1.3 III 12. *MLC* (163) reconstructs the line. For further consideration of the reconstruction, see lines 14-23 below.

Line 1. *m̊*: The lower half of the vertical wedge of the sign is visible.
ẙ: One of the three left-hand wedges is not visible.
p̊: The lower horizontal wedge is clear. The upper horizontal wedge shows a clear head and little evidence for the rest of the sign. The tablet breaks along the upper horizontal sign.
ʿ̊: There is room for this sign on the tablet, but this space is so damaged that the reading is based on context.
n̊: Two horizontal wedges are barely visible. A third may lie in the preceding damaged space in which the ʿ is assumed to be. Context requires *n* rather than *ʾa*.
k̊: Context assumes the reading of *k*, but only the head of the lower left-hand horizontal wedge of *k* is visible.

Line 2. *ḥ̊*: Only the winkelhocken (connected to the assumed horizontal wedge of *h*) is visible. Otherwise, the sign is unreadable, and other readings are possible, such as *q*.
d: The tails of the second and third vertical wedges do not go down as far as the first vertical wedge.

Line 3. *r*: For the most part this sign is visible. The left-hand edge of the tablet breaks along the edge of the heads of the most left of the upper and lower wedges of the *r*.
[. . .]: There is a lacuna between *r* and the next legible sign. The space is sufficient for reading two shorter signs as well as for one longer sign. V reconstructs *[. l]*. CTA has a word divider (which is not visible) and *[l]*. KTU also reads word divider plus *[ ]*.

ḥ: The lower part of the vertical wedge falls on a crack.
t: The form is poor compared to other examples of the letter.

Line 4. *ẓ*: So CTA and KTU. The lack of space between the horizontal wedges and the winkelhocken shows that the reading cannot be *p* as read by V. One may compare *pʿ* in KTU 1.1 IV 17, 19 and 29 where there is considerable space between the two letters. The angle of the winkelhocken also excludes the reading ʿ. The heads of the two horizontal wedges are damaged slightly, but still visible.
[. . .]: The lacuna between *ẓ* and the next legible sign is larger than the comparable lacuna in the preceding line. V reads space perhaps enough for two signs. CTA is more explicit leaving two dashes inside brackets, and KTU has left room enough to read two signs within its brackets.
°:There are remains of a sign on the right-hand side of the break, but they are illegible.

Line 5. *q*: The left-hand part of the horizontal wedge is unclear.

Line 6. *š̊*: The middle and right-hand wedges are visible, but the left-hand winkelhocken is barely visible.

Line 7. °: CTA and KTU read a word divider before the next clear sign whereas V does not. There may be a word-divider here. Before *ʾa* there are two vertical "nicks." KTU's *x* is based on this; i.e., they read the one closest to *ʾa* as the word-divider and the left-hand one as the end of the vertical wedge of an uncertain letter. The first one may be a word divider and the second simply damage to the surface. The KTU reading would require the divider to be very close to the following letters.

Line 8. KTU read an *m*. V's drawing has no letter. The so-called wedges fall in the damaged area where the writing surface no longer exists. (On the horizontal-looking "wedge," compare a similar looking crack in the area directly above the *m* at the beginning of line 10.) This so-called *m* is off the line and stands somewhat below it.

Line 9. KTU reads *]x[* in the lacuna on the left-hand side of the tablet.
k: The left lower wedge and the right-hand wedge are visible. The upper left wedge can hardly be seen. The head of the upper left wedge lies on the broken edge of the lacuna on the left-hand side of the tablet. Between the left bottom wedge and the clear horizontal wedge of the letter is a "chip" in the surface roughly shaped like a right-angle triangle (with 90° angle on the left). This partially obscures the bottom wedge.

Line 10. *m*: All of this sign can be seen except the head of the vertical wedge.
ʿ̊: For this barely visisble letter, V, CTA and KTU read ʿ. Other readings may be possible.
ʾarṣ: The letters are written closely to one another.

Line 11. .: The sign lies on the very left-hand edge of the tablet. CTA and KTU reads nothing. V records a word divider, which is possible. Compared to the word-divider after *m* in the same line, the wedge here is about the same size and in about the same position relative to the other letters.
p: The body of the upper horizontal wedge is slightly damaged.
.: This word divider is read by V, CTA and KTU. Compared to the word divider in line 10 (and others in the immediate vicinity of line 11), the word divider in line 11 lacks a substantial head.

Line 12. *n*: V, CTA and KTU all read *n*. The head of the left-hand horizontal wedge is clear. There are two internal "dents" which show the beginning of the second and third wedges.

Lines 13b-17a. The formulas are reconstructed on the basis of 1.4 IV 20-26 and 1.6 I 32-38. See also the less well-preserved versions in 1.1 III 21b-25, 1.2 III 4-6, 1.3 V 5-8 and 1.17 VI 46b-51.

Line 13. *š*: V reads *š*, KTU has *š** and CTA records *(ʿ/š)*. If one compares the stances of *š* in the preceding line and *š* in line 11, the sign here is not an ʿ, but *š*. What remains at the beginning of line 13 is the right-hand wedge of *š* which otherwise lies in the lacuna on the left- hand side of the tablet.
l: This wedge is recognized overwhelmingly by scholars as a scribal error for *d*. The form *ʾilk* is otherwise unknown in Ugaritic, whereas *ʾidk* is relatively common.

Line 14. *ʾi*: Only the bodies of the three horizontal wedges of the *ʾi* are visible. Neither the heads of these three wedges, nor the small vertical wedge of the *ʾi* sign can be seen. This sign could be an *h* instead of *ʾi*.
.: The word divider after *n* is read by V, CTA and KTU. Compared to the other word divider in this line, and the word divider almost directly below in the next line, this word divider is somewhat damaged.
ẓ: The two horizontal wedges before the winkelhocken are not clear. There appears to be either an area which has been chipped between the wedges or the scribe ran the wedges together (the writing is small and above the line, off to an angle). This results in what appears to be one large, fat wedge. Still, *ẓ* is the only likely reading.

Line 15. The beginning of the line presents problems for reconstruction. The idiom elsewhere for obeisance from a distance (1.1 III 2; cf. 1.3 IV 38; 1.4 V 24; 1.17 V 10) uses the expressions *šd* and *kmn* whereas the extent portion of the poetic line (in line 14) uses *ḥẓr*. The normal parallel term for *ḥẓr* is *bt* (Avishur 1984:540-41), though in the reversed order. The reconstruction here is offered most tentatively.
n: KTU reads *p]ʿ** before *m*, but V and CTA read *pʿ]n*. The tablet is broken right before *n* and shows neither room nor evidence for an ʿ according to the WSRP photograph.
ʿ: All read ʿ as required by context. The sign differs from ʿ in line 11 or 12. The top of the letter is damaged.

Line 16. *ḥ*: The right winkelhocken and the right-hand portion of the head of the vertical wedge are all that survive. The remaining wedges conform to the shape of the wedges of *ḥ* in line 17. All read *ḥ*, as required by context.
ẙ: This letter has only five wedges.

Line 17. *ṣ̊*: CTA and KTU read *ṣ*. V reads the letter within the reconstructed portion of this line. The WSRP photograph shows most of the right-hand vertical wedge of the *ṣ* sign. The top left- hand corner of the right-hand vertical wedge of *ṣ* is missing.

Lines 17b-23 are reconstructed largely on the basis of 1.3 III 13-17, 29 and IV 7-10 (see also line 27b-31a).
Line 18. *ṭ*: All read *ṭ* without difficulty. The end of the horizontal wedge touches the winkelhocken at about the middle of the lower diagonal as in the other instances of this letter. The reading is also indicated by context.

Line 19. *m̊*: Only the right-hand vertical wedge of *m* can be seen. The head is clear from the WSRP photo whereas the body of the right-hand vertical wedge is less clear. V includes *m* within the reconstructed portion of the line. CTA reads *m*

without qualification. KTU records *m**. The reading *m* is also required by context.
.: This word divider is large compared to those in lines 18 and 20.

Line 20. .: All read a word divider at the beginning of the visible portion of this line, but it is faint.
ʾa: The wedges are bunched together as at the end of 1.1 II 16.

Line 22. *n*: V reads the *n* as part of the reconstructed portion of the line. CTA reads *n* without qualification, and KTU has *n**. Only the right-hand horizontal wedge is clear (cf. the *n* at the end of the same line). The reading *n* is favored by context.

Line 23. *k̊*: V reads this sign as reconstructed, CTA has the sign without qualification, and KTU reads *k**. All that remains of the sign is the right hand tip of the body of the right-hand wedge. Context requires the reading.

Line 24. *b̊*: V read *by (?)]dk*, CTA *]bdk*, and KTU *]b*dk*. The signs *d* and *k* are clear. Before the *d* sign are the head of a vertical sign and part of the right-hand portion of the head of a horizontal wedge. Therefore, *b* is a possible reading.
d: There are only two horizontal wedges.
s̊: The top left-hand wedge is damaged.

Line 25. °: V reads *ym (?)]nk*, CTA *]nk*, and KTU *]m*nk*. The *n* and *k* signs are clear, but only the head of the vertical wedge is visible. Readings beside *m*, such as *g*, are possible.

Translation and Vocalized Text

El's Tells His Messengers The Message for Anat

[Then you shall surely head toward Inbb]	[ʾiddaka tatinā panima tôka ʾinb$_{v}$bi[144]]
[Across a thousand courts, ten thousand houses (?)].	[bi-ʾalpi ḥaẓiri[145] rabbati bahatīma (?)]
[At the feet of Anat bow low and fall,]	[lê-paʿnê ʿanati huburā wa-qîlā]
[Prostrate yourselves and honor her.]	[tištaḥwiyā wa-kabbidā hiyata]
[And speak to Adolescent Anat,]	[wa-rugumā lê-batulati[146] ʿanati[147]]

---

[144] The precise derivation of the name of the mountain is unknown. Dietrich, Loretz and Sanmartín relate it to Hurrian *en*, "Gott," + *paba*, "Berg," while Margalit derives the name from **nbb*, "to be hollow." See Pardee 1989-90b:482.

[145] The noun is used presumably as a collective.

[146] See above pp. 8-9 n. 20.

[147] The *Ugaritica V* deity-list provides the spelling *^{d}a-na-tu$_{4}$*, vocalized as *ʿanatu* (Huehnergard 1987b:161). Opinions regarding the etymology of Anat's name differ. Wood (1916:263) suggested that her name be related to **ʿny*, "to afflict," since this meaning accords with her martial character. Gray (1979:321) compares Arabic *ʿanwat*, "violence." Albright (1925:95-97) relates Anat's name to Arabic *ʿinâya*, "solicitude, providence," and other forms which he considers cognate. Following Albright's later views, McCarter (1987:148) connects her name with Akadian *ittu*, "sign"; hence the goddess is the sign of the presence of the god (for discussion, see Gray 1979:321-22 n. 42). Deem (1978:30) relates the goddess' name to a putative BH root **ʿnh*, "to love, to make love," and with an agricultural term *mʿnh/mʿnt*, "a turn of the plow, a furrow." On the basis of Anat's sexual activities,

[Address the In-law of the Peoples:]	[ṯanniyā lê-yabimati[148] liʾamīma[149]]
["Message of Bull El, your Father,] [Word of the Beneficent One, your Scion:]	[taḥmu ṯôri ʾili ʾabī-ka] [hawatu laṭipāni ḥatiki[150]-ka]
['Place in the earth war,] [Set in the dust love;]	[qiriyi(y)[151] bi-ʾarṣi malḥamata] [šīti bi-ʿapari-ma dûdayama]
[Pour peace amidst the earth,] [Tranquility amidst the fields.]	[saki šalama lê-kabidi ʾarṣi] [ʾarabb$_v$dadi lê-kabidi šadīma]
1 [You hurry! You hasten! You rush!]	[ḥūšu-ka ʿāṣu-ka ʿabāṣu-ka]
2 [T]o me let your feet [run], [To me let] your legs [haste]n...	[ʿi]mma-ya paʿnā-ka [talsumāni] [ʿimma-ya tiwta]ḥā ʾišdā-ka

3 ....
...your [f]ood (?) and drink (?)...
4 ....
5 .... [la]pis...
6 ...raise in the middle of...
....

Deem (1978:26) concludes: "It would appear, therefore, appropriate to seek an etymology of her name to reflect this aspect of love and fecundity." While a sexual connotation may be found in some passages with the root **ʿnh*, the passages cited in support of this view (Exod 21:10, 23:6, 18; Hos 2:16-17, 23-25) are difficult and have been interpreted in other ways. Finally, the apparently secondary connection between the name of the goddess and *ʿn*, "spring," in KTU 1.96.5-14 may be noted (for Anat and the springs, see Bordreuil 1990). On Anat, see P. L. Day 1991, 1992; Walls 1992. For further opinions, see Pardee 1989-90b:464-66.

[148] Many commentators render *ybmt* by "sister-in-law" (e.g., *CML*² 49; see *TO* 90-92). Noting that BH **yābāmâ* refers to a "widowed sister-in-law" while **yābām* refers to a "brother of a deceased husband," Walls (1992:94-96, 157) takes *ybmt* as a kinship term referring to "a non-blood related female living in the household—a female affine." He compares other terms of family relations which appear in DNs (see *CMHE* 11, 14). Without citing supporting evidence, P. L. Day (1991:145) suggests that *ybmt*, like *btlt*, expresses "the notion of childlessness."

[149] See Akk *līmu*, "clan" (including Emar 373.164 and 378.14; Fleming 1992:74; *CAD* L:198); BH *lĕʾōm*, "people" (*BDB* 522). See the parallelism with *hmlt* in 1.5 VI 23-24 and 1.6 I 6-7 (Walls 1992:96). As a result, the suggestion that *lʾim* is a divine name (cf. the PN Zimri-Lim, etc.) seems less likely. For opinions, see Pardee 1989-90b:459.

[150] See *CMHE* 15; Ullendorff 1962:341; Healey 1980.

[151] The consonantal form is *qryy*. The question is whether or not the final *-y* is a *mater lectionis* (as represented in this vocalization) or some other ending. So Blau and Loewenstamm (1970:27) argue that final *-y* is a "kohortativen Suffix" like BH *-â*. For discussion of **qry*, see below p. 203.

7 . . . bind . . .
8 . . . he will die . . .
9 . . . . like spittle[152] . . .
10 . . . . prepare (?) for the earth (?) . . .
11 . . . .
12 . . . . They/You will pass . . .
13 . . . .

El's Messengers Journey to Anat's Home

14 Then [they surely head toward] Inbb,	ʾiddaka [la-yatina panīma [tôka] ʾinb$_{v}$bi
15 Across a thousand courts, [ten thousand houses ?].	bi-ʾalpi ḥaẓiri [rabbati ba-hatīma(?)]
16 [At the fe]et of Anat [they bend over and fall,]	[lê-paʿ]nê ʿanati [yahburā wa-yaqîlā]
17 [They prostrate them]selves and honor her.	[yišta]ḥwiyāna wa-ya[kabbidāna-ha]

El's Messengers Delivers His Message to Anat

[And they lift their voice and de]clare,	[yiššāʾā gā-humā wa-ya]ṣūḥā
18 "Message [of Bull El, your Father,]	taḥmu [tôri ʾili ʾabī-ka]
[Word of the Bene]ficent One, your Scion:	[hawatu la]ṭipāni ḥatiki-ka
19 ['Place in the earth wa]r,	[qiriyî(y) bi-ʾarṣi malḥa]mata
20 [Set in the du]st love;	šīti bi-ʿapa[ri-ma dûdayama]
[Pour peace] amidst the earth,	[saki šalāma] lê-kabidi ʾarṣi
21 [Tranquility amidst the fie]lds.	[ʾarabb$_{v}$dadi lê-kabidi ša]dīma
22 You hurry! [You hasten! You rush!]	ḥūšu-ka [ʿāṣu-ka ʿabāṣu-ka]
[To me] let your [fe]et run,	[ʿimma-ya paʿ]nā-ka talsumāni
23 [To me let] your [legs hurry]	[ʿimma-ya tiwtaḥā ʾišdā]-ka
24 To the mountain [. . .]	tôka ḫuršāni [. . .]

. . . .

25 . . . .

Commentary

Poetic Parallelism and Word/Syllable Counts

	semantic parallelism	word/syllable count
[ʾiddaka tatina panīma tôka ʾinb$_{v}$bi]	a b c	5/14
[bi-ʾalpi ḥaẓiri rabbati bahatīma (?)]	d e	4/13

[152] De Moor (1965:363-64) compares Hittite *iššali-*, "saliva, spittle."

The first two lines are quite disparate on all levels of parallelism. Only the repetition of consonants *t* and *b* is somewhat impressive. It might be possible to view the second line as the first in a tricolon with the following two lines, as in 1.4 VIII 24-29, but the basic pattern operative in this bicolon appears in 1.3 IV 38.[153]

[lê-paʿnê ʿanati huburā wa-qîlā]	a′ b b′	4/12
[tištaḥwiyā wa-kabbidā hiyata]	b″ b‴ a′	3/11

The longer verbs and the independent pronoun in the second line balance the shorter verbs and the prepositional phrase in the first line. The repetition of *wa-* plus imperative heightens the syntactical parallelism. Connection between the previous bicolon and this one appears in the prepositional phrase *[bi-ʾalpi]* and *[lê-paʿnê]* which show considerable sonant parallelism.

[wa-rugumā lê-batulati ʿanati]	a b	3/12
[ṯanniyā lê-yabimati liʾamīma]	a′ b′	3/12

Besides the general syntactical parallelism, the consonants *m* and *l* especially bind the unit.

[taḥmu ṯôri ʾili ʾabī-ka]	a b c	4/9
[hawatu laṭipāni ḥatiki-ka]	a′ b′ c′	3/11

Apart from the virtual identical syntactical parallelism, *[ḥatiki-ka]* forms sonant parallelism with both *[taḥmu]* and *[ʾabī-ka]*.

[qiriyî(y) bi-ʾarṣi malḥamata]	a b c	3/10
[šīti bi-ʿapari-ma dûdayama]	a′ b′ c′	3/11

The bilabials, *b*, *m* and *p*, are especially prominent. The close syntactical parallelism is sharpened by the presence of preposition *b-* plus gutteral plus *r* in the prepositional phrase of each line.

[saki šalāma lê-kabidi ʾarṣi]	a b c d	4/11
[ʾarabb$_{v}$dadi lê-kabidi šadima]	b′ c d′	4/12

The long noun in the second line balances the verb and first noun in the first line. The identical phrase *[lê-kabidi]* in each line heightens the semantic parallelism. *[šalāmi]* and *[šadīma]* form sonant paral-

---

153 See above pp. 161, 168-169.

lelism and with *[lê-kabidi]* constitute an example of semantic-sonant chiasm.

This bicolon belongs thematically with the previous bicolon, and perhaps the direct objects and prepositional phrases in all four lines and the imperatives in the first three lines as well as the double *d*'s in *[dûdayima]* and *[ʾarabb$_v$dadi]* highlight the relationship.

1 [ḥūšu-ka ᶜāṣu-ka ᶜabāṣu-ka]	a a′ a″	3/10
2 [ᶜi]mma-ya paᶜnā-ka [tal-sumāni]	a b c	3/10
[ᶜimma-ya tiwta]ḥā ʾišdā-ka	a′ c′ b′	3/9

This apparent tricolon consists of a monocolon and a bicolon, as suggested by lines 22-23 below.

14 ʾiddaka [la-yatinā panīma tôka] ʾinb$_v$bi	a b c d	5/15
15 bi-ʾalpi ḥaẓiri [rabbati baha-tīma(?)]	e f g h	4/13
16 [lê-paᶜ]nê ᶜanati [yahburā wa-yaqîlā]	a b b′	4/13
17 [yišta]ḥwiyāna wa-ya[kab-bidānu-ha]	b″ b‴ a	2/12

[yiššaʾā gā-humā wa-ya]ṣūḥā

This line appears to be extra-colonic.

18 taḥmu [ṯôri ʾili ʻabī-ka]	a b c	4/9
[hawatu la]ṭipāni ḥatiki-ka	a′ b′ c′	3/11
19 [qiriyî(y) bi-ʾarṣi malḥa]mata	a b c	3/10
20 šīti bi-ᶜapa[ri-ma dûdayama]	a′ b′ c′	3/11
[saki šalāma] lê-kabidi ʾarṣi	a b c	4/11
21 [ʾarabb$_v$dadi lê-kabidi ša]dīma	b′ c′	3/12
22 ḥūšu-ka [ᶜaṣu-ka ᶜabāṣu-ka]	a a′ a″	3/10
[ᶜimma-ya paᶜ]nā-ka talsumāni	b c d	3/10
23 [ᶜimma-ya tiwtaḥā ʾišdā]-ka	b d′ c′	3/9

tôka ḫuršāni[

Introduction

The extant portion of this column has two main parts, El's instructions to his messengers for Anat and the messengers' execution of the instructions. The greatest problem in this column revolves around the nature of lines 3b-13b, which may or may not be part of the message. If it is, it is unparalleled, unlike the rest of the message which closely replicates 1.3 III 11-20 and 1.3 IV 7-12. Given the lack of parallel to the message in 1.3, it may be suspected that some piece of direct speech or narrative intervenes between the instructions to the messengers and their execution of the instructions. Some of the language in lines 3b-13b recalls 1.1 V-IV. Perhaps these lines contain a message informing Anat of Baal's status, presumably in a shorter form in constrast with messages given in 1.1 V-IV.

Lines 1-3a

These lines present El in mid-sentence, delivering instructions to his messengers to tell Anat to travel to his mountain. Following conventions well-known from other passages and based on the narrative description paralleling the speech in lines 14-21 in this column, del Olmo Lete (*MLC* 163) reconstructs the beginning of the column with one tricolon and five bicola in which El gives to his messengers directions to Anat's mountain, his commands to speak to her and the beginning of the message which resumes in the extant text in line 1.

Lines 3b-13a

These lines are very difficult. Although it is usually assumed that these lines continue El's speech to be delivered before Anat, there are no parallels which help to illuminate this section. Indeed, the parallel narrative of lines 24-25 in this column provides no help, as they are also extremely fragmentary. Rather, guesses are hazarded on the basis of the few preserved words.

Virolleaud and Cassuto reconstructed *[l]ḥmk*, "your food," in line 3, mostly because the following word, *wšt*, could be an imperative to drink; the reconstruction remains unsure.

Line 4 is unintelligible.

Line 5 may contain the word *[ʾi]qnʾim*, lapis lazuli, an opaque azure-blue semi-precious stone of lazurite. It was considered so valuable that the Ugaritic monarch ʿAmmiṯtamru once attempted to pass off fake lapis lazuli to his Hittite overlord, Tudhalias IV, who was understandably angry (see *PRU IV*:105; KTU 4.318; Pardee 1977:13). Real lapis was imported from Afghanistan (Herrmann 1968; Majidzadeh 1982). In 1.4 V 19 it serves with other materials for building Baal's palace, and here it may refer to material for Yamm's palace.

Line 6 contains **nš*ʾ *bqrb*, literally "to raise in the midst," assuming the two words belong together syntactically. If this phrase as well as line 5 concern the construction of a palace, they would belong to Yamm's palace mentioned more fully in 1.1 III and 1.2 III.

Line 7 contains a single word, ʾ*asr*, "to bind," also attested in 1.1 IV 9, 22.

The only intelligible word of line 8 is *ymtm*, which could be a verbal form of **mwt*, perhaps to be rendered "he will die" (cf. *TO* 302 n. f). Taken with *k*ʾ*i*ṯ*l* in line 9, used in 1.18 IV 24-25 to describe the death of Aqhat at the hands of Anat's henchman, Yṭpn, lines 7-9 here perhaps refer to El's intentions toward Baal; this is only a guess.

Lines 10-11 are unclear.

Line 12 betrays no clear idea unless the verb *t*ʿ*tqn* alludes to the passing of time as it does in 1.6 II 5, 26 and reconstructed for 1.1 V 3 and 16.

Line 13 is likewise unclear except for the final word which begins the next section.

De Moor (1987:20) interprets the section:

> . . . it seems that ʿAnatu has complained about other gods harassing her, presumably in connection with the building plans of her husband Baʿlu, which understandably excited envy. Ilu promises help and asks ʿAnatu to come to him with a list of materials needed for Baal's palace.

This view depends largely on reconstructed lines. It seems unlikely given El's support of Yamm in 1.1 IV that El would offer Baal help at this point in the narrative.

Lines 13b-17a

Line 13b begins the narrative describing the travel of El's messengers to Anat's abode, ʾ*inbb*. In the stereotypical language largely used in 1.1 III 1-3, 21-25, El's servants come to Anat and perform obeisance before her. The passage shows little departure from the usual language for the travel of divine messengers to, and prostration before, a superior deity. There is one difference in that this passage uses *ḥẓr*, "court," where the other exemples of this type-scene have *šd*, "field."[154] This passage uses an architectural term instead of the customary agricultural term.

Lines 17b-25

El's speech to Anat in this section has two parts. The first, lines 17b-21, commands Anat to desist from war, an activity characteristic of the goddess (1.3 II 5-16; 1.13.3-7; cf. 1.96.4-5). The second part of this passage, lines 21-23, orders her to hurry to El's abode. This second passage closely parallels lines 1-3 above and 1.1 III 10-12. Yet, unlike Baal's message to Anat in the fuller parallel passages, 1.3 III 13-31 and 1.3 IV 8-20, or El's message to Kothar in 1.1 III 12b-16, El here does not describe the cosmic importance of the message.

The first part is specifically addressed only to Anat, as in 1.3 III 14b-17 and IV 8b-10. There are two general approaches to the two bicola in this unit calling for cosmic peace. 1.1 II 19-21 is understood either as a rite leading to peace or as a call for Anat to desist from war. In accordance with the first view, Gibson (*CML*[2] 49; cf. *SPUMB* 102) translates:

> Put an offering of loaves in the earth,
> Set mandrakes in the ground,
> Pour a peace-offering in the heart of the earth,
> honey from a pot in the heart of the fields.

In this translation the two bicola are parallel and the objects of verbs represent consummable items.

The second view is exemplified in the translation of Goetze (1944):

> Remove war from the earth,
> Do away with passion!
> Pour out peace over the earth,
> Loving-kindness over the fields!

In this view the first bicolon is taken to contrast with the first one and the nouns constitute abstract qualities (Levine 1974:12).

According to Goetze and other scholars,[155] *mlḥmt*, *ddym* and *šlm* are abstractions, but for de Moor and others, they are consumable

---

[154] See above p. 195. On *šd*, see above p. 169.

[155] *ANET* 136; *GA* 91, 124-25; Goetze 1944; Levine 1974:12; Pope 1977:600; *MLC* 164, 183, 186.

items.[156] The first word is the only instance of the *m*- preformative of **lḥm* which otherwise means "to eat" in Ugaritic.[157] It is taken also as "war" on the basis of cognates in other Semitic languages (e.g., BH *milḥāmâ*). Under this view the line represents a summons to desist from battle (cf. Watson 1980:9). The parallelism of the verb **qry* with **šyt*, "to set," in the next line seems to suggest a comparable meaning, perhaps "put" (so *CML*² 49). The verb is parallel to the *C*-stem of **ᶜly*, "to go up," used for a sacrifice in 1.19 IV 22, 29.[158]

The second term, *ddym*, is unattested in Ugaritic literature apart from this message to Anat here and in 1.3 III 15, IV 9, 24, 29 (to be reconstructed possibly in 1.7.27; so *CUL* 182). The only other contextual parallel may be found in the Leiden Magical Papyrus dating to a New Kingdom period: "...ᶜAnat of ᵓ*Iddkn*; she bringeth seven jugs of silver and eight jugs of bronze and she poureth the blood upon the ground..." (Massart 1954). This passage may illustrate a ritual corresponding to the mythological description of Anat's setting *ddym* into the earth. Otherwise, *ddym* is attested only in myth. The word has been related to *ddyt* in the Egyptian myth of the "Deliverance of Humanity from Destruction" (see *ANET* 10-11; Fensham 1965). This story details how in the aftermath of creation, Re punishes the humanity's rebelliousness by unleashing the violent goddess Hathor. She is, however, too success-

---

156 *SPUMB* 102-04, with older commentators listed. See also *CML*² 51; cf. *TO* 163-64.

157 According to Swiggers (1981) nominal forms of this root often indicate the chief staple of various Semitic cultures: BH *leḥem*, "food, bread"; Arm *lḥm*, "food, victuals, fowl"; Syr *lḥam*, "cake, loaf of bread"; Arb *laḥm*, "flesh, meat"; Geᶜez *lahem*, "ox, cow"; Tigre *laḥmi*, "cow"; *laḥam*, a tree with edible fruit; South Arabic dialect of the island, Soqotra, *leḥem*, "fish, shark." For these forms, see also Krotkoff 1969; Ellenbogen 1977:93.

158 Rabin 1961:399; *SPUMB* 103; *MLC* 621. For this interpretation of the verb commentators appeal to Ethiopic ᵓ*aqāraya*, "to bear towards, offer" (Leslau 445; Fisher 1969:180-81) and Sabean **qrw*, "offer, dedicate (?)" (Biella 466) as well as Arabic **qry*, "to invite, receive as a guest." See Leslau 445; *SPUMB* 103; Pardee 1975:368; 1976:266; *CML*² 157; *MLC* 621. Pardee suggests that the *G*-stem of the root means "to meet" and the *D*-stem means "to offer." De Moor takes the meaning of the *D*-stem as "to bring (a sacrifice) to". The setting of a meal underlies the attestations of the root in the derived stems, with the Ugaritic usage showing a nuance of "offering" (as opposed to "invitation" or "banquet"). Rabin (1961:399) also compares Akk *karû*, "invite, summon," and *keretu*, "banquet." He takes **kry* in 2 Kgs 6:23 as an Akkadian loan.

ful, almost destroying humanity. In order to prevent humanity's utter annihilation, the other deities seek to trick her. The servants of Re add to beer[159] a red substance called *ddyt*, giving it the appearance of human blood. Seven thousand jars of the mixture are prepared, and Re has it poured out in the fields where the goddess is expected to appear the next day. At dawn she goes to the place and mistaking the liquid for human blood, she drinks it until she is drunk.

The character of *ddyt* has been debated. Earlier commentators such as Wilson agreed about the red color of the substance, but left open the question of whether it was a mineral or vegetable (*ANET* 11 n. 11). More recent discussion leans to the former view. According to Harris (1961:156-57), *ddyt* is a blood red mineral that was used as an astrigent or emollient. In his study of Egyptian materials, Lucas (1948:22) likewise identifies *ddyt* as a mineral. It would appear Ugaritic *ddym* is an item, perhaps a consummable intoxicant which one can "set in the dust" (*št bʿprt*) just as the Egyptian drink containing *ddyt* can be poured in the fields. The gemination of the first two consonants of Ugaritic *ddym* and BH *dûdāʾîm*, generally rare for Semitic languages, might suggest a non-Semitic origin (Greenberg 1950). In contrast, *ddyt* was indigenous to Egypt as shown by Re's instructions (*ANET* 11): "'Go ye to Elephantine and bring me red ochre (*ddyt*) very abundantly.' Then this red ochre was brought to him." Moreover, the form of the word is standard in Egyptian. In view of these facts, it would appear that Ugaritic *ddym* may be a loanword from Egyptian *ddyt*.[160]

BH *dûdāʾîm*, identified as "mandrakes" in the versions to Gen 30:14-16 and Song of Songs 7:14, is sometimes invoked in the discussion of Ugaritic *ddym*, despite the difference of spelling.[161] The biblical word may have no direct connection with either Ugaritic

---

159 For beer in ancient Egypt, see Lucas 1948:16-23 who compares it in both composition and method of preparation to modern Nubian drink called "bouza."

160 The difference in the spellings of the final consonant in *ddyt* and *ddym* (Harris 1961:156) requires explanation. Professor Robert Ritner informs me that the final *-t* ending was unpronounced during the New Kingdom period. Borrowed into West Semitic as *ddy-*, the final consonant of Ugaritic *ddym* may be either an enclitic mem or a dual/plural ending (marking abstraction?). I wish to thank Professor Ritner for his help in this discussion.

161 *SPUMB* 103-04; Pope 1977:648; Batto 1987:197-98; de Moor 1987:9 n. 44.

ddym or Egyptian *ddyt*,[162] and the account of *dûdāʾîm* in Gen 30: 14-16 would suggest a plant rather than a mineral. It has been assumed that both Ugaritic *ddym* and BH *dûdāʾîm* may be related to the Hebrew and Ugaritic root **d(w)d*, "to love." The association between the verb "to love" and a sexual stimulant such as mandrakes appears natural enough, but the unusual formation of *ddym* as well as *dûdāʾîm* may suggest that the semantic connection with this root is secondary. Perhaps due to either paranomasia or a folk etymology with **dwd*, "to love," Ugaritic *ddym* could connote either a love-inducing agent or love more generally.

The Egyptian myth of the "Deliverance of Humanity from Destruction" is connected to El's message to Anat not only by *ddyt/ddym*, but also in the larger type-scene. In both texts, a switch from the goddess' warring behavior to a peaceable one involves the pouring or placing of *ddym/ddyt* in the earth, despite some differences in how this outcome is achieved. Both goddesses manifest a warring disposition which has been viewed against the wider ancient Near Eastern background of battling goddesses (Fensham 1965; Pope 1977:648; P. L. Day 1991; Walls 1991). Like Anat and Hathor-Sekhmet, Indian Kali and Sumerian Inanna[163] are warrior goddess who battle humans, and in some passages they stand deep in their blood. These religious traditions differ in their treatment of this theme. The Egyptian version places this scene in the context of human origins, unlike the Ugaritic passage (cf. Batto 1987). Rather, El calls Anat to desist from combat in order to prevent her interference in his plans to elevate Baal's foe, Yamm, to the level of the cosmic kingship.

The third direct object in El's speech is *šlm*, rendered either "peace" in general or "peace offerings." While the first translation is based on the common Semitic **šalāmu*, "peace" (Goetze 1944; Levine 1974:12-13),[164] the second accords with *šlmm* attested in Ugaritic ritual texts (de Moor 1970b; Dietrich and Loretz 1981:84;

---

162 See the older discussions cited by Harris (1916:156-57) as to whether Egyptian *ddyt* was to be derived from BH *dûdāʾîm*.

163 Perhaps under the influence of the warrior-goddess Ishtar; see Hallo and van Dijk 1968.

164 Perhaps compare also Akk *šulmānu*, "greeting gift," a sign of homage to royalty as attested in Enuma Elish 4.134 (Levine 1974:16; Anderson 1987:36-39; cf. Weinfeld 1983b:99 n. 14).

cf. Janowski 1981). This derivation suits de Moor's view (1987:9 n. 44): "This is probably the mythological prototype of a ritual act performed in connection with the season of late ploughing (late autumn)." For de Moor (1987:9 n. 45) this line is "probably corresponding to the pouring of the oil of pacification in the actual ritual."

In accordance with the different views of the other direct objects in the two bicola, interpretations of *ʾarbdd* divide over whether it is an abstract quality or a consummable item (del Olmo Lete 1984:153). On the one hand, Goetze (1944) and Pope (1977:600) take *ʾarbdd* as "love," based on the parallelism with *šlm*, rendered as "peace" (Levine 1974:12-13). On the other hand, de Moor (1975; *SPUMB* 104) takes *ʾarbdd* as three words, *ʾar*, "honey," *b*- "from," and *dd*, "pot." Accordingly Gibson (*CML*² 49) translates *ʾarbdd* "honey from a pot." The word *ʾarbdd* has been interpreted also as an *ʾaqtilal* formation of *rbd*, "calm" (so del Olmo Lete 1978:40-42; 1984:154-55; for criticism see Renfroe 1992:83); as two words, *ʾarb*, either as a *C*-stem formation with ʾ ("the aphel") or an ʾ-preformative (elative) form of **rb(y)*,"to be much" and *dd*, "love," meaning "much love" (Dietrich and Loretz 1981:84)[165]; or as a Hurrian loan-word meaning "Liebes-Opfer" (Sanmartín 1976). While the *C*-stem formation with ʾ is generally not recognized as an Ugaritic conjugation, Ugaritic attests to both other ʾ-preformative substantives including *ʾalʾiy*, *ʾalʾiyn*, *ʾanhb* and perhaps *ʾamrr* and to double-words, such as *blmt*, literally "non-death." The interpretation of *ʾarbdd* as "much love" comports with the translation of *šlm* as "peace," and unlike other suggestions incurs no grammatical problems.

Given the wide divergence of the two main approaches to the objects in the two bicola, it would appear difficult to adjudicate their general meaning within the larger context of El's speech to Anat. On the one hand, the first three direct objects as well as the verbs which govern them may reflect consumable goods. Indeed, the parallel of Egyptian *ddyt* with Ugaritic *ddym* seems to require this view. Furthermore, Levine's suggestion that the first bicolon contrasts with the second bicolon appears unlikely; such contrasts are generally

---

165 Rather than a *C*-stem form with ʾ-prefix, the so-called "*ʾaphel*"; see del Olmo Lete 1978:40-42 for proposals.

rare in the Ugaritic poetry. On the other hand, the context suggests a more general call to peace. Given the apparent disparity between vocabulary and context, a third proposal may be suggested, namely that the vocabulary reflecting material items has been recast into a message of peace. While the modern philological enterprise chooses between consumable items or abstract meanings according to etymological grounds, the words may have connoted multiple senses despite the etymologically different origins of these senses; hence a term such as *mlḥmt* in this context perhaps connoted warfare as well as food. Likewise, *ddym* may evoke ritualistic connotations all the while expressing a call to peace. The same may be true of *šlm*, although the singular form of the noun is never used for peace-offerings in Ugaritic ritual texts. Similarly, *ʾarbdd* may mean "much love," perhaps constituting an abstract noun without any ritual connotations.

The message of peace to Anat should perhaps not be viewed only as a cessation of hostilities. Rather, the prevention of war anticipates and serves as prelude to the emergence of cosmic fertility, and it may be that the ritualistic connotations of the nouns may heighten the sense of impending fructification. The biblical parallels describing "the planting of peace" cited by Batto (1987) illuminate the dimension of fertility expressed in El's speech to Anat.[166] The biblical passages which Batto discusses herald a new era of peace to be established by Yahweh, much as the communiqués to Anat from El and Baal announce an impending epoch of cosmic harmony and well-being. Ezek 34:25-30 describes the removal of hostilities from the earth and the concomitant advent of paradisial conditions. Verse 29 (MT) reads: *wahăqīmōtî lāhem maṭṭaʿ lĕšēm*, "and I will raise up for them a famous plantation"; but LXX reads *phuton eirēnēs*, suggesting a Hebrew Vorlage **maṭṭaʿ šālôm*, "a planting of peace." Lev 26:3-6 speaks of nature cooperating to produce abundant harvests and elimination of conflict: *wĕnātattî šālôm bāʾāreṣ*, "And I will set peace in the earth" (verse 6). More explicit is Zech 8:10-12 which proclaims the idyllic future age when Yahweh will exercise definitive rule over the earth:

> For before those days there was no wage for man nor any wage for beast. To him leaving and to him entering there was no peace from the adversary, as I [Yahweh] set every man against his fellow. But I

---

166 Cf. the royal language of "the plant of righteousness" in Isa 11:1, etc. For a reversal of this theme in a royal context, see Jer 34:26.

> am not to the remnant of this people now as in those former days, oracle of Yhwh of hosts. For I will sow peace [Batto reading *ʾezrĕʿâ šālôm on the basis of LXX *deichō eirēnēn*]. The vine will give its fruit; and the earth will give its yield; and the heavens will give their dew.

Batto also cites intertestamental and NT parallels. 1 Enoch 10:16 God gives the order to the angel Michael: "Destroy injustice from the face of the earth. And every iniquitous deed will end, and the plant of righteousness will appear, and plant eternal truth and joy." In Matt 10:34 (cf. Luke 12:51) Jesus is quoted as saying: "Do not think that I have come to cast peace on the earth" (*balein eirēnēn epi tēn gēn*); I have not come to cast peace, but a sword" (see also James 3:8). According to Goetze (1944) the words to Anat are echoed in Luke 2:14 which heralds the era of Jesus:

doxa en hupsistois theō	Glory to God in the highest
kai epi gēs eirēnē	and on earth peace,
en anthrōpois eudokias	Among men goodwill.

Goetze proposed that Ugaritic *ʾarbdd* is semantically similar to Greek *eudokias*, "goodwill." In view of the biblical parallels cited by Batto, Goetze's interpretation is plausible, although the terms in Luke 2:14 do not use the specific language of the planting of peace.

Batto also notes biblical parallels to the motif of removing war from the earth (so also de Moor 1987:9 n. 45). Hos 2:20 describes how Yahweh "will break the bow and the sword and the battle (*milḥāmâ*) out of the land (*min hāʾāreṣ*)." Batto suggests that the latter prepositional phrase echoes the summons to Anat, *qryy bʾarṣ mlḥmt*. The biblical verse belongs to a longer passage, Hos 2:20-24, which contains other items paralleled in the speech to Anat in 1.1 II 12b-16. These include the motif of the heavens and earth answering (*ʿny), which corresponds thematically to *tʾaʾunt šmm ʿm ʾarṣ*, "the converse of the Heavens to the Earth" in 1.1 III 14, 1.3 III 24, IV 16. Both Dahood (1965:281) and Batto compare Ps 46:10 which also describes the cessation of war: *mašbît milḥāmôt ʿad-qĕṣēh hāʾāreṣ*, "he makes war to cease to the ends of the earth" (cf. Waldman 1978:84-85 n. 14). Zech 9:10 likewise promises "peace unto the nations." The biblical parallels illustrate the force of the announcement of peace: it calls for the end of conflict and anticipates the advent of tremendous human well-being and cosmic fertility.

The end of El's speech in lines 21b-24 calls Anat to hurry to his abode, just as he summons Kothar to hasten to his abode in 1.1 III 11-12a. She is to come to *ḫršn*, generally taken to mean "mountain." De Moor (1987:20 n. 103) suggests the possibility "mountain-range." In 1.2 III 12 El's mountain is called *ks*, which would indicate that *ḫršn* itself is not the name of El's mountain. This is apparently the reason for del Olmo Lete's reconstruction following *ḫršn* here (*MLC* 165):

[mi montana divina (?)],
[hacia el montre Kasu〉〉].

Little is understood of lines 24-25. Structurally they fall in the section of El's speech parallel in lines 3b-13a. It is unclear whether all of these lines continue El's speech or begin a response of the addressee or perhaps a short piece of narrative.

KTU 1.2 III

Other Numbers: CTA 2.3 = UT 129 = III AB C = RS 3.346 = AO 16.640 (bis).

Measurements: 60 by 69 by 9 millimeters.

Condition: This text consists of three fragments. It shows several large cracks as well as numerous smaller cracks and chips. The surface is chipped and effaced throughout. Some of the surface is blackened, a condition which, P. Bordreuil informs me, may be natural and not due to fire. The signs in some areas have deteriorated to such a point that some readings, though visible to Virolleaud, are presently unclear.

Find Spot: house of the Great Priest, "tranchée" B 3, point topographique 3, 5, 7 at a depth of .30-.40 cm. = point topographique 338, 343, 341 (Bordreuil and Pardee 1989:31).

KTU 1.2 III

Bibliography

Text Editions: Virolleaud 1944-45:1-12; CTA pp. 8-10 + figure 5 and plate II; KTU pp. 7-8.

Studies and Translations: Caquot and Sznycer, *TO* 121-26; Driver, *CML*[1] 76-79; Gibson, *CML*[2] 37-38; de Moor 1987:35-38; del Olmo Lete 1977; *MLC* 165-68.

Text

1]°°[ ]n[
2 kpt]r.lr[ḥ]q̊[.̥ʾilm ḥkpt.lrḥq]
3 [ʾilnym.ṯn.mṯ]p̊dm.t[ḥt.ʿnt.ʾarṣ.ṯlṯ.mtḥ.ǵyrm]
4 [ʾidk.]l̊ytn[.]pnm.ʿm[.ʾi]l.mbk[.nhrm.qrb.ʾapq.thmtm]
5 [ygly.]ḏlʾi[l].wyb̥ʾu[.q]r̊š̊.mlk[.ʾab.šnm.lpʿn.ʾil]
6 [yhbr̥.]wyql[.y]š̊tḥw[y.]ẘykb[dnh]ᵅ y[
7 [ ]k̊ṯr.wḫ[ss.]tbʿ.bn[.]bht.ym[.rm]m.hkl.ṯpṭ.[nhr]
8 [ ]°rt°.°[ ]tb°.kṯr[wḫss.t(?)]bn.bht[z]blym
9 [t(?)r]m̊m.hk[l.ṯpṭ].nhr.bt.k[ ]p°[
10 [ḥš.bḥ]th.tbn[n.ḥ]š.trm[mn.hklm.ʾalp.šd.ʾaḫd.]bt
11 [rbt.̥]k̊mn.hk[l]šbš̥°°°°lm[ ]lšdt[ ]mm
12 [ ]b̊ym.ym.y[ ]t.yʾ°°[ ]°°°.ʿṯtr̊.d°°[ ]
13 [ ]ḥrḥrtm.w°[ ]n.[ ]ʾiš[̥]h[ ]ʾišt
14 [ ]y.yblmm.ʾu[ ]°[̥]k.yr̊d̊[ ]ʾi[ ]n.bn̊
15 [tʿ?]nnnrt[.]ʾilm[.]š̊pš̊.tšʾu.gh.w[tṣḥ.šm]ʿ.mʿ[ʿṯ]
16 [tr.yṯ]ʾir.ṯr.ʾil.ʾabkl.pn.zbl.ym.lpn.[ṯ]pṭ[.nh]r
17 [ʾik.ʾa]l.yšmʿk.ṯr.[ʾi]l.ʾabk.lysʿ°°l°ṯ°[tk.lyh]p̊[k]
18 [ksʾa.]mlkk.lyṯbr.ḫṭ[.]mṯpṭk.wyʿn[.ʿṯtr].d[ ]k[ ]
19 [ ]°ḥ.by.ṯr.ʾil.ʾab[y].ʾank.ʾin.bt[.l]y[.km.ʾi]lm[.w]ḥ̊ẓr̊[.kbn]
20 [qd]šlbʾum.ʾard.bn[p]šny.trḥṣn.kṯrm[ ]bb[ht]
21 [zbl.]ym.bhkl.ṯpṭ.nh[r].yṯʾir.ṯr.ʾilʾåbhlpn̊[z]bly[m]
22 [lpn.ṯp]ṭ̊[.nhr.]mlkt.[ ]°m.lmlkt.wn[.]ʾin.ʾaṯt[.l]k.km]
23 [ ]°°zbl.ym.y°[ ]ṯpṭ.nhr
24 [ ]yšlḥn.wyʿnʿṯtr
25 [ ]°[ ]

Textual Notes

Line 1. V reads two horizontal wedges at the beginning of the line. Three are visible.
°: V's hand-copy reads *b*, CTA *b/d*, UT *]ab[* and KTU xd*. As the two right-hand wedges of *d* would fall in the lacuna, either *b* or *d* is possible.

Lines 2-3 are reconstructed on the basis of 1.3 IV 32-36 (*MLC* 165). See also the poorly preserved version in 1.1 III 17-21a.
Line 2. *r[ḥ]q̊*: CTA reads *r[ḥq]* while KTU has r*ḥ*q*[.i]l. One horizontal wedge

after *r* is clear. Judging from the position of the visible wedge, it belongs to *q*; hence *r[ḫ]q* may be read.
The wedge represented by KTU's reading *]l*[* is not visible to my eye.
Line 3. *]p̊dm.t[*: V's hand-copy shows a sign with two or more horizontal wedges, *ṯ*, a word-divider, *t* and *p*. KTU reads no signs in this line. CTA has *]m.t[* The heads of two vertical wedges are barely visible. The two horizontal wedges seen by V could belong to *b*, *d*, *ʾa* or *n*. The top of the vertical wedge of *m* is visible (presumably what V read as *ṯ*). The left-hand side of *t* is also visible. The readings are suggested also from parallel contexts.

Lines 4-6 are reconstructed on the basis of 1.4 IV 20-26 and 1.6 I 32-38. See also the less well-preserved versions in 1.1 III 21b-25, 1.3 V 5-8 and 1.17 VI 46b-51. Cf. the formulaic language in 1.1 II 13b-17a.
Line 4. *l̊*: V records only one horizontal wedge for *l*.
y: The letter is largely damaged now; V recorded all six wedges.
pnm: For the first letter the lower wedge is clear, but only the tail of the upper horizontal wedge can be seen. It is hard to distinguish the three wedges in *n* (so too V's hand-copy). The *m* is clear.
.: The word-divider following *pnm* falls in a blackened area.
ʿ: The letter is obscure on the right-hand side, but the rest of the wedge and its stance are standard for ʿ.
m: The top of the head of the vertical wedge is the only visible part of *m*.
Unlike KTU's reading *n[hrm.]*, V and CTA put *[nhrm.]* entirely in the lacuna. The wedges read by KTU are not visible. The word-divider before *[nhrm.]* read by V and KTU is also no longer visible.

Line 5. *ḏ*: Only the right-hand wedge is visible (so too V's hand-copy).
l: V's hand-copy shows three vertical wedges, but only two are presently visible. All commentators, including V, CTA and KTU, read *ḏd* for *ḏl* based on the parallel passages. The error is due to haplography of the three horizontal wedges.
r̊: Only the right-hand horizontal wedge is visible (in contrast to V's hand-copy where all five wedges are recorded).
k̊: Only the heads of the two left-hand horizontal wedges are visible (V's hand-copy shows only the bottom wedge). The head of the top horizontal wedge is smaller than that of the lower horizontal wedge.

Line 6. *l*: The bottom of the vertical wedges and one of its heads are obscure.
š̊: This wedge is blackened. The signs appear bunched together
w: V's hand-copy recorded all the wedges of *w* in *[y]štḥw[y]*, but now only the heads and part of the tails of the left-hand wedges are visible.
]°y[: CTA and KTU read *r* and *y* (KTU places a question-mark after *r*). CTA (p. 9 n. 4) notes the deterioration which these letters have apparently suffered since the time of V's hand-copy. CTA reconstructs the end of line 6 and the beginning of line 7: (6) *[ʾaḫ]r y[ʿn ṯr ʾil ʾabh (7) šmʿ lk]ṯr wḫ[ss]*.

Lines 7b-9 are reconstructed on the basis of 1.4 V 53-54.[1]
Line 7. *k̊*: CTA reads *k]ṯr* while KTU reads *]k*ṯr*. The very end of the most right-hand horizontal wedge is visible (so too in V's hand-copy) which justifies KTU's reading.
h: V records three wedges, but now only two are visible.
°: CTA reads *t]bʿ* (see CTA, p. 9 n. 5) while KTU reads *]t*b*ʿ*. V reads *ḥš[.t]b[n*

[1] See below pp. 235-37 for further discussion.

?]. The head of a vertical wedge along the left-hand edge of the tablet is followed by a winkelhocken. V takes these two wedges as the middle and right-hand wedges of *š*, while CTA and KTU regards them as the top right- hand vertical wedge of *b* and the winkelhocken of ᶜ. The angle of the stance of the latter fits an ᶜ and is not part of *š* (cf. the winkelhocken of these letters in lines 6, 8 and 10).
[ ]: CTA reads *b[n.]* while KTU reads *bn*[.]*. The second letter is not visible.
⟨*zbl*⟩?: It is tempting to emend *zbl* before *ym* due to the otherwise parallel wording in line 8 and on the basis of line-length ("*metri causa*").
[nhr]: At the end of the line V's hand-copy shows *]r*. CTA (p. 9 n. 7) notes that the letters of *nhr* are no longer visible. Cf. KTU's reading *n[hr]*. None of the wedges of *n* are visible to me.

Line 8. °: CTA has *(h/ʾi)rn.w[ʾ* closely followed by Gibson (*CML*[2] 37)'s reading *[-] hrn. w*. V and Driver (*CML*[1] 77 n. 9) read *[b]ʾirtk*, "[in] thy despite" (literally, "[against] thy breast"). KTU has *h*/i*rtx.w[*. The reading of the first letter cannot be adjudicated; the visible tails of the three horizontal wedges could suit either *h* or *ʾi*.
°: After *r* either *ʾa* or *n* is possible; the heads of at least two horizontal wedges are visible. Context suggests *tb*ᶜ.
°: Either *k* or *w* could be read on the basis of the heads of the two wedges following the first word-divider.
°: CTA and KTU read *tb*ᶜ while V has *tbr[k?]*. CTA (p. 9 n. 9) expresses doubts about reading ᶜ. The stance of the wedge would be uncharacteristic for ᶜ and accords better with a large horizontal wedge. Moreover, the two preceding horizontal wedges recorded in V's hand-copy are visible. Context suggests *tb*ᶜ.
ṯ̊: CTA reads *k[ṯ]r* while KTU reads *kṯ*r**. There is small circular chip in the surface on the right-hand side of *k* which extends to the space where *ṯ* is to be reconstructed. However, the heads of the vertical wedge and the left-hand point of the winkelhocken are partially visible, thus justifying KTU's reading.
[w]: V's hand-copy does not show *w*, and it is not presently visible although CTA reads *w[ḫss]* and KTU has *w*[ḫss]*.
[ ]bn: Both CTA and KTU reconstruct *[t(?)]bn* (KTU's reading of *b* is marked with *).
[z]: Though read by all, *z* is not visible to me. Context requires the reconstruction.
l: Only the heads are presently visible.
y: The left-hand wedges are unclear.

Lines 9-10a. These lines are reconstructed primarily on the basis of 1.4 V 53-54 (*MLC* 166).[2]
Line 9. *m̊*: Unnoted by V, CTA and KTU, the right-hand corner of the head of a vertical wedge precedes *m*. Given the parallel text, *m* is a most plausible reading.
.: There is a word-divider after *nhr* as read by KTU (against CTA).
.: V's hand-copy has no word-divider after *bt*, while CTA, Gibson (*CML*[2] 37) and KTU rightly read *bt.k*. CTA (p. 10 n. 2) expresses some doubts about the word-divider, but it is visible.
k[: After *k*, V reads the left-hand vertical and horizontal wedges of *b* or *d*, while CTA has a word-divider and KTU read no wedges. No wedges are now visible.
]p°[: For the end of the line CTA reads *[šp[*. The initial wedges presently visible are two small horizontal ones, which reflects the *p* read by CTA and KTU. These are the only wedges in V's hand-copy. What CTA reads as *š* seems to be some small damage on the tablet. Part of the head of a single horizontal wedge is visible after

---

2 See below p. 237 for further discussion.

p, providing some basis for KTU's reading *n**. According to KTU the final letters are *]p*n**. KTU reconstructs *[ṣrrt.ṣ]pn*, implying that Yamm's palace is to be built on Mount Sapan.[3] Or, the end of the line could be reconstructed equally well as *[ǵr.ʾil.lṭ]pn*.

Line 10. *h*: V reads the second letter as *h*, CTA gives either *h* or *m* as possibilities and KTU has *m* (for the difficulty of the reading, see CTA p. 10 n. 3). The three horizontal wedges of *h* are visible, and the letter perhaps represents the 3 masc. sg. pronominal suffix.
.: As seen by V, there is a word-divider after *h* (against CTA and KTU).
Lines 10b-11a. These lines are plausibly reconstructed on the basis of 1.4 V 56-57 (so KTU; *MLC* 166).
š: The right-hand edge of the middle vertical wedge and the head of the right-hand wedge are visible.
m: Most of the vertical wedge and part of the left-hand side of the head are visible.
t: Most of the head remains visible (cf. CTA p. 10 n. 4).

Line 11. *k̊*: All read *k*, which has suffered badly from a crack. Most of the heads of the wedges are no longer visible.
CTA reads a word-divider after *k* while KTU rightly does not.
mn.h: CTA reads *mnh[– –]* while KTU reads *mn[.]h*k*[l]s*. For *n* V reads only a single wedge, but two wedges are visible. After them is the head of a vertical wedge, possibly a word-divider. The tails of the three horizontal wedges of *h* are visible.
Lines 11b-14a. For this very difficult section, see the different readings listed in del Olmo Lete 1977:45-46.
šbš: KTU adds a word-divider after *š*, while V and CTA do not. No word-divider is presently visible.
°°°°: The signs after *šbš* are very difficult to read. V read *[. . .]bt b(?)*. CTA and KTU read only *t*. I see a single horizontal wedge (*t*?), then *ʾu*, another single horizontal wedge (*t*?) and the right-hand side of a wedge. The sign which V read as a *b* and I see as *ʾu* lacks two of the three horizontal wedges of *d*, but the sign is very damaged and it is impossible to be sure.
°: While V, CTA and KTU all read *ǵlm*, the first sign is very unclear. CTA and KTU both place a question-mark after the word-divider following *°lm*. V's hand-copy shows no wedge, but a damaged space.
[ ]: CTA and KTU read *y*, while V records a single vertical wedge. The wedge is not visible.
m: The present remains of the first *m* is the very end of the horizontal wedge and all of the vertical wedge.

Line 12. *b̊*: All read *b* as the first letter in the line. The sign falls on the left-hand edge of a lacuna, and it would be possible to read instead *d̊*.
y: The second *y* has a vertical crack on the right-hand side and is obscured due to blackening.
y: The third *y* is badly damaged. The top two left-hand wedges and the top right-hand wedge are visible.
ṯ: Unlike KTU, CTA does not read *t* after *y[ ]*. The wedge is partially visible.
ʿ: V reads *ʿ* where CTA and KTU has *š*. The angle of the stance approximates *ʿ* more than the winkelhocken of *š* (cf. *š* in the preceding line). Furthermore, there

[3] On the basis of content, this reconstruction would seem unlikely. For discussion, see below p. 237.

is room on the surface of the tablet before the lacuna for at least the middle vertical wedge of *š*. Hence ͑ is the better reading.
°: Following ͑ V read parts of two other wedges, the head of a horizontal wedge followed by the head of a vertical wedge; both fall along the damaged edge of the lacuna. CTA and KTU read *[ ]n*. The surface of the tablet is very damaged, and the readings cannot be adjudicated. It remains theoretically possible that *y͑n* was the original reading.
°°: V's hand-copy shows a single horizontal wedge followed by *pk.*, which CTA and KTU take as *ʾapk.*, regarded as an error for *ʾapnk* (so *CML*[2] 37). The damage to the heads of these wedges is so great that these readings canot be confirmed. For the initial sign after *[ ]*, I see the heads of two horizontal wedges, the upper one slightly to the right of the lower one. For the second sign, I see the heads of two vertical wedges with the head of a lower horizontal wedge preceding them (*b*, *d* or *ʾu*?). A diagonal crack runs through this sign which badly obscures the reading.
r̊: Only the heads of two horizontal wedges are clear.
d°°: V's hand-copy has *dt* and a single horizontal wedge at the right-hand edge of the tablet. CTA reads *d(t/m)*, while KTU has *dm*[*. The letter *d* has suffered damage. The heads of the vertical wedges are written closely together, and the horizontal wedges are lost in a large crack. The wedge following *d* is a single horizontal wedge. The tablet has room for another wedge, but the area is damaged, and it is possible that *m* is to be read. A single horizontal wedge follows. As V's hand-copy shows, this wedge is higher than the preceding *t* like the horizontal wedges of the letter *m* (as in *bym ym* at the beginning of line 12). Hence *dm°[*, *dt°[* and *dtm[* are possible readings. The first reading could be reconciled with the common reconstruction *dm[lk]* (see CTA p. 10 n. 6), but it is by no means clear or required by context.

Line 13. °: Before the second lacuna V and KTU read *u*/d**, while CTA gives *l*, *ʾu* and *d* as alternatives. The tops of three vertical wedges are visible while no horizontal wedge is visible. Any of the three possibilities given by CTA might be read.
n: After the second lacuna all read *n*; the letter is poorly preserved.
h: The heads of the wedges are not visible.
ʾi: The heads of the wedges are not visible. For the end of the line, see CTA p. 10 n. 7.

Line 14. *]°[*: Between *ʾu* and *k* V's hand-copy has *ṯ*, CTA reads no letters and KTU gives *xḫ**. Part of a wedge, apparently the right-hand side of a vertical wedge, is visible.
.: After *k*, CTA and KTU read a word-divider which V's hand-copy does not record. Part of the head of the word-divider is visible.
r: The upper left-hand horizontal wedge is not visible.
d: The left-hand and middle vertical wedges are not visible.
ʾi: The heads of the horizontal wedges are not visible.

Line 15. *[t͑?]nn*: The initial lacuna might be reconstructed with a form of the verb **͑ny*, "to speak up, answer," perhaps *[t͑]nn*, a 3 f. sg. indicative-energic prefix form given the following fem. sg. subject, *nrt ʾilm špš*. A large horizontal crack runs through the first three letters. As a result, only the upper ridges of the three *n*'s wedges are visible. CTA and KTU reconstruct a word-divider between the second and third *n*'s, but there is no space for the head of such a word-divider.
ʾi: Only two of the horizontal wedges and none of the little vertical wedge are visible.
m̥: Only the horizontal wedge is visible.
s̊ps̊: Only the right-hand wedges of the two *š*'s are visible.

.: CTA reads with a question-mark a word-divider after *špš*. V and KTU read the word-divider.
t: Only the tail of the horizontal wedge of *t* in *tšʾu* is visible.
The lacuna in the second half of the line is partially reconstructed on the basis of context. The name of the addressee follows the invocation *šmʿ mʿ* in other passages (e.g., 1.4 VI 4).

Line 16. The lacuna at the beginning of the line is reconstructed partially on the basis of the putative parallel of line 21 (so CTA 10 n. 9 following V).
V's hand-copy does not read a word-divider after *ʾabk*. CTA reconstructs *[.]* after *ʾabk*, while KTU reads the word-divider.
.: V and CTA read a word-divider before the initial occurrence of *pn* in this line, while KTU does not. CTA would delete the word-divider. Given the occasional attestation of word-divider in the middle of words, the emendation is unnecessary.
]r: V's hand-copy reads *]r*, CTA *[n]hr* and KTU *]n*h*r*. Only the wedges of the final letter are visible. The reconstruction is likely given the formulaic character of the epithets (see CTA p. 10 n. 10).

Lines 17-18 may be reconstructed partially on the basis of 1.6 VI 26-29.
Line 17. *lysʿ°°l°ṯ°[*: On the basis of the parallel CTA reconstructs *.[ʾalt.]* while KTU has *.[ʾa]l*t[.]*. V does not read any of these letters or word-dividers. The top of the head of one vertical wedge is visible as is the right-hand corner of a second vertical wedge to its right. Hence following KTU *l* may be read. The letter *t* is not visible. On the basis of the parallel *lysʿ.ʾalṯtb[* may be read.
p: For the end of the line CTA reads *ṯ[btk.ly]hpk*, KTU has *ṯbtk[.]ly*[hpk]*. V reads only two sets of double horizontal wedges at the end of the line (presumably the reading *p* and the beginning of *k* in CTA's reading). One set of double horizontal wedges is presently visible. My guess is that this letter is *p*.

Line 18. *mṯpṭk*: The reading is feasible, but the letters run closely together and some wedges are rather unclear.
[ʿṯtr]: CTA reconstructs *[ʿṯtr]* while KTU reads *ʿ*ṯ*[t]r**. V has no signs in his hand-copy.
.d[: For the end of the line CTA reads *.d(t/m)[-]k[?]*, and KTU has *.d*[m].k*x[ ]*. V's hand-copy has the word-divider and *d* followed by a lacuna about two letters in length, followed by *k* and a short lacuna. V's hand-copy represents well what is presently visible. It might be considered whether CTA's reading of line 12 (in CTA p. 10 n. 6) played any role in its fuller reading of the end of line 18 (see CTA p. 10 nn. 6 and 13).

Line 19. *°ḥ*: For the beginning of this line V reads *[l(?)]qḥ*, CTA has *[- -?]ḥ* and KTU reads *[ ]q*(?)ḥ*. The winkelhocken read by V and KTU is partially visible.
ʾab[y]: V's hand-copy and CTA read *ʾaby*, while KTU has *ab[y]*. The letter *b* shows only the left-hand vertical wedge and the head of the left-hand horizontal wedge. The rest of the letter and *y* presently fall in a crack. See further CTA p. 10 n. 15; cf. KTU p. 8 n. 15.
ʾa: One head is clear while the other falls in a crack.
bt: The letters are obscure.
[ʾi]lm: V read the tails of the two lower horizontal wedges of *ʾi* and all of its vertical wedge of *ʾi* as well as all of *l*. Following suit, CTA read *ʾilm*, while KTU has *i*l*m*. The wedges of *ʾi* are no longer visible, nor are the heads of *l*.
[.w]: CTA reconstructs *[.w]* while KTU reads *.w*. V's hand-copy has no wedges in the lacuna. The wedges are not presently visible.

ḥ̊: Only the right-hand side of the head of the vertical wedge is visible. Only the edge of the winkelhocken is evident.
r̊: Only the heads of the two left-hand horizontal wedges are preserved.

Line 20. *lbʾum*: V reads *lbʾum*, CTA reads *lb-m* and emends to *lbdm* (p. 10 n. 17), and KTU has *lb*d*m**. There is no evidence of a second or third head of horizontal wedges of a putative *d* although it must be noted that this wedge is admittedly unclear. CTA's emendation in unnecessary in terms of content.[4]
ʾa: V and KTU read *ʾard*. CTA gives *t* as an alternative for the first letter of *ʾard*. As best as I can make out, there are two wedges.
bn[p]šy: V's hand-copy shows *n*, two horizontal wedges followed by damage on the surface followed by the right-hand wedge of *š*. CTA reads *bn[p]šny* which would suggest deterioration of the tablet relative to the time of V's reading. At present the wedges of *p* are not visible. KTU gives *bn š*(?)nq*. KTU questions the reading *š*, but the stance of the right-hand wedge suits this reading. KTU's reading of *q* for V's and CTA's *y* has no basis (is it a typographical error?).
]bb[ht]: For the end of the line V's hand-copy shows two *b*'s and accordingly CTA reconstructs *b b[ht]* while KTU has *b*/d* bh*[t]*. KTU's listing *d* as a possible alternative to *b* presumes that some wedges may be lost on the left-hand side of the lacuna. No part of *h* is presently visible. The reconstruction of CTA and KTU is possible and is based on the parallel expression *bhkl* in line 21.

Line 21. The lacuna is reconstructed partially on the basis of the extant parallel of line 16.
ʾå: Corresponding to CTA and KTU's reading of the first letter of *ʾabh*, V's hand-copy shows a horizontal wedge and possibly the bottom tip of a vertical wedge after *ʾil*. In view of the parallels the damaged letter would appear to be *ʾa*. Several cracks obscure the reading. According to CTA and KTU the damaged area containing *ʾa* in *ʾabh* is large enough to reconstruct further a word-divider before the word. There is a crack in the surface which obscures reading.
After *ʾabh*, KTU reads a word-divider against CTA. V's hand-copy shows the reading, *ṯpṭ*, an epigraphically and thematically problematic interpretation.
lpn̊[z]bly[m]: For the end of the line CTA reads *lpn [.zb]l y[m]* while KTU has *l p*[n.z]b*l y[m]*. The upper horizontal wedge of *p* is unclear. The top edges of the heads of *n* are visible. Unlike V and CTA, KTU reads rather than reconstructs *b**. Two horizontal wedges are partially visible, justifying KTU's reading.

Line 22. *ṯ̊*: V and CTA read *ṯ* while KTU places the letter in the lacuna, but reconstructs it. The head of the vertical wedge is visible; so is the upper edge of the head of the horizontal wedge as well as the upper part of the winkelhocken.
[ ]: V's hand-copy shows *nhr*, which is reconstructed by CTA and KTU as part of the lacuna. The letters are not presently visible.
°: Following a short lacuna CTA gives *p* and *h* as alternative readings while V (with a question-mark) and KTU read *h*. V's hand-copy gives the tails of three horizontal wedges. CTA (p. 10 n. 22) notes that the reading materially would appear to be *p*. Presently a third horizontal wedge is not visible although there is room both above and below the other two horizontal wedges for it. Either the third tail is no longer visible, or *p* is possibly a scribal error for *h*.
m: V's hand-copy shows the whole sign. Only parts of the heads and none of the tails of the two wedges are visible.
ʾa: Two heads are visible, although the sign is otherwise obscure.

---

[4] See pp. 253-54 below for further discussion.

Line 23. °°: At the beginning of the line, V's hand-copy reads *tp*. CTA reconstructs and reads *[wǵlmt.kbn.qdš] wy[–]*. See CTA 11 n. 2 for the difficulty of the readings. KTU reads no wedges before *zbl*. The head of a one horizontal wedge stands above the upper edge of the head of a second horizontal wedge. These wedges are followed by the head of a single vertical wedge.
°: V and KTU reads yᶜ*(?) while CTA records no wedge after *y*. There is some wedge to the right of *y*, but it is right on the edge of the broken edge of the tablet and it is very difficult now to read.

Line 25. °: CTA reads no letters in this line. KTU reads l*/d*. V read some wedge below *š* in *yšlḥn* in line 24. There is a head of a vertical wedge below *š* in line 24.

Translation and Vocalized Text

1 . . .
2 . . .
3 . . .

Kothar Travels to El's Abode

4	[Then] he heads	[ʾiddaka] la-yatinu panīma
	Toward [E]l at the springs of the [Double-Rivers,]	ᶜimma [ʾi]li mabbikī na[harêmi]
	[Amidst the channels of the Double-Deeps.]	[qirba ʾappiqī tahāmatêmi]
5	[He comes to] the mountain of E[l] and enters	[yagliyu] ḏada ʾi[li] wa-yabuʾu
	The [te]nt of the King, [the Father of Years.]	[qa]rša malki [ʾabī šanīma]
6	[At El's feet he bends over] and falls,	[lê-paᶜnê ʾili yahburu] wa-yaqîlu
	[He] prostrates himself and honor[s him.]	[yi]štaḥwi[yu] wa-yakabbi[duna-hu]

El Speaks to Kothar

7	. . .	
	"[Ko]thar wa-Ha[sis], depart!	kôṯaru wa-ḫa[sīsu] tabaᶜ(?)[5]
	Build the palace of Yamm,	banī bahatī yammi
	[Erec]t the palace of Judge Rive[r,]	[rām]im hêkali ṯāpiṭi na[hari]
8	[In the hea]rt (?). . .	[bi-]ʾi(?)rti . . .
	"Depart (?), Kothar [wa-Hasis!]	tabaᶜ (?) kôṯaru [wa-ḫasīsu]
	[May you] build the palace of [Pr]ince Yamm,	[ta]bnê bahatī [za]buli yammi
9	[May you er]ect the pala[ce of Judge] River.	[tarā]mim hêka[li ṯāpiṭi] nahari
	Amidst [the mountain of Bull El the Bene]ficent (?)	bi-tôka [ǵūri ṯôri ʾili laṭi(?)]pāni (?)
10	[Hurry, the pa]lace let it be bui[lt,]	[ḥūšu baha]tūma tubnû[na]
	[Hur]ry, [may there be er]ected [a palace].	[ḥū]šu turāmi[muna hêkalū-ma]
	[A thousand acres may] the house [cover],	[ʾalpa šidda ʾaḫada] bêtu

---

[5] Cognates of Ug *tb*ᶜ include Syr *tba*ᶜ, Arb *tabi*ᶜ*a*, "to follow," and Akk *tebû*, "to depart" (*UgM* 76 n. 84; *UT* 19.2517).

11 [A thousand] hectares the pala[ce]."	[rabbata] kumāna hêka[lu]

Athtar Acts

11 . . .
. . . boys at (?) the field(s?) of Yamm . . .
12 . . . in the sea . . .
Sea/Yamm (?) . . .
13 Then Athtar . . .
. . .
14 . . . fire . . . he carries . . .
He descends . . .

Shapshu Speaks

15 The divine lamp, Shapshu, [spea(?)]ks	[taʿ(?)]nîna niratu ʾilīma šapšu
She raises her voice and [cries out]:	tiššaʾu gā-ha wa-[taṣūḥu]
"[Hea]r now, [O Athtar]:	[šama]ʿ maʿ [ʿaṯṯaru]
16 Bull El, your Father, [will take ven]geance (?)	[yaṯ]ʾiru ṯôru ʾilu ʾabū-ka
Before Prince Yamm,	lê-panê zabuli yammi
Before [Ju]dge River.	lê-panê [ṯā]piṭi nahari
17 [How] will he hear you,	[ʾêka ʾa]l yišmaʿu-ka
Bull [E]l, your Father?	ṯôru [ʾi]lu ʾabū-ka
Surely he will remove the [sup]port of your seat,	la-yissaʿu [ʾā]lata ṯibti-ka
18 Surely he will [overturn the throne] of your kingship,	la-ya[hpuku kussiʾa] mulki-ka
Surely he will break the sceptre of your rule."	la-yaṯabbiru ḫuṭṭa maṯpaṭi-ka

Athtar Answers

And Athtar [the kin]g (?) answers:	wa-yaʿnî ʿaṯ[ta]ru du-[mal?]ku (?)
19 ". . . me, Bull El, [my Father],	[ ]ḥ bi-ya ṯôru ʾilu ʾabū[-ya]
As for me, I have no house [like] the gods,	ʾanāku ʾênu bêtu [lê-]ya [kama] ʾilīma
20 Nor a court [like the holy on]es.	wa-ḥaẓiru [ka-binī qud]ši
(Like) a lion I will descend with my desire.	labiʾu-ma[6] ʾarida bi-napši-niya[7]
Kothar shall wash me	tirḥaṣu-nī kôṯaru-ma
21 In the h[ouse of Prince] Yamm,	bi-ba[hatī zabuli] yammi
In the palace of Judge River.	bi-hêkali ṯāpiṭi naha[ri]

---

[6] In addition to Semitic cognates (e.g., BH *lābî'*, "lion"; *BDB* 522), Ward (1961:35) cites Demotic *lby*, "lion" and Coptic *laboi*, "lioness" which he takes as possible Semitic loans.

[7] The status of the ending *-ny* is problematic. Gibson (*CML*² 38) takes the ending as dual, but this view does not seem to square with the context. See *PU* 1.61; Pardee 1980:271.

	May Bull El his Father take vengeance	yaṯʾiru ṯôru ʾilu ʾabū-hu
	Befo[re Pr]ince Ya[mm],	lê-pa[nê za]buli ya[mmi]
22	[Before Judge River.]	[lê-panê ṯāpiṭi nahari]
	Am I king... or not king (?)?	malaktu...himu lā-malaktu (?)
	But [y]ou have no wife li[ke the gods...]	wa-na ʾênu ʾaṯṯatu [lê-]ka ka[ma ʾilīma]
23	...(?) Prince Yamm...	zabul$_{v}$ yamm$_{v}$...
	Judge River... (?)	ṯāpiṭ$_{v}$ nahar$_{v}$

Speech

24	"...he will send me (?)..."	...yišlaḥu-ni

Athtar Responds

	Athtar answers:...	wa-yaʿnî ʿaṯtaru
25	...	

Commentary

Poetic Parallelism and Word/Syllable Counts

		semantic parallelism	word/syllable count
4	[ʾiddaka] la-yatinu panīma	a b c	3/10
	ʿimma [ʾi]li mabbikī na[harêmi]	d e f	4/11
	[qirba ʾappiqī tahāmatêmi]	d′ f′	3/10

The third line repeats many syntactical features of the second line. Both lines show an initial preposition formed from a tri-litteral base. Both lines use a construct phrase consisting of plural noun in construct to a dual form. The dual morphology also creates a limited sonant parallelism between the final nouns in the second and third lines, and one may sense sonant parallelism between *mabbikī* and *[ʾappiqī]* especially betwen the bilabials and the palatals. The two lines also show some contrasts. The most conspicuous contrast is syntactical: *[ʾi]li* is the object of the preposition in the second line, while *[ʾappiqī tahāmatêmi]* is the object in the third line. The first line lacks syntactical and morphological parallelism with the other lines. Sonant parallelism may be discerned between the particle *la-* in the first line and *[ʾi]li* in the second line and between *panīma* in the first line and *na[harêmi]* in the second line.

5	[yagliyu] ḏada ʾi[li] wa-yabuʾu	a b c a′	4/11
	[qa]rša malki [ʾabī šanīma]	b′ c′ [= x + y]	4/9

Semantic and syntactical parallelism dictates that *wa-yabuʾu* be taken as the first word in the second line (Parker 1989:9-10). The word and syllable counts resulting from placing *wa-yabuʾu* in the second line, i. e. 3/7 and 5/13, would appear to preclude this option. Given the logic of placing the two verbs in the first line, does the imbalace represent a way to emphasize the dwelling of El? The two major units of the second line correspond syntactically and semantically with an element in the first line. Sonant parallelism is limited to the otherwise unparallel elements *wa-yabuʾu* and *[ʾabī]*.

6	[lê-paᶜnê ʾili yahburu] wa-yaqîlu	a b c c′	4/12
	[yi]štaḥwi[yu] wa-yakabbi[duna-hu]	c″ c‴	2/11

With respect to length, the verbal forms in the second line balance the prepositional phrase in the first line. The two prefix forms of the verbs linked by *wa-* in both lines provide morphological and syntactical parallelism. With the root letter *b* and the ending *-hu*, *yakabbi[duna-hu]* forms sonant paralelism with *yahburu*.

7	. . .		
	kôṯaru wa-ḫa[sīsu] tabaᶜ	a b c	3/9
	banī bahatī yammi	a b c	3/7
	[rām]im hêkali ṯāpiṭi na[hari]	a′ b′ c′	4/11
8	[bi-]ʾi(?)rti (?) . . .	d (?)	

The syntactical, morphological and semantical parallelism of the second and third lines is patent, and perhaps the second and third lines formed part of a standard colon to which the first line was prefixed. (This view appears born out by the next unit if it is understood correctly.) Although the syntax of the first line departs markedly from the second and third lines, *b* in *tabaᶜ banī bahatī* forms an alliterative link between the first and second lines.

8	. . .		
	tabaᶜ (?) kôṯaru [wa-ḫasīsu]	a (?) b c	3/9
	[ta]bnê bahatī [za]buli yammi	a b c	4/10
9	[tarā]mim hêka[li ṯāpiṭi] nahari	a′ b′ c′	4/12
	bi-tôka [ǵūri ṯôri ʾili laṭi]pāni (?)	d e f (?)	5/13 (?)

Like the last unit, this one shows an initial command to Kothar followed by two lines commanding the building of the palace followed by yet a fourth line perhaps supplying the location for the construction. If the fourth line is reconstructed correctly even in its general outlines, then the first line appears to be prefixed to a tricolon. As in the preceding unit, the second and third lines manifest multiple levels of parallelism. The prefix element *[ta-]*, if correctly reconstructed in initial position in the second and third lines, would form a link with the initial syllable of the first line, but this depends on the reading *tb*^{c}. The fourth line shows a divine name and two epithets which would provide semantic parallelism with the second and third lines. Furthermore, a noun of place stands in construct to these divine names and epithets in the second, third and fourth lines. Finally, *[ṯāpiṭi]* in the third line and *[laṭi]pāni* in the fourth line would form sonant parallelism. These observations depend, however, on the correctness of the reconstruction of these lines.

10 [ḥūšu baha]tūma tubnû[na]	a b c	3/9
[ḥū]šu turāmi[muna hêkalu-ma]	a c′ b′	3/11

This bicolon exhibits highly proximate morphological, syntactical and semantic parallelism, assuming the correctness of the reconstructions. Moreover, the second words in the two lines show a limited sonant parallelism with *t* and *m*.

[ʾalpa šidda ʾaḫada] bêtu	a b c d	4/9
11 [rabbata] kumāna hêka[lu]	a′ b′ d′	3/9

Besides the conspicuous morphological, syntactical and semantic parallelism in the bicolon, *bêtu* and *[rabbata]* show sonant parallelism.

. . .

15 [ta^{c}(?)]nîna niratu ʾilīma šapšu	a b c	4/11
tiššaʾu gā-ha wa-[taṣūḥu]	a′ a″	3/9

These speech-opening formulas constitute a poetic bicolon. The *ta-* verbal prefixes in conjunction with the feminine ending on *niratu* link the two lines; otherwise, the sonant parallelism is restricted to sibilants.

[šama]^{c} ma^{c} [^{c}aṯtaru]	a b c	3/6
16 [yaṯ]ʾiru ṯôru ʾilu ʾabū-ka	a b c	4/10
lê-panê zabuli yammi	d e f	3/8
lê-panê [ṯā]piṭi nahari	d e′ f′	3/9

In these four lines a monocolon precedes a tricolon. Nonetheless, on the semantic level, divine titles bind the two first lines. The name of *^{c}aṯtaru* and the *[yaṯ]ʾiru ṯôru* form strong sonant parallelism. Gutterals have a high profile providing contrast between the two lines.

While ʿ and to a lesser extent *m* dominate the first line, ʾ is strong in the second line. Apart from sonant parallelism, the third and four lines exhibit nearly perfect parallelism and balance in line-length.

17 [ʾêka ʾa]l yišmaʿu-ka	a b c d	3/7
ṯôru [ʾi]lu ʾabū-ka	e [= x + y] d′	3/7

Although they are semantically and syntactically divergent, the lines are balanced in length, and they end with the same pronominal element. Moreover, there is sonant parallelism between *[ʾa]l* and *[ʾi]lu* and the alliteration of ʾ in both lines.

la-yissaʿu [ʾā]lata ṯibti-ka	a b c	3/10
18 la-ya[hpuku kussiʾa] mulki-ka	a′ b′ c′	3/10
la-yaṯabbiru ḫuṭṭa maṯpaṭi-ka	a″ b″ c″	3/11

All three lines have nearly perfect syntactical and morphological parallelism including identical initial syllables with the asseverative *la-* and closing syllables with the suffix *-ka*. Sonant parallelism, beyond that generated by morphological parallelism, is found in *ṯibti-//yaṯabbiru. . . maṯpaṭi-*.

wa-yaʿnî ʿaṯ[ta]ru du-[mal?]ku

The line appears to be extra-colonic.

19 [ ]ḥ (?) bi-ya ṯôru ʾilu ʾabū[-ya]	a (?) b c (= x + y)	5/10

ʾanāku ʾênu bêtu [lê-]ya [kama] ʾilīma	a b c a′ d	6/14
20 wa-ḥaẓiru [ka-binī qud]ši	c′ d′	3/9
labiʾu-ma ʾarida bi-napši-niya	e f g	3/12

Within these four lines the second and third lines represent a formulaic bicolon known elsewhere, and the first line is prefixed to the other two lines. Some morphological parallelism and semantic parallelism links the first and second lines. These features include *bi-ya and ʾabī[-ya]//[lê-]ya*; and *ʾilu* and *ʾilīma*. The fourth line appears to have built onto the preceding bicolon. The enclitic *-ma*, the preposition *bi-* and the suffix *-niya* echo forms in the preceding bicolon.

tirḫaṣu-nī kôṯaru-ma	a b	2/8
21 bi-ba[hatī zabuli] yammi	c d e	3/9
bi-hêkali ṯāpiṭi naha[ri]	c′ d′ e′	3/10

yaṯʾiru ṯôru ʾilu ʾabū-hu	a b c	4/10
lê-pa[nê za]buli ya[mmi]	d e f	3/8
22 [lê-panê ṯāpiṭi nahari]	d′ e′ f′	3/9

malaktu...himu lā-malaktu (?)
wa-na ʾênu ʾat̠t̠atu [lê-]ka ka[ma ʾilima]

23 zabul$_v$ yamm$_v$...
t̠āpit$_v$ nahar$_v$

Introduction

The placement of this fragment at this point in this study has been addressed in the Introduction.[8] The column is terribly damaged. Two basic parts can be discerned. The contents of the first part of the fragment, lines 2-11a, appear in a variant form in the latter portion of 1.1 III 19-29, specifically the travel to El's abode and his commands to Kothar to construct a palace for Yamm. More specifically, assuming the general correctness of the reconstructions of Virolleaud (followed in CTA and KTU), 1.2 III 2-3 corresponds generally to 1.1 III 19-21, 1.2 III 4-6 to 1.1 III 21-26, and 1.2 III 9b-10 to 1.1 III 27-29. It would appear then that 1.2 III overlaps with 1.1 III. The question is how precise the overlap is. For many commentators (Gibson, del Olmo Lete and de Moor, for example), 1.2 III 2-6 replicate Kothar's journey to El's abode, and lines 6 (or 7?)-11a give El's commission to Kothar in somewhat clearer terms than in 1.1 III 26-30. Caquot and Sznycer would not see two discrete parts; rather, Athtar is the subject of both parts.[9] In the first part, he and not Kothar travels to El to register his complaints about a house for Yamm. The references to Kothar in this section are taken by Caquot and Sznycer as part of El's speech detailing his decision to commission a palace for the Sea-god. There is unfortunately no reference to Athtar to indicate that he is the one who travels to El. Moreover, the formulas involved with Kothar in this section appear in 1.4 V 51-54 as commands to the craftsman-god. It is impossible to prove the point either way and any reconstruction is provisional, but Kothar seems the more likely referent.

The second portion, lines 11b-25, may treat a separate incident involving Athtar and his recognition of his lack of kingship. This section contains an action, or less likely a speech (11b-14), followed by a series of speeches, perhaps responses to El's support for Yamm. If so, it would imply that several members of the pantheon are

---

8 See above pp. 21-25.
9 *TO* 121 n. a; cf. *CML*² 37 textual note to lines 7-10.

present for El's commission and thus the scene would constitute an example of the divine council at El's abode and thus demonstrate that the divine council meets at El's abode. Unfortunately, 1.2 III 11b-25 does not give the exact location of the speakers.

Lines 1-6a

In lines 2-3 Kothar[10] perhaps tells El's messengers how far his abode is. The missing section preceding lines 2-3 may give more of Kothar's response as found in 1.1 III 17-18. Lines 4-6 adds further information to the description of El's abode found in 1.1 III. 1.2 III 4-6 details the location of El's home "at the springs of the Two-Rivers, Amidst the channels of the Double-Deeps" (*EUT* 61). The word *mbk* is a *m*-preformative noun from the root **nbk*.[11] The dual form of the noun, *n[hrm]*, is suggested by the dual form of the parallel word, *thmtm* (Pardee 1980:270).[12]

Excursus 2: The Homes of El and the Divine Council

The watery character of El's home is evident from both iconographic and literary sources. Pope (1971) demonstrates that a drinking mug excavated at Ugarit represents El in his abode, specifically Athirat's standing before El with Anat in the background (in the form of a bird) described in 1.4 IV. Behind the throne of El are fish, signifying the water of his abode. The precise location vis-à-vis the waters remains somewhat unclear. From the iconography of the mug, it might be inferred that El's abode sits in the waters, as the literary description says, "amidst the channels of the Double-Deeps." One Ugaritic incantation against the bite of the snake (KTU 1.100.3) locates El's abode at *mbk nhrm bᶜdt thmtm*, "at the springs of the Two-Rivers, at the meeting-place of the Double-Deeps." In using *bᶜdt* instead of *ʾapq*, this description perhaps locates locates El's abode at the meeting place of the two cosmic oceans, the upper waters and the lower waters (Gaster 1935:474; de Moor 1987:15 n. 81). KTU 1.100.3 apparently departs from the terrestrial sort of description provided in the poetic narrative of the Baal Cycle and renders El's domicile in cosmological terms.

---

10 For *TO* 121 n. a, Athtar; cf. *CML*² 37 textual note to lines 7-10.

11 See Fronzaroli 1955:48, 52; *EUT* 73-74; Oden 1977:30-36. For the variation between the bilabials in *mbk* and *npk* (KTU 1.14 VI 1 and III 9), see Garr 1986:46.

12 For a possible Eblaite background to the divine "deeps" (*thmtm*), see *tì-'à-ma-tum*, equated with Sumerian *AB.A*, "sea" (Stieglitz 1990:88).

Further iconographic evidence adds evidence pertaining to the description of El's mountain. A seal from the Akkadian period at Mari (Keel 1978:fig. 42; 1986:309) depicts, in Keel's words (1986: 309), "a god of the type of El enthroned, between the springs of two streams, on a mountain. He is flanked by two vegetation goddesses who grow out from the waters." Uehlinger (1993) has published an Old Assyrian seal which depicts the weather-god and two goddesses standing before an enthroned El-type figure with two attendants.[13] Concerning the El-figure and his throne Uehlinger (1993:345-46) comments:

> In der "rechten" Hand hält der Gott ein Gefäss, aus dem in einem bis etwas über Kniehöhe verlaufenden Bogen Wasser fliesst. Der Thronende ist also als Gott des frischen Quelwassers bzw. des Süsswassers charakterisiert.

As perhaps suggested by the water in this seal, the two streams in the Mari seal apparently correspond to the two channels of El's abode.[14] Albright and Pope suggest that the Quranic *majmaʿ al-bahrein*, "junction of the two oceans" in the Quran (sura 18:59-63) also represents a reflex of the cosmic abode of El, situated at the periphery of the cosmos.[15] The dual form of *bahrein* perhaps reflects, like *thmtm*, the two cosmic seas at whose meeting-point the divine home lies.[16] Finally, a geological formation called *ᵈKAŠKAL.KUR*, "underground water-course" (E. Gordon 1967: 70-88) may pertain to the Ugaritic descriptions of El's abode.[17] In an OB itinerary, a place is called *[a]p-qum ša KAŠKAL.KUR* (Goetze 1953:53) which in another itinerary is called *Ap-qú-ú sa Ba-li-ḫa-a* (Hallo 1964:58-64). According to Gordon, this equivalence suggests that *ᵈKAŠKAL.KUR* represents a hydrological feature of the Balih river. Gordon discusses in some detail how one of these underground water-courses emerges at the Nahr Ibrahim near the site

[13] I wish to thank Dr. Uehlinger for bringing this seal to my attention.

[14] For other possible iconographic representations of El in his abode, see Lambert 1985b:449-50.

[15] Albright 1932:12 n. 35; *EUT* 78. So also Lipiński 1971:47, 65; de Moor 1987:15 n. 81. Cf. Wensinck 1978:902.

[16] Lipiński (1983:309) argues that a Palmyrene-Greek bilingual identifies the sea-god Poseidon with Semitic *ʾlqwndʿ ʾlhʾ ṭbʾ*, "*ʾlqwndʿ*, the good god," whom Lipiński takes to be El. If Lipiński's interpretation were correct, then this equation of deities might be viewed as a function of El's aqueous home.

[17] See above pp. 183-84.

which Pope proposes for the home of El (see below). In this connection the Akkadian term *ʾapqum* from the itineraries echoes the cognate phrasc *ʾapq* as it is used in descriptions of El's abode. In sum, El's abode lies at the confluence of the two cosmic oceans at the distant horizon. This home was also located in terrestial terms at the confluence of two underground channels at El's mountain.

Where these waters were thought to be located at El's mountain here and in 1.1 III 23 remains unclear. Ginsberg (*KU* 20) and Pope (*EUT* 61) compare Ugaritic *mbk nhrm* and *ʾapq thmtm* on the one hand, and BH expressions *mibbĕkê nĕhārôt* (Job 28:11), *nibkê yām//tĕhôm* (Job 38:16) and *ʾappîqê yām* (2 Sam 22:16; cf. Ps 18:16) used in connection with the underworld. It might be surmised from the biblical references that the subterranean waters associated with El's home in Ugaritic myth came to be associated with the waters of the Netherworld in Israelite tradition (cf. Pope 1977:673; Weinfeld 1983a:137 n. 79; *CML*^{2} 53 n. 3). Cross (*CMHE* 38) relates the watery depths of El's abode to the waters which emerge from beneath Mount Zion.[18] Cross asserts that these are the fresh waters unlike the waters of the Abyss or Netherworld, but there is no evidence indicating this aspect of the waters' character (cf. *EUT* 63). On the contrary, the word, *ḫrš[n]*, "mountain" in 1.1 III 22 may indicate that his home stands at the headwaters of the Netherworld, as Pope (*EUT* 69-72), Cross (*CMHE* 39) and McCarter (1973) suggest. This view would accord with the biblical references to the Netherworld with terminological ties to the description of El's abode.

Terrestrial identifications for El's mountain have been proposed. Pope (*EUT* 72-81) suggests the site of Khirbet Afqa in the Lebanon (Josh 13:14). Nestled in a majestic mountainous setting, the Nahr Ibrahim emerges from a cavern to plunge into a deep and verdant gorge. Only seven and a half miles away, on the other side of the mountain, another spring feeds the lake called Birket el-Yammuneh, "the Little Sea."[19] Cross (*CMHE* 38) proposes an

---

[18] Isa 33:20-22; Ezek 47:1-22; Joel 4:18; Zech 14:8; cf. 1 Enoch 17:1-7 and 26:1-2. The waters of paradise in Gen 2:10 may likewise be based on the imagery of waters emerging from the house of El (perhaps indicating a relation between the two sets of oracular material in Ezekiel 28 (see *CMHE* 38 n. 151; cf. Wilson 1987).

[19] For discussion and a picture of the waters at Afqa, the source of the Nahr Ibrahim, also the Adonis river, see Jidejian 1968:119-30, plate 123.

alternative locale, Mount Haman, situated on the north Syrian coast. Cross (*CMHE* 26-28) sees the name of El's mountain behind the Punic epithet *bʿl ḥmn*, "lord of the Amanus," and follows Landsberger in viewing it as a title of El. As apparent support, the iconography of Baal Hamon comports with the iconography of El known at Ugarit.[20] Cross identifies Punic *ḥmn* with Ugaritic *ḫmn*, used as a theophoric element in proper names and in alphabetic Hurrian texts from Ras Shamra, but Cross distinguishes this peak from Ugaritic *ʾamn* in KTU 2.33.16. For Cross (*CMHE* 27) the former refers to the particular Mount Amanus while the latter is a different mountain, although both are "in the same general region." Given the difference of spelling, it is understandable that some commentators take *ʾamn* as Mount Amanus (Yadin 1970:215-16, 228 n. 67; Cogan 1984; Xella 1991:163).

Citing Cross' view, Stager (1991:42, 45, 72 n. 19) takes the throne-name of the Roman emperor, Elegabalus (203-222 C. E.), as a Latinized form of the West Semitic *ʾĒl Jebel*, "El of the mountain." Elegabalus, a Syrian, brought a statue of Tanit to Rome. He took a vestal virgin for a wife and identified her with the goddess Tannit and himself with the god, Elagabal. Stager (1991:45) suggests:

> Their marriage, then, replicated that of the heavenly couple, Baʿal Hamon (alias Elagabal) and Tanit. Thus these Phoenician deities became part of the imperial cult in Rome.

The name Elegabalus does not give the specific name of El's mountain, but indicates only that El has a mountain named *ḫmn*. It would appear that the simplest solution is to understand Ugaritic *ʾamn* as Mount Amanus. However, this conclusion does not exclude the possibility that Ugaritic *ḫmn* could too refer to Amanus, especially since the place-name *pʿrḥmn* appears in a Phoenician seal dating to the eighth century. According to Bordreuil (1986:21-22), *pʿrḥmn* is to be understood as the town "Pʿr of the Amanus" which corresponds to the modern village of Bağras situated in the Amanus range. Hence, El's mountain could be *ḫmn* (Amanus); perhaps *ʾamn* and *ḫmn* are two spellings for the same place.

Lipiński (1971:40) places El's abode at the sources of the Jordan river near Mount Hermon and cites rabbinic evidence from

---

[20] J. Day (1989:37-40) raises several difficulties with the putative iconographic evidence.

Midrash Rabbah on Genesis 33 (67a) that the cavern of Banias was one of the outlets of the Deep or Ocean. He also cites Testament of Levi 2:7 which locates a great sea above, i.e., the celestial ocean, above Mount Hermon. According to Lipiński, the phrase, "Deep to deep calls" (*tĕhōm-ʾel-tĕhōm qōrēʾ*) in Ps 42:8 draws on the cosmological idea of the divine watery abode and may be traced to El's abode. There may be older evidence as well which points to Mount Hermon as the seat of the divine assembly. According to a late recension of Gilgamesh, Mount Hermon was the seat of the Sumerian pantheon, reflecting a West Semitic idea regarding the home of the divine assembly (Lambert 1960:12). This tradition likely provides the background for the descent of the Watchers to earth at Mount Hermon in the book of Enoch (1 Enoch 6:6; cf. 13:7). Lipiński's proposal suits both the home of the divine assembly and the site of El's abode, and it might be argued that the evidence of the traditions about Mount Hermon and Banias militates in favor of identifying the sites of El's abode and the divine assembly, although these two may not be the same place in some West Semitic traditions and may have been associated secondarily.[21]

The only explicit literary information describing the location of El's abode comes from the West Semitic narrative of Elkunirsa (*ANET* 519; Hoffner 1990:69). This text places the home of Elkunirsa at the Mala river, that is, the upper Euphrates before Carchemish where the river assumes its name of Euphrates (Otten 1958:83 n. 28; del Monte and Tischler 1978:537). According to Albright and others (see Mullen 1980:152-53; de Moor 1987:15 n. 81), Gilgamesh 11.194-96 (*ANET* 95) is reminiscent of the rivers of El's abode (*mbk nhrm*, "the springs of the Two-Rivers"):

> "Now, let Utnapishtim and his wife be like the gods;
> let Utnapishtim dwell in the distance (*ina rūqi*)
> at the mouth of the rivers (*ina pî nārāti*)."
> So they took me and made me dwell in the distance
> at the mouth of the rivers.

The directions, *ina rūqi, ina pî nārāti*, "in the distance, at the mouth of the rivers" have been compared with the description of the location of El's abode (see Mullen 1980:152-53). If the information from the Elkunirsa story and Gilgamesh 11 pertains to the terrestrial loca-

21 For the difficulties, see above pp. 174, 230-31. See below p. 285.

tion of El's abode, it may be located not on the coast, as proposed by Pope and Cross, nor in the Hermon range, pace Lipiński. Rather, a location in inland Syrian would represent another alternative (cf. *EUT* 75 for northern Mesopotamian candidates). Other elements in the Ugaritic literature may reflect a northern Mesopotamian background.[22] In sum, the various proposals comport topographically with the Ugaritic descriptions of El's abode. They would also be ideal candidates for cultic sites; indeed, both Khirbet Afqa and Mount Hermon functioned as cult places for hundreds of years. It seems quite possible that various sites were known as El's abode as presupposed by different pieces of evidence.

Some scholars assume an identification between the mountains of El and the divine council (*CMHE* 45-46; Mullen 1980:281-83; see Roberts, *IDBS* 977). As Pope (*EUT* 94-95) long ago observed, major differences in the descriptions of the mountain of El and the mount of the divine council urge caution against identifying the two sites. First, while the name of El's mountain is given as *ks*, the mount of the assembly is *ll* according to KTU 1.2 I 20. In order to obviate this contradictory evidence, some scholars change the name of the site of the assembly from *ll* to *ʾil*.[23] Mullen (1980:130 n. 32, 167-68) refrains from the emendation, but identifies the two mountains.

Second, significant differences between the descriptions of El's abode and the scenes of the divine council might militate against making such an identification. While explicit scenes of the assembly involve feasting, explicit descriptions of El's abode do not. Explicit descriptions of El's abode mention the architectural features of his home as well as the cosmic waters, but explicit descriptions of the divine assembly do not contain these features. Explicit descriptions never use the terms for the general divine council. It must be said, however, that in some cases, it is difficult to determine whether action takes place in El's abode or at the divine assembly or neither. According to Cross (*CMHE* 183-84), the scenes in 1.3 V and 1.4 IV depicting one or two deities with El constitute occasions of the divine council.[24] These two instances are not explicitly scenes of the divine assembly, however. Indeed, unlike explicit descriptions of the divine

---

[22] See above pp. 89-90.
[23] *CMHE* 37, 183; *CMCOT* 42; 1979:145; Wyatt 1986:381; cf. *EUT* 68-69.
[24] For further remarks on 1.3 V, see Pope 1971.

assembly, neither of these two scenes occasions a feast. It might be suggested that when the deities are mentioned in general, an assembly of the pantheon seems intended; KTU 1.2 I, 1.4 VI, 1.15 II and 1.16 VI meet this criterion for the company of the pantheon. Intercession before El may take place either within the confines of the entire assembly (1.15 II), or under the aegis of what may be his own assembly—whether explicitly at his abode (1.3 V and 1.4 IV) or not (1.17 I). In these and other instances (such as 1.6 I), it is impossible to determine the precise setting. However, based on parallels with Mesopotamian literature, some of these cases would appear to represent meetings of the divine council. For example, when El discusses with Anat and Athirat the question of permission for the construction of a palace for Baal, it appears to compare with divine council scenes in Mesopotamian literature where the topic of divine palace-building is addressed (Hurowitz 1992:140). In Enuma Elish 6.47-81 (*ANET* 68-69), the decision to build a palace for Marduk involves the deliberations of the divine assembly.

Third, the different terminology for the various divine assemblies in ritual texts might militate against identifying El's abode with the home of the divine assembly.[25] The juxtaposition of *dr ʾil* with *pḫr bʿl* in KTU 1.40, and the equation of *pḫr ʾilm* with ^{d}*pu-ḫur ilānī*^{meš} would weigh against the identification of El's council with the general divine assembly. The terminology of *dr ʾil* with *pḫr bʿl* in 1.40 suggests that El's council was represented in terms differing from either the assembly of Baal or the divine council embracing the pantheon as a whole. The ritual and literary texts may contain differing notions regarding divine councils, but if these differences are pertinent, the ritual texts would provide further, albeit indirect, evidence against identifying El's abode with the site of the general assembly of the pantheon in the mythological texts.

Finally, the description of El's tent has also played a major role in the identification of his home with the site of the divine assembly. On the one hand, the tent tradition belongs to the imagery associated with the abode of El and the biblical "tent of meeting" (*ʾōhel môʿēd*), as Cross, Clifford and others observe. The use of the terms Ugaritic *qrš* and BH *qereš* and the independent witness of the narrative of Elkunirsa (*ANET* 519) establish the tent traditions of El in

---

[25] See Pardee 1986:65-66.

West Semitic literature. On the other hand, the linguistic term *mᶜd* describing the divine assembly in Ugaritic literature is also associated with Yahweh's abode. Cross (*CMHE* 37-39;1981:173), Clifford (*CMCOT* 43, 55) and Greenfield (1987b:548) take *mᶜd* as an indication of the Ugaritic identification of the mountain of assembly with the abode of El, but the evidence may be read in the opposite manner, namely that Israelite tradition amalgamated language associated with El, Baal and the divine council. Roberts (1976b:977) argues this position in his comments on Isa 14:13:

> This passage contains a strangely confused mixture of Canaanite mythology, since it assigns Zaphon, Baal's mountain in the Ugaritic texts, to El and identifies it with the mount where the divine council meets. Such confusion seems to reflect Yahwistic appropriation of both El and Baal material.

As mentioned above, this point may apply to the mount of assembly as well.[26] In sum, El's abode, Baal's home and possibly the home

---

[26] According to Greenfield (1987:551-54), Ps 27:5-6 refers to the tent of Yahweh which by means of word-play evokes language associated with Baal's home in Ugaritic tradition, specifically *yiṣpĕnēnî* (*ṣpn; cf. *yaʾaṣpenî* in verse 10). Greenfield (1987b:553-54; cf. Smith 1988:172 n. 6) also argues that like 1.3 III 31 where *nᶜm*, "the pleasant (place)," parallels other terms for Baal's abode, *bĕnōᶜam* in Ps 27:4 denotes a location and stands in parallelism with *bĕhêkālô*, "in his temple" (the parallelism of form with verse 13 might indicate a comparable interpretation of *bĕṭūb* in this verse although this term is not applied to Baal's home in Ugaritic literature). There may be other signs of Israelite amalgamation of language for the divine abode which Ugaritic literature distinguishes. The language for Baal's abode may lie behind some descriptions of the divine mountain in biblical literature. Two difficult passages, Ps 48:3 and Isa 14:13, have provoked widely divergent interpretations regarding the divine mountain. Ps 48:3 refers to Mount Zion as *yarkĕtê ṣapôn*, "in the recesses of Sapan" or "in the far north" (RSV; *CMHE* 38). As commentators have long suggested (see Smith 1989b), the description of Zion involves a mountain, and the tradition concerning Baal's mountain echoes in the use of *ṣāpôn* in this passage. Rather than draw any parallel to Baal's peak, Mount Sapan, Cross (*CMHE* 38) equates this mountain with the home of the divine council: "Perhaps the most extraordinary case of identification of Zion with the cosmic mount of assembly is in Psalm 48:3 where Zion, Yahweh's holy mountain, is given the name, *Yarkĕtê Ṣāpōn*, 'the Far North'." This passage does not use language specific to the divine assembly, yet Cross identifies the peak described in this verse with the mount of assembly; at the same time, there is one term specific to Baal's mountainous abode in this passage, but Cross does not relate the two in this context. To locate Zion in the "far north"—even if the passage were to require such a translation—is not the only point of the expression; rather, the location evokes a divine abode related at least by name to Baal's mountain. As Clifford (*CMCOT* 142-44) notes, the Ugaritic parallel to be drawn with *yarkĕtê ṣāpôn* in Ps 48:3 is Baal's home. Isa 14:13 presents another difficult case of the amalgamation of Baal's mountain with the

of the divine assembly may represent separate mountains in the Ugaritic texts, but in biblical tradition the language and imagery associated with all three are attributed to the mountain of Yahweh.[27]

In sum, the evidence regarding the homes of El and the divine assembly is problematic, and final judgement on the relation of El's abode to the mountain of the council and El's council to the general divine assembly may be reserved. While language and context distinguish between the two sites, the extant texts bearing on these is-

---

home of the divine assembly. Commentators agree that this passage refers to the mount of assembly, but otherwise there is sharp disagreement. On the one hand, Cross identifies this mountain of divine assembly with the mountain of El. This identification was rejected by Albright (1945:31 n. 88), Scott (*IDB* 5:262), Dahood (1966:289-90), McKay (1970:452, 461-62) and Kaiser (1974:39). On the other hand, Cross rejects any identification of this mountain with the peak of Baal's abode, *ṣapān*, despite the presence of this term in this verse as in Ps 48:3. Cross, Clifford (*CMCOT* 161-62 n. 85), and Mullen (1980) render *ṣāpôn* in Isa 14:13 as "north." This translation genericizes the name of mountain which may have either specifically refered to or reflected the influence of the title of Baal's mountain. Critical of the translation "north," Roberts (1973:334-35; 1975:556) renders *ṣāpôn* as "Zaphon," the name of Baal's mountain. He also notes the mixture of language associated with El and Baal in Isa 14:13. Roberts renders *ṣāpôn* in Job 26:7 also as the name of Baal's mountain. As a result of Israelite convergence of language for divine abodes, the imagery associated separately with El, Baal and the divine assembly came to be applied to the divine abode of Yahweh.

The convergence of these traditions was perhaps enhanced by some overlap between them. For example, the divine assembly, El and Baal appear atop their mountains. As the Mari seal suggests (see p. 226 above), El dwells, in the midst of waters which are on the mountain (cf. *CMHE* 37-38). These waters appear in two different ways in biblical tradition. On the one hand, these waters flow from Jerusalem and have healing properties. The first aspect of the waters of El's abode continued in biblical tradition as part of the language of the temple-dwelling of Yahweh (so *CMHE* 38). On the other hand, as Pope (*EUT* 62) observes, the terminology of waters associated with El's abode appear in biblical tradition as the waters of the Netherworld (see pp. 186-87). The word, *ḫršn*, "mountain" to 1.1 III 22 may indicate that El's abode stands at the headwaters of the Netherworld, as Pope (*EUT* 69-72), Cross (*CMHE* 39) and McCarter (1973) suggest despite criticism of the etymological connection between Akkadian *ḫuršānu*, "mountain" and *ḫuršānu*, "underworld" (see p. 186). The motif of the waters indicates that amalgamation in biblical tradition also produced displacment of motifs. It may be that the notion of El dwelling in the waters of the deep did not comport with other descriptions of Yahweh, because the realm of Yahweh was thought, at least in some circles, to be removed from the underworld. Hence the idea of the waters of the underworld survived in biblical writings, but not in conjunction with notions of the divine abode. Similarly, the notion of the divine assembly and Baal feasting atop their mountains appears to have displaced descriptions of El enthroned at the watery deeps from descriptions of either Yahweh enthroned in the heavenly realm or corresponding temple imagery.

[27] For further discussion of the amalgamation of divine mountains in biblical tradition, see Smith 1990:21-22, 23-24.

sues may not provide the entire picture, and despite substantial evidence to the contrary, it remains possible that the sites of El and the divine council were considered one and the same.

Lines 6b-11a

In these lines, Kothar receives from El three sets of commands concerning the construction of Yamm's palace, explicitly mentioned lines 8-9. According to Caquot and Sznycer (*TO* 121 n. a and 122 n. h), Athtar is told by El of his instructions to Kothar. It may be noted that Ugaritic poetic narrative frequently relates instructions and their execution by the one to whom the instructions are addressed, but the relating of instructions to a third party by the one who gave the instructions would be rare, if not unique to 1.2 III 7-10. This fact would cast doubt on the notion that this passage describes Athtar being informed by El of his instructions to Kothar. Line 6b introduces the speech of El, perhaps with some introductory formula, such as *[wyᶜn.?] ṯr ᵓil ᵓabh*, which is attested in the parallel position in 1.1 III 26. Other introductory phrases introducing speech of El following obeisance before him include *yšᵓu gh wyṣḥ* in 1.4 IV 30 (cf. *wyᶜn lṭpn ᵓil dpᵓid* in 1.4 IV 58).

The parallels among the three sets of commands in lines 7-10 may be partially indicated in schematic form:

Line 7: (a) kṯr wḫ[ss] tbᶜ, "Kothar wa-Ha[sis], depart"
(b) bn bht ym, "build the house of Yamm"
(c) [rm]m hkl ṯpṭ n[hr], "[erec]t the palace of Judge R[iver]"

Lines 8-9:(a) tbᶜ (?)[28] kṯr w[ḫss], "depart (?), Kothar wa-[Hasis]"
(b′) [t(?)]bn/bn bht zbl ym, "[may you (?)] build/build the house of Prince Yamm"
(c′) [tr]mm/[r]mm hk[l ṯpṭ] nhr, "[may you ere]ct/[ere]ct the pala[ce of Judge] River

Line 10: (b′) [ḥš bh]tm tbn[n], "[hurry], may [a hou]se be buil[t]" or "[hurry], may you buil[d] [a hou]se"
(c′) [ḥ]š trm[mn hklm], "[hur]ry, may there be erec[ted a palace]" or "[hur]ry, may you erec[t a palace]"

These three sets of orders to Kothar reinforce El's message and indicates its urgency, at least to El. There is no other such sequence

---

[28] The reading of ᶜ in this word is problematic, however. See above p. 213.

known elsewhere in the Ugaritic corpus, the closest parallel being 1.4 V 51-55. The verbs in the first set in line 7 are imperatives, indicated by the lack of a prefix to *bn*.

The form *bht* in line 7 is plural construct.[29] Loewenstamm (*CS* 71 n. 85) compares *bhtm* to the plural use of South Arabian ʾ*byt* also for the god's house and notes Gordon's point (*UT* 19.463) that the god's house is composed of various buildings. The same plural usage occurs with BH *miškĕnôt* for the Jerusalem temple, the house of Yahweh (*CMHE* 97 n. 24).

The third line in line 7 uses the *D*-stem (or "polel") of **rwm* in the sense of "cause to be high, exalted." In this context the form is parallel with **bny*, "to build," and means "to construct, erect." Ezra 9:9 and Ben Sira 49:12 use this idiom for the construction of the temple in Jerusalem.[30] The third poetic line in line 7 also adds Yamm's standard epithet, *ṯpṭ nhr*, "Judge River."[31] This title may not constitute evidence of specifically judicial functions. Rather, in view of the broader use of the root **ṯpṭ*, some commentators argue that the epithet means "ruler,"[32] especially as this root elsewhere parallels **mlk* and here parallels **zbl* used also as a term for leadership (Held 1968; von Soden 1972; Mendenhall 1973:84; see Stol 1972). Despite these parallels, Albright (1936:17-20) and McCarter (1973:412 n. 33) view *ṯpṭ nhr* as a reflex of the judicial river ordeal (see Fensham 1984:66-67, 69).[33] Curtis (1988:8-9) criticizes this approach to *ṯpṭ nhr* because there is no clear West Semitic evidence for the river ordeal. Yamm was viewed perhaps as a ruler, in which case "Ruler River" would be a more apt translation of *ṯpṭ nhr*.

---

[29] The infix *-h-* is not a *mater lectionis* (cf. Dietrich and Loretz 1973:73, 1975: 559), but a pluralizing element surviving in words with largely biconsonantal or weak root bases such as BH ʾ*ĕlōhîm* (cf. Ugaritic ʾ*ilhm*) and its back-formation, ʾ*ĕlōah*; Ugaritic ʾ*amht* and BH ʾ*ămāhôt*, "(female) servants"; BA *ʾ*ăbāhātāʾ*, "fathers"; Jewish Aram ʾ*immāhātāʾ*, "mothers" (see Huehnergard 1987a:182 for further discussion). Like *bhtm*, BH *battîm* is highly irregular.

[30] So Loewenstamm 1971:94; Avishur 1980-81; 1984:16, 612. Weinfeld (1983c:108) notes that Akkadian *šaqû*, "to be high" is used also for the construction of buildings (*AHw* 1180, under *šaqû* II D 7a).

[31] The root **nhr* means "to flow." See Arb *nahara*; BH **nhr* in Isa 2:2; Jer 51:44; and Egyptian **nhr*, "to wander," possibly a loan from Semitic (Ward 1963:420-23). For the noun, cf. Ak *nâru*, BH *nāhār*, BA *nĕhar*, Syr *nahrāʾ*, all meaning "river" (*UT* 19.1623).

[32] *CS* 349; Gevirtz 1980; Fensham 1984; Curtis 1988:1988:8-9; Pardee 1980:271; cf. Cazelles 1984.

[33] See above p. 187.

An OB text, LB 1000 (*CAD* Ḫ:255; Frymer-Kensky 1977:1.156), provides a parallel supporting the standard translation "Judge River," however. This text invokes two deities, ᵈ*ID* and ᵈ*ḫuršānu*. While the former is clearly the divinized River, the latter would seem to be the divinized River Ordeal. Roberts (1972:46) notes further that the Akkadian river-god Naru "received a social character primarily from the role the river played in the river ordeal, so it is primarily thought of as a judge, just as in Ugarit."[34] In view of this background, one might wonder whether Baal's battle with Yamm reflects, albeit distantly, the background of a water ordeal, although the West Semitic evidence for the water ordeal is weak. It would appear, however, that the judicial function of Yamm is only vestigial in the form of his epithet *ṯpṭ*. It remains possible that Yamm's functions included a judicial one, even if it was not primary.

The verbal forms of lines 8b-9a pose problems. The question is whether they represent active or passive forms. In view of the preceding imperative to Kothar, they would appear to constitute active forms. The final line of the tricolon of lines 8b-9a contains Yamm's epithet *zbl ym*, "Prince Sea."[35] This designation has no clear counterpart in biblical sources, but as Cassuto (*BOS* 285) and Jacobs (1977:2) observe, the Talmud witnesses to later echoes of this title. b. B. Bat. 74b attests the title in the form, *śrʾ šl ym*, "Prince of the sea":

> When God desired to create the world, He said to the Prince of the sea, "Open your mouth and swallow up all the waters of the world!" The latter answered, "Lord of the universe, I have enough with my own!" Whereupon God trampled on him and slew him, as it is said, "By his power He beat down the sea, and by his understanding He smote Rahab."

B. Hul. 41b also attests the title, *śrʾ dym* (Tsevat 1954:47).[36] Jacobs notes that the divine antipathy toward Leviathan and Behemoth as well as other motifs in rabbinic aggadah indicate that like biblical apocalyptic and other Second Temple literature, rabbinic sources preserve and elaborate older versions of the West Semitic conflict myth.

---

[34] Like Ugaritic *ṯpṭ nhr*, the divine river ᵈ*ID*, well-attested in Old Babylonian texts from Mari, is male (see Gelb 1992:134; Lambert 1985a:535). Cf. Mari PN *I-ti* ᵈ*Naru*ᵐ , "The divine River knows" discussed in Curtis 1988:8.

[35] Literally, "raised one" and therefore "exalted one"; cf. BH *nāśîʾ*. See von Soden 1972.

[36] See above p. 151.

Line 9 presumably ends with a specification of the building site, if the parallel in 1.4 V 55 is any indication. The name of the location is obscured by the lacuna at the end of line 9. The only surviving letters are *]pn*, plausibly reconstructed as *[lṭ]pn*, a title of El. If this is correct, Yamm's house is to be erected at El's mountain and the rest of the line is perhaps to be reconstructed: *btk [ǵr ṯr ʾil lṭ]pn*.

The morphology of the verbs in line 10 is more difficult to interpret than the corresponding forms in lines 8-9. Like the verbs in lines 8-9, the verbs in line 10 consist of an order to depart plus invocation of the god (though varied in position compared to line 7), plus two commands to build the palace, following by a specification of the location of the building site (see below). The verbs are either second person voluntives (so *CML*² 37) or imperatives (Held 1965:274), as the lacunas are amenable to either view. Passive jussive forms might be considered as or more likely, as it might be argued that the verbs vary in each of the three sets in order to make each set more compelling.

The third set of commands to Kothar offers yet further variation. Taken with lines 10b-11a (see below), this set forms two bicola. It omits the order to depart, perhaps indicating that the forms are passive. This bicolon adds *ḥš* in each line; this variation is attested also in 1.4 V 51-54, a series of commands to Kothar to build the palace of Baal. The form is technically an imperative (Gordon 1977:97) or an infinitive functioning as an imperative and forming hendiadys with the verbs to build; it has been translated adverbially, "quickly" (Held 1965:274, 277 n. 26). The verbs in the third set possibly vary as well; they could be either second person singular active volitives addressed to Kothar, or third person plural passive jussives. According to Held (1965:274; cf. *BOS* 133 n. 81), the verbs in line 10 and 1.4 V 53-54 are passive in voice and the nouns are plural, thus agreeing with the verbal forms in gender and number. Since the verbs of the second set appear possibly as second person volitives, the verbs of the third set may offer a further variation, in this case internal passives.

The lines following each of the three sets of commands offer numerous problems due to the fragmentary condition of the text. The line following the orders in line 7 is most difficult; the word *ʾirt*, "breast," if read correctly (*MLC* 166), might approximate the formula in the parallel position in the following line. Just as *bt.k* may indicate the place of Yamm's palace, so perhaps *ʾirt* belongs to a prepositional phrase denoting the locale of his house, an expression found in 1.22 I 25: *bʾirt lbnn*, "in the heart of Lebanon." The line following the verbs in line 8 perhaps concerns the location of the palace, as the parallel to *bt.k* in 1.4 V 55 would indicate. This section of 1.4 V, specifically lines 56-57, also provides a parallel with lines 10b-11 as plausibly reconstructed by del Olmo Lete (*MLC* 166): *[ʾalp šd ʾaḫd]bt//[rbt]kmn hk[l]*, "[A thousand acres may] the house [cover]// [ten thousand] hectares the pala[ce]." The parallel from 1.4 V 56-57 fits the little extant remains of 1.2 III 10b-11a and the lacuna in these lines can accomodate the rest of the reconstruction as well.

Lines 11b-14

These lines are extremely fragmentary and generally lack parallels in the Ugaritic mythological corpus. It is not entirely evident that these lines form a single unit. Line 11b seems to refer "to the fields of Yamm," *lšdt ymm*, and line 12 begins a section concerning Athtar. Gibson (*CML*² 37-38) takes lines 11b-14 as narrative followed by two speeches by Shapshu (15-18a, 21b-23) and two responses by Athtar (18b-21a, and 24b). Del Olmo Lete (*MLC* 166-68; 1984:50, 51-52) differs in taking lines 11b-14 as an initial speech of Athtar rather than narrative. De Moor (1987:36-38) takes lines 11b-21a somewhat differently: El finishes his speech in line 12a and then Athtar speaks first in lines 12-14, then Shapshu in lines 15-18a, with Athtar's response in lines 18b-21a.

It is difficult to assess these differences of interpretation, largely because of the many and substantial lacunas. For this reason Ginsberg (*ANET* 129) perhaps wisely prescinded from translating little of this section except the explicitly marked speeches of Shapshu and Athtar in lines 15-20. Both del Olmo Lete (1977:44; cf. *MLC* 166-67; 1984:50) and de Moor (1987:36) offer highly suggestive reconstructions of lines 11b-14a. The many differences in their translations of these lines show the gravity of the difficulties. The left-hand column provides del Olmo Lete's translation and the right gives de Moor's:

He hurried [to light fire],

the servant in the fields (?) of *Yammu*;
in the abode of *Yammu*

one day [after another] he set it.
Thereupon *ᶜAṯtaru* the [pretender shouted]:

"Burning flames and [conflagration (?)],
[also] fire [has been kindled for my palace],

I will set [your] pa[lace on] fire,

For [Yammu] desires a house in the dark,
in the bitter field of the sea!"
Let [Baᶜlu (?)] die in the deepest sea!"

ᶜAthtaru confronted him.
Because you have become k[ing, Yammu,]

fever and r[ui]n [are yours]!

fire they brought [to my house]".
[in the middle of] the fire my [lads] will carry it!

There is no evidence presently available to determine whether lines 11b-14 constitute narrative or direct discourse. Although the extant verbal forms are in the third person (line 14), this information is insufficient to resolve the difficulty. There are no first or second person forms of any sort, and the third person forms could belong to either narrative or speech. There is a piece of highly circumstantial evidence which might serve to support the view that lines 11b-14 are narrative. In the Introduction,[37] it is suggested that KTU 1.4 VIII-1.6 was modelled to a certain extent on 1.1-1.2. Specifically, correspondences noted between the two sections include the place of Athtar in both 1.2 III and 1.6 I as noted by del Olmo Lete (1977:44-46). The latter passage includes first Athtar's attempt to measure up to the size of Baal's throne and then failing to do so, he descends (*yrd*) in line 63 and retracts his claim to Baal's kingship. Similarly, the interlude of 1.2 III 11b-14 contains very little explicit information, but one clear form is *yrd* in line 14 perhaps indicating, as in 1.6 I 63, that Athtar descends, thereby ceding claims to universal kingship. This is a guess, however, based on hardly any evidence.

Line 11b provides little information; perhaps it reports that a messenger (*ǵlm*) went to Yamm and told him the news of El's exchange with Kothar. Line 11b might then provide a transition between Kothar's commission from El and "the Athtar interlude." Based on

---

37 For discussion, see pp. 18–19.

the few extant words in this passage, it might be guessed that in lines 12-13 a fire (*ʾišt* in line 13) is set in, or possibly carried (*yblmm*) into, a palace of Yamm perhaps in order to fire the bricks as in 1.4 VI 22-35. It is commonly supposed that in line 12 Athtar receives the title *dm[lk]*, literally "the one of ki[ngship]." In the translations quoted above, del Olmo Lete accepts this reconstruction and translates the phrase as Athtar's title "the Pretender" (i.e., to the throne) while de Moor takes this reconstructed word as a verb, "to become king." This reconstruction is often connected with the putative attestation of the expression *ʿṯtr d[ml]k* in line 18.[38] While this reconstruction for line 18 is feasible, the same reconstruction for line 12 is dubious, given the possible reading *dt*°.

Line 13 contains the word, *ḥrḥrtm* (plural, dual or with mimation?), unless another letter is to be reconstructed before the attested portion of this word such as *[š]ḥrḥrtm* (so del Olmo Lete). The word *ḫurḫur(r)atu* occurs in an Akkadian text from Ugarit (see van Soldt 1990:346-47; Huehnergard 1987b:126), and is cognate with *ḫurḫuratu*, a word for a red dye (*CAD* Ḫ:250-51), but the relevance of such a word in this context is unclear. Line 14 contains one other complete word, *yrd*, perhaps indicating Athtar's descent as in 1.6 I 63. Line 18 may support the notion of Athtar's descent as he laments his plight.

Excursus 3: The God Athtar

The character and role of Athtar in the Ugaritic texts have not been well understood.[39] Given the general lack of Ugaritic evidence, it would appear germane to present it in concert with other ancient Near Eastern sources bearing on this god.

In the texts from Farah dating to the twenty-sixth century, Athtar is attested in a Sumerian proper name *ur. ᵈaš-tár*, according to Lambert (1985b:537; Farah III 110 i 3). At Ebla *aš-dár* is equated with Inanna (Heimpel 1982:14-15; Krebernik 183:31; Xella 1985: 290). Xella assumes that Eblaite *aš-dár* is Astarte because of this equation,[40] but Archi (1979-80:168) and Heimpel (1982:14-15)

---

38 See below pp. 252-53.

39 See Caquot 1958; Garbini 1974 ; Gray 1949b; du Mesnil du Boisson 1945-48; *TO* 95. For general surveys of Athtar, see Pope, *WdM* 249-50; *CEBCR* 39-45.

40 Cf. *ᶠAstar-ummi* in text 45 in Arnaud 1991:85; Ugaritic *ʿṯtrʾum* (*PTU* 46, 113). It is on the basis of this name as well as the female-male interpretation of the Venus

identify *aš-dár* with Athtar. According to Heimpel the basis of the equation is not anthropomorphic as Athtar and Inanna belong to different sexes. He suggests that the two are equated because they both represent the Venus star, the male in the morning and the female at evening.[41] According to Archi (1979-80:171), the name of the god appears frequently as a theophoric element in personal names from Ebla, but is relatively rare in sacrificial lists.

The Mari texts refer to Astar as *ᵈMUŠ.ZA.(ZA)* (Lambert 1985b: 529-30). In distinction, the name *ᵈMUŠ.ZA.ZA* may be Astarte (see Gelb 1992:133). At Mari *ᵈMUŠ.ZA.(ZA)* is attested as a "male Ishtar" (Heimpel 1982:14). An inscription of Puzur-Astar includes curses by *ᵈMUŠ.ZA.(ZA)*, that is Astar, with Dagan and "Enki, lord of the assembly."[42] Mari texts witness also to *ᵈas-tár-ṣa-ar-ba-at*, apparently Ashtar plus a geographical name (Lambert 1985b:529-30).

The astral character of Athtar during second millennium Syria is evident from Emar 378.39′ which attests to *ᵈAš-tar MUL*, "Astar des étoiles." This occurrence is representative of the understanding of the god, as the other entries in Emar 378.36′-39′ also present other deities in ways characteristic of them: "Ea of scribes, Nabu of schols, Ea of the forges." Arnaud (1991:15) argues that *ᵈNIN.URTA* in the Emar texts is to be read as *ᵈAš-tar*, based on the double equation Ninurta = Aštabi and Aštabi = Aštar (see below). According to Arnaud, Athtar then was the city god of Emar. If so, the equation with Ninurta would also suggest Athtar's martial character at Emar. However, the equation is not secure since as Fleming (1992:248-52, esp. 249 n. 186) observes, Emar 378 contains *ᵈNIN.URTA* (lines 7; 47′-48′ [partially reconstructed]) as well as *ᵈAš-tar MUL* (line 39′). The name of Athtar appears also as a theophoric element in several proper names (Fleming 1992:221 n. 70).

Ugaritic texts add further information about Athtar. As in 1.2 III, in 1.6 I Athtar is presented as a warrior, albeit one who is inadequate for kingship. His epithet *ʿrẓ* is cognate with BH *ʿārîṣ*,

---

star that some scholars consider Athtar to be androgynous. However, the referent of these names may be Athtart just as the male Ishtar at Mari is Athtar. Or, the names may refer to Athtar and the usage was considered metaphorical (see Smith 1990:99). For the issue of Athtar's putative androgyny, see further pp. 257-58.

41 Jacobsen 1976:140; Roberts 1972: 39-40; Caquot 1958:51. See Enuma Anu Enlil 50-51, VI 5 (Reiner 1981:48-49).

42 Lambert (1985b:537) takes this reference to Enki as El.

"powerful," which is applied to Yahweh in Jer 20:11 (Caquot 1958:47). The Ugaritic title need not be rendered "terrible," but "powerful" or the like.[43] This martial aspect is also reflected in the correspondence of the war-gods Sumerian *^{d}L[UGAR.MÁ]R?.DA* (as restored by Huehnergard 1987b:164), the Hurrian Ashtabi (read *aš-ta-bi-[n]i?* by Huehnergard 1987b:164; cf. Stern 1991:35) and the syllabic Akkadian spelling of Athtar's name as *aš-ta-ru* in *UgV*, 137 iv b 16.

Athtar also appears in KTU 1.24, the hymn of the moon-goddess Nikkal. Given the astral character of some of the other deities in this text such as Nikkal and Yarih, the mention of Athtar in 1.24.28 may be due to his astral character (Caquot 1958:47-49). Gray (1949:91) and Oldenburg (*CEBCR* 41) suggest the further possibility that the "lion" mentioned in line 30 may be Athtar. Gray suggests this equation, as the lion is the animal of Ishtar and Ishtar was derived from Athtar. This reasoning is quite speculative and the reading *lbʾu* is debated (*TO* 394-95 n. w). Gibson (*CML*^{2} 129) reads *lbb*, "heart," but lists *lbʾu* as a second possibility. The evidence of 1.24.28 is consistent with the evidence from Ebla and Emar: Athtar was associated with the planet Venus or "the Venus star."[44]

Caquot deduces from 1.24.28 that Athtar once held a high place in the pantheon otherwise unattested in the Ugaritic myths. The Baal Cycle would reflect Baal's displacement of Athtar in impor-

---

[43] J. C. Greenfield, personal communication. *UT* 19.1919 translates *ʿrẓ* "terrible, majestic," and de Moor (*SPUMB* 204-05) renders "tyrant, mighty."

[44] See Gray 1949b; *LC*^{2} 170; Pope, *WdM* 249-50; *CEBCR* 130; Roberts 1972:39; *TO* 95. The decline of Athtar in 1.2 III and 1.6 I has been compared also with the fate of the stary figure, Shahar ben Helal, who falls from the heavens to the depths according to Isa 14:12-15 (see Grelot 1956a; McKay 1970; Craigie 1973; Loretz 1976; Hanson 1977:206). Comparison has been made also between Athtar and the two gods, named Shahar wa-Shalim, "Dawn and Dusk" in 1.23.52-53 (see Gray 1949b; Pope, *WdM*, 250; *YGC* 187). It has been argued that these two deities correspond to the morning and evening Venus star and are to be identified with *ʾilm nʿmm* in KTU 1.23.60 and 67 (Gray 1949b; cf. *CML*^{2} 30). Attridge and Oden (1981:88 n. 96) suggest that the descent of Athtar from heaven is reflected in PE 1.10.31: "Astarte placed upon her own head a bull's head as an emblem of kingship. While travelling around the world, she discovered a star which had fallen from the sky. She took it up and consecrated it in Tyre." The suggestion by Attridge and Oden assumes a misidentification on the part of Philo of his source.

tance (*YGC* 231-32; Caquot 1958:58), a reconstruction which might explain why Athtart seems to be Baal's consort. Arnaud (1981: 34)[45] posits a reconstruction at Emar which may apply as well at Ugarit: perhaps at one time Athtart was Athtar's consort, and Athtart subsequently became Baal's consort.

The name of Athtar appears in the ninth century Mesha stele (KAI 181:17) as the first element in the double-name *ʿštrkmš*, "Ashtar-Kemosh," a Moabite god. The name *ʿštrkmš* has been thought to belong to DNs which Gordon characterizes as a "fusing of two different names"[46] belonging to two originally separate deities. Stern (1991:37-38) treats **ʿštr* as an epithet, "as a generalized form of the deity meaning, 'the warrior,' or the like," but such a sense is otherwise unattested unless **ʿštr* in the Deir ʿAlla inscription (Combination I, line 14) were to be understood in this manner. Unfortunately, this line is poorly understood and consequently left untranslated in the edition of J. A. Hackett.[47] The Aramaic Sefire inscription likewise contains a compound name, 'Attarsamak who is said to be the king of Arpad (*ANET* 659; KAI 222-224). This name is attested also on an Aramaic seal dating to about 800 (Bordreuil 1986:76 # 86). Another Aramaic seal of about the same date preserves the name *brʿtr*, meaning either "son of Athtar" or less likely "Athtar is pure" (Bordreuil 1986:80 # 93). Naveh (1979:115- 16) notes the personal names *ʿtrdmry* at Hermapolis, *ʿtrmlky* at Elephantine, and *ʿtrswry* at Elephantine and Palmyra. Caquot (1958: 51) observes that the name of Athtar survives in Palmyrene PNs *ʿstwr* (CIS II:3933), *ʿstwrgʾ* (4199) and *ʿbdʿstwr* (4418) and in the name of an ancestor of a family of converts called *barʿaštōr* (b. Bikk. 64a).[48]

The name *ʿtršmn*, "Athtar of the heavens" appears on an Aramaic seal dated to the end of the ninth century (Bordreuil 1986:75 # 85). The second element of Atarsamain's name has been taken as an indication of his astral status.[49] Cross (1983b:61) regards the owner

---

45 This publication came to my attention via Pardee 1979-80b:466. I wish to thank Professor Pardee for supplying me with a copy of the original publication.

46 *UT* 8.61 n. 1; Barstad 1984:173; Olyan 1988:55.

47 Hackett 1980:29. McCarter (1980) translates *ʿštr* as "young." If this word were related to the name of the god, then it would militate in favor of the non-Aramaic character of the dialect.

48 For further Aramaic proper names with *ʿtr* as the theophoric element, see Bordreuil 1986:80.

49 *YGC* 228; for criticisms of Albright's other identifications with Athtar, see *CMHE* 7 n. 13.

of the seal as an Aramaized Arab since "the god bears a favorite epithet of a North Arabian league." The same name appears also in NA sources which provide some information about Athtar among the northern Arabs (Ebeling 1932; Weippert 1972:44-45 n. 24; Teixidor 1977:68-69). According to Esarhaddon, his father Sennacherib took as war booty the images of Arab gods, including that of Atarsamain, and Esarhaddon returned them (*ANET* 291). Assurbanipal also mentions that he "rounded up the confederation of Atarsamain (*^{lu}a*ʾ*lu ša ^{d}Ataršamain*)."[50] Most commentators translate *a*ʾ*lu* as "people" (Weippert 1972:44-45; Barré 1983:161 n. 47) which may be supported by appeal to Arabic ʾ*ahl*, ESA ʾ*hl* and Lihyanite ʾ*l*, "people" (Biella 7; Cross 1983a:36 n. 63). Cross (*CMHE* 7 n. 13; 105 n. 49; 1983:36 n. 63) argues that the context, however, favors the translation, "league," or "sacral confederation." Sabean witnesses to the linguistic equivalent ʾ*hl* ʿ*ṯtr*, "community/clan of Athtar," attested in a number of inscriptions (e.g., CIH 434.1; 547:1; see G. Ryckmans 1934:27-28; Biella 7).[51] Ashurbanipal also addresses a prayer to Atarsamain (Cogan 1974:15-20; Barré 1983:161 n. 47). North Arabian sources also attest to the names ʿAttar and ʿAttarsamin (Höfner in Gese, Höfner and Rudolph 1970:377; G. Ryckmans 1951:23).

The Phoenician evidence is minimal at best. In a fourth century Byblian inscription Garbini (1960:322) reads *l*ʿ*štrḥn* and claims that the theophoric element belongs to Ashtar.

ESA inscriptions, hailing from the kingdoms of Hadramout, Maʿin, Qataban and Sabaʾ and dating from the eighth century B. C. E. to the sixth century C. E., witness to Athtar (G. Ryckmans 1934:27; 1951:41-42; 1962; Jamme 1947:85-97; 1956:264-65; Höfner in Gese, Höfner and Rudolph 1970:268-70).[52] According to Jamme (1947:85-86), the name of Athtar is most frequently written ʿ*ṯtr*, but sometimes it appears as (ʿ)*str*, ʿ*tr* and (ʿ)*ṯt* in Sabaʾ and as ʿ*śtrm* and (ʿ)*ṯt* in Hadramout (Jamme 1947:85-97; *ANET* 663-69).

---

50 For a critical translation of Prism A, VIII, line 124 (cf. line 112), see Weippert 1972:44-45, 68-69; *ANET* 299.

51 Weippert regards ʾ*hl* in this phrase as the "Priester- oder Kultgenossenschaft" of Athtar (cf. G. Ryckmans 1934:27-28). *AHw* (39a) takes the Akkadian phrase as "Beduinenstamm" and raises the possibility that the Akkadian word may be a loanword from Arabic ʾ*ahl*.

52 I owe many details in the following discussion (noted below) to Professor A. Jamme who most graciously commented on my notes.

The god is well-attested. J. Ryckmans (1992:172) regards him as the most important god of the South Arabian pantheon: "all the South Arabian nations venerated him under the same name and he takes first place in enumerations of several gods."

ESA inscriptions suggest that Athtar is an astral deity (Jamme 1947:88-89; *ANET* 663 n. 5; J. Ryckmans 1992:172). Scholars generally take Athtar's title Šarqân as an epithet characterizing the star-god as "the eastern" (G. Ryckmans 1934:29; Jamme 1947:88; *ANET* 666, 667)[53] In one Sabean inscription (CIH 149.2-3) Jamme (1947:88) reconstructs *[šr]qn/wǵrbn*, "[the ea]st and the west," which "marque les deux stades opposés de Vénus."

Athtar shows a number of other features and titles. Athtar is also called *yǵl*, "avenger" (RES 3978.1), *ʾb*, "father" (RES 2693.5) and *rfʾn* (RES 3978.1). G. Ryckmans takes the third form as a sanctuary or an epithet, but Höfner (*WdM* 498) and Jamme (1947:89 n. 257) regard it as an epithet meaning "protector." Jamme suggests also the possibility of a place-name. Jamme (1956:265) notes three further characteristics of the god: (1) *ʿṯtr* is the deity to whom people **rṯd*, "entrusted" things because they believed that he was strong enough to protect their property; (2) the deity is mentioned commonly in the imprecations on tombs; and (3) the deity is qualified by the epithet *ʿzz*, "strong."

According to Jamme (1947:89; 1956:264-65), RES 4194.5 and CIH 47.2 suggest that Athtar was a god of irrigation.[54] These inscriptions call Athtar *mnḍḥhmw*, which Jamme translates as "leur divinité d'irrigation." There is some disagreement over the value of this evidence. It should be noted that **nḍḥ* shows no specific association with irrigation, only with watering. Höfner (*WdM* 515) understands the epithet as "Bewässerungsgottheit," and translates the root **nḍḥ*, "mit Wasser bespregen, befeuchten." Van den Branden (1959:184) examines the context where this title occurs and concludes that it may not refer to the role of irrigation as such, but to

---

53 Jamme 1947:88; *ANET* 666 n. 5. It has been supposed that Athtar has the epithet *ḏ-yhrq*, "he who sets," implying that Athtar was the evening star (*CMHE* 68). According to Jamme (1947:92 n. 284), RES 4176.9 attests *byhrq* which is to be interpreted not as an epithet but as a place-name. It is also claimed that in South Arabian inscriptions he is said also to be the first-born of moon-god (Höfner, *WdM* 249), but Jamme (1947) disputes this view.

54 The name of the god has been related to Arb *ʿaṯtarî* (see below), which refers to natural irrigation of water found on the surface running in channels or the like (Lane 1952).

divine protection, another meaning known for the Arabic root **nḍḥ*. The meaning of "protection," however, stands outside the development of the basic fundamental meaning of the root. Hence, Athtar may have been attributed the role of waterer.

Jamme also notes the pertinence of an inscription, Fakhry 71.4-5 (G. Ryckmans 1951:62). In this inscription Athtar receives a gift "in gratitude because he has vouchsa[fed] the spring storm [which was] an abundant irrigation" *ḥmdm/bḏt/[wr]y/brq/ḏṯʾn/sqym/mhšfqm* (translation and transcription, courtesy of Jamme). G. Ryckmans (1951:41) suggests that this feature of Athtar was a secondary development: "c'est-à-dire remplaçent les divinités d'irrigation." Jamme (1947:89) views the presentation of Athtar as "une reproduction fautive imputable au lapicide de l'énumération *habituelle* des noms divin" (Jamme's italics). It would appear then Athtar was viewed occasionally as a provider of waters, but J. Ryckmans (1992:172) offers a more generous view:

> ʿAṯtar was the god of natural irrigation by rain, in contrast to the artificial irrigation of of the arid zones, which depended on rainwater fallen elsewhere and conveyed and distributed by an irrigation network. This could explain a distinction between two kinds of Sabaean lands in the first centuries A.D.: the "domain (*mulk*) of ʿAṯtar," in contrast to that "of Almaqah," the national god of Saba."

The issue remains open.

The etymology of the god's name is debated. G. Ryckmans (1962:190) takes the root to be **ʿṯr*, "être riche, irriguer." The third consonant is often explained as an infix *-t-* with metathesis.[55] Krebernik identifies the form with the Akkadian *PitRāS* form "mit begriffsintensivierender Bedeutung" (*GAG*, para. 56n). This infix is unusual at best for a divine name.

Krebernik (1983:31) cites BH **ʿšr* and Aram **ʿtr* as cognates. Akk *ešēru*, "to thrive, prosper" (of crops, animals, persons) may be related as well (*CAD* E:354), but it is possible that BH **ʿšr* and Aram **ʿtr*, as well as Akk *ešēru*, are related instead to Arab **ǵṯr*, "to flourish" (used of land) and the noun *ǵaṯaran*, "abundance" (Lane 2230). Delcor (1974:13) relates the name of the god to this root, but given the Ugaritic attestation of both ʿ and *ǵ*, this view is unwarranted. Kre-

---

[55] G. Ryckmans 1934:27; Delcor 1974:13; Krebernik 1983:31. This view may be traced to Delitzsch 1889:181 (reference courtesy of A. Jamme).

bernik also cites South Arabian *ʿṯr based on two dubious citations.[56]

Robertson Smith (1972:100 n.2), Gaster (*Thespis* 133 n. 35),[57] Gray (1949), G. Ryckmans (1951:41, 62), Oldenburg (*CEBCR* 39) and de Moor (*SPUMB* 205) relate the name of Athtar to Arabic *ʿaṯṯarî*, which ancient authorities define as "soil artificially irrigated." Robertson Smith (1972:99 n. 2), Caquot (1958:59) and de Moor (*SPUMB* 205 n. 4) observe that the authorities for this interpretation of this Arabic word are problematic. However, in support of this view, G. Ryckmans (1962:190) relates this word to a Yemeni term, *ʿanṯari*, "land thriving on rain supply" (Piamenta 1991:2.316, 324).[58] G. Ryckmans (1962:190 n. 31) cites van Arendonk to the effect that in Arabic sources "*ʿiḏy baʿl* et *ʿaṯṯari* ont également été parfois employés indifféremment pour les terrains abreuvés par la pluie." According to Robertson Smith (1972:99 n. 2), *ʿaṯṯari* may have been originally distinguished as land watered by an artificial channel. It appears unlikely, however, that this word was the basis for the god's name, since the basic meaning of the Arabic root is "to stumble, fall, trip." Arabic *ʿaṯṯarî* apparently derived secondarily from the god's name.

Leslau (73) relates the god's name to Tigre *ʿastär*, "heaven," Geʿez *ʿastar*, "sky," Amharic *astär*, "star" (from Geʿez), and Bilin *astär*, "sky." These nouns could have derived from the god's name and may indicate that Athtar was considered an astral god. Finally, Jamme (1956:265) relates *ʿṯtr* to Arb *ʿattâr*, "strong," based on his understanding of the god (noted above). Jamme (1956:265) explains the linguistic issue: "le changement de la dentale *t* en spirante *th* paraissant *dû* à l'influence de la gutterale ʿ". This unusual linguistic condition has not met with general acceptance (G. Ryckmans 1962:191). In sum, the South Semitic evidence suggests that Athtar was an important astral god who was considered a strong protector

---

[56] Conti Rossini 1931:214. The first alleged attestation was based on a mistaken reading as shown by Höfner (1936:84; see also Biella 389); the correct reading is *wtr*. The other alleged attestation, RES 3306.405, is fragmentary and the text is poorly understood. The South Semitic evidence for *ʿtr in this meaning is dubious. Information courtesy of A. Jamme.

[57] Gaster (*Thespis* 133 n. 35) suggests that *ʿšr in Ps 65:10 also shows this meaning, but this is disputed.

[58] Piamenta takes the word from *ʿaṯṯarî*. Note also the Arabic *ʿaṯirat ʾarḍ*, land (without herbage) that has *ʿiṯyar*, "dust" (Lane 1952).

and at least occasionally a provider of water through natural irrigation.

Given the ancient Near Eastern evidence, approaches to the question of why Athtar represents an unsuitable candidate for kingship in 1.2 III and 1.6 I have gravitated in two directions. First, scholars including Jacobsen, Gaster and Gray propose that Athtar represents irrigation and therefore serves as an apt foil to Baal's rains.[59] The limited etymological evidence would support this view. The comparative evidence for Athtar as a god of irrigation is also late and meager, and it is unclear whether it represents a development specific to Arabia. Moreover, no Ugaritic text explicitly attributes this function to Athtar. However, the notion may be old, and Ugarit could have known the notion of Athtar as a producer of water. If so, Athtar's control over the earth, attested in *wymlk bʾarṣ ʾil klh*, "and he will rule in all the great earth" (KTU 1.6 I 65), may reflect his ability to provide water (cf. Wyatt 1986; Waterston 1988). Second, the closest comparative evidence from Emar as well as the little Ugaritic information (1.24.28) would support the view that Athtar was an old astral deity. That he was considered a divine warrior displaced by Baal is reflected in 1.6 I (Caquot 1958:55; Gese in Gese, Höfner and Rudolph 1961:138).

The two views may be related environmentally. The geographical distribution of the cults of Athtar and Baal may constitute part of the larger problem in the picture of Athtar at Ugarit. The cult of Athtar appears largely restricted to inland areas.[60] Apart from the Ugaritic texts, there is no clear evidence for the cult of Athtar on the coast. There is no mention of Athtar in either the Amarna letters, Egyptian sources mentioning West Semitic deities, the Bible or Philo of Byblos. The value of the single Phoenician attestation for establishing the cult of Athtar is questionable. In contrast, the cult of Baal was at home on the coast. Within the Ugaritic texts, the representation of Athtar as a weak god may reflect his cult's absence from coastal areas.

Accordingly, it is tempting to follow W. R. Smith (1972:99-100 n. 2) in viewing the difference between Baal and Athtar in agricul-

---

[59] Jacobsen 1976:140; *Thespis* 127, 219; *LC*[2] 170. For other scholars who hold this view, see *SPUMB* 205 n. 3.

[60] Cf. the remarks of Gray (*LC*[2] 170 n. 2): "The fertility function of the deity is not to be doubted, but in view of the pre-eminence of the cult of Aṯtar in oases and lands bordering on the desert it seems more natural than the fertility-function of the deity in the settled lands."

tural terms, especially as the later use of these gods' names for land fed by water. Smith remarks that m. B. Bat. 3:1 reflects the older use of *baʿl* as land wholly dependent on rain, and argues that the original contrast lay between land wholly dependent on rain as opposed to irrigated land.[61] The coastal regions received heavy rainfall which precluded the need for either dry farming or irrigation. At Ugarit for example the rains fall over seven or eight months and exceed 800 mm. each year (Yon 1992:698). In contrast, many of the inland sites where Athtar is attested practiced either dry farming or natural irrigation. It might be argued that in the environment of Ugarit, the god of the storm would naturally supplant the god of natural irrigation.

An additional consideration deserves notice. The Baal Cycle indicates that unlike Baal, Athtar belongs to the family of El and Athirat, but the basis for this familial relationship is unclear.[62] Given the wide attestation of Athtar as an astral deity, the basis for his relationship to El and Athirat may lie in the astral character of this family unit. Unfortunately, the evidence for the astral character of El or Athirat is extremely meager. In KTU 1.23.48-54 El is the father of Shahar and Shalim. Job 38:7 may preserve an old notion about the family of El (*CEBCR* 18) in the parallel phrases *kôkĕbê bōqer*, "morning stars"//*kol-bĕnê ʾĕlōhîm*, "all the divine sons" (or "all the sons of God"). ESA sources may support this point. Athirat is the name of a Qatabanian solar goddess and spouse of the moon-god (Jamme 1956:266). El survives in South Arabian religion as well (Oldenburg 1970; J. Ryckmans 1992:172). It must be emphasized that the Ugaritic evidence for the astral character of El and Athirat's family is minimal. By the same token, this paucity of information may be due to the displacement of the family of El and Athirat by the Ugaritic cult of Baal who does not belong to this family. Similarly, the South Arabian cult of El appears to have been displaced by the cult of Athtar (so J. Ryckmans 1992:172).

In sum, the Ugaritic texts as well as the most proximate compara-

---

[61] W. R. Smith 1972:102 n. 2. For subsequent modifications of this contrast in rabbinic and Arabic sources, see Smith 1972:95-113, esp. 100, 102 n. 2.

[62] For the problem of Baal's paternity, see above pp. 91-94. The contrast between the family line of Athtar and that of Baal is explicit in 1.24.25-30, if the approach taken by Gibson (*CML*[2] 129) and others (*TO* 393-94) is generally correct. This approach is not followed, however, by de Moor (1987:144).

tive evidence from Emar indicate that Athtar was an astral god who was considered a warrior. It would appear that at Ugarit Baal supplanted Athtar as the divine warrior and provider of water. The narratives of KTU 1.2 III and 1.6 I stress that Athtar is not powerful enough to serve as divine king. Indeed, some scholars have understood Athtar as a foil to Baal in the Baal Cycle (Greenfield 1985). Oberman (*UgM* 19) regarded Athtar as Baal's "alter ego."

Lines 15-18a

As recognized by the commentators, lines 15-18a constitute Shapshu's speech. This goddess confirms El's support of Yamm's kingship as she does in 1.6 VI 23-29. Following most commentators, Watson (1983:254) notes that the formula represented by *tšʾu gh w[tṣḥ]*, "she raises her voice and [cries out]" in line 15, constitutes a narrative introduction to speeches in the Ugaritic mythological texts.

The first part of the speech to Athtar in lines 15b-16 opens with an invocation to him to hear the following message of Shapshu. The formula, **šmʿ mʿ* + DN, opens a number of speeches (e.g., 1.4 VI 4; 1.6 VI 23-24; cf. 1.4 V 59). Following the invocation is a tricolon which is clear, except for the verb *[yṯ]ʾir*. Based on context Ginsberg (*ANET* 129) suggests "favor," Driver (*CML*[1] 79) translates "confirmed," and van Selms (1970:255-56) renders the same verb as "bestow favor." De Moor (1987:37) likewise translates *yṯʾir ṯr ʾil ʾabk*, "Bull El has granted his favor...". According to Gibson (*CML*[2] 38), Ugaritic *yṯʾir* means "he will arrange" as in 1.3 II 36-37 (cf. 20-21).[63] In 1.3 II 36-37, **ṯʾr* belongs to a description of a feast. In view of syntax and context, **ṯʾr* might refer to setting a table before Yamm as a sign of El's favor, but this appears unlikely as no such object appears in the text. Gibson accordingly compensates with a parenthetical addition: "the bull El your father [will indeed] cause (the table) to be set." It would seem that **ṯʾr* in 1.2 III

[63] Apparently following *SPUMB* 69 where de Moor takes the forms of **ṯʾr* as variants of the root **ṯʿr*, "to set." De Moor interprets *tṯʾar* in 1.3 II 37 as a *G*-stem impf., and *yṯʾir* as an *N*-stem of the same verb.

16 and 21 is unrelated to the usage in 1.3 II 36-37.[64] Relying on the Arabic cognate *ṯʾr, "to avenge" (*CEBCR* 132, 191; Mullen 1980:109), it may be preferable to translate that Bull El "will take vengeance before Prince Yamm."[65] (In this manner El might be viewed as "favoring" Yamm.)

The second part of Shapshu's speech is paralleled fully in 1.6 VI 26-29. It begins with a question to Athtar in the form of a bicolon: how shall El hear or pay heed (**šmᶜ*) to him. The use of **šmᶜ* in this line balances with the invocation **šmᶜ* at the beginning of the first section in line 15. The use of El's title, "Bull" *ṯr*, in lines 16 and 17, likewise gives some further balance to the two parts of Shapshu's speech as does the appearance of **ṯpṭ* at the end of both parts, in lines 16 and 18.[66] Shapshu's question in line 17 seems to presuppose a protasis that if Athtar opposes El's wishes to make Yamm the monarch of the pantheon and cosmos, how shall (or perhaps better, why should) El hearken to Athtar. Indeed, the use of **šmᶜ* in lines 15 and 17 would reinforce this reading, for Shapshu commands Athtar to "listen," to her words (line 15), in which case El "will listen" to Athtar (line 17).

The next statement in lines 17b-18 (//1.6 VI 27b-29) contains only one major philological difficulty, namely *ʾalt*. Assuming Arb *ʾalah*, "tool, implement," some commentators take *ʾalt* as "furniture" on the basis of the parallelism with *ksʾa mlkk* (see *SPUMB* 236). Based on the same etymology, Gordon (*UT* 19.211) suggests "platform" also as a possibility. De Moor prefers "door-jamb of your residence" (*SPUMB* 230, 236-37) on the basis of BH *ʾayil*, "door-jamb." This view, however, assumes the meaning of "residence" for *ṯbt*. While possible philologically, *ṯbt* refers literally in other poetic instances to the throne or seat of "sitting." Oldenburg (*CEBCR* 190 n. 8) takes *ʾalt* as a noun meaning "support," based on the middle weak root which is attested in Ugaritic (cf. *ʾawl* in 1.12 II 5b; *MLC* 511). In this context it would be an attractive solution if it were to be understood as an abstract noun used for a concrete referent.[67]

---

[64] Especially if *ṯʾr in 1.3 II is to be considered a text-critical error for *ṯᶜr (see the previous note).

[65] Not necessarily with the sense of "blood-vengeance" supposed by Oldenburg (*CEBCR* 132, 191).

[66] Perhaps the second person sg. suffixes in lines 16, 17 and 18 and the various instances of *l* in lines 16, 17 and 18 likewise give some unity to the two parts.

[67] For another Ugaritic example, see *dᶜtk* in 1.6 VI 50. For BH cases see *GKC* 83c.

Although the etymological basis of the translation "support" is superior to the gloss, "furniture," either would suit the context and literary parallels to *ʾalt ṯbtk*. The motifs of the royal throne and sceptre appear in a variety of Near Eastern curses (Greenfield 1971:254-58; de Moor and van der Lugt 1974:4 n. 8; Demsky 1978:8) beginning with the epilogue to the Code of Hammurapi (*ANET* 179, xxvi rev. 50-51, xxvii rev. 45-46):

> May he (Anu) break his sceptre...
> May he (Sin) deprive him of the crown (and) throne of sovereignty...

The Ahiram sarcophagus (KAI 1:2) contains the same cliché:

tḥtsp ḥṭr mšpṭh	May his staff of judgement be broken,
thtpk ksʾ mlkh	May the seat of his kingship be overturned.

Greenfield also notes a parallel in b. Git 35a, which cites a curse against Rabbi bar Huna: *lyhpkwh lkwrsyh*, "may they overturn his chair." These passages reflect the original setting of the formula in 1.2 III 17b-18//1.6 VI 26-29. In all of these curses, except the Talmudic one, a king uses this motif against a potential successor: if he commits certain named acts against the person of the speaker, the curse is in force. The setting of these curses is specifically royal, and suits the royal issues at stake in 1.2 III and 1.6 VI. In the case of 1.2 III, the question of kingship is raised specifically in line 22. Set in the speech of Shapshu, the curse assumes the sort of protasis explicit in the parallel passages cited above, namely that if Athtar opposes the will of El, he may not support Athtar. Furthermore, the curse is altered slightly in 1.2 III 17b-18: the particle *l-* indicates that the verbs are not jussives, but asseverative statements. In sum, Shapshu's speech shows that El now supports Yamm for kingship and Athtar cannot oppose this state of affairs lest he risk El's loss of support for his kingship over his domain. There is nothing in the lines to suggest that Athtar does not remain king over his own realm, just as the same speech to Mot in 1.6 VI 23-29 does not indicate that Mot has lost kingship over his realm of the Underworld to Baal, except in the sense that Baal is sovereign over the entire cosmos.

Lines 18b-25

The beginning of the unit is evident from the introductory speech formula of line 18a. Line 18b opens the speech of Athtar with a title which according to Gibson (*CML*² 3) describes Athtar "as possessing the kingship." This view of Athtar's status, which assumes the problematic reconstruction *dmlk* in both lines 12 and 18,[68] is unclear. It may refer to either Athtar's dominion over his own realm, like Yamm and Mot (so Wyatt 1986, 1988), or kingship beyond his own realm. The former appears more likely, but so little is understood of this scene that either view remains a possibility. Del Olmo Lete (*MLC* 167) views the putative title *dmlk* as an expression of Athtar's pretensions to the throne which Yamm and Baal also claim. This view may be overreading the title; it may simply reflect Athtar's royal character. In any case, these interpretations hinge on a debatable reconstruction.

Athtar apparently complains in lines 18b-20a not that he is the king of the pantheon, but that he has no house like the gods and being a king, too, he deserves a palace. The opening of the first line of the speech in line 19 has often interpreted as the imperative of the root **lqḥ*, "to take," plus prepositional phrase, *ly*.[69] Some commentators wisely refrain from interpreting what may or may not be a verb here (so *TO* 124; *CML*² 38). In his invocation Athtar calls El his father, a common motif in the Baal Cycle; many deities call El their father. In lines 19b-20a Athtar expresses the sentiment that he has no palace like the other gods, a lament which echoes Baal's complaint expressed in 1.3 IV 46-48, V 38-39, 1.4 I 9-10 and IV 50-51 (cf. 1.3 V 3-4). The lacuna at the beginning of line 19 may hide some further meaning. It would seem that despite this gap, the bicolon expresses Athtar's recognition that he lacks a royal palace, a sign of royal power.

The next bicolon, line 20b, is exceptionally problematic. The first line might reflect Athtar's recognition that he must descend from kingship, but the interpretations of the line vary a great deal. Taking *npš* as "tomb" and emending *lbʾum* to *lbdm*,[70] Gibson (*CML*² 38) renders: "Alone I shall go down into the grave of us both." Gibson (*CML*² 38 n. 5) comments that this line reflects an

> ... extension of the metaphor whereby the entrance to the underworld is compared to the throat of the god of death Mot (cp. 5 i 17). The reference here is perhaps to drowning in the sea; the sun of course sank into the sea west of Ugarit.

---

[68] CTA p. 10 n. 6; *CML*² 38, textual note to line 18. See above p. 240.

[69] So Virolleaud; see CTA p. 10 n. 14. For discussion, see above p. 216.

[70] So also CTA, KTU, *TO* 124 and *MLC* 168.

One difficulty with this view is that *npš* does not mean "grave" in Ugaritic (Pope 1978:28). Another problem is whether the emendation is warranted. Like Gibson, *TO* (124) emends *lbʾum* to *lbdm* and takes *bn[p]šny* with the next line, creating two unbalanced lines. Clapham (1968:152) translates the bicolon: "When I am (re-)born Kothar will wash me." The subordinate clause in this translation assumes an idiom, "to descend as the son of my life," but such an idiom is otherwise unknown. The collocation of *npš* and *lbʾim* found in 1.5 I 14 may clarify Athtar's statement (Smith 1985:60). In 1.5 I 14 Mot, another rival claimant to kingship, declares *pnpš npš lbʾim*, "my desire is the desire of the lion." The parallel line in 1.2 III 20 may be rendered analogously: *lbʾum ʾard bn[p]šny*, (like) a lion I will descend with my appetite."

The sense of the metaphor in 1.2 III 20, if the line is understood correctly, is unclear. The word *lbʾum* might reflect the use of an animal not to represent high human rank as in 1.15 IV 6-8 (Miller 1970a), but to signify a warrior. This usage, though rare for "lion" (*lbʾu*), may have some textual basis. A. Mazar (1992:300; cf. *CMHE* 33) argues that the inscriptions on the El-Khadr arrowheads containing *lbʾt*, "the one of the lion" or "Lion Lady," may refer to a class of professional bowmen. He also suggests that Ps 57:5 is relevant to this title: "I lie down in the midst of lions that greedily devour the sons of men; their teeth are spears and arrows, their tongues sharp swords." The usage involved may be metaphorical for a warrior, in the case of Athtar for a fallen warrior. If Athtar's descent involves the underworld, the motif perhaps is echoed in Eccles 9:4: "for a living dog is better than a dead lion." Finally, it is possible that *lbʾu* may be a title of Athtar which reflects his martial character.[71] In any case, Athtar's desire of 1.2 III 20 is directed toward kingship, as the rest of the passage suggests.

In the next clause of line 20, *trḥṣn kṯrm* is notoriously difficult to interpret, not least because of the short lacuna following it. It is understandable that the clause has met with a variety of interpretations. Obermann (*UgM* 18-19 n. 25b) translates "they will wash me

---

[71] See *TO* 125 n. o. The reading of the relevant Ugaritic passage cited by Caquot and Sznycer (*TO* 394-95 n. w'), 1.24.30, is difficult. KTU reads *lb*u**. Gibson (*CML*[2] 129, textual note to line 30) insteads reads *lbb*.

skillfully,'' reflecting **kṯr* in the sense of ''skill.'' As support appeal might be made to *mkṯr*, ''skilled work,'' a meaning of the root attested in Akkadian, Aramaic and Hebrew (Smith 1985:51-79). Another translation is: ''the *kṯrm*/skillful ones will wash me.''[72] Gibson (*CML*² 38 n. 6) views these figures as attendants of Yamm. The difficulty with this approach involves the identity of these figures who are otherwise unknown in West Semitic texts. Stern (1991:34) divides *kṯrm* into two words, *k*-, ''like'' and *ṯrm*, ''bulls.'' The parallelism with the image of the lion in the first line might be invoked as support for this view. Clapham (1968:152) and Smith (1985:60) argue that the name of the craftsman-god is attested here. Clapham translates ''Kothar will wash me.'' As noted by Obermann (*UgM* 18 n. 25b), the *t*- prefix of the imperfect form of **rḥṣ* would seem to require either a plural or dual subject; in the latter case, *kṯrm* could be the name of Kothar (with mimation) serving as the subject of the verb.[73]

The role of washing assigned to Kothar, if correctly understood, might be viewed against the background of various witnesses to this god. In Ugaritic Kothar was known to dwell at an island abode, *kptr* (1.1 III 18), variously identifed with Crete or Cyprus. Accordingly, his epithets include the titles, *bn ym*, ''Son of Sea,'' and *bnm ʿdt*, ''Son of the Confluence'' in KTU 1.4 VII 15-16.[74] This maritime background comports with the difficult description of Kothar as accompanying Shapshu in the sea and Underworld in KTU 1.6 VI 48-53. Perhaps as Gaster notes (*IDB* 1:787-88), the location of the underworld converged on the western sea. PE 1.10.11 (Attridge and Oden 1981:44-45) describes Chousor: ''He is, in fact, Hephaistos and he invented the hook, lure, line, and raft, and was the first of all men to sail'' (*einai de touton ton Hephaiston, eurein de agkistron kai delear kai hormian kai skedian prōton te pantōn anthropōn pleusai*). In Ptolemy's History (Book IV, Chapter VI, line 26), Chousaris is the name

---

[72] Caquot 1958:46; *CML*² 38; van Selms 1979:742; Cooper, *RSP III* 386; *MLC* 168.

[73] Cf. the use of the dual pronoun, *hmt*, for Kothar in 1.17 V 30. The *t*- prefix appears on the apparently masculine dual imperfect verbal forms in KTU 1.5 II alternating between *y*- prefix forms (*ytn* in line 14) and *t*- prefix forms (*tšʾa* and *wtṣḥ* in lines 16-17) in depicting Baal's two messengers going to Mot (*UT* 9.15; cf. Ginsberg 1944). The verbs, *tšbʿn* in 1.23.64, *ttlkn* in 1.23.67 and *tṣdn* in 1.23.68 are apparently duals governed by *ʾilmy nʿmm* in 1.23.60 and *ʾilm nʿmm* in 1.23.67; the *-y* on *ʾilmy* would suggest a dual form.

[74] *TO* 98, 216; Smith 1985:105-18.

of a river on the Atlantic coast of Africa. Over sixty-five years before the discovery of the Ugaritic texts, Falbe and Lindberg (1862:159) argued that this river was named after the Phoenician god Chousar. Various traditions concerning surah 108 of the Quran record that kawthar is the name of a river in paradise (Horovitz and Gardet 1978:806). In modern Bedouin tradition, kawthar is said to be invoked at the washing of new-born children (Pope, *RSP III* 386). These highly diverse witnesses apparently reflect Kothar's western, watery reputation (for further discussion, see Smith 1985:105-14). Given these diverse witnesses to Kothar, it would be possible only to guess the meaning of 1.2 III 20: Athtar exclaims that he is like one going to the Netherworld, and like others on their way to this destination, he will be washed by Kothar; or, Athtar will be washed "in the house of Yamm"(?) in lines 20b-21, located in the sea which contains the abode of Kothar. These options are at best guesses.

In lines 21b-22 Athtar seems to accept El's support for Yamm's kingship. Just as Athtar's lament in lines 19-20a anticipates Baal's complaint in 1.3 IV 47-54, V 35-43 and 1.4 I 4-18, and IV 47-57, so Athtar's final words in line 22 resemble the dilemma, possibly a question like the one posed in 1.4 VII 43: *ʾumlk ʾublmlk*, "king or not king (am I)?" (cf. *SPUMB* 167). The differences between the two sentences seem to be restricted to form: the words in 1.4 VII 43 may constitute a declaration while the utterance in 1.2 III 22 may reflect the form of the double rhetorical question noted by Held (1969), namely no particle ("zero element") preceding the first question and *hm* preceding the second one. Furthermore, the former's third person statement uses nouns where Athtar's first person declaration utilizes verbal forms. The similarities between the two passages might appear to militate in favor of the reconstruction of the first person independent pronoun, *ʾan*, in 1.2 III 22 (V reads *ʾa(?)n*, Gibson *ʾan*, CTA *wn*, and KTU *w*n**). In this case the first question would balance with the second question: *mlkt ʾan//lmlkt ʾan*. In either instance, the use of the pronoun is not absolutely necessary as the verb also reflects the first person character of the line; rather, the pronoun would underline the speaker's self-elevation. The question *mlkt. . . hm mlkt* in line 22[75] could represent not an objection to Yamm's kingship (so de Moor 1987:37), but Athtar's claim that he,

---

[75] Assuming the correctness of reading *h* (as opposed to *p*). For discussion of the reading, see above p. 217.

too, is a king (as in 1.6 I 65) and thus deserving of a house like the one which El commissions for Yamm in the first half of 1.2 III. Athtar then offers the counterclaim that Yamm lacks a consort like the other gods.

According to Caquot and Sznycer (*TO* 126 n. u), Gibson (*CML*[2] 38) and del Olmo Lete (*MLC* 167, 168), line 22 closes Athtar's speech and then presents Shapshu's response to Athtar. Gibson (*CML*[2] 38) reconstructs a narrative introduction to Shapshu's speech: "⟨And Shapash luminary of the gods answered:⟩".[76] This reconstruction would be unnecessary as the speech assumes mention of the Shapshu from lines 15-16. Indeed, the phenomenon of omitting a narrative introduction to speech appears in 1.5 II 7 (*ANET* 138 n. 6) and 1.6 I 5, although in these cases the preceding narrative refers explicitly to the speaker of the speech that follows. In the case of 1.2 III 22, no immediately preceding narrative mentions Shapshu. Another possibility is to see the beginning of Shapshu's speech as early as line 21 (*SPUMB* 12, 167; van Selms 1970:257; Gordon 1977:69). Oldenburg (*CEBCR* 191) and de Moor (*SPUMB* 121) present Yamm as a speaker in the conversation, but there is no evidence for this reconstruction.

There are varying interpretations resulting from the assumption that Shapshu is the speaker. Following a number of commentators, Gibson (*CML*[2] 38) takes Shapshu's objection to Athtar's desire for kingship because of his lack of a wife. The word *wn* belongs to the beginning of this line to judge from analogous formulas.[77] While Baal complains in these lines that he has no house like the other gods, Shapshu tells Athtar that "you have no wife like. . ." The objection posed by Shapshu lacks explicit parallels. Gibson (*CML*[2] 38 n. 7) takes the objection as a lack of a wife and therefore of an heir, a requirement for a proper king. Why Athtar has no wife is unclear. Gaster (*Thespis* 126, 219; cf *UgM* 19) argues that Athtar lacks a wife because he is too young. Oldenburg (*CEBCR* 130) argues that his lack of a wife may be traced to his androgynous character. This view

---

76 Cf. the proposal in *CML*[1] 78-79 to reconstruct a formula introducing a speech of El in the middle of line 22, just before *mlkt*. . .*hm mlkt*.

77 The particle *wn* in line 22b seems to provide connection to a preceding sentence. So 1.3 IV 46 = 1.3 V 38 = 1.4 I 9; 1.4 IV 50; 1.14 III 14; 1.17 V 3. For the grammar of this particle, see Garr 1986:52 n. 50.

of Athtar hinges on parallels which would suggest that Athtar was associated with the Venus star. According to Stern (1991:35) the absence of an explicit reference to Athtar's androgyny militates against the importance of this motif here: "just such an attribute would be seized on for the myth of his rivalry with Baal". There is no textual support for Oldenburg's interpretation. Furthermore, the putative notion of Athtar's androgyny arises from a dubious view of his association with the Venus star. There is no evidence that Athtar symbolized both male and female aspects associated with the Venus star. Rather, it stands to reason that Athtar and Athtart together symbolized these two aspects.[78]

These interpretations assume, however, that Athtar is the one described in line 22b, but de Moor proposes a more economic interpretation of line 22. De Moor's proposal eliminates the need to assume a switch in speaker without a narrative marker for direct discourse. De Moor sees Athtar's speech continuing to line 23, thus explaining the absence of an introductory formula to Shapshu's speech in line 22 as assumed by del Olmo Lete and reconstructed by Gibson (*CML*² 38). The objection in line 22b is aimed then not at Athtar by Shapshu, but at Yamm by Athtar himself. Yamm is not said to have a consort, and he could be the object of the retort in line 22. De Moor also differs in the identification of the speakers of the following lines: line 23 contains a short response by Yamm to Athtar (mostly reconstructed), and like Gibson and del Olmo Lete, de Moor sees lines 24-25 as a speech of Athtart surviving only with the formula introducing direct discourse. Whether or not line 23 constitutes a separate speech as argued by de Moor cannot be verified. In de Moor's favor, lines 23-24a cannot continue Athtar's speech as others argue, since line 24b begins Athtar's response. For this reason de Moor's judgment that line 23 contains a brief speech by Yamm is reasonable and has the further merit of avoiding the assumption of lines 22b-23 as Shapshu's speech (so del Olmo Lete and Gibson). Line 24b contains another introductory speech formula, which would indicate that this unit does not exceed this line, but it is possible that the unit ends prior to line 24, possibly in line 23. This question cannot be adjudicated, given the fragmentary condition of lines 23-24a. In view of the incomplete character of lines 23-24a, it

---

78 See the discussion above p. 241.

is impossible to determine with confidence the character of these lines although de Moor's view is the least problematic.

Line 24a signals the close of one speech and the beginning of another through the formula introducing discourse, *wyʿn ʿṯtr*, "And Athtar answered". The ending of the speech in line 23 concerns Yamm; in what way is unknown. Only a form of the verb **šlḥ* remains. The point of Athtar's retort is likewise a mystery. The only extant letters in line 25 read by KTU do not appear in CTA.

KTU 1.2 I-II-IV

Other numbers: CTA 2.1, 2.2 and 2.4 = UT 137 = III AB A and B = RS 3.367 = AO 16.640 (museum number).

Measurements: 125 by 101 by 29 millimeters.

Condition: The upper portion of the obverse of the tablet (1.2 I and II) is generally in good condition. The surface is smooth and the signs are well-preserved. The lower portion of tablet of the tablet's obverse has a rough, damaged surface. The reverse of the tablet (1.2 IV) shows a corresponding condition, poorly preserved on the upper portion and well-preserved on the lower portion. The tablet is blackened in some areas (like 1.2 III).

Find Spot: house of the Great Priest, "tranchée" N 3, point topographique 3 at a depth of 2.10, "p-ê [peut-être] de la terre ramenée" = point topographique 203 (Bordreuil and Pardee 1989:32).

KTU 1.2 I

Bibliography

Text Editions: CTA pp. 6-8 + figure 3 and plates II, III; KTU pp. 6-7; *UH* 167-68 = *UM* 167-68.

Studies and Translations: Aistleitner 1964:48-50; Caquot and Sznycer, *TO* 27-33; Clifford, *CMCOT* 42-48; Cross, *CMHE* 37, 114, 118; Driver, *CML*[1] 78-81; Gaster, *Thespis* 155-60; Gibson, *CML*[2] 40-43; Ginsberg, *ANET* 130; Gordon, *UL* 12-14; 1977:69-72; Herdner 1949; Jirku 1962:21-23; Miller 1965; *DW* 28-33; de Moor, *SPUMB* 124-25, 128-33, 140-42; 1987:29-35; del Olmo Lete, *MLC* 168-73; Stuart 1976:63-71; van Zijl, *Baal* 13-30.

Text

1 [ ]
2 °°°°[ ]
3 ʾ̥at.ẙpʿtb̊[ ]
4 ʾalʾiynbʿl[̥]
5 d̊rk.tk.m̊šl̊[ ]
6 b̊r̊ʾ̊išk.ʾaymr̊[ ]
7 ṯ̊pṭ.nhr.yṯb[ ]
8 r̊ʾišk.ʿṯtrt.[šm.bʿl.qdqdk.]
9 °°t.mṭ.tpln.bg[bl]
10 [ʾab.]šnmʾaṯtm.t[ ]
11 [m]lʾakm.ylʾak.ym.[ ]
12 [b]ʿlṣʿlṣmnpr.š°[ ]
13 [ ]ṭ.ṯbr.ʾaphm.tbʿ.ġlm̊[m.ʾal.tṯb.ʾidk.pnm]
14 [ʾa]l̊ ttn.ʿm.pḫ̥r.mʿd.t̊[k.ġr.ʾil.lpʿn.ʾil]
15 ʾal̥̊.tpl.ʾal.tšthwy.pḫr[mʿd.qmm.ʾamr.ʾam]
16 rṯny.dʿtkm.wrgm.lṯr.ʾa[by.ṯny.lpḫr]
17 mʿd.tḥm.ym.bʿlkm.ʾadnkm.ṯpṭ[ṭ.nhr]
18 tn.ʾilm.dtqh.dtqyn.hmlt.tn.bʿl[.wʿnnh]
19 bn.dgn.ʾarṯm.pḏh.tbʿ.ġlmm.lyṯb.[ʾidk.pnm]
20 lytn.tk.ġr.ll.ʿm.phr.mʿd.ʾap.ʾilm.lḥ[m]
21 yṯb.bn.qdš.lṯrm.bʿl.qm.ʿl.ʾil.hlm
22 ʾilm.tphhm.tphn.mlʾak.ym.tʿdt.ṯpṭ[.nhr]
23 t°ly.hlmrʾišthm.lẓr.brkthm.wlkḥṯ[.]
24 zblhm.bhm.ygʿrbʿl.lm.ġltm.ʾilm.rʾišt
25 kmlẓrbrktkm.wln.kḥṯ.zblkm.ʾaḥd
26 ʾilm.tʿnylḥt.mlʾak.ym.tʿdt.ṯpṭ.nh̥
27 šʾu[.]ʾilm.rʾaštkm.lẓr.brktkm.lnkḥ̊ṯ
28 zblkm.wʾank.ʿny.mlʾak.ym.tʿdt.ṯpṭ.nhr
29 tšʾuʾilm.rʾašthm.lẓr.brkthm.lnkḥṯ[.]zblhm
30 ʾaḫr.tmġyn.mlʾak.ym[.]tʿdt.ṯpṭ.nhr.lpʿn.ʾil
31 [lt]pl.ltšthwy.pḫr.mʿd.qmm.ʾa°°.ʾamr
32 [ṯn]ẙ.dʿthm.ʾišt.ʾištm.yʾitmr.ḥrb.lṭšt
33 [ ]nhmrgm.lṯr.ʾabh.ʾil.tḥm.ym.bʿlkm
34 [ʾadn]km.ṯpṭ.nhr.tn.ʾilm.dtqh.dtqynh
35 [hml]t.tn.bʿl.wʿnnh.bn.dgn.ʾarṯm.pḏh
36 [ ]°.ṯr.ʾabh.ʾil̊[.]ʿbdk.bʿl.yymm.ʿbdk.bʿl
37 [nhr]m.bn.dgn.ʾa[s]rkm.hw.ybl.ʾargmnk.kʾil̊m
38 [ ]ybl.wbn.qdš.mnḥykʾap.ʾanš.zbl.bʿ[l]
39 [yʾuḫ]d.byd.mšḫṭ̊.bm.ymn.mḫṣ.ġlmm.yš[ḫṭ(?)]
40 [ymnh.ʿn]t.tʾuḫd.šmʾalh.tʾuḫd.ʿṯtrt.ʾik.m[ḫṣt.mlʾak]
41 [.ym.tʿ]dt.ṯpṭ̊.nhr.mlʾak.mṭḫr.yḥb[ ]
42 [ ]mlʾak.bn.ktpm.rgm.bʿlh.w.ẙ[ ]
43 [ ].ʾap.ʾanš.zbl.bʿl.šdmt.bg[ ]
44 [ ]dm.mlʾak.ym.tʿdt.ṯpṭ.nh̥[r]
45 [ ]̥.ʾan.rgmt.lym.bʿlkm.ʾad[nkm.ṯpṭ]
46 [nhr]h̊wt.gmr.hd.lw°y[ ]
47 [ ]ʾi̊yrh[.]°thbr°[ ]
48 [ ]°°°[ ]°[ ]

Textual Notes

Line 1. V's hand-copy shows a bit of a wedge. CTA reads no sign while KTU has *]x[*. The surface of the first three lines is badly damaged.

Line 2. °°°°: V reads a number of wedges which could fit with KTU's reading *w*(?) ṯb*.x*[. CTA reads no letters for this line. Four very damaged wedges are visible.

Line 3. *ẙ*: The heads of the top four wedges are visible.
b̊: The reading is conjectural as only the two horizontal wedges are presently visible (so too V's hand-copy). KTU reads *x* after *b**. CTA reads nothing after *b*.

Line 4. KTU reads a word-divider at the end of the line while CTA does not.

Line 5. CTA and *CML*² 40 unnecessarily emend *drk.tk* to *drktk*.
m̊: The reading is problematic as the vertical wedge is not visible (so too V's hand-copy).
l̊: The reading is a guess, as V's hand-copy shows only the head of the left-hand wedge. Now only the left-hand edge of the head of the wedge is clearly visible.

Line 6. *r̊*: The sign shows only three of the wedges (so too V's hand-copy).
Lines 6-7. KTU signals some sort of damaged wedge with an asterisk at the end of these two lines, but these putative wedges are not visible.

Line 8. V reads no word-divider after *rʾišk*, while CTA, KTU and Horwitz (1972:48) do.
[šm]: KTU reads *š*[m]* while CTA has *[šm]*. Neither the word-divider nor any part of *š* is visible.

Line 9. °°*t*: CTA reads *[–]t*. KTU has *l*(?)t*t* (V's hand-copy is not compatible with this reading). A diagonal indentation into the surface of the tablet starts at the beginning of line 9, runs through *š* in *šnm* in line 10 and down to *k* in *mlʾakm* in line 11.
CTA reads *bg[bl]* while KTU questions the reading with *b g*(?)[bl]*.

Line 10. *[ʾab]*: CTA shows the lacuna *[–]* where KTU reads *a*(?)b**. The space containing KTU's readings is very damaged. If they were accurate, they would sit somewhat above the other signs in this line.
CTA and KTU read a word-divider after *šnm* while V and Horwitz (1972:48) do not.
[ ]: KTU reads *]x[* at the end of the line.

Line 11. *[m]*: CTA reconstructs *[m]lʾakm* where KTU reads *m*lakm*. See line 9 for a description of the damage to the space. There may be space for another letter before *[m]*.
[ ]: KTU reads *x[* at the end of the line.

Line 12. *[b]ʿlṣ*: CTA reads *bʿlṣ* while KTU reconstructs *[b]ʿlṣ*.
V, KTU and Horwitz (1972:48) read no word-dividers after *bʿlṣ* and *ʿlṣm*, while CTA does.
.: V reads no word-divider after *npr* while CTA, KTU and Horwitz (1972:48) do.
°: The left-hand edge of the head of a horizontal wedge appears after *š*.

Line 13a. *[ ]*: KTU and *CML*² 40 reconstruct *[ʾu]ṭ* and CTA reads *ʾuṭ*.
h: Two of the three wedges are visible; there is some damage to the sign which may obscure the third wedge.

m̊: Only the head of the horizontal wedge is preserved.

Lines 13b-19a may be reconstructed partially on the basis of lines 30-35.

Line 14: *l̊*: The left-hand wedge is not preserved.
t̊: The head is visible despite a crack. Context also suggests the reading.

Line 15˚: A crack obscures the reading.
ḥ̊: The letter falls in a crack which begins at the first sign in line 14 and runs horizontally through several signs down to line 20.
KTU reads a word-divider at the end of the line.

Line 16. CTA has *ʾa[b]* and KTU reads *ab*[*.
It is common to reconstruct *ʾil* in the lacuna (so CTA, KTU, *CML*[2] 41, *MLC* 170, etc.). Elsewhere (e.g., 1.3 V 35, 1.4 I 5 [reconstructed], IV 47) *ʾil* intervenes between *ṯr* and **ʾab* in this formula, which might suggest that *ʾil* is not to be reconstructed after *ʾa[by]*. If any emendation is to be made, it is to reconstruct ⟨*ʾil*⟩ between *ṯr* and *ʾa[by]*. If emendation were resisted, the syllable count would be also more balanced, i.e. 10/9 (see commentary below). For these reasons no emendation is accepted here.

Line 17. *p̊*: CTA reconstructs *ṯ[pṭ* while KTU reads *ṯp*[ṭ]*. Part of thc head of a horizontal wedge is apparently the basis of KTU's reading.

Line 19. *[ʾi]*: CTA reconstructs *[ʾidk]* while KTU has *i*[dk]*.

Line 20. *h*: an error for ḫ as recognized by all.
ḥ̣: V's hand-copy shows the the head of the horizontal wedge as well as the bottom of the vertical wedge. *ḥ* is a scribal error for *ḫ* noted by CTA, KTU, etc.; see Horwitz 1977:124 n. 10.
⟨*l*⟩: Following CTA and *CML*[2] 41, *llḥm* is read for *lḥm* by haplography on the basis of the parallels in 1.18 IV 18b-19, 29b-30 (cf. 1.16 IV 11-12). Grammatically the infinitive does not require the prefixed *l*-, but the parallels suggest it. KTU dispenses with the emendation.

Line 21. *ʾi*: This letter is less clear than the following letters.

Line 23. °: CTA reads *t[ǵ]ly*. *UT*, *MLC* and KTU read *ttly*, and they emend to *tǵly*, on the basis of the parallel wording in line 24. The diagonal wedge is not visible, and what has been taken as a horizontal wedge was not evident to V or CTA. The damage to the space so obscures the reading that original sign cannot be read with confidence.
h: Following CTA, KTU, etc., *ʾilm* is read for *hlm* based on the parallel in line 24. The word *hlm* does not otherwise appear in second position in a line (see Brown 1987:203). Perhaps it represents vertical scribal error from line 21b-22a (*hlm ʾilm*).

Lines 23 and 24. *ʾi*: Some commentators take the two occurrences of *rʾišt*- in these lines as errors for *rʾašt*- (see Segert 1961:197; *MLC* 170-71) because *rʾašt*- occurs in lines 27 and 29. CTA puts a question-mark on the reading of *rʾišt*- in line 24. If the alphabetic form, *rʾišthm*, does not constitute a text-critical error, it may represent a singular collective if the noun is used both in the feminine and masculine, as the collective use of the singular in 1.3 II 9 is masculine in form. Dahood (1965:37) compared this example of the collective use with the singular BH *rōʾš* attested as a collective in Num 24:18, Hab 3:13, Pss 68:22, 110:6 and Job 22:12. Sivan (1992:236) explains the base *rʾišt*- as a fem. pl. qatl base, i.e. **raʾšatu*. The other examples which Sivan cites are relatively few. In any case, various grammatical proposals to the issue warrant caution against making an unnecessary text-critical "correction."

Line 26. *ʾi̊*: CTA has *ʾilm* and KTU reads *i*lm*. V's hand-copy clearly shows the sign, but it is now very difficult to read.
m: The letter has two cracks.
⟨r⟩: There is room for a letter after *nh* as shown in V's drawing. Following CTA, KTU, *CML*² 41, etc., read *nh⟨r⟩*. For the omission of *r* on the end of words elsewhere, see *UT* 5.27, esp. n. 1, but the grammatical explanation is unnecessary.

Line 27. *s̊*: The visible right-hand wedge fits the stance of this letter.
[.]: After *s̊ʾu* KTU reads a word-divider which CTA reconstructs. There is space for the word-divider, but a vertical crack obscures the reading.
ḥ̊: While the vertical wedge is visible, the rest of the sign is obscure.

Line 28. *z*: The head of the bottom wedge is damaged like the first sign in many lines in this column.
r: Some of the heads are difficult to see except the upper left-hand one.

Line 29. .: After *ts̊ʾu* KTU reads a word-divider which CTA lacks.
br: Three cracks obscure the end of *b* and the beginning of *r*.
h: One horizontal wedge is not visible. The top of the visible wedges are blackened. There are some small cracks on the bottom of the wedges.
k̊: The right-hand wedge is not visible.
ṯ̊: The winkelhocken is not visible.

Line 30. After *ym* KTU reads a word-divider which CTA reconstructs. There appears to be a vertical crack.

Line 31. *[l]*: CTA reconstructs *[lt]pl* while KTU has *[l]t*pl*.
ʾa°°: CTA reads *ʾa[–]* while KTU reads *ʾa*ṯ*r**. A large horizontal crack obscures the reading (see V's drawing). If the crack broke along the wedges, the head of the wedge before the vertical wedge would appears to belong not to a winkelhocken, but to a horizontal wedge. This would suggest the reading *ʾamr* rather than *ʾaṯr*. Given the extent of the damage, this suggestion is conjectural. Despite the continuation of the crack to through the remaining wedges in the line, the reading of the final word in the line is not disputed.

Line 32: *ẙ*: Only the right-hand wedges are visible. Context suggests the reading.

Line 33: *l̊*: This sign shows only two wedges as noted by V's drawing and Horwitz. A vertical crack obscures the reading.

Lines 34-35. Following CTA, KTU, etc., the lacunas at the beginning of these lines are reconstructed on the basis of lines 17-18.

Line 36. *[ ]°*: CTA reconstructs *[wyʿn.]* while KTU reads *[wyʿ]n**. Some (two?) wedges are visible, but they are unclear. V reads the heads of two vertical wedges while KTU's reading presumes the top edges of the heads of horizontal wedges. The preceding lacuna would appear to fit three letters.
.: The word-divider is obscured by a crack.
l̊: A large crack obscures all but the tail of the left-hand vertical wedge.

Line 37. *[ ]*: Many reconstruct *[nhr]m* (so CTA; KTU; *MLC* 37); others favor *[yy]m* (see also *MLC* 37); and still others prefer *[lʿl]m* (*ANET* 130; *CMHE* 114; Stuart 1976:67). To judge from the space missing in the previous and following lines, three letters are to be reconstructed.
ʾi̊l̊m: The letters are read by all, but they are damaged greatly. The heads of the middle and lower horizontal wedges of *ʾi* are not visible; and *l* shows only parts of the heads of its wedges.

Line 38. *[ ]*: There appears to be room for three letters. For the reconstruction *[ṯʿyk]* at the beginning of the line, see Cross cited in Stuart 1976:67, 71 n. 30. *[hw]* has also been proposed (*SPUMB* 125; *CML*² 42).
k: Some read *w* as a possibility instead of *k* (UT; CTA; KTU).
ʿ: KTU reads *bʿl** while CTA has *bʿ[l]*.

Line 39. *[ ]*: CTA, KTU, etc. reconstruct *[yʾu]ḫd* at the beginning of the line.
ṭ: The heads of all the wedges (except for the winkelhocken) are mostly visible.
[ ]: Perhaps reconstruct *yš[ḫṭ]* or *yš[kl]* at the end of the line. A verb of violence, "to attack," "to strike" or the like appears indicated by the parallelism. The only I-*š* verbs that seem contextually suitable are **šḫṭ* and **škl* (**šql*, "to slay," the *C*-stem of **qyl*, is reserved for the slaughtering of animals.)

Line 40. CTA reconstructs *[ymnh.ʿn]t* while KTU reads *[ʿ]n*t*. *[ydh.ʿ]nt* may better suit the lacuna, but *ymn* and *šmʾal* are a parallel pair while *yd* and *šmʾal* are not (see Avishur 1984:588-89).
m[: At the end of the line CTA reads *[.]m[ḫṣt.ml]* while KTU has *.m*ḫ*[ṣt]*.

Line 41. The beginning of the line is reconstructed following CTA. KTU has *[tʿ]dt*.
ṭ: Only parts of the heads of the wedges (except for the winkelhocken) are visible.

Line 42. *]*: Before *mlʾak* KTU reads a word-divider which CTA lacks. The surface is damaged.
ẙ[: Only the head of the top left-hand wedge is visible.

Line 43. *]*: Before the first word-divider KTU reads *]x* which CTA lacks.
[: At the end of the line CTA reads *bg[* while KTU has *b g* x[*.

Lines 45-46. *d̊*: Only the head of the left-hand vertical wedge is visible. Following CTA, KTU, etc., *ʾad[nkm.ṯpṭ nhr]* is reconstructed.
Line 46. *]*: At the beginning of the line KTU reads *]xx*.
h̊: The heads of the wedges of this sign are not visible.
°: V reads *n*, while KTU has *n**. CTA and *CML*² 43 read *lwʾay* or *lwny*. Due to damage, it is impossible to clarify the number of heads.
[: At the end of the line KTU reads a word-divider which CTA lacks.

Line 47. *ʾi̊*: Though faint, the tails are visible.
°*thbr*°: CTA has . *(?) g[-] thbr[* whereas KTU has *[.]xx thbr xx[*.

Line 48. CTA reads nothing for this line; KTU has *]xxx[*.

Translation and Vocalized Text

Baal's Messengers Deliver Their Message to Yamm (?)

1 . . . .
2 And (?) they return. . .
3 "You, you rose against. . .
4 Mightiest Baal. . .
5 Your dominion (?). . .

6 On your head be Ayyamarri, [Prince Yamm],	bi-raʾši-ka ʾayyamarrī [zabulu[79] yammu?]
7 [Between your hands (?)], Judge River.	[bêna yadê-ka (?)] ṯāpiṭu naharu
May [Horon] bre[ak, O Yamm],	yaṯabbi[ra ḥôranu yā-yammu[80]]
8 [May Horon break] your head,	[yaṯabbira ḥôranu] raʾša-ka
Athtart, the Na[me of Baal, your crown.]	ʿaṯtartu ši[mu[81] baʿli qudquda-ka]
9 Staff...	
May you fall at the he[ight of your years].	
10 Like the Father of Years (?), two women..."	

Yamm Instructs His Messengers

11 Yamm sends messengers,	malʾakêmi yilʾaku yammu
[Judge River, a legation].	[taʿudata yilʾaku naharu]
12 They rejoice exceedingly,	
13 [Their heart] re[joices?],	
Their nose breaks (?).	
"Go, you boy[s; do not sit still];	tabaʿā ǵalmā[mi ʾal taṯibā]
14 [Now] head	[ʾiddaka panīma] ʾal tatinā
To the Assembled Council,	ʿimma puḫri môʿidi
T[o Mount Lalu].	tô[ka ǵūri lali]
15 Do not bow [at El's feet],	[lê-paʿnê ʾili] ʾal tappulā
Do not kowtow before the [Assembled] Council.	ʾal tištaḥwiyā puḫra [môʿidi]
16 [Standing, make your spee]ch,	[qāmāmi ʾamāru ʾama]rā
Repeat your instructions.	ṯanniyā daʿta-kumā
So tell Bull [(?) my] father,	wa-rugumā lê-ṯôri ʾa[bī-ya (?)]
17 [Repeat to the] Assembled [Council]:	[ṯanniyā lê-puḫri] môʿidi
'Decree of Yamm, your Master,	taḥmu yammi baʿli-kumu
Your Lord, Ju[dge River]:	ʾadāni-kumu ṯāpi[ṭi nahari]
18 "Give up, O Gods, the one you obey,	tinū ʾilīmu dā-taquhū
The one you obey, O Multitude;	dā-taqiyūna hamulatu

---

79 The *G*-stem passive **zabulu*, is a conventional vocalization. See von Soden 1972 for the basis of the vocalization *zubulu*. If correct, the form shows a form of regressive assimilation known for other words (*UT* 5.19).

80 The case of nouns in the vocative in Ugaritic is unclear. In Arabic, a particular person addressed in the vocative takes the nominative case, including examples with vocative particle *yā* (Wright 2.85).

81 It is possible that the vocalization is /*šumu*/.

Give up Baal [that I may humble him],	tinū baʿla [wa-⟨ʾ⟩aʿannîna[82]-hu]
19 The Son of Dagan that I may seize his gold.'''	bina dagani[83] ʾariṯa[84]-mi paḏa-hu

The Assembly Reacts to the Sight of Yamm's Messengers

The boys depart, they do not sit still.	tabaʿā ǵalmāmi lā-yaṯibā
20 I[mmediately they he]ad	ʾi[ddaka panīma] lā-yatinā
To Mount Lalu.	tôka ǵūri lali
To the Assembled Council	ʿimma puḫri môʿidi
21 Meanwhile the Gods sit down to fea[st],	ʾap ʾilūma ⟨lê-⟩laḥā[mi] yaṯibū
The Holy Ones to dine,	banū qudši lê-ṯarāmi[85]
Baal waits on El.	baʿlu qāma ʿal ʾili
22 There! the Gods perceive them,	halum ʾilūma tipahū-humā
They perceive Yamm's messengers,	tipahūna malʾakê yammi
The legation of Judge [River].	taʿudata ṯápiṭi [nahari]
23 They lower their heads,	taǵliyu ʾilūma riʾšāti[86]-humu
On top of their knees,	lê-ẓāri[87] birakāti-humu
24 On their royal thrones.	wa-lê-kaḥaṯī zabuli-humu
Them Baal rebukes:	bi-humu yigʿaru baʿlu
25 "Why do you lower, O Gods, your heads	lama ǵalîtumu ʾilūma riʾšāti-kumu
On top of your knees,	lê-ẓāri birakāti-kumu
On your royal thrones?	wa-la-na kaḥaṯī zabuli-kumu
26 In unison will the Gods answer	ʾaḥda ʾilūma taʿniyū
The tablet of Yamm's messengers,	lūḥata malʾakê yammi
The legation of Judge Riv⟨er⟩?	taʿudati ṯāpiṭi naha⟨ri⟩

---

82 ⟨ʾ⟩ to indicate sandhi. See below pp. 291-92 for discussion. Cross (1979:43) calls the form an "indicative-emphatic ('energic')," which he vocalizes **yaqtuluna*. Rainey (1986:4, 10-12) labels the same form as an "indicative energic," which he vocalizes **yaqtulun(n)a*. It is unclear how to resolve the final weakness of the verbal root and the initial vowel of the "indicative energic" ending.

83 The form appears syllabically, but due to the absence of a case-ending, Huehnergard (1987b:10, 118) understands the syllabic spelling as Akk *dagan* rather than Ugaritic */*dagan(u)*/. For the etymology of the name, see above p. 91.

84 Taking the form as **yaqtula* volitive.

85 Gordon (*UT* 19.2745) cites Iraqi Arb *ṯarama*, "to cut to pieces" (e.g. meat or opinions) and Akk *šarāmu*, "to cut up, off." See also Rainey 1971:166; 1973:52. For a possible Akkadian nominal cognate, see Geller 1992:207. Cf. the Ug sacrificial offering called *ṯrmn* to which de Tarrago n (1980:67) compares Hittite *NINDAšaram(m)a(n)*, "pain" or "un gateau."

86 See above p. 262.

87 Translating *ẓr* as "back, top," Held (1965:406) cites as cognates EA *zuḫru*, Akk *ṣēru* and Arb *ẓahr* with the original root **ẓhr*. Gordon (*UT* 19.1047) cites also BH *ṣōhar*, which he translates as "roof" or "skylight" (Gen 6:16).

27 Raise, O Gods, your heads	šaʾū ʾilūma raʾašāti-kumu
From the tops of your knees,	lê-ẓāri birakāti-kumu
28 On your royal thrones.	lê-na kaḥaṯī zabuli-kumu
And I myself will answer Yamm's messengers,	wa-ʾanāku ⟨ʾ⟩aʿniyu[88] malʾakê yammi
The legation of Judge Riv⟨er⟩."	taʿudata ṯāpiṭi nahari
29 The gods raise their heads	tiššaʾū ʾilūma raʾašāti-humu
From the tops of their knees,	lê-ẓāri birakāti-humu
On their royal thrones.	lê-na kaḥaṯī zabuli-humu

The Messengers Deliver Yamm's Message

30 Then Yamm's messengers arrive,	ʾaḫra timǵayāni malʾakā yammi
The legation of Judge River.	taʿudatu ṯāpiṭi nahari
31 At El's feet they [do not] fall,	lê-paʿnê ʾili [lā-]tappulā
They do not kowtow before the Assembled Council.	lā-tištaḥwiyā puḫra môʿidi
Standing, they speak a speech,	qāmā ʾamāru (?) ʾamarā
32 [Repe]at their instructions.	[ṯanni]yā daʿta-humā
A flame, two flames they appear,	ʾišitu[89] ʾišitāmi yiʾtamarā
33 Their [ton]gue a sharp sword.	ḥarbu laṭūštu [lašā]nu-humā
They tell Bull El his Father:	ragamā lê-ṯôri ʾabī-hu ʾili
"Word of Yamm, your Lord,	taḥmu yammi baʿli-kumu
34 Your [Master], Judge River:	[ʾadāni-]kumu ṯāpiṭi nahari
'Give up, O Gods, the One you obey,	tinū ʾilūma da-taquhū
35 The One you obey, [O Multitu]de;	dā-taqiyūna-hu [hamula]tu
Give up Baal that I may humble him,	tinū baʿla wa-⟨ʾ⟩aʿannina-hu
The Son of Dagan, that I may possess his gold.'"	bina dagani ʾariṯa-mi paḏa-hu

El Responds

36 [And] Bull El his Father [answers ?]:	[wa-yaʿ]nî (?) ṯôru ʾabū-hu ʾilu
"Your slave is Baal, O Yamm,	ʿabdu-ka baʿlu yā-yammu-ma

---

[88] ⟨ʾ⟩ to indicate sandhi. Gibson (*CML*² 41 n. 9) takes the verb as a ptcp. It has also been interpreted as an infinitive or 1 c. sg. prefix form with elision of ʾ before ʿ (Pardee 1980:272). In the construction of independent pronoun with infinitive, the infinitive usually precedes the pronoun. The participle is rarely used as the main verb in an independent clause. For the third option, adopted here, see also *wʿnnh* in line 18//35. It may be noted that of the three options, this vocalization most closely approximates the form of the verb in Baal's corresponding question in line 26.

[89] For the second vowel, see the syllabic form *i-ši-t[u₄]* (Huehnergard 1987b: 110). Cf. Ak *išatu*, Syr *ʾeššātāʾ*, BH *ʾēš*, *ʾiššô* (with 3 masc. sg. suffix) ⟨ *ʾišš-. For discussion, see Huehnergard 1987b:63.

37	Your slave is Baal, [O River], The Son of Dagan, your captive.	ʿabdu-ka baʿlu [naharu-]m bina dagani ʾasīru-ka-ma
38	He will bring tribute to you, Like the Gods, [a gift to you] he will bring, Like the Holy Ones, offerings to you."	huwa yabilu ʾargamana-ka ka[91]-ʾilīma [ṯaʿaya-ka] yabi wa-binī qudši minaḥī(y)[92]-

Baal Responds

	Then Prince Baal is shaken.	ʾap ʾanaša zabulu baʿlu
39	[He seize]s with his hand a striker, In his right hand a slayer. The lads he st[rikes (?)].	[yuʾḫu]du[93] bi-yadi mašḫa bi-mi yamīni miḫīṣa[94] ǵalmêmi yiš[ḫaṭu?]
40	[His right hand A]nat seizes, His left hand Athtart seizes.	[yamīna-hu ʿa]natu tuʾḫud šamʾāla-hu tuʾḫudu ʿaṯtart
41	"Why did [you st]rike [Yamm's messengers,] [The lega]tion of Judge River?"	ʾêka maḫa[sṭa malʾakê yan [taʿu]data ṯāpiṭi nahari

The messenger(s?) . . . he . . .
42 . . . the messengers . .
Between the shoulders . . . his lord's word (?) and . . .
43 . . .

---

[90] The suffix is dative (see Tuttle 1978:268 n. 89).

[91] For this syntax, see Pardee 1980:272; cf. Stuart 1976: 67, 71 n. 30.

[92] According to Blau and Loewenstamm (1970:28-29), *y* in *mnḥyk* may be a *mater lectionis* for the plural construct oblique case-ending comparable to *ʾaḫyk* (**ʾaḫī-ka*) in 1.12 II 50. For other opinions, see Pardee 1980:272; for **mnḥ*, see below on pp. 308-09.

[93] The source of the *ʾu* in these and similar *G*-stem prefix forms rather than a syllable-closing *ʾi* represents a grammatical conundrum. Some commentators suggest that the *G*-stem prefix forms of the type **yʾu/tʾu-* of this root (as well as those of **ʾhb*, "to love" and **ʾkl*, "to eat, consume") represent instances of the "Canaanite shift" in Ugaritic following quiescence of ʾ and lengthening of the initial vowel (Pope 1966:456; for essentially the same view, see Tropper 1990:364, 367). For criticism of this view, see Marcus 1968:59-60 citing Ginsberg 1936:175. Gordon (*UT* 4.8, n. 2) views these forms as vestiges of an old *G*-stem active prefix. Rainey (1971:158) takes these forms as internal passives with active meaning. Huehnergard (1987c:279-80 n. 58) suggests the possibility that these forms are historical spellings reflecting the assimilation of the initial vowel to the second vowel and the assimilation of the ʾ to the following gutteral, i.e. "[t/yuḫḫud-] ‹ [t/yaḫḫud-] ‹ /t/yaʾḫud". While these explanations are of necessity *ad hoc*, the last has the merit of parallels for the proposed changes elsewhere in Ugaritic. None of these proposals answers the question of why the unusual *ʾu* is not extended to other *G*-stem prefix verbal forms. In any case, the vocalization does not affect either a scanning of the parallelism or word or syllable counts.

[94] For this vocalization, see below p. 310.

Baal Responds a Second Time

Then Prince Baal is shaken.
The terraces in . . .
44 . . . Yamm's messengers,
The legation of Judge Riv[er].

45 "I myself say to Yamm, your lord,	ʾana ragamtu lê-yammi baʿli-kumu
46 [Your] mast[er, Judge] River,	ʾadā[ni-kumu ṯāpiṭi nahari]

'[Hear?] the word of the Annihilator
Haddu . . .' . . ."
47 . . . you (?) bow down . . .
48 . . .

Commentary

Poetic Parallelism and Word/Syllable Counts

		semantic parallelism	word/syllable count
6	bi-raʾši-ka ʾayyamarrī [zabulu yammu?]	a b c (?)	4/13
7	[bêna yadê-ka?] ṯāpiṭu naharu	a′ (?) c′	4/12

The syntactical and semantic parallelism assumed by the reconstructions is highly pronounced. In addition, *b*- stands in the initial position at the head of prepositional phrases with body parts, thus forming sonant-semantic parallelism. The first line is demarcated from the second by the marked alliteration *ʾayyamarrī [. . . yammu]*.

	yaṯabbi[ra ḥôranu yā-yammu]	a b c	3/10
8	[yaṯabbira ḥôranu] raʾša-ka	a b d	3/10
	ʿaṯtartu ši[mu baʿli qudquda-ka]	b′ (= x + y) d′	4/11

This tricolon exhibits beautiful climactic parallelism on every level. The sonant parallelism is generated by morphology.

11	malʾakêmi yilʾaku yammu	a b c	3/9
	[taʿudata yilʾaku naharu]	a′ b c′	3/10

Any observations regarding the poetics of this bicolon rely on the reliability of the reconstruction of the second line. Indeed, any remarks would be purely circular, as the reconstruction is posited on the basis of poetic considerations.

13	tabaʿā ǵalmā[mi ʾal taṯibā]	a b c	4/10

14 [ʾiddaka panīma] ʾal tatinā	a b′	4/10
ʿimma puḫri môʿidi	c d	3/7
tô[ka ǵūri lali]	c′d′	3/6

The second line begins a tricolon with the following two lines. Despite the semantic differences, the first two lines contain some morphological and sonant parallelism. *[ʾal taṯibā]* and *ʾal tatinā* show a highly marked morphological, syntactical and sonant parallelism. The two bilabials and the nasals in *ǵalmā[mi]* and *[panīma]* likewise create sonant parallelism in the absence of other levels of parallelism.

In the third and fourth lines the syntax of preposition plus construct phrase provides the most pronounced parallelism. The syntax generates some sonant parallelism in the genitive endings of the nouns and the accusative endings in the prepositions. Otherwise, sonant parallelism is limited to the gutteral plus *r* in *puḫri* and *[ǵūri]* as well as the internal vowel /u/. The latter feature is all the more prounounced as these words are the only ones in the two lines with the vowel /u/.

15 [lê-paʿnê ʾili] ʾal tappulā	a b	4/9
ʾal tištaḥwiyā puḫra [môʿidi]	b′ a′	4/10

The particle plus prefix verb as well as the adverbial phrases are the most marked parallel features of this bicolon.

16 [qāmāmi ʾamāru ʾama]rā	a b c	3/9
ṯanniyā daʿta-kumā	b′ c′	2/7

The consonant *m* resonates through the first line, and in the second line it is picked up only in the final syllable. The /a/ vowel resonates throughout this unit.

wa-rugumā lê-ṯôri ʾabī-[ya (?)]	a b	2/10
17 ṯanniyā lê-puḫri môʿidi	a′ b′	2/9

The morphology, syntax and semantics are quite parallel.

taḥmu yammi baʿli-kumu	a b c	3/8
ʾadāni-kumu ṯāpi[ṭi nahari]	c′ b′ (= x + y)	3/11

The unit displays a standard parallelism generated largely by morphology.

18 tinū ʾilīmu dā-taquhū	a b c	3/9
dā-taqiyūna hamulatu	c′ b′	3/9

The longer forms of the dependent verb and noun in the second line balance the independent verb in the first line. The repetition of **yqy* provides balance between the two lines. The nouns are equally bound together by syntax as vocatives referring to deities and by the sonant balance of *l* and *m*. The two nouns are not found together elsewhere, and their unusual collocation may stress the collectivity of the council (at Baal's expense?). On the sonant level, /u/ resonates through both lines.

tinū baʿla [wa-⟨ʾ⟩aʿannîna-hu]	a b c	3/10
19 bina dagani ʾariṯa-mi paḏa-hu	b′ c′ (= x + y)	4/12

The syntax and semantics strongly link the two lines. Moreover, the first person form of the verbs, the energic/volitive *-a* ending, and the final suffixes connect the two lines. These similarities produce sonant parallelism heightened further by the consonants, *tiṉū ḇaʿla//ḇiṉa*.

tabaʿā ǵalmāmi lā-yaṯibā	a b c	3/10
20 ʾi[ddaka panīma] lā-yatinā	a′ c′	3/10
tôka ǵūri lali	a b	3/6
ʿimma puḫri môʿidi	a′ b′	3/7
21 ʾap ʾilūma ⟨lê-⟩laḥā[mi] yaṯibū	a b c d	4/11
banū qudši lê-ṯarāmi	b′ c′	3/8
baʿlu qāma ʿal ʾili	b″ d e	4/7

The parallel bicolon in 1.18 IV 18b-19, 29b-30 (cf. 1.16 IV 11-12) would suggest that the first two lines constitute an original bicolon and the third line has been suffixed secondarily. By the same token this addition has been made in accordance with the general syntax of the first two lines. Like the first line (which the second largely echoes), the third line includes divine referent and verb of posture. Alliteration of *b* and *q* in the first two words of the third line echoes the same consonants in the second line. Furthermore, the final noun in the third line echoes sonantly the prepositions in the first two lines.

22 halum ʾilūma tipahū-humā	a b c	3/10
tipahūna malʾakê yammi	c d e	3/9
taʿudata ṯāpiṭi [nahari]	d′ e′ (= x + y)	3/10

The suffix on the initial verb connects semantically with the objects in the next two lines. Indeed, the objects of the three lines form climactic parallelism: "them"//"the messengers of Yamm"//"the legation of Judge River." All three lines are linked by divine elements, reinforced sonantly by the bilabials and vowels in *ʾilūma* and *yammi* (although the divine element in the first line functions in semantically and syntactically different ways from those in the last two lines). The dental in initial position likewise links the last two lines.

23 taǵliyu ʾilūma riʾšāti-humu	a b c	3/11
lê-ẓāri birakāti-humu	d e	2/9
24 wa-lê-kaḥaṯī zabuli-humu	d′ e′	2/10

As in line 21, the noun in the first line echoes sonantly with the prepositions in the last two lines; the order of these elements in this tricolon is reversed relative to those of line 21. The suffixes at the end of the three lines (as well as the preceding oblique pl. case ending) provide strong end-rhyme. This conspicuous linkage heightens the sonant similarities between the nouns which govern these suffixes: *r* and *-āti* in *riʾšāti-*//*birakāti-*; and *k* and *b* in *birakāti-*//*kaḥaṯī zabuli-*.

bi-humu yigʿaru baʿlu

This speech-opening formula is extra-colonic.

25 lama ǵalîtumu ʾilūma riʾšāti-kumu	a b c d	4/14
lê-ẓāri birakāti-kumu	e f	2/9
wa-lê-na kaḥaṯī zabuli-kumu	e′ f′	3/11
26 ʾaḥda ʾilūma taʿniyū	a b c	3/8
lūḥata malʾakê yammi	d e	3/8
taʿudati ṯāpiṭi naha⟨ri⟩	e′ (= x + y)	3/10
27 šaʾū ʾilūma raʾašāti-kumu	a b c	3/11
lê-ẓāri birakāti-kumu	d e	2/9
28 lê-na kaḥaṯī zabuli-kumu	d′ e′	2/10
wa-ʾanāku ⟨ʾ⟩aʿniyu malʾakê yammi	a b c	4/12
taʿudata ṯāpiṭi nahari	b′ c′ (= x + y)	3/10

Given the tendency to replicate colas parallel in direct discourse and narrative, one might suspect that ⟨*lḥt*⟩ has been omitted from this unit (cf. line 26) and that a tricolon is involved. However, the resulting word count would be 2/3/3 and the resulting syllable count would be 8/8/10. Though possible, the first lines of Ugaritic cola tend to be longer than the second or third lines.

29	tiššaʾū ʾilūma raʾašāti-humu	a b c	3/12
	lê-ẓāri birakāti-humu	d e	2/9
	lê-na kaḥaṯī zabuli-humu	d′ e′	3/10
30	ʾaḫra timǵayāni malʾakā yammi	a b c	4/11
	taʿudatu ṯāpiṭi nahari	b′ c′ (= x + y)	3/10
31	lê-paʿnê ʾili [lā-]tappulā	a b	3/9
	la-tištaḥwiyā puḫra môʿidi	b′ a′	3/10
	qāmā ʾamāru (?) ʾamarā	a b c	3/8
32	[ṯanni]yā daʿta-humā	b′ c′	2/7
	ʾišitu ʾišitāmi yiʾtamarā	a a b	3/11
33	ḥarbu laṭūštu [lašā]nu-humā	c d b′	3/10

The lines appear divergent in content as well as in syntax, morphology and sound. The first line repeats the consonants *ʾi*, *t* and *m* while the second shows nasals and sibilants and repeats the vowels /a/-/u/. What further connects the lines is the referent of the two semantically divergent metaphors as well as their potentially destructive character.

ragamā lê-ṯôri ʾabī-hu ʾili

This speech-opening formula might be read as the first line of a tricolon with the following unit. If so, all three lines would share divine elements as well as a term expressing the relationship of the divine figures to either the speaker or the addressee. Given the formulaic character of the following bicolon as well as the extra-colonic character of most one-line speech introductions, this line would appear to be extra-colonic.

	taḥmu yammi baʿli-kumu	a b c	3/8
34	[ʾadāni-]kumu ṯāpiṭi nahari	c′ b′ (= x + y)	3/11
	tinū ʾilūma dā-taquhū	a b c	3/9
35	dā-taqiyūna-hu [hamula]tu	c b′	2/10
	tinū baʿla wa-⟨ʾ⟩aʿannîna-hu	a b c	3/10
	bina dagani ʾariṯa-mi paḏa-hu	b′ c′	3/12

36 [wa-yaʿ]nî (?) ṯôru ʾabū-hu ʾilu

This speech-opening formula is not integrated poetically into this passage and appears as an extra-colonic rubric.

	ʿabdu-ka baʿlu yā-yammu-ma	a b c	3/9
37	ʿabdu-ka baʿlu [naharu-]ma	a b c′	3/9
	bina dagani ʾasīru-ka-ma	b′ a′	3/10

The optional restoration *[lʿl]m*, "forever" in the second line would produce a b c//a b d//b' a (*CMHE* 114, 183 n. 162; Pardee 1980:272). Of all the reconstructions, *[nhr]m* produces the most congruent parallelism, but *[lʿl]m* also forms suitable parallelism, and it would correspond more precisely to the terminology of Baal's surrender to Mot in 1.5 II 12. The repetition of the first two words link the first two lines, while the second person suffixes and the enclitic -*m* connect all three lines.

	huwa yabilu ʾargamana-ka	a b	3/10
38	ka-ʾilīma [ṯaʿaya-ka] yabilu	c b′ a	3/11
	wa-binī qudši minaḥī(y)-ka	c′ (= x + y) b′	3/9

This unit is rendered here as a tricolon (Stuart 1976:67, 71; Pardee 1980:272), but several commentators (*ANET* 130; *CML*² 42; de Moor 1987:33 n. 146) understand it as a long bicolon, since the parallelism resulting from taking the unit as a tricolon is unusual (de Moor 1987:33 n. 146). Viewing the unit as a bicolon would result in unusually long lines, however. Furthermore, the *w* preceding *bn qdš* suggests the beginning of a new line unless it were to be taken as pleonastic; this difficulty perhaps caused some commentators to read *w* for *k* (*UT*; KTU; cf. CTA *w/k*). The comparative *k*- may serve as a double-duty particle (Pardee 1980:272), but only if *wbn qdš* represents the beginning of a line.

	ʾap ʾanaša zabulu baʿlu	a b c	4/9
39	[yuʾḫu]du bi-yadi mašḫaṭa	b′ c d	3/9
	bi-mi yamīni miḫīṣa	c′ d′	3/8
	galamêmi yiš[ḫaṭu?]	e f (?)	2?/7?

Like some other units, this one apparently consists of a bicolon augmented by a line on either side. The semantics militate in favor of placing the fourth line with this unit rather than with the following one. The bilabials reinforce the connection among all the lines despite the general semantic disparities among them.

40	[yamīna-hu ʿa]natu tuʾḫudu	a b c	3/10
	šamʾāla-hu tuʾḫudu ʿaṯtartu	a′ c b	3/10

The morphological, syntactical and semantic parallelism between the lines are quite pronounced. Sonant parallelism obtains in the nasal and *m* in the first word in the two lines.

41	ʾêka maḫa[ṣta malʾakê yammi]	a b c d	4/10
	[taʿu]data ṯāpiṭi nahari	c′ d′ (= x + y)	3/10
	. . .		
45	ʾana ragamtu lê-yammi baʿli-kumu	a b c	4/12
46	ʾadā[ni-kumu ṯāpiṭi nahari]	c′ b (= x + y)	3/11

Introduction

The main section of the extant portion of 1.2 I, namely lines 11-46, exhibits a general symmetry:

A Yamm's instructions to his messengers (lines 11-19)
  B Divine assembly cowed by the messengers' appearance (lines 19-24)
    C Baal rebukes the assembly (lines 24-29)
A′ Yamm's messengers carry out his instructions (lines 30-35)
  B′ El submits to the demands of the messengers (lines 36-37)
    C′ Baal reacts to the demands (lines 38-46)

The column present a number of other symmetries within lines 11-35. The description of the council's reaction to the sighting of Yamm's messengers in lines 19-24 is matched generally by the words of Baal's speech in lines 24-29. These sections might be understood in chiastic terms in relation to Yamm's speech in lines 11-19 and its execution in largely the same wording in lines 30-35.

The roots *ʿ*ny* and their variants figure repeatedly connecting disparate parts of the divine council scene (lines 18 [reconstructed], 26, 28, 35, 36 [partially reconstructed]). The two homonymous roots play a role in contrasting Baal and Yamm's messengers. In his speech Baal asks if the gods will answer the messengers and then declares that he will answer (*ʿ*ny*) them (lines 26, 28). For their part, the messengers of Yamm declare their master's intentions to humble (*ʿ*ny*) Baal (lines 18// 35). El answers (line 37) in support of the messengers. Furthermore, Baal and Yamm's messengers stand before the seated assembly of the pantheon, but their postures, though identical, signify a marked contrast in their status. In line 21 Baal stands like a servant before his master while the messengers in line 31 stand as an expression of defiance as they forego the traditional obeisance expected of their lesser rank.

Lines 1-10

These lines represent direct discourse, indicated by *ʾat*, "you," in line 3 and *-k*, "your," in line 6. Line 1 has no legible letters. In line 2 KTU reads *wṯb*, which could represent the conjunction *w-* plus a verbal form, either from the root **ṯ(w)b*, "to turn, return," or **yṯb*, "to sit, dwell." Without context there is no way to adjudicate between the alternatives. If this word belongs to a speech between enemies (Baal and Yamm) or at least opposing parties (Kothar and Yamm), then the middle weak root would seem preferable as a command for the hostile party "to return" and not "to sit." The verb **yṯb* often connotes enthronement, a sentiment which opposing parties rarely express to one another. However, if *wṯb* belongs to narrative, it may indicate the return of messengers to the addressee of the following lines.

Line 3 represents direct address to a second party: "You, you have risen (against me?)" (so *MLC* 168). The verb **ypʿ* in 1.3 III 37 refers precisely to the opposition of one warrior against another. When Anat first glimpses Baal's two messengers in this passage, she asks:

mn ʾib ypʿ lbʿl	What foe has risen against Baal,
ṣrt lrkb ʿrpt	(What) enemy against the Cloudrider?

Given Yamm's position as the front runner for kingship at the end of KTU 1.1, 1.2 I 1-3a might represent one enemy's complaint about the other's behavior; which figure is Baal and which one is Yamm cannot be easily resolved. However, given that this language applies in 1.3 III 37 to a foe of Baal, it may also be addressed to an enemy of the Cloudrider in this context as well.

Scholars divide over the speaker in line 4. Ginsberg (*ANET* 130) and de Moor (1987:29-30) plausibly reconstruct the extant words of line 4 as a narrative introduction, "[And] Baʿlu the Almighty [answered:]". Lines 6-7 would then represent Baal's curse of Yamm. Gibson (*CML*^{2} 4) suggests Kothar as the speaker in line 4f., given that the name of the weapon invoked against Yamm is the very one empowered by the craftman god's incantation in 1.2 IV 18-26 (Obermann 1948). According to Philo of Byblos, Chousor practiced "verbal arts including spells and prophecies," *logous askēsai kai epōdas kai manteias* (PE 1.10.11; Attridge and Oden 1981:44-45). Though noteworthy, the connection constitutes a tenuous basis for establishing the speaker of this section. Baal could utter the same curse against Yamm.

Del Olmo Lete (*MLC* 108-09, 168) reconstructs *ʾalʾiyn bʿl* at the beginning of a second speech directed against Yamm and pronounced in the midst of the divine assembly mentioned explicitly in lines 10f. Most scholars agree that lines 7-9 involve an imprecation against an enemy, and Ginsberg (*ANET* 130) and del Olmo Lete view the speech from line 4b-9 as an "Imprecación de Baʿlu." Del Olmo Lete's translation assumes partial parallels from 1.1 IV 24-25//1.2 IV 12, 19b-20 for line 5 and parallelism between the names of the weapons in 1.2 IV 11-22 for lines 6-7a:

[ ] 4 ʾalʾiyn bʿl	[Y respondió] *Baʿlu*, el Victorioso:
[ ]	[‹‹ ! De tu trono regio seas arrojado],
[ ] 5 drk.tk.mšl[ ]	[del solio de] tu poder [expulsado(?)!].
[ ]	[! En tu mollera *Yagruš* golpee],
6 brʾišk.ʾaymr[ ]	en tu cabeza *Ayyamur*, [Príncipe *Yammu*],
[ ]7 ṯpṭ nhr	[en tu mollera], Juez *Naharu*!

The other words in lines 4-7a are compatible with a struggle between Yamm and Baal. The terms of conflict concern "dominion" (line 5) and the weapon of battle is invoked upon the head (line 6) just as it acts in the narrative of 1.2 IV 24-25. It may be that this broken section anticipates the battle of Baal against Yamm in 1.2 IV.

Lines 7b-9 contain imprecations reconstructed on the basis of 1.16 VI 54-57 (so CTA and many others). Following the consensus on these lines, del Olmo Lete (*MLC* 169) reconstructs lines 7b-9 as follows:

yṯb[ ]	! Rompa [*Ḥôranu*, !oh *Yammu*!],
[ ]8rʾišk	[rompa *Ḥôranu*] tu cabeza,
ʿṯtrt.š[m.bʿl.qdqdk.]	*ʿAṯtartu*, [Nombre de *Baʿlu*, tu mollera!].
[ ]9l(?)tt.mṭ.tpln.	. . . tambaleándote caigas
bg(?)[bl.]	en el [límite de tus años y seas humillado (?)].

This reconstruction is based on the two curses more fully known in the parallel passage, 1.16 VI 54-57.[95] The first curse reads:

yṯbr ḥrn ybn	May Horon smash, O son,
yṯbr ḥrn rʾišk	May Horon smash your head,
ʿṯtrt šm bʿl qdqdk	Athtart, Baal's Name, your crown!

---

95 As is generally recognized. See O'Callaghan 1952:43-46; *WdM* 295; Parker 1977:168-69.

The addressees vary in the different curses. In 1.2 I 7 the name of the addressee falls in the lacuna. It is presumed to be *yymm*, "O Yamm," like *ybn* in 1.16 VI 55 (cf. van Selms 1970:258) and paralleled in form in 1.2 I 36 (Pardee 1980:271). Young (1979:841 n. 8) equates this curse with the English expression, "to go to hell," an interpretation which suits Keret's curse in 1.16 VI 54-57 and presumably the setting of 1.2 I 7b-8 as well. The invocation of Horon suits a curse against a foe. The Ugaritic corpus attests to Horan's power incantations against snake bites (KTU 1.100; Pardee 1988b:223-25) as well as demons (RIH 78/20.8-9; Caquot 1979-80, 1982; Fleming 1991). The Magical Papyrus Harris (Harris 501) invokes Horan and Anat in an Egyptian curse against a wolf: "Haurôn make thy fangs impotent, thy foreleg is cut off by Arsaphes, after ᶜAnat has cut thee down."[96] The invocation of Astarte is likewise suitable to an imprecation. Astarte's martial power was well-known in Emar especially by way of her title *ᵈIš₈-tár ME* (*Aštartu taḫazi*), "Athtart of the battle" (Emar 370.20; Fleming 1992:213, 229) as well as in Egypt (Leclant 1960; Stadelmann 1967:101-102). She is invoked also in the treaty of Esarhaddon (*ANET* 534).

The designation *[šm bᶜl]*, "Name of Baal," is reconstructed in line 8 on the basis of KTU 1.16 VI 56. It refers to Astarte in these passages and KAI 14:18. The element *šm* is a deity at Ebla (Pomponio 1983:152; Xella 1983:290; Stieglitz 1990:81). It is common in second and first millennium PNs, including Amorite names (Huffmon 1965:248-49), Akkadian names from Ugarit (*PTU* 193- 94), and Phoenician and Hebrew names (Cross 1980:3). It might be argued from this evidence that *šm* originally represented a separate Semitic deity which was identified secondarily with the goddess as an expression of her relationship to the god with whom she was most commonly associated.[97] In the Ugaritic and Phoenician contexts, the meaning of this expression is unclear. Coogan (1978:74) translates *šm bᶜl* as "Baal's other self," perhaps approximating the English phrase, "alter ego." Olyan (1988:48) calls Astarte the "name essence" of Baal: "we should also mention her epithet **šimu baᶜli*, 'the name of Baal,' an early example of hypostatization in Ca-

---

[96] For this text, see Albright 1936:3; Stadelmann 1967:87. On Horon, see also Gray 1949a.

[97] The same view might apply to *kbd*, "glory," attested at Ebla and in Amorite personal names as a deity and in later West Semitic tradition as an hypostasis (see below pp. 279-80).

naanite religion, which directly associates her with Baal, as a manifestation of his name essence.'' Caquot and Sznycer (*TO* 94) suggests her roles as ''chasseresse et guerrier'' as a possibility, perhaps since both Baal and Astarte are divine warriors. Astarte as warrior is well attested in Egyptian sources (Leclant 1960).

The association between the two deities is based on more than a shared role. Baal and Astarte are associated in second millennium iconography and texts. Frankfort (1939:289) notes that a seal from Bethel depicts a storm-god and a goddess and a hieroglyphic inscription with the name of Astarte. In the twelfth century Egyptian story, ''The Contest of Horus and Seth for the Rule,'' Anat and Astarte appear together as the daughters of Re and the wives of Seth (*ANET* 15); the latter god was identified with Baal, for example in the thirteenth century treaty of Ramesses II with Hattusilis.[98] A single figure from Memphis served as the prophet of Baal and Astarte (*ANET* 250 n. 13), which perhaps also illustrates the close relationship between Baal and Astarte and their cult in Memphis during New Kingdom times.

Later sources also support the relationship between Baal and Astarte. Philo of Byblos states that Astarte and Baal (*Zeus Dēmarous kai Adōdos*), ''king of the gods'' (*basileus theōn*), ruled the land together under the consent of El (*kronou*) (PE 1.10.31; Attridge and Oden 1981:54-55; Olyan 1988:48). Olyan comments: ''This suggests clearly that she is queen alongside Baal who is king, though the word 'queen' does not occur in the text.'' Olyan concludes (1988: 48) from Philo of Byblos' remarks that Astarte was the queen, consort and ally of Baal. Olyan also offers the suggestion that as part of her relationship with Baal, manifest in 1.2 I 40 and 1.2 IV 28, Astarte ''is attentive to Baal's best interests.''

The Israelite hypostasis of the name also appears in martial contexts (Isa 30:27; *Thespis* 156). Unlike the Ugaritic and Phoenician evidence, Israelite texts (Ps 29:2[99]; Isa 30:27) attest a theophanic

---

[98] *ANET* 200-01. For further examples of the identification of Seth with Baal in New Kingdom Egypt, see *ANET* 249.

[99] In Ps 29:1-2 the *bĕnê ʾēlîm* are called to acknowledge the *kābôd* and *ʿōz* of Yahweh and the *kĕbôd šĕmô*. The qualities involved are not general abstractions, but constitute features of the divine appearance in the storm described in the verses 3-9. The ''appearance of his glory'' is the theophanous appearance in the storm. ''Glory'' has been compared with Akk *melammu*, the theophanous radiance or sheen accompanying the procession of the deity (*CAD* M/2:10; see *CMHE* 153, 165-67). Similarly, ''the glory of his name'' may be no abstraction, but the theophanous

use of the divine name[100] and in Ps 29:2, a cultic setting is provided explicitly for this theophany. These biblical attestations may reflect some original cultic or theophanic aspect of the name hypostasis in other West Semitic cultures. Furthermore, the designation of the goddess as the name of the god in West Semitic texts may reflect some dimension of its original polytheistic setting in early Israelite culture. In the immediate context of 1.2 I 8, it is clear that it is an enemy of Baal which is addressed since *ʿṯtrt š[m bʿl]* is the ally of Baal. The larger context of lines 11f. would suggest that Yamm is the object of Baal's curse.

A second curse follows in lines 8b-9. The word *mṭ*, "staff" (?), does not appear in the curses of 1.16 VI 57-58, and it may be surmised that it represents part of a further curse, perhaps involving either the breaking of the enemy's staff or the destruction of the enemy by means of a staff (cf. 1.3 II 15-16). De Moor (1986:257; 1987:30) proposes: *[trd m]mt*, "[May you go] down [to the p]lace of death." This view assumes a text-critical error of *ṭ* for *t*. Given the little attested of this line and the lack of parallels for it, an emendation seems unduly speculative. Lines 8b-9a would seem to constitute the first line in the tricolon. Its second and third lines in line 9b are paralleled in 1.16 VI 57-58 (see *CML*² 102; de Moor and Spronk 1982b:190; de Moor 1986:257; 1987:30):

tqln bgbl šntk	May you fall at the peak of your years,
bḥpnk[101] wtʿn	At your end (?) may you be humbled.

---

glory manifested by the appearance of the hypostasis of the name as in Isa 30:27. The divine name is also an element in the divine procession of Exod 23:20f. These texts show both Deuteronomic and non-Deuteronomic notions of hypostases as warrior which echo the role of Astarte as the name and face of Baal.

100 A derivative usage appears in Exod 23:20-21; cf. Isa 63:9; for discussion, see Smith 1990:100-01.

101 The word *bḥpnk* is a well-known difficulty. It is often rendered "with your hands empty" or the like (*CML*² 102). Taking **ḥpn* from **ḥpp* and comparing Arb **ḥff*, "to delimit, border," Renfroe (1992:49-50) suggests the translation: "Within your *limit/term* may you be brought down" (Renfroe's italics). A translation "at your end" perhaps accords better with the apparently parallel *bgbl šntk*. The prepositional phrase may represent a sentence adverbial, sometimes connected by *w* before the main clause, in this case *tʿn*. Blau (1977:90, para. 4:3:2) lists some examples of this phenomenon in Ugaritic. A lesser possibility is that *bḥpnk* constitutes either an infinitival or prepositional phrase serving as the protasis of a temporal sentence: "when you come (or, in your coming) to the end, may you be humbled." Pope (*EUT* 40 n. 74) discusses "nouns serving as the apodoses of temporal sentences." One of his examples, *nhmmt wyqmṣ* (KTU 1.14 I 34-35), represents a noun functioning as the protasis of a temporal sentence. Furthermore, the first phrase in

It is possible to fit at least the first line of this bicolon into the lacuna of 1.2 I 9. If this reconstruction of 1.2 I 9 is correct (see CTA 3 n. 7; KTU 6 nn. 3-4; *TO* 126; *CML*² 40; *MLC* 169; de Moor 1986:257), then 1.2 I 9 and 1.16 VI 58 vary in their synonyms for "fall": 1.2 I 9 has **npl* while 1.16 VI 58 has **q(y)l*. Margalit (1979:545) attributes the difference in word-choice to a greater alliterative effect with the following word in 1.2 I 9 which he signals by capitalizing the letters in question: *tPLn BgBL* (if alliteration was the guiding principle for word-choice, one can only wonder why the poet of 1.16 VI 58 failed to attempt the same effect).

The significance of *]šnm ᵓaṯtm* in line 10 is unclear. It is possible that it continues the curses of the previous lines (so de Moor 1987:30). Taking *šnm ᵓaṯtm* as "two women," Gibson (*CML*² 40 n. 2) asserts that "Yam appears to have had two wives unlike Athtar who had none (2 iii 22)." The word *ᵓaṯtm* is dual in form and would suggest that *šnm* is not a numeral. Del Olmo Lete does not translate this line, but the reconstruction of KTU in *MLC* (169), *a*(?)b*.šnm.aṯtm*, could refer to El's epithet, *ᵓab šnm*, and *ᵓaṯtm* could be El's two wives known from 1.23.37-49 (see de Moor 1987:30 n. 132). 1.2 I 10 may allude to these two wives in passing. It is possible to imagine that line 10 refers to El in the assembly with his two women. De Moor (1987:30) offers a logical translation: [Like the F]ather of Years you [take] two wives". According to de Moor, lines 3-6 presents Baal's speech to Yamm while lines 7-10 constitute Yamm's response. However, the notion that the addressee should take "like the Father of Years, two wives" would seem to apply more aptly to Yamm than to Baal, in view of Athtar's complaint about Yamm in 1.2 III 22. It might be more logical to assume that a single message from Baal to Yamm is involved in lines 2-10, and that lines 11f. represent Yamm's response to Baal's effrontery. There is no indication of a change in speakers, although such a transition may fall in the lacuna; de Moor reconstructs a change of speakers in the lacuna at the end of line 6. Furthermore, the invocation of Athtart, Baal's consort and ally, seems misplaced in a curse against Baal. It seems more suitable in a curse spoken by Baal against Yamm. Therefore, lines 2-10 more likely represent a single message sent by Baal to Yamm than two speeches between them.

---

bdmᶜh nhmmt in 1.14 I 32, which Pope renders, "As he shed tears, (comes) slumber" could represent the same syntactical construction as *bḥpnk*.

Lines 11-19a

The reconstructions for lines 11-19a are based largely on the parallels with lines 19b-35. Yamm's instructions begin in line 12 (cf. line 30), as line 11 seems to represent a narrative introduction: "messengers Yamm sent," with "messengers" fronted perhaps for emphasis. Yamm's "messengers" (*mlʾakm*[102]) are called *tʿdt ṯpṭ nhr* in lines 22, 26, 28 and 30, and *tʿdt nhr* may be reconstructed as the second half of the bicolon in line 11. The word *tʿdt* is often understood as a synonym such as "envoys" (*ANET* 130; de Moor 1987:32) or the like. As a feminine singular noun (< **ʿwd*[103]), *tʿdt* calls for a translation reflecting an "abstract for concrete" (*CML*² 159), such as "legation." These servants of Yamm (called *ǵlmm* in line 13) are not ambassadors, but messengers; "embassy" (*TO* 128 n. g′; *CML*² 41; *MLC* 170) is therefore not quite accurate. The word *tʿdt* has been compared also with *ʿddn* in KAI 202:12 (Ginsberg 1958:62*; Ross 1970; cf. Greenfield 1969c:176). In this passage the gods are said to answer Zakkur *[b]yd ḥzyn wbyd ʿddn*, "[by] the hand of seers and by the hand of legates." *Ḥzyn* and *ʿddn* are prophets who convey the divine word to Zakkur. The term *ʿddn* reflects their role as prophetic messengers just as Yamm's *tʿdt* functions as the intermediary of his message to El and the divine council.[104]

Lines 12-13a are not repeated in the parallel section on lines 19b-35, and it is unclear whether it belongs to Yamm's speech or not. As in line 11, both lines 12 and 13 are apparently missing a poetic line. As a result, it would seem that two bicola are to be reconstructed in these lines. Many commentators take *ʿlṣ ʿlṣm* in line 12

---

102 For the semantic development of this root, see Greenstein 1979; Cohen 1989b:17.

103 BH *ʿēd*, "witness"; Geez *ʿawwadi*, "herald," the active ptcp. of *ʿawwada*, "to proclaim, issue a decree" (Leslau 1966; Leslau 77). Pardee (1978a:206) comments that if *tʿdt* means "messenger," then "it would be the literary term for 'witness'." Commentators generally compare BH feminine singular collective, *tĕʿûdâ*, "testimony."

104 While *ʿddn* has been taken from a geminate root, Ginsberg (1958:62*) derives *tʿdt*, *ʿddn* and *ytʿdd* (1.4 III 11) from **ʿwd*; *ʿddn* could be the *D*-stem formation of the middle weak verb like the Ugaritic *tD*-stem *ytʿdd* (*UT* 19.1819; cf. Ugaritic *knn* and BH *kōnēn* < **kwn*) while *tʿdt* is based on the *G*-stem of the same root. Cf. the name of the Israelite prophet, *ʿōdēd* (2 Chron 28:9). For further discussion, see *SPUMB* 130-31. It should be remembered that the reading of *ytʿdd* in 1.4 III 11 is uncertain (see Renfroe 1992:87).

as an expression of the messengers' joy. Assuming Akk *eleṣu*, "to rejoice,"[105] Driver renders: "with the jubilation of jubilant men."[106] The meaning of *npr* is controversial. De Moor (1990:133 n. 151) translates the line: "with jubilant cries they flew heavenwards" (reconstructing *š[mm])*, assuming Syriac *nfar* and Tigrina *neferè*, "to fly" (*UT* 19.1680; cf. *MLC* 592) as cognates for *npr*. This view may be supported from other Ugaritic occurrences of **npr*. In 1.6 II 37 the plural nominal form is parallel with *ᶜṣrm*, "birds" (de Moor and van der Lugt 1974:20), and in 1.19 III 28 the verb is applied to birds and occurs with **dʾy*, "to fly." The root **npr* would therefore fall in the semantic field of avian flight. De Moor (1987:31 n. 133) comments further that "The messengers took the form of birds." The main problem with this view is contextual: the messengers do not depart, but remain to hear the message of their master. Gaster (*Thespis* 156) takes a different approach. He translates lines 12-13: "let us shatter [their]****, ******break their****!" This translation presupposes that *npr*, parallel to *ṯbr* in the next line, derives from the root **prr*. Given the length of the lacuna at the end of line 12, Pardee (1980:271) doubts that **npr* and **ṯbr* are parallel unless they belong to a tricolon.

Caquot and Sznycer (*TO* 128) translate *npr* in yet a third way: "Dans l'allégresse, le coeur jo[yeux...]". J. B. Bauer (1957:130; noted by de Moor and van der Lugt 1974:20) and Caquot (1974:204) reconstruct *npr š[mḫ]* on the basis of Akk *ú-ša-li-ṣa nu-pa-ar-šú-un* (Nin A VI 51; Borger 1956:63) which Bauer renders "ich liess jauchzen Gemur." Caquot and Sznycer (*TO* 128 n. l) therefore compare *npr* with Akk *nupāru*, "coeur (siège du sentiment)" and reconstruct *š[mḫ]*, "happy." This approach suits the context. It is to be noted that **ᶜlṣ* and **śmḥ* constitute a BH parallel pair (see 1 Sam 2:1; 2 Sam 1:20; Zeph 3:14; Pss 5:12; 9:3; 68:4; Prov 23:15-16; see Avishur 1984:72, 147-48). Like the proposed reconstruction, Zeph 3:14 uses **śmḥ* and **ᶜlṣ* with *lb*, "heart" (see also **ᶜlṣ lb* in 1 Sam 2:1; **śmḥ lb* and **ᶜlṣ klyt* in Prov 23:15-16).

---

105 Commentators have also compared ESA *mᶜlṣ*, "joy" (Rabin 1961:396), but according to Beeston (1979:267) some ESA contexts exclude this meaning (e.g., Sabean *mᶜlṣ*, "wheatland," cited in Biella 370).

106 *CML*[1] 79; cf. *CML*[2] 40. For further discussion of this root, see Millard 1975.

The meaning of line 13a and its relationship to line 12 is unclear. As *ʾap* is a part of the body, *]ṭ*, has been read *ʾuṭ* or reconstructed *[ʾu]ṭ*,[107] and *ṯbr* is perhaps the verb "to break" (one of those parts?). Accordingly, de Moor (1987:31) believes that Yamm's messengers are described in the form of birds: "the bills of their beaks (open) to a span." Another approach has been suggested. Based on Arabic *ʾṯṯ, "to emit a moaning or creaking sound" (Lane 66) and BH *ʾēṭ*, "gentle sound, murmur," Oldenburg (*CEBCR* 191) renders: "snorting are their nostrils." Del Olmo Lete (1978:44-45) likewise cites Arb *ʾṯṯ in its meaning "to creak, split." Does the line *]ṭ ṯbr ʾaphm* refer to some physical gesture (e.g., snorting) which is idiomatic for joy? Or, is *ʾaphm* a particle (see *PU* 1.59, 71; *PU* 2.89-90) and the referent of *ṯbr* simply lost in the lacuna? Perhaps the best guess about this colon is that the messengers rejoice at the prospect of receiving instructions from their master Yamm and then they receive these instructions in the following lines.

Lines 13b-14a command the messengers to depart. Commentators take the second verb *ṯṯb* from either **ṯwb*, "to return" or **yṯb*, "to sit" (see *SPUMB* 128). In taking *ṯṯb* from **yṯb* and not **ṯwb*, Ginsberg (1950:160) reversed his earlier view (1941:13) that this form in other passages might mean "to return":

> "They do return"... is inapposite, since the place they depart for—El's assembly—is not their base of operations. As "the messengers of Yamm, the emissaries of Judge Nahar," they necessarily reside on the latter's premises. From this it follows that altho "they do return" would not be non-sensical in other passages, *lyṯb* must in these too be rendered by "they tarry not".

In Gen 45:9 *ʾal taʿămōd*, literally "do not stand," idiomatically expresses the command not to delay and would parallel the semantic development of **yṯb* from "sit" to "delay" in line 13. The third expression for departure *[ʾidk pnm] ʾal ttn* is well-attested in the Ugaritic mythological corpus, including 1.1 III 1*, 21.[108]

In line 14 Yamm tells the messengers to go to the home of the

---

[107] Cf. *ʾuṭm* in 1.5 I 5 (and reconstructed in line 32) and 1.18 IV 3. For different views, see *TO* 241 n. j.; Emerton 1978:75; *MLC* 524; del Olmo Lete 1984:159; Renfroe 1992:84-85. As Cohen (1978:34 n. 150) observes, the context of *ʾuṭm* in 1.5 I 4-6 is likewise obscure.

[108] For this formula, see p. 165.

divine assembly, the Olympus of the Ugaritic pantheon. The goal of the journey of Yamm's messengers is said to be *ll*, reconstructed on the basis of the parallel in line 20. The meaning of the mountain's name is highly debated, "night" perhaps the most frequently cited opinion.[109] Assuming this etymology, de Moor (1987:31 n. 136) remarks: "Probably the god of the night who acted as nominal president of the assembly of the gods, like Nusku in some Mesopotamian traditions". If the mountain of the divine assembly is not identical with El's abode,[110] then the evidence suggests two possible sites for the divine assembly. The first site lies south of Ugarit. According to an OB fragment of Gilgamesh and the Cedar Forest (Gilgamesh 5), the divine assembly called *mu-ša-ab e-nu-na-ki*, "the dwelling-place of the Anunnaki" is in the area of *sa-ri-a ù la-ab-na-na*, "the Sirion (Anti-Lebanon or Hermon range) and the Lebanon (range)" (T. Bauer 1957:255-56, rev. lines 13, 20; Lambert 1960a:12; 1982: 313-14; *ANET* 504, OB version, tablet 5, fragment C, rev., line 13). This tradition may provide the background for the descent of the divine Watchers to earth at Mount Hermon in the book of Enoch (1 Enoch 6:6; cf. 13:7). For Lipiński (1971:15-26) this tradition locates El's abode at the sources of the Jordan river near Mount Hermon, but the passages in Enoch appear more appropriate to the home of the divine assembly. Or, perhaps the locales, though not identical, were thought to be near one another.[111] Another site proposed for the home of the divine council is a mountain to the north of Ugarit mentioned in the records of Shalmanezer III (*ANET* 278). According to this evidence, Mount Lallar located in the southern extremity of the Amanus range.[112] The name of Mount Lallar may be related to *ll* in KTU 1.2 I 19, although the difference in spelling remains to be explained. There is no means presently available to adjudicate between these two sites; indeed, more than one site may have been known in different traditions as the mount of divine assembly.

The pantheon is mentioned in spare terms in 1.2 I 14-15, but the corresponding section in lines 20b-21 constitutes the most explicit

---

109 *CML*[1] 5 n. 1; Lipiński 1971:43-44; *TO* 128-29 n. l; *SPUMB* 129; Gordon 1977:70. Pope (*EUT* 68-69, 94) compares also Hittite *luli-*, "pond."

110 See the discussion above on pp. 230-34.

111 For discussion, see above p. 229.

112 For further discussion, see Smith 1988b; independently noted by J. C. Greenfield (personal communication).

description of the divine council in Ugaritic literature.[113] The council is called *pḫr mʿd*, "the assembled council" in lines 15, 16-17 and 20.[114] In this expression the divine council apparently includes the deities in general. The general divine council is also called *ʿdt ʾilm*, "the gathering of the gods," in 1.15 II 7 and 11. KTU 1.15 II 1-6 provides a partial listing of the great deities who belong to this assembly: El, Baal, Yarhu, Kothar wa-Hasis, Rahmay (probably Anat) and Reshep. The expression, *p[ḫ]r bn ʾilm* in 1.4 III 14, would seem to refer to the divine council, given the plural form of *ʾil*. The poetic texts attest to *dr ʾil* in KTU 1.15 III 19 in parallelism with "the gods," *ʾilm*, which might be construed as an indication that *dr*

---

[113] See Mullen 1980; Pardee 1986:65-66; cf. MacDonald 1979:521-26.

[114] The root of *mʿd* is **wʿd*, as indicated by Ugaritic *mwʿd*, "council," and Arb *mawʿid* which refers to an appointed time or place (Wehr 1081). The word apparently is a West Semitic loan-form in the Wen-Amun story (*ANET* 29; Wilson 1945:245; Clifford 1971:225; *TDOT* 6:136): "When morning came, he [Zakar-Baal] had his assembly (*mwʿd*) summoned, and he stood in their midst and said to Tjeker, "What have you come (for)?". Clifford considers *mʿd* "the native Canaanite word" and *puḫru* the "less familiar. . .epic word." It has been argued that the related BH form *môʿēd* refer to the divine assembly in Isa 14:13 and Lam 2:6 (*EUT* 49). The speaker in Isa 14:13 brags: "I will sit in "mount of gathering" (*har môʿēd*), located "in the far north" (*yarkĕtê ṣāpôn*), possibly a generic designation for the distant northern site of the assembly (*CMHE* 37-38, 180 n. 148), but quite possibly an echo of the location of Baal's abode. Miller (*DW* 187 n. 35; cf. *EUT* 90) sees Ugaritic *p[ḫ]r bʿl*, "the as[sem]bly of Baal," in KTU 1.39.7 as a development of Baal's assembly on his own mountain; it may be this motif or *pḫr k⟨b⟩kbm//dr dt šmm* in 1.10 I 4-5 which provides some background to the description of the assembly in Isa 14:13. In this verse, the speaker also boasts that "I will ascend to heaven, above the highest stars" (*kôkĕbê ʾēl*; for the interpretation of *ʾēl* in this verse as a superlative, see *EUT* 13 n. 79). The iconographic evidence for the home of the divine assembly would comport with this further detail regarding the home of the divine assembly. According to Barnett (1935:203 n. 7; 1969:8), a bronze bowl in the British Museum (no. 65) shows the pantheon above a range of mountains among the stars. Lam 2:6 uses **wʿd* in a description of the Temple's destruction: "He has broken down his booth like that of a garden,/laid in ruins the place of his appointed feasts (*môʿădô*)." RSV's interpretation of *môʿădô* as feasts goes back at least to the Targum of Lamentations (Hillers 1972:37). Hillers (1972:32) takes this word in its literal sense of "his assembly." It might appear to constitute a usage of the old term for divine assembly (*EUT* 49), here applied to Yahweh's abode manifest on the terrestrial level in the Temple. However, Provan (1990) defends the traditional view of *môʿădô* as "his festival," by noting that *sukkô* suggests paranomasia on "his booths," evoking the feast of Tabernacles. While this point is valid, it does not change the fact that the verbs suggest the destruction of a place. The vestigial meaning "assembly" for BH *môʿēd*, at least in Isa 14:13, gives credence to Clifford's suggestion (1971:225, 226-27) that BH *ʾōhel môʿēd* originally referred to the meeting-place of the divine assembly, but "the sense of 'meeting' was changed by the Priestly source to 'meeting' between God and Moses."

ʾil refers to the gods as a whole. The phrase's juxtaposition to *pḫr bʿl* in the prose text 1.40 would militate against identifying *dr ʾil* as the general divine assembly, in which case the parallelism with *ʾilm* would represent a general term and not a reference to El. The poetic texts also attest once to a council of the stars, called *pḫr k⟨b⟩kbm//dr dt šmm* in 1.10 I 4-5. The feast of Baal in 1.3 I might represent a convocation of his own council, although the expression *pḫr bʿl* does not occur in this passage or in any other poetic passage.

The prose texts differ further in their terminology for the assembly. Ugaritic *pḫr ʾilm*, "the assembly of the gods" (KTU 1.118.28; cf. 1.47.29) corresponds to Akkadian ^{d}*pu-ḫur ilâni*^{meš} in a pantheon list from Ugarit (RS 20.24.28; see *UgV*:45; Herdner, *Ug VII* 3). The latter is a common designation for the divine assembly in Akkadian which embraces all the deities.[115] The prose texts further distinguish *dr ʾil w pḫr bʿl* (1.39.7; 1.41. 16; cf. 1.87.17-18; *EUT* 90; *DW* 187 n. 35), which would point to "the circle of El and the assembly of Baal." The council of El may be marked also by the expressions *mpḫrt bn ʾil* and *dr bn ʾil*, unless *ʾil* in these expressions were to mean "divine" and not "El." The former alternative appears more likely given the use of the plural forms of *ʾil* in the phrases, *pḫr ʾilm* in the prose texts, *ʿ[d]t ʾilm* in 1.15 II 11, and *p[ḫ]r bn ʾilm* in 1.4 III 14.[116] The placement of *mpḫrt bn ʾil* following *dr bn ʾil* in KTU 1.40.8, 17, 25, 33-34 and 42 might suggest their equivalence. Ugaritic prose and poetic texts use other similar expressions for other groups of deities; the dead tribal heroes are called *pḫr qbṣ dtn*.[117] These expressions are used for groups of deities in the poetic texts with less frequency.

After giving his messengers instructions for their departure and journey in lines 13b-14a//30-31, Yamm gives them orders regarding the customary act of obeisance before El in lines 14b-16a//30b-31. The normal behavior of inferiors before their superiors is to offer

---

[115] *AHw* 876; *WdM* 8; Jacobsen 1943; Clifford 1971:223-24; Mullen 1980: 114-15.

[116] See also BH *bĕnê ʾēlîm* in Pss 29:1 and 89:7; *ʾēlīm* in Exod 15:11. Phoenician expressions for the general divine council include *mpḫrt ʾl gbl qdšm*, "the assembly of the holy gods of Byblos" in KAI 4:3-5 and *kl dr bn ʾlm*, "all the circle of the divine sons" in KAI 26 III 19. The plural form is patent in *qdšm* in KAI 4:3-4 which is likely a parallel expression for *ʾlm* in KAI 26 III 19 (cf. Mullen 1980:273-74). These attestations perhaps militate against a translation "El" for Ugaritic *ʾilm* in the Ugaritic expressions for the divine assembly.

[117] 1.15 III 2-4, 13-15; cf. 1.161.3, 10. For a discussion of *ddn*/*dtn*, see above p. 89.

obeisance. In Ugaritic the formulas are regular: inferiors are to "bow low" (**hbr*) and "fall" (**qyl*) at the feet of the superior parties, "prostrate themselves" (*Št* of **ḥwy*) and "honor" (**kbd*) them as well.[118] In the Egyptian story of "Astarte and the Sea,"[119] Astarte enters before the divine assembly, and members of the pantheon offer gestures of servitude before her (*ANET* 18): "And the great ones saw her, and they stood up before her." The behavior of "the great ones" in this passage parallels Baal's posture of attention before El. Yamm commands his messengers in lines 14b-16a to forego obeisance before El and the divine council and in lines 30b-31 they act accordingly (Ginsberg 1948:140; *ANET* 130; *EUT* 28, 91; *TO* 129 n. m; Smith 1984b). The particles *ʾal* in the command in line 15 and *l-* in the corresponding bicolon in line 31 are not asseverative; rather, they negate the verbs following them, as Ginsberg, Gordon, Aistleitner, Pope, Oldenburg and Caquot and Sznycer have noted (Ginsberg 1948:140; *ANET* 130; *EUT* 28, 91; *TO* 129 n. m; Mullen 1980:125). This gesture represents "an unbelievable effrontery" (de Moor 1987:31 n. 137), as it violates the divine etiquette of inferiors performing obeisance before their superiors (Smith 1984b). This act of defiance indicates the power of the one who sends them. The importance of their standing also contrasts dramatically with Baal's position of standing: whereas theirs communicates the power of their lord, Baal's position before El conveys his inferior status. Indeed, the contrast between the subservient Baal and the defiant messengers of Yamm runs throughout this passage.

In lines 15b-16//31, the messengers are to remain standing (*qmm*) while they speak (*ʾamr*) (so *ANET* 130; *CML*[2] 40; de Moor 1987:31), assuming the reading *qmm ʾamr ʾamr*. Ea's advice to Marduk in Enuma Elish 2.100-01 may be compared to the posture to be assumed by Yamm's messengers: "When facing Anshar, approach as though in combat; Stand up as thou speakest; seeing thee, he will grow restful" (*ANET* 64).[120] KTU reads *ʾaṯr* for *ʾamr* in line 31 and implies its reconstruction for this parallel context (so also *MLC* 171). In this case, the first line would mean "stand in the place, speak" or the like. Mullen (1980:125) takes *ʾamr* to mean

118 See above pp. 189-90.
119 On the West Semitic background of this text, see above pp. 23 and 25.
120 Cf. Enuma Elish 3.11-12 (*ANET* 64).

"look, see" rather than "say." He renders the infinitive with the command adverbially "constantly stare." Though philologically defensible, this interpretation mars the parallelism with *ṯny* in the second line of this bicolon. It is to be noted that in contrast the parallel in lines 31-33 abbreviates these formulas and accomodates a new bicolon.

Lines 16a//32a use the noun **dʿt* to convey what the messengers literally "know." The root **ydʿ* refers to the content of Yamm's speech which his messengers have memorized and to relate to the divine assembly. For this reason the less literal "instructions" has been used in the translation above. Like some of the others terms in this message, **ydʿ* occurs in epistolary contexts to relate facts which the addressee already knows or to provide new information (see Pardee 1977:19). This formula for introducing speeches in this passage is stereotypical. Similar instructions appear in the Assyrian version of the myth of the Anzu bird.[121] Ea Ninigiku instructs Adad to speak to Ninurta: "Repeat [to him], to thy lord, my instructions,/ Wha[te]ver I say outline to him."

The message of Yamm in lines 17-19a//33b-35 begins with introductory formulas well-known from Ugaritic correspondence. The opening bicolon in lines 17//33b-34a announces the nature of the message and its sender. The communication is called *tḥm*, the "decree," a common term in the openings of letters. Yamm is called the pantheon's "lord" (**bʿl*) and "master."[122] These two terms derive from the realm of suzerain-vassal relationships. The treaty document, KTU 3.1.26, calls Shuppiluliumash the *bʿl* of Niqmaddu (Greenfield 1967:118; Fensham 1979:272). In a letter, KTU 2.23.2, 19 and 23, Niqmaddu acknowledges the Hittite monarch as "my lord" (*bʿly*). Later in 1.2 I 36-38 El likewise employs language from the realm of suzerain-vassal relations (see below). This use of *bʿl* as one of Yamm's titles in this greeting raises a question over Baal's identity: is he *bʿl* or is Yamm?

The aim of Yamm's speech in lines 18-19a//34b-35 is the submission of his enemy, Baal. The message is addressed to the gods (*ʾilm*)

---

121 Parker 1989b:190-91. Called Zu in *ANET* 516. Now read as Anzû (so *CAD* A/II:155; Lambert 1980a:81). For the Sumerian reading *anzu* for the logogram *AN.IM.MI.DUGUD*, see Civil 1972; Hruška 1975:35-41; J.S. Cooper 1976; for a dissenting opinion, see Lambert 1980a:81 (my thanks go to Professor Benjamin Foster for these references).

122 Concerning **ʾadn* (< **ʾad*, "father" [KTU 1.23.32] + -**ān*), see above p. 150.

and most commentators assume that *hmlt* in the parallel line is a term for the gods. The translations, sometimes presupposing BH *hămullâ*, gloss the Ugaritic word by "crowd" or the like (*CML*² 145; *MLC* 170). The term may be a social term like Arabic *hamul^ah*, "clan," suggesting not so much a multitude of deities as the group of the assembly. Caquot and Sncyzer (*TO* 129 n. p) correctly note that *hmlt* refers not to deities but humans (//*nšm*, "men") in 1.3 III 27-28,[123] but in this case it is qualified by *ʾarṣ*, "earth," presumably indicating that in other contexts *hmlt* can refer to non-terrestrial beings. Humans are not addressed in lines 18 and 35, however, and the vocative in the first half of the bicolon suggests a vocative in the second half. Hence, the collectivity of *hmlt* refers to the gods of the divine council.

N. Wyatt (1993) suggests that *ʾilm* and *hmlt* both refer to Baal. The first word would then be the singular noun *ʾil*, "god," with mimation. Interpreting *hămullâ* as "tempest, storm" in Jer 11:16 and Ezek 1:24 (*BDB* 242), Wyatt takes *hmlt* as Baal's title meaning "the Tempest." Or, if it is objected that a feminine noun is unlikely to serve as an epithet for a god, then **dhmlt* may be taken as Baal's title, "the one of the Tempest." The syntax of the line presupposed may rule out this interpretation, however. The position of the relative clause before the noun which governs it seems unlikely, although it might be regarded as a matter of poetic license. If the nouns *ʾilm* and *hmlt* were construed as vocatives and not as direct objects as in Wyatt's view, then there is no problem of syntactical dependence in the second line. Moreover, the meaning "tempest" for this root may represent an inner-Hebrew development. Finally, it appears preferable to render *hmlt* in accordance with the sense of word known elsewhere in Ugaritic. It never appears elsewhere as Baal's title, but it is attested in the more general sense for a group which in this case would be the divine council.

In lines 18-19 (//34b-35) the messengers demand that the gods "give up"[124] (*tn*) Baal who is characterized as *dtqh*//*dtqyn*. Some commentators compare the verbs in these relative clauses to Arb **wqy*, "to preserve, guard," in the I form[125] or BH **yqy* "to obey"

---

[123] Cf. 1.1 III 15-16; *UT* 19.777.

[124] For **ytn* "to give" in the sense of "give up, surrender, hand over," see also BH **ntn* in Judg 20:13.

[125] *CML*² 42; For Arb **wqy*, see Lane 3059; Wehr 1094.

and Arb **wqy*, "to fear" in the V and VII forms.[126] The noun *yiqqĕhat* in Gen 49:10 (cf. Prov 30:17) suggests the vassal status of the "obedient" toward a suzerain[127]:

> kî-yābōʾ *šay lô[128]
> wĕlô yiqqĕhat ʿammîm
>
> So that tribute shall come to him,
> and the homage of peoples be his. (NJPS)

Given the plethora of terms in 1.2 I drawn from the realm of suzerain-vassal relations, the thrust may be to show the assembly's submission not to Baal but to Yamm. The meaning, "protection," remains possible, however, as the messengers might be thought to accuse of the divine council of harboring their master's enemy.

The phrase *wʿnnh* in lines 18b//35a has been interpreted in different ways. Many commentators assume a verbal form, "to humble" or "to lord over," presumably derived from the root *ʿ*ny*, "to humble, oppress."[129] Perhaps the form is to be understood as an infinitive with the 3 masc. sg. suffix, but Held and Tsumura suggest that ʿ*nnh* is a *D*-stem verb, 1 c. sg, with 3 masc. sg. suffix. Tsumura translates the bicolon:

> Give up Baal and I will humble him!
> Dagon's Son, that I may dispossess his gold!

This suggestion presumes a type of sandhi, specifically the loss of the grapheme ʾ*a*- before ʿ. This example as well as other proposed in-

---

126 Wehr 1282. See also Arb *taqiy*, "god-fearing, devout"; *taqiya*, "fear, caution" (Wehr 1282). So see *ANET* 130; *Thespis* 156; *CMHE* 183; *MLC* 170. Caquot and Sznycer (*TO* 129 nn. o, p) take the first Ugaritic verb from **wqy*, and following Driver, they compare the second verb with BH *qāwâ*, "to wait for": the gods (ʾ*ilm*) attend Baal while humans (*hmlt*) give him homage. Since the divine council is addressed in this speech, it would seem that a vocative appears to be involved in both lines and humans are not present. Understanding the verbs similarly, Walls (1992:105 n. 32) sees the divine council as addressed by both verbs. The comparison with BH **qwh* suffers semantically: the BH root does not mean "to wait on" (like a servant), which would be the sense appropriate to this context; rather, the root means "to wait for, look eagerly for; to lie in wait for" (*BDB* 875). Cf. the nominal form *tiqwâ*, "hope."

127 For this root in West Semitic PNs, see Layton 1990:222-23.

128 For MT *šîlô*. This interpretation is an old one. De Wette, for example, suggested this possibility (see Rogerson 1992:70-71). For a more recent endorsement of this view, see Moran 1958:412.

129 *ANET* 130; *Thespis* 156; Held 1969:72 n. 15; van Selms 1970; Tsumura 1982, 1991:431. See Arb *ʿ*ny*, "to be humble, submissive, subservent, be obedient, obey"; ʿ*anin*, "humble, subservient, submissive, obedient" (Wehr 650).

stances (Fronzaroli 1955:69-70; *UT* 5.38; Tsumura 1982, 1991) have been explained, however, in other ways, sometimes as infinitives. The advantage of seeing a first person form in the first line is the resulting morphological and syntactic balance. If correct, the word *ᶜny* would not signify personal humiliation as such. Rather, it would indicate a political relationship of subservience. In KAI 202:2 Zakkur states that *ʾš ᶜny ʾnʾ*, which many translate: "I am a humble man." This expression would reflect not his personal humility, but his subservient relationship to his divine lord.[130] An analogous relationship may be expressed in Yamm's desire to humble Baal.

This view of *ᶜnnh* has not met with general acceptance. Rather, the word has been taken as a noun with a suffix. A number of scholars connect *ᶜnn* with BH *ᶜānān*, "cloud,"[131] based on Arabic *ᶜanna*, "to appear, take shape" (Lane 2162). Cross (*CMHE* 166 n. 86) speculates: "One might argue that the divine clouds were messengers of Baᶜl in the first instance, and then *ᶜnn* came to mean "messenger, errand boy'." Baal's *ᶜnn* have been thought therefore to be meteorological characters like his girl Tallay, "Dewy." This word is used also of secondary deities who are, however, not meteorological in character which would cast doubt on this view (Good 1978). Furthermore, BH *ᶜānān* is the wrong type of cloud to correspond to Baal's "cloud-helpers." According to Scott (1952: 24), BH *ᶜānān* is not a rain-bearing cloud and does not appear in a context where the rain falls.[132] Good (1978) reverts to the noun "servant," assuming the etymology of **ᶜny*, "to humble, oppress" with final *-n* ending (so also Held 1969:72 n. 15 rejecting Driver's invocation [*CML*[1] 141] of Arabic *ᶜanna*). These "servants" are perhaps the same helpers as those mentioned in 1.5 V 9; there they are called *ǵlmm*, "lads," and *ḫnzrm*, "boys." If *ᶜnnh* means "his servants," in 1.2 I 18b//35a, the word is unrelated etymologically to any meteorological phenomenon, but like Baal's attendants called *ǵlmm*, "lads," and *ḫnzrm* in 1.5 V 9, "his servants," could be associated with Baal's meteorological entourage.

---

130 So Greenfield 1969c:179; see Tawil 1974:51-55. This view assumes that *ᶜny* is not to be regarded as a place-name (so Millard 1990; reference courtesy of Dr. A. Lemaire).

131 Mann 1971; *CMCOT* 112; Mendenhall 1973:54-55; Weinfeld 1986:132; *CMHE* 17, 165-66 n. 86.

132 The closest instance would be Gen 9:13-14 which describes rained-out clouds with a shining rainbow (Professor Aloysius Fitzgerald, personal communication).

In the second line of the bicolon (line 19a//35b), Baal is called "the son of Dagan," which would occasion little comment except that in the context of the divine council headed by El, this title reflects the fact that Baal does not belong squarely within the family of El. Baal stands in the council, but not as its champion. The reference to his paternity by Dagan may hint subtly at Baal's lack of support within the assembly.[133] The syntax and meaning of the rest of line 19a//35b is debated. Cross (*CMHE* 183) renders the last two words of the line as a relative clause: "whose abundance I shall possess." A purpose clause represents the majority view (e.g., *TO* 130; *CML*² 42) and seems less awkward. The meaning of *pḏ* is debated. The word is taken commonly to mean "gold," based on BH *paz*, Talmudic Aram *pîzzûzāʾ*, and Targumic Aram *pîzzâʾ* meaning "(fine) gold" (see *CEBCR* 193 n. 4; *SPUMB* 130; *TO* 130 n. r). As the most expensive metal at Ugarit, gold would have represented an appropriate item of booty. Steiglitz (1979) estimates the relative value of gold to silver to copper to *br* (tin or electrum?) at Ugarit at a ratio of 1:4:800:800. The correspondence between Ugaritic *d* and BH *z* is unusual, however, suggesting other etymologies to commentators. All other proposals likewise involve a lack of evidence or irregular consonantal correspondences: "posessions, spoils" on the basis of context (Ginsberg 1944:27 n. 8; *ANET* 130); "abundance," based on Arabic *mafaṯṯat*, "abundance" (< **pṯṯ*, "to empty, pour out"; *CMHE* 183 n. 161); "silver" based on Arabic *fiḍḍah* (possibly a loan or Kulturwort; so de Moor, *TDOT* 4:33-35); "clothes" as in BH *kĕtōnet passîm*, "a garment of (i.e., reaching to) palms/soles" (Mendenhall 1973:55); "ax" comparing Akkadian *pāšu* and Arabic *faʿs* (*WUS* 2288); and "portion" derived from Egyptian *pss.t* (*CML*¹ 163 n. 2). Given the irregular correspondence of consonants in all of the proposals, it might be considered that the *pḏ* is a loanword.

Ugaritic and biblical examples of this type-scene would support *pḏ* as "gold" or the like. Commentators (*SPUMB* 130; *TO* 130 n. r; Pardee 1980:272) compare KTU 1.3 III 39-46 where gold is one object of the battle's spoils between enemies. Anat claims to have defeated a series of enemies and in KTU 1.3 IV 46-V 1: "I have smitten for silver, have (re)possessed the gold of Him who would

[133] See above pp. 91-94.

drive Ba‘l from the heights of Sapanu'' (Pardee 1984:253). The silver and gold reflect the ruler's wealth and the potential spoils of royal conflict. Morgenstern (1941:65) also connects Job 37:22a: ''from Saphon comes gold'' (*miṣṣāpôn zāhāb yeʾĕteh*).

The type-scene underlying both 1.2 I and 1 Kings 20 likewise favors ''gold'' as the object of Yamm's desire. In 1 Kings 20 Ben-hadad gathers his army and besieges Samaria. 1 Kgs 20:2-4 matches the language describing Yamm's delegation to the divine council in 1.2 I:

> And he sent messengers into the city to Ahab king of Israel, and said to him, ''Thus says Ben-hadad: 'Your silver and your gold are mine; your fairest wives and childen also are mine.''' And the king of Israel answered, ''As you say, my lord, O king, I am yours, and all that I have.''

There are five elements shared by this biblical text and 1.2 I. First, like Yamm, Ben-hadad sends messengers in his stead. Second, in their speech, the unnamed messengers initially quote the introductory formula, ''Thus says Ben-hadad,'' paralleled in 1.2 I 17. Third, the messengers in both texts give an oral message memorized for proclamation before the adversary. Fourth, the messengers lay claim to the possessions of the submitting foe. In 1.2 I this is ''his gold'' whereas 1 Kings 20 lists silver, gold, wives and children. Finally, both passages contain a formal expression of submission on the part of the defeated.[134] In sum, ''gold'' is highly suitable to the context of Yamm's demands.

Lines 19b-29

Lines 19b-20a repeat Yamm's instruction from lines 13-14a. The tricolon of lines 20b-21 presents the divine council feasting. The divine council is here called *ʾilm//bn qdš*. The first word is the common word for ''gods.'' The second is either a general designation, ''the holy ones'' (*EUT* 44; cf. *qdšm*, ''gods,'' in KAI 4:4-5), or ''the

---

[134] At least one difference may be noted as well. In 1 Kgs 20:4 Ahab formally declares his submission and his surrender of his possessions. In 1.2 I 36-37 it is El who on behalf of the divine assembly formally declares Baal's surrender. Baal does not express his own surrender, perhaps foreshadowing his return to battle against Yamm. In contrast, in KTU 1.5 II 19-20, Baal states his surrender to Mot via messengers in a form proximate to that of 1 Kgs 20:4: ''Your servant am I, and eternally yours'' (*ʿbdk ʾan wdʿlmk*).

sons of Qdš," i.e., Athirat (*CML*² 41, 156; de Moor 1987:32 n. 140). In the latter case, the divine council would be tantamount to the "seventy sons of Athirat" (KTU 1.4 VI 46; cf. Emar 373.37-38 for "all the seventy gods of Emar"). There is no particular warrant for seeing the goddess' epithet in this designation for the divine council, as there is no clear Ugaritic instance of *qdš* as a title for the goddess.[135] The Winchester plaque (Edwards 1955; *CMHE* 33) contains the names Qudšu-Astarte-Anat. Albright (1954:26), Cross (*CMHE* 33-34) and Olyan (1988:40 n. 6) consider Qudšu to be an epithet of Athirat by a process of elimination, since Astarte and Anat appear after Qudšu in the inscription. Olyan calls the representation on the plaque "a triple-fusion hypostasis." The evidence for *qdš* as Athirat even in this case is ambiguous, as some scholars take *qdš* as a title of either Astarte or Anat (see Olyan 1988:40 n. 6). Other views of Ugaritic *qdš* in the expression *bn qdš* treat it as epithet of El (Xella 1982).

The first two lines of the banquet scene in lines 20b-21a contain the formulaic word-pair **ʾakl//*ṯrm,* which appear as an independent bicolon in 1.18 IV 29-30, suggesting that the third line is added to form a tricolon in this context. The depiction of Baal "standing before" (*qm ʿl*) El in the third line of this tricolon characterizes a courtier before his lord.[136] Baal's attendance before El may be compared generally with Kumarbi's position before Anu: "(As long as) Anu was seated on the throne, the mighty Kumarbi would give his food. He would sink at his feet and set the drinking cup in his hand" (*EUT* 28 n. 17). Biblical parallels approximating the Ugaritic idiom include Gen 18:18, Exod 18:13, 14, Judg 3:19, 1 Sam 20:25, 1 Kgs 22:19, Zech 4:14 (cf. Jer 23:18).[137] Like other features in KTU 1.2, Baal's subservient posture before El reinforces the impression of the Storm-god's weak status.

---

135 So most recently Wiggins 1991:386-89. The word *qdš* in KTU 1.14 IV 34 is "sanctuary" and not a divine title (cf. *CMHE* 33 n. 124), and the word in the title *lṭpn w-qdš* may apply to El and not Athirat; so *EUT* 43. Redford (1973:46) takes *qi-di[-šu]* as a deity in *Ugaritica V*, text 137, iv a 14, but according to Huehnergard (1987b:173) the word means "sanctuary, shrine," given the Hurrian equivalent provided, *ḫa-ma-ar-re*, the definite form of the Hurrian noun *ḫamri*, "sanctuary."

136 *CMHE* 37 n. 147; Clifford 1979:138; Mastin 1980; Wallace 1985:96 n. 69.

137 *CMHE* 37 n. 147; Wallace 1985:96 n. 69; see also Pardee 1976:264; *PU* 2.54. For 1 Sam 20:25, see Mastin 1980. Cf. divine affirmation expressed by the idiom **qwm ʿm*, "to stand by" in KAI 202:3; 214:1, 2, 3; 215:12 (restored) (so Greenfield 1969:176)

The description of Baal standing before El has served also as one of the main supports regarding El's pre-eminent place in the pantheon.[138] Critics of this view stress El's waning status.[139] Some compromise positions stress the kingship of both El and Baal.[140] Others take El as a figure like Ea in the Enuma Elish, nominally the pantheon's head about to be superseded by Marduk (Greenfield 1985). After Marduk's kingship is firmly established, there is no sense in Enuma Elish that anyone other than Marduk—including Ea—is king of the pantheon. The same applies in the Baal Cycle: after Baal's kingship is firmly established, El's role as the old executive of the pantheon recedes into the background. Yet the situation of Enuma Elish differs from the Baal Cycle. Kingship is firmly established at a relatively earlier point in the plot of Enuma Elish, and once achieved, Marduk's place is secure. In contrast, Baal's kingship requires not only his defeat of Yamm, but also a highly protracted process of acquiring his palace. Indeed, kingship acclaimed precedes battle and temple in Enuma Elish whereas the full recognition of kingship follows battle and palace in the Baal Cycle. El emerges as a figure more fully invested with power in the Baal Cycle precisely because Baal is not predominant throughout so much of the plot. Only when El gives his authority for the palace does he recede into the background of the plot. When Baal appears weak again in the narrative of Baal-Mot, El returns to the fore of the story, first, directly to settle the matter of Baal's successor (1.6 I), and second, indirectly in Shapshu's speech to Mot (1.6 VI), voicing El's support of Baal's kingship. Threatened by Mot, Baal's dominion requires the action of El to perform his role as manager of the pantheon. KTU 1.2 I presents El in his standard role overseeing relations within the pantheon. In sum, Baal seems subservient by "standing before" (*qm ʿl*) the enthroned El, while El appears as the leader of the divine council.

Except for Baal, the deities sit on their thrones (lines 23-24, 25). The pantheon is engaged in a divine banquet, the "high life" of the pantheon. Feasting is the setting most common to the collective gathering of the gods (Jacobsen 1942:167-68). Where two or more

---

138 *CMHE* 37 n. 147, 40; L'Heureux 1979:3-49; Mullen 1980; Casadio 1987.
139 *EUT* 25-34; Kapelrud 1962:59; 1980b; *CEBCR* 123-25; Pope 1989.
140 Schmidt 1961:21-26; Casadio 1987:55; Handy 1988, 1990.

divinities are found, there a feast is often found (1.4 III 40-44, V 44-48, VI 40-59; 1.5 IV 12-16; cf. 1.3 I, II 20-37; 1.5 I 22-25, II 21-23; 1.6 V 19-22, VI 14-16). The divine life is one of satiety. This metaphor for the heavenly condition perdured as the eschatological banquet through Israelite literature (Isa 25:6-8), intertestamental texts (1 Enoch 62:14; 2 Bar 29:4), rabbinic sources (Pirke Aboth 3:20) and the New Testament (Luke 13:29; 14:15; 22:16, 29-39; Rev 3:20; see Pope 1971; Fitzmyer 1983:1026). The element of the dead participating in this heavenly feast is attested in first millennium sources in royal Aramaic inscriptions (KAI 215; see Greenfield 1968) and presumably developed independently within Israelite society by the Hellenistic period, if not earlier (see Smith and Bloch-Smith 1988).

After sighting (*tphhm*[141]) Yamm's messengers in line 22, the members of the divine council lower (*tǵly*[142]) their heads in line 23. Layton (1983) reviews the interpretations offered for the assembly's physical reaction to their sighting Yamm's messengers in lines 23-24a. The council's response has been viewed as an act of mourning based on the motif of the face or head placed on the knees in other ancient Near Eastern literatures, such as Egyptian *d3d3/tp ḥr m3st*, "head on lap," and/or BH *pnyw byn brkw*, "face between the knees" in 1 Kgs 18:42 (*UT* 19.1965; *Baal* 26; cf. de Moor 1987:32 n. 141; Layton 1983:59). Layton (1983:61) views this interpretation as incompatible with the context of the Ugaritic passsage, as the assembly has no reason to mourn. Submission or meekness is another common interpretation of the assembly's reaction (*LC*[1] 22; Gordon 1977:70), but Layton (1983:61) dismisses the idea that the sighting of the messengers would elicit such a response from the council, especially as he argues that the messengers of Yamm perform

---

141 Dahood (1965:69) and de Moor (1965:356) note The equation of the verbal root **phy* with Akkadian *i-ta-mar-ma* (**amāru*, "to see"). The third consonant appears in the form *phy* in KTU 3.1.15 (Pardee 1980:272). De Moor relates the root to Arb *bāha*, "to perceive." For further discussion of possible etymologies, see Coote 1974; Pardee 1980:272.

142 This word stands as the opposite of **nšʾ*, "to raise," in lines 27 and 29. On the basis of this contrast, commentators assume that the word means "to lower." Gruber (1980:1.353-54) also compares *ʿll bʿpr qrnw*, "to thrust one's head in the dust" in Job 16:15. *WUS* 247 cites Arb *ǵala(w)*, "das Mass überschreitenn" and translating the Ugaritic form "übermässig beugen." Rendsburg (1987:627) compares Harsusi *aǵlo*, "to throw away." For another possible attestation of the root in the Baal Cycle, see KTU's reading of 1.6 V 17.

obeisance before the council. This claim misconstrues the force of the particle *l-* in line 31. Rather than an asseverative particle, the two instances of *l-* in this bicolon in line 31 (as well as *ʾal* in the command in line 15) negate the verbs they precede, as noted above.

Another suggestion is that the reaction denotes fear (*ANET* 130; *TO* 130; *CMHE* 183). Cross (*CMHE* 93 [cf. 40, 98]) describes the divine assembly as "cowed" by the demands of Yamm's messengers: "They were cowed and despairing, sitting with heads bowed to their knees."[143] Layton (1983:62) criticizes the notion of fear in this context: "While the arrival of Yamm himself might justify fear on the part of the gods, the mere sighting of his messengers is not simply not enough to explain their behavior." However, as lines 32b-33a reveal, the appearance of the messengers is dramatic, perhaps evoking the response of submission. Why the council so reacts to Yamm's messengers may not be known, but the notion of submission may not be dismissed, as Layton also does, simply because the reason for the motif is unclear. In fact, given El's submission to the demands of Yamm's messengers in lines 36-38a, submission would seem to suit the context.

Gruber views the council's reaction as one of sadness or depression: "While fear is a reaction to impending disaster, sadness or depression is a reaction to the perception that disaster has already occurred."[144] Gruber contrasts the gesture of the council and its significance with the "lifting of the head" in KTU 1.16 III 12, signifying joy. Similarly, according to Parker (1989a:290), lowering the head expresses "fear, deference or discouragement." Layton (1983:62) criticizes Gruber's interpretation by asking "why the gods would believe that disaster has already occurred." Indeed, if the messengers come to threaten only Baal, why do the deities react negatively?

Layton (1983:59-60, 62) offers his own interpretation to the council's response to the sighting of the messengers. He compares a passage in an interlinear translation of a Sumerian text preserved on a late Babylonian bilingual describing Enlil's withdrawal in terms of laying his head on his lap (among other physical gestures). Accordingly, Layton (1983:60) sees the motif of the Ugaritic council as

---

143 Waldman (1978:191 n. 12) relates this scene to examples of "horror-struck silence."

144 Gruber 1980:1.352-53; cf. 1.350-53; 2.598; and accepted by Kruger 1989: 63. See also Marcus 1990:26 n. 28.

withdrawal or detachment, as "one who has cut himself off from the outside world." Layton (1983:62) thus reinterprets the Ugaritic scene:

> The lowering of their heads to their knees is a sign of withdrawal on the part of the gods. Perhaps they were offended that the arrival of Yamm's messengers would interrupt their banquet. Whatever the reason may be, and we can only speculate, they bowed their heads to their knees, while remaining on their thrones, and refused to respond to Yamm's request borne by his messengers. It is as if they, like Enlil, have placed their fingers in their ears so as to be inaccessible to all appeals. Their behavior stands in contrast to that of Baal, who, after rebuking them, boasts that he will answer the messengers of Yamm.

Contrary to Layton's characterization of the scene, one deity, El, is not inaccessible as he does respond to the messengers. Acting on behalf of the assembly, El answers, which contradicts Layton's interpretation.

Kruger (1989:62) further criticizes Layton's suggestion based on the differences in genres between this scene and the Sumerian parallel which he cites:

> The example which Layton quotes, belongs clearly to the literary genre of the lamentation which at times occupies itself with the whole problem of the detachment of the god. Typical in these cases is the suppliant's complaint that the god does not take notice of his needs. . . In short, Layton's proposal appears to be suspicious mainly because of the fact that he does not consider the difference in literary form and metaphorical language between these two pieces of literature sufficiently.

In other words, the relationships between the parties conveying and receiving the communication in the gesture are very different in the two texts and therefore the same gesture in the two texts does not coincide in significance.

Kruger's criticisms raise the helpful point that the physical gesture of lowering the head is to be examined specifically within the context of divine council scenes. Jacobsen (1987:388 n. 4) discusses the motif of "raising the head" in Sumerian mythic texts, including one scene involving the divine council:

> The gesture of raising the head has different meanings according to the context. Basically it is means of calling attention to oneself, but such a demand for attention may be a matter of pride, a demand for recognition, or, very differently, a plea for help. . . It can also, in an assembly, indicate a wish to be recognized by the chair, usually, it seems to volunteer for some task.

As an example of this gesture expressed in the context of the divine council, Jacobsen (1987:378) cites a temple hymn to Kesh:

> Kesh was there
>   raising the head unto him [Enlil in assembly]
> Out of all lands
>   Kesh was the one
>   raising the head,
> and (so) Enlil was moved
>   to sing the praises of Kesh.

This instance suggests that if raising the head indicates a wish to be recognized formally by the chair in order to act and offer one's services, then its opposite, to lower the head, indicates a wish not to be recognized by the chair of the assembly so that one need not act. If so, then the gods' act of lowering their heads in KTU 1.2 I may indicate their wish not to be recognized by El in the divine assembly as they do not desire to respond to Yamm's messengers. In this connection Enuma Elish 2.89 may be compared despite the difference of contexts: the news of Tiamat's plan to fight the gods inspires silence in the divine assembly: *šaptāšunu kuttumama qa[liš]ušbu*, "their lips closed, [they sat] in silence" (*ANET* 64).[145] In sum, the physical gesture of lowering the head suggests neither mourning nor fear nor dread nor depression nor withdrawal, but a desire not to be recognized and thus not to act against Yamm's messengers. This gesture is tantamount to deference or submission to Yamm. Submission coheres with El's answer to the messengers and with the description of their physical appearance.

In lines 24-29 Baal reproaches the divine council for failing to respond Yamm's messengers. The speech constitutes four parts which may be diagrammed in the following manner:

A lines 24b-25a—Baal's first question: why have the gods lowered their heads?
B lines 25b-26—Baal's second question: will the gods together answer Yamm's delegation?
A' lines 27-28a—Baal's first declaration: raise, O Gods, your heads.
B' line 28—Baal's second declaration: he will answer Yamm's delegation.

The first and second parts are questions, and constitute rhetorically the first half of the speech. Correspondingly, the third and

---

[145] Cf. Enuma Elish 2.86: "speechless was Anshar" (see Waldman 1976:191, esp. n. 12).

fourth parts represent the answers to the questions of the first and second parts, and constitute the second half of Baal's speech. The two answers largely replicate the two questions. Moreover, the two halves reflect a progression, which anticipates the action of the narrative which follows. First, the members of the divine council are asked by the Cloudrider to resume their normal dignified posture towards the legation of Yamm. Second, Baal makes a bold declaration to seize rhetorical initiative within the chambers of the divine assembly. The first question occasions no interpretive problems as it largely follows the language of the immediately preceding narrative. Baal's second question reproaching the other members of the divine council contains two major difficulties. The first involves the syntax of the clause, *ʾaḥd ʾilm tʿny*, and the second is the meaning of *lḥt*.

Many commentators render the first two words of *ʾaḥd ʾilm tʿny* as a construct phrase and the third as a verb: "Shall one of the gods answer...?"[146] Caquot and Sznycer (*TO* 130) translate the syntax in the same way, except that they take the sentence as a declaration: "L'un des dieux doit répondre...". Given the parallels to this type-scene noted below, a question seems indicated. In either case, this approach leaves unsolved the disagreement in number between the singular subject *ʾaḥd ʾilm* and the plural verb *tʿny*. Other suggestions have been made to obviate this problem. De Moor (1990:78; cf. *CML*² 41) reads *ʾaʿny* for *tʿny*. This proposal assumes haplography of a single horizontal wedge as the cause of the scribal error.[147] This approach solves the syntactical issue. It fits the syntax of El's question in 1.16 V 10-22 which is often compared to *ʾaḥd ʾilm*, namely *my ʾilm*, "who among the gods...?" (de Moor 1990:78 n. 207). De Moor's suggestion alters the form of the question as found elsewhere, however. Other passages with this type of question posed to the divine assembly frame the question in the third person. Otherwise, this solution would be attractive.

Some solutions abandon the structural parallelism between *ʾaḥd ʾilm* in lines 25b-26a and *wʾank ʿny* in line 28. A number of scholars, including Ginsberg, Driver, Jirku, Kaiser, Oldenburg and Stuart,

---

146 *ANET* 130; *CML*¹ 79; Dahood 1979:183; cf. *CML*² 41: "Will any of the gods answer...?".

147 Cf. haplography of one vertical wedge in *hlm* for *ʾilm* in line 24.

translate *ʾaḥd ʾilm tʿny* as a declarative sentence: "I see that the gods are humbled."[148] Following Aistleitner, Mullen (1980:123) takes *ʾaḥd* as the plural imperative, "unite," a meaning rarely if ever attested for Ugaritic **ʾḥd*. These interpretations seem unwarranted on a number of other grounds. This line appears to parallel Baal's declaration in the fourth part of this speech, in line 26. Baal says: *ʿny ʾank lḥt mlʾak ym*, "I will answer the message of Yamm's messengers."[149] Layton (1983:62 n. 20) correctly notes the parallel with line 26 which includes the additional word, *lḥt*, "message," indicating that the verb **ʿny* here means to "answer" and not "to oppress, humble." The pronoun, *ʾank*, in Baal's answer in the fourth section parallels *ʾaḥd* in Baal's question in the second section. Furthermore, the relation between *ʾaḥd ʾilm tʿny* and the next line appears strained, if the former line were not taken as Baal's question to the pantheon.

Given the structural similarities between *my bʾilm ydy mrṣ* in 1.16 V 10-22 and *ʾaḥd ʾilm tʿny* in 1.2 I 25-26, it would appear that both are questions put to the divine assembly. The syntactical issue remains: how can *ʾaḥd* agree with *tʿny* in number? Caquot and Sznycer (*TO* 130 n. t) and Meier (1989:185) suggest a solution to the syntactical issue by taking *ʾilm* as the subject of *tʿny* and *ʾaḥd* as an adverbial accusative: "The gods should reply as one. . ." This solution is the most satisfactory, although it should further modified; a question is probably involved given the Ugaritic, biblical and Mesopotamian examples of this type-scene.

Lichtenstein (1979:406-07) identifies three typical elements in the literary type-scene which borrows from traditional elements of the incantation genre[150]: (1) a divinely issued appeal often in the form of a question, followed by the determination of the legitimate divine agent; (2) statement of procedure; and (3) divine blessing and charge. The divine agent in the incantation genre may be a creature of the divine creator's own making, reflected in 1.16 V 10-22. In other examples, for example in the myth of Anzu, this divine agent becomes a champion or warrior who can defeat the cosmic threat. Like 1.16 V, KTU 1.2 I manifests elements of this type-scene. Like

---

148 See *TO* 130 n. t; Stuart 19876:66; Gruber 1980:2.598-99.

149 Driver (*CML*[1] 79 n. 11) considers a possible play on the meanings "to answer" and "to humble" for **ʿny* in this context although *lḥt* is explicitly the object of the verb.

150 For examples from Shurpu V-VI and CT 17, pls. 25-26, see Lichtenstein 1979:400-01 nn. 319 and 320.

Baal in 1.2 I, El poses a question to the divine assembly in 1.16 V 10-22: "Who among the gods will drive out the illness?" (*my bʾilm ydy mrṣ*). It appears evident that the construction *ʾaḥd ʾilm* in 1.2 I parallels *my bʾilm* in 1.16 V.[151]

The third person question addressed to the company of the divine council appears also in Mesopotamian literature. It is in the context of the divine assembly that decrees are handed down by the head of the pantheon. These decrees include the decision of which warrior-god will face the cosmic foe. Tablet 2.7-16 of the myth of Anzu (OB version) provides a literary example proximate to KTU 1.2 I:

> Anu opened his mouth
> Saying to the gods, his sons:
> "Which of the gods shall slay Anzu
> His name shall be greatest of all!"
> They called the Irrigator, the son of Anu;
> He who gives the orders addressed him:
> "[In] thy resolute onslaught bring lightning upon Anzu with thy weapons!
> [Thy name shall be the greatest] among the great gods,
> [Among the gods, thy brothers], thou shalt ha[ve] no equal.
> [Glorified before] thy gods, po[tent] shall be thy name!"[152]

In this passage, Anu addresses the divine council as head of the pantheon and asks who will meet the threat of Anzu. Here Adad, "the Irrigator," is summoned as the first choice. Similarly, in the myth of Labbu, Tishpak is chosen to fight on behalf of the pantheon (Lambert 1988:140). Like 1.2 I 25b-26, the myth of Anzu begins the process of selection by means of a question posed to the divine council. The storm-god, Adad, is selected as the opponent to the terrifying Anzu.[153] Both Adad and Baal, storm-gods wielding meteorological weaponry and providing fertility for the world, meet cosmic enemies threatening destruction or death. There is a further point of similarity between the myth of Anzu (1.105-09) in the Assyrian version and the Ugaritic passages, KTU 1.2 I and 1.16 V: the

---

[151] The third person usage in these cases also undermines the view of Gordon (*UT* 19.126) that *ʾaḥd* in line 25 means "I alone." While possible, it seems that the *ʾaḥd* means "one." In contrast, *ʾaḥdy* in KTU 1.4 VII 47 combines "one" and the first person singular suffix. See p. 305.

[152] The translation follows *ANET* 111-13, 514-15, except that Anzu has been substituted for Zu (see above p. 289 n. 121). For this passage, see also Lambert 1988:140; Parker 1989b:190-91.

[153] Cf. the choice of Ninurta and the role of Adad as a messenger in the Assyrian version in *ANET* 514-15.

speakers announce their own intention to respond to the challenge before the divine council.

The other problem in the second question of 1.2 I 25b-26 revolves around the meaning of *lḥt*. Scholars generally identify *lḥt* with BH *lûaḥ*, "tablet."[154] This interpretation assumes that Yamm's messengers read their master's message from a tablet. Rainey (1969: 141-42) comments:

> The southern wing of the palace produced the important body of international correspondence. Here the official diplomatic communiqués would be received and duly read before the king and/or his chief ministers of state, especially the prefect. The courier or ambassador who delivered the tablets may have, on occasion, read them aloud to the intended recipient. But this may not have always been the case. The local scribe at Ugarit probably had the task of reading the epistles before his lord. The same procedure is reflected in the poetic literature of Ugarit; the sending of messengers (*mlakm*) from one deity or dignitary to another is a recurring theme. Yamm sent his emissaries to intimidate the council of the gods; Mot sent them to threaten Baᶜl; King Keret negotiated with his besieged opponent for the hand of the latter's lovely daughter. In each case, the messengers were instructed to 'speak the word of X (the sender) to Y (the recipient)'. Nevertheless, Baᶜl urged the council of the gods to let one of their number reply to (or read aloud) the tablets (*lḥt*) of the two messengers from Yamm, even though they actually stood before the gods and delivered their announcement verbally.

De Moor (1987:32 n. 142) explains the usage in somewhat similar terms: "Messengers brought along tablets confirming their orally delivered message." This approach would appear to be confirmed by the presence of numerous clichés of royal correspondence within this scene of the divine council in 1.2 I.

Scholars have felt the difficulty raised by interpreting *lḥt* literally as "tablets," however. Gibson (*CML*² 41) renders *lḥt*, not as "tablets," but as its metaphorical equivalent,"message." In a footnote (*CML*² 4 n. 7), Gibson clarifies his translation: "Lit. 'tablets' as containing the message." Royal correspondence shows a semantic development of *lḥt* from "tablet" to "correspondence." Pardee (1977:3) translates KTU 2.72.14-16:

---

154 Rainey 1969:141-42; *TO* 130; Dahood 1979:143; Brooke 1979:69-87; Meier 1989:185.

w.lḥt.bt.	Regarding the correspondence relative to the daughter of
mlk.ʾamr	the king of Amurru
ky.tdbr.ʾumy	that you are to speak
lpn qrt	before (the assembly of) the city...

While the literal meaning of *lḥt* is "tablet" (Brooke 1979:69-87), it refers to "correspondence." In accordance with the diplomatic character of the passage, the context of 1.2 I 26 would seem to suggest a connotation of "message" for *lḥt* (*CML*² 41).[155]

As noted above, Baal's command to the council in lines 27-28a mimics his question in lines 24b-25. The wording of Baal's claim in line 28 largely replicates his question in lines 25b-26 except in two details. Baal's declaration in line 28 lacks *lḥt*, "message." Contextually little is changed by this omission. Of greater significance, line 28 reads *wʾank ʿny* compared to *ʾaḥd ʾilm* in lines 25b-26a. Baal's speech reflects a parallel structure,[156] but this structure also shows contrast. The phrase *wʾank ʿny* contrasts markedly with *ʾaḥd ʾilm*: only Baal will respond, not the gods together. Translations of *wʾank ʿny*, such as "I myself will answer" (*ANET* 130; *TO* 131; Mullen 1980:123), avoid confusion with the Ugaritic expression *ʾaḥdy*, meaning "I alone" (KTU 1.4 VII 47), and emphasize the force of *ʾank* in initial position in the sentence. This wording perhaps has the further effect of isolating Baal from the rest of the pantheon.

After Baal finishes speaking in line 28, the gods follow Baal's initial instruction to raise their heads in line 29. The immediate fulfillment of this part of Baal's speech perhaps establishes an expectation that the second part of his speech, namely that he will address Yamm's messengers and their demands, will likewise follow. As the narrative unfolds, this expectation is also fulfilled, though with some twists.

---

155 Mullen (1980:123, 127 n. 25) prefers an etymology with Arabic *laḥy/laḥw*, "insult," while Driver (*CML*¹ 79, 158) translates "harsh demands," on the dubious semantic connection with Eth *ʾalḥeḥa*, "moistened." These etymologies are otherwise unknown in Ugaritic. It appears better to seek an etymology consonant with both the attested meaning of Ugaritic *lḥt* and the diplomatic context of this passage.

156 This parallelism is overlooked in interpretations of *wʾank ʿny* as "I shall humble" or "I shall vanquish" (Gruber 1980:1.598-99 n. 2) which are defensible from a strictly philological perspective.

Lines 30-35

In accordance with Yamm's orders issued in lines 13-19, the messengers arrive before the divine council in line 30a. The beginning of the description with *ʾaḫr*, perhaps signals the temporal proximity or overlap. Pope (1986) suggests that *ʾaḫr* designates immediate temporal proximity, "then, at that very moment." This line returns the focus of the action to the messengers.

In lines 30b-31 Yamm's messengers forego obeisance and remain standing in lines 30b-32a in accordance with his orders in lines 14b-15a. Lines 32-33a abbreviate the instructions to speak reflected in the parallel lines 15b-17a, and change a few elements attested in Yamm's instructions to the messengers. Lines 31b-32a omit the bicolon *wrgm lṯr ʾaby ʾil//ṯny lpḫr mʿd* in 16b-17a. Instead, lines 32-33 contain a bicolon focusing on the messengers' fiery appearance described as "a fire, two fires."[157] Almost all verbal orders are described virtually verbatim so that this departure from the narrative is highly conspicuous. Its importance is apparent: just as they forego obeisance and inspire the silence of the assembly, their appearance in fiery form is striking, giving good reason for the pantheon's response to them. Several minor divinities embody fiery form.[158] Other fiery divine messengers or angels include the angel who appears "*as* a fiery flame" in Exod 3:2 (Garr 1992:387; my

[157] This stylistic repetition is reflected in *raḥam raḥmātayim*, "a girl, two girls" in Judg 5:30. It may be noted that just as the nouns of construct phrases may appear in poetic parallelism (Melamed 1965), so also two nouns together, the first singular, the second dual may appear in poetic parallelism as in *riqmâ//riqmatayim* in Judg 5:30.

[158] See de Moor 1987:33 n. 143. The divinity *ì-ša-tù* is known from the Ebla texts (Pomponio 1983:145, 156; Pettinato 1979:105; Fronzaroli 1984:143). Hendel (1985:674) compares *Ishum*, "Fire," in Erra 1.4-5 (Cagni 1969:58; 1977:84). Like fiery messengers of Yamm, the god of chaos, Ishum serves Nergal, the god of pestilence and death (*ANET* 110; Livingstone 1989:74). Ugaritic *ʾišt*, "fire," and *ḏbb*, "flame (?)", are two foes whom Anat is said to oppose in 1.3 III 45-46 (Cooper, *RSP III* 364), and Miller (1965:257) compares them with *pur* and *phlox* in PE 1.10.9. The divine beings envisioned in the divine council in Isa 6:2 are called *śĕrāpîm*, from the root **śrp*, "burn." One class of spirits in the Songs of the Sabbath Sacrifice from Qumran (4Q403, fragment, col. II 9; Newsom 1985:226-29, 235; cf. 4Q405, fragment 20, col. III—fragments 21-22, 10; Newsom 1985:303, 306, 313-16; Smith 1987:586) are called *bdny lhbt ʾš*, "shapes of flaming fire" to which Newsom (1985:25) compares fiery angelic figures in Num 16:22, 26:16, Ps 104:4 and 1 Enoch 14:11. Jubilees 2:2 likewise mentions *rwḥy ʾš*, "spirits of fire" (Strugnell 1959:332-33). The fiery image of divine spirits is found later in Rev 4:5: "and before the throne burn seven torches of fire, which are the seven spirits of God."

italics); the divine servant, *ʾēš lōhēṭ*, "burning fire" in Ps 104:4 (cf. Miller 1965:257; *DW* 31); and Qumranic *mlʾky ʾš*, "fiery angels" (Strugnell 1960:332-33).[159] The introduction of the image of the fiery messengers in 1.2 I is connected with the preceding narrative which describes their execution of Yamm's orders by the two attestations of **ʾmr* in lines 31-32 (Sanmartín 1973). The relationship between the messengers' orders to speak and their fiery appearance is perhaps connoted by the juxtaposition of the meanings "to speak" and "to appear" (*Gt*-stem prefix form) for **ʾmr*.

Due to the lacuna, the second half of the bicolon poses problems. A number of reconstructions are feasible: *ḥrb lṭšt [bym]/[lš]nhm/[ʿ]nhm*, "sharp swords were [in] their rig[ht hands]/ their [tong]ues/ their [ey]es." Driver, Jirku and Caquot and Sznycer (*TO* 131 n. v) favor the first reconstruction of the second line. Miller (1965:257; *DW* 31), Cross (*CMHE* 190 n. 187) and Hendel (1985) offer the first two reconstructions. Ginsberg (*ANET* 130) proposes the third. In accordance with the first reconstruction, LXX Judg 3:22 places the sword in the hand of the divine agent. The sword guarding Eden in Gen 3:24 is flaming (see Hendel 1985). Besides Ishum in the Erra Epic, Hendel (1985:674) cites depictions of divine messengers with swords in Num 22:23 and 1 Chron 21:16. Many passages attest the literary use presupposed by the second reconstruction (Pss 52:4; 57:5; Prov 16:27; Job 16:9; Psalm of Solomon 2:4; James 3:5-6; cf. Isa 30:27). The head of the heavenly armies in Rev 19:15 describes precisely a divine figure in this language: "From his mouth issues a sharp sword." This image is appropriate to the description of Yamm's messengers. Their function before the assembly is precisely to speak, and an image accenting the power of speech appears at home in this context. Either depiction would appear threatening to the divine assembly, but the next action in line 33 is **rgm*, "to speak," and so perhaps the lacuna is to be reconstructed *[lš]nhm*. In lines 33b-35 Yamm's messengers deliver their message. It is addressed specifically to El. Yamm had included *[ṯny lpḫr] mʿd* in lines 16b-17a as addressees, but this line is absent from line 33. Otherwise lines 33b-35 are identical to lines 18-19a.

---

[159] Cf. the Babylonian Jewish Aramaic incantation (Naveh and Shaked 1985:202-03, bowl 13, line 21): "angels who came to the presence of Shamash, are clad with fire and covered with fire, and a flame of fire comes out of their mouths."

Lines 36-38a

The two cola in these lines constitute the council's surrendering Baal.[160] In this passage El's response to the messengers corresponds to their demands in two ways. One way is terminological: both the demand and the response use language drawn from the realm of suzerain-vassal relations.[161] El surrenders Baal to his enemy by declaring his status as a vassal to Yamm. Baal is called Yamm's servant (*ᶜbd*) and captive (*ʾasr*) "or perhaps 'liegeman' from *ʾsr* 'to take a binding oath'" (Greenfield 1967:117). Because Yamm is Baal's new suzerain, he will pay tribute to Yamm. By joining the other deities in rendering tribute to Yamm, Baal will manifest his subservience. This sort of language punctuates this column as in lines 17-19.[162] The treaty-document KTU 3.1 bears on the languages of lines 36-38. KTU 3.1.24-26 lists *ʾargmn nqmd mlk ʾugrt dybl lšpš mlk rb bᶜlh*, "the tribute of Niqmaddu king of Ugarit which will be brought to the Sun, the Great King, his lord" (Greenfield 1967:117; Fensham 1979:272; Pardee 1974:277-78). The phrase, **ybl ʾargmn*, "to send tribute," is common to both 1.2 I 37 and 3.1.24-25.[163] In Ugaritic non-literary texts *ᶜbd* applies to the vassal of the Great King (KTU 2.23.3), just as El calls Baal the "servant" (*ᶜbd*) of Yamm in 1.2 I 36 and Baal declares himself "servant" (*ᶜbd*) of Mot in 1.5 II 12 (cf. 1 Sam 27:12). Similarly, when Niqmaddu calls upon Shuppiluliumash for help, the Ugaritic king calls himself *ardu*, "slave" (*PRU IV*:49, line 12; cf. 2 Kgs 16:7). Ugaritic **mnḥ* occurs as political tribute in KTU 4.91.1 just as it appears in 1.2 I 38.[164] The

---

160 Hoffner (1975:142 and 145 n. 8) compares Elkunirsa's handing over Baal to Ashertu in the Elkunirsa myth (*ANET* 519).

161 See especially Greenfield 1967:117; Fensham 1979:272; Kalluveettil 1982:186-87.

162 See above pp. 289-94.

163 The Ugaritic word is translated by *mandattu*, "tribute," in Akkadian at Ugarit (Rainey 1969:133; see also Pardee 1977:8). Cognates include Akk *argāmānu*, Hurrian-Hittite *argama-naa*, Luwian *arkammana-*, "tribute" (Laroche, *UgV*:521). Rabin (1963:116-18) also discusses the possible relationship with BH *ʾargaman*, Aram **ʾarg(ĕ)wānā* (including Dan 5:7, 16, 29) and its derivative, BH *ʾargĕwān* (2 Chron 2:6), "purple, red purple." The relation between the meanings, "tribute" and "purple" is debated. For opinions, see Pardee 1987c:375 (for the purple dye trade, see McGovern and Michael 1984; Spanier 1987). The word is unrelated to **rgm*, "to tell" (see above p. 169 n. 97). Given the attestation of the word in Semitic and Indo-European languages as well as its use as a trade-word, it appears to be a *Kultur-Wort* (Rabin 1963:116-18; Kaufman 1974:35-36). Ugaritic attests also *ʾirgmn*; its relationship to *ʾargmn* is debated (for opinions, see Pardee 1974:277 n. 14).

164 See Levine 1974:16; Rainey 1973:60; Dietrich and Loretz 1980:401. See

function of the tribute-gift may be gleaned by reference to Enuma Elish 4.134: after his great victory over Tiamat, Marduk receives "gifts of homage" from the gods. The opposite is the case for Baal: not only does he not receive acclamation at this point before battle, he is to join the other gods in rendering tribute to his own enemy.

The second sort of correspondence between the messengers' speech and El's answer is structural. The correspondences may be summarized accordingly:

	A: lines 34-35		B: lines 36-37
34	the one you obey, O Gods	36	your servant, O Yamm
34-35	the one you obey, O Multitude	36-37	your servant, O Nahar
35	Baal and his servants	37	the gods
35	that I may possess his gold	37	tribute to you

The initial poetic units of both sections initially name Baal's status in relation to the addressee: from the perspective of Yamm, the assembly protects Baal, while from the assembly's perspective, Baal is Yamm's servant. Furthermore, the messengers demand Baal and his gold, which El accepts in declaring Baal's tribute to Yamm just like the other gods (the suffixes on the nouns being dative; so *CML*^{2} 42 n. 3). Hence Baal, named in the messengers' demands, corresponds to the other gods, mentioned in El's response. These correspondences suggest that Baal is not the choice of the pantheon at all. Rather, the assembly has accepted the sovereignty of Yamm. The sum effect of El's speech is to represent Baal as the vassal to Yamm, the new king and head of the pantheon.

Lines 38b-43a

These lines detail Baal's initial reaction to El's speech. The first line provides the first instance of Baal's title as *zbl*. As it is a regular title of Yamm, the application of this title to Baal may suggest that Yamm and Baal have a comparable position within the pantheon. Over a millennium later, the title appears in the New Testament as a demon named Beelzebul (Matt 10:25, 12:24, 27; Mark 3:22; Luke 11:15, 18, 19).

---

also BH *minḥâ* for political tribute in 2 Sam 8:10, Ps 72:10, Zeph 3:10 as well as a common form for an offering; BA *minḥâ*, "offering" (Dan 2:46; Ezra 7:17) which may be a loan from BH; Phoenician *mnḥt* for cult offerings (KAI 69:14, 74:9-10, 145:13; 159:8, CIS 14:5, etc.); cf. Arb *minḥatu*, "gift" < **mnḥ*, "to give, to present a gift" (see Anderson 1987:27-34).

In line 29 Baal may be angry[165] or weak.[166] The strict meaning "to be weak" does not suit this context as Baal takes his weapons in the following lines. Perhaps this response involves both physical and emotional weakness. Gordon (*UT* 19.228) cites *wayyeʾānaš* in 2 Sam 12:15 which seems to render David as not only physically but also emotionally distraught over his dying child. Dietrich and Loretz (1977:47-50) likewise suggest that *ʾanš* means "ängstlich, eingeschüchtert" in the context of 1.2 I 29. This interpretation would also suit *ʾan[št]* in 1.3 V 27.[167]

Baal appears poised to take up arms in these lines, a "slaughterer" (*mšḫṭ*) in one hand and a "striker" (*mḫṣ*) in the other hand.[168] The first weapon is known from KTU 4.167 = RS 15.79 = *PRU II*:122, line 12 (*TO* 132 n. y). The word is a *m-* preformative noun from **šḫṭ*, "to destroy." Ward (1961:37-38) compares Egyptian *mshtiw*, a large metal adze used for wood-working or a ceremonial hook on a tool. The second word evidently appears as a Ugaritic loanword *miḫīṣu* in an Akkadian text from Ras Shamra (*PRU VI*:142, line 4). It refers to a type of tool or weapon.[169] The word *ǵlmm* in line 39b presumably refers to Yamm's messengers as in line 13. From this context it may be inferred that after taking up arms, Baal now attacks the *ǵlmm*. The lacuna at the end of line 39b may contain a verb for "attack" which either is a *C*-stem impf. form (e.g., *ǵlmm yš[ql]*, "the boys he fe[lled]") or has an initial root letter *š* (e.g., *glmm yš[ḫṭ]*, "the boys he st[ruck]"), according to Caquot and Sznycer (*TO* 132 n. a).[170] This sort of reconsruction would

[165] The evidence for this view of *ʾap ʾanš* might be derived from Mot's words in 1.6 V 21: *yṯb ʾap dʾanšt*, "the anger which I feel (?) will turn..." (see *SPUMB* 132-33; *Baal* 29; van Zijl 1975; Dietrich and Loretz 1977; for the probably unrelated **ʾnš* in 1.16 VI 51, see Renfroe 1990:280). According to van Zijl (1975:505), the collocation of *ʾap* and **ʾnš* in 1.2 I 38, 43 and 1.6 V 21 indicates that *ʾap* in 1.2 I 38, 43 does not mean "then," but "anger." Van Zijl's interpretation of *ʾanš* as the "*ʾaphel*" of **nšy* is unconvincing, given the uncertain existence of the "*ʾaphel*" *C*-stem in Ugaritic.

[166] On the basis of Akk *enēšu* (*AHw* 217; *CAD* E:166-67), BH *ʾnš*, "to be sick, weakly, shakey" (Dietrich and Loretz 1977; Pardee 1980:272; Renfroe 1992:63).

[167] So Walls 1992:84-85. Cf. "you are meek"; so *ANET* 149; Held 1968:93 n. 69.

[168] There is no textual basis for emending *byd* to **bm yd* as proposed by Stuart (1976:66).

[169] Huehnergard (1987b:146) attributes the first vowel to vowel assimilation in the environment of the gutteral and posits an original form **maḫīsu*.

[170] Cf. *SPUMB* 125: *bm ymn mḫṣ ǵlmm yš[ʾu]*, "in his right hand he raised a slayer of lads." De Moor therefore has a five-word second line (fifteen consonants)

comport with the alleged objection raised against Baal in lines 40-41: *ʾik mḫ[ṣt mlʾak ym]*, "how can you st[rike the messengers of Yamm]?"

In line 40 two goddesses restrain Baal. The bicolon in line 40a neatly corresponds to the bicolon of line 39: just as Baal seizes (**yʾuḫd*, if correctly reconstructed) the weapons in his hand (*byd*)//in his right hand (*bm.ymn*) in line 39, Anat seizes (*tʾuḫd*) his right hand (*ymnh*, if correctly reconstructed) and Athtart (*tʾuḫd*) his left hand (*šmʾalh*) in line 40. Anat and Astarte appear paired also in KTU 1.14 III 41-42, VI 26-28, 1.100.20, 1.107.14 and 1.114.9-10, 22-23 (Gray, *Ug VII* 88; Olyan 1988:48 n. 37; Walls 1992:111, 113 n. 36). 1.100.20 is interesting in regard to this pairing, as it names *ʾinbb* as the abode of both Anat and Athtart (Walls 1992:111). Gaster (*Thespis* 159) compares the pairing of Anat and Athtart in 1.2 I 40 to a description of Ramses III's battle: "Montu and Seth are with him in every fray; Anat and Astarte are a shield to him" (*ANET* 250). Similarly, a thirteenth century poem praises the king's war chariot, which is likenened to Anat and Astarte (*ANET* 250). In the twelfth century story, "The Contest of Horus and Seth for the Rule," Anat and Astarte appear together as the daughters of Re and the wives of Seth.[171] While Anat's martial capacities are especially manifest in 1.3 II and 1.13, Ugaritic descriptions of Athtart's bellicosity are rare. Egyptian texts betraying West Semitic influence refers to this aspect of Athtart. In a late fifteenth century text, Tutmose IV is described as "mighty in the chariot like Astarte."[172] The irony of the goddesses' action in 1.2 I 40 derives from their purported relationship with Baal as his allies.[173] Perhaps at this stage in

---

parallel to a three-word first line (twelve consonants). The lacuna at the end of line 39 would allow for a three-word clause proximate in length to the preceding lines, e.g. *ǵlmm yš[ḫṭ bʿl]* or the like.

[171] *ANET* 15. For further examples of this pairing in Egyptian sources, see *ANET* 250.

[172] *ANET* 250. For further information, see Leclant 1960; Stadelmann 1967:91-96, 101-10; Redford 1973:44-46. Albright (*YGC* 44) and Redford (1973:44) suggest that Astarte is better attested in Egypt than Anat due to the former's greater importance in Phoenicia and the coast, namely the areas where Egyptians most commonly came into contact with West Semitic peoples. Astarte is better attested in Egypt and Phoenicia than in the Ugaritic texts and Anat appears regularly in the Ugaritic texts but less so in Egypt and Phoenicia. From the distribution of evidence, it might appear that the cult of Astarte was strongest in Phoenicia and the coast south of Phoenicia while the cult of Anat was more prevalent at Ugarit and in northern Syria.

[173] And according to many commentators, his consorts as well. On the problem of Anat as Baal's consort, see above pp. xxiii n. 6, 8-9 n. 20.

his accession to kingship, Baal stands at the lowest point: no one within the pantheon supports him (cf. Walls 1992:163 n. 1). This point could hardly be made more strongly than by presenting his own allies or consorts as his restrainers.

In the initial bicolon of the speech addressed to Baal in lines 40b-41, some figure objects to his wielding arms. The rest of the speech presumably continues the theme, but it is unclear. De Moor (1987:34) offers the following reconstruction:

> "A messenger hol[ds] the staff of a free man,
> [so would you slay] a messenger?
> Between his shoulder-blades is the word of his lord,
> and he [ ]."

According to this translation Baal's action is questioned by appealing to the messenger's status. Caquot and Sznycer (*TO* 132 n. d) interpret the objection as a response to Baal's attempt to assault Yamm's messengers: the word between the shoulders refers to the pouch which the messengers carry to hold the tablets for their master's message. Caquot and Sznycer reconstruct the preceding words accordingly: "Un messager at[tache] [.........] (son) fardeau". The verb is reconstructed from **ḥbš* and *mṭḫr* is taken as burden, related to BH **ṭrḥ*, "burden" with metathesis (see *BDB* 382), but a metathesis related to Akk *ḫuṭartu*, BH *ḥōṭer*, Aram *ḥṭr* in KAI 214:3, 9, 15, 20, 25 (in later dialects *ḥuṭrāʾ*), "staff, sceptre," (*BDB* 310) may be more likely. In either interpretation Baal's action is viewed as an inappropriate assault on the diplomatic immunity of Yamm's messengers.

Some elements in this section and the next section echo motifs in 1.2 IV, perhaps anticipating the reversal of Baal's immediate fortunes. Baal takes up arms in 1.2 I 39 and 1.2 IV 7-26; the first appears furtive, the second commanding and decisive. There are also expressions common to both of these attack sections: *bn ktpm* appears in 1.2 I 42 and 1.2 IV 14, 16. Athtart's restraining Baal in 1.2 I 40 sharply contrasts with her declaration of Yamm's vassalage to Baal in 1.2 IV 28. The "Name" (*šm*), mentioned as Athtart's epithet in 1.2 I 8 and played upon by Athtart in 1.2 IV 28 likewise draws attention to her place in both columns. With these verbal parallels, KTU 1.2 I perhaps anticipates the action to come in 1.2 IV.

Lines 43b-48

This section begins by noting Baal's anger. Otherwise, the response is unclear. The passage seems to begins with a reference to terraces (*šdmt*). De Moor (1987:34) fills out the lacuna of the initial portion of this speech:

> "The terraces with the vin[es will wither],
> [the f]ields, messengers of Yamm,
> envoys of Judge Naharu!"

De Moor (1987:34 n. 150) cites the combination of *šdmt/h* with *gpn(m)* in KTU 1.23.9f., Deut 32:32 and Isa 16:8 as support for the reconstruction of *g[pn(m)]* in the initial line of the tricolon (see Stager 1982:115 n.15). Citing the same passages as de Moor, Stager (1982:118) also understands *šdmt* as "agricultural terraces especially those on which vineyards were planted". Furthermore, de Moor takes this line in accordance with his seasonal perspective: "In January the growth of the vegetation comes to a temporary halt because of the cold." While the reconstruction may be correct, it is possible that Baal refers not to such a particular time of year as de Moor proposes. Rather, Baal's loss of power could issue in the deterioration of vegetation, just as the revival of vegetation expressed by El's dream-vision in 1.6 III intimates the Cloudrider's return to life.

Line 45b presents a speech addressed by Baal to Yamm's messengers. Line 45 begins with a speech-opening formula, *ʾan rgmt lym bʿlkm*, "I tell Yamm, your lord...". These words echo the address of Yamm to Baal in lines 16b-17a, specifically *rgm lṯr ʾab[y ʾil]*, "tell Bull, my Father, El." The verb *rgmt* constitutes a performative perfect with the first person independent pronoun prefixed perhaps in order to emphasize the speaker.[174] The opening of the speech is followed by the cliché for the beginning of the message, *hwt gmr hd*, "word of the Annihilator Haddu."[175] This formula may echo the beginning of Yamm's message to El and the divine assembly in line 17b-18: *tḥm ym bʿlkm*, "word of Yamm, your lord." The title **gmr* is used of Haddu in Akkadian PNs known from Ugarit: "Haddu

---

[174] For the performative perfect, see p. 48 above. Pardee (1975:369) notes that Ugaritic *rgm l-*, "say to" is attested fifty times.

[175] For this view of the meaning, see Held 1965b:400; for other views, see Rummel, *RSP III* 444-45.

annihilates'' ^{m}*ga-mi-rad-dì*/^{m}*ga-mi-rad-du* (*PTU* 128; Knutson, *RSP III* 494; for other possible readings, see van Soldt 1991:20n.179).[176]

Only bits of Baal's message for Yamm are attested. De Moor (1987:34) reconstructs Baal's speech and the messengers' following action (with the surviving letters represented in parentheses):

> '[He]a[r] the word of Haddu, the Champion:
> [I am] a follower of Yammu (*lwny*),
> [Judge Naharu], I walk behind him! (*ʾiyrh[*)' ''
> The mes[sengers of Yammu] did not bow (*thbr*),

It is impossible to confirm the elements of this reconstruction.

In general, many elements in 1.2 I suggest Baal's diminished status. This point may be illustrated by comparing features in this column with Enuma Elish, a text which has often been compared with the Baal Cycle, especially in their exaltation of their warrior heroes.[177] Numerous general parallels between the two works are clear: both describe a cosmic enemy making threats before the divine council; both describe a combat and victory for the warrior-god and proclaim his kingship; both depict the construction of a palace for the divine warrior and a banquet celebrating the god's kingship; both describe manifestation of the divine king's theophany, his universal reign and the restoration of order (see Rummel, *RSP III* 233-77, esp. 245-47). Specifically of import for interpreting the meeting of divine council in KTU 1.2 I, Enuma Elish 1.124-4.104 shows the divine assembly's place in the struggle between two divine combatants, one the warrior-god wielding meteorological weaponry, the other the destructive cosmic ocean (*ANET* 62-67).

The differences between these scenes, as elsewhere, are equally telling. Yamm is no threat to the assembly, only to Baal. In contrast, in Enuma Elish Tiamat threatens the entire assembly, even appear-

---

176 The word *gmrm* appears in 1.6 VI 16-21 where *rʾumm*, ''buffaloes'' and *bṯnm*, ''serpents,'' have suggested the image of an animal to some scholars who accordingly take the next noun *lsmm* as ''dogs.'' So *UT* 19.592; ''depredadoras [?]'' in *MLC* 233; ''fighting-cocks'' in de Moor 1987:97; ''beasts'' in Watson 1977b:275. Cf. ''burning coals'' in *CML*^{2} 80; *MLC* 533. It would appear more likely that *lsmm* refers in this passage to human ''runners,'' perhaps parallel with *gmrm*, human warriors. See Ugaritic ⌈ma⌉ -al-sà-mu in the Ugaritic polyglot (see Blau and Greenfield 1970:17; Huehnergard 1987b:82, 143, 200). In the polyglot the word's form, though not its root, is in doubt.

177 *CMHE* 93, 113; Clifford 1971, 1979; Hanson 1973:54-58; 1975:302; Rummel, *RSP III* 233-77, esp. 245-47. See pp. 13, 34-35, 75, 79, 82, 86, 95, 96, 101, 103-05, 110-12, 130, 150, 231, 288, 296, 300, 309, 314, 335, 340, 347, 353, and 358-59.

ing to be establishing her own assembly to displace the council of the great gods (2.12). The response of the assembly in Enuma Elish is to enlist Marduk's agreement to fight Tiamat and to proclaim him as king. Marduk's exaltation as king (4.28-29) formally precedes his battle with Tiamat, but for Baal, this will follow his rebellion against Yamm's dominion and the council's incipient acceptance of that order in 1.2 IV 32, 34. Whereas Baal is degraded, Marduk is elevated by the assembly (3.13-4.72). While the chief executive of the assembly solicits the divine warrior-hero in Enuma Elish, in 1.2 I Baal, the warrior-god unchosen by the assembly, inquires whether it will respond on his behalf. El, the chief executive of the pantheon, answers, and instead of supporting Baal, El surrenders him to his enemy. Baal is not the choice of the council; rather, Yamm is, as El's response in lines 36-38 and his choice of Yamm in 1.1 V show. Indeed, El summarily hands Baal over to Yamm's messengers and the two goddesses Anat and Athtart move to subdue Baal.

Lambert (1988:140) argues that unlike Marduk in Enuma Elish, the stature of Baal recalls Tishpak in the Labbu myth and Ninurta in the Anzu myth:

> a junior god does battle with a demonic being or monster on behalf of elders unable to face the challenge themselves, but the promised reward does not include abdication in favour of the young victor.

This formulation is partially correct. In contrast to the heroes' situation in both the Myth of Anzu and Enuma Elish, the position of Baal in 1.2 I is a weakened one, as he functions without the assembly's support and fights not on its behalf, but only on his own. As this contrast suggests, the Baal Cycle uses and undermines the type-scene of the divine council's selection of a hero to do battle on its behalf.[178] In contrast to his counterpart in the myth of Anzu, Baal is not the divine champion selected by the divine executive. On the contrary, Baal puts the question to the divine council. And contrary

---

178 The literary type-scene was used also in biblical tradition. Yahweh addresses the question to the assembly of divine beings in Psalm 82. As for Baal in 1.2 I, this question represents an accusation of the other deities, but unlike Baal's predicament, Yahweh's question is followed by the divine judgement that the other deities will die like mortals. In prophetic texts, the prophet hears the proceedings of the divine council and answers the question posed by Yahweh (1 Kgs 22:5-8; Isa 6:1-12; see *EUT* 49; *CMHE* 186-90; Lichtenstein 1979:406; Parker 1989a:190-91). 2 Kgs 3:11 perhaps provides a secular variation on this type-scene: a king with his servants in attendance poses a question to them in asking for assistance, and then "one of the servants (*ʾeḥād mēʿabdê*) of the king of Israel answered."

to the conventions of the type-scene, El surrenders Baal to his enemy rather than providing him with a divine blessing and charge as he does to Shaʿtaqat in 1.16 V.

In these ways 1.2 I plays off the type-scene of the warrior-god chosen to battle on the pantheon's behalf: Baal stands without the support and acclamation of the divine council. Other aspects of this type-scene likewise reflect the presentation of a relatively weak Baal. Yamm's demands, though addressed to the council as a whole, concern only Baal; this contrasts with other divine-council scenes where the assembly, threatened corporately, chooses a warrior-god to fight on their behalf. Moreover, how Baal stands before El in 1.2 I 21, how the messengers refer to Baal as "the son of Dagan" in 1.2 I 19//35, how Baal speaks for himself in 1.2 I 24-28, how the other deities accept their rendering of tribute to Yamm, and how El announces Baal's vassalage to Yamm in 1.2 I 36-38, contribute to a picture of a warrior-god struggling toward kingship. Indeed, El's response in line 36-38b parallels structurally the subservient response to the sight of Yamm's messengers in lines 19-24, and the narrative follows with the restraining of Baal by the two goddesses who otherwise appear as his allies. At this point in the narrative Yamm is a powerful monarch ruling his subjects, the members of the divine council, and only Baal would rebel against his dominion.

KTU 1.2 II

Bibliography

Text Editions: CTA pp. 8-9 + figure 4 and plates II, III; KTU p. 7.

Studies and Editions: del Olmo Lete, *MLC* 174.

Text

1 °[
2 °°[
3 tk[
4 sʾip°[
5 wbʿ[l
6 ʾi°q°[
7 °w°[
8 ʾim̥ḫ̥ṩ.[
9 mlk̊t̊[
10 lʾåk°[

11 n̊p̊š̊°[
12 bʿ°[
13 °[
14 t[
15 ḫ°[
16 m°[

Textual Notes

Line 1. °: V read *b* or *d*. KTU reads *bx[* while CTA reads no sign after *b*. As the sign is broken on the right-hand side, the reading could be *d*.

Line 2. °°: V reads *km*, CTA offers three possibilities *(r/k/w)[* and KTU has *kx[*. All three readings witness to a single horizontal wedge after the wedges.

Line 4. °: V correctly reads a horizontal wedge following *p*, KTU reads *x[* while CTA reads no sign after *sʾip*.

Line 5. [: Correctly V reads *wbʿ[* and CTA reconstructs *wbʿ[l*, but KTU reads *wbʿl *[*.

Line 6. °: V's hand-copy has *ʾirqb/d*, CTA reads *ʾir[-] (b/ʾu/d)[* while KTU has *ik q*/g*x[*. The second sign has a large vertical crack which complicates the reading.
q: The third sign also suffers from a large crack, but the upper and lower edges of the winkelhocken of *q* are visible.
°: Whether the final sign is *b* or *d* cannot be adjudicated since the right-hand portion of the sign falls on the right-hand edge of the column.

Line 7. °: A large crack obscures the first sign in the line.
°: Following *t* V reads a single horizontal wedge, CTA has ʿ and KTU reads *t**. The single horizontal wedge could be read *t*, but it may be part of another sign such as *m* or *q*.

Line 9. *k̊t̊*: The last two signs, read *kt* by all, are now quite obscure.
[: KTU reads *x[* while V and CTA read no sign after *t*.

Line 10. *lʾåk̊*: All give this reading, but only the first letter is clear now.
°: V reads the head of a vertical wedge following *k*, CTA has *lʾak.[* and KTU reads *lak*t* x[*.

Line 11: *p̊*: As V's hand-drawing shows, the line is very damaged. The heads of this sign are not preserved.
š̊: V's hand-drawing does not show the right-hand wedge of *š* and KTU has an asterisk. At this point *š* is a fine guess as a sizable vertical crack runs through the middle wedge.
°: Part of a wedge is preserved along the right-hand edge of the tablet. V reads a horizontal wedge. The WSRP photograph shows the wedge above the line which would suggest the head of a vertical wedge.

Line 12. °: V's hand-copy reads no wedge after ʿ, CTA reconstructs *bʿ[l*, and KTU reads *bʿl *[*. There does appear to be a wedge after ʿ, but it is too difficult to read.

Line 13. °: V and CTA read *k[* and KTU reads *w*[*. The reading cannot be adjudicated, as the head of a fourth wedge is not clear.

Lines 15 and 16. °: V's hand-copy shows some wedges at the end of these two lines. Similarly, KTU reads *x[* at the end of these lines while CTA reads no signs.

Translation

1 ...
2 ...
3 Midst...
4 ...
5 And Ba[al...
6 ...
7 ...
8 ...I will strike...
9 ...King (?)...
10 ...Send...
11 ...Life/breath...
12 ...Ba[al ?...]
13 ...
14 ...
15 ...
16 ...

Commentary

The column does not contain a single complete line, and as a result, any interpretation represents guesswork based on possible ties with the better understood passages in this tablet. Lines 5 and 12 might refer to Baal. Line 8 may be a first-person declaration of battle against an enemy. Line 10 may represent the sending possibly of messengers from one enemy to another. All of these themes appear in the next column. Originally this column may have described the declaration of battle by either Yamm or Baal (or both?) via messengers, perhaps as prelude to their conflict in 1.2 IV.

KTU 1.2 IV

Bibliography

Text Editions: Virolleaud 1935:29-45; CTA pp. 11-12 + figure 6 and plates II, III; KTU p. 9; *UH* 167-68.

Studies and Translations: Aistleitner 1964:50-51; Albright 1956:17-20; Bordreuil and Pardee 1993; Caquot and Sznycer, *TO* 134-39; Cassuto, *BOS* 69-109; Cross, *CMHE* 114-16; Dietrich and Loretz 1986a; Donner 1967; Driver, *CML*[1] 80-83; Dussaud 1947:201-224; Fisher 1965; Gaster 1937; *Thespis* 160-71; Gibson, *CML*[2] 43-45; Ginsberg 1935; *ANET* 130-31; Gordon, *UL* 15-17; 1977:72-74; Greenstein 1982; Horwitz 1973; Jirku 1962:24-25; Kapelrud 1963:56-62; Montgomery 1935:268-77; de Moor, *SPUMB* 126-28, 133-42; 1987:38-43; Mullen 1980:54-59; Obermann 1947:195-208; del Olmo Lete 1982; *MLC* 174-77; Rummel, *RSP III* 233-84; van Selms 1970; Yadin 1970:211-14; Young 1950:130-31; van Zijl, *Baal* 30-46.

Text

1 [ ]y°[ ]ḫtt.mtt[ ]
2 [ ]ḥy[ ]°[ ]lʾašṣʾi.hm.ʾap.ʾamr[ ]
3 [ ].wbym.mnḫlʾabd.bym.ʾirtm.m[ ]
4 [ṯpṭ].nhr.tlʿm.ṯmḥrbm.ʾits.ʾanšq
5 [ ]h̊tm.lʾarṣ.ypl.ʾulny.wl.ʿpr.ʿẓmny
6 [b]ph.rgm.lyṣʾa.bšpth.hwth.wttn.gh.yǵr
7 tḥt.ksʾi.zbl.ym.wʿn.kṯr.wḫss.lrgmt
8 lk.lzbl.bʿl.ṯnt.lrkb.ʿrpt.ht.ʾibk
9 bʿlm.ht.ʾibk.tmḫṣ.ht.tṣmtṣrtk
10 tqḥ.mlk.ʿlmk.drktdtdrdrk.
11 kṯrṣmdm.ynḥt.wypʿr.šmthm.šmkʾat
12 ygrš.ygrš.gršymgršym.lksʾih
13 [n]hrlkḥṯdrkth.trtqṣ.bdbʿl.kmnš
14 r̊.bʾuṣbʿth.hlm.ktp.zbl.ym.bnydm
15 [ṯp]ṭnhr.yrtqṣ.ṣmd.bdbʿl.km.nšr
16 [bʾu]ṣbʿth.ylm.ktp.zblym.bn.ydm.ṯpṭ
17 [nh]r.ʿz.ym.lymk.ltnǵṣn[.]pnth.lydlp
18 tmnh.kṯr.ṣmdm.ynḥt.wpʿr.šmthm
19 šmk.ʾat.ʾaymr.ʾaymr.mr.ym.mr.ym
20 lkṣʾih.nhrlkḥṯ.drkth.trtqṣ
21 ḅd̊bʿl.km.nšrbʾuṣbʿth.hlm.qdq
22 d̊.zblym.bn.ʿnm.ṯpṭ.nhr.yprsḥym
23 ẘyql.lʾarṣ.wyrtqṣ.ṣmdbdbʿl
24 [km]nšr.bʾuṣbʿthylm.qdqd.zbl
25 [ym].bn.ʿnm.ṯpṭ.nhr.yprsḥ.ym.yql
26 lʾarṣ.tnǵṣn.pnth.wydlp.tmnh
27 yqṯbʿl.wyšt.ym.ykly.ṯpṭ.nḥr
28 bšm.tgʿrm.ʿṯtrt.bṯlʾalʾiyn.b̊[ʿl]
29 bṯ.lrkb.ʿrpt.kšbyn.zb[l.ym.k(?)]
30 šbyn.ṯpṭ.nhr.wyṣʾa.b[ ]
31 ybṯ.nn.ʾalʾiyn.bʿl.w[ ]
32 ym.lmt.bʿlm.yml[k]
33 ḥm.lšrr.w°[ ]
34 yʿn.ym.lmt°[ ]
35 lšrr.wt[ʿn]
36 bʿlm.hmt.[ ]
37 lšrr.št[ ]
38 bṛʾišh.[ ]
39 ʾib̊h.mš[ ]
40 [b]n.ʿnh[ ]
41 [ ]

Textual Notes

Line 1. °: CTA gives *(d/n)* as two options for the second letter while KTU reads *d**. The two horizontal wedges are clear, but the vertical wedges of *d* are no longer preserved.

[ ]: Based on the vertical scribal line beginning in line 4, the lacuna at the end of line 1 should accomodate three, or possibly four, signs.

Line 2. *[ ]*: Based on the distance to the left-hand edge preserved beginning in line 7, the lacuna at the beginning of this line should accomodate four signs.
]°[: Where KTU reads one sign *]x[*, CTA reads no sign. The tail of a single vertical wedge is visible.
š̊: V's hand-copy reads parts of all three wedges, but now only the winkelhocken is visible. Its stance is proper for *š* as opposed to that of ᶜ.
[ ]: Based on the vertical scribal line beginning in line 4, the lacuna at the end of this line should accomodate two, or possibly three, signs.

Line 3: *[ ]*: Based on the distance to the left-hand edge preserved beginning in line 7, the lacuna at the beginning of this line should accomodate three signs. The same argument applies to the beginning of line 4

Line 5. *h̊*: CTA reads *h* for the first letter while KTU gives two possibilities *h*/p**. The heads of the top two wedges are not clear. The letter is blackened.

Line 6. *h*: The middle wedge is somewhat indistinct compared to the other wedges.

Line 7. Is *wᶜn* an error for *wyᶜn* or a narrative infinitive?
t: The final letter runs through the vertical scribal lines.

Line 9. CTA has a word-divider after *tṣmt* while V and KTU do not.

Line 10. KTU reads a word-divider after *dt*, while V and CTA do not.

Line 13. *]*: V has *[ ]hr*, CTA reconstructs *[n]hr* while KTU reads *n*hr*. The parallels in lines 20 and 22 favor the reconstruction. Cf. line 17.
KTU posits a word-divider after *lkḥṯ*, while V and CTA show no word-divider.

Line 16. *[ʾu]*: V does not read a letter between *b* and *ṣ*, CTA reconstructs *b[ʾu]ṣbth* and KTU reads *bu*ṣbth*. The parallels in lines 13, 21 and 24 favor the reconstruction.
KTU reads a word-divider after *bn*, and V and CTA do not.

Line 17. *[nh]r*: The letters have suffered considerable damage since V's reading of *nhr*. CTA's lack of italics for the first two letters indicates some damage. KTU marks with the first letter with an asterisk. The parallels in lines 20 and 22 favor the reconstruction. Cf. line 13.
[.]: After *ltnǵṣn* CTA reads a word-divider which KTU reconstructs. There is some damage where the word-divider might be expected.

Line 20. KTU has a word-divider after *nhr*, while V and CTA do not.

Line 21: *d*: The second letter of this line has suffered some damage. Parts of the head of the right-hand horizontal as well as the tail of the left-hand vertical are not visible.

Line 23. *w*: A large horizontal crack runs through this letter and the following one. The bottom two wedges are visible.
KTU reads a word-divider after *ṣmd*, CTA places a question-mark after it, and V does not show it.

Line 24. *[km]*: CTA reconstructs *[km.]* while KTU reads *k*m*[.]*. The parallels in lines 13, 15 and 21 support the reconstruction. The room for the word-divider, which is not visible, appears lacking.

Line 25. CTA reconstructs *[ym]* while KTU reads *y*m**. The parallels in lines 14, 16 and 22 support the reconstruction.
.: V and CTA reads a word-divider after *bn*, but KTU does not.

Line 28. KTU reads a word-divider after *b* in *bšm*, but as V and CTA indicate, there is no word-divider there. There is an indentation in the surface.
b̊: CTA reads *[bˁl]* while KTU has *b*[ˁl]*. As V's hand-copy and the WSRP photo show, the head of the left-hand vertical wedge is preserved.

Line 29. CTA suggests the possible reconstruction *[k(?)]* at the end of the line based on *kšbyn* in the middle of the line. Ginsberg reconstructs [*k*] instead of V's [*w*]; the latter appears preferable on stylistic grounds (cf. 1.2 I 37-38 of *k-//w-*).

Line 32. *[*: Many scholars, including Virolleaud, Bauer, Ginsberg, de Moor (*SPUMB* 127; 1987:42), Cross (*CMHE* 116), Gibson (*CML*² 45), Dietrich, Loretz and Sanmartín (KTU), del Olmo Lete (*MLC* 177), reconstruct *yml[k]* (see CTA, p. 12 n. 4). In reading instead *ym l[*, CTA may imply that the first two letters represent the name of Yamm.

Line 33. °: After *w*, KTU reads *y*. V and CTA do not read any sign after *w*. With KTU, there appears to be the head of the upper left-hand vertical of a letter such as *y*.

Line 34. °: KTU reads a word-divider after *lmt*, while CTA does not. V has a damaged word-divider, more specifically the left-hand side of the head of a wedge.
[: Unlike Gibson (*CML*² 45), KTU, de Moor (*SPUMB* 127; 1987:42), del Olmo Lete (*MLC* 177) and others, CTA does not reconstruct *[ymlk]*, although it is noted in CTA p. 12 n. 6.

Line 35. *l*: A large horizontal crack runs through the heads of the wedges. Following Virolleaud, Bauer and Ginsberg, CTA reconstructs *wt[ˁn.ˁṯtrt]*.

Line 39. *b̊*: So CTA and KTU, but V reads *d*.

Line 40. *[b]*: V and CTA reconstruct *b*, while KTU has *b**.

Line 41. KTU reads *]x[* while V and CTA have no sign.

Translation and Vocalized Text

The First Conflict between Yamm and Baal (?)

1 . . . drive out (?). . .die(?). . .
2 . . .live(?). . .
. . . "I will surely send them out. . .
3 If then I dri[ve. . .] (?). . .
And in Yamm will be the sieve of destruction,
And in Yamm will be the breast of de[ath?] (?),
4 [. . .Judge] River will be . . . (?).
There the sword I will destroy (?).
5 I will burn the [ho]use (?)

	To the earth the noble will fall, And to the dust the mighty."	lê-ʾarṣi yappulu ʾulanuyā wa-lê-ʿapari ʿuẓmanuyā

Athtart (?) Proclaims Baal's Demise

6	[From] his mouth the word scarcely departs, From his lips his word,	[bi-]pī-hu rigmu la-yaṣaʾa bi-šiptê-hu hawatu-hu
7	And she raises her voice: "May he sink Beneath the throne of Prince Yamm."	wa-tatinu gā-hu yiǵar taḥta kussiʾi zabuli yammi

Kothar Speaks to Baal

	And Kothar wa-Hasis speaks:	wa-ʿanâ[179] kôṯaru wa-ḫasīsu
8	"Indeed, I tell you, O Prince Baal, I repeat, O Cloudrider:	la-ragamtu lê-ka la-zabulu baʿlu ṯannîtu[180] la-rākibu ʿurpati
9	Now your foe, Baal, Now your foe may you smite, Now may you vanquish your enemy.	hitta ʾiba-ka baʿlu-mi hitta ʾiba-ka timḫaṣ hitta taṣmit ṣarrata-ka
10	May you take your eternal kingship, Your everlasting dominion."	tiqqaḥ mulka ʿôlami-ka[181] darkata data dardari-ka

Kothar Prepares Two Weapons for Battle Against Yamm

11	Kothar fashions the weapons, And he proclaims their names:	kôṯaru ṣamdêmi yinḥatu wa-yapʿuru šimāti-humā
12	"Your name, yours, is Yagarrish:	šimu-ka ʾatta yagarriš
13	Yagarrish, drive Yamm, Drive Yamm from his throne, [Na]har from the seat of his dominion.	yagarriš garriš yamma garriš yamma lê-kussiʾi-hu [na]hara lê-kaḥṯi darkati-hu
14	May you leap from Baal's hand, Like a raptor from his fingers.	tirtaqiṣ bâdi[182] baʿli kama našri bi-ʾuṣbuʿāti-hu

---

179 It is possible to take this form as either a perfect or an infinitive. The former seems preferable, as infinitives more often follow a finite verbal form which indicates the sense of the infinitive (see Gai 1982).

180 The *G*-stem is also possible (see *CMHE* 114).

181 The vocalization for the first vowel of this word is given as /ô/ (< */aw/) based on BH *ʿôlām*. Cross (*CMHE* 184 n. 162) also comments: "Aramaic (> Arabic) *ʿālam* is a loan word in which there has been a back formation."

182 This vocalization is based on EA 245:35 *ba-di-ú*, glossing Akk *ina qātīšu*, "in his hand" (Ginsberg 1936:149; Held 1965b:399; Sivan 1984:209). The form represents the contraction of **bi-yadi* to **bâdi* (see Blau 1971:34; Blau and Loewenstamm 1970:30). It has been argued that original monoconsontal form **d*, "hand," underlies this form (Rabin 1955; *UT* 19.1072; cf. Tsumura 1991:434), but this putative monoconsonantal noun is unattested without the proclitic. Phoenician *bod* appears in the Poenulus in the meaning "from" (Krahmalkov 1970:73). Syriac also attests *bd*, "through, by the hand of." In this connection, the proper name Yadi-Baʿala attested at Emar and elsewhere may be noted (see Arnaud 1991:175).

	Strike the torso of Prince Yamm,	hulum katipa zabuli yammi
15	Between the hands of [Jud]ge River."	bêna yadêmi [ṯāpi]ṭi nahari
	The weapon leaps from Baal's hand,	yirtaqiṣu ṣamdu bâdi baʿli
16	Like a raptor from his [fin]gers.	kama našri [bi-ʾuṣ]buʿāti-hu
	It strikes the torso of Prince Yamm,	yalumu katipa zabuli yammi
17	Between the hands of Judge River.	bêna yadêmi ṯāpiṭi nahari
	Strong is Yamm, he does not sink.	ʿazza yammu lā-yamukku
	His joints do not shake,	la-tinnaǵuṣūna pinnātu-hu
18	His form does not sink.	lā-yadlupu tamunu-hu
	Kothar fashions the weapons,	kôṯaru ṣamdêmi yinḥatu
	And he proclaims their names:	wa-yapʿuru šimāti-humā
19	"Your name, yours, is Ayyamarri:	šimu-ka ʾatta ʾayyamarrī
	Ayyamarri, expel Yamm,	ʾayyamarrī marrī yamma
20	Expel Yamm from his throne,	marrī yamma lê-kussiʾi-hu
	Nahar from the seat of his dominion.	nahara lê-kaḥṯi darkati-hu
21	May you leap from Baal's hand,	tirtaqiṣ bâdi baʿli
	Like a raptor from his fingers.	kama našri bi-ʾuṣbuʿāti-hu
22	Strike the head of Prince Yamm,	hulum qudquda zabuli yammi
	Between the eyes of Judge River.	bêna ʿênêmi ṯāpiṭi nahari
23	May Yamm sink and fall to the earth."	yaparsiḫ[183] yammu wa-yaqîl lê-ʾarṣi
	The weapon leaps from Baal's hand,	wa-yirtaqiṣu ṣamdu bâdi baʿli
24	[Like] a raptor from his fingers,	[kama] našri bi-ʾuṣbuʿāti-hu
25	It strikes the head of Prince [Yamm],	yalumu qudquda zabuli [yammi]
	Between the eyes of Judge River.	bêna ʿênêmi ṯāpiṭi nahari
26	Yamm collapses and falls to the earth,	yaparsiḫu yammu yaqîlu lê-ʾarṣi
	His joints shake,	tinnaǵuṣūna pinnātu-hu
	And his form sinks.	wa-yadlupu tamunu-hu
27	Baal drags and dismembers (?) Yamm,	yaquṯṯu baʿlu wa-yašuttu yamma
	He destroys Judge River.	yakalliyu ṯāpiṭa nahara

183 **prsḫ* is cognate with Akk *napalsuḫu/napasuḫu*, "to squat down" in *AHw* 1578, *CAD* N/1:271-72. See Virolleaud 1935:42; Gaster 1937:29 n. 7; Farber 1977:204; *CML*^{2} 156; *MLC* 612; Watson 1982:9. Some commentators also compare Arb *faršaḫa*, "to straddle, stand with one's legs apart" (Wehr 705) despite the irregular correspondence of sibilants (*UT* 19.2112; *TO* 138 n. y; *MLC* 612).

	Athtart Rebukes Baal	
28	By name Athtart rebukes (him):	bi-šimi tigʿaru-ma ʿaṯtartu
	"Scatter, O Mighty Ba[al],	baṯ la-ʾalʾiyanu b[aʿlu]
29	Scatter, O Cloudrider.	baṯ la-rākibu ʿurpati
	For our captive is Prin[ce Yamm]	kī-šabyu-nu zabu[lu yammu]
30	[For?] our captive is Judge River. . . ."	[ki?-]šabyu-nu ṯāpiṭu naharu
	Baal Acts	
	. . . . and he goes out. . .	wa-yaṣaʾa b[
31	Mighty Baal scatters him. . .	yibaṯunanna ʾalʾiyanu baʿlu
	Proclamation of Baal's Kingship	
	. . . and [s/he answers (?):]	wa-[t/yaʿnî]
32	"Yamm surely is dead!	yammu la-mitu
	Baal rei[gns!(?)]	baʿlu-ma yaml[uk(?)]
	. . . he	
33	. . . he indeed rules!"	la-šar$_v$ru
	Kothar (?) Proclaims Baal's Kingship	
34	. . . he answers:	yaʿnî
	"Yamm surely is dead!	yammu la-mitu
	[Baal reigns (?)],	[baʿlu-ma yamluk(?)]
35	He indeed rules!"	la-šar$_v$ru
	Athtart Speaks (?)	
	. . . and she ans[wers(?):]	wa-ta[ʿnî(?)]
36	. . . may Baal [rule(?)] them (?),	baʿlu-mi himata [yamluk(?)]
37	. . . he indeed rules!	la-šar$_v$ru
38	. . . on his head. . .	bi-raʾši-hu
39	. . . his enemy. . .	ʾib$_v$-hu
40	. . . [bet]ween his eyes. . .	[bê]na ʿênê-hu
41	. . .	

Commentary

Poetic Parallelism and Word/Syllable Counts

		semantic parallelism	word/syllable count
5	lê-ʾarṣi yappulu ʾulanuyā	a b c	3/10
	wa-lê-ʿapari ʿuẓmanuyā	a′ b′ c′	2/9

The syntactical repetition of the preposition *l-* followed by substantives with the same sufformative *-ny* binds the lines. The gutterals offer a contrast between the two lines.

6	[bi-]pī-hu rigmu lā-yaṣaʾa	a b c	3/9
	bi-šiptê-hu hawatu-hu	a′ c′	2/8

Just as the initial preposition *l-* plus noun binds the two preceding lines , so the initial preposition *b-* plus noun binds these two lines. These similarities between this bicolon and the preceding one suggests poetic interlocking between the two bicola although they belong to different sections of the passage. This bicolon is connected also with the following lines syntactically as they depend on the main verb in the next line.

	wa-tatinu gā-hu yiǵar	a b c	3/8
7	taḥta kussiʾi zabuli yammi	d e f	3/10

While semantically varied, the first two lines may be viewed as weakly joined sonantly by the repetition of *t* and *y*.

wa-ʿanâ kôṯaru wa-ḫasīsu

This line is an extra-colonic rubric.

8	la-ragamtu lê-ka la-zabulu baʿlu	a b c	3/12
	ṯannîtu la-rākibu ʿurpati	a′ c′	2/10

The second line uses the consonants *b*, ʿ and *l* echoing the name in Baal in the first line. Perhaps this alliteration evoking the name of Baal may be compared with the alliteration of *y* and *m* in lines 16-17, 24-25 evoking Yamm's name or the paranomasia of *rbt* and *rbbt* in 1.4 I evoking Asherah's epithet, *rbt*. In the case of 1.2 IV 8-9, the alliteration may stress Baal's victory, and in lines 16-17, 24-25, Yamm's demise.

9	hitta ʾiba-ka baʿlu-mi	a b c	3/8
	hitta ʾiba-ka timḫaṣ	a b d	3/7
	hitta taṣmit ṣarrata-ka	a d′ b′	3/8

The suffix *-ka* provides an internal rhyming pattern with *hitta*, "now," in each line, stressing the immediacy of the event predicted. The suffix *-ka* in the preceding and following bicola loosely link the three cola of Kothar's speech. The climactic parallelism of this tricolon (*CMHE* 114 n. 10) is replicated in the use of the consonants *t* and *ṭ*. The consonant *t* is sounded at the beginning of each line in *ht*. The first line does not repeat the consonant, but the second repeats it once and the third line twice. This pattern is reiterated through the use of *ṣ*, omitted in the first line, but used once in the second line, and twice in the third line. The repetition of *t* in the following bicolon might be viewed as linking the cola.

10	tiqqaḥ mulka ʿôlami-ka	a b c	3/8
	darkata data dardari-ka	b′ c′	3/9

Cross (*CMHE* 114 n. 10) notes the strong assonance in this tricolon, especially the repetition of the syllables *-ka* and *da(r)*. Watson (1981:101-02; cf. Albright 1945:21-22) notes the reversal of consonants in each line: the consonants of *mlk* are repeated and reversed in *ʿlmk* in the first line, and *dt drdrk* rearranges and reiterates the sounds of *drkt* in the second line.[184]

11	kôṯaru ṣamdêmi yinḥatu	a b c	3/9
	wa-yapʿuru šimāti-humā	c′ b′	2/9

Despite the semantic divergence between the two lines, the syntax creates a general parallelism between the two lines. Furthermore, the parallelism of sibilant + double *m* + dental in the direct objects and their dual form more closely link the two lines.

12	šimu-ka ʾatta yagarriš	a b c	3/8
	yagarriš garriš yamma	a b c	3/7
	garriš yamma lê-kussiʾi-hu	b c d	3/9
13	[na]hara lê-kaḥṯi darkati-hu	c′ d′	3/10

The four lines appear as a tricolon prefixed by a monocolon. The monocolon shows continuity with the following line through the repetition of the name *yagarriš*. It may be noted that the pattern of consonants in *šimu-* in the first line is reversed in *garriš yamma* in the second line. Of special note in the third and fourth lines is the combination of morphological, syntactical and sonant parallelism in *lê-* plus noun (phrase) ending in the genitive plus *-hu*.

	tirtaqiṣ bâdi baʿli	a b	3/7
14	kama našri bi-ʾuṣbuʿāti-hu	c b′	3/10

Syntactical, morphological and sonant parallelism is enhanced by

[184] Cf. Ps 145:13; Dan 3:33, 4:31. See Ginsberg 1935:327; Watson 1981.

the prepositions *bâdi*//*bi*- followed by nouns with *b* and ʿ and the genitive case-ending.

	hulum katipa zabuli yammi	a b c	4/10
15	bêna yadêmi [ṯāpi]ṭi nahari	b′ c′	4/11

Parallelism is achieved on a number of levels: syntactical parallelism, especially in the nominal endings; semantic parallelism between divine titles; and chiastic, sonant parallelism between *katipa* and *[ṯāpi]ṭi* and between *yammi* and *yadêmi*.

	yirtaqiṣu ṣamdu bâdi baʿli	a b c	4/10
16	kama našri [bi-ʾu]ṣbuʿāti-hu	d c′	3/10

Compared with the corresponding bicolon in direct discourse in lines 13b-14a, this narrative form of bicolon contains further alliteration of *ṣ* due to the addition of *ṣamdu*. This word also generates sonant correspondence with *kama*. The lines are also more balanced in length, which might viewed as evidence that this form of the bicolon is more original than its counterpart in lines 13b-14a.

	yalumu katipa zabuli yammi	a b c	4/11
17	bêna yadêmi ṯāpiṭi nahari	b′ c′	4/11

The narrative form of this bicolon compared with its counterpart in lines 14b-15a contains further alliteration of *ya*-.

	ʿazza yammu lā-yamukku	a b c	3/8
	lā-tinnaǵuṣūna pinnātu-hu	c′ d	2/10
18	lā-yadlupu tamunu-hu	c′ d′	2/8

Each line contains *lā*- plus final /u/ vowel. The nasals are conspicuous in the first two lines: *m* (as well as *y*) in *yammu lā-yamukku*; and *n* in *tinnaǵuṣūna pinnātu-hu*. The juxtaposition of consonants *y* and *m* in the previous bicolon and this tricolon marks the end of this section of narrative: *ylm*. . .*ym*. . .*ydm*. . .*ym*. . . *lymk*. . . *tmnh*.

	kôṯaru ṣamdêmi yinḥatu	a b c	3/9
	wa-yapʿuru šimāti-humā	c′ b′	2/9

There is no departure between this bicolon and the bicolon in line 11.

19	šimu-ka ʾatta ʾayyamarrī	a b c	3/9
	ʾayyamarrī marrī yamma	a b c	3/8

20	marrī yamma lê-kussiʾi-hu	b c d	3/9
	nahara lê-kaḥṯi darkati-hu	c′ d′	3/10

This unit is syntactically identical to the unit in line 12b-13. The name of the second weapon affects the bicolon's alliteration in two ways, however. First, the alliteration with ʾ is more pronounced. Second and more importantly, the alliteration between Yamm and the name of this weapon is patent. Does this feature signal that this is the weapon that will achieve its goal? Furthermore, the command *marrī* heightens the alliteration with *yamma*.

21	tirtaqiṣ bâdi baʿli	a b	3/7
	kama našri bi-ʾuṣbuʿāti-hu	c b′	3/10

This bicolon duplicates that of lines 13b-14a.

22	hulum qudquda zabuli yammi	a b c	4/10
	bêna ʿênêmi ṯāpiṭi nahari	b′ c′	4/11
23	yaparsiḥ yammu wa-yaqîl lê-ʾarṣi	a b a′ d	4/11

This unit compares with the bicolon in lines 14b-15a. As a consequence, the third line in this tricolon was apparently was a secondary addition, and it might be viewed as a separate bicolon with two short lines. The word and syllable counts suggest a tricolon, however.

	wa-yirtaqiṣu ṣamdu bâdi baʿli	a b c	4/11
24	[kama] našri bi-ʾuṣbuʿāti-hu	d c′	3/10

This bicolon matches the one in lines 15b-16a with the only difference of *wa-* prefixed to the first line.

25	yalumu qudquda zabuli [yammi]	a b c	4/11
	bêna ʿênêmi ṯāpiṭi nahari	b′ c′	4/11
26	yaparsiḥu yammu yaqîlu lê-ʾarṣi	a b a′ c	4/12
	tinnaǵuṣūna pinnātu-hu	d e	2/9
	wayadlupu tamunu-hu	d′ e′	2/8

The first line is not rendered as a bicolon (so *CMHE* 115), but as a line of a tricolon in accordance with the same unit in direct discourse in line 23. By the same token, it is evident that the internal parallelism of this line continues in the shorter lines that follow. As in lines 16-17, the end of the first narrative section, the alliterative pattern of *y* and *m* appears in lines 24-25, the end of the second narrative section, perhaps signalling parallelism between the ends of the two sections: *ylm. . .ym. . .ʿnm. . .yprsḥ ym yql* (lines 24-25).

Lines 26-27 continue the alliterative pattern of *y* and *m* in lines 24-25 with the prefix conjugation: *ydlp*. . .*yqṯ*. . .*yšt*. . .*ykly*. The alliteration with *y* and *m* emphasizes the name of Yamm and perhaps sonantly signals his defeat. Yamm's fall recalls the staccato description of Sisera's demise at the hands of Jael in Judg 5:26-27: both present the staggering collapse of the warrior defeated by a weapon landed on the head (Halpern 1983:48).

27	yaquṯṯu baʿlu wa-yašuttu yamma	a b a′ d	4/11
	yakalliyu ṯāpiṭa nahara	a′ d′(= x + y)	3/10

The word and syllable counts suggest a bicolon rather than a tricolon. Given this construal of the lines, the internal parallelism of the two verbs each followed by a divine name may be noted (cf. line 26).

28 bi-šimi tigʿaru-ma ʿaṯtartu

This line appears to be extra-colonic. If the speech-opening formula were construed with the following two lines, the unit may be scanned a b c, d e, d e′, which does not especially suggest a tricolon. Furthermore, the sonant structure of the first line, especially the alliterative pattern of *tigʿaru ʿaṯtartu*, offers contrast with the other two lines. Each of the three lines, however, opens with *b*- and contains a divine name and/or title.

	baṯ la-ʾalʾiyanu b[aʿlu]	a b	2/8
29	baṯ la-rākibu ʿurpati	a b′	2/8
	kī-šabyu-nu zabu[lu yammu]	a b	3/9
30	[kī?-]šabyu-nu ṯāpiṭu naharu	a b′	3/10 (?)
	wa-yaṣaʾa b[	?	?
31	yibaṯunanna ʾalʾiyanu baʿlu	a b	3/11
	. . .		
32	yammu la-mitu	a b	2/5
	baʿlu-ma yaml[uk(?)]	a′ b′	2/5

The first half of this unit is repeated in line 34. This bicolon expresses the two basic parts of the same new royal situation. A small group of consonants are repeated: *m* is the most common, then *l* and finally *y*.

34 yaʿnî

This appears to be a prose rubric.

yammu la-mitu	a b	2/5
[baʿlu-ma yamluk(?)]	a′ b′	2/5

Introduction

The central section of this column, lines 11-27, presents the drama of Baal's defeat of Yamm. These lines contain two parallel sections each comprising a speech followed by a narrative which virtually replicates the speech. The structure of this passage has been treated in detail by Obermann (1947) and Young (1950:130-31).

The beginning of all four sections in lines 11-27, specifically lines 11-15, 15-18, 18-23, and 23-26, contains the word *ṣmd(m)*. This word marks the opening of the two commissions in lines 11-15 and 18-23, as well as the opening of the two narratives following the commissions in lines 15-18 and 23-27. This repetition appears to bear a stylistic function (see Pardee 1980:273-74). It keeps the weapons at the forefront of the narrative and by contrast the wielder of the weapons remains in the background in this section of the story. The only additions to the narrative besides the repetition of the content of the speeches are the reports of the weapons' results.

Lines 11-26 thus constitute two major sections, each with two subsections. Lines 11-27 may be schematized:

	Weapon # 1 lines 11-18	Weapon # 2 lines 18-27
Kothar's action	11	18
Kothar's speech	11-15	19-23
Weapon's action	15-17	23-25
Results	17-18	25-27

In the two sections, lines 11-18 and 18-27, Baal engages Yamm in combat. The first section is virtually repeated in the second section, except that the second section has a different name for the second weapon, it describes Baal's fight as successful and it adds material that accents this fact, specifically in lines 25b-26a and 27. Division of major scenes into two corresponding units is a feature common to Ugaritic poetic texts. Feasts sometimes divide between preparation and performance of the banquet (1.15 IV-V; cf. 1.3 I), and the preparation itself, like KTU 1.2 IV 7-17//18-22, divides into two parts of command and action (Lichtenstein 1968). Similarly, the curing of king Keret (1.16 V-VI) splits between preparation and performance, and the performance consists of two parts, command and action (Lichtenstein 1979:259). The fight and feast of Anat in 1.3 II divides into two parts which use much the same language.

The speeches of Kothar in lines 7-10 and 31-33 (?) and Athtart in lines 6-7 (?) and 28-30 might be viewed as forming an envelope around the battle in lines 11-26. In lines 6-7 Athtart proclaims Baal's demise and in 7-10 Kothar proclaims Baal's imminent victory, while in lines 27-30 Athtart encourages Baal to decimate Yamm and perhaps in lines 31-33 Kothar adds his own voice. In lines 32 and 34, perhaps part of the speech of Athtart, Baal is proclaimed king, in accord with Kothar's earlier prediction. As Baal's kingship is threatened, Kothar proclaims the Cloudrider's victory, and when Baal's kingship is confirmed, Athtart encourages Cloudrider's victory.

Lines 1-5

This opening section describes Baal falling under the power of Yamm, but the passage is generally very difficult. Detailed and sometimes speculative reconstructions have been attempted (del Olmo Lete 1982:55-59; 1984:53-58; cf. Boadt 1978:495). Lines 1-2 are very problematic. The words *yd[y]*, *ʾašṣʾi* , and perhaps *ʾamr* are verbs perhaps denoting conflict (cf. 1.18 IV 24; Ginsberg 1973). The form *lʾašṣʾi* is apparently jussive with an asseverative *l-* (Huehnergard 1983:583). The first person forms indicate that a speech is involved. Obermann (1947:197 n. 16) suggests that Baal is the speaker. Either Baal or Yamm could be the speakers, perhaps threatening the other's destruction. If lines 1-5 involve a single speech, then Baal is the speaker, perhaps denouncing Yamm and threatening his destruction.

Lines 3-4 may render Baal's further threats about the fate of Yamm. If the reconstruction *m[t]* in line 3 is correct, the motif of this line is reversed in lines 32, 34: *ym lmt*, "Yamm surely is dead!" Yamm's power is "the sieve of destruction (*mnḫl ʾabd*)"[185] in line 3. Gibson (*CML*² 43, 151) and Healey (1983b:51; 1984a:113-14) interpret *mnḫl* as a sieve based on Arb *munḫulu*. Healey also compares the expression *mnḫl ʾabd* to *bĕnāpat šāwʾ* in Isa 30:28 translated as a

[185] Held (1965b:399) noted **ʾbd*, "to put an end to" as a West Semitism in EA 244:42 and *abadat* glossed by *ḫalqat* in EA 288:52.

"sieve of destruction" (RSV). The sentiment of this expression is reversed in lines 32 and 34, as Yamm himself dies. In line 4c some take *tlʿm* in line 4a as "gnawers" (*CML*² 43) or "chest" (Watson 1980:9),[186] but the broken character of the line makes impossible to clarify the word's significance.

Line 4c contains the verb, *ʾanšq*, which Gibson (*CML*² 43 n. 3) takes as "I will kiss," an act of submission, largely on the basis of the difficult verse, Ps 2:12.[187] According to Caquot and Sznycer (*TO* 135), followed by Bordreuil and Pardee (1993:63), the verbs express the speaker's intention to destroy and burn the house (assuming the reconstruction *[b]htm*): *ʾits* in line 4b is related to BH **nts*, "to smash" (Job 30:13) and *ʾanšq* in line 4c is taken as a *D*-stem cognate with the BH *C*-stem form **hiśśîq*, "to burn" (Isa 44:15; Ezek 39:9). This sense fits the context better than an expression of submission which is otherwise absent from the context. Other interpretations have been offered for lines 3-4.[188]

Line 5 could refer to the two protagonists by means of a dual first person pronominal suffix, *-ny*, or *-ny* consists of sufformative elements.[189] The nouns may refer either to their "strength" or "might" (*CML*² 43),[190] or the adversaries themselves (Ginsberg 1935:331 nn. 4-5; Obermann 1947:197 n. 11). In line 5 perhaps Baal predicts that either a standoff between Yamm and him is to result or the battle will continue.[191] A standoff is incongruent with the rest of the narrative, but a battle transpires in a matter of lines. Appeal might be made to a similar description in 1.6 VI 21-22: *mt ql bʿl ql ʿln*, "Mot falls; Baal falls upon him." It is also possible, but

---

186 Based on Ethiopic *tlʿ*, "breast, chest"; cf. *AHw* 1369. For a range of opinins, see further *MLC* 636.

187 This view of Ps 2:12 assumes a text-critical change from the MT reading *bar* ("purely") to *lĕraglāyw* (cf. Akk *našāqu šēpe*; see Holladay 1978; von Mutius 1981).

188 See van Selms 1970:265; *TO* 134-35; *CML*² 43; *MLC* 174-75; del Olmo Lete 1982:56.

189 Either the *-anu* "adjectival morpheme" (*CMHE* 28 n. 87) plus *-y* "adjectival suffix" or a compound suffix *-ny*. Cross (*CMHE* 56 n. 45) comments: "In view of Ugaritic and Amorite data we are inclined to posit closely related adjectival suffixes in two series: *-i/a/u-ya* and *-ī/ā/ū-ya* which appear also in the compound suffixes *-yānu*, *-uyānu*, etc. Certain members of the series specialized in certain uses, gentilics, hypocoristics, etc., varying according to dialect." Cf. *PU* 1.61; Boadt 1978:495.

190 De Moor and Spronk (1982:164) compare RIH 78/3:rev. 2: *ʾul ly*, "a force for me" (?).

191 For alternative views of line 5, see Boadt 1978:495.

less likely, that the sense of *ʾarṣ* and *ʿpr* is not a terrestrial one, but rather a reference to the underworld. In either case, the lines allude to the mutual destruction of the two foes. KTU 1.10 II 24-25 uses the word-pair, *ʾarṣ//ʿpr*, in this manner:

ntʿn bʾarṣ ʾiby	We will plant in the earth my enemies,
wbʿpr qm ʾaḫk	And in the dust the foes of your brother.

While lines 1-5 bear numerous difficulties, some parallels may illuminate the general context. According to Philo of Byblos (PE 1.10.28), Pontis ("Sea" = Yamm) defeats Demarous (Attridge and Oden 1981:52-53), a title long recognized as a modification of Baal's epithet *dmrn*, "Warrior," in KTU 1.4 VII 39 (Cassuto 1949:140-45). It is my guess that lines 1-5 render Baal's apparently futile curses against Yamm who stands here at the apogee of his power.

Lines 6-7a

The first bicolon in lines 6-7a contains formulas well-known from Aqhat. 1.19 II 26-27 illustrates both the division of the lines and their temporal relationship with the following bicolon in 1.2 IV 6-7a:

bph rgm lyṣʾa	From his mouth word had not departed,
bšpth [hwth]	From his lips [his word],
bnšʾi ʿnh wtphn	When he raised his eyes, he looked.

The final line with its initial element *b-* is a clause (cf. 1.19 III 14) dependent on the preceding bicolon. In 1.19 III 7-8 the line division is the same, but the syntax varies slightly:

bph rgm lyṣʾa	From his mouth word did not depart,
bšpth hwt[h]	From his lips [his] word,
knp nšrm bʿl yṯbr	(Then) the wings of the raptor Baal broke.

In 1.19 II 26-27 and 1.19 III 7-8 (and its parallels, 1.19 III 21-22, 35-36; for further parallels, see Parker 1989b:125), a tricolon is involved. The Ugaritic parallels indicate that the word had "scarcely" left the mouth when the next action transpires; the only ambiguous aspect of this picture is the grammar of the particle *l-* which might be construed either as a negative (*TO* 135) or an emphatic (*PU* 1.35). Different BH wordings of the same motif, for example in Gen 24:15, 45, 29:9 and Dan 4:28, would suggest that the word had not

yet left his mouth when the following action takes place; hence *l-* is the negative particle.

The first two lines represent speech-closing formulas (Watson 1983a:260), which provide a transition to the next narrative unit. It is often assumed that the next unit is a description of the apparently defeated Baal groaning (*TO* 135; Bordreuil and Pardee 1993:63) or falling (*CML*[2] 43) beneath the throne of Yamm. However, *wttn gh* belongs to the narrative, as Ginsberg (1935:331; *ANET* 130) observed, and the action may be a speech (Renfroe 1992:110), as *wttn gh* may be a speech-opening formula like *tš*ˀ*u gh* in 1.2 III 15. Ginsberg supposes that a third party, perhaps Athtart, is present and notes her appearance in line 28 of this column. The speech would appear to be a curse that "he sink" (*yǵr*, to be derived from the middle weak root meaning "to sink") which governs the following prepositional phrase, *tḥt ks*ˀ*i zbl ym* (*UT* 19.1985; Rainey 1969:172). Perhaps following Baal's words uttered against Yamm, Athtart speaks, but this time to affirm Baal's defeat. The poetic arrangement presupposed by this interpretation creates an imbalanced bicolon, which is possible to obviate by taking the first word of the curse, *yǵr*, as the final word of the first line of the bicolon.

Two other suggestions for the syntax for the second bicolon of lines 6-7a are inferior to Ginsberg's interpretation.[192] First, *Yǵr* as a person could be the feminine singular subject of the verb *ttn*: "*yǵr* cries out."[193] Such a personage is otherwise unknown, and given the preceding verbs of speaking and no following speech by *yǵr*, this interpretation appears unlikely. Second, perhaps the verb *ttn* is passive,[194] agreeing in gender with *g-* "voice," as Baal is otherwise the figure described by the preceding verbs (*UT* 19. 547). In sum, the parallels to the first two lines noted above and Ginsberg's insight about the third and fourth lines suggest that after Baal speaks (rather than a female personage as Ginsberg presupposes in his translation), Athtart or some female proclaims: "May he sink under the throne of Prince Yamm." The point of this motif of Baal's sinking under Yamm's throne may be compared with Kumarbi's position before Anu: "(As long as) Anu was seated on the throne, the mighty

---

192 For alternatives views, see del Olmo Lete 1984:53-54 n. 95.

193 Suggested as a possibility by Pardee 1980:273. See also van Selms 1970:265; cf. Hoftijzer 1972:156; del Olmo Lete 1982:56.

194 *TO* 135; cf. *CML*[2] 148; *SPUMB* 124, 134: infinitive with energic ending.

Kumarbi would give his food. He would sink at his feet and set the drinking cup in his hand'' (*EUT* 28 n. 17).

Although there is no difficulty with taking *yǵr* in line 6b from the root **ǵwr*, ''to sink,'' Renfroe (1992:111) disputes this derivation and instead takes the verb from the attested Ugaritic root, **nǵr*, ''to guard'' (1.4 VII 14). Renfroe translates: ''*Let him beware* (?) under Prince Sea's throne!'' (Renfroe's italics). Renfroe criticizes the picture of Baal lying beneath Yamm's throne: ''the prospect of the divine craftman Kothar handing over cunning weapons of battle to the Lord [Baal] while the later is cowering under the throne of his opponent taxes credibility.'' One might similarly wonder why Baal is under the throne of Yamm if he is not in a defeated or submissive posture. Moreover, comparative evidence may mitigate Renfroe's objection to the picture of Baal fallen beneath throne of Yamm. Some folklorists[195] note in both Enuma Elish and the Baal Cycle an initial conflict or first encounter between the divine hero and the enemy, which issues in the temporary setback for the hero, only to be reversed in a second engagement. In the conflict between Baal and Yamm, KTU 1.2 IV 1-7 would constitute the initial episode and 1.2 IV 7b-27 its reversal (del Olmo Lete 1982:55-59). Similarly, in Enuma Elish 4.67-68 Marduk falls back in disarray following his first meeting with Tiamat (Lambert 1986:56 n. 4). A number of parallels follow suit (*Thespis* 150). In the first round of conflict between the storm-god and Illuyanka ends in the dragon's victory (*ANET* 125-26; Beckman 1982). Ninurta likewise meets initial adversity in battle (Kramer 1972:80). In the Rgveda, the storm-god Indra initially flees before the serpent, Vrtra.[196] Philo of Byblos (PE 1.10.28; Attridge and Oden 1981:52-53) records Sea's victory over Demarous, although this account may represent a different version (cf. Attridge and Oden 1981:90 n. 119). Later reflexes of the old West Semitic conflict myth include the motif of the divine hero's initial defeat by the cosmic enemy. According to b. B. Bat. 74b-75a, the angel Gabriel meets defeat in his initial meeting against Leviathan (Jacobs 1977:8). The beast of Rev 13:1-10 receives power and victory for a limited time before his final defeat in Rev 19:20.

Although not made explicit in 1.2 IV, the location of conflict on Mount Sapan seems likely in view of the reference to battle,

---

[195] Jason 1977:32; Milne 1988:169-70; see above p. 26.

[196] This story has been traced to a Near Eastern antecedent, though not without controversy; see above p. 113.

probably between Yamm and Baal, on Mount Sapan in 1.1 IV 5 and 18. The final clash between Baal and Mot likewise occurs on Mount Sapan (1.6 VI 12-13). Zeus attacks Typhon at mons Cassius. Mount Hazzi, the Hittite equivalent of Mount Sapan, is the site where the Storm-god first views his enemy, Ullikumi (*ANET* 123).[197] The final goal of KTU 1.2 IV is Baal's defeat of Yamm, perhaps on Mount Sapan, and the call for Baal to sink beneath Yamm's throne need not be viewed as transfering this scene to Yamm's abode.

Lines 7b-10

The speech of Kothar is arranged in three units, a tricolon enveloped by two bicolons. The speech sets the stage for Baal's victory. On the surface, the initial bicolon first emphasizes Kothar's speaking, but this unit may amount to more than a matter of emphasis. Like his incantations over the weapons in the following section, Kothar's prediction may have some further force to them. According to Philo of Byblos, Chousor is said to have "practiced verbal arts including spells and prophecies," *logous askēsai kai epōdas kai manteias* (PE 1.10.11; Attridge and Oden 1981:44-45). The incantations in the following section resemble Chousor's spells, and perhaps Kothar's prediction—in this case about Baal's kingship—is echoed in Philo of Byblos' attribution of prophecy to Chousor. The best example of Kothar's predictions is found in 1.4 VI. In 1.4 VI 1-9 Kothar insists in installing a window in the heavenly palace of Baal, and in 1.4 VI 14-15 the craftsman-god predicts that Baal will reverse his decision and asks Kothar to put in the window after all (cf. 1.4 VII 14-19).

The initial bicolon in lines 7b-8 addresses Baal with two epithets which are highly congruent with the scene at hand. The first is the stock epithet *zbl bʿl*, "Prince Baal," acknowledging Baal's royal status. The second is *rkb ʿrpt*, "Cloudrider," pointing to the meteorological character of the conflict at hand (Weinfeld 1973).[198]

---

[197] See above pp. 122-23. Cf. Joel 3:9-17, 19-21; Zech 14:4; 2 Esdras 13:35; cf. Isa 66:18-21; Ezek 38-39. In Ps 48:3 Mount Zion is called Saphon. Similarly, the Aramaic version of Psalm 20 written in Demotic has Saphon for Mount Zion (Nims and Steiner 1983; for further discussion of biblical parallels, see Smith 1990:53-54).

[198] Cf. BH *rōkēb baʿărābôt* in Deut 33:26; Pss 68:5, 104:3, perhaps a modification of the old epithet *rkb ʿrpt*; so Gray 1977:7, 9, 21 n. 4. For other options and discussion, see Cooper, *RSP III* 458-60.

Boadt (1978:9) compares the setting and general content of the following tricolon of lines 8b-9 with biblical prophetic oracles against the nations. Both issue judgement against the enemy or enemies of the main deity. As with the first bicolon in this section, the terms of battle are specifically royal, and in this tricolon divine kingship is expresed as an eternal reality. Ps 92:10 [E 9] is commonly compared to this tricolon (Ginsberg 1935:327; *Baal* 33; *SPUMB* 135):

kî hinnē ᵓōyĕbêkā yhwh	For, lo, thy enemies, O Yahweh
kî-hinnē ᵓōyĕbêkā yōᵓbēdû	For, lo, thy enemies shall perish;
yitpārĕrû kol-pōᶜălê ᵓāwen	All evildoers shall be scattered.

Both tricola contain a punctuating particle at the start of the first two lines, which also have cognates words for "enemy," based on the root *ᵓyb (for the form of Ugaritic *ᵓib*, cf. BH *ᵓebâ*, "emnity"). The vocative in the first line, followed by the verb delayed in the second line also appears in both tricola. Both tricola delay the introduction of a verb until the second line and introduce a second verb in the third line. Following the direct discourse of the first two lines, the third line shifts to indirect address. The differences between the two passages highlight distinctive aspects of both texts. Baal's victory is won through a cosmic struggle waged against Yamm, but Yahweh's battle is cast in moral terms; it is directed specifically against evildoers. A contrast might be drawn also between the particles in the two passages. The temporal particle, *ht*, in 1.2 IV 8-9 emphasizes the temporal immediacy of Baal's victory while the possibly related[199] particle *hinnē* may be either temporal or spatial (see Jer 17:18-19). In Ps 92:10 *hinnē* perhaps stresses the physical immediacy of the enemies' demise (Donner 1967:344-46). Despite these differences, the theme as well as the pace and punctuation by particles nonetheless compare closely in 1.2 IV 8-9 and Ps 92:10.

Lines 11a//18

Line 11 introduces the action central to this column. Kothar is said to "fashion" (*ynḥt*) a weapon, an interpretation based on Arabic *naḥata*, "to sculpt stone, work wood."[200] The act of fashioning

---

199 The base of Ug *ht* and BH *hinnē* has been related to **hēn*, "when, if" (*UgM* 71 n. 81).

200 Lane 2773-74. Obermann 1947:199; *UgM* 15 n. 23; *LC*[1] 24; *WUS* 1771; *TO* 136 n. n; McCarter 1984:459-60.

accords with Kothar's craftsmanship. This view has not met with general acceptance, however. The verb *nḥt* has been frequently understood on the basis of BH **nḥt*, "to descend."[201] A *C*-stem form might be expected, were the cognate West Semitic root **nḥt*, "to descend," although it may be a *D*-stem form. The notion of bringing down a club leaves unanswered the locale from which the club descends. Such a description would lack a parallel as well. Good (1986:153) suggests a third possibility that *nḥt* specifically means "to strengthen" the weapons through incantations. This view suits the context well, although the sense of *nḥt*, "fashion," comports equally well with Kothar's craftsmanship. The etymological basis of Good's suggestion depends mostly on some highly controverted Ugaritic and biblical passages,[202] but Joel 4:11 is suggestive (Pope 1989: 226): *hanḥat yhwh gibbôrêkā*, "strengthen, O Yahweh, your warriors."

Kothar fashions *ṣmdm*, the dual form, hence two **ṣmd*. Obermann (*UgM* 15 n. 23, 94; 1947:202) denied that *ṣmdm* is dual, prefering to see the terminations *-km* and *-hm* as singular suffixes with mimation. Ginsberg (1948:141) "could not find it in his heart to deny salvation to" Obermann for this interpretation, but as the plural base for "names," **šmt-*, in lines 11 and 18 indicates, *ṣmdm* is dual. The second occurence of the dual form in line 18 is technically superfluous. The repetition of the dual form represents poetic usage that need not conform to the logic of prose according to some scholars (see Gordon 1977:73; Pardee 1980:273-74). As noted above, the word *ṣmd(m)* serves a stylistic function of marking the opening of the four major sections in this unit. This repetition places the weapons at the foreground of the action and de-emphasizes Baal's role in the victory over Yamm.

The word *ṣmd(m)* refers to a weapon of some sort (also attested in 1.6 V 3, 1.65.14 and 1.82.16; cf. Healey 1983b:48). The nature of the weapon is not clearly understood although attempts to resolve the difficulty have been made on the basis of a variety of etymologies. Albright (1941:16 n. 24a; *TO* 136 b. o) compared Arabic *ṣamada*, "to strike" (Lane 1726-27). Neuberg (1950:164) suggests

---

[201] Ginsberg 1935: 332; *UT* 19.1635; *CMHE* 23 n. 16; *SPUMB* 135-36; *CML*[2] 152; *MLC* 509.

[202] KTU 1.23.37; 2 Sam 22:35 = Ps 18:35; cf. Isa 30:30; see *SPUMB* 136.

the root **ṣmt*, "to destroy," and assuming Neuberg's view, Garr (1986:52) explains the variation in the final consonant as a phonological shift involving voicing. Ginsberg (1935: 328) and Rosenthal (1953:72-83; cf. Good 1984:80-81) relate the word to the root *ḍamada* which refers to binding or tying. Ginsberg (1935: 328) identified *ṣmdm* with the two-pieced maces excavated at Ugarit. The weapon consists of two pieces, a head latched onto a handle, specifically in Ginsberg's words (1935:328) "a mace with a stone head drilled through to adjust the wooden shaft, to which it is lashed tightly with thongs; and hence the name from the root *ṣmd*, 'to bind.' Such mace heads are found frequently in excavations."

Yadin (1970: 211-14) also relates *ṣmdm* to iconographic evidence. According to Yadin, the two *ṣmdm* symbolize double-lightning bound at the middle. Yadin appeals to depictions of the storm-god holding double-lightning in his right hand (*ANEP* #501), known for Adad in Mesopotamia from the Old Babylonian period onwards. The god holding double-lightning sometimes stands atop either his enemy, the dragon, or his symbol, the bull (cf. Williams-Forte 1983:24-27). Many of the seals with these depictions bear an inscription with the name of the owner who describes himself as the "servant of the god Adad," the apparent subject of the iconography (van Buren 1933: 70-73).

A famous stele from Ugarit, sometimes called the "Baal au foudre" stele and housed in the Louvre, depicts Baal wielding two weapons.[203] The weapon in his right hand is sometimes characterized as a mace (Amiet 1980:201).[204] In his left hand Baal holds "tree-lightning" (Vanel 1965:84; Williams-Forte 1983:28, 30).

---

203 For further discussion of the iconography of this stele, see above pp. 106-07.

204 In this connection, the weapon mentioned in the Emar installation ritual for the priestess of ^{d}IM (Emar 362) might be viewed as the West Semitic Storm-god's weapon. According to Dietrich (1990), the ^{giš}*TUKUL DINGIR.MEŠ* is not a weapon but a divine emblem. Fleming (1992:50 n. 7) observes, however: "In lines 45, 46, and 63 ^{giš}*TUKUL* varies with the syllabic spellings of *ḫaṣṣinnu*, and both terms should represent the same item in the ritual. Thus the actual weapon is apparently an axe, though it is often called simply 'the weapon' (*kakku*)." Fleming argues, however, that the weapon "is not the particular weapon of . . . the storm-god" (see Fleming 1992:165-66; see also 1992:206 n.12). Fleming's conclusion leaves open the possibility that this is not necessarily the case: "Perhaps it is best to guess that there is more than one divine weapon, and the scribes do not deem it necessary to identify the particular weapon required, since it would be obvious to those involved." If so, then perhaps the weapon which the West Semitic Storm-god wields in the conflict myth was indeed celebrated ritually at Emar.

Other examples of second millennium iconography of the storm-god depict him with a weapon (Vanel 1965:esp. 108; Seeden 1980:esp. 102), which appears at times as "branch-like lightning" (Williams-Forte 1983:26). KTU 1.4 VII 41 may refer to this representation of Baal's lightning as *ʾarz bymnh*, "the cedar in his right hand." A New Kingdom Egyptian text (Papyrus Leiden 345) states that "Baal smites thee with the cedar tree which is in his hand" (*ANET* 249; Williams-Forte 1983:36). According to Williams-Forte, Baal is not yet in possession of a cedar-weapon in 1.2 IV, since he does not brandish his cedar-weapon until 1.4 VII 41. Therefore, Williams-Forte reasons, Baal does not wield this weapon against Yamm, but against Mot. The narrative assumes that Baal does have access to the weapon prior to 1.4 VII 41, and as Keel (1986:309) notes, the *ʾarz* is wielded not against Mot, but against unnamed enemies in 1.4 VII. *Ṣmd* may be a general term for weapon, while *ʾarz* may be a more specific type of weapon.

Comparative evidence drawn from Mediterranean and Near Eastern myths comports with the meteorological character of *ṣmdm* (*Thespis* 164-65). Zeus pelts Typhon with thunderbolts at Mons Cassius, the Latin name for Mount Sapan (Apollodorus, *The Library*, 1.6.3; Frazer 1921:48-49). Zeus' thunderbolts made by Cyclopes, the son of the craftsman-god Hephaistos, have been compared with Baal's weapons fashioned by Kothar (Walcot 1969:115). Hadjioannou (1978:109) notes that Zeus' epithet, *labranios*, deriving from *labrus*, the double-axe, has been understood as a thunderbolt. Like Baal, Marduk in Enuma Elish 4.39, 49-50 and the Storm-god in the Song of Ullikumi (*ANET* 123) are armed with the storm. In the Rgveda Indra defeats Vrtra with thunderbolts, forged by the divine craftsman, Tvashtr.[205] Finally, it should be noted that the name of Baal's weapon apparently lies behind the expression *bʿl ṣmd*, literally "Baal/lord of the *ṣmd*," in the Phoenician Kilamu inscription (KAI 24:15; Yadin 1970:211-14). This title perhaps survived vestigially in the Quran (surah 112), where the word appears as a title of Allah: *allahu ṣ-ṣamadu*, "Allah is Al-Ṣamad."[206] Rosenthal (1953:83) had the Ugaritic and Phoenician evidence in mind in characterizing

---

205 See above pp. 113-114 n. 224.
206 See Rosenthal 1953:82-83; Rubin 1984; Ambrose 1986.

the title as "a survival of a Northwest Semitic religious term, although its original sense was not understood."[207]

Kothar's naming (*ypʿr*) of the weapons in line 11b does not represent a simple act of providing a general label. The expression may be more complicated. Giving a name in this context provides an identity or identification of function (see Cohen 1968). The precise connotation of the idiom varies. Applied to a person or character as in 1.1 IV 13-20, it refers to naming for the purpose of a special task. This sense is made most explicit in Kothar's naming of the weapons.[208] Obermann (1947) notes further that the two acts of naming represent magical incantations uttered by Kothar to empower the weapons. This interpretation has gained wide acceptance and apparently has a reflex in the description of Chousor in Philos of Byblos' *Phoenician History* (PE 1.10.11).[209] De Moor's comparison of KTU 1.82 extends Obermann's insight. De Moor (1984) interprets KTU 1.82 as a series of incantations against demons, some of which are identified with cosmic monsters (such as *tnn*). These incantations invoke Baal's help against the demonic forces. These incantations mirror on the human level the cosmic battle between Baal and his adversaries. Furthermore, incantational language directed against demons perhaps served as a model for describing Baal's weapons against his adversaries in KTU 1.2 IV. Connotations of the language of incantation may be perceived futher in the use of the verb **grš*, "to expel" (1.2 IV 11, 18), a verb which is used for the expulsion of illness in KTU 1.16 V 10-28 (cf. RIH 78/20) and in **mkk* (1.2 IV 17, 26), used for the desired demise of a demon in RIH 78/20.11 (for this text see Fleming 1991). Similarly, it may be noted that **tmnt* in KTU 1.2 IV 26 might evoke the incantational usage of this word in RIH 78/20.6. It goes beyond the evidence to suggest that the sort of weapons used in the exorcism in RIH 78/20.5a is connoted in the *ṣmdm* in KTU 1.2 IV. Nonetheless, the

---

207 For later theological interpretations, see Rubin 1984; Ambrose 1986; van Ess 1989:4-5; Schub 1990.

208 Cohen (1968:34) also tentatively suggests the possibility that "speaking the name" (**pʿr šm*) applied to inanimate objects in this passage may refer to an act of creation like the Akkadian idioms *šuma nabû*, *šuma zakāru* and *zikra nabû*. This suggestion fits the immediate poetic context as the parallel verb *nḥt* quite likely refers to creation in the form of Kothar's craftsmanship. However, other instances of Ugaritic **pʿr šm* do not suggest creation (1.1 IV 15; 1.12 I 28-29; see above pp. 149-50 for further discussion).

209 See above p. 336.

incantational language might be viewed as informing the scene as a whole. Verbal magic produced by a craftsman-god shows general parallels among other Near Eastern and Mediterranean divine craftsmen. Ea, like Kothar a house-maker and weapon-maker, is also a patron of magic and *bel šiptu*, "lord of incantations" (Tallqvist 1938:289-90). According to the "Memphite Theology" (*ANET* 4-6), Ptah created the world through his powerful word.[210] Hephaistos forms many objects with magical qualities, including three-legged tables with gold wheels able to work on their own (Iliad 18:373f.) and gold and silver watch dogs (Odyssey 7:91f.).

Lines 11b-15a//19-23a

Kothar's introductory words in lines 11b-12 and 19 give a high profile to the weapons. The expression, "your name" stands in initial position. Furthermore, the name is stressed by the addition of the independent pronoun standing in apposition.[211] The independent pronoun heightens the direct address to the weapon. It may argued further that the grammatical apposition between each name and the second person pronoun communicates not only emphasis, but it also expresses an identity between them. The phrase *ûšĕmî yhwh lōʾ nôdaʿtî*, "but by my name the Lord I did not make myself known" (RSV),[212] in Exod 6:3 also uses the word, "name" (**šēm*) with the pronominal (suffixal) subject. According to Garr (1992: 396) the grammatical apposition between the deity and the name in Exod 6:3 expresses a relationship of identity. The same relationship applies to the weapons and their names. In sum, the lines emphasize the identity of the weapons as revealed through their names. In contrast, the assumed wielder of the weapons remains in the background throughout this section.

The names of the two weapons, *ygrš* (line 12) and *ʾaymr* (line 19), are emblematic of their functions. The name of the first weapon

---

210 See Allen 1988:12-13; Černý 1952:58. For a general treatment of Ptah, see Holmberg 1946.

211 See above pp. 181, 305. BH contains examples with the second person (Muraoka 1985:61-66). In 1 Kgs 21:19 Elijah dramatically describes the ultimate fate of Ahab: "the dogs will lick your blood, indeed yours" (*yālōqqū hakkĕlābîm ʾet dāmmĕkā gam-ʾattâ*). For another case of the second person pronoun in an invocation, see Jer 12:3; 15:15. See further Garr 1992:389-96.

212 NJPS has essentially the same translation also reading the *N*-stem form as reflexive. Garr (1992:385) renders: "But, I, my name Yahweh, was not known to them."

means "may it drive" (*D*-stem jussive).[213] The weapon works precisely toward the purpose that its name designates. The image of the driven Sea is applied as an image for Yahweh's enemies. Isa 57:20 applies *yām nigrāš*, "the driven Sea," to the wicked (*SPUMB* 136). Amos 8:8 describes how the land of Israel will be "driven" (*nigrĕšâ*) like the Nile on the day of judgement (Scullion 1972:114-15). The second weapon, *ʾaymr*, consists of two elements: *ʾay*, "all" or "any" as in 1.23.6 (*bis*)[214]; and **mry*, "expel" (Obermann 1947:203 n. 31; cf. *LC*¹ 25 n. 3). Albright, followed by Ginsberg (1935:328 n. 2), compares the weapons of Ningirsu, *ŠÁR.UR*, "Nivelant-tout," and *ŠÁR.GAZ*, "Brisant-tout."[215]

Lines 12-15 and 19-23 both contain three commissions to the weapons. The general purpose of both weapons is stated in the initial commission, literally to "expel/drive Yamm from his throne"// "Nahar from the seat of his dominion." Kingship is the terms of the battle between the two divine adversaries. These stakes are named at the beginning of the Baal-Yamm narrative, in 1.1 IV 24-25. The throne is emblematic of Baal's kingship later in the cycle as well (1.6 I 58).

The second commission orders the weapons to attack "like a *nšr*." 1.18 IV 16-27 presents Anat flying among the *nšrm*. Moreover, she tells Yṭpn in 1.18 IV 17-18 (cf. 28-29):

ʾaštk km nšr bḥb[šy]	I will set you as a *nšr* on [my right h]and (?)[216]
km dʾiy btʿrty	Like a hawk (?) in my sheath.

It is also assumed that this image presupposes the practice of

[213] So *UT* 19.624; *CMHE* 115; cf. *CML*² 44; *MLC* 176, 557. Pardee (1974:277 n. 9) suggests that **grš l-* is poetic while **grš b-* is prosaic.

[214] Some commentators relate the initial element in the name *ʾaymr* to BH *ʾôy* or *hôy* (*UT* 19.142; *CML*¹ 137; *CMHE* 115 n. 12). The evidence in Ugaritic, specifically in 1.23.6 (*UT* 19.142; Huehnergard 1987b:276) militates against this view. Gordon (*UT* 19.142) cites *ʾēw* [Qere *ʾê*] *šēkār*, "any liquor" in Prov 31:4. Leslau (49) relates this particle to interrogative particles and indefinite pronouns in a number of Semitic languages. Huehnergard (1987b:276) compares Ak *ayyu* and Eth *ʾayy* for the meanings "which, any."

[215] Lipiński's translation (1967:281-82). Jacobsen (1987:237 n. 7, 400 n. 46) renders *ŠAR.UR* as "the one who who lays low multitudes." For the two weapons of Ningirsu, see Falkenstein 1959:139. For the account of Gudea's creation of these weapons for Ningirsu in Gudea Statue B, see *ANET* 269. For *ŠAR.UR* in Lugale-e, see J. J. M. van Dijk 1983:65f. (lines 109f.); Jacobsen 1987:237f. Lipiński compares the meaning of the initial elements in these names with the element **ʾay* in the name of the weapon, *ʾaymr*.

[216] Or possibly "wristlet" (so *CML*² 112). Firmage (1992:1146) notes EA 147:12 where "*ḫabši* glosses ZAG, 'right hand'."

falconry[217] despite the claim that evidence for falconry in the ancient Near East is minimal at best.[218] This passage assumes that *nšr* is used for hunting purposes. However, eagles are not known to have been used for hunting, which casts some doubt on glossing *nšr* as "eagle" in either this context or in 1.2 IV 13-14 and 21. The same problem attends the other common translation for *nšr*, namely "vulture." Indeed, in the most recent study of this problem, Firmage concludes: "The precise identification of the species indicated by Ug *nšr* is not possible on the basis of our texts."

Cognate languages do not show an uniform view of the bird in question. Arabic *nasr* is translated "eagle" by Lane (2790), and *minsar/mansir* is the beak of a bird of prey. Akkadian *našru* is a late replacement for *erû*, "eagle" (*CAD* N/II:79; *CAD* E:324). *BDB* (676-77) allows both "eagle" and "vulture" as possiblities for BH *nešer*. According to Driver (1955:129; see also King 1988: 132), BH *nešer* refers to the griffon vulture rather than the eagle, although the word is commonly translated "eagle." The griffon vulture stands between three and four feet in length, with a wing-span of almost eight feet; it has a bald spot and it eats carrion, prey unfit for food. The white patch on an eagle gives an impression of baldness; in fact the spot consists of white feathers. It is sometimes claimed that eagles also eat carrion (*BDB* 677). BH *nešer* seems to conform better to the griffon-vulture than to the eagle, as *nešer* has a bald spot (Mic 1:16) and a long wing-span (Ezek 17:3), and eats carrion (Job 39:27-30). Some biblical passages referring to *nešer* are sufficiently imprecise that they could refer to the eagle. In sum, etymological evidence does not resolve the question (Firmage 1992:1158 n. 44; see also Riede 1993:378).

As some Semitic languages use the root for either the eagle or the vulture or both, the word in Ugaritic may represent a wider category, perhaps a large bird of prey. A more general rubric for *nšr* may be suggested also by the context of 1.18 IV 17-18 (cf. 28-29). In this bicolon, *nšr* is parallel with *dʾiy*. If the A-word here is the more general term while the B-word is the more specific one as is commonly the case in Ugaritic poetry, then a term more general than

---

[217] LaSor in Young 1950:130 n. 22; *Baal* 35-36; *CML*^{2} 44 n. 2; *TO* 137 n. r; Gordon 1977:9 n. 8; Watson 1977b:273-74; Firmage 1992:1146.

[218] See Firmage 1992:1146; cf. Reiter 1988, 1990.

dᵓiy may be indicated for *nšr*. As a possible translation, R. Fuller (personal communication) suggests "raptor," which has been adopted in the translation above.

In the context of the second commission, **rqṣ* has been rendered as "dance" (*CML*[2] 44) or "swoop" (*Baal* 35-36), based on Ginsberg's etymological comparison (1935:331) with Arabic *raqaṣa*, "dance" (Lane 1136). The translation, "dance," appears out of place with the image of a bird's movement in the second line of the bicolon. The translation, "swoop" for **rqṣ* conveys the general flight of the bird, while "jump" or "leap" might represent the initial action of the bird taking flight.[219] The syntactic construction with *bd*, either "in" (Pardee 1976:370; 1980:274) or "from" (Watson 1977b:273), suggests the weapon's departure from the position of Baal's hand. Hence "leaping" would appear to be more accurate than "swooping." Young (1950:130 n. 22) and de Moor (*SPUMB* 136; cf. *Thespis* 168) suggest that the weapons act independently of Baal. Citing the iconographic evidence presented by Vanel (1965: 108; see also Seeden 1980:102), Pardee suggests that the weapons remain in the Storm-god's hand. In a sense both views are correct: it is assumed that Baal fights Yamm with weapons in hand, but the power conferred on the weapons is magnified through the image of their flight "from" Baal's hand. It may be argued that this depiction serves a larger literary function. Like the repetition of *ṣmd(m)* noted above, the metaphorical independence of the weapons, conveyed through the comparison with the hunting bird, places them in the foreground of the story while Baal stands in the background.

The third commission to the weapons specifies the goal of their attack. Lines 14-15 and 21-22 differ only in the parts of Yamm's body to suffer attack. In lines 14-15 the first weapon is commanded to "strike the *ktp* of Prince Yamm, the *bn ydm* of Judge River." Here the flight-plan goes from Baal's hand to the area of Yamm called literally "between the hands" (*bn ydm*). In contrast, in lines 21-22 the second weapon is commissioned "to strike the *qdqd* of Prince Yamm, *bn ᶜnm* of Judge River." Syntactically and morphologically *ktp* parallels *qdqd*, and *bn ydm* parallels *bn ᶜnm*. The terms *ktp* and *qdqd* apparently are general in character, and the following construct phrases are more specific. Commentators agree on the meaning of the body-terms mentioned in the command to the second weapon: *qdqd* refers to the crown or cranium while *bn ᶜnm*, literally "between

---

219 My thanks go to Mr. Richard Whitekettle on this point.

the eyes," refers to the front of the head.[220] In contrast, the words for the body-parts attacked by the first weapon are disputed. Many scholars agree that *ktp* means "shoulders," based on BH *kātep* and Syriac *katpāʾ*,"shoulder, shoulder-blade" (*LS* 353). Complicating the appeal to etymology, Akkadian *katappātu* meaning "sternum or parts of the ribs" (*CAD* K:303a; *AHw* 465a). Cross and Freedman (1948:205 n. 40) translate "bosom," although there is little or no evidence for this particular option. The general quality of the parallel term *qdqd*, "crown," used for the second weapon suggests that *ktp*, though attested elsewhere in the sense of shoulder, may refer to a part of the body more general than "shoulder," perhaps "torso." The parallel term for *ktp*, *bn ydm* has been interpreted as "the back," largely based on arguments involving Zech 13:6.[221] The prophet is whipped **bên yadayim*, presumably on the "back." Similarly, in 2 Kgs 9:24 a man is shot from behind, *bên zĕrōʿāyw*, "between the arms." Despite these apparent parallels, appeals have been made to Akkadian *birti aḫīya*, "between my arms," for chest (*LC*[2] 27 n. 2; Driver 1967:108; de Moor 1973:98-99) and Arabic *bayna yadaihi*, "in front of" (Wehr 87), to indicate chest (Cross and Freedman 1948:205 n. 40), or more generally, the front of Yamm's body (Montgomery 1935:275; *CML*[1] 83; *Baal* 37; *SPUMB* 136). The parallels are not decisive for either solution. The BH parallels cited indicate that the precise meaning of Ugaritic *bn ydm* may be conditioned by context. Furthermore, arguments against the Arabic parallel[222] are misplaced. While the phrase *baina yadaihi* does not specify a part of the body, it does means the front of something or someone; the semantic development from a specific part of the body to the front of the body is plausible, as the development of West Semitic *pn*, "face," to *lpn*, "before," would suggest.

An iconographic parallel contained in the Tel Asmar seal (*ANEP* #691; Frankfort 1934) may help to break the impasse posed by the etymological alternatives. The Tel Asmar seal depicts a battle between a warrior figure and a seven-headed dragon. Rendsburg (1984:451) argues that the seven-headed dragon is to be identified

---

220 Cf. the English expression: "hit right between the eyes."

221 Ginsberg 1935:327; 1948:140; *CS* 410-11; Marcus 1978:111-17; Avishur 1980:129-30; Rendsburg 1984:450 n. 11.

222 So made in most of the works cited in the previous note.

with Yamm, an assumption which the Baal Cycle itself vitiates, since it distinguishes between Yamm and the seven-headed beast. Some insight may be gained from Rendsburg's proposal, nonetheless. He notes that the Tel Asmar seal depicts not one, but two scenes of conflict: in the first scene the hero attacks the beast on the back and in the second he attacks the beast on the front. If the seal represents a parallel to the warfare between Baal and Yamm, it would imply that the first weapon attacks Yamm on the back and the second strikes Yamm on the front. Hence the movement would involve not only a shift in point of attack from the body to the cranium, but also from the back to the front of the body.

On the surface the battle involves two warriors, but it also evokes the lightning of Baal. As with other passages in the Baal Cycle (see 1.4 V 6-9; VII 25-31; 1.6 III; see also 1.16 III), the meteorological background has been emphasized in many discussions of 1.2 IV (see *SPUMB* 141; *Baal* 40). The image of the *ṣmdm* as *nšr* in lines 13-14 and 24 evokes the image of lightning according to many scholars (*Thespis* 168; *SPUMB* 136; Watson 1977a). Such an image is more explicit with the meteorological weapons *IM. DUGUD*, "flashing storm," and *IM.GIG*, "dark storm," which are compared to eagles (*ANET* 584, 585; *Thespis* 168; *SPUMB* 136). While meteorological language lies at most in the background of KTU 1.2 IV, its many ancient Near Eastern parallels suggest that the weapons connote the god's thunderbolt and lightning. In contrast with 1.2 IV, meteorological imagery is considerably more explicit in the account of Marduk's conflict with Tiamat in Enuma Elish 4.39-40, 47-50 (*ANET* 66; Mann 1977:48-49):

> In front of him he set the lightning,
> With a blazing flame he filled his body.
> Then he set forth the winds he had brought, the seven of them.
> To stir up the inside of Tiamat they rose behind him.
> Then the lord raised up the flood-storm, his mighty weapon.
> He mounted the storm-chariot irresistible [and] terrifying.

Similarly, Israelite texts presenting divine battle render it in terms of a storm theophany.

From Israelite parallels including Psalm 29[223] and its prosaic counterparts in 1 Kings 19 and 2 Esdras 13:1-4, it might be inferred

---

[223] Psalm 29 is such a clear instance of this type that Ginsberg, Gaster, Cross and Fitzgerald have suggested that Psalm 29 was originally a "Canaanite" hymn to Baal (for discussion, see Cunchillos 1976:163-68; Fitzgerald 1974; J. Day 1985a;

that Baal's conflict with Yamm derives ultimately from the natural conditions prevailing along the Levantine coast, specifically the rainstorm moving eastward across the Mediterranean Sea onto land. The phenomenon has been documented for its force and impact (*SPUMB* 108) and has numerous Israelite reflexes.[224] While the meteorological dimension in Baal's conflict with Yamm is muted in comparison with many Mesopotamian and Israelite parallels, it apparently lies behind Baal's conflict with Yamm. In the transformation from nature myth to court drama (Clifford 1984), the thunderbolt of the storm-god has become the weapon of the warrior-god. As Loewenstamm (1978 = *CS* 346-61) and Clifford (1984) note, KTU 1.2 IV presents two warriors locked in combat and not two forces of nature. This battle narrated by Philo of Byblos (PE 1.10.28; Attridge and Oden 1981: 52-55) as the conflict between Demarous (= Baal) and Pontos (= Yamm) also reads as a story of personal conflict.

1985b:58). According to Fitzgerald (1974), the higher level of alliteration achieved by substituting the name of Baal for Yahweh in this psalm shows that it was originally a "Canaanite" psalm. Furthermore, the location of *midbar qādēš* in Ps 29:8 recalls *tk mdbr qdš*, possibly translated either as "in the midst of the holy outback" or "in the outback a sanctuary," in KTU 1.23.65. This evidence apparently suggests a Syrian site for *midbar qādēš* in Ps 29:8 better than the traditional Israelite place name Kadesh (noted by many commentators; see *CMHE* 154 n. 37; J. Day 1985b:60 n. 169; *MLC* 617), although the reference could have been understood secondarily in this way in Israelite tradition (an alternative not entertained by some commentators who acknowledge the importance of the Ugaritic evidence; see J. Day 1985b:60). If so, the storm theophany in Psalm 29 might have been viewed originally as a storm moving from the Mediterranean across the Lebanon, the Anti-Lebanon and into the Syrian desert; this view may indicate a non-Israelite West Semitic provenience for the description. The storm theophany of the psalm, the archaic form of the language and the northern referents made in the psalm would suit either a non-Israelite background or a northern Israelite provenience. The prepositional phrase *lammabbûl* in Ps 29:10 may be pertinent to this issue. The phrase would appear to refer to time past based on the contrastive parallelism with *lĕʿôlām* (rather than the location of enthronement according to most commentators; see *CMHE* 147 n. 4; Cunchillos 1976:111-21). It did not correspond originally, however, either to primeval flood traditions described in Genesis 6-9 (so Cohen 1989a; 1989b:18-20), or precisely to the ancient West Semitic conflict, attested primarily in this passage of the Baal Cycle (so Dahood 1966:180). Rather, Psalm 29 celebrates the present experience of the divine theophany resembling the conflict of old. And perhaps KTU 1.2 IV celebrates both the ancient victory of Baal as well as its present experience of the Cloudrider's power over the Sea. The use of *ʾaḥar hammabbûl* (Gen 9:28; 10:1, 32; 11:1) and *(mê ham)mabbûl* (Gen 6:17; 7:6, 7, 10, 17; 9:11 [twice], 15) as temporal expressions may have inspired a secondary interpretation of Ps 29:10 along the lines of the biblical flood traditions.

224 E.g., Isa 51:10; Nahum 1:3, 8-9, 12; Hab 3:8; Pss 29, 74:13-14, 89:9-10, 93, 96-99; Job 7:12, 26:12-13. See Rummel, *RSP III* 233-84; J. Day 1985b; Kloos 1986. For the thunderbolt presaging the arrival of the autumnal rains from the Mediterranean Sea, see pp. 98, 347.

Lines 15b-18a//23b-26

These lines largely repeat in narrative form the content of the second and third commissions. Lines 15-18a do not depart from the commissions except in the form of the verbs. The desired result is not immediately realized, however. Yamm remains "strong" (*ʿz*) following the attack by *ygrš*. In his battle against Baal in KTU 1.6 VI 17, 18, 20, Mot is also "strong" (*ʿz*), indicating that Baal's victory over Mot is less than definitive. Lines 19-23 finally reverse the place of the protagonists: now it is Yamm who has slumped to the ground in contrast to the sentiment expressed of Baal in lines 6-7. Yamm's collapsing parallels the shaking of his joints, and his falling parallels the sinking of his form. The third commission in lines 19-23 adds a detail absent from lines 12-15. The jussives in lines 19-22a echo the narrative of lines 17-18, and then lines 22-23 add the wish: "May Yamm collapse and fall to the earth." Lines 25-26 follow lines 15-17 in wording, but in accordance with the additional instruction given to the second weapon in lines 22-23, the narrative relates how "Yamm collapses, and falls to the earth," how "his joints (*pnth*) shake, and his form (*tmnth*) sinks."

The word *pnth* in lines 17//26 is a matter of some dispute. The word-pair, *pnth*//*tmnth*, is commonly compared with *pānêkā*//*tĕmûnātekā* in Ps 17:15,[225] leading some scholars to interpret *pnth* as "his face."[226] While comparison with Ps 17:15 would seem compelling, 1.3 III 33-34 (cf. 1.4 II 19) disproves this interpretation for Ugaritic *pnt*. In this passage *pn* and *pnt* are distinguished: Anat's face (*pn*) sweats while the sinews (*ksl*) of her *pnt* "loosen" (**nǵṣ*).[227] Held (1965b:415) compares Dan 5:6: "and the joints of his loins are loosened" (*wĕqitrê ḥarṣēh mištārayin*). Following Ginsberg (*ANET* 131) and Held, Ugaritic **pnt* may be explained as "joints" or the like, perhaps on semantic analogy with BH *pinnâ*, "corner," which constitutes an architectural feature.[228] That this analogy underlies the

---

[225] *CMHE* 33 n. 151; *CML*[2] 44 n. 5; intimated by Ginsberg 1935:332 nn. 18-19.

[226] Dietrich and Loretz 1978:432-33; Baldacci 1978:417-18.

[227] Held 1965b:401-06, 415; de Moor 1980a:425-26; *SPUMB* 137. Renfroe (1992:64) argues that the root means "to shake, be in commotion."

[228] Obermann 1947:204 n. 26; *SPUMB* 137; *CML*[2] 156; *TO* 137 n. u; *MLC* 611; Segert 1984:198; see also Renfroe 1992:63. Other Semitic roots including **ʾnp*, **rgl*, and **ṯǵr* are used for both body-parts and architectural features; for discussion see above on pp. 189-90 n. 141.

description of Yamm's fall may be inferred from the parallel verbs *ymk//ydlp* in lines 17-18 (cf. line 26) which Eccles 10:18 uses for the collapse of a building.[229] The notion of "joints" or the like fits the use of *nǵṣ* in 1.3 III 33-34 and 1.4 II 19, and a similar notion could underlie 1.2 IV 17, 26.[230] However, there may be a further connotation involved, at least for the verb *ymk* in line 17. As noted above, this verb may echo the incantational language more explicitly attested by the spells pronounced by Kothar in lines 11-15 and 19-23, as this root conveys the desired demise of the demon exorcized in RIH 78/20.11 (see Fleming 1991:152).

Like **pnt*, **tmn* appears in lines 17//26 to describe Yamm's buckling figure (see Dietrich and Loretz 1978). Most commentators compare BH *tĕmûnâ*, "form," sometimes used in a cultic or religious sense of vision of a deity. A temple setting of BH *tĕmûnâ* is evident in Ps 17:15 and the same or a similar cultic background may lie behind Exod 33:7-8 as well.[231] Job 4:16 uses the word in the context of a noctural vision. The late Egyptian tale of Setne Khamwas and Si-osire describes Thoth's form in a temple at night (Lichtheim 1980:146; Parker 1989b:101-05, 155):

> He went to the temple of Khmun, [made his] offerings and libations before Thoth. . . made a prayer before him. . . lay down in the temple. That night he dreamed a dream in which the mysterious form of the great god Thoth spoke to him.

From these occurrences it might be inferred that West Semitic **tmn* was originally a term for vision of the divine in a cultic setting and was secondarily used to describe the description of the deity in 1.2 IV 17 and 26. Based on the architectural sense of *pnt* and the verbs,

---

[229] See Driver 1949; Speiser 1951; Greenfield 1958:208-09. Cognates include BH **dlp* in Eccles 10:18 and Ps 119:28, Akk *dalāpu* and Arb *dalafa*, all meaning "to totter. Speiser and Driver argue that the meaning "to drip" attested in Syr *dlap* and BH noun *delep*, "drip," is to be associated also under the general rubric of "spasmodic movement." Greenfield (1958:209 n. 13) finds "the attempt to bridge the semantic gaps unconvincing."

[230] Akk *panatu*, "front side," might provide a more proximate cognate for 1.2 IV 17 and 26. If so, the verbal form *tnǵṣn* could be feminine singular with nunation (cf. *tmǵyn* in 1.3 II 17). The use of *pnt* in 1.3 III 33-34 (cf. 1.4 II 19) would militate against this view, however, unless two words are involved. It is possible that the original WS word-pair, **pnt//*tmn*, was replaced by **pānîm/*tĕmûnâ* in Ps 17:15 under the influence of the common BH word, *pānîm*, "face."

[231] See Tournay 1991:80. See also Num 12:8; cf. Deut 4:12, 15.

ymk and *ydlp*, de Moor (1980a:425-26) compares **tmn* with Akkadian *temēnu*, "foundation." Another occurrence of Ugaritic **tmn* may suggest a rather different background or at least connotation. In the context of an incantation against a demon, RIH 78/20.5b-6a attests to **tmn* in parallelism with *gb*, "back" (Fleming 1991:150). The possibility that an incantational background resonates in 1.2 IV 17//26 is enhanced by the more explicit language of spells and incantational language found in this column noted above.

Line 27

This line marks the formal end of the battle section. While lines 7-26 emphasize the help of the magical weapons made by Kothar, line 27 returns Baal to the action of the narrative. The verbs of line 27 have caused no little difficulty (*SPUMB* 138-39; Kloos 1986: 87-88). The first two verbs have inspired numerous suggestions which are philologically and thematically defensible. All of them share the view that the verbs represent actions taken by Baal against Yamm. The root of *yqṯ* has been derived from **qṯṯ*, "to drag out, pull out,"[232] **yqṯ*, "to ensnare,"[233] or **nqṯ*, "to strike." The interpretion *yqṯ* based on Arabic **qṯṯ*, "to draw, drag," is possible. The etymology **qṯṯ* is sometimes based on a disputed view of *yqṯqṯ* in KTU 1.114.5 which is evidently different from *yqṯ* at least insofar as the former is intransitive.[234] If so, Arb **qṯṯ* could be cognate. The parallels for dragging the cosmic enemies are somewhat rare, however. Gaster (*Thespis* 169) cites Job 40:25 (E 41:1) which depicts Leviathan drawn with a fish-hook. No such weapon is explicit in 1.2 IV 27 and may vitiate the parallel.

Greenstein connects Ugaritic **yqṯ* in 1.2 IV 27 with BH **yqš*, "to ensnare." The sense of "snaring" might be preferable here, given the parallels in the use of the verbs as well as the many parallels for the motif. BH **yqš*, has been related, however, to Ugaritic **yqš* which appears in a Ugaritic list of professions (meaning "fowler"?). Again it is possible to argue that two differents roots are involved. A derivation from **nqṯ*, "to strike" incurs no apparent philologi-

---

232 *Thespis* 169; *SPUMB* 138; *CML*² 44, 157; Dietrich and Loretz 1986a:118-19.

233 Greenstein 1982.

234 Greenstein 1982; Pardee 1988b:13-48; Cooper 1991:834; cf. Dietrich and Loretz 1986a:118.

cal problems,[235] and it fits the context unless it were objected that the action of the weapons in lines 19-23 renders such an interpretation superfluous. Applied to human enemies in the *G*-stem (Ps 9:17), the BH root **nqš* means "to knock, strike" (*BDB* 669). The sequence of "striking" (**nkh*) and "destroying" (**klh*) an enemy occurs also in 2 Kgs 13:19.

For the second verb *yšt*, there are four possibilities: **nšt*, "to dry up,"[236] **šyt*, "to set,"[237] **šty*, "to drink,"[238] or **štt*, "to separate, disperse."[239] Few BH passages with **nšt*[240] refer precisely to the drying sea, with the possible exception of Isa 19:5 which describes the divine drying of the Nile. As further support for the notion of drying up the waters, though without any bearing on the etymology of **nšt* for *yšt* in 1.2 IV 27, passages such as Exod 14:21-22, Isa 11:15 and 51:9-11 might be invoked. The blowing of the wind in Exod 15:8, 10 comes from the **ʾap*, "nose" of Yahweh. Exod 14:21 interprets this wind as a "strong east wind," which "made the sea dry land." Isa 44:27 uses the word-pair **ḥrb//*ybš* for the drying of the primordial deep, which represents the most proximate Israelite parallel to Baal's putative drying of Yamm (see Avishur 1984:643, 651). Yahweh says: "[I,] who said to the deep, 'Be dry; I will dry up your floods'" (NJPS). However, the BH word-pair **ybš//*ḥrb* appears not in a storm theophany, but in the scirocco (e.g., Isa 19:5-6; 50:2; 51:10; Jer 51:36; Hos 13:15; Nah 1:4; Joel 1:20), an unlikely reflex of the storm-god's battle against Yamm.[241] Furthermore, *tnn* as Yahweh's enemies appears largely, if not exclusively, in the context of the scirocco.[242] This is not to say that Anat's claim to defeat of *tnn* in 1.3 III 40 reflects the scirocco, only that Israelite material with either the theme of drying the Sea or defeating *tnn* may not derive from the meteorological imagery of Baal's stormy character. This sort of language is not applied otherwise to the West

---

235 According to *BDB* 669, Arb *naqaša*, "strike in, carve," is a loanword.

236 Montgomery 1935:276; Hoftijzer 1981:166 n. 539; Kloos 1986:87-88.

237 *SPUMB* 138-39; Fenton 1978:344; Greenstein 1982:201.

238 *CMHE* 115; Mullen 1980:57.

239 Obermann 1947:205; *CML*[1] 143 n. 26; *TO* 138 n. a. See *SPUMB* 138 for further authorities. See also Bordreuil and Pardee 1993:64.

240 Isa 41:17. Greenstein (1982:201) reads *wnštw* for MT *wntšw* in Jer 18:14.

241 Professor A. Fitzgerald, private communication.

242 E.g., Isa 51:9-11; Jer 51:34-37, 42-45; Ezek 29:1-16; 32:3-15; so A. Fitzgerald, private communication.

Semitic storm god, which may indicate that the "drying up" of the cosmic waters may not have belonged originally to the repertoire of martial acts associated with the West Semitic storm-god. The theme of drying Yamm in Isa 51:9-11 may reflect Yahwistic assimilation of the imagery of the east wind, which could have derived mythically from Mot (Smith 1990:53). In Hos 13:14-15 the imagery of the east wind and death stand together, perhaps reversing the association of the east wind with Death; the east wind is Yahweh's weapon. Baal has "winds" (**rḥ*) in his meteorological entourage in 1.5 V 7, but these winds do not "dry up" watery enemies. The notion that Baal dries Yamm is possible, if the language is figurative rather than an indication of Baal's character as a storm-god. However, the other verbs imply an action which one warrior-god inflicts on another, which would seem to discount the sense "to dry up."

Gibson takes the verb from the middle weak root, **šyt*, usually "to put, place," and he translates "laid him down" (*CML*[2] 44, 159). The translation appears to stretch unduly the semantic range of the root. De Moor (*SPUMB* 139) also accepts this view and understands the sequence of verbs as "dragging Yamm out of the sea (*qṯṯ*), putting him down on the shore (*šyt*) and dealing him the death-blow (*kly*)." Greenstein (1982) also takes *yšt* from **šyt*, and understands the meaning with the verb *yqṯ* as "to ensnare." He reads the verbs as three actions in a sequence and he appeals to ancient Near Eastern parallels to the Storm-god's battle against the cosmic foe. As noted by Pope (1973:181, 185-86), snaring the cosmic foe occurs in Illuyanka (*ANET* 126; Beckman 1982), Enuma Elish 4.95, Ezek 32:3 and Job 26:13.[243] Jacobs (1977:9 n. 47) argues that "the great net" in the poem by the Palestinian poet Qallir describing an encounter between angels and Leviathan derives from the ancient motif of divine snaring known also from Enuma Elish 4.95. KTU 1.2 IV 27 may attest this motif. Ugaritic parallels to "snaring" are also manifest. In 1.3 III 38-42 Anat states that she surely "harnessed" (?) (*lʾištbm*) Tunnanu, a divine enemy, and in 1.83.8-10, she places him in a harness: *tnn lšbm tšt trks lmrym*, "She places Tunnanu in a harness (?), She binds (him) to the heights."[244] As with the verbs in

243 See also Prayer of Manasseh verses 2-3; cf. the capture of the enemy with a net in Ezek 32:3 (cf. 12:13).
244 For the problems with **šbm*, see Barr 1973; Loewenstamm 1959, 1975.

1.2 IV 27, the verbs, *tšt* and *trks*, in 1.83.8-10 clearly presuppose Tunnanu as their object. KTU 1.83.8-10 is *prima facie* the most relevant parallel for interpreting *yšt* and *yqṯ* in 1.2 IV 27, as the two verbs *tšt* and *trks* would semantically parallel them. The verbs *yšt* and *tšt* would convey the same notion of setting up a cosmic enemy for trapping, expressed by "snaring," **yqṯ*, in 1.2 IV 27 and "harnessing," **rks*, in 1.83.8-10. However, the possible etymological difficulty noted above may vitiate Greenstein's thematically insightful proposal.

Assuming an interpretation of **šty*, "to drink," for *yšt*, Cross (*CMHE* 155 n. 13) finds the alternation of the short impf. *yšt* with the long imperfect verbal forms "puzzling." Another etymological suggestion is probably indicated given this grammatical conundrum. Moreover, parallels for the "drinking" of Sea are rare at best. At with the proposal, "to dry up," the meaning "to drink" appears misplaced in a series of verb describing the destruction of one warrior upon another.

Finally, **štt* as derived from Arabic *šatta*, "separate," is taken as an expression for dispersing or dismembering Yamm (Oberman 1948; *CML*[1] 143 n. 26; *TO* 138 n. a; Bordreuil and Pardee 1993:64). This view may be compared semantically with Anat's dispersal of Mot in 1.6 II 35. In this context scattering" (**drʾ*) Mot is followed by his consumption by birds, expressed by the verb **kly*, the root that likewise follows *yšt* here. According to de Moor (*SPUMB* 138), the *G*-stem means "to become dissolved" and hence a *D*-stem form **yštt* would be required. It is unclear that the *G*-stem could not be transitive, however.

The meaning of the third verb, *ykly*, "to destroy," is not in dispute (3 masc. sg. *D*-stem impf.).[245] Ugaritic literary tradition reflects some diversity of opinion over Yamm's conqueror. 1.3 III 38-42 includes Yamm in a list of cosmic foes which Anat states that she destroyed. Indeed, the verb used of Anat and Yamm is precisely **kly*, "destroy," the third of the three verbs attributed to Baal in 1.2 IV 27. 1.3 III 38-42, which probably reflects an older tradition casting Anat in the role of divine warrior. The Baal Cycle expresses the exaltation of Baal; one way it achieves this purpose is to attribute to Baal roles elsewhere associated with other deities, or perhaps the role was attributed to a number of deities. In connection with Baal's defeat of Yamm, it should be noted that a seal of the Akkadian

---

245 See Dietrich and Loretz 1981b; Fensham 1979b.

period from Mari shows a warlike god thrusting a spear into a stream with a spear (Vanel 1965:73-74; Keel 1978:fig. 42; 1986:309).

The verbal mood of *ykly* is more problematic. Commentators routinely interpret this verb as a narrative action that Baal destroyed Yamm (*CMHE* 115 n. 13). According to Ginsberg (*ANET* 131) and Greenstein (1982:205), the fact that Yamm reappears in 1.4 VII 3-4 (*mdd ʾil y[m]*, "the beloved of El, Ya[mm]") indicates that some modal interpretation of *ykly* is necessary. Baal "would destroy" Yamm, implying that Baal does not do so at this particular time. Driver (*CML*[1] 83) and Gaster (*Thespis* 169) obviate this problem by a different view of the syntax. Driver translates lines 27-28: "Baal was drawing up Yam and scattering (him), was making an end of Judge Nahar (when) Athtart rebuked him by name...". Gaster proposes: "He is about to hack him to pieces (?), to make a full end of that Ruler of the Stream(s) when ʿAshtart [calls him] by name...". Despite the modal modification suggested by Ginsberg and Greenstein and the syntactic proposal advanced by Driver and Gaster, two other possible explanations might be cited in favor of the indicative force of *ykly*. First, Yamm could indeed "die" in this passage, only to reappear in 1.4 VII. This view may be defended by appealing to the parallel sequence for Mot: he appears to be destroyed by Anat in 1.6 II, only to reappear in 1.6 VI (*SPUMB* 140). In this regard Yamm's death in 1.2 IV 32, 34 may not have constituted a great narrative difficulty for the ancient audience of the Baal Cycle. Second, the verb could reflect a redactional tension on the final form of the text.[246] In an older, traditional version of this story, Baal did exterminate Yamm once and for all, but when this traditional material was redacted into the longer saga of the Baal Cycle, the verb *ykly* remained although Yamm re-appears later in the narrative.

Yamm's destruction in line 27 marks some closure in the extant column, as it finally fulfills the curse which seems to be uttered in line 3. Yahweh's defeat of the Sea is cast most commonly in terms of "confining" or "defeating," but rarely is Sea destroyed. The Testament of Moses 10:6 reads: "And Sea all the way to the abyss will retire, to the sources of waters which fail, Yea, the river will vanish away." Similarly, Rev 21:1 expresses the disappearance of Sea

---

[246] See above pp. 33-35.

as an eschatological reality: "Then I saw a new heaven and a new earth; for the first heaven and the first earth had passed away, and sea was no more."

Lines 28-40

The division of lines 28-40 is problematic, although it is clear that line 28 begins a speech. The line has a speech opening formula, though with a twist. Athtart rebukes Baal, either "by name" (*ANET* 131; *CML*¹ 83; Pardee 1980:274), "by his name" (*TO* 94; Greenstein 1982:204), or most literally, "the Name" (*CML*² 44). The idiom, "rebuke," is elsewhere attested as **gᶜr b-*,[247] which would indicate that *šm* is the object of the verb-preposition combination in this case. De Moor (*SPUMB* 139) takes the sentence literally, "ᶜAṯtartu rebuked the Name." Pardee (1980:274) labels such a rendering as "hyper-literalism." He takes the syntax as representing *bšm tgᶜrm bh ᶜṯtrt*, "Athtart rebukes him by name," with deletion of *bh* "for reasons of concision."[248] While Pardee may be correct, paronomasia may be seen in this usage,[249] as Athtart appears as "the Name of Baal" in 1.2 I 8.[250] This paranomasia in 1.2 IV 28 is perhaps heightened further by the emphasis which "name" obtains by standing in initial position. Athtart's rebuke of Baal regarding Yamm may represent an ironic play on a traditional notion of the storm-god rebuking Yamm.[251]

---

[247] KTU 1.2 I 24; 1.114.14; Gen 37:10; Zech 3:2. See Greenstein 1982:204; van Zijl 1969; Kennedy 1987:50, 62; Caquot, *TDOT* 3.49-53. Macintosh (1969:472-73) cites Eth *geᶜera*, "to cry, groan"; *jaᶜara* in Syrian Arb "to bellow" and in colloquial Egyptian Arb "to snarl"; and Arm **gᶜr*, "to rebuke." Macintosh (1969:473) suggests that the root does not denote only an act of speech but a manner of speech involving passionate anger as suggested by *miggaᶜărat yhwh minnišmat rûaḥ ʾappô* in 2 Sam 22:16//Ps 18:16. The root "signifies the expulsion of sound denoting disgust or anger." Macintosh notes Arb *jaᶜara*, "to void dung" (Lane 429) as well as the association of BH **gᶜr* with *pereš*, "dung," in Mal 2:3. The root in one of the Ugaritic hippiatric texts (1.85.2) has been interpreted as "roaring," a horse ailment (for views along these lines, see Renfroe 1988:181-83). Since the other maladies in this text involve defecation or urination, Renfroe (1988:182-83) connects this instance of **gᶜr* to Arb *jaᶜara*, "to void dung." Whatever the interpretation of the root in this passage, the various meanings of the root in Arabic and the other languages involve physical passage from orifices, whether of words, roaring or excrement.

[248] Greenstein (1982:204) translates "His name she rebukes, does ᶜAṯtartu."

[249] Ginsberg 1945b:10 n. 19b; *TO* 94; cf. Olyan 1988:48.

[250] Reconstructed in accordance with the parallel text, KTU 1.16 VI 56; see above pp. 278-79.

[251] Cf. Yahweh's rebuke of *tehôm* in Ps 104:6-7 (cf. Isa 50:2; Nah 1:4; Ps 106:9).

In lines 28-29a Athtart commands Baal *bṯ*, either to "scatter" Yamm[252] or "to be ashamed."[253] Olley (1976:233-34) suggests that "Ashtart is reproaching Baal for thinking to take the life of a captive." This usage accords with BH examples of **bwš* for a wrong act although Olley notes that the forensic emphasis is missing from the Ugaritic passage. There are some questions about this approach. First, grammatical considerations weigh against the translation, "shame." The verb *ybṯnn*, "he scatters," in line 31 apparently has an object suffix indicating a transitive verb, although paranomasia involving the two meanings could be involved. De Moor (*SPUMB* 139) obviates this difficulty by taking the suffix as dative. Second, shaming the hero following his victory might appear unlikely (*TO* 139 n. b), but the speech-opening formula does indicate that Athtart is rebuking Baal, in which case the cry, "shame on you," may not be out of place. In contrast, the command to scatter Yamm would fit both the sense and the grammar of the verb. Furthermore, the action of scattering resembles the more developed image of Anat's scattering Mot in 1.6 II 30-35 (*TO* 139 n. b) and Yahweh's scattering Leviathan in Ps 74:14 and *tnn* in Ezek 29:5 (cf. Greenstein 1982:202-03).

Athtart next proclaims in a nominal sentence that Yamm is "our captive."[254] This proclamation reverses the fortunes of Baal pronounced by El in 1.2 I 37. Baal was Yamm's prisoner (*ʾasr*) in 1.2 I 37; now Yamm is Baal's captive (*šby*). The remaining lines proclaim Baal's kingship and Yamm's "death." Lines 32 and 34 proclaim that *ym lmt*, "Yamm is surely dead" (*CMHE* 116; Gordon 1977:74; *CML*[1] 83). The obvious difficulty that Yamm reappears later in the narrative of the cycle (KTU 1.4 VII) has led some interpreters to diminish the sense of *mt*. Yamm is "vanquished" (Obermann 1947:198 n. 16) or "dying" (*ANET* 131; cf. Greenstein 1982:205). Obermann's attempt (1947:198 n. 17) to argue that the meaning of *mt* in lines 32, 34, is "undone," also obviates the apparent difficulty that *mdd ʾil y[m]* appears later in the Baal Cycle. A further possibility would be to reject the reconstruction of *mdd ʾil y[m]*

---

252 *UgM* 16 n. 23; *CML*[2] 44; for further commentators, see *SPUMB* 139. Based on Arb *baṯṯa*, "to spread; scatter, disperse" (Wehr 41).

253 *ANET* 131; *CML*[1] 83; Dahood 1965:9; *SPUMB* 139; Greenstein 1982:204; Olley 1976:233-34; cf. *CML*[2] 44 n. 11.

254 Obermann (1947:198) translates *šbyn* as "he [Prince Yamm)] has made us captives," but the syntax and context do not suggest Yamm's subjugation of deities. See *SPUMB* 139.

in 1.4 VII 3-4, but this alternative lacks textual grounds. As noted above, it would appear that the "death" of a god does not necessarily preclude his appearance later in the narrative. Furthermore, conflicting literary traditions regarding the defeat of Yamm may underlie this textual tension. While the word may have originally indicated Yamm's death and final end in the narrative, the placement of this conflict into the larger cycle of material may have caused a redactional tension.

The end of line 28 seems to continue the affirmation of Baal's victory over Yamm. Commentators including KTU reconstruct *yml[k]*. Unlike KTU, CTA does not reconstruct the end of the line in this manner, but leaves the reading as *ym l[*. This reading would perhaps suggest that *ym* refers to the god and is not part of a verb. Unlike CTA's reading, KTU's reconstruction provides sensible syntax with *bʿlm*, but it should be cautioned that the reconstruction is not certain. If the reconstruction is correct, Baal is proclaimed king, reversing El's proclamation of Yamm in 1.1 IV 13f. (cf. 1.6 I 55). The divine council similarly proclaims Marduk as king in Enuma Elish 4.28 : "Marduk is king," *ᵈmarduk-ma šar-ru* (*ANET* 66). Middle Assyrian and Neo-Assyrian coronation ceremonies also included the proclamation of Assur's kingship, for example in Assurbanipal's Coronation Hymn (VAT 13831:15): "Assur is king—indeed Assur is king!" *ᵈaš-šur LUGAL ᵈaš-šur-ma LUGAL* (Livingstone 1989:xxiii, 26). Upon his accession to the Israelite throne in 2 Kgs 9:13, Jehu is acclaimed: "Jehu reigns!" *mālak yēhûʾ*. In a conclusion to the poem of Exodus 15, Yahweh is acclaimed as king: *yhwh yimlōk lĕʿōlām wāʿed*, "may Yahweh reign forever and ever" (verse 18). The exact tense of *bʿl ymlk* has been discussed at great length, especially in connection with the biblical parallels (Rummel, *RSP III* 234). The form of the verb, the context and the parallels with VAT 13831:15, Enuma Elish 4.28 and 2 Kgs 9:13 would suggest a present meaning (*CMHE* 116).

The repetition of phrases in lines 32-33 and 34-35 perhaps suggest two further proclamations of Baal's kingship (*TO* 139 n. f). One of the speakers is masculine, given the form of *yʿn* as 3 masc. sg. form; one may be feminine if the reconstruction of *wt[ʿn]* in line 35 is correct. Kothar's speeches and possibly that of Athtart at the beginning of the extant column may suggest them as possible speakers at the end as well (van Selms 1970: 266-67). Accordingly, van Selms (1970:267) introduces Kothar as the speaker:

...w[yšmḫ kṯr wḫss w]yʿn	Then Kathir-and-Khasis rejoiced and answered:
ym lmt	Yamm has died;
[bʿlm ymlk	it is Baal who will reign.
ʾašlh lʾil tḥm] lšrr	I shall forward the decree to El for confirmation.

In support of the reconstruction in the first line, KTU 1.4 V 20 and 35 may be invoked; these lines use **šmḫ* to describe the initial reactions of Anat and Baal upon learning of El's permission for the construction of Baal's palace. The reconstruction of van Selm's final line is questionable because of its inordinate length. The first word *]ḥm* has been interpreted as "heat," based on this meaning of *ḥm* in 1.19 I 40 (*CML*^{2} 45 n. 2). Van Selms (1970:267) reconstructs *[t]ḥm lšrr*, "decree for confirmation," presuming a scene depicting the deliverance of the news of Baal's victory to El. This notion is otherwise unknown, but it could accord with the following phrase, *lšrr*. This may be a further statement of kingship, comparable to the proclamation of Marduk in Enuma Elish 4.28. Perhaps *šrr* is cognate with Akkadian *šarru*, "king" and Hebrew *śar*, "leader" (*CEBCR* 196 n. 5), although an Ugaritic geminated form would require a different morphological base. The word seems to be otherwise attested in Ugaritic (cf. *UT* 19.2477). Driver (*CML*^{1} 83) takes the phrase as a commentary on Baal's desires to rule: "(he) burns to hold rule." Gibson (*CML*^{2} 45 n. 2) translates the phrase *ḥm šrr*: "heat is indeed assured." Gibson compares Gen 8:22 to this phrase, perhaps as an expression of the natural order symbolizing divine order achieved by the kingship of the warrior-god. De Moor (1987:42) offers a seasonal view as well in translating: "heat for the stalks." In view of the larger context, van Selm's approach is the most appealing. A "decree" or confirmation of Baal's kingship, perhaps in the context of the divine council, would be well-suited to the context. Given the difficulties of this section, it must be judged that other proposals remain plausible.

The word *šrr* appears a third time in line 37, though with a different word following it. The third occurrence of this word suggests the possibility that its context represents a third proclamation of Baal. Van Selms (1970:267) reconstructs lines 35b-37a on the basis of his interpretation of lines 33b-35a:

. . . wtˁ[n ˁ*t*trt	And Athtartu answered:
mt ym	Yamm has died;
mlk] bˁlm	it is Baal who will reign.
hmt [tšlḥn lʾil tḥm] lšrr	Let it be them who forward the decree to El for confirmation.

Other words of lines 35-40 can be ascertained, though without further clarifying the context. *TO* (139 n. f) makes the plausible suggestion that *št* in line 37 refers to an act of coronation. "On his head" (*brʾišh*) in line 38 and "[be]tween his eyes" (*[b?]n ˁnh*) in line 40 would fit either a recounting of victory over Yamm, specifically how Baal struck him on these body parts (*ktpm*) or with a *ktp*, a weapon,[255] or perhaps a description of a coronation.

The political language in KTU 1.2 IV as well as some of its parallels may be taken as evidence for the political setting of Baal's victory over Yamm. As noted above in the Introduction,[256] a number of second millennium Levantine texts apply the language of the West Semitic conflict myth to human monarchs. The most dramatic example bears mention again as it highlights the relationship between human and divine kingship involved in the use of the West Semitic conflict myth. Durand (1993:45; cf. Charpin and Durand 1986:174) presents a Mari text (A.1968. lines 1′-4′) that quotes the words of Nur-Sin of Aleppo to Zimri-lim of Mari:"I s[et] you on the thr[one of your father]; the weapons with which I had battled against Sea (*tâmtum*) I gave to you" (*lu-t[e-e]r-ka a-na giš-[gu-za é a-bi-ka] ú-te-er-ka giš-tukul-[meš] ša it-ti te-em-tim am-ta-aḫ-ṣu ad-di-na-ak-kum*). That this text is parallel with the 1.2 IV is patent (Charpin and Durand 1986:174; Bordreuil and Pardee 1993). This text also indicates the political character which this myth assumed: if the political character of myth is in evidence at Mari, how much more so at Ugarit where the myth was so much at home. Both the victory and coronation in KTU 1.2 IV suggest the great importance attached to divine kingship and may hint at a corresponding significance for the Ugaritic dynasty.

---

[255] O'Callaghan (1952:40) argued that the word refers to Baal's weapon both in this passage and in 1.6 V 3 on the strength of the West Semitic loan in the Egyptian Papyrus Leiden I 343, obverse II, lines 2-4: *p3 ktp Bˁr m ḏ3ḏ3k*, "the *ktp* of Baal is (stuck) in thy head" (Massart 1954:52).

[256] See above pp. 106-10. See also Smith 1990:56-58.

If A.1968 helps to indicate the political character of 1.2 IV, the parallels between Baal and Marduk help to indicate the limits of this political portrait of Baal. Although Baal emerges as king in 1.2 IV, his victory is not an overwhelming one compared to that of Marduk or Yahweh.[257] Rather, this text provides evidence of Baal's limited exaltation. Baal requires the assistance of Kothar's magical weapons. Even so, Yamm withstands the first weapon, and only the second magical weapon gives victory to Baal. Baal's victory and later the explicit proclamation of his kingship by the other deities apparently represent tenuous achievements. The divine order represented in Baal's kingship has value: it provides rains and, to a limited degree, order. Yet this order, while precious, is precarious. Baal's defeat of Yamm is achieved only with the help of Kothar and with the support of Athtart (1.1-1.2). His palace, the sign of his kingship, is gained later only through the aid of Anat and Asherah and the permission of El (1.3-1.4). Threatened by Mot, Baal's royal status is saved by Anat and Shapshu's intervention (1.5-1.6). In sum, Baal's kingship requires the energies of other major deities. Without them Baal has no kingship, and without them there is no order or fertility in the cosmos.

---

[257] Features common to the Baal Cycle and Enuma Elish are discussed above on pp. b, 13, 35, 75, 79, 81-82, 86, 95, 96, 101, 103-05, 110-12, 114, 130, 150, 231, 296, 300, 309, 314-15, 335, 340, 347, 353 and 358.

BIBLIOGRAPHY

Ackerman, S.
1992 *Under Every Green Tree; Popular Religion in Sixth Century Judah*. HSM 46. Atlanta, GA: Scholars.

Aistleitner, J.
1964 *Die mythologischen und kultischen Texte aus Ras Shamra*. Sec. ed. Budapest: Akadémiai Kiadó.

Albright, W. F.
1920 "Gilgames and Engidu, Mesopotamian Genii of Fecundity." *JAOS* 40:307-35.
1924 "Contributions to Biblical Archaeology and Philology." *JBL* 43:363-93.
1926 "The Egyptian Empire in Asia in the Twenty-First Century B.C." *JPOS* 8:223-56.
1933 "More Light on the Canaanite Epic of Aleyan Baal and Mot." *BASOR* 50:13-20.
1934 *Vocalization of the Egyptian Syllabic Orthography*. New Haven: American Oriental Society.
1936a "The Canaanite God Hauron (Horon)." *AJSL* 53:1-12.
1936b "Zabul Yam and Thapiṭ Nahar in the Combat between Baal and the Sea." *JPOS* 16:17-20.
1938 "Recent Progress in North-Canaanite Research." *BASOR* 70:18-20.
1940 "Islam and the Religion of the Ancient Orient." *JAOS* 60:283-301.
1941 "Anath and the Dragon." *BASOR* 84:14-17.
1945 "The Old Testament and Canaanite Language and Literature." *CBQ* 7:5-31.
1954 "Some Observations on the New Material for the History of the Alphabet." *BASOR* 134:26.
1956 *Archaeology and the Religion of Israel*. Sec. ed. Baltimore: Johns Hopkins.
1958 "Specimens of Late Ugaritic Prose." *BASOR* 150:36-38.
1961 "The Old Testament and the Archaeology of the Ancient East." *The Old Testament and Modern Study; A Generation of Discovery and Research*. Oxford Paperbacks 18. Ed. H. H. Rowley. Oxford: At the Clarendon. 27-47.

Albright, W. F., and T. O. Lambdin
1957 "New Material for the Egyptian Syllabic Orthography." *JSS* 2:113-27.

Allen, J. P.
1988 *Genesis in Egypt; the Philosophy of Ancient Egyptian Creation Accounts*. Yale Egyptological Studies 2. New Haven, CT: Yale Egyptological Seminar.

Al-Yasin, I.
1952 *The Lexical Relationship between Ugaritic and Arabic*. Shelton Semitic Monograph Series. New York: Department of Semitics of Shelton College.

Ambrose, A. A.
1986 "Die Analyse von Sure 112." *Der Islam* 63:219-47.

Amiet, P.
1980 *Art of the Ancient Near East*. Trans. J. Shepley and C. Choquet. New York: Abrams.

Anderson, G. A.
1987 *Sacrifices and Offerings in Ancient Israel; Studies in their Social and Political Importance*. HSM 41. Atlanta: Scholars.

Archi, A.
1979-80 "Les dieux d'Ebla au IIIe millennaire avant J.C. et les dieux d'Ugarit." *Les annales archéologiques arabes syriennes* 29-30:161-71.

Arnaud, D.
1981 "La Religion à Emar." *Le Monde de la Bible* 20:34.
1991 *Textes syriens de l'âge du bronze récent*. Aula Orientalis Supplements 1. Barcelona: Editorial AUSA.
Astour, M. C.
1973 "A North Mesopotamian Locale for the Keret Epic?" *UF* 5:29-39.
1982 Review of J. Strange, *Caphtor/Keftiu; A New Investigation*. *JAOS* 102:395-96.
1989 *Hittite History and Absolute Chronology of the Bronze Age*. Partille: Paul Åströms förlag.
Attridge, H. W., and R. A. Oden
1981 *Philo of Byblos. The Phoenician History; Introduction, Critical Text, Translation, Notes*. CBQMS 9. Washington: The Catholic Biblical Association of America.
Avigad, N., and J. C. Greenfield
1982 "A Bronze *phiale* with a Phoenician Dedicatory Inscription." *IEJ* 32:118-28.
Avinery, I.
1976 "The Position of the Declined *kl* in Syriac." *Afro-Asiastic Linguistics* 3/5:25.
Avishur, Y.
1980 "Expressions of the Type *byn ydm* in the Bible and Semitic Languages." *UF* 12:125-33.
1980-81 "*RWM* (*RMM*)—'Build' in Ugaritic and the Bible." *Leshonenu* 45:270-79.
1984 *Stylistic Studies of Word-Pairs in Biblical and Ancient Semitic Literatures*. AOAT 210. Kevelaer: Butzon & Bercker; Neukirchen-Vluyn: Neukirchener Verlag.
Baldacci, M.
1978 "A Lexical Question Concerning the Ugaritic Anath's Text." *UF* 10:417-18.
Barnett, R.D.
1935 "The Nimrud Ivories and the Art of the Phoenicians." *Iraq* 2:179-210.
1969 "Ezekiel and Tyre." *EI* 9 (The W.F. Albright Festschrift):6-13.
1982 "Assurbanipal's Feast." *EI* 18 (N. Avigad Volume):1*-6*.
Barr, J.
1973 "Ugaritic and Hebrew *šbm*." *JSS* 18:17-39.
1974 "Philo of Byblos and his 'Phoenician History'." *Bulletin of the Johns Rylanders Library* 58:17-68.
Barré, M. L.
1983 *The God-List in the Treaty between Hannibal and Philip V of Macedonia: A Study in Light of the Ancient Near Eastern Treaty Tradition*. The Johns Hopkins Near Eastern Studies. Baltimore/London: Johns Hopkins.
Barré, M. L, and J. Kselman
1983 "New Exodus Covenant and Restoration in Psalm 23." *The Word of the Lord Shall Go Forth; Essays in Honor of David Noel Freedman in Celebration of his Sixtieth Birthday*. Ed. C. L. Meyers and M. O'Connor. American Schools of Oriental Research Special Volume Series No. 1. Winona Lake, IN: Eisenbrauns. 97-127.
Barstad, H.
1984 *The Religious Polemics of Amos; Studies in the Preaching of Am 2, 7B-8, 4, 1-13, 5, 1-27, 6, 4-7, 8, 14*. SVT 34. Leiden: Brill.
Batto, B.
1987 "The Covenant of Peace: A Neglected Ancient Near Eastern Motif." *CBQ* 49:187-211.
1992 *Slaying the Dragon; Mythmaking in the Biblical Tradition*. Louisville, KY: Westminster/John Knox.

Bauer, H.
1933 "Die Gottheiten von Ras Schamra." *ZAW* 51:81-101.
1934 Review of C. F. A. Schaeffer, *La deuxième campagne de fouilles à Ras Shamra*. *OLZ* 37:238-47.
Bauer, J. B.
1957 "Ugaritisch *npr* und *ʿlṣ*." *AfO* 18:130.
Bauer, T.
1957 "Ein viertes altbabylonisches Fragment des Gilgames-Epos." *JNES* 16:254-62.
Baumgarten, A. I.
1981 *The Phoenician History of Philo of Byblos; A Commentary*. Études préliminaires aux religions orientales dans l'Empire Romain 89. Leiden: Brill.
Beckman, G. M.
1982 "The Anatolian Myth of Illuyanka." *JANES* 14:11-25.
1986 "Inheritance and Royal Succesion among the Hittites." *Kaniššuwar; A Tribute to Hans Güterbock on his Seventy-fifth Birthday May 27, 1983*. Ed. H.A. Hoffner, Jr. and G.M. Beckman. Assyriological Studies 23. Chicago: The Oriental Institute of the University of Chicago. 13-31.
Beeston, A. F. L.
1979 Review of R. Steiner, *The Case for Fricative Laterals in Proto-Semitic*, *JSS* 24:265-67.
Berlin, A.
1985 *The Dynamics of Biblical Parallelism*. Bloomington, IN: Indiana University.
Betlyon, J. W.
1991 "Canaanite Myth and Early Coinage of the Phoenician City-States." *Ancient Economy in Mythology: East and West*. Ed. M. Silver. New York: Rowman & Littlefield. 135-61.
Binger, T.
1992 "Fighting the Dragon. Another Look at the Theme in the Ugaritic Texts." *SJOT* 6:139-49.
Blake, F. R.
1951 *A Resurvey of the Hebrew Tenses*. Rome: Pontifical Biblical Institute.
Blau, J.
1957 "*Hōbrē šāmājim* (Jes. xlvii 13) = Himmelsanbeter." *VT* 7:183-84.
1968 "On Problems of Polyphony and Archaism in Ugaritic Spelling." *JAOS* 88:523-26.
1971 "Marginalia Semitica II." *IOS* 1:1-35.
1977 *An Adverbial Construction in Hebrew and Arabic; Sentence Adverbials in Frontal Position Separated from the Rest of the Sentence*. The Israel Academy of Sciences and Humanities Proceedings VI/1. Jerusalem: The Israel Academy of Sciences and Humanities.
Blau, J., and J. C. Greenfield
1976 "Ugaritic Glosses." *BASOR* 200:11-17.
Blau, J. and S. E. Loewenstamm
1970 "Zur Frage der scriptio plena im Ugaritischen und Verwandtes." *UF* 2:19-33.
Boadt, L.
1978 "Textual Problems in Ezekiel and Poetic Analysis of Paired Words." *JBL* 97:489-99.
1980 *Ezekiel's Oracles against Egypt; A Literary and Philological Study of Ezekiel* 29-32. BibetOr 37. Rome: Biblical Institute Press.
Böhl, F. M. Th.
1936 "Die fünfzig Namen des Marduk." *AfO* 11:191-218.

Bonnet, C.

1988 *Melqart; Cultes et mythes de l'Héraclès tyrien en méditerranée*. Studia Phoenicia VIII. Bibliothèque de la faculté de philosophie et lettres de Namur 69. Leuven: Uitgeverij Peeters/Presses universitaires de Namur.

Bordreuil, P.

1986 *Catalogue des sceaux ouest-sémitiques inscrits de la Bibliothéque Nationale, du Musée du Louvre et du Musée biblique et Terre Sainte*. Paris: Bibliothéque Nationale.

1989 "À propos de la topographie économique de l'Ougarit: Jardins du midi et pâsturages du nord." *Syria* 66:263-74.

1990 "La déesse ᶜAnat et les sources du Ṣapon." *Techniques et pratiques hydro-agricoles traditionelles en domaine irrigué; Approache pluridisciplinaire des modes de culture avant la motorisation en Syrie. Tome 2. Actes du Colloque de Damas 27 juin – 1er juillet 1987*. Ed. B. Geyer. Institut français d'archéologie du proche orient. Bibliothèque archéologique et historique 136. Paris: Geuthner. 257-69.

1991 "Recherches Ougaritiques." *Sem* 40:17-30.

Bordreuil, P., and D. Pardee

1982 "Le ritucl funeraire ougaritique RS 34.126." *Syria* 59:121-28.

1989 *La Trouvaille épigraphique de l'Ougarit; 1. Concordance*. Ras Shamra-Ougarit V. Paris: Éditions Recherche sur les civilizations.

1990 "Le papyrus du marzeaḥ." *Semitica* 38 (Hommages à Maurice Sznycer I):49-68, plates VII-X.

1991-92 "Textes ougaritiques oubliés et ⟨⟨transfuges⟩⟩." *Semitica* 41-42:23-58.

1993 "Le combat de *Baᶜlu* avec *Yammu* d'après les textes ougaritiques." *MARI* 7:63-70.

Borger, R.

1956 *Die Inschriften Asarhaddons Königs von Assyrien*. AfO Beiheft 9. Graz: Weidner. Reprinted: Osnabrück: Biblio-Verlag, 1967.

Bottéro, J., and S. N. Kramer

1989 *Lorsque les dieux faisaient l'homme; Mythologie mésopotamienne*. Paris: Éditions Gallimard.

van der Branden, A.

1959 "Les divinités sub-arabes *mnḏḥ* et *wrfw*." *BiOr* 16:183-84.

Brooke, G. J.

1979 "The Textual, Formal and Historical Significance of Ugaritic Letter RS 34.124 (= KTU 2.72)." *UF* 11 (Festschrift für C. F. A. Schaeffer):69-87.

Bryan, D. B.

1973 "Texts relating to the Marzeaḥ. A Study of an Ancient Semitic Institution." Ph.D. diss., The Johns Hopkins University, Baltimore, MD.

van Buren, E. D.

1933 *The Flowing Vase and the God with Streams*. Berlin: Hans Schoetz & Co., GMBH.

Burkert, W.

1979 *Structure and History in Greek Mythology and Ritual*. Berkeley/Los Angeles/London: University of California.

Cagni, L.

1969 *L'epopea di Erra*. Rome: Istituto di Studi del Vicino Oriente.

1977 *The Poem of Erra*. SANE 1/3. Malibu, CA: Undena.

Caquot, A.

1958 "Le dieu ᶜAthtar et les textes de Ras Shamra." *Syria* 35:45-60.

1959 "La naissance du Monde selon Canaan." *La naissance du monde*. Sources orientale 1. Paris: Éditions du Seuil. 175-84.

1974 "Notes de lexicographiques ougaritiques." *Actes du premier congrès international sémitique et chamito-sémitique, Paris, 16-19 juillet 1969*. Ed. A. Caquot and D. Cohen. Janua Linguarum 159. The Hague: Mouton. 203-08

1979-80 ''Horon: Revue Critique et Données Nouvelles.'' *Les annales archeologiques arabes syriennes* 19-20:173-80.
1982 ''Le dieu Horon, bilan critique et données nouvelles.'' *RHR* 199:243-44.
1988 ''Un recueil ougaritique de formules magiques: KTU 1.82.'' *SEL* 5 = *Cananea Selecta; Festschrift für Oswald Loretz zum 60. Geburstag*. 31-45

Caquot, A., and M. Sznycer.
1980 *Ugaritic Religion*. Iconography of Religion 15/8. Leiden: Brill.

Caquot, A., J. M. de Tarragon and J. L. Cunchillos
1989 *Textes ougaritiques; Tome II. Textes religieux. Rituels. Correspondance*. LAPO 14. Paris: Cerf.

Casadio, G.
1987 ''El and Cosmic Order: is the Ugaritic Supreme God a *deus otiosus*?'' *Studia Fennica* 32:45-58.

Cassuto, U.
1938 ''The Palace of Baal in Tablet II AB of Ras Shamra.'' *Or* 7:265-90 = *BOS* 113-39.
1949 ''Zeus Demarous in the Ugaritic Texts.'' *Sepher Dinaburg*. Ed. Y. F. Baer. Jerusalem. 65-67 = *BOS* 188-92.
1967 *A Commentary on the Books of Exodus*. Trans. I. Abrahams. Jerusalem: Magnes. First published in Hebrew in 1956.

Cazelles, H.
1947 ''Note sur l'origine des temps convertis hébreux (d'après quelques texts Ugaritiques).'' *RB* 54:388-93.
1984 ''*mṯpṭ* à Ugarit.'' *Or* 53 (Mitchell Dahood Memorial Volume):177-82.

Černý, J.
1952 *Ancient Egyptian Religion*. London: Hutchinson House.

Charpin, D.
1987 ''De la Joie à l'Orage.'' *MARI* 5:661.

Charpin, D., and J. Durand
1986 ''⟨⟨Fils de Simʾal⟩⟩: Les origines tribales des rois de Mari.'' *RA* 80:141-83.

Civil, M.
1972 ''The Anzu-Bird and Scribal Whimsies.'' *JAOS* 92:271.

Clapham, L.
1969 ''Sanchuniaton: the First Two Cycles.'' Ph.D. diss., Harvard University, Cambridge, MA.

Clifford, R. J.
1971 ''The Tent of El and the Israelite Tent of Meeting.'' *CBQ* 33:221-27.
1979 ''The Temple in the Ugaritic Myth of Baal.'' *Symposia Celebrating the Seventy-fifth Anniversary of the Founding of the American Schools of Oriental Research (1900-1975)*. Ed. F. M. Cross. Cambridge, MA: American Schools of Oriental Research. 137-45.
1984 ''Cosmogonies in the Ugaritic Texts and in the Bible.'' *Or* 53 (Mitchell J. Dahood Memorial Volume):183-201.
1987 ''Mot Invites Baal to a Feast: Observations on a Difficult Text (CTA 5.i = KTU 1.5 I).'' *''Working with No Data''; Semitic and Egyptian Studies Presented to Thomas O. Lambdin*. Ed. D. M. Golomb. Winona Lake, IN: Eisnebrauns. 55-65.

Cogan, M.
1974 *Imperialism and Religion: Assyria, Judah and Israel in the Eighth and Seventh Centuries B. C. E.* SBLMS 19. Missoula, MT: Scholars.
1984 '''...From the Peak of Amanah'.'' *IEJ* 34:255-59.

Cohen, H. R.
1968 ''The Idiom קרא בשם in Second Isaiah.'' *JANES* 1/1:32-34.
1978 *Biblical Hapax Legomena in the Light of Akkadian and Ugaritic*. SBLDS 37. Missoula, MT: Scholars.

1989a "'*Ha(Shem) lammabbûl yāšab*' (Tehillîm 29:10)—pîrûš ḥādāš." *Leshonenu* 53/3-4:193-201.
1989b "The 'Held Method' for Comparative Semitic Philology." *JANES* 19:9-23.

Conti Rossini, K.
1931 *Chrestomathia arabica meridionalis epigraphica*. Rome: Istituto per l'Oriente.

Coogan, M. D.
1978 *Stories from Ancient Canaan*. Philadelphia: Westminster.

Cooper, A.
1991 Review of D. Pardee, *Les Textes paramythologiques de la 24e campagne (1961)*. *JAOS* 111:833-36.

Cooper, J. S.
1976 "More Heat on the AN.IM.DUGUD Bird." *JCS* 26:121.

Coote, R. B.
1974 "Ugaritic *PH(Y)*, 'see'." *UF* 6:1-5.
1981 *Amos Among the Prophets; Composition and Theology*. Philadelphia: Fortress.

Courtois, J. C.
1974 "Ugarit Grid, Strata, and Find Localizations: A Reassessment." *ZDPV* 90:97-114.

Craigie, P. K.
1973 "Helal, Athtar and Phaeton (Jes 14, 12-15)." *ZAW* 85:223-25.
1977 "Three Ugaritic Notes on the Song of Deborah." *JSOT* 2:33-49.

Cross, F. M.
1968 "The Song of the Sea and Canaanite Myth." *Journal for Theology and Church* 5:1-25.
1976 "The 'Olden Gods' in Ancient Near Easatern Creation Myths." *Magnalia Dei. The Mighty Acts of God. Essays on the Bible and Archaeology in Memory of G. Ernest Wright*. Ed. F. M. Cross, W. E. Lemke and P. D. Miller, Jr. Garden City, NY: Doubleday. 328-38.
1979 "A Recently Published Phoenician Inscription of the Persan Period from Byblos." *IEJ* 29:40-44.
1980 "Newly Found Inscriptions in Old Canaanite and Early Phoenician Scripts." *BASOR* 238:1-20.
1981 "The Priestly Tabernacle in Light of Recent Research." *Temple and High Places in Biblical Times; Proceedings of the Colloquium in Honor of the Centennial of Hebrew Union College—Jewish Institute of Religion. Jerusalem, 14-16 March, 1977*. Ed. A. Biran. Jerusalem: The Nelson Glueck School of Biblical Archaeology of Hebrew Union College—Jewish Institute of Religion. 169-78.
1983a "The Epic Traditions of Early Israel: Epic Narrative and the Reconstructions of Early Israelite Institutions." *The Poet and the Historian; Essays in Literary and Historical Biblical Criticism*. Ed. R. E. Friedman. HSS 26; Chico, CA: Scholars. 13-39.
1983b "The Seal of Miqnêyaw, Servant of Yahweh." *Ancient Seals and the Bible*. Ed. L. Gorelick and E. Williams-Forte. Malibu, CA: Undena. 55-63.

Cross, F. M., and D. N. Freedman
1948 "The Blessing of Moses." *JBL* 67:191-210.

Cunchillos, J. L.
1976 *Estudio des Salmo 29; Canto al Dos de la fertilidad-fecundidad. Aportación al conocimiento de la Fe de Israel a su entrada en Canaan*. Valencia: La Institución San Jerónimo.
1984-85 "Le Temple de Baᶜal à Ugarit et la Maison du Grande Prêtre." *École pratique des hautes études Vᵉ Section—Sciences Religieuses. Annuaire* 103: 231-44.
1985 "Le dieu Mut, guerrier de El." *Syria* 62:205-18.

1986 "Que tout aille bien auprès de ma mère! Un qatala optatif en ougaritique?" *Salvacion en la Palabra. Targum—Deerash—Berith; En memoria del professor Alejandro Diez Macho*. Ed. D. M. Leon. Madrid: Ediciones Cristiandad. 259-66.
1987 "Peut-on parler de mythes de création à Ugarit." *La Création dans l'orient ancien*. Lectio divina 127. Paris: Cerf. 79-96.

Curtis, A. H. W.
1978 "The 'Subjugation of the Waters' Motif in the Psalms; Imagery or Polemic?" *JSS* 23:245-56.
1988 "God as 'Judge' in Ugaritic and Hebrew Thought." *Law and Religion: Essays on the Place of the Law in Israel and Early Christianity*. Ed. B. Lindars. Cambridge: James Clark & Co. 3-12, 159-61.
1990 "Some Observations on 'Bull' Terminology in the Ugaritic Texts and the Old Testament." *OTS* 26:17-31.

Dahood, M. J.
1965 *Ugaritic-Hebrew Philology; Marginal Notes on Recent Publications*. BeO 17. Rome: Pontifical Biblical Institute. Photomechanical Reproduction, 1976.
1966 *Psalms I. 1-50*. AB 16. Garden City, NY: Doubleday.
1969 "Ugaritic-Hebrew Syntax and Style." *UF* 1:15-36.
1979 "Eblaite, Ugaritic, and Hebrew Lexical Notes." *UF* 11 (Festschrift für C.F.A. Schaeffer):141-46.
1981 "Ut ʿ*nt*: III: 25-26 and Isaiah 21, 12." *Or* 50:194-96.

Dalley, S.
1989 *Myths from Mesopotamia; Creation, the Flood, Gilgamesh and Others*. Oxford/New York: Oxford University.

Dalman, G.
1929 *Arbeit und Sitte in Palästina. Vol. I*. Gütersloh: Evangelischer Verlag.

Damrosch, D.
1987 *The Narrative Covenant; Transformations of Genre in the Growth of Biblical Literature*. San Francisco: Harper and Row.

Davies, G. I.
1979 "A Note on the Etymology of *hištaḥᵃwāh*." *VT* 29:493-95.

Day, J.
1985a "Echoes of Baal's Seven Thunders and Lightnings in Psalm XXIX and Habakkuk III 9 and the Identity of the Seraphim in Isaiah VI." *VT* 29:143-51.
1985b *God's Conflict with the Dragon and the Sea. Echoes of a Canaanite Myth in the Old Testament*. University of Cambridge Oriental Publ. 35. Cambridge: Cambridge University.
1989 *Molech: A god of human sacrifice in the Old Testament*. University of Cambridge Oriental Publications 41. Cambridge: University of Cambridge.
1992 "Baal." *The Anchor Bible Dictionary; Volume 1. A-C*. Ed. D. N. Freedman. New York: Doubleday. 545-49.

Day, P. L.
1991 "Why is Anat a Warrior and Hunter?" *The Bible and the Politics of Exegesis. Essays in Honor of Norman K. Gottwald on His Sixty-Fifth Birthday*. Ed. D. Jobling, P. L. Day and G. T. Sheppard. Cleveland: Pilgrim. 141-46, 329-32.

Deem, A.
1978 "Anath and Some Biblical Hebrew Cruces," *JSS* 23:25-30.

Delcor, M.
1974 "Astarté et le fécondité des troupeaux en Deut. 7,13 et parallèles." *UF* 6:7-14.

Delitzsch, F.
1889 *Assyrische Grammatik*. Porta linguarum orientalium 10. Berlin: H. Reuther.

Demsky, A.
1978 "Mesopotamian and Canaanite Literary Traditions in the Ahiram Formula." *EI* 14:7-11.
Diest, F. E.
1971 "A note on *ṣḥrrt* in the Ugaritic text 51 viii 22." *JNWSL* 1:68-70.
Dietrich, M.
1990 "Das Einsetzungsritual der Entu von Emar (Emar VI/3, 369)." *UF* 21:47-100.
Dietrich, M., and O. Loretz
1973 "Untersuchungen zur Schrift- und Lautlehre des Ugaritischen (II); Lesehilfen in der ugaritischen Orthographie." *UF* 5:71-77.
1977 "*anš(t)* und *(m)inš(t)* im Ugaritischen." *UF* 9:47-50.
1978 Ug. *tmn* 'Gestalt'." *UF* 10:432-33.
1980 "Baal *rpu* in KTU 1.108; 1.113 und nach 1.17 VI 25-33." *UF* 12:171-82.
1981a "Neue Studien zu den Ritualtexten aus Ugarit." *UF* 13:63-100.
1981b "Ugaritic *kly* 'aufbrauchen, ausgehen'." *UF* 13:294-96.
1984 "*kl* 'ganz, alle' mit Suffixen in Ug. Texten." *UF* 16:351-52.
1986a "Baal Vernichtet Jammu (KTU 1.2 IV 23-30)." *UF* 17:117-21.
1986b "Ug. *ngš* und *ngṯ*, *mgṯ*." *UF* 18:451-52.
1989 "The Cuneiform Alphabets of Ugarit." *UF* 21:101-112.
Dietrich, M., O. Loretz, and J. Sanmartín
1973 "Zur ugaritischen Lexicographie (VII); Lexikographische Einzelbemerkungen." *UF* 5:79-104.
1974 "Zur ugaritischen Lexicographie (XI); Lexikographische Einzelbemerkungen." *UF* 6:19-38.
van Dijk, Jacobus
1986 "ᶜAnat, Seth and the Seed of Preᶜ." *Scripta Signa Vocis; Studies about Scripts, Scriptures, Scribes and Languages in the Near East, presented to J. H. Hospers by his pupils, colleagues and friends*. Ed. H. L. J. Vantiphout et al. Groningen: Egbert Forsten. 31-51.
van Dijk, Jan
1983 *LUGAL. UD ME-LÁM-bi NIR-G̃ÁL; La récit épique et didactiques des Travaux de Ninurta du Déluge et de la nouvelle Création. Texte, traduction et introduction*. 2 vols. Leiden: Brill.
Dijkstra, M.
1974 "*Baᶜlu* and his Protagonists: Some Remarks in CTA 6 V 1-6." *JANES* 6:59-68.
1983 "Contributions to the Reconstruction of the Myth of Baᶜal." *UF* 15:25-32.
1986 "Once Again: The Closing Lines of the Baᶜal-Cycle." *UF* 17:147-52.
1987 "Epigraphical Evidence for the Determination of the Column Order of the Tablets KTU 1.1 and KTU 1.20-22." *UF* 19:49-60.
1989 "Marginalia to the Ugaritic Letters (II)." *UF* 21:141-52.
1991 "The Weather-God on Two Mountains." *UF* 23:127-40.
Dijkstra, M. and J. C. de Moor
1975 "Problematic Passages in the Legend of Aqhâtu." *UF* 7:171-216.
Dobrusin, D.
1981 "The Third Masculine Plural of the Prefixed Form of the Verb in Ugaritic." *JANES* 13:3-10.
Donner, H.
1967 "Ugaritismen in der Psalmenforschung." *ZAW* 79:322-50.
Driver, G.R.
1955 "Birds in the Old Testament: 1. Birds in Life." *PEQ* 87:129.
1967 Review of *CAD* II B. *JSS* 12:105-09.

Drower, M. S.
1975 "Ugarit." *CAH* II/2:130-60.
Durand, J. M.
1993 "Le mythologème du combat entre le dieu de l'orage et la mer en Mésopotamie." *MARI* 7:41-61.
Dussaud, R.
1932 "Le sanctuaire et les dieux pheniciens de Ras Shamra." *RHR* 105:245-302.
1941 *Les découvertes de Ras Shamra (Ugarit) et l'Ancien Testament*. Sec. ed. Paris: Geuthner.
1947 "Astarté, Pontos et Baᶜal." *CRAIBL*: 201-24.
Ebeling, E.
1932 "Attar." *Reallexikon der Assyriologie I. A-Bepašte*. Berlin/Leipzig: de Gruyter. 312.
Edwards, I. E. S.
1955 "A Relief of Qudshu-Astarte-Anath in the Winchester College Collection." *JNES* 14:49-51.
Eissfeldt, O.
1940 "Zum geographischen Horizent der Ras-Schamra-Texte." *ZDMG* 94:59-85.
1944 "Ugaritisches." *ZDMG* 98:84-100.
1952 *Sanchunjaton von Berut und Ilimilku von Ugarit*. Beiträge zur Religionsgeschichte des Altertums 5. Halle: Max Niemeyer.
1963 *Kleine Schriften II*. Ed. R. Selheim and F. Maass. Tübingen: Mohr (Siebeck).
1965 *The Old Testament; an Introduction*. Trans. P. R. Ackroyd. New York/Evanston, IL: Harper and Row.
Eliade, M.
1991 "Toward a Definition of Myth." *Mythologies*. Compiled by. Y. Bonnefoy. Directed by W. Doniger. Trans. G. Honigsblum. vol. 1. Chicago/London: University of Chicago. 3-5.
Ellenbogen, M.
1977 "Linguistic Archaeology, Semantic Integration, and the Recovery of Lost Meanings." *Proceedings of the Sixth World Congress of Jewish Studies*. Volume I. Ed. A. Shinan. Jerusalem: World Union of Jewish Studies. 93-95
Emerton, J.A.
1977 "The Etymology of *hištaḥᵃwāh*." *OTS* 20:41-55.
1978 "A Further Note on CTA 5 I 4-6." *UF* 10:73-77.
Engnell, I.
1943 *Studies in Divine Kingship in the Ancient Near East*. Upsala: Almqvist & Wiksells.
1969 *A Rigid Scrutiny. Critical Essays on the Old Testament*. Trans. and ed. J.T. Willis. Nashville, TN: Vanderbilt University.
van Ess, J.
1989 *The Youthful God: Anthropomorphism in Early Islam*. The University Lecture in Religion at Arizona State University. Tempe, AZ: Department of Religious Studies, Arizona State University.
Falbe, T., and J. C. Lindberg
1862 *Numismatique de l'ancienne Afrique*. Vol. 3. Ed. L. Müller. Copenhagen: Imprimerie de Bianco Luno.
Falkenstein, A.
1959 *Sumerische Götterlieder Teil I*. Heidelberg: Carl Winter/Universitätsverlag.
Farbe, W.
1977 *Beschwörungsrituale an Istar und Dumuzi*. Wiesbaden: Franz Steiner.

Faulkner, R. O.

1976 *A Concise Dictionary of Middle Egyptian*. Oxford: Griffith Institute.

Fauth, W.

1990 "Das Kasios-Gebirge and Zeus Kasios. Die antike Tradition und ihre vorder orientalischen Grundlagen." *UF* 22:105-18.

Fensham, F. C.

1965 "The Destruction of Mankind in the Near East." *AION* 15:31-37.

1966 "Winged Gods and Goddesses in the Ugaritic Tablets." *OA* 5:157-64.

1977 "The Numeral Seventy in the Old Testament and the Family of Jerubbaal, Ahab, Panammuwa and Athirat." *PEQ* 109:113-15.

1978 "The Use of the Suffix Conjugation and the Prefix Conjugation in a Few Old Hebrew Poems." *JNWSL* 6:9-18.

1979a "Notes on Treaty Terminology in Ugaritic Epics." *UF* 11 (Festschrift für C. F. A. Schaeffer):265-74.

1979b "The Semantic Field of *kly* in Ugaritic." *JNWSL* 7:27-30.

1984 "The Ugaritic Root *ṯpṭ*." *JNWSL* 12:63-69.

Fenton, T. H.

1969a "Command and Fulfillment in Ugaritic—'tqtl : yqtl' and 'qtl : qtl'." *JSS* 14:34-38.

1969b "Passages in Ugaritic Discourse—Restorations and Observations." *UF* 1:199-200.

1973 "The Hebrew 'Tenses' in the Light of Ugaritic." *Proceedings of the Fifth World Congress of Jewish Studies*. Volume 4. Jerusalem: World Union of Jewish Studies. 31-39.

1977 "The Claremont 'MRZḤ' Tablet, Its Text and Meaning." *UF* 9:7-75.

1978 "Differing Approaches to the Theomachy Myth in Old Testament Writers." *Studies in the Bible and the Ancient Near East Presented to Samuel E. Loewenstamm on His Seventieth Birthday*. Ed. Y. Avishur and J. Blau. Jerusalem: E. Rubinstein's Publishing House. 2 vols. 2. 337-87 (Hebrew), 1.191-93 (English Summary).

Firmage, E.

1992 "Zoology." *The Anchor Bible Dictionary; Volume 6. Si-Z*. Ed. D. N. Freedman. New York: Doubleday. 1109-67.

Fisher (Mack-Fisher), L.

1963 "The Temple Quarter." *JSS* 8:34-41.

1965 "Creation at Ugarit and in the Old Testament." *VT* 15:313-24.

1969 "An Ugaritic Ritual and Genesis I, 1-5." *Ugaritica VI*. Mission de Ras Shamra XVII. Paris: Mission archéologique de Ras Shamra/Paul Geuthner. 197-205.

1990 "A Survey and Reading Guide to the Didactic Literature of Ugarit: Prolegomenon to a Study on the Sage." *The Sage in Israel and the Ancient Near East*. Ed. J. G. Gammie and L. G. Perdue. Winona Lake: Eisenbrauns. 67-80.

Fisher, M.

1969 "Lexical Relations between Ethiopic and Ugaritic." Ph.D. diss., Brandeis University, Waltham, MA.

Fitzgerald, A.

1974 "A Note on Psalm 29." *BASOR* 215:61-63.

Fitzmyer, J. A.

1983 *The Gospel According to Luke X-XXIV*. AB 28A. Garden City, NY: Doubleday.

Fleming, D.

1991 "The Voice of the Ugaritic Incantation Priest (RIH 78/20)." *UF* 23:141-54.

1992 *The Installation of Baal's High Priestess at Emar; A Window on Ancient Syrian Religion*. HSS 42. Atlanta, GA: Scholars.
Fontenrose, J. E.
1966 *The Ritual Theory of Myth*. Berkeley/Los Angeles: University of California.
1980 *Python; A Study of the Delphic Myth and Its Origins*. Sec. ed. Berkeley/Los Angeles: University of California.
Forshey, H. O.
1973 "The Hebrew Root *NḤL* and its Semitic Cognates." Th.D. diss., Harvard University, Cambridge, MA.
Frankfort, H.
1934 "Gods and Myths on Sargonid Seals." *Iraq* 1:1-29.
1939 *Cyclinder Seals; A Documentary Essay on the Art and Religion of the Ancient Near East*. London: Macmillan.
1970 *The Art and Architecture of the Ancient Orient*. The Pelican History of Art. First paperback edition based on the fourth hardback impression of 1970. New York: Penguin Books.
Frazer, J. G.
1921 *Apollodorus. The Library; in two volumes*. Vol. 1. Loeb Classical Library. London: William Heineman; New York: G.P. Putnam's Sons.
Fredericks, D.C.
1988 *Qoheleth's Language: Re-evaluating its Nature and Date*. Ancient Near Eastern Texts and Studies 3. Lewiston, NY/Queenston, Ontario: Edwin Mellen.
Freedman, D.
1970-71 "Counting Formulas in Akkadian Epics." *JANES* 3/2:65-81.
Freedman, D. N.
1980 *Pottery, Poetry, and Prophecy; Studies in Early Hebrew Poetry*. Winona Lake, IN: Eisenbrauns.
1981 "Temples without Hands." *Temple and High Places in Biblical Times; Proceedings of the Colloquium in Honor of the Centennial of Hebrew Union College—Jewish Institute of Religion. Jerusalem, 14-16 March, 1977*. Ed. A. Biran. Jerusalem: The Nelson Glueck School of Biblical Archaeology of Hebrew Union College—Jewish Institute of Religion. 21-30.
Friedman, R. E.
1980 "The *MRZḤ* Tablet from Ugarit." *MAARAV* 2/2:187-206.
Fronzaroli, P.
1955 *La Fonetica Ugaritica*. Sussidi Eruditi 7. Rome: Edizioni di Storia e Letteratura.
1984 "Eblaic Lexicon." *Studies on the Language of Ebla*. Ed. P. Fronzaroli. Quaderni di Semitistica 13. Florence: Istituto di Linguistica e di Lingue Oreintali, Universita' di Firenze. 117-57.
Frymer-Kensky, T.
1977 "The Judicial Ordeal in the Ancient Near East." Two vols. Ph.D. diss, Yale University, New Haven, CT.
Gaál, E.
1977 "Tuthmosis III as Storm-God?" *Studia Aegyptiaca* 3:29-38.
Gai, A.
1982 "The Reduction of Tenses (and Other Categories) of the Consequent Verb in North-west Semitic." *Or* 51:254-56.
Garbini, G.
1960 "The God ᶜAštar in an Inscription from Byblos." *Or* 29:322.
1974 "Sul nome ᶜAthtar—ᶜAshtar." *AION* 24:409-10.
1983 "Note sui testi rituali Ugaritici." *OrAnt* 22:53-60.

Gardiner, A.
1932 "The Astarte Papyrus." *Studies Presented to F.L. Griffiths*. London: Egypt Exploration Society. 74-85.
Garr, W. R.
1985 *Dialect Geography of Syria-Palestine, 1000-586 B.C.E.* Philadelphia: University of Pennsylvania.
1986 "On Voicing and Devoicing in Ugaritic." *JNES* 45:45-52.
1992 "The Grammar and Interpretation of Exodus 6:3." *JBL* 111:385-408.
Gaselee, S.
1917 *Achilles Tatius*. Loeb Classical Library. London: William Heinemann; New York: G.P. Putnam's Sons.
Gaster, T. H.
1933 "The Ritual Pattern of a Ras-Šamra Epic." *ArchOr* 5:118-23.
1937 "The Battle between the Rain and the Sea. An Ancient Semitic Nature-Myth." *Iraq* 4:21-32.
1946 "A King without a Castle. Baal's Appeal to Asherat." *BASOR* 101:21-30.
1946-47 "The Canaanite Epic of Keret." *JQR* 37:285-93.
1950 "The Religion of the Canaanites." *Forgotten Religions*. Ed. V. T. A. Ferm. New York: Philosophical Library. 13-43.
1952 "The Egyptian 'Story of Astarte' and the Ugaritic Poem of Baal." *BO* 9:82-85.
Gelb, I.J.
1980 *A Computer-Aided Analysis of Amorite*. AS 21. Chicago: The Oriental Institute of the University of Chicago.
1992 "Mari and the Kish Civilization." *Mari in Retrospect; Fifty Years of Mari and Mari Studies*. Ed. G. D. Young. Winona Lake, IN: Eisenbrauns. 121-202.
Geller, M. J.
1992 "A Vocabulary of Rare Words." *Or* 61:205-07.
Gese, H., M. Höfner and K. Rudolph
1970 *Die Religionen Altsyriens, Altarabiens under der Mandäer*. Die Religionen der Menschheit X/II. Stuttgart: Kohlhammer.
Gevirtz, S.
1973 "Parallelization of Selfsame Verbs in the Amarna Letters." *JNES* 32:99-104.
1980 "On Hebrew *šebeṭ* = 'Judge'." *The Bible World. Essays in Honor of Cyrus H. Gordon*. Ed. G. Rendsburg, A. Adler, M. Arfa and N.H. Winter. New York: KTAV. 61-66.
Gibson, J. C. L.
1975 "Myth, legend and folklore in the Ugaritic Keret and Aqhat Texts." *VTS* 28:60-68.
1984 "The Theology of the Ugaritic Baal Cycle." *Or* 53 (= Mitchell J. Dahood Memorial Volume):202-19.
Ginsberg, H. L.
1935 "The Victory of the Land-God over the Sea-God." *JPOS* 15:327-33.
1936 "Baᶜlu and his Brethren." *JPOS* 16:138-49.
1940 "Two Religious Borrowings in Ugaritic Literature II." *Or* 9:39-44.
1941 "Did Anath Fight the Dragon?" *BASOR* 84:12-14.
1944 "Baal's Two Messengers." *BASOR* 95:25-30.
1945a "Ugaritic Studies and the Bible." *BA* 8:21-58.
1945b "The North-Canaanite Myth of Anath and Aqhat I." *BASOR* 97:3-10.
1946 *The Legend of King Keret*. BASOR Sup. 2-3. New Haven, CT: The American Schools of Oriental Research.
1948 Review of J. Obermann, *Ugaritic Mythology*. *JCS* 2:139-44.

1950 "Interpreting Ugaritic Texts." *JAOS* 70:156-60.
1955 "Ugaritic Myths and Legends." *Religions of the Ancient Near East: Sumero-Akkadian Religious Texts and Ugaritic Epics*. Ed. I. Mendelsohn. New York: The Liberal Arts Press. 221-79.
1958 "An Unrecognized Allusion to King Pekah and Hoshea of Israel." *EI* 5:61*-65*.
1973 "Ugaritico-Phoenicia." *JANES* 5 (T. H. Gaster Festschrift):131-47.
1978 "The Oldest Record of Hysteria with Physical Stigmata, Zech 13:2-6." In *Studies in the Bible and the Ancient Near East Presented to Samuel E. Loewenstamm on His Seventieth Birthday*. Ed. Y. Avishur and J. Blau. Jerusalem: E. Rubinstein's Publishing House. vol. 1.23-27.

Ginsberg, H. L., and B. Maisler (Mazar)
1934 "Semitised Hurrians in Syria and Palestine." *JPOS* 14:243-67.

Goetze, A.
1944 "Peace on Earth." *BASOR* 93:17-20.
1953 "An Old Babylonian Itinerary." *JCS* 7:51-72.
1958 "Remarks on Some Names Occurring in the Execration Texts." *BASOR* 151:28-33.
1975 "The Struggle for the Domination of Syria (1400-1300 B.C.)." *Cambridge Ancient History; Third Edition. Volume II Part 2. History of the Middle East and the Aegean Region c. 1380-1000 B.C.* Ed. I. E. S. Edwards, C. J. Gadd, N. G. L. Hammond and E. Sollberger. Cambridge: At the University Press. 1-20.

Good, R. M.
1978 "Clouds Messengers?" *UF* 10:436-37.
1984 "Some Ugaritic Terms Relating to Draught and Riding Animals." *UF* 16:77-81.
1986 "Hebrew and Ugaritic *nḥt*." *UF* 17:153-56.

Gordon, C. H.
1943a *The Loves and Wars of Baal and Anat*. Princeton: Princeton University; London: Humphrey Milford, Oxford University Press.
1943b "The Poetic Literature of Ugarit." *Or* 12:49-51.
1953 "Sabbatical Cycle or Seasonal Pattern?" *Or* 22:79-81.
1958 *The World of the Old Testament*. Garden City, NY: Doubleday.
1966 "Leviathan: Symbol of Evil." *Biblical Motifs; Origins and Transformations*. Ed. A. Altmann. Cambridge, MA: Harvard University. 1-9.
1976 "El, Father of Šnm." *JNES* 35:261-62.
1977 "Poetic Myths and Legends." *Berytus* 25:5-133.
1982 "Khnum and El." *Scripta Hierosolymitana* 28:203-14.

Gordon, E. I.
1967 "The Meaning of the Ideogram ᵈ*KAŠKAL.KUR* = 'Underground Water-Course' and its Significance for Bronze Age Historical Geogaphy." *JCS* 21:70-88.

Grabbe, L. L.
1976 "The Seasonal Pattern and the Baal Cycle." *UF* 8:57-63.
1982 "Ugaritic *ṯlṯ* and Plowing: On the Proper Cultivation of Semitic Etymologies." *UF* 14:89-92.

Grave, C .
1980 "The Etymology of Northwest Semitic *ṣapānu*." *UF* 12:221-29.
1982 "Northwest Semitic *ṣapānu* in a Breakup of an Egyptian Stereotype Phrase in EA 147." *Or* 51:161-82.

Gray, J.
1949a "The Canaanite God Horon." *JNES* 8:27-34.
1949b "The Desert God ᶜAṯtr in the Literature and Religion of Canaan." *JNES* 8:72- 83.

1953 "The God Yw in the Religion of Canaan." *JNES* 12:278-83.
1956 "The Hebrew Conception of the Kingship of God: Its Origins and Development." *VT* 6:268-85.
1977 "A Cantata of the Autumn Festival: Psalm LXXVIII." *JSS* 22:2-26.
1979 "The Blood Bath of the Goddess Anat in the Ras Shamra Texts." *UF* 11 (Festschrift für C.F.A. Schaeffer):315-24.

Greenberg, J. H.
1950 "The Patterning of Root Morphemes in Semitic." *Word* 6:162-81.

Greenfield, J. C.
1958 "Lexicographical Notes." *HUCA* 29:203-28.
1961 Review of O. Kaiser, *Die mythische Bedeutung des Meeres von Ägypten, Ugarit und Israel. JBL* 80:91-92.
1967 "Some Aspects of Treaty Terminology in the Bible." *Fourth World Congress of Jewish Studies. Papers. Vol. 1.* Jerusalem: World Union of Jewish Studies. 117-19.
1969a "Amurrite, Ugaritic and Canaanite." *Proceedings of the International Conference on Semitic Studies, Held in Jerusalem, 19-23 July 1965.* Jerusalem: The Israel Academy of Sciences and Humanities. 92-101.
1969b Review of M. Dahood, *Ugaritic-Hebrew Philology. JAOS* 89:174-78.
1969c "The Zakir Inscription and the Danklied." *Proceedings of the Fifth World Congress of Jewish Studies. Volume 1.* Ed. P. Peli. Jerusalem: World Union of Jewish Studies. 174-91.
1971 "Scripture and Inscription: The Literary and Rhetorical Element in Some Early Phoenician Inscriptions." *Near Eastern Studies in Honor of William Foxwell Albright.* Ed. H. Goedicke. Baltimore/London: Johns Hopkins. 253-68.
1973 "Un rite religieux araméen et ses parallèles." *RB* 80:46-52.
1974 "The Marzeaḥ as a Social Institution." *Acta Antiqua Academiae Scientarum Hungaricae* 22:452-55.
1976 "The Aramean God *Ramman/Rimmon.*" *IEJ* 26:195-98.
1979 "The Root *ŠQL* in Akkadian, Ugaritic and Aramaic." *UF* 11 (Festschrift für C.F.A. Schaeffer):325-27.
1984 "A Touch of Eden." *Acta Iranica deuxième série, volume IX. Orientalia J. Duchesne-Guillemin Emerito-oblata.* Leiden: Brill. 219-24.
1985 "Baʿal's Throne and Isa. 6:1." *Mélanges bibliques et orientaux en l'honneur de M. Mathias Delcor.* Ed. A. Caquot, S. Légasse and M. Tardieu. AOAT 215. Kevelaer: Butzon & Bercker; Neukirchen-Vluyn: Neukirchener Verlag. 193-98.
1987 "The Hebrew Bible and Canaanite Literature." *The Literary Guide to the Bible.* Ed. R. Alter and F. Kermode. Cambridge, MA: The Belknap Press of the Harvard University Press. 545-60.

Greenstein, E. L.
1979 "Trans-Semitic Idiomatic Equivalency and the Derivation of Hebrew *mlʾkh.*" *UF* 11 (Festschrift für C.F.A. Schaeffer):329-36.
1982 "The Snaring of Seal in the Baal Epic." *MAARAV* 3:195-216.
1986-87 "Aspects of Biblical Poetry." *Jewish Book Annual* 44:33-42.
1988 "On the Prefixed Preterite in Biblical Hebrew." *Hebrew Studies* 29:7-17.
1993 "Between Ugaritic Epic and Biblical Narrative: The Role of Direct Discourse." Annual Meeting of the Society of Biblical Literature.

Grelot, P.
1956a "Isaïe XIV 12-15 et son arrière-plan mythologique." *RHR* 149:18-48.
1956b "On the Root עבק/עבץ in Ancient Aramaic and in Ugarit." *JSS* 1:202-05.
1957 "Complementary Note on the Semitic Root עבק/עבץ." *JSS* 2:195.

Griffiths, J. G.
1970 *Plutarch's De Iside et Osiride.* Cambridge: Cambridge University.

Grønboek, J.H.
1985 "Baal's Battle with Yam—A Canaanite Creation Fight." *JSOT* 33:27-44.
Gruber, M.
1980 *Aspects of Nonverbal Communication in the Ancient Near East*. Studia Pohl 12. Rome: Biblical Institute Press.
Güterbock, H. G.
1951 "The Song of Ullikumi." *JCS* 5:135-61.
Haas, V., and G. Wilhelm
1974 *Hurritische und luwische Riten aus Kizzuwatna; Hurritologische Studien I*. AOATS 3. Kevelaer: Verlag: Butzon & Bercker; Neukirchen-Vluyn: Neukirchener Verlag.
Hackett, J. A.
1980 *The Balaam Text from Deir ᶜAlla*. HSM 31; Chico, CA: Scholars.
Hadjioannou, K.
1978 "On Some Disputed Matters of the Ancient Religon of Cyprus." *RDAC*:103-10.
Hallo, W. W.
1964 "The Road to Emar." *JCS* 18:58-64.
Hallo, W. W., and J. J. A. van Dijk
1968 *The Exaltation of Inanna*. Yale Near Eastern Researches 3. New Haven/London: Yale University.
Halpern, B.
1981 *The Constitution of the Monarchy in Israel*. HSM 25. Chico, CA: Scholars.
1983 "Doctrine by Misadventure: Between the Israelite Source and the Biblical Historian." *The Poet and the Historian; Essays in Literary and Historical Biblical Criticism*. Ed. R. E. Friedman. HSS 26. Chico, CA: Scholars. 41-73.
1991 "Jerusalem and the Lineages in the Seventh Century BCE: Kinship and the Rise of Individual Liability." *Law and Ideology in Monarchic Israel*. Ed. B. Halpern and D. W. Hobson. JSOTSup 124; Sheffield: JSOT. 11-107.
Handy, L.K.
1988 "A Solution for Many *MLKM*." *UF* 20:57-59.
1990 "Dissenting Deities or Obediant Angels: Divine Hierarchies in Ugarit and the Bible." *Biblical Research* 35:18-35.
Hanson, P.D.
1973 "Zechariah 9 and the Recapitulation of an Ancient Ritual Pattern." *JBL* 92:37-59.
1975 *The Dawn of Apocalyptic*. Philadelphia: Fortress.
1977 "Rebellion in Heaven, Azazel, and Euhemeristic Heroes in I Enoch 6-11." *JBL* 96:195-233.
Harris, J. R.
1961 *Lexicographical Studies in Ancient Egyptian Minerals*. Deutsche Akademie der Wissenschaften zu Berlin Institut für Orientforschung 54. Berlin: Akademie-Verlag.
Healey, J. F.
1977 "The Underworld Character of the God Dagan." *JNWSL* 5:43-51.
1980 "The Sun Deity and the Underworld. Mesopotamia and Ugarit." *Death in Mesopotamia; Papers read at the XXVIe Rencontre assyriologique internationale*. Ed. B. Alster. Copenhagen Studies in Assyriology 8. Copenhagen: Academisk Forlag. 239-42.
1980 "Ugaritic *ḥtk*: A Note." *UF* 12:408-09.
1983a "Burning the Corn: New Light on the Killing of Motu." *Or* 52:248-51.
1983b "Swords and Plowshares: Some Ugaritic Terminology." *UF* 15:47-52.
1984a "Ancient Agriculture and the Old Testament (with special reference to Isaiah XXVIII 23-29." *OTS* 23:108-19.

1984b "The Immortality of the King: Ugarit and the Psalms." *Or* 53 (Mitchell Dahood Memorial Volume): 245-54.

Hecker, K.

1974 *Untersuchungen zur akkadischen Epik*. AOAT 8. Kevelaer: Butzon & Bercker; Neukirchen-Vluyn: Neukirchener Verlag.

Heidel, A.

1949 "A Special Usage of the Akkadian Term *Šadû*." JNES 8:233-35.

Heimpel, W.

1982 "A Catalog of Near Eastern Venus Deities." *Syro-Mesopotamian Studies* 4/3:9-22 [59-72].

1987 "The Natural History of the Tigris according to the Sumerian Literary Composition LUGAL." *JNES* 46:309-17.

Held, M.

1959 "*mḫṣ*/**mḫš* in Ugaritic and Other Semitic Languages (A Study in Comparative Lexicography)." *JAOS* 79:169-76.

1962 "The YQTL-QTL (QTL-YQTL) Sequence of Identical Verbs in Biblical Hebrew and in Ugaritic." *Studies and Essays in Honor of A. A. Neumann*. Ed. M. Ben-Horin, B. D. Weinryb and S. Zeitlin. Leiden: Brill for the Dropsie College, Philadelphia. 281-90.

1965a "The Action-Result (Factitive-Passive) Sequence of Identical Verbs in Biblical Hebrew and Ugaritic." *JBL* 84:272-82.

1965b "Studies in Comparative Semitic Lexicography." In *Studies in Honor of Benno Landsberger on his Seventy-Fifth Birthday April 21, 1965*. AS 16. Chicago: The Oriental Institute of the University of Chicago. 395-406.

1968 "The Root *ZBL*/*SBL* in Akkadian, Ugaritic and Biblical Hebrew." *JAOS* 88/1 (= Essays in Memory of E.A. Speiser. Ed. W.W. Hallo. American Oriental Series 53):90-96.

1969 "Rhetorical Questions in Ugaritic and Biblical Hebrew." *EI* 9 (W. F. Albright Volume):71-79.

1973 "Pits and Pitfalls in Akkadian and Biblical Hebrew." *JANES* 5 (T. H. Gaster Festschrift):173-90.

Hendel, R.

1985 "'The Flame of the Whirling Sword': A Note on Genesis 3:24." *JBL* 104:671-74.

Herdner, A.

1949 "Le Poème de Ras Shamra III AB, B." *Actes du XXIe Congrès international des orientalistes. Paris, 23-31 juillet 1948*. Paris: Société asiatique de Paris. 102-03.

Herrmann, G.

1968 "Lapis Lazuli: The Early Phases of Its Trade." *Iraq* 30:21-57.

Herrmann, W.

1969 "Aštart." *MIOF* 15:6-55.

Hess, R. S.

1991 "The Divine Name in Late Bronze Age Sources?" *UF* 23:181-88.

Hill, G. F.

1914 *Catalogue of Greek Coins of Palestine in the British Museum (Galilee, Samaria and Judea)*. London: British Museum.

Hillers, D. R.

1972 *Lamentations*. AB 7A. Garden City, NY: Doubleday.

1985 "Analyzing the Abominable: Our Understanding of Canaanite Religion." *JQR* 75:253-69.

Hoffner, H. A., Jr.

1965 "The Elkunirsa Myth Reconsidered." *RHA* 23/76:5-16.

1975 Hittite Mythological Texts: A Survey." *Unity and Diversity; Essays in the History, Literature, and Religion of the Ancient Near East*. Ed. H. Goedicke and J. J. M. Roberts. Baltimore/London: Johns Hopkins. 136-45.
1990 *Hittite Myths*. Ed. G. M. Beckman. SBL Writings from the Ancient World Series 2. Atlanta, GA: Scholars.

Höfner, M.
1936 "Zur Interpretation altsüdarabischer Inschriften II." *WZKM* 43:77-108.

Hoftijzer, J.
1972 "Two Notes on the Baal Cycle." *UF* 4:155-58.
1981 *A Search for Method. A Study in the Syntactic Use of H-Locale in Classical Hebrew*. Leiden: Brill.

Holladay, W. F.
1978 "A New Proposal for the Crux of Psalm II 12." *VT* 28:110-12.

Holmberg, M. S.
1946 *The God Ptah*. Lund: C. W. K. Gleerup.

Hornung, E.
1982 *Conceptions of God in Ancient Egypt; the One and the Many*. Trans. J. Baines. Ithaca, NY: Cornell University Press.

Horovitz, J., and L. Gardet
1978 "Kawthar." *The Encyclopaedia of Islam (New Edition). Volume IV*. Leiden: Brill. 805-06.

Horwitz, W. J.
1972 "Discrepancies in an Important Publication of Ugaritic." *UF* 4:47-52.
1973 "A Study of Ugaritic Scribal Practices and Prosody in CTA 2:4." *UF* 5:165-73.
1974 "Some Possible Results of Rudimentary Scribal Training." *UF* 6:75-83.
1977 "Our Ugaritic Mythological Texts: Copied or Dictated?" *UF* 9:123-30.
1979 "The Ugaritic Scribe." *UF* 11 (Festschrift für C.F.A. Schaeffer):389-94.

Hrushovski (Harshav), B.
1971 "Hebrew Prosody." *Enc Jud* 13:1195-1240.

Hruška, B.
1975 *Der Mythenadler Anzu im Literatur und Vorstellung des alten Mesopotamien*. Assyriologia 2. Budapest: [Eötrös Lo ránd Tudományegyetem].

Huehnergard, J.
1983 "Asseverative **la* and Hypothetical **lu/law* in Semitic." *JAOS* 103:569-93.
1987a "Three Notes on Akkadian Morphology." *"Working with No Data"; Semitic and Egyptian Studies Presented to Thomas O. Lambdin*. Ed. D. M. Golomb. Winona Lake, IN: Eisenbrauns. 181-93.
1987b *Ugaritic Vocabulary in Syllabic Transcription*. HSS 32. Atlanta: Scholars.

Huffmon, H.
1965 *Amorite Personal Names in the Mari Texts: A Structural and Lexical Study*. Baltimore/London: Johns Hopkins.

Hunt, N.
1991 "Mount Saphon in Myth and Fact." *Phoenicia in the Bible; Proceedings of the Conference held at the University of Leuven on the 15th and 16th of March 1990*. Ed. E. Lipiński. Leuven: Departement Oriëntalistiek/Utigeverij Peeters. 103-05.

Hurowitz, V.
1985 "The Priestly Account of Building the Tabernacle." *JAOS* 105:21-30.
1992 *I Have Built You an Exalted House; Temple Building in the Bible in the Light of Mesopotamian and Northwest Semitic Writings*. JSOTS 115. Sheffield: JSOT.

Hutter, M.
1985 *Altorientalische Vorstellungen von der Unterwelt. Literar- und religionsgeschichtliche Uberlegungen zu "Nergal und Ereškigal"*. Göttingen: Vandenhoeck & Ruprecht; Freiburg: Universitätsverlag.

Hvidberg, F. F.
1962 *Weeping and Laughter in the Old Testament; A Study of Canaanite-Israelite Religion*. Ed. F. Løkkegaard. Leiden: Brill; Copenhagen: Nyt Nordisk Forlag-A. Busck.
Hvidberg-Hansen, O.
1971 "Die Vernichtung des goldenen Kalbes und der ugaritische Ernteritus." *Acta Or* 33:5-46.
Ingholt, H., et al.
1955 *Recueil des tessères de Palymyre*. Paris: Geuthner.
Isaksson, B.
1987 *Studies in the Language of Qohelet With Special Emphasis on the Verbal System*. Studia Semitica Upsaliensia 10. Uppsala: Acta Universitatis Upsaliensis.
Jacobs, I.
1977 "Elements of Near-Eastern Mythology in Rabbinic Aggadah." *JJS* 28:1-11.
Jacobsen, T.
1943 "Primitive Democracy in Ancient Mesopotamia." *JNES* 2:159-72 (= *Towards the Image of Tammuz* 157-72).
1968 "The Battle between Marduk and Tiamat." *JAOS* 88:104-08.
1975 "Religious Drama in Ancient Mesopotamia." *Unity and Diversity; Essays in the History, Literature and Religion of the Ancient Near East*. Ed. H. Goedicke and J. J. M. Roberts. Baltimore/London: Johns Hopkins. 65-97.
1976 *The Treasures of Darkness; a History of Mesopotamian Religion*. New Haven/London: Yale University.
1984 *The Harab Myth*. Sources from the Ancient Near East 2/3. Malibu: Undena.
1987 *The Harps that once. . . : Sumerian Poetry in Translation*. New Haven/London: Yale University.
1988 "The Asakku in Lugal-e." *A Scientific Humanist; Studies in Memory of Abraham Sachs*. Ed. E. Leichty, M. de J. Ellis and P. Gerardi. Occasional Publications of the Samuel Noah Kramer Fund, 9. Philadelphia: The University Museum. 225-32.
Janowski, B.
1980 "Erwägungen zur Vorgeschichte des israelitischen *šᵉlāmîm*-Opfers." *UF* 12:231-59.
James, E. O.
1969 *Creation and Cosmology: A Historical and Comparative Inquiry*. Studies in the History of Religions XVI. Leiden: Brill.
Jamme, A.
1947 "Le Panthéon sub-arabe préislamique d'après les sources epigraphiques." *Le Muséon* 60:57-147.
1956 "La religion sud-arabe préislamiques." *Histoire des religions 4*. Publié sous la direction de M. Brillant and R. Aigrain. Paris: Bloud et Gay. 264-72.
Jason, H.
1977 *Ethnopoetry. Form, Content, Function*. Forum Theologicae Linguisticae 11. Bonn: Linguistica Biblica.
Jidejian, N.
1968 *Byblos Through the Ages*. Beirut: Dar el-Machreq Publishers.
Jirku, A.
1951 "Die Sprache der Gottheit in der Natur." *TLZ* 76:637.
1962 *Kanaanäische Mythen und Epen aus Ras Schamra-Ugarit*. Gütersloh: Gütersloher Verlaghaus Gerd Mohn.
1970 "Šnm (Schunama), der Sohn des Gottes 'Il." *ZAW* 82:278-79.

Joüon, P.
1991 *A Grammar of Biblical Hebrew*. Trans. and rev. T. Muraoka. 2 vols. Subsidia biblica 14/I and II. Rome: Editrice Pontificio Istituto Biblico.
Kaiser, O.
1959 *Die mythische Bedeutung des Meeres in Ägypten, Ugarit und Israel*. BZAW 78. Berlin: Töpelmann.
1974 *Isaiah 13-39; A Commentary*. OTL. Philadelphia: Westminster.
Kalluveettil, P.
1982 *Declaration and Covenant; A comprehensive Review of Covenant Formulae from the Old Testament and the Ancient Near East*. Rome: Pontifical Biblical Institute.
Kapelrud, A.
1952 *Baal in the Ras Shamra Texts*. Copenhagen: Gad.
1962 "Temple Building, a Task for Gods and Kings." *Or* 32:56-72.
1963 "Baal and Mot in the Ugaritic Texts." *IEJ* 13:127-29.
1979 "Ba^cal, Schopfung und Chaos." *UF* 11 (Festschrift für C.F.A. Schaeffer):407-12.
1980a "Creation in the Ras Shamra Texts." *Studia Theologica* 34:1-11.
1980b "The Relationship between El and Baal in the Ras Shamra Texts." *The Biblical World; Essays in Honor of Cyrus H. Gordon*. Ed. G. Rendsburg, R. Adler, M. Arfa and N. H. Winter. New York: KTAV. 79-85.
Kaplan, M. F.
1976 "Another Slaying of Tiamat?" *IEJ* 26:174-77.
Kaufman, S.
1974 *The Akkadian Influences on Aramaic*. Assyriological Studies 19. Chicago: University of Chicago.
1978-79 "The Structure of the Deuteronomic Law." *MAARAV* 1/2:105-58.
Keel, O.
1978 *The Symbolism of the Biblical World. Ancient Near Eastern Iconography and the Book of Psalms*. New York: Seabury.
1986 "Ancient Seals and the Bible." *JAOS* 106:307-11.
Kennedy, J. M.
1987 "The Root *G^cR* in the Light of Semantic Analysis." *JBL* 106:47-64.
Kinet, D.
1978 "Theologische Reflexion im ugaritischen Ba^cal-Zyklus." *BZ* 22:236-44.
1981 *Ugarit—Geschichte und Kultur einer Stadt in der Umwelt des Alten Testamentes*. Stuttgarter Bibelstudien 104. Stuttgart: Verlag Katholisches Bibelwerk GmbH.
King, P. J.
1988 *Amos, Hosea, Micah—An Archaeological Commentary*. Philadelphia: Westminster.
Kirk, G. S.
1970 *Myth; Its Meaning and Functions in Ancient and Other Cultures*. London: Cambridge University; Berkeley/Los Angeles: University of California.
Kitchen, K. A.
1962 *Suppiluliuma and the Amarna Pharaohs. A Study in Relative Chronology*. Liverpool Monographs in Archaeological and Oriental Studies 5. Liverpool: University Press.
1977 "The King List of Ugarit." *UF* 9:131-42.
1982 Review of J. Strange, *Caphtor/Keftiu; A New Investigation*, *PEQ* 114:155-56.
Kloos, C. J. L.
1982 "The Flood on Speaking Terms with God." *ZAW* 94:639-42.
1986 *Yhwh's Combat in the Sea; A Canaanite Tradition in the Religion of Ancient Israel*. Amsterdam: G.A. van Oorschot; Leiden: Brill.

Knudtzon, J. A.

1915 *Die El-Amarna-Tafeln*. Two vols. Leipzig: J. C. Hinrichs'sche Buchhandlung.

Koch, K.

1988 *Studien zur alttestamentlichen und altorientalischen Religionsgeschichte, Zum 60. Geburtstag von Klaus Koch*. Ed. E. Otto. Göttingen: Vandenhoeck & Ruprecht.

Komoróczy, G.

1973 "'The Separation of Sky and Earth'. The Cycle of Kumarbi and the Myths of Cosmogony in Mesopotamia." *Acta Antiqua Academiae Scientarum Hungaricae* 21:21-45.

Kopf, L.

1955 Review of I. Al-Yasin, *The Lexical Relationship between Ugaritic and Arabic*. *BO* 12:134-36.

Korpel, M. C. A. and J. C. de Moor

1986 Review of J. Day, *God's Conflict with the Dragon and the Sea*, *JSS* 31:243-45.

Kraemer, J. H. Gatje and M. Ullman, eds.

1960 *Wörterbuch der klassischen arabischen Sprache, Vol. K*. Wiesbaden: Harrassowitz.

Krahmalkov, C.

1970 "The Punic Speech of Hanno." *Or* 39:52-74.

Kramer, S. N.

1966 "Dumuzi's Annual Resurrection: An Important Correction to 'Inanna's Descent'." *BASOR* 183:31.

1972 *Sumerian Mythology; A Study of the Spiritual and Literary Achievement in the Third Millennium*. Rev. ed. Philadelphia: University of Pennsylvania.

1982 "BM 98396: A Sumerian Prototype of the Mater-Dolorosa." *EI* 16 (H. M. Orlinsky Volume):141*-46*.

1983 "The Weeping Goddess: Sumerian Prototypes of the Mater Dolorosa." *BA* 46:69-80.

Krebernik, M.

1983 "Zur Syllabar und Orthographie des lexikalischen Texte aus Ebla. Teil 2 (Glossar)." *ZA* 73:1-47.

Kreuzer, S.

1985 "Zur Bedeutung und Etymologie von *HIŠTAḤ*^{A}*WĀH/YŠTḤWY*." *VT* 35:39-60.

Kristensen, A. L.

1977 "Ugaritic Epistolary Formulas: A Comparative Study of the Ugaritic Epistolary Formulas in the Context of Contemporary Akkadian Formulas in the Letters from Ugarit and Amarna." *UF* 9:143-58.

Krotkoff, G.

1969 "*laḥm* 'Fleisch' und *lehem* 'Brot'." *WZKM* 62:76-82.

Kruger, P. A.

1989 "On non-verbal communication in the Baal epic." *Tydskrif vir Semitistiek/Journal for Semitics* 1/1:54-69.

Kutler, L. B.

1987 "Features of the Battle Challenge in Biblical Hebrew, Akkadian and Ugaritic." *UF* 19:95-99.

Lahiri, A. K.

1984 *Vedic Vrtra*. Dehli: Motital Banarsidass.

Lambdin, T. O.

1971 *Introduction to Biblical Hebrew*. New York: Scribner's.

Lambert, W. G.

1960a *Babylonian Wisdom Literature*. Oxford: Clarendon.

1960b "The Domesticated Camel in the Second Millennium—Evidence from Alalakh and Ugarit." *BASOR* 160:42-43.

1964 "The Reign of Nebuchadnezzar I: A Turning Point in the History of Ancient Mesopotamian Religion." *The Seed of Wisdom: Essays in Honor of T. J. Meek*. Ed. W. S. Cullough. Toronto: University of Toronto. 3-13.
1965 "A New Look at the Babylonian Background of Genesis." *Journal of Theological Studies* 16:287-300.
1968a "Literary Style in First Millennium Mesopotamia." *JAOS* 88 (E. A. Speiser Memorial Volume. Ed. W. W. Hallo. American Oriental Series 53):123-32.
1968b "Myth and Ritual as Conceived by the Babylonians." *JSS* 13:104-12.
1975a "The Cosmology of Sumer and Babylon." *Ancient Cosmologies*. Ed. C. Blacker and M. Loewe. London: George Allen & Unwin Ltd. 42-62.
1975b "The Historical Development of the Mesopotamian Pantheon: A Study in Sophisticated Polytheism." *Unity and Diversity; Essays in the History, Literature and Religion of the Ancient Near East*. Ed. H. Goedicke and J. J. M. Roberts. Baltimore/London. 191-200.
1977 "Zum Forschungsstand der Sumerisch-Babylonischen Literatur-Geschichte." *ZDMG Supplement III XIX. Deutscher Orientalischentag von 28. September bis 4. Oktober 1975 in Freiburg im Breisgau*. Ed. W. Voigt. Wiesbaden: Franz Steiner Verlag GmbH. 64-73.
1980a "New Fragments of Babylonian Epics." *AfO* 27:71-82.
1980b "The Theology of Death." *Death in Mesopotamia; Papers read at the XXVI[e] Rencontre Assyriologique internationale*. Ed. B. Alster. Mesopotamia. Copenhagen Studies in Assyriology 8. Kopenhagen: Akademisk forlag. 3-66.
1982 "Interchange of Ideas between Southern Mesopotamia and Syria-Palestine as Seen in Literature." *Mesopotamien und seine Nachbaren*. Ed. H. Kuhne, H. J. Nissen and J. Rengler. Berliner Beitrage zum Vorderen Orient 1/1. Berlin: Dietrich Reimer. 311-15.
1985a "The Pantheon of Mari." *MARI* 4:525-38.
1985b "Trees, Snakes and Gods in Ancient Syria and Anatolia." *BSOAS* 48:435-51.
1986 "Ninurta Mythology in the Babylonian Epic of Creation." *Keilschriftliche Literaturen*. Ed. K. Hecker and W. Sommerfeld. XXII Rencontre Assyriologique. Berliner Beitrage zum Vorderen Orient 6. Berlin: Dietrich Reimer. 55-60.
1988 "Old Testament Mythology in its Ancient Near Eastern Context." *Congress Volume; Jerusalem 1986*. Ed. J. A. Emerton. SVT 40. Leiden: Brill. 126-43.

Lambert, W. G., and A. R. Millard
1965 *Cuneiform Texts from Babylonian Tablets, Part XLVI*. London: Trustees of the British Museum.

Lambert, W. G., and P. Walcot
1965 "A New Babylonian Theogony and Hesiod." *Kadmos* 4:64-72.

Lambrechts, P.
1952 "Les fêtes phrygiennes de Cybèle et d'Attis." *Bulletin de l'Institut belge de Rom* 27:141-70.
1955 "La resurrection d'Adonis." *Annuaire de l'Institut de philologie et d'histoire orientales et slaves* 13:207-40.
1967 *Attis, van herdersknaap tot god*. Amsterdam: Noord-Hollandische Uitg. Mij.

Laroche, E.
1968 "Notes sur le Panthéon hourrite de Ras Shamra." *JAOS* 88:148-50.
1975 Review of H. Klengel, *Keilschrifturkunden aus Boghazköi, Heft XLIV*, *RHA* 33:63-64.

Layton, S. C.
1983 "'Head on Lap' in Sumero-Akkadian Literature." *JANES* 15:59-62.
1986 "Biblical Hebrew 'To Set the Face,' in Light of Akkadian and Ugaritic." *UF* 16:169-81.

1990 *Archaic Features of Canaanite Personal Names in the Hebrew Bible*. HSM 47. Atlanta: Scholars.
Leclant, J.
1960 "Astarté à cheval d'aprés les représentations égyptiennes." *Syria* 37:1-67.
Leslau, W.
1966 "The Origin of Geez *ʿAwadi* 'Herald'." *JSS* 11:226-27.
Levenson, J.D.
1988 *Creation and the Persistence of Evil; The Jewish Drama of Divine Omnipotence*. San Francisco: Harper & Row.
Levine, B.A.
1963 "Ugaritic Descriptive Rituals." *JCS* 17:105-11.
1974 *In the Presence of the Lord; A Study of Cult and Some Cultic Terms in Ancient Israel*. Studies in Judaism in Late Antiquity 5. Leiden: Brill.
Levine, B.A. and J.M. de Tarragon
1984 "Dead Kings and Rephaim: the Patrons of the Ugaritic Dynasty." *JAOS* 104:649-59.
Lewis, T. J.
1989 *Cults of the Dead in Ancient Israel and Ugarit*. HSM 39. Atlanta, GA: Scholars.
1991 "The Ancestral Estate (נַחֲלַת אֱלֹהִים) in 2 Samuel 14:16." *JBL* 110:597-612.
L'Heureux, C.E.
1979 *Rank Among the Canaanite Gods. El, Baʿal, and the Rephaʾim*. HSM 21. Missoula, MT: Scholars.
Lichtenstein, M.
1968-69 "The Banquet Motifs in Keret and Proverbs 9." *JANES* 1/1:19-31.
1972 "Psalm 68:7 Revisited." *JANES* 4/2:97-112.
1979 "Episodic Structure in the Ugaritic Keret Legend: Comparative Studies in Compositional Technique." Ph.D. diss., Columbia University.
Lichtheim, M.
1973 *Ancient Egyptian Literature. Volume I: The Old and Middle Kingdom*. Berkeley/Los Angeles/London: University of California.
1976 *Ancient Egyptian Literature. Volume II: The New Kingdom*. Berkeley/Los Angeles/London: University of California.
1980 *Ancient Egyptian Literature. Volume III: The Late Period*. Berkeley/Los Angeles/London: University of California.
Lipiński, E.
1967 "Recherches Ugaritiques." *Syria* 44:253-82.
1970 "Banquet en l'honneur de Baal: CTA 3 (V AB), A, 4-22." *UF* 2:75-88.
1971 "El's Abode. Mythological Traditions related to Mt. Hermon and the Mountains of Armenia." *OLP* 2:13-69.
1978 "Ditanu." *Studies in the Bible and the Ancient Near East Presented to Samuel E. Loewenstamm*. Ed Y. Avishur and J. Blau. 2 vols. Jerusalem: E. Rubinstein's Publishing House. 1.91-98-110.
1983 "The 'Phoenician History' of Philo of Byblos." *BiOr* 40:305-10.
Livingstone, A.
1986 *Mystical and Mythological Explanatory Works of Assyrian and Babylonian Scholars*. Oxford: Clarendon.
1989 *Court Poetry and Literary Miscellanea*. State Archives of Assyria III. Helsinki: Helsinki University Press.
Loewenstamm, S.E.
1959 "The Muzzling of the Tannin in Ugaritic Mythology." *IEJ* 9:260-61 = *CS* 91-92.
1962 "The Ugaritic Fertility Myth—the Result of a Mistranslation." *IEJ* 12:87-88 = *CS* 160-61.

1969a "The Numerals in Ugaritic." *Proceedings of the International Conference on Semitic Studies held in Jerusalem, 19-23 July 1965*. Jerusalem: The Israel Academy of Sciences and Humanities. 172-79.
1969b "Remarks upon the Infinitive Absolute in Ugaritic and Phoenician." *JANES* 2/1:53.
1971 "Grenzgebiete Ugaritischer Sprach- und Stilvergleichung." *UF* 3:93-100.
1972 "The Killing of Mot in the Ugaritic Text." *Or* 41:378-82 = *CS* 426-32.
1973 "Lexicographical Notes on 1. *ṭbḫ*; 2. *hnny/hlny*." *UF* 5:209-11 = *CS* 449-58.
1975 "Anat's Victory over Tunnanu." *JSS* 20:22-27 = *CS* 465-70.
1978 "The Ugaritic Myth of the Sea and its Biblical Counterparts." *EI* 14: 96-101 = *CS* 346-61.

Loretz, O.
1976 "Der kanaanäische Mythos vom Sturz des Šaḥar-Sohnes Hêlel (Jes. 14, 12-15)." *UF* 8:133-36.
1980 "Vom Baal-Epitheton *adn* zu Adonis und Adonij." *UF* 12:287-92.

Lucas, A.
1948 *Ancient Egyptian Materials & Industries*. Third ed. London: Edward Arnold.

Luft, U.
1978 *Beiträge zur Historisierung der Götterwelt und der Mythenschreibung*. Az eötvös loránd tudományegyetem ókori történeti tanszékeinek kiadványai 22. Studia Aegyptiaca IV. Budapest: n.p.

MacDonald, J.
1979 "An Assembly at Ugarit?" *UF* 11 (Festschrift für C.F.A. Schaeffer): 515-26.

Macintosh, A. A.
1969 "A Consideration of Hebrew נער." *VT* 19:471-79.

Mack-Fisher, L. (see Fisher, L.)

Majidzadeh, Y.
1982 "Lapis Lazuli and the Great Khorasan Road." *Paléorient* 8/1:59-69.

Malamat, A.
1965 "Campaigns to the Mediterranean by Iahdunlim and Early Mesopotamian Rulers." *Studies in Honor of Benno Landsberger on his Seventy-fifth Birthday April 21, 1965*. Assyriological Studies 16. Chicago: University of Chicago. 367-73.
1987 "'ʾlhwtw šl hym htykwn ktqst prg-ʾwgryty" ("The God of the Mediterranean Sea in a pre-Ugaritic text"). *Mhqrym bmqrʾ: ywsʾym lʾwr bmlʾt mʾh šnh lhwdldtw šl m"d qʾswtw* (*Researches in the Bible: . . . the Hundredth Birthday of M.D. Cassuto*). Jerusalem: Magnes. 184-88.
1992 "The Divine Nature of the Mediterranean Sea in the Foundation Inscription of Yahdunlim." *Mari in Retrospect: Fifty Years of Mari and Mari Studies*. Ed. G. D. Young. Winona Lake, IN: Eisenbrauns. 211-15.

Mallon, E. D.
1982 "The Ugaritic Verb in the Letters and Administrative Documents." Ph.D. diss., The Catholic University of America, Washington, D. C.

Mann, T.
1971 "The Pillar of Cloud in the Red Sea Narrative." *JBL* 90:15-30.
1977 *Divine Presence and Guidance in Israelite Traditions: The Typology of Exaltation*. Baltimore/London: Johns Hopkins.

Marcus, D.
1968 "The Three Alephs in Ugaritic." *JANES* 1:50-60.
1969a "The Stative and the Waw Consecutive." *JANES* 2/1:37-40.
1969b "Studies in Ugaritic Grammar I." *JANES* 1/2:55-61.
1970a "Aspects of the Ugaritic Verb in the Light of Comparative Semitic Grammar." Ph.D. diss., Columbia University, New York City.

1970b Review of A. S. Kapelrud, *The Violent Goddess; Anat in the Ras Shamra Texts*. *JANES* 2/1:111-14.
1972 "The Verb 'To Live' in Ugaritic." *JSS* 17:76-82.
1973 Review of J. C. de Moor, *New Year with Canaanites and Israelites*. *JAOS* 93:589-91.
1978 "Ugaritic *BN YDM*: 'Chest' or 'Back'." *Studies in Bible and the Ancient Near East Presented to Samuel E. Loewenstamm*. Ed. Y. Avishur and J. Blau. 2 vols. Jerusalem: E. Rubinstein's Publishing House. 1.111-17
1990 "'Lifting up the Head': On the Trail of a Word Play in Genesis 40." *Prooftexts* 10:17-27.

Margalit (Margulis), B.
1979 "Alliteration in Ugaritic Poetry: Its Rôle in Composition and Analysis." *UF* 11 (Festschrift für C.F.A. Schaeffer):537-57.
1980 *A Matter of ›Life‹ and ›Death‹: A Study of the Baal-Mot Epic (CTA 4-5-6)*. AOAT 206. Kevelaer: Verlag Butzon & Bercker; Neukirchen-Vluyn: Neukirchener Verlag.
1981 "The Ugaritic Creation Myth: Fact or Fiction?" *UF* 13:137-45.

Margulis, B. (see Margalit, B.)

Massart, A.
1954 *The Leiden Magical Papyrus I 343 + I 345*. Leiden: Brill.

Mastin, B. A.
1980 "Jonathan at the Feast. A Note on the Text of I Sam. 20:25." *VT* 30:113-24.

Matouš, L.
1961 "Zur Dattierung von Enuma Elish." *Archiv Orientální* 29:30-34.

Mazar, A.
1992 "The Iron Age I." *The Archaeology of Ancient Israel*. Ed. A. Ben-Tor. Trans. R. Greenberg. New Haven, CT: Yale. 258-301.

McCarter, P. K., Jr.
1973 "The River Ordeal in Israelite Literature." *HTR* 66:403-12.
1980 "The Balaam Texts from Deir ʿAlla: The First Combination," *BASOR* 239:49-60.
1984 *II Samuel*. AB 9. Garden City, NY: Doubleday.

McCarthy, D. J.
1967 "'Creation' Motifs in Ancient Hebrew Poetry." *CBQ* 29:393-406.

McGovern, P. E. and R. H. Michael
1984 "Royal Purple and the Pre-Phoenician Dye Industry of Lebanon." *MASCA Journal* 3/3:67-70.

McKay, J. W.
1970 "Helal and the Dawn-Goddess: A Re-examination of the Myth in Isaiah XIV 12-15." *VT* 20:454-64.

McLaughlin, J. L.
1991 "The *marzeah* at Ugarit. A Textual and Contextual Study." *UF* 23:265-81.

Meier, S.
1986 "Baal's Fight with Yam (KTU 1.2.I, IV). A Part of the Baal Myth as Known in KTU 1.1, 3-6?" *UF* 18:241-54.
1989 *The Messenger in the Ancient Semitic World*. HSM 45. Atlanta: Scholars.

Melamed, E. Z.
1961 "Break-up of Stereotype Phrases as an Artistic Device in Biblical Poetry." *Studies in the Bible*. Ed. C. Rabin. Scripta Hierosolymitana VIII. Jerusalem: Magnes. 115-53.

Mendenhall, G.E.
1973 *The Tenth Generation; the Origins of the Biblical Tradition*. Baltimore/London: Johns Hopkins.

1992 "Thc Amoritc Migrations." *Mari in Retrospect; Fifty Years of Mari and Mari Studies*. Ed. G. D. Young. Winona Lake, IN: Eisenbrauns. 233-41.
du Mesnil du Buisson, R.
1945-48 "ᶜAshtart et ᶜAshtar à Ras-Shamra." *JEOL* 10:406.
Mettinger, T. N. D.
1976 *King and Messiah; The Civil and Sacral Legitimization of the Israelite Kings*. Coniectanea Biblica, Old Testament Series 8. Lund: C. W. K. Gleerup.
1988 *In Search of God; The Meaning and Message of the Everlasting Names*. Trans. F. H. Cryer. Philadelphia: Fortress.
1990 "The Elusive Essence; YHWH, El and Baal and the Distinctiveness of Israelite Faith." *Die Hebräische Bibel und ihre zweifache Nachgeschichte; Festschrift für Rolf Rendtorff zum 65. Geburstag*. Ed. E. Blum, C. Macholz and E. W. Stegemann. Neukirchen-Vluyn: Neukirchener Verlag. 393-417.
Millard, A.
1974 Review of J. J. M. Roberts, *The Earliest Semitic Pantheon*, *JSS* 19:87-90.
1975 "עלץ 'To Exult'." *JTS* 26:87-89.
1984 "The Meaning of Eden." *VT* 34:103-06.
1990 "The Homeland of Zakkur." *Semitica* 39:47-52
Miller, P. D.
1965 "Fire in the Mythology of Canaan and Israel." *CBQ* 27:256-61.
1967 "El the Warrior." *HTR* 60:411-31.
1970 "Animal Names as Designations in Ugaritic and Hebrew." *UF* 2:177-86.
1980 "El, the Creator of the Earth." *BASOR* 239:43-46.
1981 "Ugarit and the History of Religions." *JNWSL* 9:119-28. Repr. with little change as "Aspects of the Religion of Ugarit." *Ancient Israelite Religion; Essays in Honor of Frank Moore Cross*. Ed. P. D. Miller, Jr., P. D. Hanson and S. D. McBride; Philadelphia: Fortress, 1988. 55-66.
1985 "Eridu, Dunnu, and Babel: A Study in Comparative Mythology." *Hebrew Annual Review* 9 (Biblical and Other Studies in memory of S. D. Goitein):227-51.
Milne, P. J.
1988 *Vladimir Propp and the Study of the Structure in Hebrew Biblical Narrative*. Bible and Literature Series, 13. Sheffield: Sheffield Academic Press.
del Monte, G. F. and J. Tischler
1978 *Répertoire Géographique des Textes Cunéiformes VI; Die Orts- und Gewässernamen der hethischen Texte*. Wiesbaden: Dr. Ludwig Reichert Verlag.
Montgomery, J. A.
1933 "Notes on the Mythological Epic Texts from Ras Shamra." *JAOS* 53:97-123, 283-84.
1935 "Ras Shamra Notes IV: The Conflict of Baal and the Waters." *JAOS* 55:268-77.
de Moor, J. C.
1965 "Frustula Ugaritica," *JNES* 24:355-64.
1968 "*Rapiʾuma*—Rephaim." *ZAW* 88:323-45.
1969 "Studies in the New Alphabetic Texts from Ras Shamra I." *UF* 1:167-88.
1970a "B. Margulis on RS 24.258." *UF* 2:347-50.
1970b "The Peace-offering in Ugarit and Israel." *Schrift en Uitleg*. Kampen: J.H. Kok. 112-17.
1971 "The Semitic Pantheon of Ugarit." *UF* 3:187-228.
1972 *New Year with Canaanites and Israelites. Pts. I and II*. Kamper Cahiers 21 and 22. Kampen: J. H. Kok.
1973 "Ugaritic Lexicography." *Quaderni di Semitistica* 2:61-102.
1975 "*ʾar* 'Honey-Dew'." *UF* 7:590-91.

1979 "Contributions to the Ugaritic Lexicon." *UF* 11 (Festschrift für C.F.A. Schaeffer):639-53.
1980a "The Anatomy of the Back." *UF* 12:425-26.
1980b "El, the Creator." *The Biblical World; Essays in Honor of Cyrus H. Gordon.* Ed. G. Rendsburg, R. Adler, M. Arfa and N. H. Winter. New York: KTAV. 171-87.
1981 "Donkey-Packs and Geology." *UF* 13: 303-04.
1984 "More on Demons in Ugarit (KTU 1.82)." *UF* 16:237-50.
1986 "Ugaritic Lexicographical Notes I." *UF* 18:255-61.
1987 *An Anthology of Religious Texts from Ugarit.* Nisaba 16. Leiden: Brill.
1990 *The Rise of Yahwism; the Roots of Israelite Monotheism.* Bibliotheca Ephemeridum Theologicarum Lovaniensium XCI. Leuven: University Press/Uitgeverij Peeters.

de Moor, J. C. and K. Spronk
1982 "Problematical Passages in the Legend of Kirtu (II)." *UF* 14:173-90.

de Moor, J. C. and P. van der Lugt
1974 "The Spectre of Pan-Ugaritism." *BO* 31:3-26.

Moran, W. L.
1958 "Gen 49:10 and its Use in Ez 21:32." *Bib* 39:405-25.
1961 "The Hebrew Language in its Northwest Semitic Background." *The Bible and the Ancient Near East; Essays in honor of William Foxwell Albright.* Ed. G. E. Wright. Garden City, NY: Doubleday. 54-72.
1970 "The Creation of Man in Atrahasis I 192-248." *BASOR* 200:48-56.
1992 *The Amarna Letters.* Baltimore/London: Johns Hopkins. (Translation and revision of Moran, *Les lettres d'El-Amarna.* Trans. D. Collon and H. Cazelles. LAPO 13. Paris: Les Éditions du Cerf, 1987).

Morgenstern, J.
1941 "Psalm 48." *HUCA* 16:1-95.

Mosca, P.
1986 "Ugarit and Daniel 7: A Missing Link." *Bib* 67:496-517.

Mowinckel, S.
1962 *The Psalms in Israel's Worship.* Two vols. Trans. D. R. Ap-Thomas. Oxford: Basil Blackwell. Repr. as The Biblical Seminar no. 14; Sheffield: JSOT, 1992.

Mulder, M. J.
1972 "Hat man in Ugarit die Sonnenwende begangen?" *UF* 4:79-96.

Mullen, E. T.
1980 *The Assembly of the Gods. The Divine Council in Canaanite and Early Hebrew Literature.* HSM 24. Chico, CA: Scholars.

Müller, H. P.
1970 "Notizen zu althbräischen Inschriften I." *UF* 2:229-42.

Muntingh, L. M.
1984 "The Conception of Ancient Syro-Palestinian Kingship in the Light of Contemporary Royal Archives with Special Reference to the Recent Discoveries at Tell Mardikh (Ebla) in Syria." *Monarchies and Socio-Religious Traditions in the Ancient Near East (Papers read at the 31st International Congress of Human Sciences in Asia and North Africa).* Ed. H. I. H. Prince Takahito Mikasa. Wiesbaden: Harrassowitz. 1-10.

Muraoka, T.
1985 *Emphatic Words and Structures in Biblical Hebrew.* Jerusalem: Magnes; Leiden: Brill.

Murtonen, A.
1952 *A Philological and Literary Treatise on the Old Testament Divine Names* אל,אלוה,אלהים, and יהוה. Studia Orientalia 18:1. Helsinki: Societas Orientalis Fennica.

von Mutius, H. G.
1981 "Die Bezeugung einer aussertiberiensischen Punktationsform in Ps 2,12 durch mittelalterliche judische Gelehrte." *BZ* 15:44-45.
Nakata, I.
1968 "Problems of the Babylonian Akītu Festival." *JANES* 1/1:41-49.
Nash, K. S.
1989 "The Palestinian Agricultural Year and the Book of Joel." Ph.D. diss, The Catholic University of America, Washington, D. C.
Naveh, J.
1979 "A Nabatean Incantation Text." *IEJ* 29:111-19.
Naveh, J., and S. Shaked
1985 *Amulets and Magic Bowls; Aramaic Incantations of Late Antiquity*. Jerusalem: Magnes; Leiden: Brill.
Neuberg, F. J.
1950 "Ugaritic and the Book of Isaiah." Ph.D. diss., The Johns Hopkins University, Baltimore, MD.
Neumann, E.
1970 *The Origins and History of Consciousness*. Bollingen Series XLII. Princeton: Princeton University.
Newsom, C.
1985 *The Songs of the Sabbath Sacrifice: A Critical Edition*. HSS 27. Atlanta, GA: Scholars.
Niehr, H.
1992 "Ein umstrittenes Detail der El-Stele aus Ugarit." *UF* 24:293-300.
Nims, C. F., and R. C. Steiner
1983 "A Paganized Version of Psalm 20:2-6 from the Aramaic Text in Demotic Script." *JAOS* 103 (S. N. Framer Festschrift):261-74.
North, R.
1973 "Ugarit Grid, Strata and Find Localizations." *ZDPV* 89:113-60.
Obermann, J.
1946 "Sentence Negation in Ugaritic." *JBL* 65:233-48.
1947 "How Baal Destroyed a Rival. A Magical Incantation Scene." *JAOS* 67:195-208.
O'Callaghan, R. T.
1952 "The Word *ktp* in Ugaritic and Egypto-Canaanite Mythology." *Or* 21:37-46.
Oden, R. A., Jr.
1977 *Studies in Lucian's De Syria Dea*. HSM 15. Missoula, MT: Scholars.
1987 *The Bible Without Theology; The Theological Tradition and Alternatives To It*. San Francisco: Harper & Row.
O'Flaherty, W.
1981 *The Rig Veda; An Anthology*. Middlesex: Penguin.
Oldenburg, U.
1970 "Above the Stars of El. El in Ancient South Arabic Religion." *ZAW* 82:187-208.
Olley, J. W.
1976 "A Forensic Connoṭation of *bôš*." *VT* 26:230-34.
del Olmo Lete, G.
1977 "Notes on Ugaritic Semantics III." *UF* 9:31-46.
1978 "Notes on Ugaritic Semantics IV." *UF* 10:37-46.
1982 "Notes on Ugaritic Semantics V." *UF* 14:55-69.
1983 "Athiratu's Entreaty and the Order of the Ugaritic Tablets KTU 1.2/3." *AO* 1:67-71.

1984 *Interpretación de la Mitología Cananea; Estudios de Semántica Ugarítica*. Valencia: Institución San Jerónimo.

del Olmo Lete, G. and J. Sanmartín

1988 "A New Ugaritic Dictionary. Its Lexicographical and Semantic Structure." *AO* 6:255-74.

Olyan, S. M.

1988 *Asherah and the Cult of Yahweh*. SBLMS 34. Atlanta: Scholars.

Oppenheim, L.

1936 "Arrapḫäisch mala = 'Hälfte'." *AfO* 11:237-39.

Otten, H.

1958 "Keilschriftexte." *MDOG* 91:73-84.

Pardee, D.

1973 "A Note on the Root ʿ*tq* in CTA 16. I 2, 5 (*UT* 125, KRT 125)." *UF* 5:229-54.

1974 "The Ugaritic Text 147 (90)." *UF* 6:275-82.

1975 "The Preposition in Ugaritic." *UF* 7:329-78.

1976 "The Preposition in Ugaritic." *UF* 8:215-322.

1977 "A New Ugaritic Letter." *BO* 34:3-20.

1978a "*Yp*ḥ 'Witness' in Hebrew and Ugaritic." *VT* 28:204-13.

1978b "A Philological and Prosodic Analysis of the Ugaritic Serpent Incantation." *JANES* 10:73-108.

1980 "The New Canaanite Myths and Legends." *BO* 37:269-91.

1981a "Ugaritic and Hebrew Metrics." *Ugarit in Retrospect; Fifty Years of Ugarit and Ugaritic*. Ed. G. D. Young. Winona Lake, IN: Eisenbrauns. 113-30.

1981b "Visiting Ditanu—The Text of RS 24.272." *UF* 15:127-40.

1984 "Will the Dragon Never Be Muzzled?" *UF* 16:251-55.

1986 Review of E. T. Mullen, *The Assembly of the Gods: The Divine Council in Canaanite and Early Hebrew Literature*; B. Halpern, *The Constitution of the Monarchy in Israel*; R. E. Friedman, *Exile and Biblical Narrative*; R. E. Friedman, ed., *The Creation of Sacred Literature*. *JNES* 45:64-67.

1987a "'As Strong as Death.'" *Love and Death in the Ancient Near East: Essays in Honor of Marvin H. Pope*. Ed. J. Marks and R.M. Good. Guilford, CT: Four Quarters. 65-69.

1987b "Epigraphic and Philological Notes." *UF* 19:199-217.

1987c "Ugaritic Bibliography." *AfO* 34:366-471.

1988a "A New Datum for the Meaning of the Divine Name Milkashtart." *Ascribe to the Lord; Biblical & other studies in memory of Peter C. Craigie*. Ed. L. Eslinger & G. Taylor. JSOTSup 67. Sheffield: JSOT. 55-67.

1988b *Les textes para-mythologiques de la campagne (1961)*. Ras Shamra-Ougarit IV. Éditions Recherche sur les Civilizations, Mémoire no. 77. Paris: Éditions Recherche sur les Civilizations.

1988c "*Tukamuna wa Sunama*." *UF* 20:195-200.

1988d *Ugaritic and Hebrew Poetic Parallelism; A Trial Cut (*ʿ*nt* I and Proverbs 2). SVT 39. Leiden: Brill.

1989-90a Review of J. C. de Moor, *An Anthology of Religious Texts from Ugarit*, *AfO* 37-37:177-79.

1989-90b "Ugaritic Proper Names." *AfO* 36-37:390-513.

Pardee, D., and R. M. Whiting

1987 "Aspects of epistolary verbal usage in Ugaritic and Akkadian." *BSOAS* 50:1-31.

Parker, S. B.

1977 "The Historical Composition of *KRT* and the Cult of El." *ZAW* 89:161-75.

1989a "KTU 1.16 III, the Myth of the Absent God and 1 Kings 18." *UF* 21:283-96.

1989b *The Pre-biblical Narrative Tradition; Essays on the Ugaritic Poems Keret* and *Aqhat*. SBL Resources for Biblical Study 24. Atlanta, GA: Scholars.
1990a Review of D. Pardee, *Ugaritic and Hebrew Poetic Parallelism*. *JBL* 109:503-04.
1990b "Toward Literary Translation of Ugaritic Poetry." *UF* 22:257-70.
1992 "Middle Eastern Religions." *Encyclopaedia Brittanica Volume M*:111-15

Paul, S.
1968 "Cuneiform Light on Jer 9,20." *Bib* 49:373-76.
1980 "Adoption Formulae: A Study of Cuneiform and Biblical Legal Clauses." *MAARAV* 2/2:173-85.

Perlman, A. L.
1978 "Asherah and Astarte in the Old Testament." Ph.D. diss., Graduate Theological Union, Berkeley, CA.

Petersen, D. L., and M. Woodward
1977 "Northwest Semitic Religion: A Study of Relational Structures." *UF* 9:237-43.

Pettinato, G.
1979 *Culto ufficiale ad Ebla durante il regno di Ibbi-Sipis*. Orientis Antiqui Collectio - XV. Rome: Instituto per l'oriente/Centro per le Antichità e la Storia dell'arte del vicino oriente.
1980 "Pre-Ugaritic Documentation of Ba^{c}al." *The Biblical World; Essays in Honor of Cyrus H. Gordon*. Ed. G. Rendsburg, R. Adler, M. Arfa and N. H. Winter. New York: KTAV. 203-09.

Piamenta, M.
1991 *Dictionary of Post-Classical Yemeni Arabic*. Two vols. Leiden: Brill.

Pitard, W.
1987 "RS 34.126: Notes on the Text." *MAARAV* 4/1:75-86.

Plumley, J. M.
1975 "The Cosmology of Ancient Egypt." *Ancient Cosmologies*. Ed. C. Blacker and M. Loewe. London: George Allen & Unwin Ltd. 17-41.

Pomponio, F.
1983 "I nomi divini nei testi di Ebla." *UF* 15:141-56.

Pope, M. H.
1952 Review of U. Cassuto, *The Goddess Anath* (Heb.), *JCS* 6:133-36.
1966 "Marginalia to M. Dahood's Ugaritic-Hebrew Philology." *JBL* 85:455-66
1971 "The Scene on the Drinking Mug from Ugarit." *Near Eastern Studies in Honor of William Foxwell Albright*. Ed. H. Goedicke. Baltimore/London: Johns Hopkins. 393-405.
1972 "A Divine Banquet at Ugarit." *The Use of the Old Testament in the New and Other Essays: Studies in Honor of W. F. Stinespring*. Ed. J. M. Efird. Chapel Hill, NC: Duke University. 170-203.
1973 *Job*. AB 15. Garden City, NY: Doubleday.
1977a "Notes on the Ugaritic Rephaim Texts." *Essays on the Ancient Near in Memory of Jacob Joel Finkelstein*. Ed. M. de Jong Ellis. Memoirs of the Connecticut Academy of Arts & Sciences 19. Hamden, CT: Archon Books. 163-82.
1977b *Song of Songs*. AB 7C. New York: Doubleday.
1978 "A Little Soul-Searching." *MAARAV* 1/1:25-31.
1981 "The Cult of the Dead at Ugarit." *Ugarit in Retrospect. Fifty Years of Ugarit and Ugaritic*. Ed. G.D. Young. Winona Lake, IN: Eisenbrauns. 159-79.
1986 "The Timing of the Snagging of the Ram, Genesis 22:13." *BA* 49:115-17.
1989 "The Status of El at Ugarit." *UF* 19:219-30.

Porten, B.
1968 *Archives from Elephantine*. Berkeley/Los Angeles: University of California.

Posener, G.

1953 "La legende egyptienne de la mer insatiable." *Annuaire de l'Institut de Philologie et d'Histoire orientales et slaves* 13:461-78.

Provan, I.

1990 "Feasts, Booths and Gardens (Thr 2,6a)." *ZAW* 102:254-55.

1991 "Past, Present and Future in Lamentations III 52-66: The Case for a Precative Perfect Re-examined." *VT* 41:164-75.

Rabin, C.

1955 "Hebrew *D* = 'Hand'." *JJS* 6:111-15.

1961 "Etymological Miscellanea." *Studies in the Bible*. Ed. C. Rabin. Scripta Hierosolymitana VIII. Jerusalem: Magnes. 384-400.

1963 "Hittite Words in Hebrew." *Or* 32:113-39.

1977 "Hamitic Languages as a Source of Semitic Etymologies." *Proceedings of the Sixth World Congress of Jewish Studies; held at the Hebrew University of Jerusalem 13-19 August 1973 under the auspices of the Israel Academy of Sciences and Humanities*. Volumc I. Division A. Ed. A. Shinan. Jerusalem: World Union of Jewish Studies. 329-40.

Rainey, A.

1962 "The Social Stratification of Ugarit." Ph.D. diss., Brandeis University, Waltham, MA.

1969 "The Scribe at Ugarit: His Position and Influence." *Proceedings of the Israel Academy of Sciences and Humanities (Jerusalem)* 3:126-47.

1971 "Observations on Ugaritic Grammar." *UF* 3:151-72.

1973 "Gleanings from Ugarit." *IOS* 3:34-62.

1974 "El-ᶜAmârna Notes." *UF* 6:295-312.

1986 "The Ancient Hebrew Prefix Conjugation in the Light of Amarnah Canaanite." *Hebrew Studies* 27:4-19.

Recanati, F.

1987 *Meaning and Force; The Pragmatics of Performative Utterances*. Cambridge Studies in Philosophy. Cambridge: Cambridge University.

Redford, D. B.

1973 "New Light on the Asiatic Campaign of Horemheb." *BASOR* 211:36-49.

1990 "The Sea and the Goddess." *Studies in Egyptology Presented to Miriam Lichtheim*. Volume II. Ed. S. Israelit-Groll. Jerusalem: Magnes. 824-35.

1992 *Egypt, Canaan, and Israel in Ancient Times*. Princeton: Princeton University.

Reiner, E.

1981 *Babylonian Planetary Omens, 2, Enuma Anu Enlil (EAE), Tablets 50-51*. In colloboration with D. Pingrie. Bibliotheca Mesopotamica 2/2. Malibu, CA: Undena.

Reiter, K.

1988 "Falknerei im Alten Testament? Ein Beitrag zur Geschichte der Falknerei." *MDOG* 120:189-206.

1990 "Falknerei in Ugarit." *UF* 22:271-78.

Rendsburg, G. A.

1984 "UT 68 and the Tell Asmar Seal." *Or* 53:448-52.

1987a "Gen 10:13-14: An Authentic Hebrew Tradition Concerning the Origins of the Philistines." *JNWSL* 13:89-96.

1987b "Modern South Arabian as a Source for Ugaritic Etymologies." *JAOS* 107:623-28.

Renfroe, F.

1988 "Diagnosing Long-Dead Patients: The Equine Ailments in KTU 1.85." *Or* 57:181-91.

1990 "The Foibles of a Feeble Monarch." *UF* 22:279-84.

1992 *Arabic-Ugaritic Lexical Studies*. Abhandlungen zur Literatur Alt-Syrien-Palästinas 5. Münster: UGARIT-Verlag.

Ribichini, S.

1981 *Adonis. Aspetti 'Orientali' di un mito greco*. Studi Semitici 55. Rome: Consiglio Nazionale di Ricerche.

Riede, P.

1993 "Register." *Gefährten und Feinde des Menschen; Das Tier in der Lebenswelt*. Ed. B. Janowski, U. Neumann-Gorsolke and U. Glessmer. Neukirchen-Vluyn: Neukirchener Verlag. 377-86.

Rin, S. and S.

1967 "Ugaritic-Old Testament Affinities." *BZ* 11:174-92.

Roberts, J. J. M.

1972 *The Earliest Semitic Pantheon; A Study of the Semitic Deities Attested in Mesopotamia before Ur III*. Baltimore/London: Johns Hopkins.

1973 "The Davidic Origin of the Zion Tradition." *JBL* 92:329-44.

1975 "*Ṣāpôn* in Job 26, 7." *Bib* 56:554-57.

Robertson, N.

1982 "The Ritual Background of the Dying God in Cyprus and Syro-Palestine." *HTR* 75:314-59.

Rogerson, J. W.

1974 *Myth in Old Testament Interpretation*. BZAW 134. Berlin: de Gruyter.

1992 *W. M. L. de Wette Founder of Modern Biblical Criticism; An Intellectual Biography*. JSOTSup 126. Sheffield: JSOT.

van Rooy, H. F.

1979 "The Relation between Anat and Baal." *JNWSL* 7:85-95.

Rosenthal, F. R.

1939 "Die Parallelstellen in den Texten von Ugarit." *Or* 8:213-37.

1953 "Some Minor Problems in the Qurʾân." *The Joshua Starr Memorial Volume; Studies in History and Philology*. Jewish Social Studies, Publications No. 5. New York: Conference on Jewish Relations. 67-84.

Ross, J. F.

1970 "Prophecy in Hamath, Israel and Mari." *HTR* 63:1-28.

Rubin, U.

1984 "*Al-Ṣamad* and the high God. An Interpretation of *sura* CXII." *Der Islam* 61:197-217.

Rummel, S.

1978 "The *ʿnt* Text: A Critical Translation." Ph. D. diss., Claremont Graduate School, Claremont, CA.

Ryckmans, G.

1934 *Les nom propres sub-sémitiques; Tome I. Répertoire analytique*. Bibliothèque du Muséon 2. Louvain: Bureaux du Muséon.

1951 *Les religions arabes préislamiques*. Sec. ed. Bibliothèque de Muséon XXVI. Louvain: Publications universitaires.

1962 "ʿAṯtar-Ištar: Nom sumérien ou sémitique?" *Herrmann von Wissmann-Festschrift*. Ed. A. Leidlmair. Tübingen: Geographischen Instituts der Universität Tübingen. 186-92.

Ryckmans, J.

1992 "South Arabia, Religion of." *The Anchor Bible Dictionary; Volume 6. Si-Z*. Ed. D. N. Freedman. New York: Doubleday. 171-76.

Sanmartín, J.

1973 "Semantisches über *ʾmr* 'sehen' und *ʾmr* 'sagen' im Ugaritischen." *UF* 5:263-70.

1976 "*arbdd* 'Liebes-Opfer': ein hurrisches Lehnwort im Ugaritischen." *UF* 8:461-64.

Santucci, J. A.
1988 Review of A. J. Lahiri, *Vedic Vrtra. Religious Studies Review* 14/1:89.

Sarna, N. H.
1993 *Songs of the Heart; An Introduction to the Book of Psalms*. New York: Schocken.

Sass, B.
1991 "The Beth Shemesh Tablet and the Early History of the Proto-Canaanite, Cuneiform and South Semitic Alphabets." *UF* 23:315-26.

Sasson, J. M.
1981 "Literary Criticism, Folklore and Ugaritic Literature." *Ugarit in Retrospect: Fifty Years of Ugarit and Ugaritic*. Ed. G. D. Young. Winona Lake, IN: Eisenbrauns. 81-98.

de Savignac, J.
1986 "Le sens du terme Sâphôn." *UF* 16:273-78.

Schaeffer, C. F. A.
1932 "Les fouilles de Minet el-Bheida et de Ras-Shamra. Trosième campagne (printemps 1931); rapport sommaire." *Syria* 13:1-27.
1939 *The Cuneiform Texts of Ras Shamra Ugarit*. The Schweich Lectures, 1936. London: Oxford University.
1956 *Ugaritica III*. Mission de Ras Shamra VIII. Paris: Geuthner.

Schaeffer-Forrer, C. F. A.
1979 *Ras Shamra 1929-1979*. Collection Maison de l'Orient (CMO), Hors serie No 3. Lyon: Maison de l'orient Mediterranean.

Schloen, J. D.
1993 "The Exile of Disinherited Kin in *KTU* 1.12 and *KTU* 1.23." *JNES* 52:209-20.

Schmidt, W. H.
1961 *Königtum Gottes in Ugarit und Israel*. BZAW 80. Berlin: Töpelmann.

Schub, M.
1990 "Ibn Yaʿiš's Comment on a 'Balanced-Comitative' Sentence." *Zeitschrift für arabische Linguistik* 22:79-82.

Scott, R. B. Y.
1952 "Meteorological Phenomena and Terminology in the Old Testament." *ZAW* 64:11-25.

Scurlock, J. A.
1992 "K 164 (*BA* 2, P. 635): New Light on the Mourning Rites for Dumuzi." *RA* 86:53-67.

Scullion, J. J.
1972 "Some Difficult Texts in Isaiah cc. 55-66 in the Light of Modern Scholarship." *UF* 4:105-28.

Seeden, H.
1980 *The Standing Armed Figurines in the Levant*. Prähistorische Bronzefunde I/1. Munich: C. H. Beck.

Segert, S.
1958 "Die Screibfehler in den ugaritischen literarischen Keilschrifttexten." *Von Ugarit nach Qumran; Beitrage zur alttestamentlichen und altorientalischen Forschung. Otto Eissfeldt zum 1. September 1957*. Ed. J. Hempel and L. Rost. BZAW 77. Berlin: Töpelmann. 193-212.
1971 "Ugaritic Texts and Textual Criticism of the Hebrew Bible." *Near Eastern Studies in Honor of W. F. Albright*. Ed. H. Goedicke. Baltimore/London: Johns Hopkins. 413-20.
1979 "Ugaritic Poetry and Poetics: Some Preliminary Observations." *UF* 11 (Festschrift für C.F.A. Schaeffer):729-38.
1984 *A Basic Grammar of the Ugaritic Language with selected texts and glossary*. Berkeley: University of California.

1993 "Cuneiform Alphabets from Syria and Palestine." *JAOS* 113:82-91.
van Selms, A.
1970 "Yammu's Dethronement by Baal; An attempt to reconstruct texts UT 129, 137 and 68." *UF* 2:251-68.
Sethe, K.
1926 *Die Ächtung fiendlicher Fürsten, Völker und Dinge auf Altägyptischen tongefässcherden des mitteleren Reiches*. Berlin: Verlag der Akademie der Wissenschaften in Kommission bei Walter de Gruyter.
Siegelová, J.
1971 *Appu-Märchen und Ḫedammu-Mythus*. StBoT 14. Wiesbaden: O. Harrassowitz.
Simpson, W. K., et al.
1973 *The Literature of Ancient Egypt*. New ed. New Haven/London: Yale University.
Sivan, D.
1984 *Grammatical Analysis and Glossary of the Northwest Semitic Vocables in Akkadian Texts of the 15th-13th C.B.C. from Canaan and Syria*. AOAT 214. Kevelaer: Bercker & Butzon; Neukirchen-Vluyn: Neukirchener Verlag.
1986 "Problematic Lengthenings in North West Semitic Spellings of the Middle of the Second Millennium B. C. E." *UF* 18:301-12.
1992 "Notes on the Use of the Form Qatal as the Plural Base for the Form Qatl in Ugaritic." *IOS* 12:235-38.
Smith, J. Z.
1982 *Imagining Religion; from Babylon to Jonestown*. Chicago/London: University of Chicago.
Smith, M. S.
1984a "Baal's Cosmic Secret." *UF* 16:295-98.
1984b "Divine Travel as a Token of Divine Rank." *UF* 16:359.
1985 "Kothar wa-Hasis, the Ugaritic Craftsman God." Ph.D. diss., Yale University, New Haven, CT.
1986a "Baal in the Land of Death." *UF* 17:311-14.
1986b "Interpreting the Baal Cycle." *UF* 18:313-39.
1986c "Mt. Ll in KTU 1.2 I 19-20." *UF* 18:458.
1987 "Biblical and Canaanite Notes to the Songs of the Sabbath Sacrifice." *RdQ* 12/4:585-88.
1988 "Death in Jeremiah IX, 20." *UF* 19:289-93.
1989 "God and Zion: Form and Meaning in Psalm 48." *SEL* 6:67-77.
1990 *The Early History of God; Yahweh and the Other Deities in Ancient Israel*. San Francisco: Harper & Row.
1991 *The Origins and Development of the Waw-Consecutive; Northwest Semitic Evidence from Ugarit to Qumran*. HSS 39. Atlanta, GA: Scholars.
Smith, M. S. and E. M. Bloch-Smith
1988 "Death and Afterlife in Ugarit and Israel." *JAOS* 108:277-84.
Smith, W. R.
1972 *The Religion of the Semites; The Fundamental Institutions*. New York: Schocken.
von Soden, W.
1967 "Kleine Beitrage zum Ugaritischen und Hebraischen." *Hebraische Wortforschung: Festschrift zum 80. Geburtstag von Walter Baumgartner*. SVT 16. Leiden: Brill. 291-300.
1970 "Zur Stellung des 'Geweihten' (*qdš*) in Ugarit." *UF* 2:329-30.
1972 "Due Fürstin (*zubultum*) von Ugarit in Mari." *UF* 4:159-60.
1982 "Mottoverse zu Beginn babylonischer und Antiker Epos, Mottosätze in der Bible." *UF* 14:235-39.

van Soldt, W. H.
1990 "Fabrics and Dyes at Ugarit." *UF* 22:321-57.
1991 *Studies in the Akkadian of Ugarit: Dating and Grammar*. AOAT 40. Kevelaer: Butzon & Bercker; Neukirchen-Vluyn: Neukirchener Verlag.
Spanier, E. (ed.)
1987 *The Royal Purple and the Biblical Blue, ARGAMAN and TEKHELET*. Jerusalem: Keter.
Speiser, E. A.
1935 "Notes to Recently Published Nuzi Texts." *JAOS* 55:432-43.
1951 "The Semantic Range of *dalāpu*." *JCS* 5:64-66.
Spronk, K.
1986 *Beatific Afterlife in Ancient Israel and in the Ancient Near East*. AOAT 219. Kevelaer: Verlag Butzon & Bercker; Neukirchen-Vluyn: Neukirchener Verlag.
Stadelmann, R.
1967 *Syrisch-palastinensische Gottheiten in Ägypten*. Probleme der Ägyptologie 5. Leiden: Brill.
Stager, L. E.
1982 "The Archaeology of the East Slope of Jerusalem and the Terraces of the Kidron." *JNES* 41:111-21.
1991 "Eroticism & Infanticide at Ashkelon." *Biblical Archaeology Review* 17/4:35-53, 72.
Stannard, B.
1992 *The Cosmic Contest: A Systems Study in Indo-European Epic, Myth, Cult and Cosmogony*. Southport: Carib.
Steiner, R. C., and C. F. Nims
1984 "You Can't Offer Your Sacrifice and Eat It Too; A Polemical Poem from the Aramaic Text in Demotic." *JNES* 43:89-114.
Stern, P. D.
1991 *The Biblical Ḥerem; A Window on Israel's Religious Experience*. Brown Judaic Series 211. Atlanta, GA: Scholars.
Stieglitz, R. R.
1979 "Commodity Prices at Ugarit." *JAOS* 99:15-23.
1990 "Ebla and the Gods of Canaan." *Eblaitica: Essays on the Ebla Archives and Eblaite Language*. Volume 2. Ed. C. H. Gordon. Winona Lake, IN: Eisenbrauns. 79-89.
Stol, M.
1972 "Akkadische *šāpiṭum*, *šapāṭum* und westsemitisches *špṭ*." *BiOr* 29:276-77.
Stolz, F.
1982 "Funktionen und Bedeutungsbereiche des ugaritischen Baᶜalmythos." *Funktionen und Leistungen des Mythos; Drei altorientalische Beispiele*. Ed. J. Assman et al. OBO 48. Freiburg: Universitatsverlag; Göttingen: Vandenhoeck & Ruprecht. 83-118.
Strange, J.
1980 *Caphtor/Keftiu; A New Investigation*. Acta Theologica Danica 14. Leiden: Brill.
Strugnell, J.
1960 "The Angelic Liturgy at Qumran—4QSerek Šîrôt ᶜOlat Haššabat." *Congress Volume; Oxford 1959*. SVT 7. Leiden: Brill. 318-45.
Stuart, D.
1976 *Studies in Early Hebrew Meter*. HSM 13. Missoula, MT: Scholars.
Swiggers, P.
1981 "The Meaning of the Root *lḥm* 'Food' in the Semitic Languages." *UF* 13:307-08.

Talmon, S.
1963 "The Gezer Calendar and the Seasonal Cycle of Ancient Canaan." *JAOS* 83:177-87.
Tallqvist, K.
1938 *Akkadische Götterepitheta*. Helsinki: Societas Orientalia Gernica.
de Tarragon, J. M.
1980 *Le cult à Ugarit d'après les textes de la pratique en cunéiformes alphabétiques*. Cahiers de la Revue Biblique 19. Paris: Gabalda.
Tawil, H.
1974 "Some Literary Elements in the Opening Sections of the Hadad, Zākir, and the Nērab II Inscriptions in the Light of East and West Semitic Royal Inscriptions." *Or* 43:40-65.
1980 "Azazel, the Prince of the Steppe." *ZAW* 92:43-49.
Teixidor, J.
1977 *The Pagan God: Popular Religion in the Greco-Roman Near East*. Princeton, NJ: Princeton University.
Tessier, B.
1984 *Ancient Near Eastern Cylinder Seals from the Marcopoli Collection*. Berkeley/Los Angeles/London: University of California; Beverly Hills, CA: Summa Publications.
Te Velde, H.
1967 *Seth, God of Confusion. A Study of his Role in Egyptian Mythology and Religion*. Problem der Ägyptologie 6. Leiden: Brill.
1977 "The Theme of the Separation of Heaven and Earth." *Studia Aegyptiaca* 3:161-70.
Thomas, D. W.
1953 "A Consideration of Some Ununusual Ways of Expressing the Superlative in Hebrew." *VT* 3:209-24.
1968 "Some Further Remarks on Unusual Ways of the Expressing the Superlative in Hebrew." *VT* 18:120-24.
Thompson, S.
1965 "Myths and Folktales." *Myth; A Symposium*. Ed. T. A. Sebeok. Bloomington, IN: Indiana University. 169-80.
Thureau-Dangin, F.
1907 *Die sumerischen und akkadischen Köningsinschriften*. Leipzig: J. C. Hinrichs'sche Buchhandlung.
Toombs, L.
1983 "Baal, Lord of the Earth." *The Word of the Lord Shall Go Forth; Essays in Honor of D.N. Freedman in Celebration of His Sixtieth Birthday*. Ed. C. L. Meyers and M. O'Connor. ASOR Special Volume Series 1. Winona Lake, IN: Eisenbrauns (for ASOR). 613-23.
van der Toorn, K.
1991a "The Babylonian New Year Festival: New Insights from the Cuneiform Texts and Their Bearing on Old Testament Study." *Congress Volume; Leuven 1989*. Ed. J. Emerton. SVT 43. Leiden: Brill. 331-44.
1991b "Funerary Rituals and Beatific Afterlife in Ugaritic Texts and in the Bible." *BiOr* 48:40-66.
1992 "Anat-Yahu, Some Other Deities, and the Jews of Elephantine." *Numen* 39:80-101.
Tournay, R. J.
1991 *Seeing and Hearing God with the Psalms; The Prophetic Liturgy of the Second Temple in Jerusalem*. Trans. J. E. Crowley. JSOTSup 118. Sheffield: JSOT.

Tromp, N. J.
1969 *Primitive Conceptions of Death and the Nether World in the Old Testament*. BeO 21. Rome: Pontifical Biblical Institute.
Tropper, J.
1990 "Silbenschliessendes Aleph im Ugaritischen." *UF* 22:359-69.
Tsevat, M.
1954 "The Canaanite God Šälaḥ." *VT* 4:41-49.
Tsumura, D. T.
1982 "*Sandhi* in the Ugaritic Language." *Bungei-Gengo Kenyu* (*Studies in Language and Literature: Language*) 7:111-26 (Japanese; summarized in *Old Testament Abstracts* 6 [1983] 246-47 # 773).
1991 "Vowel Sandhi in Ugaritic." *Near Eastern Studies; Dedicated to H. I. H. Prince Takahito Mikasa on the Occasion of His Seventy-Fifth Birthday*. Bulletin of the Middle Eastern Culture Center in Japan. Ed. Masao Mori. Wiesbaden: Harrassowitz. 427-35.
Tuell, S. S.
1993 "A Riddle Resolved by an Enigma: Hebrew גלש and Ugaritic *GLṮ*." *JBL* 112:99-104.
Tuttle, G. A.
1978 "Case Vowels on Masculine Singular Nouns in Construct in Ugaritic." *Biblical and Near Eastern Studies in Honor of William Sanford LaSor*. Ed. G. Tuttle. Grand Rapids, MI: Eerdmans. 253-68.
Uehlinger, C.
1993 "Audienz in der Gotterwelt; Anthropomorphismus und Soziomorphismus in der Ikonographie eines altsyrischen Zylindersiegels." *UF* 24:339-59.
Ullendorff, E.
1962 "Ugaritic Marginalia II." *JSS* 7:39-51.
1972 "Ugaritic Marginalia III." *IOS* 2:463-69.
1978 "Ugaritic Marginalia IV." *EI* 14 (H. L. Ginsberg Volume):19*-23*.
Vanel, A.
1965 *L'iconographie du dieu l'orage*. Cahiers de la Revue Biblique 3. Paris: Gabalda.
de Vaux, R.
1940 Review of C. F. A. Schaeffer, *Ugaritica*. *RB* 49: 248-58.
1965 *Ancient Israel*. 2 vols. Trans. Darton, Longman and Todd, Ltd. New York/Toronto: McGraw-Hill.
Velankar, H. D.
1950 "Hymns to Indra in Mandala I." *Journal of Bombay University* 20/2:7-34.
Verreet, E.
1988 *Modi Ugaritici; Eine morpho-syntaktische Abhandlung über das Modalsystem im Ugaritischen*. OLA 27. Leuven: Department Oriëntalistiek/Uitgeverij Peeters.
Vine, K.
1965 "The Establishment of Baal at Ugarit." Ph.D. diss., University of Michigan, Ann Arbor, MI.
Virolleaud, C.
1935 "La revolte de Košer contre Baal. Poème de Ras Shamra (III AB A)." *Syria* 16:29-45.
1938 *La déesse ᶜAnat*. Paris: Geuthner.
1944-45 "Fragments mythologiques de Ras-Shamra." *Syria* 24:1-23.
1946 "Le dieu de la Mer dans la mythologie de Ras Shamra." *CRAIBL*:498-509.
Wakeman, M.
1969 "The Biblical Earth Monster in the Cosmogonic Combat Myth." *JBL* 88:313-20.

1973 *God's Battle with the Monster; A Study in Biblical Imagery*. Leiden: Brill.
Waldman, N. M.
1976 "A Comparative Note on Exodus 15:14-16." *JQR* 66:189-92.
1978 "The Breaking of the Bow." *JQR* 69:82-88.
Wallace, H. N.
1985 *The Eden Narrative*. HSM 32. Atlanta, GA: Scholars.
Walls, N. H., Jr.
1992 *The Goddess Anat in the Ugaritic Texts*. SBLDS 135. Atlanta, GA: Scholars.
Ward, W. A.
1961 "Comparative Studies in Egyptian and Ugaritic." *JNES* 20:31-40.
1962 "Some Egypto-Semitic Roots." *Or* 31:397-412.
1963 "Notes on Some Semitic Loan-words and Personal Names in Late Egyptian." *Or* 32:413-36.
1969 "The Semitic Root *ḥwy* in Ugaritic and Derived Stems in Egyptian." *JNES* 28:265-67.
Waterston, A.
1988 "The Kingdom of ᶜAṯtar and his Role in the AB Cycle." *UF* 20:357-64.
1989 "Death and Resurrection in the A. B. Cycle." *UF* 21:425-34.
Watson, W. G. E.
1977a "The Falcon Episode in the Aqhat Tale." *JNWSL* 5:69-75.
1977b "Ugaritic and Mesopotamian Literary Texts." *UF* 9:273-84.
1978a "Notes on Ugaritic Lexicography." *Newsletter for Ugaritic Studies* 16:61.
1978b "Parallels to Some Passages in Ugaritic." *UF* 10:397-401.
1980 "Philological Notes." *Newsletter for Ugaritic Studies* 21:8-9.
1981a "Reversed Rootplay in Psalm 145." *Bib* 62:101-02.
1981b "Reversed Word-pairs in Ugaritic Poetry." *UF* 13:189-92.
1982 "Lexical Notes." *Newsletter for Ugaritic Studies* 28:9.
1983a "Introduction to Discourse in Ugaritic." *AO* 1:253-61.
1983b "Lexical Notes." *Newsletter for Ugaritic Studies* 30:12.
1984 "Middle-Eastern Forerunners to a Folktale Motif." *Or* 53:333-36.
1988 "More on Metathetic Parallelism." *WO* 19:40-44.
1989 "Parallelism with *Qtl* in Ugaritic." *UF* 21:435-442.
Wieder, A. A.
1974 "Three Philological Notes." *Bulletin of the Institute of Jewish Studies* 2:103-09.
Weinfeld, M.
1973 "'Rider of the Clouds' and 'Gatherer of the Clouds'." *JANES* 5 (= T.H. Gaster Festschrift):421-26.
1977-78 "Gen. 7:11, 8:1-2 against the Background of Ancient Near Eastern Tradition." *WO* 9:242-48.
1983a "Divine Intervention in War in Ancient Israel and in the Ancient Near East." *History, Historiography and Interpretation; Studies in Biblical and Cuneiform Literature*. Ed. H. Tadmor and M. Weinfeld. Jerusalem: Magnes. 121-47.
1983b "Social and Cultic Institutions in the Priestly Source against their Ancient Near Eastern Background." *Proceedings of the Eighth World Congress of Jewish Studies. Jerusalem, August 16-21, 1981; Panel Sessions. Bible Studies and Hebrew Language*. Jerusalem: World Union of Jewish Studies—The Perry Foundation for Biblical Research. 95-129.
1983c "Zion and Jerusalem as Religious and Political Capital: Ideology and Utopia." *The Poet and the Historian; Essays in Literary and Historical Biblical Criticism*. Ed. R. E. Friedman. HSS 26. Chico, CA: Scholars.
Weippert, M.
1973-74 "Die Kämpfe des assyrischen Königs Assurbanipal gegen die Araber; Redaktionskritische Untersuchung des Berichts in Prisma A." *WO* 7:39-85.

Wensinck, A. J.
1978 "Al-Khadir." *Encyclopaedia of Islam* 4:902-05.
Whitaker, R. E.
1970 "A Formulaic Analysis of Ugaritic Poetry." Ph.D. diss., Harvard University, Cambridge, MA.
Wiggins, S. A.
1991 "The Myth of Asherah: Lion Lady and Serpent Goddess." *UF* 23:383-89.
Wilson, R. R.
1987 "The Death of the King of Tyre: The Editorial History of Ezekiel 28." *Love and Death in the Ancient Near East: Essays in Honor of Marvin H. Pope*. Ed. J. Marks and R. M. Good. Guilford, CT: Four Quarters. 211-18.
Wood, W. C.
1916 "The Religion of Canaan." *JBL* 35:163-279.
Wyatt, N.
1979 "Some Observations on the Idea of History among the West Semitic Peoples." *UF* 11:825-32.
1980 "The Relationship of the Deities Dagan and Hadad." *UF* 12:375-79.
1985 "'Jedidiah' and Cognate Forms as a Title of Royal Legitimization." *Bib* 66:112-25.
1986 "The AB Cycle and Kingship in Ugaritic Thought." *Cosmos* 2:136-42.
1987a "Baal's Boars." *UF* 19:391-98.
1987b "Killing and Cosmogony in Canaanite and Biblical Thought." *UF* 17:375-81.
1987c "Who Killed the Dragon?" *AO* 5:185-98.
1988 "The Source of the Ugaritic Myth of the Conflict of Ba^{c}al and Yam." *UF* 20:375-85.
1989 "Quaternities in the Mythology of Ba^{c}al." *UF* 21:451-60.
1993 "The Titles of the Ugaritic Storm-god." *UF* 24:403-24.
Xella, P.
1982 "*QDŠ*. Semantica del 'Sacro' ad Ugarit." *Materiali Lessicali ed Epigrafici—I*. Collezione di Studi Fenici 13. Rome: Consiglio Nazionale delle Ricerche. 9-17
1983 "Aspekte religiöser Vorstellungen in Syrien nach den Ebla- und Ugarit-Texten." *UF* 15:279-90.
1991 *Baal Hammon; Recherches sur l'identité et histoire d'un dieu phénico-punique*. Collezione di Studi Fenici 32. Rome: Consiglio Nazionale delle Ricerche.
Yadin, Y.
1968 "'And Dan, why did he remain in Ships?'" *AJBA* 1/1:9-13.
1970 "Symbols of Deities at Zinjirli, Carthage and Hazor." *Near Eastern Archaeology in the Twentieth Century; Essays in Honor of Nelson Glueck*. Ed. J. A. Sanders. Garden City, NY: Doubleday. 199-231.
Yon, M.
1985 "Baal et le roi." *De l'Indus aux Balkans; Recueil à la mémoire de Jean Deshayes*. Ed. J. L. Huot, M. Yon and Y. Calvet. Paris: Éditions Recherche sur les Civilisations. 177-90.
1989 "*Ṣḥr mt*, la chaleur de Mot." *UF* 21:461-66.
1991 "Stèles de pierres." *Arts et industrie de la pierre*. Ras Shamra-Ougarit VI. Ed. M. Yon. Paris: Éditions sur les Civilisations. 273-343.
1992 "Ugarit; History and Archaeology." *The Anchor Bible Dictionary; Volume 6. Si-Z*. Ed. D. N. Freedman. New York: Doubleday. 695-706.
Young, D. W.
1979 "The Ugaritic Myth of the God Horan and the Mare." *UF* 11 (Festschrift für C. F. A. Schaeffer):839-48.

Young, G. D.
1950 "Ugaritic Prosody." *JNES* 9:124-33.
Young, I.
1993 *Diversity in Pre-Exilic Hebrew*. Forschungen zum Alten Testament 5. Tübingen: Mohr (Siebeck).
Zaccagnini, C.
1970 "Note sulla terminologia metallurgica di Ugarit." *OA* 9:315-24.
Zevit, Z.
1976 "The Priestly Redaction and Interpretation of the Plague Narrative in Exodus." *JQR* 66:193-211.
van Zijl, P. J.
1969 "A Discussion of the Root *gaʿar*." *Biblical Essays: Proceedings of the 12th Meeting of De Ou Testamentiese Werkgemeenskap in Suid Afrika*. Pretoria: Pro-Rege-Pers Baperk. 56-63.
1975 "A Discussion of the Words *anš* and *nšy* in the Ugaritic Texts." *UF* 7:503-14.

INDEXES

INDEXES

Ugaritic Citations

Ugaritic Texts

The references to KTU 1.1 and 1.2 are selective.

Ugaritic Grammar

Ugaritic Vocabulary

Other Texts Cited

Akkadian and Sumerian Texts

Arabic texts

Bible, Inscriptions, Intertestamental literature and Dead Sea Scrolls, and Rabbinic sources

Bible

Hittite Texts

Indian Texts

General Index

The references to Ugaritic deities are selective.

AUTHORS CITED

PLATES

Plate 1 KTU 1.1 II and III (Photograph by Bruce and Kenneth Zuckerman, West Semitic Research; used by permission of the Musée du Louvre).

Plate 2 KTU 1.1 II 1-5 (Photograph by Bruce and Kenneth Zuckerman, West Semitic Research; used by permission of the Musée du Louvre).

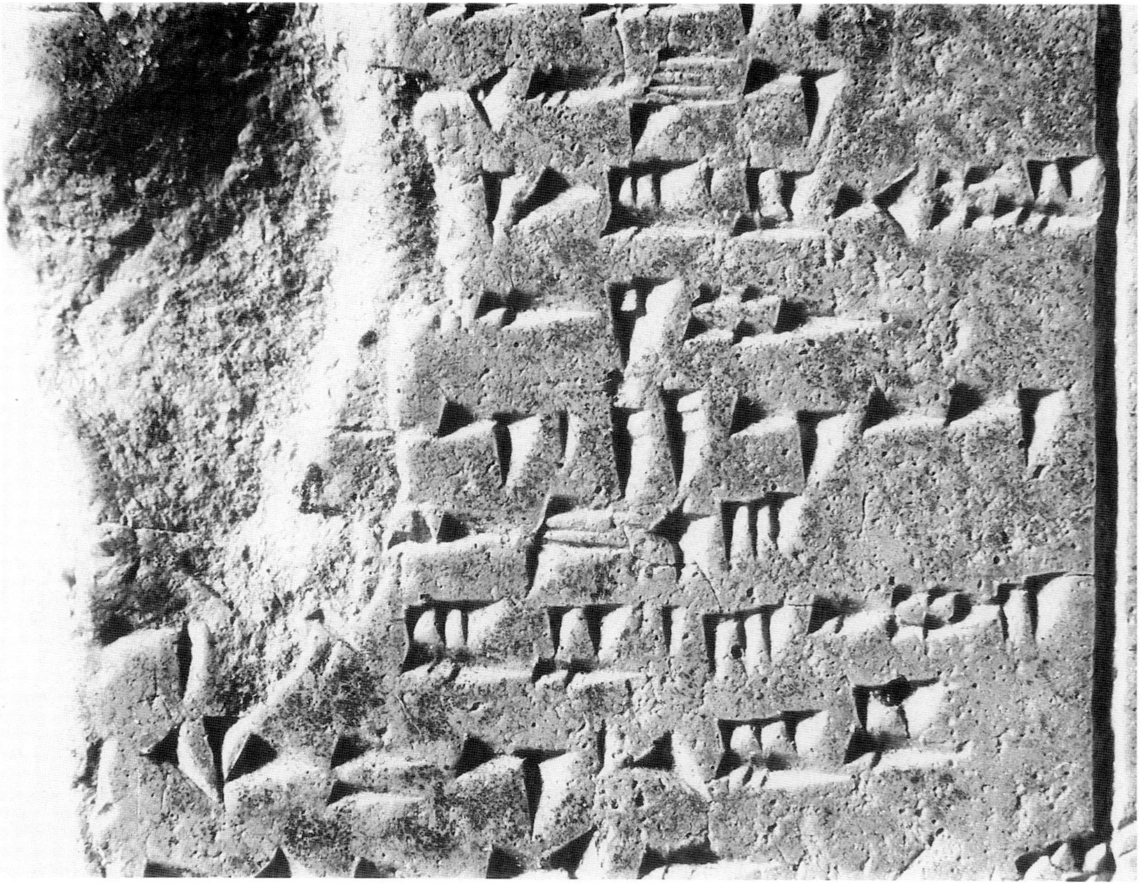

Plate 3 KTU 1.1 II 5-11 (Photograph by Bruce and Kenneth Zuckerman, West Semitic Research; used by permission of the Musée du Louvre).

Plate 4 KTU 1.1 II 10-16 (Photograph by Bruce and Kenneth Zuckerman, West Semitic Research; used by permission of the Musée du Louvre).

Plate 5 KTU 1.1 II 15-21 (Photograph by Bruce and Kenneth Zuckerman, West Semitic Research; used by permission of the Musée du Louvre).

Plate 6 KTU 1.1 II 21-25 (Photograph by Bruce and Kenneth Zuckerman, West Semitic Research; used by permission of the Musée du Louvre).

Plate 7 KTU 1.1 III 1-7 (Photograph by Bruce and Kenneth Zuckerman, West Semitic Research; used by permission of the Musée du Louvre).

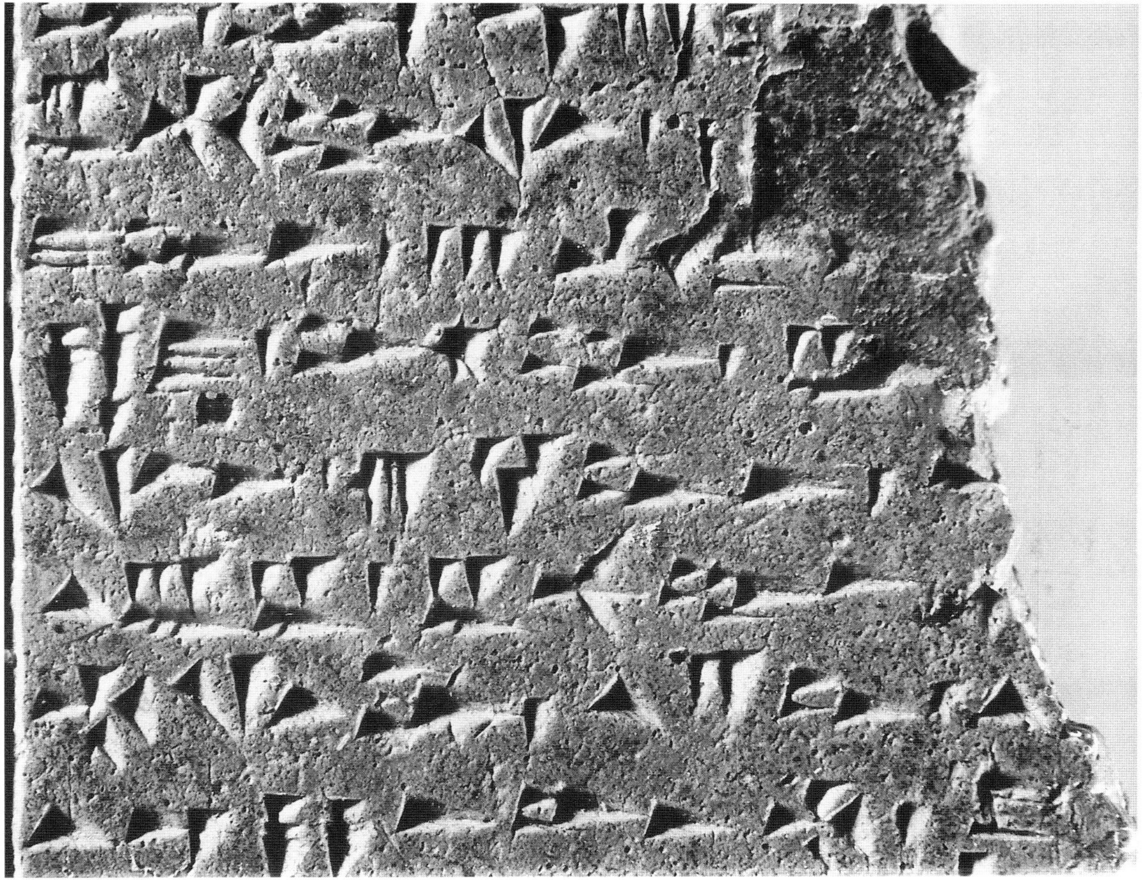

Plate 8 KTU 1.1 III 5-11 (Photograph by Bruce and Kenneth Zuckerman, West Semitic Research; used by permission of the Musée du Louvre).

Plate 9 KTU 1.1 III 10-17 (Photograph by Bruce and Kenneth Zuckerman, West Semitic Research; used by permission of the Musée du Louvre).

Plate 10 KTU 1.1 III 16-23 (Photograph by Bruce and Kenneth Zuckerman, West Semitic Research; used by permission of the Musée du Louvre).

Plate 11 KTU 1.1 III 20-27 (Photograph by Bruce and Kenneth Zuckerman, West Semitic Research; used by permission of the Musée du Louvre).

Plate 12 KTU 1.1 III 24-30 (Photograph by Bruce and Kenneth Zuckerman, West Semitic Research; used by permission of the Musée du Louvre).

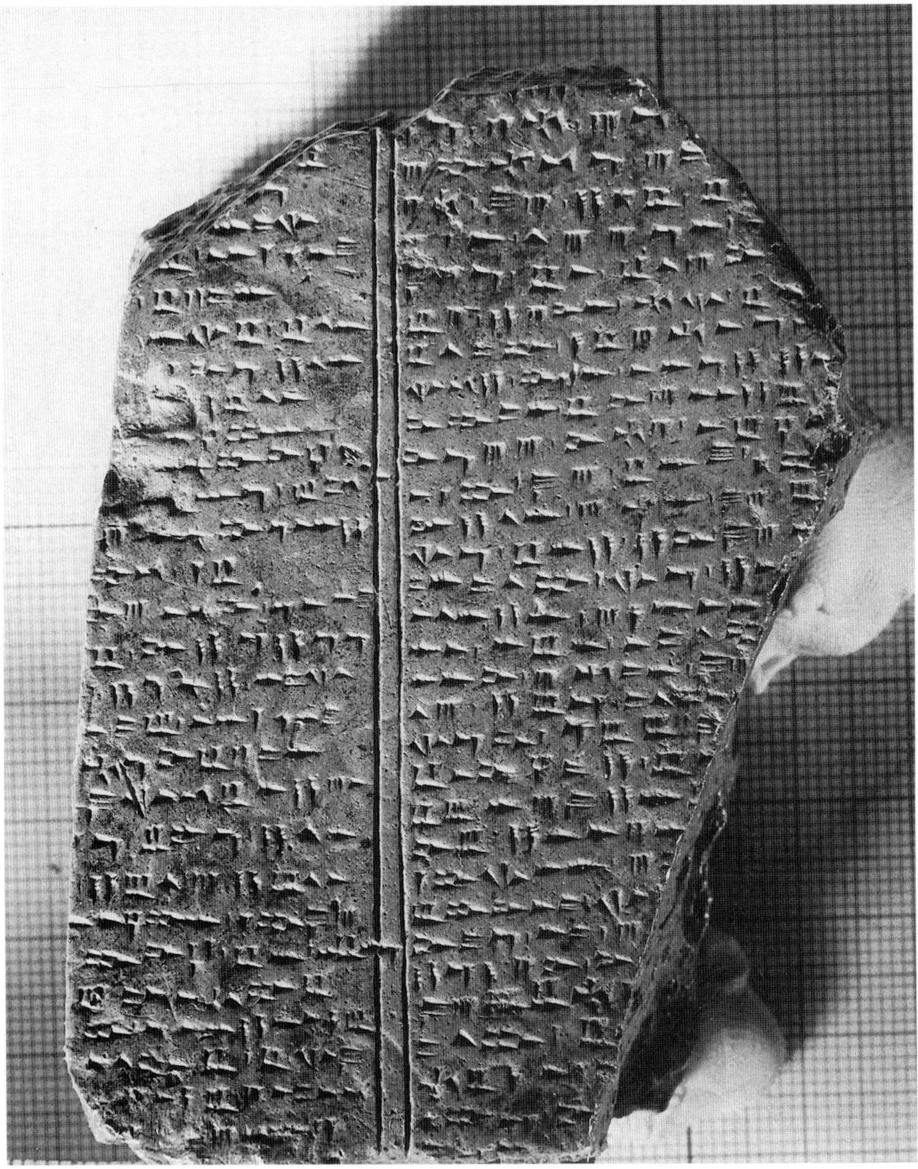

Plate 13 KTU 1.1 V and IV (Photograph by Bruce and Kenneth Zuckerman, West Semitic Research; used by permission of the Musée du Louvre).

Plate 14 KTU 1.1 IV 1-10 (Photograph by Bruce and Kenneth Zuckerman, West Semitic Research; used by permission of the Musée du Louvre).

Plate 15 KTU 1.1 IV 9-19 (Photograph by Bruce and Kenneth Zuckerman, West Semitic Research; used by permission of the Musée du Louvre).

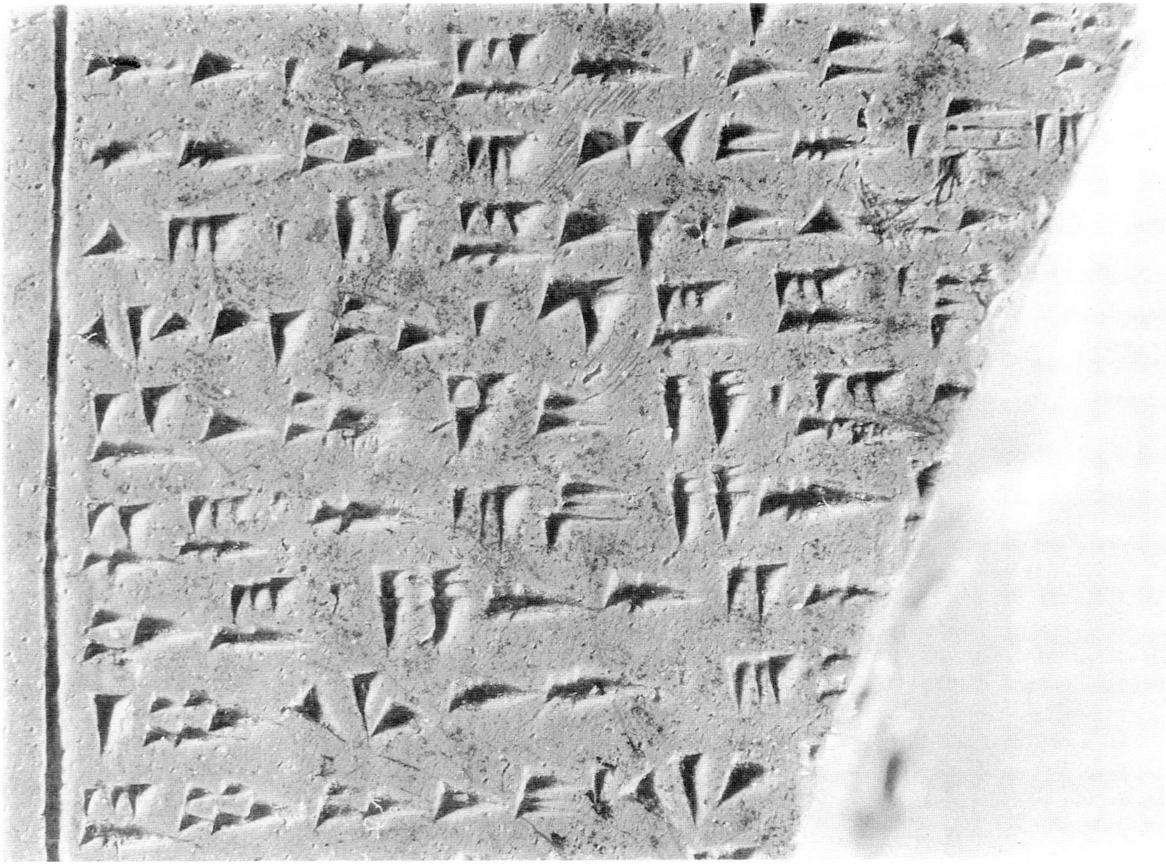

Plate 16 KTU 1.1 IV 17-25 (Photograph by Bruce and Kenneth Zuckerman, West Semitic Research; used by permission of the Musée du Louvre).

Plate 17 KTU 1.1 IV 24-30 (Photograph by Bruce and Kenneth Zuckerman, West Semitic Research; used by permission of the Musée du Louvre).

Plate 18 KTU 1.1 IV 27-32 (Photograph by Bruce and Kenneth Zuckerman, West Semitic Research; used by permission of the Musée du Louvre).

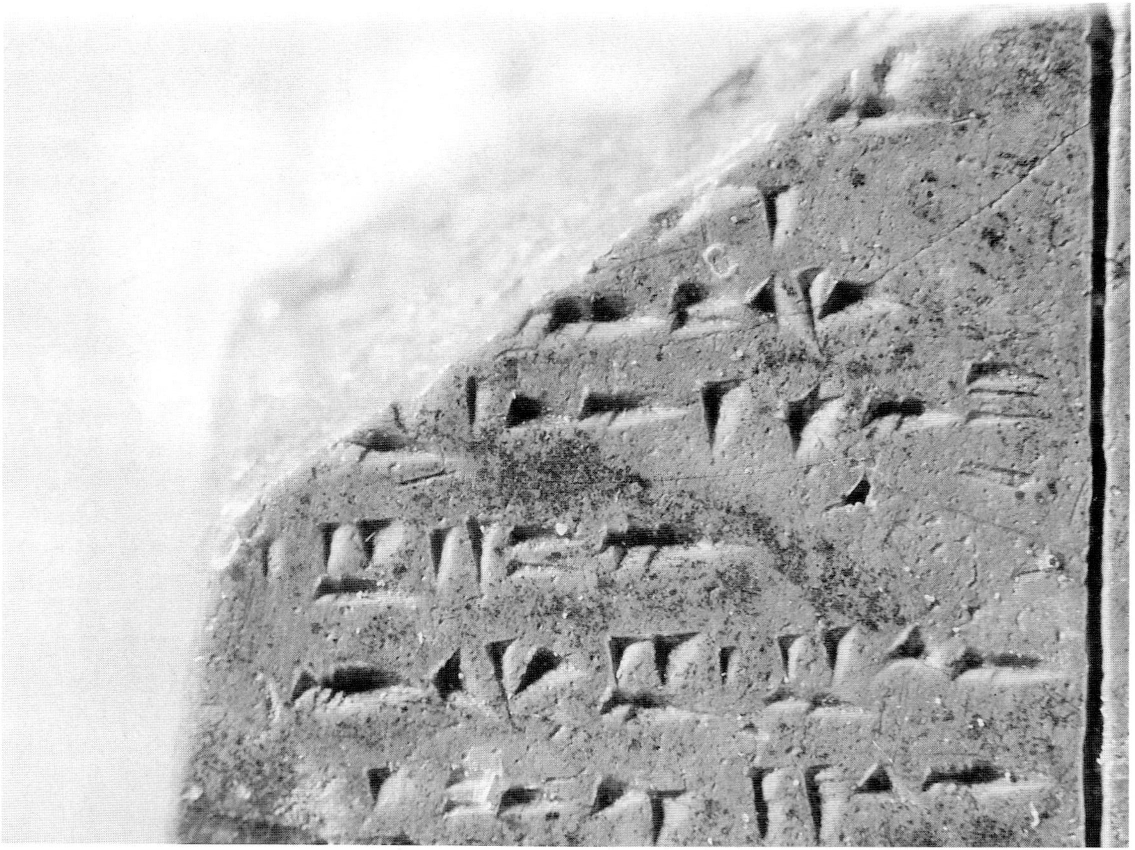

Plate 19 KTU 1.1 V 1-7 (Photograph by Bruce and Kenneth Zuckerman, West Semitic Research; used by permission of the Musée du Louvre).

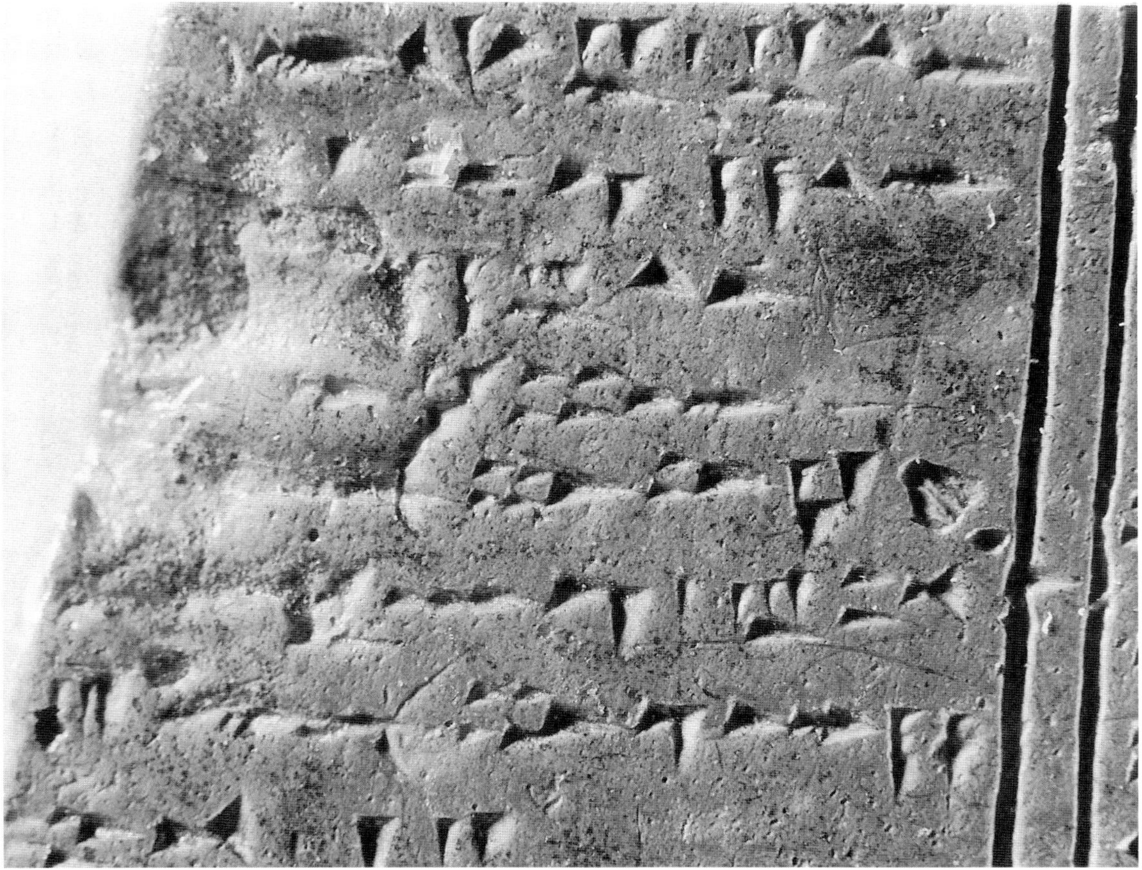

Plate 20 KTU 1.1 V 6-13 (Photograph by Bruce and Kenneth Zuckerman, West Semitic Research; used by permission of the Musée du Louvre).

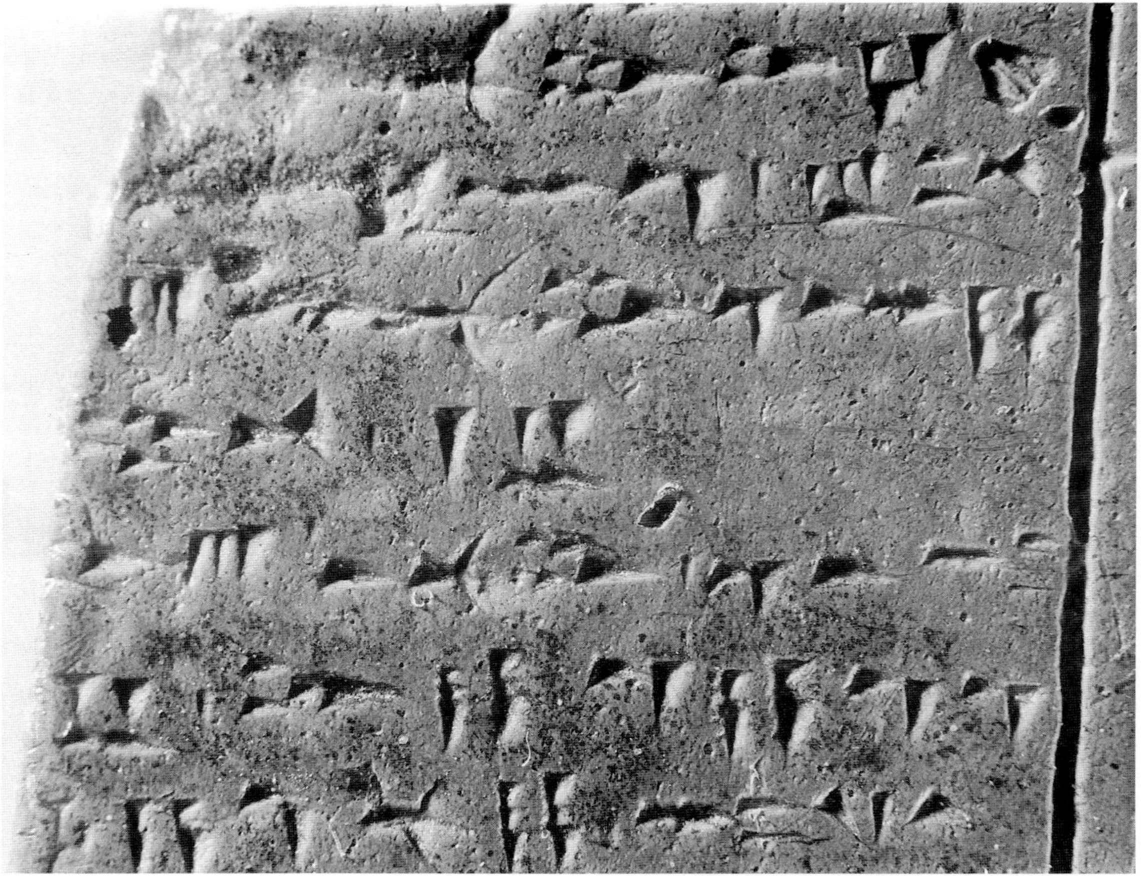

Plate 21 KTU 1.1 V 10-16 (Photograph by Bruce and Kenneth Zuckerman, West Semitic Research; used by permission of the Musée du Louvre).

Plate 22 KTU 1.1 V 15-21 (Photograph by Bruce and Kenneth Zuckerman, West Semitic Research; used by permission of the Musée du Louvre).

Plate 23 KTU 1.1 V 20-26 (Photograph by Bruce and Kenneth Zuckerman, West Semitic Research; used by permission of the Musée du Louvre).

Plate 24 KTU 1.1 V 24-29 (Photograph by Bruce and Kenneth Zuckerman, West Semitic Research; used by permission of the Musée du Louvre).

Plate 25 KTU 1.2 III (Photograph by Bruce and Kenneth Zuckerman, West Semitic Research; used by permission of the Musée du Louvre).

Plate 26 KTU 1.2 III right-hand edge (Photograph by Bruce and Kenneth Zuckerman, West Semitic Research; used by permission of the Musée du Louvre).

Plate 27 KTU 1.2 III 2-7 left-hand side (Photograph by Bruce and Kenneth Zuckerman, West Semitic Research; used by permission of the Musée du Louvre).

Plate 28 KTU 1.2 III 3-9 middle (Photograph by Bruce and Kenneth Zuckerman, West Semitic Research; used by permission of the Musée du Louvre).

Plate 29 KTU 1.2 III 4-10 middle (Photograph by Bruce and Kenneth Zuckerman, West Semitic Research; used by permission of the Musée du Louvre).

Plate 30 KTU 1.2 III 6-11 right-hand side (Photograph by Bruce and Kenneth Zuckerman, West Semitic Research; used by permission of the Musée du Louvre).

Plate 31 KTU 1.2 III 8-14 left-hand side (Photograph by Bruce and Kenneth Zuckerman, West Semitic Research; used by permission of the Musée du Louvre).

Plate 32 KTU 1.2 III 10-17 middle (Photograph by Bruce and Kenneth Zuckerman, West Semitic Research; used by permission of the Musée du Louvre).

Plate 33 KTU 1.2 III 11-17 right-hand side (Photograph by Bruce and Kenneth Zuckerman, West Semitic Research; used by permission of the Musée du Louvre).

Plate 34 KTU 1.2 III 16-21 left-hand side (Photograph by Bruce and Kenneth Zuckerman, West Semitic Research; used by permission of the Musée du Louvre).

Plate 35 KTU 1.2 III 14-21 middle (Photograph by Bruce and Kenneth Zuckerman, West Semitic Research; used by permission of the Musée du Louvre).

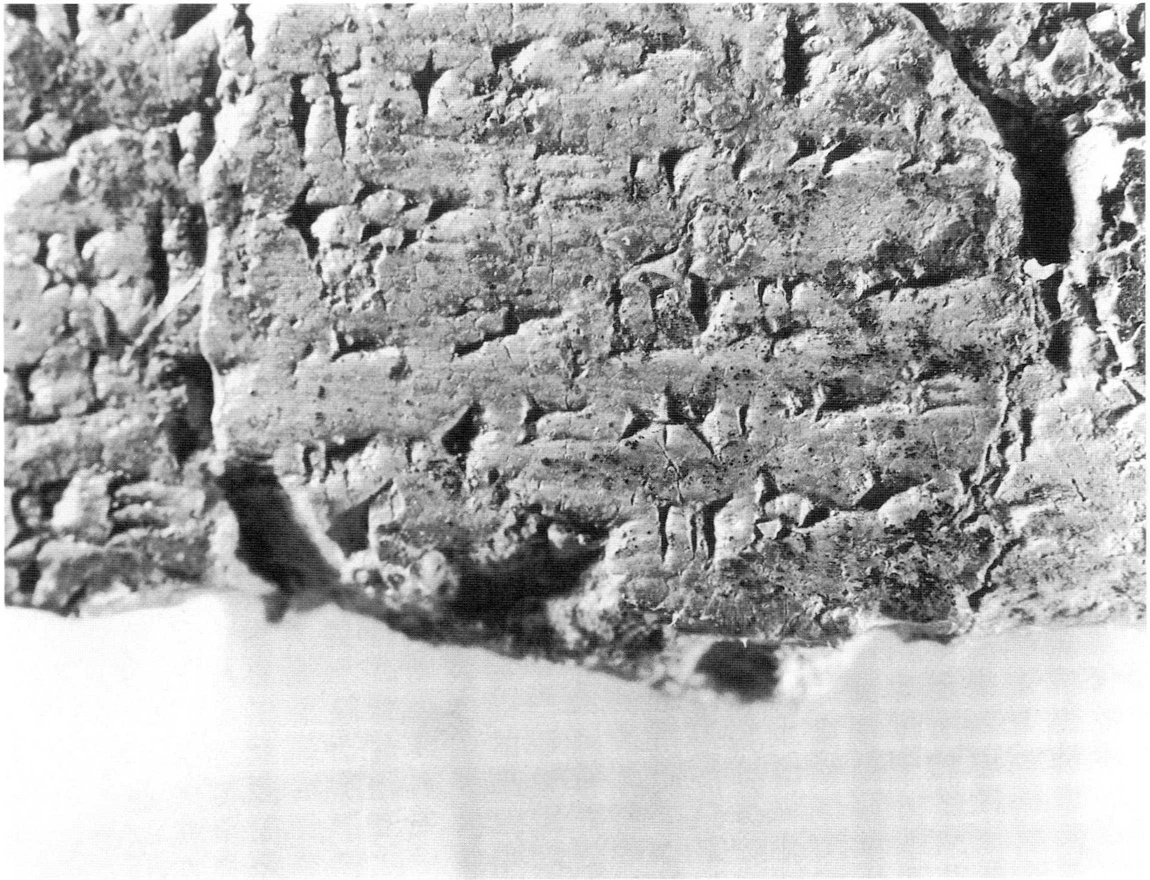

Plate 36 KTU 1.2 III 18-22 left-hand side middle (Photograph by Bruce and Kenneth Zuckerman, West Semitic Research; used by permission of the Musée du Louvre).

Plate 37 KTU 1.2 III 19-25 middle (Photograph by Bruce and Kenneth Zuckerman, West Semitic Research; used by permission of the Musée du Louvre).

Plate 38 KTU 1.2 III 19-25 right-hand side (Photograph by Bruce and Kenneth Zuckerman, West Semitic Research; used by permission of the Musée du Louvre).

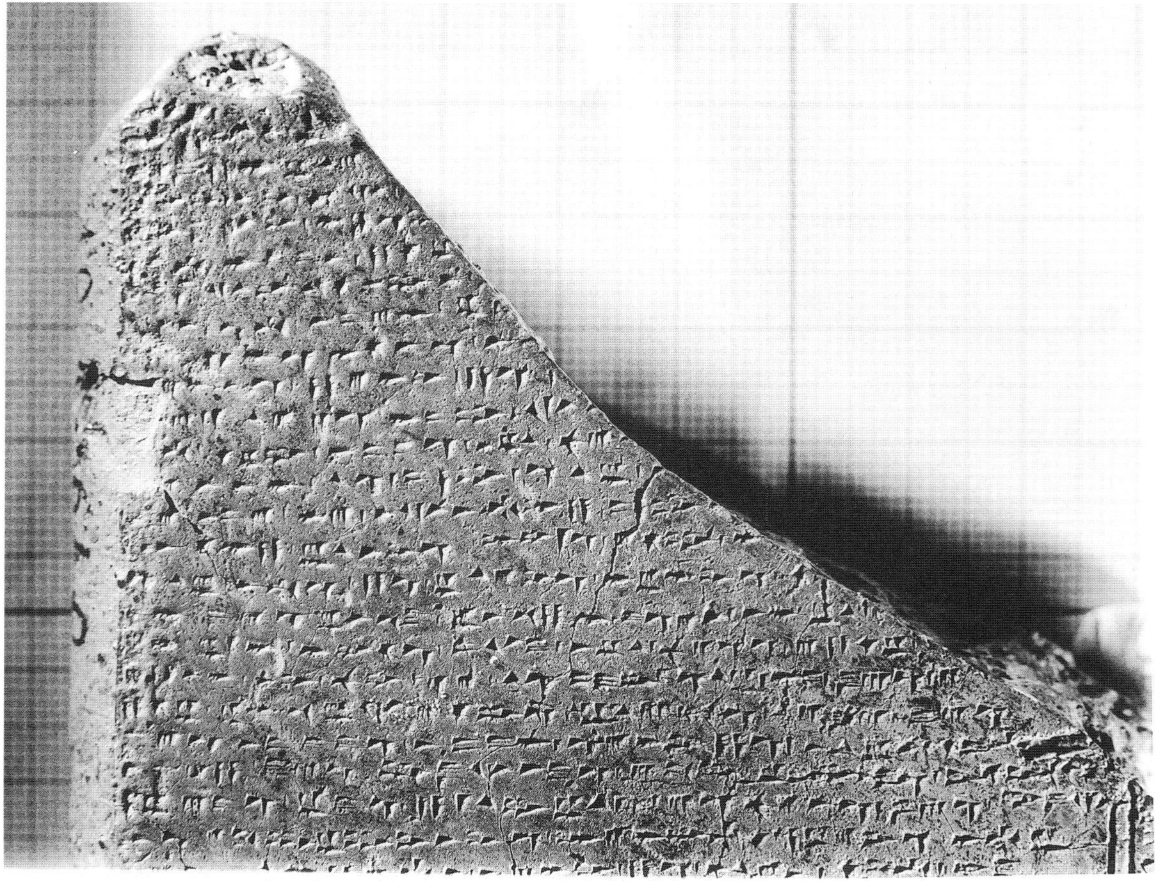

Plate 39 KTU 1.2 I 1-25 (Photograph by Bruce and Kenneth Zuckerman, West Semitic Research; used by permission of the Musée du Louvre).

Plate 40 KTU 1.2 I 21-47 middle and right-hand side + 1.2 II (Photograph by Bruce and Kenneth Zuckerman, West Semitic Research; used by permission of the Musée du Louvre).

Plate 41 KTU 1.2 I 22-48 left-hand side and middle (Photograph by Bruce and Kenneth Zuckerman, West Semitic Research; used by permission of the Musée du Louvre).

Plate 42 KTU 1.2 IV 1-23 (Photograph by Bruce and Kenneth Zuckerman, West Semitic Research; used by permission of the Musée du Louvre).

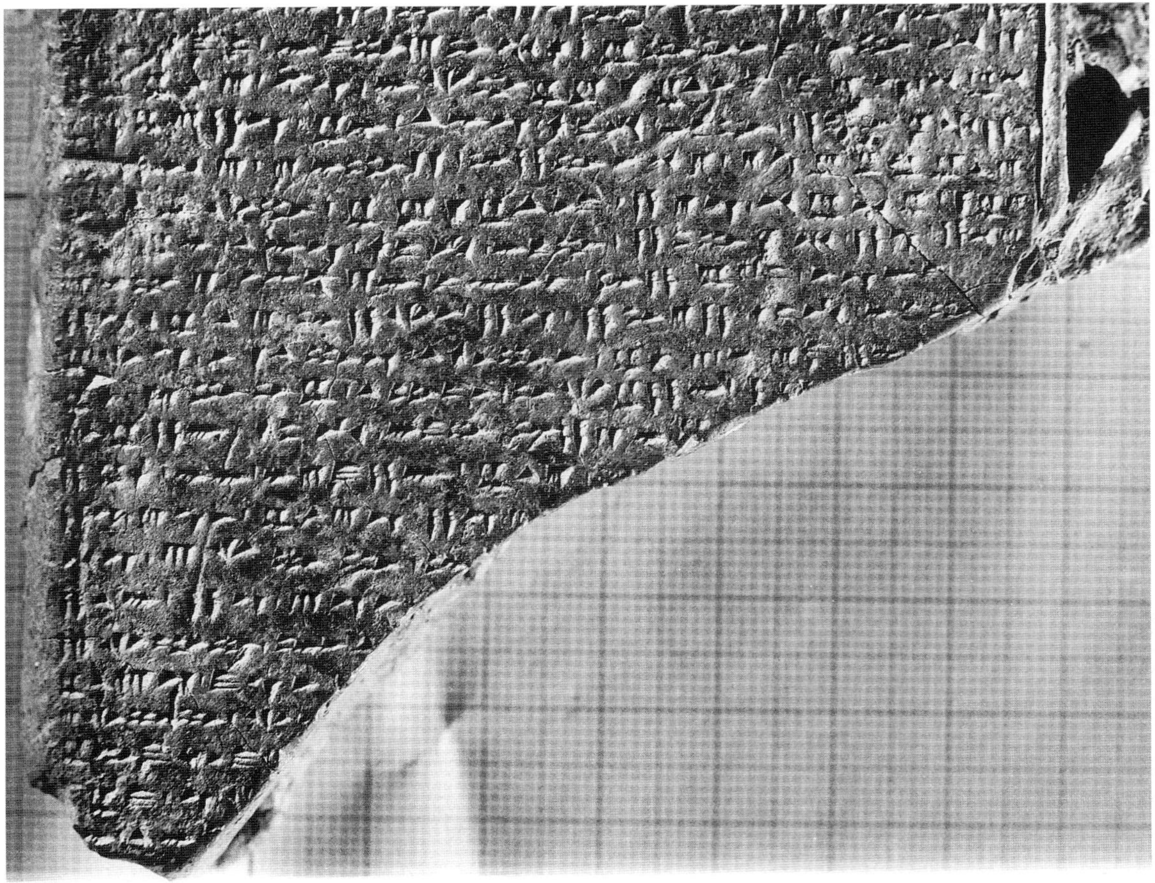

Plate 43 KTU 1.2 IV 20-40 (Photograph by Bruce and Kenneth Zuckerman, West Semitic Research; used by permission of the Musée du Louvre).

Plate 44 KTU 1.2 IV 1-6 left-hand side (Photograph by Bruce and Kenneth Zuckerman, West Semitic Research; used by permission of the Musée du Louvre).

Plate 45 KTU 1.2 IV 1-6 middle left-hand side (Photograph by Bruce and Kenneth Zuckerman, West Semitic Research; used by permission of the Musée du Louvre).

Plate 46 KTU 1.2 IV 1-6 middle right-hand side (Photograph by Bruce and Kenneth Zuckerman, West Semitic Research; used by permission of the Musée du Louvre).

Plate 47 KTU 1.2 IV 1-6 right-hand side (Photograph by Bruce and Kenneth Zuckerman, West Semitic Research; used by permission of the Musée du Louvre).